WORLD FOOD

An Encyclopedia of
History, Culture, and
Social Influence from
Hunter-Gatherers to the
Age of Globalization

FOOD

— Volume 2 —

Mary Ellen Snodgrass

SHARPE REFERENCE
an imprint of M.E. Sharpe, Inc.

SHARPE REFERENCE

Sharpe Reference is an imprint of M.E. Sharpe, Inc.

M.E. Sharpe, Inc.
80 Business Park Drive
Armonk, NY 10504

Cover images (clockwise from top left) provided by: De Agostini/Getty Images; Stringer/AFP/Getty Images; The Granger Collection, New York; Bachrach/Getty Images; Vincent Thian/Associated Press.

Library of Congress Cataloging-in-Publication Data

Snodgrass, Mary Ellen.
World food: an encyclopedia of history, culture, and social influence from hunter-gatherers to the age of globalization / Mary Ellen Snodgrass.
     p. cm.
Includes bibliographical references and index.
ISBN 978-0-7656-8278-9 (cloth: alk. paper)
1. Food—History—Encyclopedias. 2. Cooking—History—Encyclopedias. I. Title.

TX349.S66 2013
641.303—dc23
                                                              2012014375

Publisher: Myron E. Sharpe
Vice President and Director of New Product Development: Donna Sanzone
Vice President and Production Director: Carmen Chetti
Executive Development Editor: Jeff Hacker
Project Manager: Laura Brengelman
Program Coordinator: Cathleen Prisco
Editorial Assistant: Lauren LoPinto
Text Design and Cover Design: Jesse Sanchez

Contents

WORLD FOOD

— Volume 2 —

Mail-Order Food

Mail-order convenience has benefited both homemakers and vendors by adding variety and speed to food shopping. Beginning in 1852 with wines from Aristide Boucicaut's Paris store Au Bon Marché, advances in rotary printing made catalog advertising profitable and adaptable to a variety of commerce. The concept of home grocery shopping met with public approval, especially with Montgomery Ward of Chicago beginning in 1875. As advertised in *Farm Journal, Machinists' Monthly Journal, Missions,* and *Santa Fe Employees Magazine,* the firm guaranteed goods offered in a grocery list, including Alaska salmon, Campbell's soup, coffee, Cracker Jack, Domino sugar, Jell-O, Norwegian herring, pure extracts, raisins, Royal baking powder, and Van Houten's Cocoa. Kays of Worcester, organized in Worcestershire, England, by William Kilbourne Kay in 1890, offered the British shopper gourmet teas by mail. In the United States, the explosive personal wealth of pioneers in northern California inspired merchandisers to ship to the West the luxury foods of the East.

In 1893, Richard Warren Sears of Stewartville, Minnesota, printed the first Sears, Roebuck catalog, the world's most successful groceries-by-mail service. The corporation grew from its Chicago headquarters to some 800 stores in North America. Guarantees printed in English, German, and Swedish promised ease of ordering and returns. Sears supplied isolated farmwives with pantry needs, including crackers, dried and canned fruit, flour, meat, mustard, salt cod, sauces, and vinegar. After the success of a brownie recipe in the 1897 catalog, Sears created a house-brand brownie mix.

Factory-processed foods succeeded with a large customer base. The 1900 Sears catalog listed 18 types of sugar and a broad choice of beverages—four varieties of coffee, two of root beer, three of cocoa, and 22 of tea. Stock ranged from the familiar—egg noodles, gelatin, ground pepper, peas, spaghetti, and Spanish peanuts—to shredded coconut and sliced Hawaiian pineapple from the company's island plantations. For baking, the homemaker could select chocolate, cracked wheat, raisins and currants, spices, vanilla, and yeast cakes. By fall 1907, the Sears catalog reached 3 million addresses.

In the same era, England's postal service shipped some 130 million parcels annually, many of them in direct response to food ads in magazines and newspapers. The growing use of potatoes buoyed mail orders from female shoppers, typically aged 25–45.

After Richard Sears's retirement in 1908, Sears expanded its food offerings under the aegis of Julius Rosenwald, a Jewish immigrant from Germany. The company's 1923 catalog listed a book on diet and health with a key to calorie counting, along with canned seafood, 25 varieties of canned vegetables, and fruit pie mix. For quick meals, Sears warehoused clams, kippered herring, mock turtle soup, sardines in oil, shrimp, smoked haddock, and tinned salmon. Following the Great Depression, the Great Atlantic and Pacific Tea Company (A&P), Piggly Wiggly, and other grocery chains cut into demand for Sears mail-order grocery line, and the company abandoned food sales in 1941.

Famous stores offered convenience and peace of mind to purchasers of high-priced specialty items for holiday and hostess gifts. Begun by Ray Kubly in 1926 in Monroe, Wisconsin, Swiss Colony advertised bulk cheese, petits fours, and sausage by mail. In Medford, Oregon, Harry & David Holmes featured a Fruit-of-the-Month Club, a marketing ploy introduced in 1938. In 1947, the company's gift-wrapped Tower of Treats extended from pears to baklava, cheese, chocolate truffles, and shortbread. In 1950 in New Orleans, Gambino's Bakery earned a reputation for its Doberge butter cakes and Lenten king cakes containing a plastic Baby Jesus doll. In Nebraska in 1952, Omaha Steaks began vacuum packing prime cuts of beef—filet mignon, porterhouse, and T-bone—and cheesecake. From 1956, Williams-Sonoma in San Francisco mailed out stir-fry sauces, steakhouse rubs, and waffle mixes; Hickory Farms in northwestern Ohio specialized in summer sausage gift boxes. In 1968, for a Yule catalog from Dallas, Texas, Neiman Marcus featured mint candies shaped like green peas. The company's request for 20,000 jars swamped the Italian village where workers hand rolled the candies.

In the 1980s, when department stores lost out to discount shopping malls, mail-order groceries rose in profitability through store credit cards. Later, Internet commerce aided workingwomen as well as diabetics and sufferers of allergies to dairy, eggs, gluten, and nuts. Bill and Ruth Penzey opened a spice business in Milwaukee, Wisconsin, in 1986, showcasing Tahitian vanilla beans, Vietnamese cinnamon, and Turkish herb blends.

Zingerman's in Ann Arbor, Michigan, teased the palate with pistachio cream, Purim pastries, and wild oats granola. Otto's in Burbank, California, distributed Magyar goulash mix and marzipan from Hungary. Paxton & Whitfield, a cheesemonger in Gloucestershire, England, packed hampers of chutneys and patés; Forman & Field of London stocked Alderton ham and *porchetta*.

Today, online send-a-meal sites cater everything from Carolina barbecue to Italian lasagna to live lobster. Corporations reward clients with Collin Street Bakery fruitcakes and Dean & Deluca premium-grade chocolates and nuts wrapped in colored foil and nestled in baskets. Shippers in California, Florida, and Texas pack and ship clementines, honeybells, satsumas, and valencia oranges in time for Christmas and Hanukkah. The Vermont Country Store in Rutland focuses on hard-to-find items—Austrian wafers, navy bean soup, pierogis, stollen, and wild rice—and such nostalgic treats as Garibaldi biscuits, ribbon candy, Sen-Sen, and Walnettos.

Shoppers worldwide enjoy eel fillets and scallops from Medallion in Charlottetown, Prince Edward Island; Ardtaraig rock oysters and smoked duck from Annbank, Scotland; and jelly and vinaigrette from Saskatoon, Saskatchewan. Australian shippers in New South Wales created a market niche for organic crocodile, lime leaves, and salad mixes. Customers buy artisan cheese, Jamaican jerk spices, Russian caviar, peanut-free sweets, and gourmet desserts and wines from glossy catalogs and online sites, for example, Ontario's www.canadianfavourites.com and England's www.africanfoods.co.uk, www.marksand spencer.com, and www.waitrose.com. In the first decade of the twenty-first century, the U.S. market for mail-order foods was estimated to exceed $6 billion annually.

See also: Exotic Food Clubs; Hudson's Bay Company.

Further Reading

Benson, John, and Laura Ugolini. *A Nation of Shopkeepers: Five Centuries of British Retailing.* London: I.B. Tauris, 2003.

Cherry, Robin. *Catalog: An Illustrated History of Mail-Order Shopping.* New York: Princeton Architectural, 2008.

Coopey, Richard, Sean O'Connell, and Dilwyn Porter. *Mail Order Retailing in Britain: A Business and Social History.* Oxford, UK: Oxford University Press, 2005.

Sohn, Mark F. *Appalachian Home Cooking: History, Culture, and Recipes.* Lexington: University Press of Kentucky, 2005.

Maize
See Corn and Maize

Malnutrition

Malnutrition, the result of eating too little or consuming an unbalanced diet, threatens the immune system and longevity of more than 2 billion people. The rates worldwide are startlingly varied: Only 7 percent of Chinese children are underweight, compared with 28 percent in sub-Saharan Africa and 43 percent in India. An estimated 58 percent of deaths worldwide result from hunger.

Half of fetal and child mortality derives from insufficient nutrition, which besets 30 percent of the global population. Those children who survive the first 24 months in poor conditions suffer underweight and irreversible damage to body and intellect from insufficient protein during growth spurts. In addition to struggling to maintain body temperature and to heal from injuries, the malnourished have a limited chance of overcoming contagious disease, especially enteritis, the number one child killer.

The variety of suffering depends on the type of undernutrition. Pregnant women deprived of vitamin B6 can produce malnourished infants at risk for spina bifida and other birth defects. As a child's weight sinks below 80 percent of normal, marasmus, a lack of protein, deprives the body of musculature and energy. A similar protein and micronutrient shortage produces kwashiorkor, a wasting of tissue accompanied by edema and ulceration that is common among children in parts of Africa in which cassava dominates the diet.

Specific inadequacies afflict small populations. Iodine deficiency causes cretinism and goiter, a throat tumor associated with the populations of Russia and Siberia. Zinc deficiency leaves children vulnerable to enteritis. A lack of iron results in anemia from insufficient hemoglobin, which produces malaise and listlessness. Anemic women tend to die in childbirth or produce anemic infants. Pernicious anemia, a terminal illness caused by an insufficiency of vitamin B12, produces jaundice and numbness. In 1934, George Richards Minot, William Parry Murphy, and George Hoyt Whipple shared the Nobel Prize in Medicine for discovering that iron in raw liver counters the effects of a poor diet, Helen Keller International and UNICEF distribute iron and zinc supplements in Mozambique and Uganda.

Vitamin deprivation results in identifiable body anomalies, such as infection and night blindness from a lack of vitamin A. In 1884, Japanese naval physician Takaki Kanehiro treated beri-beri from too little thiamine, or vitamin B1, in the rice-heavy diet of sailors. The deficiency caused heart arrhythmia and swelling. An American doctor, Edward Bright Vedder, began treating beri-beri in 1910 with rice bran, the husk removed from grains of polished rice. The treatment also aided chronic alcoholics and victims of arsenic poisoning.

A deficiency of niacin, or vitamin B3, in the diet can cause pellagra, a severe scaling of the skin and formation of lesions. The disease resulted from the importation of corn to Europe, where farmers neglected to mix the grain with lime. A prime killer in Alabama, Mississippi, and South Carolina in the early 1900s, pellagra remained lethal until 1926, when Joseph Goldberg, a researcher for the U.S. Public Health Service, discovered the value of brewer's yeast in combating the resultant gum disease and porous bones.

For sailors during the Renaissance, scurvy resulted from a lack of vitamin C in shipboard meals. Over three centuries, some 2 million victims succumbed to hemorrhaging from mucous membranes and wounds. Although recognized in Egypt since 1550 B.C.E., the nutritional deficiency received anecdotal treatment from sea captains who fed their crews citrus juice, fresh fruits and vegetables, and pickles, all sources of vitamin C. John Woodall, a surgeon for the East India Company, issued a simple solution in 1614, when he prescribed artemisia, horseradish, scurvy grass, or sorrel as remedies. In 1747, James Lind, a researcher of naval nutrition, offered citrus fruit as the most practical antiscorbutic.

A common scourge among children of developing countries or institutionalized children, rickets results from insufficient vitamin D and calcium in the diet. A lack of nutrients, as from breast feeding by malnourished mothers, results in stunting—twisted bones and skeletal deformity of skull and spine. Treatment begins with increased exposure to sunlight as an antirachitic (antidote to rickets) and also may include consumption of butter and milk, eggs, and fish oil from herring, salmon, or tuna.

Less common deficiencies involve inadequate vitamin K, a risk for older Thai females, who tend to suffer internal bleeding. For newborns, a lack of vitamin K can cause lethal hemorrhaging. An ailment that affects women worldwide, osteoporosis, a thinning of connective bone tissue, results from deficient calcium in the diet. The fragility of bones may result in serious fractures of the hip and spine, catastrophic losses to mobility for the elderly.

Science has intervened in the effects of malnutrition on the populations of developing countries. A biofortified sweet potato high in vitamin A reduces incidences of blindness and child death. With the aid of the Bill and Melinda Gates Foundation and the World Bank, HarvestPlus in Washington, D.C., is producing zinc-enriched rice and wheat and iron-packed beans and millet. Another project elevates vitamin A in bananas, cassava, and corn. In France, pediatrician André Briend concocted Plumpy'Nut, a nutritive peanut paste of milk, oil, peanuts, and sugar. The efficient nutrient delivery system emptied hospitals of patients on intravenous feeding in Malawi and helped to relieve the underfed in Ethiopia, Haiti, Nicaragua, Niger, Somalia, and Yemen.

See also: African Diet and Cuisine, Sub-Saharan; Airlifts, Food; Famine; International Food Aid; Liebig, Justus von; Lind, James; Linnaeus, Carolus; Rumford, Count; Russian Diet and Cuisine; Seaman's Diet and Cuisine; Soup Kitchens; Yeast.

Further Reading

Druett, Joan. *Rough Medicine: Surgeons at Sea in the Age of Sail.* New York: Routledge, 2000.

Hayes, Dayle, and Rachel Laudan, eds. *Food and Nutrition.* New York: Marshall Cavendish, 2009.

Levitt, Emily, Kees Kostermans, Luc Laviolette, and Nkosinathi Mbuya. *Malnutrition in Afghanistan: Scale, Scope, Causes, and Potential Response.* Washington, DC: World Bank, 2011.

Nardo, Don. *Malnutrition.* Detroit, MI: Gale, 2007.

Winkler, Peter. *Feeding the World.* Washington, DC: National Geographic, 2003.

Mandarin Diet and Cuisine

The diet of Shandong Province, Mandarin cuisine has refined much of Chinese cookery with elegant touches. From a repertoire of 4,000 recipes, heavily sauced dishes from the royal table in the Forbidden City satisfied the expectations of the imperial family and Manchurian noblemen for centuries. In Beijing's streets, shoppers munched on skewers of lamb or mutton grilled in the open air and wrapped in wheat pancakes. Vendors offered Mandarin snacks, notably, Mongolian barbecue and fried chicken seasoned with fermented tofu, garlic, scallions, sesame, soy paste, and vinegar.

During the Ming dynasty (1368–1644), imperial food service required a cadre of 5,000 kitchen workers. Regional Huaiyang specialists opened restaurants featuring mildly flavored delicacies from north of the Yangtze River based on fresh water fish and pork. The subsequent Qing dynasty, which ruled until 1912, countenanced the monopoly of catering guilds, which stratified foods and dishes by social and economic class. At the imperial compound, the main meal of the day, presented around 2 P.M., featured two or three tables of entrées, three of cakes and cereals, and a small side table of preserved vegetables.

Recipe: Peking Duck

Defat a duck by removing the tail and feet and suspending the carcass with string in a constant airflow for four hours. Place the fowl in a strainer and salt the surface. Bathe in a sauce of 3 tablespoons of honey, 1 tablespoon each of sherry and rice vinegar, one slice of ginger, one chopped scallion, and 4 teaspoons of cornstarch whisked in water. Suspend the duck for an additional six-hour period.

Bake the duck, spine side up, at medium heat for 30 minutes on an oiled oven rack above a bain-marie (double boiler). Turn the duck and bake it for another half hour. Crisp the duck in 4 inches of oil in a wok for three minutes. Serve the sliced meat with its crisp skin and hoisin sauce.

Chefs at a Beijing restaurant fill buns with pork and place them in bamboo steamers. Mandarin cuisine, the food of China's northern imperial courts, features wheat rather than rice. Steamed buns and noodles are preferred side dishes. *(Liu Jin/AFP/Getty Images)*

Until the coming of nationalism in the 1920s, which rid halls of feasting as a politically incorrect extravagance, the Manchu-Han Complete Banquet flourished among the wealthy and privileged; coordinated wait staff displayed hundreds of dishes. From the time of the Emperor Qianlong (1735–1796), event planners featured classical opera as a backdrop for the exquisite presentation of bear, bird's nests, and lily roots, prepared by 400 chefs.

Imperial cooks created such exotica as duck webs and cold fish maw (stomach) and the stand-alone highlights moo shu pork in crepes and crisp Peking duck, an imperial favorite from the mid-fourteenth century. Similar showcasing of a single staple advanced the popularity of tea eggs and chicken velvet, a forcemeat of chicken breast stabilized by egg whites. Chefs de-emphasized rice and carved vegetables, while stressing distinct tastes of dumplings and steamed buns.

Often compared to French cuisine, Mandarin dining lets such entrées as lemon chicken and lion's head pork set the tone of a meal. Skill at battering and temperature control produces such specialties as crispy shrimp hors d'oeuvres and flowering peanuts. "Red cooking" braises poultry with an aromatic liquid combining ginger and wine with soy sauce. Glacéed bananas, which American Mandarin specialist Cecilia Sun Yun Chiang introduced at San Francisco's Ghirardelli Square in the 1960s, arrive at table coated in a crackled caramel.

In contrast to Cantonese and Szechuan Chinese steamed vegetables and rice, Mandarin food stresses an aristocratic approach to cooking. Table service dramatizes expensive meats and such rare ingredients as shark's fin and sea cucumber. Under these high standards, minced squab and beggar's chicken wrapped in lotus leaves and baked in hot ash emphasize light and tender meaty flavor over the salty or spicy tastes of peasant fare. Unique combinations—double-fried walnuts and mayonnaise shrimp, for example—appeal to the tastes of China's elite.

See also: Aphrodisiacs; Noodles; Polo, Marco; Poultry; Silk Road.

Further Reading

Chiang, Cecilia, and Lisa Weiss. *The Seventh Daughter: My Culinary Journey from Beijing to San Francisco.* Berkeley, CA: Ten Speed, 2007.

Coe, Andrew. *Chop Suey: A Cultural History of Chinese Food in the United States.* New York: Oxford University Press, 2009.

Geraci, Victor W., and Elizabeth S. Demers. *Icons of American Cooking.* Santa Barbara, CA: Greenwood, 2011.

Gong, Rosemary. *Good Luck Life: The Essential Guide to Chinese American Celebrations and Culture.* New York: HarperCollins, 2005.

Jung, John. *Sweet and Sour; Life in Chinese Family Restaurants.* Cypress, CA: Yin and Yang, 2010.

Manioc

A cheap, drought-tolerant famine crop, South American manioc (also called cassava or yuca) provides much of the tropics and subtropics with a chief source of carbohydrates. Originating in Guatemalan vegeculture, manioc (*Manihot esculenta*) flourished in sweet and bitter varieties. When sieved and squeezed, it produced a liquid starch for use on bark paper and fabric.

Brazilians and eastern Peruvians first encountered the 5- to 12-foot (1.52- to 3.66-meter) plant in 10,000 B.C.E.

and elevated it to a trade commodity along the Lower Amazon, Orinoco, and Guiana rivers. Neolithic, or New Stone Age, food technology around 8000 B.C.E. shifted emphasis from raw meat to cooked beans, grain, and manioc.

In the Western Hemisphere, the tuber grew wild in Venezuela in 5000 B.C.E., in Central America and the Mexican lowlands from 4600 B.C.E., and in Puerto Rico from 1300 B.C.E. With hoe and machete, the Maya of El Salvador cultivated manioc as early as 600 C.E. and cooked the pulp on clay griddles.

All manioc is toxic. The Tupi of Brazil pulped bitter manioc on stone graters and removed prussic acid, a poisonous hydrocyanide. Without proper soaking to remove the cyanide, the tuber caused goiter and a shambling gait from neuropathy. The Tupi processed the detoxified fiber into meal, pancake-shaped loaves, tapioca, and a table dip or sauce called *tucupi,* which tenderized servings of fish and game in a pepper pot stew.

Across northern South America, the tuber generated a common menu item, appearing in Peruvian earth ovens alongside roasting ears and pork, and as *carimañolas* at the breakfast buffet and *enyucado* at lunch in Cartagena, Colombia. Manioc also supplied South Americans with *chicha,* a coconut-flavored beer made from fiber chewed by brewers and fermented with salivary enzymes.

The Americas and Europe

In the Caribbean on November 16, 1492, Christopher Columbus first saw the Taíno grating manioc for flatbread and porridge. As a food store for hard times and supplies for voyagers, they planted uninhabited parts of the Lucayan Islands with the tubers, which could remain in the ground unharvested until needed. Native cooks peeled the root with clam, conch, mussel, and whelk shell tools; the spine of the stingray served as a grater. Cuban natives made graters by permeating hardwood slabs with stone chips and setting the apparatus in a trough. In the Bahamas and Cayman Islands, the Carib fermented manioc pulp into beer.

In the early 1500s, natives on St. Thomas introduced members of the Danish West India Company to manioc as well as to arrowroot and sweet potatoes. Enslaved Arawak and Carib farmers in the West Indies managed two annual harvests of corn and manioc. In this same period, on Hispaniola (present-day Dominican Republic), the Spaniards shackled some 2 million aborigines and forced them to mine gold. Without opportunities to cultivate manioc fields, they survived on a starvation diet of beans and herbs.

Bernal Díaz del Castillo, a Spanish chronicler of Hernán de Cortés's conquest of Mexico, described manioc flour in the 1520s as an essential of shipboard staples because of its three-year shelf life and resistance to weevils. To ensure supplies, the Spanish accepted manioc tubers and bread from the Taíno as taxes.

After Portuguese settlers encountered manioc in Brazil in the 1530s, the tuber bolstered New World cuisine

with a substitute for European wheat, which required a drier climate and six times more ground for planting than manioc. The Spanish elite demeaned the vegetables as pagan, but, in 1539, explorer Hernando de Soto accepted manioc as a portable form of nutrition for his military expedition from Cuba into Florida and the American South. In the 1660s, laborers for the French West India Company on Martinique renewed past croplands by piercing each manioc mound with digging sticks and inserting manioc cuttings. Bread makers dried and cooked the tubers into loaves on inch-thick clay griddles.

Africa

In the late 1600s, at the same time that nutritionists studied the chemical properties of manioc grown in London's Chelsea Physic Garden, Portuguese traders introduced the tuber to Angola and the Congo. Traditional foodways slowly admitted manioc to the staple crops of bananas, millet, and yams. By 1650, after losing their familiar food crops to baboons, drought, and locusts, the Bushongo accepted manioc as a source of meal for bread. East of the Zambezi River, the Southern Lunda depended on manioc as their staple carbohydrate, which Scots missionary David Livingstone called the native "staff of life."

While European colonists established the tuber as a source of silage for livestock, manioc remained a staple of native cuisine centered on the Gulf of Guinea and was familiarly known as *foufou,* a pounded paste. For homeless people, common custom in Madagascar allowed the poor to chop pieces of sweet manioc in the field to munch like raw turnip. In 1739, the tuber became slave food at Réunion after the governor introduced the tuber as a continuous monoculture.

In 1786, vegetable dissemination passed the tuber and its tasty foliage from Mauritius and Madagascar to India. For former slaves who founded Freetown, Sierra Leone, on March 11, 1792, the flexibility of manioc cookery extended its use to boiling, frying, grating, liquefying, pureeing, roasting, and stewing and fermenting into beer. Domesticated in 40 countries, in the 1800s, manioc became Africa's primary food.

Manioc in Modern Times

English naturalist Charles Darwin found widespread cultivation of manioc in April 1832 in Chile, where its leaves enriched the soil as green manure. In Brazil and on Floreana Island off Peru, he ate *farinha* (manioc bread), which natives made from pounded roots. In Mozambique in 1893, the Portuguese Nyassa Company headquartered at Porto Amélia (present-day Pemba) and began developing commerce between the Rovuma and Lurio rivers. Manganja women superintended manioc beds and dried the tubers to make porridge, the national dish. On arrival at East Africa, Norwegian missionaries adapted their waffle recipes to native manioc flour and buttermilk.

At the rate of more than 230 million tons (209 million metric tons) annually, manioc in China, Costa Rica, Ghana, Guyana, Indonesia, Nigeria, the Philippines, Thailand, and Vietnam fortifies the diet with calcium, iron, phosphorus, vitamin C, and zinc, but little protein or other micronutrients. It remains a common breakfast food in South America; in Ecuador, manioc-based drinks refresh consumers with their sweet, fruity taste. In the mid-1980s, northern Vietnamese farmers began a four-year swidden cycle with upland rice and concluded with manioc planting before returning to slash and burn methods to revitalize the soil. In the Philippines, the Hanunóo of southern Mindoro Island broadened their swidden cultivation with manioc as well as millet, papaya, and yams.

Today, manioc nourishes some 500 million people worldwide as farina, greens, tapioca, and fried strips comparable to french fried potatoes. Fermented manioc bread is a reliable pack food because it needs no refrigeration.

See also: Beer; Columbus, Christopher; French East India Company; Hybridization; Poisonous Foods.

Further Reading

Duiker, William J., and Jackson J. Spielvogel. *The Essential World History*. Boston: Wadsworth/Cengage Learning, 2010.

Keegan, William F., and Lisabeth A. Carlson. *Talking Taíno: Essays on Caribbean Natural History from a Native Perspective*. Tuscaloosa: University of Alabama Press, 2008.

Keoke, Emory Dean, and Kay Marie Porterfield. *American Indian Contributions to the World: 15,000 Years of Inventions and Innovations*. New York: Checkmark, 2003.

Staller, John E. *Maize Cobs and Cultures: History of* Zea mays L. New York: Springer, 2010.

Ucko, Peter J., and G.W. Dimbleby, eds. *The Domestication and Exploitation of Plants and Animals*. New Brunswick, NJ: Aldine Transaction, 2008.

Maritime Trade Routes

Until the advent of railroads and airways in the mid-1800s, water routes for the food trade extended over time from rivers to sea-lanes, becoming the fastest intercontinental conveyance for edibles. The first maritime network, formed in 3000 B.C.E., carried dates, grain, and oil from Babylon in Mesopotamia southeast from the Euphrates and Tigris rivers. Planked keelboats traveled along the Arabian Gulf to the island of Bahrain and the Harappan culture on the Indus River to barter for sorghum and millet.

Ancient Food Trade

The beginning of spice trading around 1600 B.C.E. involved Egyptians, 90 percent of it at Alexandria, in larger cargo ventures. Freight masters carried oil and wine to central Africa and introduced the chicken to Tanzania.

With the coronation of Hatshepsut as pharaoh in 1479 B.C.E., trading networks down the Red Sea to Punt (present-day Somalia and Eritrea) enriched Egypt with ebony, spices, and table aromatics. Exotic fare from Africa, India, and Malaysia turned Alexandria's harbor market into a world-class food bazaar.

Farther north, the Phoenicians (or Canaanites), the adventurers and cross-carriers (interharbor transporters) of the ancient world, traversed coastal waters and the Atlantic Ocean in cedar plank ships to trade honey, oil, and wine from Aleppo and Tyre to Cornwall, England. A Semitic merchant culture at Byblos, Sidon, and Tyre in present-day Lebanon, from 1200 to 333 B.C.E., Phoenicia bought and sold barley and wheat from Palestine and Syria and traded dates, figs, and pomegranates and salted eels, sturgeon, and tuna. The Phoenicians imported livestock and bags of grain and sea salt, chests of saffron, and cardoons, olives, olive oil, and wine from Egypt, Greece, Mesopotamia, Sardinia, Sicily, and the Atlantic coast of Iberia.

Around 1000 B.C.E., the Chinese paralleled Phoenician mercantilism with varied routes to cassia merchants in Southeast Asia. The arrival of the sweet potato from South America to Hawaii and Rapa Nui added a trade item to lure Chinese freighters eastward. Profitability increased during the Eastern Han dynasty at the beginning of the current era from lengthy oceanic merchandizing from Hanoi and through the Strait of Malacca to Sri Lanka, India, the Persian Gulf, and Axum, the capital of Ethiopia on the Red Sea. Chinese traders also sailed east to the Solomon Islands to buy the meat of dolphins, pigs, sharks, and turtles.

Because sea transport outpaced overland hauling over desert or mountainous terrain, Athenian and Egyptian food dealers also preferred ships to caravans. Greek navigators, carrying oil, olives, and wine, outlined Mediterranean passages through the Dodecanese to Pontus, a source of caviar, fish, and grain on the Black Sea and the Sea of Azov. Greek explorers steered west toward Crete, Cyprus, Delos, and Magna Graecia, the Greek colonies in Sicily and lower Italy.

Farther south, from 250 B.C.E. to 250 C.E., Egyptian and Roman coasters dominated Red Sea routes to Ethiopia, Zanzibar in Africa, Mocha in southern Arabia, coastal India, the Dong Song Kingdom in Vietnam, and China. North Africa competed with Mediterranean grain depots by offering stocks of corn. For maximum income, the Romans exacted a 25 percent tax on such luxury imports as sea urchins.

By emulating Phoenician navigation systems, Italy's sea merchants cut the cost of shipping, as compared to land routes, by some 85 percent. A heavily traveled sea course carried routine grain deliveries from Egypt to the Roman warehouses of Ostia, which the Emperor Claudius expanded in 42 C.E. The harbor, originally plotted by Julius Caesar, enhanced food distribution up the Tiber River by limited draft vessels and barges.

Extending their reach to western India, Roman shippers traveled the Red Sea, calling at ports along the east coast of Africa and the southern tip of Arabia to load coconuts, drugs, rice, and sugar. The split of the empire into Western Rome and Byzantium resulted in 490 in commercial fragmentation. During the Dark Ages, sea trade in the waters of the Middle East declined until Arab caliphs cleared them of piracy, around 700, and restored corn routes from the Black Sea.

Medieval Freight Magnates

In the seventh and eighth centuries, the Chinese exploited travel to India via monsoon winds. At the Bay of Bengal, they bought coconuts, a popular aphrodisiac. While caravans carried exotic foodstuffs—caraway, coriander, eggplant, figs, sugar beets, and wines—over land, the maneuverable seagoing junk, equipped with rotating sails, moved into the wind to carry bulk rice and tea to less profitable ports. Ships carrying cotton, pepper, sesame, wheat, and yellow beans connected Denzhou in eastern China with Korea and Japan by way of the Yellow Sea. To the south, Cantonese shippers crossed the South China Sea to reach the Malay Peninsula and Sumatra, a major depot for Indonesian cinnamon and cloves. By 850, Muscat dominated the trade route between Oman over the Sea of Oman and the Arabian Sea to India and Sri Lanka. From there, traders ventured over the spice route to the Strait of Malacca and north to Singapore.

Late medieval shipping, envigorated by the Hanseatic League, a twelfth- through sixteenth-century trade alliance in northern Europe, carried grain from Novgorod, Russia, southeast over the Baltic Sea through Riga and Danzig to Lübeck and Hamburg and over the North Sea to Bergen and Bruges. A thriving market in London, home to 100,000 in 1299, retailed 27,000 tons (24,500 metric tons) of beer and grain, much of it from Lübeck. London maintained its end of the trade by dispatching grain and sheep. Up the Scots coast, Newcastle markets reciprocated with wood for cooking and heating. Flanders shippers quickly broke cargoes of grocery staples from Ireland into small deliveries for Bruges, Ghent, and Ypres in Belgium, which had populations of more than 150,000 before the Black Death of 1348.

Simultaneously, Varangian and Viking voyagers carried dried cod and mead from Russia and Scandinavia as far as Byzantium. The wealth pouring in from Arabian herbs, opium, and spices arriving from Jeddah and sugar from Iberia to Mediterranean ports elevated Genoa and Venice to city-states. Venice, the queen of the Mediterranean trading routes, distributed goods to Bruges and Flanders, to ports north of the Danube River delta, and along the Rhine River to Augsburg and Cologne.

The fullest late medieval account of ocean routes comes from *Tuhfat al-Nuzzar fi Ghara'ib al-Amsar wa'Ajaib al'Asfar* (*On Curiosities of Cities and Wonders of Travel*, 1354), a travelogue by Moroccan cleric and traveler Ibn Battuta.

Among his perusals of world shipping, he appended a lengthy description of the Chinese junk, which he admired for its adaptability to varied oceanic conditions. In 1405, Ming Emperor Zhu Di replaced fishing fleets with a flotilla of 300 ships crewed by 27,000 sailors, who explored food markets over 35,000 miles (56,000 kilometers) in Arabia, India, Malaysia, and Mogadishu, Somalia.

In 1497, five years after Christopher Columbus pioneered a route to the New World, long-distance navigator and colonizer Vasco da Gama of Sines, Portugal, made short hops to Cape Verde in the Atlantic Ocean and longer voyages to eastern South America. He veered east around the Cape of Good Hope to Mozambique to provision his fleet with fresh vegetables and water. In Calicut, India, he tested barter with vegetarian Hindus and learned by trial and error why they rejected beef. He returned via Malindi (present-day Mombasa, Kenya) to Lisbon in July 1499 with cinnamon, citrus fruit, cloves, dates, melons, dairy products, palm wine, and rice. On the route back to Iberia around South Africa, his men paid the price of lengthy sea journeys in shipboard deaths from scurvy and tuberculosis.

The Race for Speed

The Dutch revolutionized maritime trade with the flyboat, a merchantman that carried 20 percent more cargo with a 30 percent smaller crew. The competitive fleet conveyed corn, salt, and sugar as well as Baltic grain. From 1550 to 1610, increased commerce in Ionian currants, nutmeg, pepper, rye and wheat, and salt fish boosted Antwerp to a major player along shipping lanes from Asia to England and the Baltics. Increasing demand and raising prices to the south, crop failures in Italy heightened the need for rapid navigation via the shortest routes to such dependent overpopulated cities as Genoa and Livorno. In Venice, importers registered grain at warehouses in Rialto and San Marco and sold it directly to traders, who dispatched outgoing ships to North Africa and the Levant with anchovies and olive oil.

By 1620, despite high insurance rates to offset pirate raids, global shippers conveyed an annual load of 3,500 tons (3,200 metric tons) of pepper, 245 tons (222 metric tons) of cloves, 225 tons (204 metric tons) of nutmeg, and 90 tons (82 metric tons) of mace. For laborers, Venetian docks employed some 5,000 Greeks as sailors and overseers. Grocers' prices remained so high that even the loss of merchantmen from the Indian Ocean around Africa's Cape Horn failed to dent the profits on the spice trade. Foodstuffs—fish from Newfoundland, cotton and molasses from Virginia, sugar and rum from Cuba and Hispaniola, cocoa from Mexico—redirected investments from Old World fleets to deep-sea vessels servicing New World shores. Competition from English merchant fleets and international wars drove small Asia-based colonial companies out of business, including, in 1799, the Dutch East India Company.

From the late 1770s to 1869, captains of hydrodynamically efficient clipper ships sped global food distribution by navigating courses along parallel ocean currents and trade winds. They made the most of expenditures for men and craft by carrying coffee, spices, and tea from Canton and Java around Cape Horn and across the Atlantic and by returning with American apples and ice slabs cut from ponds and packed in straw. After 1813, steady traffic along sea-lanes from Peru and the West Indies to Honolulu provided Andalusian horticulturist Francisco de Paula Marín with 65 fruit, nut, and vegetable seeds and slips that turned Hawaii into a food paradise.

Sea-to-sea freighting to the California goldfields during the 1849 gold rush transported food staples, building supplies, and whiskey and laudanum via steamer around the Four Evangels at Tierra del Fuego, the dividing point between Atlantic and Pacific. Up the South American coast, traders made for the Pacific hub at San Francisco to load gold dust and coins. Other perishables, particularly coffee, rice, and tea, traveled Pacific sea-lanes from Australia, China, the East Indies, and Hawaii to Portland, Seattle, and the California shore. By 1880, American vessels dominated the maritime food and fuel trade.

Modern Shipping

Since the opening of the Panama Canal in August 1914, oceangoing vessels have ringed the world with cheap, dependable, and speedy food delivery. The evening out of distribution from have to have-not nations has simplified famine and emergency relief and lowered the death rate from spoiled food and starvation, a looming disaster following two world wars.

In the latter 1970s, when South Korea emerged as a commercial power, Japanese and American cargo liners traveled at 12 knots, and smaller tramp steamers traveled at 10 knots. Through the improvements to food packaging and ship technology, major companies competed directly with air freight for regular contracts based on speed, sanitation, and efficiency. Gantry cranes and derricks maneuvered unit loads—bananas, bulk grain, champagne, copra, poppy seeds, rapeseed, shrimp, tea, tilapia, and wheat—directly into holds. Tankers loaded linseed, molasses, potable water, soybeans, vegetable oil, and wine by hose directly from storage tanks on shore. The replacement of individual casks and bottles for syrups and vinegars lowered cost due to breakage from cargo shifting. Reefers (refrigerated ships) sped dairy products and vegetables from holds and tweendecks directly to food suppliers in small harbor towns.

Improvements in containerized freight refrigerated with liquid nitrogen or dry ice allowed machinery to do the tedious work once relegated to longshoremen, who previously stacked case goods on hand trucks for rolling up gangways to pallets. Self-loading conveyor belts, both covered and open-air, reduced the chance of human error from fatigue and overheating in airless holds. Reduction

of time in marine humidity ensured the freshness of coffee beans and prevented the clumping of granular salt and sugar.

During the shipping boom of 2004, specialized vessels increased the profits for investors in the food trade and enhanced the market for crews and ships. As economist Adam Smith explained in *The Wealth of Nations* (1776), the key to merchandising is transport. To guarantee the safe arrival of lobster and shrimp, seafood vessels backed up refrigerated units with their own chillers and compressors. For difficult navigation in island clusters and among reefs, larger vessels off-loaded goods broken down into smaller batches for coasters to deliver to wharfs, such as the harbor wharf/farmer's market at St. Bart's and through the choke point between India and Sri Lanka on the Palk Strait. Quicker intermodal passage from shore to hold slashed losses from defrosted meats from Sydney, Australia, and limited travel damage to blood oranges and tomatoes from Haifa, Israel.

See also: Australian Food Trade; Clipper Ships; Ibn Battuta; Sanitation; Trade Routes; Trading Vessels; World Trade.

Further Reading

Berggren, Lars, Nils Hybel, and Annette Landen, eds. *Cogs, Cargoes, and Commerce: Maritime Bulk Trade in Northern Europe, 1150–1400.* Toronto: Pontifical Institute of Mediaeval Studies, 2002.

Junker, Laura Lee. *Raiding, Trading, and Feasting: The Political Economy of Philippine Chiefdoms.* Quezon City, Philippines: Ateneo de Manila University Press, 2000.

Stopford, Martin. *Maritime Economics.* 3rd ed. New York: Taylor & Francis, 2009.

Van Gelder, Maartje. *Trading Places: The Netherlandish Merchants in Early Modern Venice.* Boston: Brill, 2009.

Markets and Marketing

The methods and strategies of food marketers determine how companies develop interest in new or obscure products and regenerate enthusiasm for flagging commodities. To create a reciprocal exchange—satisfaction in consumers and profits for companies—marketing begins with research into the reception of diversity in traditional cuisine, such as Crisco to Southern cooks, instant coffee to the French, and Kentucky Fried Chicken in the seafood-rich diet of Bermudans. Once a company targets a prospect, the details of how to package, transport, and present an unfamiliar foodstuff require additional analysis, such as how to distribute Greek yogurt in Bali and whether to post billboards to advertise feta cheese in South Africa. Individual obstacles require understanding of social patterns, as in explaining the convenience of a self-service cafeteria or the etiquette of eating blood oranges, popcorn, shish kebab, sushi, and tacos.

Historically, the media familiarized shoppers with new products, connecting canned milk, cod liver oil, and iceberg lettuce with nutritional advances and Quaker Instant Oats with the grandfatherly figure of the Quaker on the box. In 1693, John Dunton's *The Ladies' Mercury* offered Englishwomen a site that answered questions about foods with a personalized reply. The Q&A set a standard still popular in women's magazines and newspapers.

In 1843, Eliza Leslie of Philadelphia, the food maven of *Miss Leslie's Magazine,* applied the individual approach to consumer queries. Also in Philadelphia, writer Finley Acker's *Table Talk* magazine offered consumer advice in 1886 by championing packaged biscuits and brand names—Baker's Cocoa, Pettijohn's Breakfast Food, and Purity Dried Fruit. Author Sarah Tyson Rorer contributed food articles to *Table Talk* that endorsed Fleischmann's yeast cakes and Niagara corn starch, a tasteless thickening agent for gravy.

After 1912, American home economist Christine Frederick, a champion of female consumerism, established the League of Advertising Women to identify and squelch false advertising claims, especially those directed at new mothers by Heinz, Nestlé, and von Liebig. Frederick wrote a column for *Ladies' Home Journal* that introduced consumers to processed foods, notably Fry's Premium Cocoa, a source of quick energy and warmth for Canadians. In 1913, the British Commercial Gas Association hired Maud Brereton to promote gas as a cooking fuel through store demonstrations and free recipe pamphlets. Because women tended to trust female advertisers, marketing became a lucrative field for female writers.

In 1930, full-page ads in *Good Housekeeping* presented photos of actual salesmen and customer testimony about worthy products, notably Birds Eye frozen fish fillets and home canning in glass jars processed in a pressure cooker. Detailed journal recipes initiated the success of rotisserie chicken and Toll House chocolate chip cookies. Radio broadcasts glorified processed foods as necessities for the busy housewife, for example, canned pineapple rings for fruit salads, condensed soups as bases for meat and vegetable combinations, peanut butter as a quick and easy sandwich filler for bag lunches, and Reddi-wip aerosol whipped cream.

Exemplary figures in food marketing indicated the need for innovation and psychological assessment of consumers, such as American engineer Lillian Gilbreth's 1945 studies of pantry needs for disabled and elderly cooks. Gilbreth focused on ingredients for such ordinary meals as meat loaf with mashed potatoes and green salad and chocolate pudding for dessert. In 1948, J.I. Rodale's *Prevention* magazine issued testimonials for the organic diet, which he elevated to a food cult. Euell Gibbons's *Stalking the Wild Asparagus* (1962), which advocated foraging for greens and herbs, preceded his 1974 commercials for Grape-Nuts, a natural food cereal. In 1963, Julia Child showcased French utensils and Mediterranean foodstuffs

on *The French Chef,* a televised cooking demonstration on Boston's WGBH that survived in syndication into 2010.

Television advertising, especially programs geared to children, came under the scrutiny of the Center for Science in the Public Interest (CSPI). In 1971, the nonprofit organization examined televised marketing of controlled substances, shoddy nutrition, and unhealthful foods. To promote sensible diet and physical activity, advisers analyzed the impact of films, magazines, sporting events, television advertising, and toy and video games on the rising obesity rate among American children. Because half of the 65 television ads that children see daily relate to food, the CSPI warned of misleading persuasive techniques for the K–3 range. The most insidious marketing for caffeinated drinks, low-nutrition beverages, salty snacks, and sweetened cereals lured children with coupons, games, toys, and trading cards, incentives that avoided the issue of quality choices for growing bodies. More troubling to analysts, the hyping of empty calories on school buses and in textbooks and in-school television promoted false logic about the elements of wholesome meals.

In 1989, the World Fair Trade Organization promoted food production and unbiased trading conditions in 70 developing nations in Africa, Asia, and Latin America by giving isolated growers access to the global market. The effort boosted sales of bananas, chocolate, coffee, honey, sugar, tea, and wine planted, harvested, or produced by poor farmers and workers. In 2010, according to *The New York Times,* sales of fair-trade foods reached $1.3 billion in the United States, or 22.4 percent of global food sales. Seventy percent of fair-trade marketing involves coffee and coffee products.

Electronic advancement after the 1980s skewed food-marketing maneuvers from billboards and print copy toward the home computer. *Better Homes and Gardens* expanded marketing ploys with *The Healthy Cooking CD Cookbook* (2000) on CD-ROM. Early-twenty-first-century food marketing favors pop-up ads that demand the attention of Internet users, particularly those looking for diet pills or skimming recipes. In November 2011, the Australian Food and Grocery Council pushed for a ban on cartoons, e-mail, Internet sites, and pay television ads that promote junk food.

See also: Adulterated Food; African Food Trade; Agribusiness; Fast Food; Mail-Order Food; Maritime Trade Routes; Marshall, Agnes; McDonald's; Packaging; Street Food; Supermarkets; Trading Vessels; World Trade.

Further Reading

McGinnis, J. Michael, Jennifer Appleton Gootman, and Vivica I. Kraak, eds. *Food Marketing to Children and Youth: Threat or Opportunity?* Washington, DC: National Academies Press, 2006.

Wright, Simon, and Diane McCrea, eds. *The Handbook of Organic and Fair Trade Food Marketing.* Ames, IA: Blackwell, 2007.

Marshall, Agnes (1855–1905)

An eclectic British caterer and author, Agnes Bertha Smith Marshall gained fame as an authority on elegant European cookery and fancy ices and as a diversified cooking entrepreneur.

Marshall was born at Walthamstow, Essex, on August 24, 1855. Educated in the Cordon Bleu style in haute cuisine, she expressed contempt for unsanitary railroad cafés, street snacks, and canned food. To upgrade common tables, she introduced the English to the ornate glories of French chef Auguste Escoffier that adorned the tables of assemblies and receptions. To heighten sensual pleasure, she devised savory pairings—chestnut with citron, tangerine with rum, and banana with citrus fruits.

As an entrepreneur, Marshall prepared women for cooking in aristocratic kitchens and enabled middle-class wives to build reputations for fine cooking. She marketed cast-iron kitchenware, cutlery, and utensils, such as the caramel cutter, chafing dish, duck crusher, forcing bag, ice breaker, raisin seeder, and saccharometer (for testing the degree of sweetness). On Regent Street in London, she demonstrated culinary techniques for up to 600 including the shaping of chicken, egg, ham, onion, and tongue into breakfast cutlets and the larding of an Easter rabbit with bacon. Her instant freezing of ice cream at the table with liquid nitrogen astonished diners.

Among the foodstuffs that Marshall sold at her residential showroom, baking powder, curry, flavorings, food dye and fragrances, fruit liqueurs, leaf gelatin, and vinegars established her expertise in quality goods. She distributed coralline pepper, refined sugar, and Luxette, her brand of fish canapé spread for hors d'oeuvres and picnics. Her 1,000 tin molds turned out frozen bombes (frozen semi-spherical desserts), sorbets, and soufflés in geometric shapes and imitations of fish and swans, flowers and leaves, fruit, grain shocks, horseshoes, nuts, shells, and vegetables, such as artichokes, asparagus, and cauliflower.

Marshall turned food preparation into a successful conglomerate. From operating a domestic staffing registry, she extended her investment to a culinary institute, the Mortimer Street School of Cookery in London, which earned £880 from her first 40 pupils. From 10:30 A.M. to 4 P.M., she taught classes to mold such dishes as a beef and mushroom mélange for serving with piped mashed potatoes. She employed a military colonel retired from a posting in India to demonstrate curry making. Marshall garnished her masterworks with flowers made from colored gels, egg, and foie gras. Her students traveled to special events to perform and won a silver medal at the 1885 exposition in Antwerp, Belgium, for their display. In addition, she stocked a warehouse with domestic ice caves, freezers, refrigerators, and jelly bags, all her own inventions. Her lace paper doilies and ice cups simplified serving of and cleaning dishes for such specialties as custards and *crème panachée,* her version of a three-layered Neapolitan ice cream cake.

Also in 1885, Marshall published *Ices Plain and Fancy: The Book of Ices,* followed in 1894 by *Fancy Ices,* both illustrated with line drawings and recipes. In addition, she edited a weekly magazine, *The Table* (1886–1905), which published new recipes and menus and offered prize competitions to caterers, hoteliers, and housewives in Britain, the colonies, and the United States. She also shaped ground almonds into an ice cream cone, which she called "cornet à la crème." Her editorials encouraged the training and social respect of kitchen staff. Her *Mrs. A.B. Marshall's Cookery Book* (1888) became a best seller.

The Martha Stewart of her day, Agnes Marshall was a forerunner of the modern television chef and domestic entrepreneur. Before her death at Brighton on July 29, 1905, following a fall from a horse, she took her table ideas on tour to the United States. For her contribution to chilled desserts, she earned the sobriquet "Queen of Cream."

See also: Escoffier, Georges Auguste; Ice Cream.

Further Reading

Clendenning, Anne. *Demons of Domesticity: Women and the English Gas Industry, 1889–1939.* Burlington, VT: Ashgate, 2004.

Katz, Solomon H., and William Woys Weaver, eds. *Encyclopedia of Food and Culture.* New York: Charles Scribner's Sons, 2003.

Quinzio, Jeri. *Of Sugar and Snow: A History of Ice Cream Making.* Berkeley: University of California Press, 2009.

Trubek, Amy B. *Haute Cuisine: How the French Invented the Culinary Profession.* Philadelphia: University of Pennsylvania Press, 2000.

McDonald's

An American food service phenomenon, McDonald's has impacted eating styles, family relationships, and foreign impressions of U.S. capitalism. In 1940, brothers Maurice James and Richard James McDonald opened the anchor restaurant in San Bernardino, California. After launching a franchising effort in 1953, they allied with Ray Kroc, a milkshake machine seller from Chicago. Eight years later, Kroc bought out the brothers and began building the McDonald's empire into a world presence. He intended to overcome the kickback and corruption of the 1950s that he had observed firsthand at Tastee Freez.

A factory system of ingredient purchase and storage, preparation, portion size, and cooking times preceded the standardizing of customer service to a wait of less than five minutes for food and drink. In addition to family-oriented presentation, Kroc made available water fountains and clean restrooms at all franchise locations. Beginning with burgers, fries, and cola, the menu expanded to chicken, breakfast items, desserts, salads, wraps, and fruit smoothies.

Kroc invested in television advertisement and roadside recognition. Paired golden arches implanted along highways and city streets the *M* of McDonald's against a cheerful red rectangle. The public relations gimmicks of on-site playgrounds, toys in Happy Meals, and a company clown, Ronald McDonald, entertained children at birthday parties and introduced the concept of the Ronald McDonald House, a charity directed at the health and treatment of sick children worldwide.

After 1990, when the company announced a switch from frying french fries in beef fat to all-vegetable oil, religious ascetics and other vegetarians patronized the restaurants to eat what they thought were fries untainted by animal fats. When editors of *India West* newspaper revealed McDonald's duplicity in April 2001, Hindus raged at misrepresentation that violated the ethics of vegetarians. On May 1, 2001, Hindu attorney Harish Bharti and others in Lynnwood and Seattle, Washington, filed a class-action suit against the McDonald's fast-food chain in the state as well as in California and British Columbia. Joined by Jewish, Muslim, and Sikh groups, Bharti charged false advertisement that desecrated holy norms.

In India, protesters smashed McDonald's restaurant windows; Hindu politicians demanded that the government oust the chain. Company official Walt Riker denied the charge of fraud and declared that french fries sold in India and Fiji were all vegetable. He added that the franchise never publicized itself as a vegetarian restaurant. The company requited the claims in 2005 with checks ranging from $50,000 to $1.4 million.

Late-twentieth-century furor targeted the iconic fast-food chain with a multitude of ethical violations. Protesters pictured the corporation as a promoter of child obesity and underage labor and a torturer of animals. Greenpeace claimed that the conglomerate denuded world rain forests and tribal lands for growing soybeans and creating pastures for raising beef cattle. As franchises opened in 119 countries, grassroots efforts blamed American fast food for destabilizing family mealtime and for spreading litter from milkshake cups and burger wrappers.

The combined assault of Erich Schlosser's *Fast Food Nation: The Dark Side of the All-American Meal* (2001), Morgan Spurlock's *Super Size Me* (2004), and Scott Ingram's *Want Fries with That? Obesity and the Supersizing of America* (2005) slowed corporate growth. Company officials fought back by balancing fast foods with vegetarian meals, abandoning polystyrene clamshell boxes, recycling cooking oil for diesel engines, promoting bioplastics, pumping syrup directly into underground cola tanks, and building new locations from recycled fiberboard and glass.

See also: Fast Food; Slow Food; Vegetarianism.

Further Reading

Gilbert, Sara. *The Story of McDonald's.* Mankato, MN: Creative Education, 2009.

Kinchloe, Joe L. *The Sign of the Burger: McDonald's and the Culture of Power.* Philadelphia: Temple University Press, 2002.

Love, John F. *McDonald's: Behind the Arches.* Wake Forest, NC: Paw Prints, 2008.

Schlosser Eric. *Fast Food Nation: The Dark Side of the All-American Meal.* Boston: Houghton Mifflin, 2001.

Médici, Catherine de' (1519–1589)

As a royal bride, Catherine de' Médici introduced Tuscan cuisine to the French in the sixteenth century.

The daughter of Lorenzo II de' Médici, Duke of Urbino, and Madeleine de La Tour d'Auvergne and the niece of Pope Leo X and Pope Clement VII, she was born in Florence, the cultural core of Renaissance Italy and the center of Médici family influence. She lost both parents in infancy and passed to the care of aunts and nuns. Training at the papal court sparked her worldliness and sophisticated manners.

After her engagement to King Henry II of France at age 14, she traveled to her new home on September 2, 1533, with a staff of Florentine *capi cuochi* (head chefs), confectioners, cupbearers, distillers, gardeners, pastry cooks, and waiters. An apocryphal story asserts that Canon Pietro Valeriano tucked into the princess's luggage a packet of *fagioli* (beans), the foundation of the Provençal cassoulet.

At Marseilles on October 28, 1533, Catherine's wedding banquet included two pasta entrées. The first, a savory version, was topped with cheese and meat drippings. The second took the form of a dessert pasta flavored with butter, cinnamon, honey, saffron, and sugar. Henry treated her to grand posthunt feasts, for which chefs gilded and roasted whole beasts. Teams of waiters carried the kill to the head table on oversized platters.

Because Catherine's family were renowned Italian financiers who grew rich on trade in cloves, ginger, nutmeg, pepper, saffron, and salt, the French mocked her as "the grocer's daughter." Soon, however, they reevaluated her broad-mindedness about serious dining and health, such as the grilling of songbirds and the use of tobacco powder to cure headache.

After her coronation on June 10, 1549, at the Royal Abbey of Saint Denis, the city of Paris hosted a dinner in Catherine's honor featuring a floor covering of strewn herbs and service of four vegetables—artichokes, asparagus, broad beans, and peas—to accompany 24 bird and game entrées, an elitist snub of butcher's cuts. The meats included 132 boiled chickens, 99 pigeons and turtledoves, 90 spring chickens, 66 turkeys, 33 ducks and egrets, 33 goslings and herons, 33 hares and pheasants, 30 capons and kids, 30 peacocks, 21 swans, 13 geese and partridges, nine cranes, and three bustards.

Dining with Catherine

As queen, Catherine concealed her squat shape with corsets, high-heeled shoes, and hoop skirts. She superintended the provisioning and arming of the military as well as plans for the royal *villeggiatura,* the withdrawal of the royal family to rural estates to partake of more rustic fare. As a wife and mother of ten, she broke the pattern of court excess with sojourns in the countryside for fresh vegetables. In the style of her great-grandfather, Lorenzo the Magnificent, she grew and ate fruits and vegetables, planted new crops, and made cheese. She lavished attention on her most prominent sons, Francis II, Charles IX, and Henry III, engineered their marriages, and bolstered their reigns. Two of her daughters, Elizabeth and Margaret, became queens.

Widowhood at age 40, afforded Catherine power and luxury she had never before controlled and increased her impact on haute cuisine. She evicted the royal mistress, Diane de Poitiers, from Chenonceau Castle on the Loire and began cultivating a splendid vegetable garden. During religious turmoil between Catholics and Huguenots in the 1570s, she elevated the Valois dynasty by patronizing the arts. At the Royal Palace at Fontainebleau, her dedication to humanistic advancement updated northern European cuisine and rid dining of its déclassé medievalism. Her cooks perfumed *choux* pastry, eclairs, gelati, and macaroons. At state fêtes, she introduced the carved goblet, Murano glassware, and the table fork to place settings of knives and spoons. The refined diner began carrying a personal fork along to soirees as a symbol of elegance and savoir faire.

Catherine's arrangement of dishes into courses pioneered an appreciation of foods as members of gustatory groupings. In place of mundane soup and stew, her staff arrayed continental specialties—aspic, candied vegetables, milk-fed veal and liver, pasta, scaloppine—along with ices and ice cream, sherbet, and zabaglione for dessert. For the nuptial dinner of Charles IX and Elizabeth of Austria in 1570, Catherine's staff served two barrels of oysters, 1,000 pairs of frog legs, 400 herring, 200 crayfish, 68 carp, 50 pounds of whale meat, 28 salmon, 18 brill, and ten turbot, as well as platters of lobsters and mussels.

At the queen's direction, French gastronomy embraced *carabaccia* (onion soup), duck *à l'orange,* grated Parmesan cheese over gratins, guinea hens, heated hippocras (spiced wine) and the chilling of cordials and wine Roman style with ice or snow. Her name attached to artful dishes, such as steak à la Médici, a slice of beef adorned with artichoke heart, carrots and peas, tomatoes, and turnips.

Table Art

Catherine valued the look of food on its way from kitchen to table to plate. In the formal dining rooms at the Tuileries palace, she preferred elegant Limoges and Wedgwood place settings, silverware, and embroidered linens. Her entertainments paired feasting with ballets and masques. For variety, she balanced sumptuous court meals with picnics.

The French embraced artichokes, her favorite food, as the latest fad vegetable and declared it an aphrodisiac. Her menus featured asparagus, baby peas, broccoli, cardoons, cucumbers, custard, marmalade, melon seeds, mushrooms, parsley, quenelles of poultry, spinach, sweetbreads, and truffles. In 1564, morning banquets at her ornamental dairies at Fontainebleau and outside Paris at Saint-Maur symbolized respect for bucolic values, fertility, and motherhood as well as a love of French soil.

In a return to the splendor of the court of Francis I, the queen's extravagance demanded huge expenditures to support a court of 10,000. The progress from one palace to another relieved her home district of food shortages and placed new demands on other dairies, hunting grounds, orchards, and produce farms. Staffing required appointments of bread waiters and spit turners. Meat carvers introduced tournedos of beef, a new take on the cutting and arrangement of meat on a plate. When court jealousies raised questions of safety, she added a food taster to her personal staff.

Although gout, migraines, and toothache ended her late-in-life food debauchery with a limited regimen of pureed foods, her style found favor with her nephew, Henry IV. Catherine cast new light on food complements, particularly the separation of salted entrées from sweet desserts and the service of eggs Florentine over sautéed spinach and topped with mornay sauce. With the addition of broth, extracts, garlic and onion, herbs and spices, and sauces, French gastronomy reached a height in the grandeur and profusion of Louis XIV's table at Versailles. European restaurants continue to display portraits of Catherine de' Médici, the Florentine gourmand.

See also: Aphrodisiacs; Beans and Legumes; Feasting; French Diet and Cuisine; Grilling; Ice; Pan-European Diet and Cuisine; Shellfish; Symbolism, Food.

Further Reading

Courtright, Nicola. "A Garden and a Gallery at Fontainebleau: Imagery of Rule for Medici Queens." *Court Historian* 10:1 (December 2005): 55–84.

Frieda, Leonie. *Catherine de Medici: Renaissance Queen of France.* New York: Harper Perennial, 2003.

Knecht, R.J. *Catherine de' Medici.* London and New York: Longman, 1998.

Recipe: French Onion Soup

Slice five white onions paper thin. Sauté them in butter in a covered saucepan. Boil the onions in 3 cups of boiling water or beef stock for one-half hour with one bay leaf. Crumble three slices of stale French bread into the mixture. Top with 1/2 cup of grated Gruyère, 1 tablespoon of capers, one chopped sprig of thyme, sea salt, pepper, and a sprinkle of red wine vinegar.

Medieval Diet and Cuisine

From 400 to 1400 C.E., the tastes of the Middle Ages bore historical significance as the first period cuisine reported in Arabic, British, Catalan, French, Italian, Mongolian, Polish, and Spanish sources. For information on the cultivation of plants, honey, and pond fish for the table, farmers turned to the Latin masters—Cato, Columella, Crescentius, Palladius, Varro, and Virgil—whose opinions held sway over agriculture, apiculture, and pisciculture during the first millennium C.E.

In illumination and text, scrolls revealed the stirring of barley and wheat into coarse gruel, an inelegant staple perpetuated from ancient Rome into the Dark Ages. Additional pictorial proof of lively food chores derives from tapestry, which captures the daily activities of communal ovens, farmer's markets, kitchens, and pantries. Because Catholic monks from Egypt to Ireland dominated period scriptoria and scholarship, their libraries contained up-to-date evidence of kitchen uses of such daily fare as cabbage and fava beans and chamomile and sage for remedies and wellness.

Religion and Medieval Customs

Eastern Orthodox and Roman Catholic prelates condemned a meat- and wine-rich diet for its association with social prominence and wealth. They advocated sacred self-control at table. After concurrence by St. Jerome and St. John Chrysostom in the fourth century C.E., the monastic hierarchy vilified alcohol and red meat as sins of the flesh. Around 515, St. Benedict the Great of Nursia, Italy, the fount of Christian hospitality, denounced food extremes that violated vows of poverty and that encouraged drunkenness, gambling, and licentious behavior.

On meatless days, the Benedictines followed a regimen of eggs, frogs, smelts, snails, and unborn rabbits, which were technically considered undeveloped meat. Communion bread took on a mystic power for medieval Italian bakers, who marked loaves with religious symbols—crosses, stars, pentecostal flames—and the Chi-Rho, the first Greek letters of "Christos" (the anointed one). Bread baked on Good Friday remained on the kitchen shelf as a medicine to be grated into water as a panada, a thickened remedy for enteritis.

Christian restraints on food during the 40 days each of Advent, Lent, Epiphany, and Pentecost inspired clever ways of circumventing ecclesiastical law forbidding the consumption of butter, cheese, fat, meat, and milk. On meatless days, Irish children went house to house begging for the eggs that fasting families had not eaten. Cooks made food substitutions, such as fish roe baked in eggshells or in *soumada* (almond milk) to emulate a meat dish. The daring cook extended the definition of *seafood* to include coastal geese and puffins.

Medieval wall art features Cistercian monks stoking the hearth, an embodiment of the Benedictine rule re-

A medieval lord dines on the bounty of his estate, prepared and served by a large staff. In feudal Europe, the laboring classes produced their own carbohydrate-rich foods and ate few of the meats and delicacies enjoyed by the wealthy. *(North Wind Picture Archives/Associated Press)*

quiring daily cookery and domestic chores that welcomed wayfarers to warmth and a hearty meal. For the suppression of gluttony and sexual debauchery, religious houses relied on monk's pepper (*Vitex agnus castus*), a gastronomic antidote to natural reproductive urges.

For the sick and weary, monasteries stocked kitchen restoratives derived from curative herbs and vegetables grown in the physic garden. In the late 500s at Lake Zurich, Switzerland, evangelist St. Gall raised 16 beds of cabbage, chard, garlic, leeks, lettuce, onions, parsnips, radishes, shallots, and watercress for the daily pottage, a vegetable ragout. Although low in fat and high in fiber, such medieval peasant fare lacked protein as well as vitamins A, C, and D.

Exchange and Experimentation

The elegant bounty of Persian cuisine influenced cookery in India and Turkey and spread flavored pilaus to the royal courts of medieval Europe. After William the Conqueror seized Saxon England for Normandy in fall 1066, the average yeoman gained a broader view of sophisticated cuisine. Because of the subsequent Crusades in the Holy Lands, the Middle Ages experienced the swap of advanced agriculture and produce, including Lombardy chestnuts, Maltese figs, and Syrian raisins and sugarcane.

Among German grain dealers in Lübeck in 1159, formation of the Hanseatic League by Henry the Lion of Saxony stabilized prices by evening out food gluts of salt perch and tuna and compensating for crop failures of rye and wheat. Harbor towns, which dominated food importation, developed reputations for mealtime exoticism—for example, the cinnamon, cloves, ginger, nutmeg, pepper, and saffron that Portuguese traders introduced in Lisbon and Porto.

Under the dominance of European Catholicism, Corsican, Iberian, Italian, and Provençal vineyards aged wine for the Eucharist. For good reason, medieval brewers fermented robust ales by building their vats next to bakeries. By reusing starter from successful batches, they preserved zesty beer with flavorful yeast that initiated microorganisms in the next batch. Both ale and wine supported a healthy trade among nations.

Food by Social Rank

In a broadly stratified society, workers packed a simple plowman's lunch of bread with cheese, a pickled vegetable, and perhaps a boiled egg. Increasing respect for community baking elevated the craft to municipal importance. The loss of a baker to accident or epidemic devastated villagers until a replacement trained for the job. The laboring classes raised pond fish and poultry and sold fresh plaice (flatfish) and eggs to the moneyed class. The rich lengthened the shelf life of their *garde mangers* (pantries) by excavating them underground. For home dining, commoners bartered daily for affordable supplies and consumed little produce from livestock. They ate legumes and rye crusts from wood bowls and filled their horn cups with water, cider, mead, or perry (fermented pear juice).

The affluent bourgeois supped on manchet (soft wheat loaves), pork, eel and lark pies, and the pheasants and venison field-dressed by hunters. From trained vines and espaliered fruit and nut trees along the sun-warmed stone walls of manses and abbeys, the gardeners of dukes and bishops ensured quality almonds, grapes, and peaches for baking tarts and for sweetening stuffed goose and other complex dishes. As the focus of banquets, the carver turned into an art the slicing of meat into "gobbets" (bite-sized pieces). To avoid criticism by the Roman Catholic Church for such luxury foods as whole stuffed carp and suckling pig, the wealthy allowed the poor to carry off from late dinners and feasts the leftover sops and trenchers of bread, the flat surfaces that doubled as plates.

In a class-oriented hierarchy, the intermarriage of noble families introduced acculturation via international feasts, such as the three-day nuptial reception on May 12, 1192, for Richard I, the Lionheart, of England and Berengaria of Navarre. Hosts honored guests at Limassol, Cyprus, with platters of spiced hash meat, painted marzipan, sugared fruits, and taro, an unusual menu for an English wedding feast.

Discriminating Tastes

Influenced by the Greek physician Galen's studies of the four body humors to cookery around 180 C.E., the medieval menu advanced nutrition and eating for health and longevity. The classic lore of curatives passed orally from one apothecary to another during apprenticeship, conveying such advice as the eating of pure white sugar to benefit the bladder, blood, chest, and kidneys. Additional gastronomic aid came from a balance of sweet with sour, as in vinegary meat sauces made from dates and currants.

Mediterranean savories teased the palate of late medieval gourmands. Based on Syrian cuisine, the contrast of sour with sweet required knowledge of vinegar and verjuice, an acidic flavoring pressed from unripe grapes or crab apples. Street vendors offered ready-to-eat condiments, including green sauce and garam masala, a preblended Indian spice. Monastic cooks studied Apicius, the Roman cookbook author, for advice on holiday specialties and the ladling of wassail (mulled cider) at Yule gatherings.

The issuance of nutritive standards by al-Majusi of Persia around 980, German abbess Hildegard of Bingen in 1152, and German philosopher Albertus Magnus in 1259 identified foods such as anise comfits (candy), wild bird brains, and turmeric that sustained strength and cured debility. Mustard helped quell the overwhelming brine of meat preserved in vinegar and salt and enlivened the flavor of eels in gelatine. Gardening research offered solutions to failing appetite during rehabilitation and to infirmary dietetics for surgical patients and amputees, particularly soldiers recuperating from the Crusades. In Asia, Chinese herbalism expanded in the 1200s C.E. with Chia Ming's guidebook on dining well to stay healthy. Among the foods suspected of threatening health, authors listed cucumbers, melons, pumpkins, and raw pears, all considered difficult to digest.

A Stimulating Diet

After years of leaving home for manual toil unfed, workers began taking fresh-air snacks of barley beer and oatcakes for breakfast, elevating the day's intake from two meals to three. Chinese plowmen stopped work at midmorning for a meager repast of an onion bulb or garlic clove wrapped in unleavened flatbread. For Scandinavian artisans, meals of salt-fermented gravlax (buried salmon) presented a savory blend of dill and sugar in thin slices served on *flatbrød* (crackers) with capers and lemon. Crafters halted daily toil for "nuncheons," work breaks of cheese or mutton pasties (turnovers), which they could eat without utensils.

In contrast to foods readily available to commoners, upscale cookbooks revealed the profusion of dishes served to royalty and aristocrats. The recipes mentioned in Huou's three-volume 1330 survey of table delights enjoyed by Mongolian Emperor Kublai Khan indicated tastes for body-strengthening meats and produce delivered by caravan and junk to China's imperial chef.

In addition to titillating new flavors and aromas—asafetida, candied hazelnuts, pomegranates, and quince—food specialists throughout the late Middle Ages searched for the magic curative and libido enhancer, such as antler soup, composed of chopped stag antlers, gingerbread, honey, and wine. Moroccan traveler Ibn Battuta preferred coconuts as a stimulant to romance. Marco Polo reported that Chinese males courted women with bowls of fragrant Mandarin duck soup.

By the mid 1300s, as the liberality of the coming Renaissance defeated ignorance and superstition, diners achieved some choice in their food intake. At Krakow, Casimir II of Poland initiated urbanism by inviting German Jews to migrate east from the Rhineland, bringing with them ethnic cookery and foodways. For variety, an icehouse provided the table with fish roe and seafood as well as fresh dairy products.

Period cooks added the chilling of steamed vegetables to lengthy rotisserie cooking and basting of meats at the hearth, a culinary technique described in detail in *Forme of Cury (Forms of Cookery,* ca. 1390), compiled by the chef of Richard II. The salting of fish extended the shelf life of coastal goods to the provisioning of armies, press gangs, and ships' galleys. The era's sausage recipes preserved for winter the meat from livestock and equipped communities for famine during military siege. The increased use of ground almonds and almond milk and the importation of rice contributed a basis for the subtle tarts and sickroom capon blancmanges of the Renaissance.

See also: Charlemagne; Condiments; Crusaders' Diet and Cuisine; Feasting; Grilling; Huou; Maritime Trade Routes; Nuts and Seeds; Polo, Marco; Salad and Salad Bars; Taillevent; Trade Routes; Vegetarianism; Vinegar; Yeast.

Further Reading

Adamson, Melitta Weiss, ed. *Regional Cuisines of Medieval Europe: A Book of Essays.* New York: Routledge, 2002.

Newman, Paul B. *Daily Life in the Middle Ages.* Jefferson, NC: McFarland, 2001.

Scully, D. Eleanor, and Terence Scully. *Early French Cookery: Sources, History, Original Recipes, and Modern Adaptations.* Ann Arbor: University of Michigan Press, 2002.

Scully, Terence. *The Art of Cookery in the Middle Ages.* Rochester, NY: Woodbridge, 2005.

Mediterranean Diet and Cuisine

A model of healthful food choices and lifestyle, the Mediterranean diet and cuisine yields measurable improvements to wellness and longevity. From Roman times, families in Crete, Greece, Italy, the Levant, and Magna Graecia (Sicily and southern Italy) burned charcoal in braziers, portable burners that also cooked spitted salmon, sardines, and herbed game and lamb. Diners dressed their salads with olive oil and lemon juice and consumed the entrée along with bread and honey, whole grains, legumes and vegetables, almonds and walnuts, and watered table wine.

Central to daily consumption, nuts and fruit—apricots, berries, dates, grapes, melons, olives, oranges, peaches, pears—added variety and roughage to bolster health. For Rome's legionaries, a light ration of watered wine accompanied heavy consumption of bread and gruel made from barley, oats, spelt, and wheat. More complex recipes introduced wheat flatbread, barley cakes, and combinations of chickpeas and lentils, elements still favored in twenty-first-century Italian diet and cuisine.

Following World War II, American physiologist Ancel Benjamin Keys, the developer of K-rations for the U.S. military, researched cholesterol and coronary disease. From 1958 to 1964, he monitored results of the Seven Countries Study among 12,000 men in Finland, Greece, Holland, Italy, Japan, the United States, and Yugoslavia. The results indicated that Greeks and Italians promoted wellness by eating relatively large quantities of fresh produce and olive oil, while Americans and Finns courted heart disease, obesity, and stroke by smoking and eating butter, lard, and meat. The differences were reflected in heart attack rates among males in the 1960s: Greeks averaged 33 per 100,000, compared with 189—5.7 times as many—for U.S. men. Based on his findings, Keys campaigned for a reduction of saturated fat in the American intake by advocating the Mediterranean diet. With his wife, biochemist Margaret Haney Keys, he compiled *How to Eat Well and Stay Well the Mediterranean Way* (1975), a commentary on degenerative ills. The text identifies sources of omega-3 fatty acids, antioxidants, and fiber, the indigestible ingredients that promote thorough metabolism and beneficial flora in the gut. The text outlined shopping and cookery for educated families seeking longer untroubled lives.

A widely publicized examination of French eating habits in 1991 pointed to the health benefits deriving from the consumption of red wine, including lower incidence of cardiac disease than in countries that consume less animal fat—the French Paradox. The Oldways Preservation Trust, convened by the Harvard School of Public Health and the World Health Organization in January 1993, championed the Mediterranean ideal of wholesome, satisfying fresh foods consumed in pleasurable company. In 1995, the Association for the Advancement of the Mediterranean Diet dispatched a diet bus to educate children in Catalonia and Valencia on the worth of regional eating styles.

Late in the 1990s, medical research linked antioxidants in the Mediterranean diet with positive physiological effects, including a reduction in diabetes, melanoma (skin cancer), and obesity. The traditional Mediterranean regimen stressed moderate consumption of cheese, eggs, and yogurt and daily intake of olive oil, a less inhibitive fat to the cardiovascular system than butter or lard. In a followup to the Keys fieldwork, nutritionist Walter Willett, on staff with Harvard University's School of Public Health, and Patrick J. Skerritt recommended restructuring the American diet in *Eat, Drink and Be Healthy: The Harvard Medical School Guide to Healthy Eating* (2001, 2005), which crusaded for evidence-based advice and weight control. Willett and Skerritt proposed that other heritage diets contain heart-healthy food combinations, such as Japanese and Latin American gastronomy.

Additional benefits from the Mediterranean model emerged from further research. Related suggestions ranged from regular exercise and less between-meal snacking on processed foods to slower eating of small portions of healthful foods, multi-course meals, and higher water intake, resulting in improved digestion and metabolism. Locavores and supporters of farmer's markets acclaimed abundant seasonal fruit and vegetables. Vegetarians approved Greek yogurt and the standard *macedoine de fruit* (mixed fruit) offered at the end of the meal rather than sugary desserts.

Subsequent kudos for the Mediterranean diet from the *American Journal of Epidemiology* and the Mayo Clinic in 2008 and 2009 announced reduced risk for Alzheimer's disease, breast cancer, and Parkinson's disease, in part owing to the lower intake of animal protein. Additional studies have linked the diet with protection from arthritis, asthma, autoimmune disease, gum disease, and hyperglycemia. In 2010, the United Nations Educational, Scientific and Cultural Organization (UNESCO) honored the Mediterranean dietary pattern as an integral element of Cretan, Greek, and southern Italian heritage.

See also: Egyptian Diet and Cuisine, Ancient; Greek Diet and Cuisine, Ancient; Israeli Diet and Cuisine; Italian Diet and Cuisine; Maritime Trade Routes; Olives and Olive Oil; Pan-European Diet and Cuisine; Pasta; Roman Diet and Cuisine, Ancient; Theophrastus; Trade Routes; Trading Vessels.

Further Reading

Cloutier, Marissa, and Eve Adamson. *The Mediterranean Diet.* New York: Avon, 2004.

Hoffman, Richard, and Mariette Gerber. *The Mediterranean Diet: Health and Science.* Ames, IA: Wiley-Blackwell, 2012.

Mariani, John F. *How Italian Food Conquered the World.* Foreword by Lidia Bastianich. New York: Palgrave Macmillan, 2011.

Matalas, Antonia-Leda. *The Mediterranean Diet: Constituents and Health Promotion.* Boca Raton, FL: CRC, 2000.

Mexican Diet and Cuisine

Mexican gastronomy exhibits a hybridization of ancient Mayan and medieval Aztec diet with Renaissance Spanish delicacies.

In pre-Columbian Mexico, after 7000 B.C.E., Mayan tastes preceded Aztec culinary developments with a corn-centric diet in the form of corn on the cob, dumplings, griddle cakes, and popcorn. Women prepared kernels by macerating them with stone rollers and mixing the results into a multipurpose paste. In addition to corn in bread and gruel, Mayans drank corn in *atole* (a hot beverage) and posole, a liquid gruel sweetened with honey. Pit roasting and barbecuing readied for the table deer, iguana, peccary, and turkey as well as armadillo, manatee, monkey, and tapir. Additional wild stocks of agave, fish, manioc, papaya, plums, prickly pear, *ramón* (breadnut) seeds, turtles, and yucca varied meals of garden produce.

Aztec Tradition

In central Mexico from the sixth century C.E., the Aztec of Tenochtitlán served indigenous species—algae, frogs and newts, tacos wrapped around live crickets, and roasted caiman or turkey as a specialty. Intercropping on *chinampas* (floating gardens) boosted corn yields with companion plantings of beans, a nitrogen fixer. Cultivation of wild herbs suppressed invasive insects and provided piquant flavorings for corn and bean dishes. Traditional kitchen work involved women in the daily five-hour processes of grinding of corn on a mano and metate (grinding stones), the toasting of corn cakes on *comals,* and the cooking of stews in a clay *olla.*

Upon the arrival of Hernán de Cortés, the conqueror of Aztecan Mexico, on November 8, 1519, the Spanish snubbed Aztec staples—amaranth greens, chia seeds, custard apples, ground seeds and insects, jicama, maguey worms, nopal leaves, and quinoa—as primitive. Witness accounts of cannibalism on native altars attested to the Spanish revulsion of native ways; however, the soldiers readily adopted avocados, beans, corn, pineapples, squash, sweet potatoes, tomatoes, and tomatillos. They also relished foaming mugs of hot chocolate, spiced with chilies and vanilla. Conquistadors took the tamale recipe (chopped meat, vegetables, and cornmeal steamed in cornhusks) home to Spain as evidence of Aztec civilization.

Ibero-Mexican Fusion

The Amerindian foods of Mexico combined well with those of the Spanish and Portuguese. When Iberians colonized the land in the 1500s, they introduced domestic cattle, goats, oxen, sheep, and swine, leading to a significant change in local diets from vegetable to animal protein. Unlike native Puerto Ricans, whose population declined from epidemics and enslavement, Mexicans remained vigorous and open to the hybridization of table fare. Surviving are the unique dishes of indigenous Mixtec, Nahua, and Zapotec speakers—stewed *espirulina* (algae), mountain lion, roasted grasshoppers and quail, and venison meatballs—but they had little significance in the post-Columbian diet. By the late 1500s, farmers were planting wheat, which developed into a lucrative export throughout Caribbean military installations.

A mother and daughter present a sampling of regional food from Michoacán state in west-central Mexico. Regional differences in climate, geography, indigenous culture, and history contribute to a rich and diverse cooking heritage across the country. *(Adalberto Rios Szalay/LatinContent/Getty Images)*

The new Mexican diet featured Spanish touches in the addition of almonds, cheese, cinnamon, citrus fruit, coffee, garlic, lettuce, nutmeg, olive oil, onions, parsley, rice, and wheat to dishes of beans, chicken, ostrich, and pork. The novelty of European fare precipitated a decline in indigenous cuisine. For the moneyed consumer, cattle herding in Sonora generated a surplus of fat, which replaced butter and olive oil in Spanish recipes for *carnitas* (roasted meats), tacos, tamales, and *tortas* (flatbread). Cane sugar gained a place in Mexican cuisine once dominated by honey and maguey sap. By the late 1500s, fruit farming balanced heavy entrées with the light touch of cherries, citrus fruit, figs, grapefruit, melons, and peaches. Nonetheless, poor Mexica clung to their traditional vegetarian diet as the only food they could afford.

Roman Catholicism imposed European foods for celebration. On Epiphany each January 6, the devout served sweet yeast bread. For All Souls' Day on November 2, remembrances of the dead included empanadas, a Span-

ish meat turnover, and tamales, a national dish. The Spanish preference for sugar over honey at Christmas called for *buñuelos* (fried pastry) topped with sugar and served with fruit punch.

In 1699, the addition of sweet wine as a part of the Eucharist justified Dominican and Jesuit viticulture. In Baja, the source of 90 percent of Mexican wine, Spanish grape species provided a basis for sangria, a fruity Spanish table beverage. The abortive Mexican Empire of Maximilian I from 1864 to 1867 introduced barley beer, which evolved into a national staple alongside mescal and *pulque,* two alcoholic drinks fermented from maguey.

Postcolonial Fare

The collapse of colonialism and the rise of commercial coffee, cotton, sorghum, and sugar plantations for export left native peons in a poorer nutritional state than they had achieved before European conquest. Social inequalities between exacerbated chronic disease and high mortality rates for newborns. Those reduced to consumption of limited calories per day shared the hardship of Indians, Kenyans, and Vietnamese.

In 1980, under the *Sistema Alimentario Mexicano* (Mexican feeding system), the Mexican government directed food surpluses toward a fairer distribution. The Otomi of the Mezquital Valley created their own solution to poor nutrition by reviving ancient reliance on native greens. The Tarahumara of Copper Canyon continued to lose 70 percent of their offspring. From those who survived, they produced a race of runners from a meatless diet rich in chia seeds and *pinole* (trail mix).

Currently, Mexican fare features fresh, unprocessed ingredients in quantity, notably raw milk cheese and ceviche, seafood marinated in lime juice. Entrées slow-roasted in banana leaves or goat and pork grilled or fried in lard come to the table with guacamole, *pico de gallo,* and salsas made with cilantro, lime, onion, peppers, tomatoes, and tomatillos. Other *moles* (sauces) combine herbs and spices—chipotle, cinnamon, cumin, *epazote,* oregano—with chocolate, nuts, seeds, and vegetables. Margaritas and other specialty drinks begin with tequila, made from the blue agave.

See also: Aztec Diet and Cuisine; Corn and Maize; Díaz, Bernal; Las Casas, Bartolomé de; Manioc; Peppers; Tex-Mex Diet and Cuisine; Tortillas.

Further Reading

Cantú, Norma Elia, ed. *Moctezuma's Table: Rolando Briseño's Mexican and Chicano Tablescapes.* College Station: Texas A&M University Press, 2010.

Janer, Zilkia. *Latino Food Culture.* Westport, CT: Greenwood, 2008.

Staller, John E., and Michael Carrasco, eds. *Pre-Columbian Foodways: Interdisciplinary Approaches to Food, Culture, and Markets in Ancient Mesoamerica.* New York: Springer, 2010.

Middens

A garbage pile, shell mound, kitchen dump, or ritual heap, a midden provides archaeologists with data on past human habitations and seasonal campsites. Items open a window on daily life and diet as well as on the harvesting of food plants and animals, such as the predominance of sea mammals to the Inuit and the Greenland Norse; the mix of land and sea mammals in the diet at Nukdo, Korea; fresh water mussels along the Nile River in Egypt; palm fruit among Nubians of ancient Sudan; and hazelnuts in Mesolithic Colonsay, Scotland. Whether nomadic or sedentary, people rid their surroundings of unwanted or offensive materials, including clay pipes, medicine containers, fishhooks, rock fragments, unusable skins and animal dung, and human feces. From their storehouses and fires come charcoal, cooking rocks, nutshells and seashells, animal bones, the remains of pests and vermin, and broken grinding tools and pot shards, all evidence of the history and development of paleo-cuisine.

The study of refuse heaps began in the early twentieth century, notably with the amateur investigation by Captain George Comer, an Irish Canadian whaler in Hudson's Bay. His two-year excavation of a Dorset culture dumpsite in Thule, Greenland, in 1916–1917 contributed to Arctic Eskimo ethnology. From subsequent studies of remnants of food preparation, specialists have determined the range of diet, nutritional deficiencies, and sophistication of cookery, preservation methods, and food storage among ancient peoples throughout the world.

Nutritional analysis of a people's limited longevity and the results of malnutrition, such as the conditions of pellagra among the grain-fed Nubians of Sudan and scurvy among early Egyptians, helps to illuminate the limitations of ancient societies and explain their eventual overthrow or demise.

See also: Beef; Coprolites; Fertile Crescent Diet and Food Trade; Fish and Fishing; Hunter-Gatherers; Royal Greenland Trade Department; Shellfish.

Further Reading

Milner, Nicky, Oliver E. Craig, and Geoffrey N. Bailey, eds. *Shell-Middens in Atlantic Europe.* Oakville, CT: Oxbow, 2007.

Midden Sites and Dietary Evidence

People	Refuse Location	Time Period	Diet
Abenaki	Damariscotta River, Maine	50 C.E.	alewife, clam, cod, deer, eider, oyster, shad, and sturgeon
Aborigines	Hunter Island, Tasmania	4600 B.C.E.	abalone, albatross, crayfish, egg, fish, limpet, lizard, muttonbird, penguin, periwinkle, rat, and seal
Andamanese	Andaman, India	58,000 B.C.E.	fish, mangrove, oysters, rat, and wild pig
Ertebolle	Logstor, Denmark	5400 B.C.E.	cod, deer, dolphin, eel, ling, pike, raspberry, seal, shark, strawberry, whale, and whitefish
Homo sapiens	Klasies River, South Africa	118,000 B.C.E.	antelope, corms, limpet, penguin, roots, seal, whelk, and winkle
Huaca Prieta	Chicama Valley, Peru	3500 B.C.E.	bean, clam, crab, cucumber, fish, mussel, pepper, sea urchin, snail, and tomato
American Indians	Camp Bowie, Texas	750 C.E.	acorn, agave, bird, bison, camas bulb, deer, lechuguilla, rabbit, sotol, turtle, violet bulb, and wild onion
Innu	Port au Choix, Labrador	2900 B.C.E.	egg, fish, grass seed, mussel, narwhal, polar bear, seal, seaweed, sedge, sorrel, and walrus
Jomon	Natsushima, Japan	9000 B.C.E.	Asian bean, bird, clam, deer, dog, duck, oyster, and salmon
Lapita	Wairau Bar, Tahiti	1500 B.C.E.	dog, eagle, eel, kuri, moa, rat, shark, skate, sunfish, and swan
Maori	Waiotahi, New Zealand	1350 C.E.	eel, fern, kumara, lily, moa, mussel, pigeon, pipi, sweet potato, and yam
Ohlone	Emeryville, California	500 C.E.	abalone, acorn, clam, cockle, duck, fish, goose, grass seed, mussel, otter, oyster, and whale
Timucua	Daytona Beach, Florida	2500 B.C.E.	clam, duck, mussel, oyster, seal, snail, tortoise, and turkey
Tlingit	Castle Hill, Alaska	3000 B.C.E.	buttersole, cod, duck, halibut, rat, rockfish, salmon, seal, sea lion, and walrus
Vedda	Pallemalala, Sri Lanka	4000 B.C.E.	buffalo, deer, hare, mollusk, monkey, mouse, tuna, and wild pig
Wathaurong	Victoria, Australia	23,000 B.C.E.	duck, fish, greens, murnong, possum, raspberry, wallaby, and yam

Mithen, Steven. *After the Ice: A Global Human History, 20,000–5,000 B.C.E.* Cambridge, MA: Harvard University Press, 2006.

Stein, Julie. *Deciphering a Shell Midden.* San Diego, CA: Academic Press, 1992.

Milling

The world's oldest food industry—dating to Paleolithic times—milling, or the separating of kernels from husks, increases the taste and digestibility of beans or grains for use in bread and porridge. Agrarian exploitation of grain began with the Nepalese and Sumerian cultivation of millet and wheat in 8000 B.C.E., the Andean sowing of quinoa near Lake Titicaca around 7000 B.C.E., and teff growing in Ethiopia from 4000 B.C.E. The grinding process advanced from the Latin American mano and metate (grinding stones), African mortar and pestle, and Egyptian saddle querns (concave grinding stones) to mills powered by dray animal, wind, water, steam, and gas and electricity.

In Babylon, Greece, India, Mycenae, the Sahel, Scandinavia, Sudan, and Turkey, the cumbersome nature of hand pounding and grinding with stones forced an end to nomadism and anchored farmers to one agrarian area, including the buckwheat- and rice-growing and milling areas of China, Indonesia, the Philippines, and Thailand. Like the Pueblo corn processing of the North American Great Basin, in the earliest era of acorn, barley, and oats refinement in England around 1050 B.C.E., hand-grinding dominated much of the homemaker's day, followed by sifting flour through hair or reed baskets.

Early Industry

In 500 B.C.E., Roman technology simplified the miller's job with slave- or animal-driven grinding of soft wheat that bakers sifted through linen. After the Roman invasion of Britain in 55 B.C.E., Britons in the Wey Valley of south-central England accepted the use of watermills as a shortcut to producing flour. As populations increased, growers sold their harvests to professional corn factors. Millers pulverized the kernels and distributed to bakeries three basic grades of flour—wholemeal (whole wheat), sifted brown, and sifted white. The highest grade produced the whitest, lightest bread, the food of the privileged. In Gaul in the 300s C.E., mechanized milling spread to Barbégal, where an aqueduct made snowmelt available year-round. Additional sites in Caesarea, Palestine; Leptis Magna, Libya; and Zama, Tunisia, applied Roman engineering to the problem of feeding growing populations. In the Christian era, monasteries operated mills, such as the tidal mill in Nendrum, Ireland, built in 619 C.E.

Medieval milling concentrated food control in the hands of the feudal squire. In the eleventh century, English, Irish, Orkney, and Shetland millers adapted grinders to water and wind power, often retaining the original building on a manor as the distribution point of food supplies to serfs and yeomen. According to *The Domesday Book* (1086), England alone supported 6,000 milling operations. East Anglians experimented with harnessing wind power in brick and stone tower structures in 1180. Even with more complex flour industries, however, milling remained a family skill, passed from father to son.

The Miller's Job

Villages such as Murcia, Spain, promoted the construction of mills to ensure a supply of bread. Millwrights specialized in designing frames and hoists suited to individual locations. The miller also relied on the skills of the blacksmith, carpenter, cooper, and machinist, all of whom kept flour and meal production in operation. Additional skill in leathercraft maintained elevator belts that lifted barrels, tubs, and three-bushel sacks to the loft. Because river locations exposed grain and flour storage to perennial threat of flash flood, dam and weir builders deflected rushes of water.

Grooved millstones crushed kernels by pressure and friction generated by gravity. Two-stage systems also threshed stalks and sorted and removed chaff from grain. Each mill offered loft space for storage in the driest location of the unheated building. Millers kept cats or hired rat catchers to rid the garner of vermin. Another threat to milling, the fine dust generated by the mechanism could explode and set fire to wooden shafts and rotors. Depending on the quality of the millstones, each grain run generated stone particles in the product. Cloth or woven metal sieves and sifting reels separated the grit and bran. Patrons could choose to keep the bran in a product, called unbolted (unsieved) meal, and to retrieve the middlings (coarse particles) for cereal or grits. The process concluded with days of drying the flour to prevent souring and to hasten whitening. Unscrupulous millers enhanced natural bleaching by adding alum, ground bones, powdered chalk, and white lead.

At community facilities, millers contracted individually with growers and ground corn or grain to the required fineness in exchange for a percentage of the flour and meal. The standard toll was 12.5 percent for corn and 16.7 percent for buckwheat, oats, rye, and wheat. In Louisiana, rice brokers determined the toll by bidding on the finished product.

Automation

In 1771, wheelwright Oliver Evans of Newport, Delaware, author of *The Young Mill-Wright & Miller's Guide* (1795) devised an automated water-powered gristmill on Red Clay Creek, where he charged 30 shillings to grind 100 bushels. Imitators of Evans's structure abandoned Dutch and German lava millstones and equipped their mills with French quartz millstones. Among Quakers, such as Amos and Mahlon Janney of Catoctin Creek, Virginia, and Isaiah Linton in Bucks County, Pennsylvania, mechanization encouraged merchant milling for profit and export at the standard rate of £196 per barrel. From 1803 to 1815, the Napoleonic Wars increased demand and doubled prices for milled goods. In Hungary, milling adapted in 1865 to a roller method, a gradual reduction of grain kernels through sequential applications of pressure. The use of rollers suited the region's hard wheat with a more labor-intensive method than those developed in France, England, and North America.

In the century between 1850 and 1950, American milling achieved a finer product by a shift of technology to metal and roller mills and by adding an air stream that blew chaff from kernels of corn, oats, soybeans, and wheat. U.S. food producers increased productivity and flour sanitation significantly, as mechanization accounted for an ever-increasing portion of milling labor—reaching 98.5 percent in 1950. Refinements enabled westerers to migrate over the frontier with flour that remained edible despite extremes of weather and open-air cookery. However, the loss of bran from the diet resulted in starchier, less elastic dough that caused intestinal fermentation, microbial growth, and flatulence as well as a decline in calcium, iron, and vitamins A and B1. Brown rice alone retained much of its lysine but lost some 80 percent of its thiamine and iron and further dropped in food value with washing before grinding. During the same period, Melbourne, Australia, acquired its first mechanized roller mill.

Post–World War I demand for rice and soy flour and meal produced a similar milling boom in Borneo, China, India, Japan, Korea, and Thailand. Simultaneously, Minneapolis, Minnesota, became the world's grain processing center, earning it the name "mill city." Until a decline in the mid-1960s, Minneapolis's flour and meal traveled by barge and rail from warehouses to Canada and the Atlantic Coast and by ship to England and Wales.

A mid-1970s backlash against carbohydrate-rich flour products informed the public of the loss of nutrition and fiber in daily bread through milling. The media issued warnings about the addition of ascorbic acid and potassium bromate to replace natural aging and of chloride and peroxide bleaches that whitened the yellow grain endosperm. Synthetic vitamins, added to rice and wheat flour since World War II, alarmed artisanal baker Andrew Whitley, spokesman for the Real Bread Campaign. Public outcry demanded wholemeal grain, which some bakeries, such as Backhaus in Germany and Wheatberry in Massachusetts, milled in-house. By validating whole-kernel milling, food processors supported global tastes for brioche, ciabatta, focaccia, naan, pita, rice cakes, and whole grain pasta.

See also: Asian Food Trade; Bread; Cereal; Charlemagne; Einkorn Wheat; Industrial Food Processing; Linnaeus, Carolus; Olives and Olive Oil.

Further Reading

Cauvain, Stanley P. *Bread Making: Improving Quality.* Boca Raton, FL: CRC, 2003.

Chakraverty, Amalendu, ed. *Handbook of Postharvest Technology: Cereals, Fruits, Vegetables, Tea, and Spices.* New York: Marcel Dekker, 2003.

Pennefeather, Shannon M. *Mill City: A Visual History of the Minneapolis Mill District.* St. Paul: Minnesota Historical Society Press, 2003.

Smith, Andrew F. *Eating History: 30 Turning Points in the Making of American Cuisine.* New York: Columbia University Press, 2009.

Monoculture

From the beginning of farming and aquaculture, monoculture encouraged clear-cutting, heavy plowing, and soil compacting for the production of a single food crop or the stocking of ponds with one fish variety. Common to Central American cacti, New England orchardry, Hungarian vineyards, Jamaican sugarcane, North American soy, and Australian wheat fields, intensive monoculture simplifies the annual pattern of cultivation and harvest within one region's range of moisture and temperature, such as Washington State apples and Israeli blood oranges.

The one-plant philosophy unifies methods of irrigation and pest control by tailoring techniques to a single seed or tuber, particularly potatoes or yams. Seedlings emerge simultaneously; seed heads mature at the same time, yielding, for instance, a mass harvest of oats or a single crop of walnuts. All maintain a uniform size. For corn growers, weeds underfoot never reach enough height to infringe on corn stalks.

Similarly, the limiting of ponds to a common fish has served fresh water East German carp and Canadian rainbow trout and the milkfish raised in the brackish waters of the Philippines. Japanese pisciculture has flourished for centuries in the breeding of eel, sea bream, salmon, and yellowtail as well as growing seaweed such as nori. The focus on a single product reduces educational demands for farm labor and the need to equip a fishery with a variety of nets and weirs.

The reduction of biotic competition for nutrients and space ensures appropriate light and root room for plants and environmental controls for fish breeding. Large-scale monoculture yields one crop for harvesting and marketing, thus concentrating labor on the ramifications of a single task, such as threshing rice from chaff or netting edible tilapia from fingerlings. Farmers suffice on one type of machinery and a single method of storage in a barn or silo.

In the 1940s, plant geneticist Norman Ernest Borlaug introduced semidwarf, thick-stemmed wheat in Chapingo, Mexico, as a means of shortening growing seasons and boosting yield. Borlaug's experiment in the tropics and semitropics reduced crop disease. By introducing shuttle breeding, he encouraged double wheat seasons at different altitudes and latitudes. Thus, plantation monoculture reduced the need for importing grain and provided Mexican farmers with an export crop.

On the downside, one-crop systems leave farmers at the mercy of nature and external forces, especially crop gluts, food fads, and wars. The liabilities of monoculture resound in serious crop failures, notably, the Irish Potato Famine of 1845–1848, a tragic period of starvation for the island's peasants. A single fungus or pest, particularly stem rust in Kenyan and Ugandan wheat fields, can destroy an entire season's crops and infest soil for years to come, as with nematodes in southeastern American tomato beds and gypsy moths in Moroccan plum trees.

The pursuit of a single crop forces the grower to rely more heavily on pesticides and fewer varieties of resistant strains, thereby raising the price of Silver Queen corn seed and Meyer lemons from China. Diners lose the diversity of heirloom Doorknob peppers and Arran potatoes. Children acclimate to predictable flavors and textures, such as McDonald's french fries, made from the Russet Burbank potato. Foods grown in set parts of the country require more fuel for trucking to distribution centers. The fresh taste of local herbs and greens gives place to the tasteless head of commercially grown iceberg lettuce.

Current thinking favors mixed cropping for introducing varied legume seeds and heirloom edibles to truck farms. Crop diversity in cucumbers and strawberries increases sustainability and avoids the depletion of soil nutrients, a common occurrence in the production of corn and cotton. Deeper-rooted plants, including eggplant and tomatillos, stabilize soil, preventing erosion, and requiring less fertilizer. More economical use of cropland benefits the poor by lowering food prices, particularly the varied yields from Japanese rice beds.

For fish growers, full use of a pond requires varieties that feed on aquatic vegetation as well as aquatic insects and zooplankton. By stocking tilapia with catfish in a planted pond, the grower makes use of bottom gleaners and top feeders. This variety achieves population and weed control and produces a higher yield of edible meat. Taiwanese growers mix flora and fauna by cultivating seaweed with crab and shrimp, thus producing three times the harvest in comparison with that of monoculture.

See also: Famine; Fish and Fishing; Honey; Local Food Movement; Plant Disease and Prevention; Potatoes.

Further Reading

James, Glyn. *Sugarcane.* Oxford, UK: Blackwell Science, 2004.
Vinton, Sherri Brooks, and Ann Clark Espuelas. *The Real Food Revival: Aisle by Aisles, Morsel by Morsel.* New York: Jeremy P. Tarcher/Penguin, 2005.
Wojtkowski, Paul Anthony. *Introduction to Agroecology: Principles and Practices.* Binghamton, NY: Food Products, 2006.

Monosodium Glutamate

A controversial food additive, monosodium glutamate (MSG), an odorless crystal resembling table salt, accentuates natural flavors. The Romans turned the taste into a food fad by fermenting fish entrails and heads into *garum,* the era's popular condiment. The Japanese achieved a similar flavor boost from a broth of *Laminaria japonica,* a seaweed that contained natural glutamate.

First isolated in 1908 by Japanese chemist Kikunae Ikeda, MSG mimicked the savor of meat, a taste called *umami* (deliciousness). Manufacturers synthesized the salt from vegetables and peelings boiled in acid and neutralized in caustic soda. The taste, first marketed in 1909 by the Ajinomoto Company, enters the human diet in breast milk. It joins bitter, salty, sour, and sweet to form a quintet of human mouth responses to palatability.

As a culinary condiment sometimes identified as hydrolyzed vegetable protein, MSG gained regard in China and Korea as an excitotoxin, a stimulant to brain neurons. The U.S. Food and Drug Administration (FDA) cleared the additive for use in 1947 after testing the production of Ac'cent, a carbohydrate fermented by bacteria or yeast. MSG currently adds zest to bacon, jerky, and sausage; barbecue, chili, spaghetti, soy, and Worcestershire sauces; beer and other beverages; bouillons and soups; canned vegetables; corn oil, salad dressing, and spreads; and such snack foods as corn, potato, and tortilla chips.

In May 1968, anecdotal evidence of the MSG complex, or "Chinese restaurant syndrome," arose among American diners. Complaints of asthma, chest tightness, flushed skin, heart palpitations, hyperactivity, migraine headache, and mouth and throat numbness or swelling were reported in extensive testing in 1995. The activation of the pancreas appeared to threaten insulin balance in diabetics. Health specialists drew ominous conclusions from the fact that Japan, the nation that consumes the most MSG, also had the world's highest rate of stomach cancer.

Because of inconclusive results, the FDA placed no ban on MSG, which appears safe in normal proportions. Food producers in Australia, New Zealand, and the United States require the identification of MSG on food labels but allow heavy saturation of fast foods with the additive. Fringe health groups continue to blame MSG for neurotoxicity that causes amyotrophic lateral sclerosis (ALS), Alzheimer's disease, autism, food addictions, Huntington's chorea, and Parkinson's disease.

See also: Additives, Food; Industrial Food Processing; Organic Foods.

Further Reading

Lipkowitz, Myron A., and Tova Navarra. *Encyclopedia of Allergies.* New York: Facts on File, 2001.

L'Orange, Darlena, and Gary Dolowich. *Ancient Roots, Many Branches: Energetics of Healing Across Cultures and Through Time.* Twin Lakes, WI: Lotus, 2002.

Metcalfe, Dean D., Hugh A. Sampson, and Ronald A. Simon, eds. *Food Allergy: Adverse Reactions to Food and Food Additives.* Malden, MA: Blackwell Science, 2003.

Moravian Diet and Cuisine

Hospitality from the eastern third of the Czech Republic centers on entrées and artisanal beers and wines that have influenced the cuisines of Austria, eastern Bohemia, Silesia, and western Slovakia. From the second century C.E., Moravian cuisine earned a negative reputation from the Roman historian Tacitus for relying on berries, black bread, milk, porridge, and wild game. The grim diet altered significantly during the next half millennium toward rich aromas and sweet-spicy delicacies, including mead and honey cakes. Moravian cooks gained a reputation that outranked neighboring specialists.

Lacking in financial primacy, farmers cooperated with the food industry to produce a series of seasonal specialties—asparagus, beets, cabbage, carrots, celery, onions, peas, potatoes, radishes, and turnips and harvests of buckwheat, corn, rye, spelt, and wheat. From the 800s C.E., growers shielded their grain supply away from flooding and near the community gristmill. Their pubs and inns gained fame for hearty pork with cabbage and dumplings, garlic soup, roast beef with sour cream, white wines, and dark beer, all at a reasonable price.

Moravian Christian idealism placed food at the heart of *agape,* the Greek concept of giving without expecting any return. Women embraced the task of the congregation kitchen with fervor, whether stuffing pork sausage into casings, filling aromatic cakes with plums and walnuts, drying plums for fruit leather, or soaking sour milk cheese in beer. At Christmas, they celebrated the central religious holiday with a Yuletide carp and a cookie pyramid. At Easter, a ham baked in chopped herbs covered with crust centered the movable feast.

The eighteenth-century Moravian pietists who settled Bethlehem, Lititz, and Nazareth, Pennsylvania, and Winston-Salem, North Carolina, adapted rapidly to New World gardening with beans, corn, pumpkins, squash, and sweet potatoes. They insisted on pure water from cisterns and wells. During fellowship with Indians in Georgia, missionaries gratefully accept dried venison and grouse as gifts and reciprocated with meals whenever natives visited their homes. During the singing of hymns with the Carolina Cherokee, evangelists passed baskets of sugar buns and mugs of coffee. In Alaskan missions, Moravians bought char from the Inuit and stocked dried fish as famine food for the Indians.

For group meals and bake sales, Moravians imported unique baking recipes enriched with allspice, brown sugar, butter, cloves, molasses, and yeast. In North American missions, Moravian food relief promoted hygiene, nutrition, and the spiritual welfare of the needy, notably in their Labrador and Newfoundland outreaches to the Inuit and in East End, the typhoid-ridden Creole community of St. John in the Danish West Indies. In a ministry to the Delaware Indians of the Ohio River valley, Moravians made rapid conversions among hungry pregnant women and widows, who had no social support system to supply food.

Farther south, holiday sweets introduced in the 1740s at the *Christkindlmarkt* (Christmas craft fair) stressed the aroma of cinnamon and ginger in scotch cakes, sweet buns, and spice cookies, the star ethnic treat in Old Salem's Moravian bakeries. Distributed at Christmas love feasts, paper-thin spice cookies served with hot coffee competed with beeswax candles in Yuletide perfume. Today, via direct sales, charities, and the Internet, the sharing of the holiday with worshippers emphasizes the concept of one Earthly family, joined in love by Moravian delicacies.

Current Moravian cookery showcases intense flavors, from pickled gherkins, potato cakes sizzled in lard, and savoy cabbage to stuffed rabbit, fried carp with caraway seeds, smoked trout with dill, and braised pork knees and roast goose. Much of the fare is labor intensive, such as herbed meat rolls, potato turnovers with sauerkraut, and wedding tarts. Side dishes perpetuate heritage flavor blends—sweet noodles with poppy seeds, lentils baked with millet, plum jam with cottage cheese, Černá Hora and Kelt beers, and apricot brandy.

See also: Beer; Hearth Cookery; Pennsylvania Dutch Diet and Cuisine; Royal Greenland Trade Department.

Recipe: Moravian Spice Cookies

Heat 1 cup of molasses and 1 cup of corn syrup with 1/2 cup each of lard and margarine. Stir in 1 cup of dark brown sugar. Add 6 cups of flour, 1 tablespoon of cinnamon, and 1/2 teaspoon each of allspice, ground cloves, and nutmeg. Knead the dough and let it rest for 72 hours. Atop 2 cups of flour, roll out cookies extra thin before cutting. Bake at 360 degrees Fahrenheit on greased cookie sheets for a scant 15 minutes.

Further Reading

Engel, Katherine Carté. *Religion and Profit: Moravians in Early America.* Philadelphia: University of Pennsylvania Press, 2009.

Oliver, Sandra Louise. *Food in Colonial and Federal America.* Westport, CT: Greenwood, 2005.

Zibart, Eve. *The Ethnic Food Lover's Companion.* Birmingham, AL: Menasha Ridge, 2001.

Mozambique Company

A semifeudal firm that ruled like a military government, the Mozambique Company (Companhia de Moçambique) transformed a Portuguese possession in Africa into a cohesive food producer between the late nineteenth and the mid-twentieth century.

The region, one of the most important agricultural sections of East Africa, exported cashews, cassava, copra, corn, fruit, mangrove bark, minerals, peanuts, potatoes, rice, rubber, sugar, wax, and wheat. Profitability lured explorers, prospectors, and speculators from Great Britain and Continental Europe. Joaquim Carlos Paiva de Andrada, the Portuguese military attaché to Paris and controller of land, mineral, and timber rights in the vicinity of Tete and Zumbo, ports on the Zambezi River, plotted an African empire.

Andrada joined land developer Manuel António de Sousa, head of the Ophir Company, and, with £40,000 in capital, organized the Mozambique Company in March 1888 in Lisbon. Because of limited resources in Portugal, further investments required selling stock to American, English, French, and German capitalists. Two months later, officials negotiated with the British the boundaries of Mozambique.

Under a 50-year royal charter in February 1891, the Mozambique Company acquired rights to minerals, fisheries, and customs and sole control over elephant hunting and human labor. Officials hired French engineers for a massive array of projects: the laying of the Beira and Mashonaland Railway to Massikessi south to the border of Zimbabwe, and the building of telegraph stations, harbors, quays, and docks.

After acquiring the province of Manica-Sofala, CEO Albert Ochs, a British national, established headquarters at the principal port of Beira and built barracks for laborers, who farmed some 60,000 square miles (155,000 square kilometers) of fertile land. At the time, male African conscript laborers, bribed by gin, worked away from their small communities. African women provided for their families by cultivating gardens and making a nourishing beer from *mealies* (corn).

Ochs rated forced African labor as his top asset and further exploited natives by wresting hut taxes of 50 pence in the region from the Sabi River to the Zambezi. By

1902, food exports moved more smoothly because of new cranes and warehouses, a lighthouse, and sea defense at Beira. The company, one of the most profitable in southern Africa, recruited farmers and gained investors and capital to dramatically enlarge the original business plan.

Headquartered on supervised native plantations, the Mozambique Company ruled agricultural territory that produced agave and sisal as well as long staple Egyptian cotton and sugarcane. Competition from the Nyassa Company, which claimed vast acreage to the north, proved weak and sporadic.

In 1910, to enhance profits, John Peter Hornung, an Anglo-Hungarian from Yorkshire married to a Portuguese wife, managed Portuguese sugar plantations, controlled Zambezi River steamers at the Chinde port in southern Mozambique, and bought Lisbon refineries. Within four years, his conglomerate produced 30,000 tons (27,000 metric tons) of sugar annually. In 1913, the value of Mozambique Company lands reached £500,000.

The strength of Portuguese administrators prevented the takeover of Mozambique by German investors and by Cecil Rhodes's British South Africa Company. The Mozambique Company excluded all foreign control until 1913. As British and French entrepreneurs proffered capital for greater exploitation of East Africa, Libert Oury, the Anglo-Belgian railroad king and director of the Mozambique Company, dominated land transport concessions and Beira port business, which added duties and licensing and transit fees to profits from food exports. Influential British capitalists upgraded company profits and began negotiations for connections at major sugar warehouses to the Trans-Zambezia Railway. Contributing to successful food production, company investments in American steam engines, English plows, threshers, corn shellers, and wagons introduced technology to Portuguese East Africa.

Trade in cotton and sugar rose in value after World War I, when the Mozambique Company built a railroad from Beira north to Nyassaland and outpaced the colony in exports. Local labor gangs, reduced in number by war losses and epidemic Spanish flu, required substitutions of migrant workers. Two companies dominated the sugar industry, Companhia Colonial de Buzi and Sena Sugar Estates, both owned by Hornung.

To supply the liquor industry, after 1920, the government required sugar planters to warehouse 10 percent of their cane in Mozambique. At least 75 percent of the cane crop went to Portugal. By 1924, one-third of the 100,000 contract laborers devoted their work to sugar. Because their real income remained at poverty levels, company peons relied on antelope and other bushmeat for subsistence.

At its height in 1925, the Mozambique Company streamlined sugar production to three times that of Angola's. The situation changed over the next year as prices tumbled and flooding reduced the cane crop. The colony as a whole exported five times the amount of food that the Mozambique Company marketed. By 1928, peanuts rose in volume to four times their former harvest.

In the 1930s, when the port of Beira handled £20 million in trade annually, tribal insurrections and banking and currency failures compromised company profits. In 1940, Mozambique laborers preferred jobs as stevedores or rail workers than as company field hands. The fascist regime of António de Oliveira Salazar curtailed the Mozambique Company's privileges in 1941, when the charter expired.

See also: African Food Trade; Portuguese Diet and Cuisine.

Further Reading

Bradshaw, York W. *The Uncertain Promise of Southern Africa.* Bloomington: Indiana University Press, 2000.
Goodwin, Stefan. *Africa's Legacies of Urbanization: Unfolding Saga of a Continent.* Lanham, MD: Lexington, 2006.
Isaacman, Allen, and Barbara Isaacman. *Mozambique: From Colonialism to Revolution, 1900–1982.* Boulder, CO: Westview, 1983.

Mustard

Foods blended with greens, oil, and seeds of the mustard plant bear vivid yellow, green, or brown color and a pungent flavor akin to horseradish. A wild family of 40 species of *Brassica* and *Sinapis* plants, mustard grew along the Mediterranean and in Himalayas, Middle East, and North Africa in Neolithic times. As a condiment, it colored the gastronomic writing of playwright William Shakespeare, Virginia gourmet Thomas Jefferson, and the soul food specialists of the Deep South. Commercial growing in Canada, Denmark, Hungary, India, Pakistan, the United Kingdom, and the United States satisfies the world's craving for a unique taste, which processors blend with lemon juice, salt, turmeric, vinegar, water, wine, and sometimes beer or whiskey. The resulting condiment, whether aged or fresh, pairs well with cheese, mushrooms, and grilled meat.

Mustard contributed to the first curry powder, which occupants of Mohenjo Daro in the Indus Valley in 4000 B.C.E. husked and winnowed before pounding the seed in mortars. A more distinctive taste derived in Bangladesh and Bengal from mustard and poppy sauce. In the Punjab, the seed, a natural hybrid, contributed to dal recipes and to a mango pickle in mustard oil. Egyptian cooks used mustard seed to dress spit-roasted geese and pigeon and mullet roe and treated fainting and seizures with therapeutic mustard seed water. Aramaic, Buddhist, Hebrew, Koranic, and Sanskrit imageries draw on the mustard seed as a metaphor for small size and zeal.

In classical history, Greek and Roman farmers turned wild mustard seed into a garden crop and a treatment for toothache and scorpion sting. Roman chefs introduced mustard to condiment history by blending the ground seed with grape must. From Julius Caesar's Gallic campaign from 58 to 51 B.C.E., soldiers learned to preserve meat in mustard brine. In the first century C.E., Campanian food writer Apicius recommended blending chicken and fish stuffing with mustard and spreading mustard sauce on the skin of roast boar. Legionaries on leave from North Africa brought home recipes for Egyptian ibis with mustard.

Medieval English cooks prepared a boar's head with crisp, brown skin and garnished it with mustard and rosemary. In 534 C.E., agroecologist Jia Sixie, a governor in Shandong Province, compiled an indexed guide to progressive Chinese farming, *Qimin Yaoshu* (*Skills for Peasants*), one of the world's oldest agricultural monographs. Among his advisories, he listed directives about growing and harvesting mustard.

Unlike imported black pepper, the condiment of the privileged, mustard cost little because it grew wild within reach of peasants. In the late 700s, mustard accompanied the Viking dead in funereal boats to a watery grave. Charlemagne's directive *Capitulare de Villis* (*The Supervision of Manors,* ca. 800) specifically ordered cleanliness in the preparation of mustard. A century later, Christian monks in Paris revived Roman technology for processing mustard. Late medieval mustard recipes from Lombardy added apples, berries, and lemon to mustard sauce as a condiment for game.

During the age of voyages in the 1600s, Portuguese mariners brightened dull ship's provisions with mustard. In the Caribbean, the standard slave diet depended on mustard greens, purchased at weekend markets in Antigua, the Bahamas, Barbados, Jamaica, and St. John. In England, naturopath Nicholas Culpeper, author of *The Complete Herbal* (1653), promoted mustard as a treatment for depression.

Mustard also accompanied diverse immigrant groups to North America. From the 1680s, Pennsylvania Dutch cooks reduced horseradish and mustard into table condiments to serve with fresh shad and oyster stew. Pioneers to Indiana added mustard greens to wild food staples. In the eighteenth century, Prussian king Frederick the Great aroused his passions with a mustard concoction from his secret recipe, which he added to his coffee.

Nor did mustard escape the influence of innovators. In 1777 in east-central France, Maurice Grey and Auguste Poupon introduced their Dijon brand, Grey-Poupon, a tangy table spread. In 1854 during the Crimean War, Scots Jamaican herbalist Mary Jane Seacole prepared mustard plasters to treat pneumonia in soldiers. At Amoy in Fukien, China, street vendors sold a regional snack pancake wrapped around cooked filling and hot mustard. Not until Isabella Mary Beeton published *Mrs. Beeton's*

Muslim women carry baskets of harvested mustard in the Kashmir Valley, in the northern Indian subcontinent. The seeds are ground and mixed with vinegar and other ingredients to make condiment mustard; the leaves can be eaten as mustard greens. *(Rouf Bhat/AFP/Getty Images)*

Book of Household Management (1861) did British curry achieve its savory boost from a blend of allspice, cayenne, cinnamon, fenugreek, and mustard.

At the New York harbor, entrepreneurs George Francis Gilman and dry goods clerk George Huntington Hartford, the original partners of the Great American Tea Company, sold cut-rate Chinese and Japanese tea and mustard on credit at bulk rates one-third that of retail cost. By the late 1890s, immigrant families across the United States supported mustard sales from the Sears, Roebuck catalog. At U.S. baseball stadiums, the purchase of a hot dog or pretzel with yellow mustard has been integral to the flavor and lore of the national pastime. South Carolina barbecuers favor mustard-based sauce over brown sugar and molasses.

In the diverse Szechuan province, Chinese vegetarians retreated from the ever-present pork and poultry with cabbage hearts and cucumbers in mustard dressing. Street peddlers served a piquant lunch or zesty snack of fragrant noodles topped with pickled mustard greens. In the 1970s, gourmet restaurants blended honey with mustard to produce a complex topping for salmon. Current research connects the mustard plant with cyanates that combat arthritis, asthma, and migraines and inhibit cancer of the colon and stomach.

See also: Adulterated Food; Barbecue; Condiments; Holiday Dishes and Festival Foods; Immigrant Diet and Cuisine; National Dishes; Oils; Pickling; Roman Diet and Cuisine, Ancient; Spices; Vinegar.

Further Reading

Antol, Marie Nadine. *The Incredible Secrets of Mustard: The Quintessential Guide to the History, Lore, Varieties, and Healthful Benefits of Mustard.* New York: Avery, 1999.

Kole, Chittaranjan. *Oilseeds.* New York: Springer, 2007.

Prance, Ghillean T., and Mark Nesbitt. *The Cultural History of Plants.* New York: Taylor & Francis, 2005.

Roberts-Dominguez, Jan. *The Mustard Book.* New York: John Wiley & Sons, 1993.

National Dishes

The food that characterizes a people and its foodways, national dishes illustrate the ingenuity of an ethnic group in readying popular local ingredients for the table. Staple foods derive from the geological and climatic constants, such as *muktuk* (whale skin and blubber) among the Inuit, flying fish in Barbados, *fufu* (a starchy paste) in Liberia, koumiss (fermented mare's milk) in Mongolia, and reindeer among Sami herders. As heritage foods and culinary tourist draws, a people's common recipes display identity and self-expression as insistent as French champagne and crepes, German bratwurst and mustard, Greek ouzo, Indian ghee (clarified butter), and New Zealand lamb.

The urge to experiment and personalize produces myriad variants on a standard theme, the reason for recipe alterations in Indonesian *satay* (spiced and grilled meat), Korean *kimchi* (fermented vegetables), Sri Lankan curried rice, and Algerian couscous. Expatriates reset memories of home with adapted foods in new lands, transferring German sauerbraten to northern Texas and Russian blini with caviar to Israel. Attempts at authentic bistro and café fare force compromise on the Ukrainian cook stirring up borscht with sour cream for diners in the Greek Isles and the Chinese chef attempting Peking duck in Sydney, Australia.

National favorites are subject to change, particularly from threat of extinction—for example, the fate of the Bactrian camel, blue whale, cayman, Hawaiian goose, and leatherback sea turtle. After European settlers destroyed the North American buffalo in the mid-1800s, the Plains Indians of Canada and the United States lost a source of pemmican, America's first international processed food. An outcry from conservationists inveighed against Chinese service of shark fins and turtle eggs and flippers.

Positive changes evolved from the introduction of technology, such as automated taco makers in Central America, the clay tagine among the Berbers of Morocco, and electric fondue pots to melt Swiss Gruyère dip. The introduction of new foodstuffs as valuable as corn to Italian polenta, rice to Portuguese paella, springbok to Boer stews, potatoes to Jewish latkes (potato pancakes), chocolate to Swiss confectioners, and coffee and tea the world over initiate lasting changes to age-old eating styles.

A nation's cuisine fits merchants and consumers as naturally as the lay of the land. Lutefisk travels well to Sweden's diverse locales; likewise, ingredients for *pot-au-feu* are available throughout France, as are tart cooking apples in the United States for apple pie, sloes for English gin, peanuts for Chadian sauces, and raw fish for Japanese sushi. For Israelis, falafel, a fried ball of ground chickpeas, suits both the home table and the street diner, as does a salad of chopped cucumber and tomato dressed with lemon juice and oil, onions, and parsley. The appeal of national dishes also spreads favorites to new locales, the destiny of English fish and chips, Taiwanese noodle soup, Nigerian kola nuts, and Turkish kebabs. Over time, ethnic gastronomic terms—*barbecue, bourbon, coffee, Danish pastry, dumplings, pilaf, pita, ramen, salsa, sangria, schnapps, yogurt*—crop up on menus worldwide.

See also: Fish and Fishing; Heritage Foods; Indonesian Diet and Cuisine; Language, Food; Manioc; Nutrition; Rice; Seaweed; Soups.

Further Reading

Corbett, John, and Scott Thornbury. *Intercultural Language Activities.* New York: Oxford University Press, 2010.

Freedman, Paul H. *Food: The History of Taste.* Berkeley: University of California Press, 2007.

Grogan, Barbara Brownell, ed. *Food Journeys of a Lifetime: 500 Extraordinary Places to Eat Around the Globe.* Washington, DC: National Geographic, 2009.

Kittler, Pamela Goyan, and Kathryn Sucher. *Food and Culture.* Belmont, CA: Wadsworth/Thomson Learning, 2004.

New World Commodities

The late-fifteenth-century exposure of Genoan sailor Christopher Columbus to North American biota introduced much of the world to a broadened palate of tastes, aromas, and textures. The first explorers of the Americas discovered beverages, fruit, meats, oils, and vegetables known for millennia to indigenous people, from *yerba maté* (leaf tea), grapefruit, and Muscovy duck to candlefish and cottonseed oil and tomatillos. Ship provisioners added to the standard peas and flour new possibilities from corn, potatoes, red beans, and sunflower oil, all staples on galley shelves for long voyages. In addition to common ingredients—arrowroot, lima beans, field peas, manioc, wild rice—Spanish explorers experienced a panoply of tastes, including the first smoking tobacco, coca, tomatoes, and the bitter taste of cinchona bark, the source of quinine, a treatment for malaria.

Over some five centuries of adjustments to standard recipe collections, the Columbian Exchange wrought lasting variety and vigor to cuisine in Africa, Asia, Australia, Europe, and Polynesia. Throughout the Western Hemisphere, avocados, bergamot, blueberries, cashews, cranberries, guavas, mangos, papayas, pecans, persimmons, and tarragon invigorated the diet with the mouthfeel and taste sensations of indigenous products. The chili pepper generated zip in Szechuan vegetable, fish, and meat dishes. The prickly pear provided a tangy desert fruit that flavored sweets and beverages. In the American colonies, jicama, pumpkins, and winter squash offered hard-shelled vegetables that could last into winter.

The pineapple spiked so many punch bowls that the prickly fruit with its perky leaf crown became a standard door carving, a colonial symbol of welcome in the Carolinas, the Caribbean, and elsewhere in the Americas. Chicle created a niche sweet with chewing gum, a treat that Mayan children had enjoyed for generations. Maple syrup offered new choices in baking and the binding of baked beans. Cacao, flavored with cane sugar and vanilla, founded a beverage and confection industry. Additional drinks from agave, corn, and greenbriar added tequila, *pulque,* and sarsaparilla to the bar list.

The infusion of interest in late Renaissance cuisine, the immediate result of the Columbian Exchange, provoked controversy as well as consumerism. Hearsay labeled the potato both an aphrodisiac and a source of leprosy and scrofula. The tomato earned bad reports for potential poisonings and, in England, as a cause of gout. The turkey, an unattractive American bird, at first provoked little enthusiasm, a fate that also befell manioc, sapodilla, and quinoa flour. More acceptable for its sweetness, the sweet potato won a place in the kitchen for its adaptability as a baked tuber and a source of pies and puddings. Nuts, including the Brazil nut and the macadamia, contributed new flavors for candies and snack food.

The variant attitudes toward New World foods precipitated a revolution in global dining. In 1521, Ferdinand Magellan took corn and tomatoes to the Philippines, where cooks accepted the new ingredients. Voyagers transported the tomato to China, India, and Japan for use in salads, sauces, and stews. Likewise, Central American chili peppers cut into the black pepper trade and sparked bite and heat in Asian, Ethiopian, and Hungarian cuisine. In Ireland, the planting of the potato in poor soil in 1625 supplied an agrarian nation with a readily grown famine food. Germans expanded their population and improved health from potato crops. Manioc, yams, and the Amazonian peanut performed a similar service for poor Africans and Asians.

Corn fed Chinese nomads fleeing the overcrowded Yangtze River area and, after 1783, sustained the American bourbon whiskey industry. Zucchini furnished French chefs a basis for ratatouille and Bulgarian, Spanish, and Turkish restaurants a source of pancakes and stuffed vegetables. The sweet potato enlivened the Filipino and Maori sea diet and supplied a new money crop to island peoples. Roast turkey cost so much in Europe that only the elite of France and Venice could afford it. The income boosted the poultry market with its first fad species.

See also: Blueberries; Cacti; Chicle and Chewing Gum; Chocolate; Columbus, Christopher; Corn and Maize; Jerky; Jiménez de Quesada, Gonzalo; London Virginia Company; Manioc; Pan-European Diet and Cuisine; Pemmican; Peppers; Potatoes; Poultry; Standish, Miles; Tudor Diet and Cuisine; Vanilla.

Further Reading

Civitello, Linda. *Cuisine and Culture: A History of Food and People.* 3rd ed. Hoboken, NJ: John Wiley & Sons, 2011.

Crosby, Alfred W. *The Columbian Exchange: Biological and Cultural Consequences of 1492.* Westport, CT: Greenwood, 2003.

Montaño, Mary Caroline. *Tradiciones Nuevomexicanas: Hispano Arts and Culture of New Mexico.* Albuquerque: University of New Mexico Press, 2001.

Smith, Andrew F., ed. *The Oxford Companion to American Food and Drink.* New York: Oxford University Press, 2007.

Nomad Diet and Cuisine

For their daily food, wandering peoples throughout history have relied on subsistence hunting of game, herd, and shore animals, gathering of wild plants, and trading with merchants and other journeyers. The constant uprooting of Tuareg cameleers in the Sahara, South African Bushmen, Chukchi walrus hunters, and Kyrgyz mountaineers limits the size and extent of the pantry and the number of metal pots and implements families can carry. Constrained resources produce predictable one-pot menus usually eaten communally, such as the goat soup served at Hmong gatherings in Southeast Asia and the milk diet of the Masai and Samburu pastoralists of Africa and the Sarakatsani of the Balkans and northern Greece.

Nomadic eating styles adapt to local exigencies. In prehistory, nomads nurtured a contempt for city dwellers' pork because constant movement prohibited transient tribes from keeping swine. For convenience, Turkish Tartars and the Bakhtiari of southern Iran cook lamb cubes as kebabs; Inuit carnivores, who lack firewood, eat whale blubber raw. Living on as limited an animal diet as the Gujjars of northern India, the Afar herders of Ethiopia subsist on milk and meat and trade salt for fruit and vegetables. The Ainu of Hokkaido, Japan, reject uncooked food in preference for the dried, roasted, or smoked meat of badger, fox, salmon, sea anemones, and wolf. They make flat dumplings from the pounded *ubayuri* lily bulb, a source of subtly flavored starch.

For wanderers, sharing is a way of life. Qatar's nomads roast whole goats, hares, and sheep and serve the meat in a communal dish along with ember-cooked truffles, buttermilk curds, dates, and dried locusts. Thin rounds of unleavened bread take the shape of a convex iron griddle, which rapidly toasts dough. Beverages served to clan members range from camel's milk to sugared coffee and spiced tea. From trades with merchants, Bedouins from Morocco to Syria and Oman add to their menus citrus fruit, dried apricots and figs, seasonings, and tahini, a sesame seed paste used in creaming crushed chickpeas into hummus.

Living with semidomesticated mammals influences diet and health. Sami reindeer herders in Scandinavia rely on dried and smoked venison as well as bear, elk, and mountain goat meat, which they relish down to the hooves, marrow, and udder. The blood and liver go into bread and black pudding. A similar husbandry with char and trout yields fish cakes and intestines and roe, eaten with potato dumplings. For flavorings, the Sami collect cloudberries and lingonberries as well as angelica buds and sorrel for mixing with reindeer milk for storage in kegs. To broaden their food choices, the Sami trade for barley flour, coffee, horse meat, and liquor.

Another meat-centered culture, Mongolian nomads focus on meals of boiled mutton with *borts* (reindeer or camel jerky), handmade noodles, and mugs of tea mixed with camel or mare's milk, a symbol of hospitality. The horse supplies *airag,* a fermented milk drink filtered through cloth and ripened in animal gut and leather bags suspended from wood frames or a yurt ceiling. For Tibetan women, yak milk processing, curd drying, and yogurt draining center daily chores along with frying bread and cooking in cauldrons and woks.

Kettle cookery, griddling, and spit-roasting over a campfire, the traditional slow food method of the so-called Gypsies—the Roma, Sinti, and others—serve the 15 million who travel Bosnia, Bulgaria, Germany, Hungary, Ireland, Romania, Russia, and Spain. Day laborers take their wages in flour and lard. Both men and women prepare and serve meals. Despite a transient existence, the Roma dine well on roasted apples and almond cakes, clay-baked hedgehog and trout, snails in broth, and fig cakes, a nourishing travel snack.

Since their migration from India through Armenia in the 1300s, the Roma acquired the nutritional and medicinal lore of berries, nettles and beech leaves, and herbs. Near the sea, they collected limpets and mussels while enhancing their grocery purchases on the proceeds of horse trading. A yen for full-flavored meat limited their consumption of beef and mutton in favor of geese, goats, pork, and wild salmon. A store of dried mushrooms flavored ragouts; dandelion roots ensured a strong ingredient for coffee, which the Roma flavored with wild honey.

Currently, the Roma treasure recipes rich in butter and eggs from free-range hens, molasses and unrefined sugar, and wholemeal flour. For luck, cooks use generous amounts of bread, garlic, pepper, salt, and vinegar. Hunting and gathering nets dulse, eels, and sea kale from the shore as well as game and seabird offal for soups and gooseberries and mulberries for boiled pudding. A favorite recipe for children involves the hollowing of a potato to hold elderberry jam before baking in embers. To avoid Gypsy taboos against impurity caused by the handling of cats and dogs, the slaughter of horses, or the contamination of menstruating women, the Roma avoid unclean strangers and the institutional kitchens of hospitals and schools. Rather than use forks and spoons polluted by *marimé* (non-Roma), they eat with their hands and a knife.

See also: Crackers; Endangered Species; Fish and Fishing; Hunter-Gatherers; Nuts and Seeds; Pit Cookery; Sicilian Diet and Cuisine; Trade Routes; Travel Food; Wild Food.

Further Reading
MacVeigh, Jeremy. *International Cuisine.* Clifton Park, NY: Delmar Cengage Learning, 2009.

Schmidt, Arno, and Paul Fieldhouse. *The World Religions Cookbook.* Westport, CT: Greenwood, 2007.

Wilson, Carol. *Gypsy Feast: Recipes and Culinary Traditions of the Romany People.* New York: Hippocrene, 2004.

Noodles

A universal staple, noodles, whether made from beans, buckwheat, corn, potatoes, rice, soy, or soft wheat, add texture and variety to broth, salads, and meat and vegetable entrées. In about 10,500 B.C.E. at Nevali Cori, Turkey, the historic transition from hunting and gathering to domesticated einkorn wheat began the shift in cookery from pit-roasted meats to bread, flour, noodles, and pasta. Noodles appear to have originated in Afghanistan, Kyrgyzstan, and Tajikistan, where cooks created *laghman* by simmering the dough strips in spices. In Guangdong, on China's southeastern shore, beginning in 4000 B.C.E., Chinese chefs flavored flour blends with alkali salt and experimented with hand-looping and stretching dough repeatedly to achieve a viscosity that held together strands.

As early as 2000 B.C.E., the northeastern Chinese of Shandong blended broomcorn and foxtail millet with soy and wheat noodles to add to dishes of mung beans and tofu for a diet rich in carbohydrates and protein. Tartar horsemen added hand-rolled noodles to mutton stews. In Singapore, to meet the demand for inexpensive food for manual laborers, noodle making became the nation's first industry. Asian diners perpetuated the Lunar New Year myth that the length of the noodle predicted longevity.

Similarly symbolic, Persian cooks welcomed the New Year with string egg noodles, a symbol of life strands and unavoidable snarls.

From ancient China, India, and Persia, cooks in the Middle East and the Mediterranean learned to break down gluten in yeast dough. In a modification of recipes for dumplings and pasta, cooks stretched thin strands into noodles for frying or adding to soup. Tibetan *thukpa,* a meaty noodle dish, spread in popularity to Nepal and India, where chili powder perked up bland egg dough with heat and piquance. On the Russian steppes, noodles complemented bread, fritters, and meat-filled *pirozhki* (dumplings). In Japan, the translucent, rubbery *shirataki* noodles began with the elephant yam, a perennial tuber high in fiber and low in calories.

Noodle aficionados pressed dough into shape with a handleless Asian rolling pin and kneaded the mass into thin blocks for cutting and oiling to prevent sticking. Cooking required high heat for a brisk boil or for a regimen of boiling, blanching in cold water, and a return to hot water. Chopsticks assisted in drainage by lifting and separating strands to keep them whole. In southern India and Ceylon, fast-food chefs used a string hopper to force rice batter into strands for *muruku,* a crisp-fried snack popularized in Fiji and Malaysia. In contrast, the Chinese made rice noodles from batter steamed and folded into accordion-pleated layers for slicing.

In the 1100s, the high cost of wheat flour made noodles a dish for the wealthy. Swabians in the late Middle Ages pushed batter through a sieve to make *spätzel,* an egg noodle served with sauerbraten and gravy or in a grated apple dessert. In colonial America, Pennsylvania Dutch egg noodles took on a vibrant yellow with the addition of saffron. By 1900, extruded noodles simplified the rigorous job of hand-pulling and -cutting dough. Chinese restaurateurs and street stall vendors profited from the inexpensive extenders of dishes made with more costly meats and fish. The invention of instant flash-fried noodles in August 1958 by Taiwanese Japanese businessman Momofuku Ando, founder of Nissin Food Products, boosted the popularity of curly or straight dough threads for hospital and school meals and factory and office lunches.

A favorite breakfast food, Taiwanese *misua* noodles, Sino-Mongolian oat curls, Japanese *champon* (pork soup) and ramen with nori (seaweed), Hong Kong milk noodles, Korean acorn starch noodles, or Vietnamese *pho* (rice vermicelli) cook rapidly in meat and vegetable broths.

Villagers in eastern China's Zhejiang Province make noodles by hand according to traditional recipes. They produce hundreds of tons annually and ship it off to sell in bigger cities. The Chinese have been making wheat noodles since about 4000 B.C.E. *(Imaginechina/Associated Press)*

Yakisoba, a Japanese dinner dish of fried noodles with pork and cabbage, enlarges on traditional Mandarin chow mein. Chinatowns in Australia, Canada, Holland, the United Kingdom, and the United States feature *lamian* as familiar tourist fare. In Singapore, cafés and wet markets offer *mee pok,* a sauced noodle that anchors servings of fish balls and chopped pork.

Noodles complement a variety of presentations and additions. Filipino diners patronize *panciterias,* restaurants specializing in *pancit* noodles. Malaysian *bakmi* (wheat noodles), boiled separate from broth, come to the table with a choice of bok choy, diced chicken, gravy, meatballs, and wonton. The Japanese udon is available in microwavable soup cups; *somen* restaurants pass noodles through cold water along a bamboo chute for diners to grasp with chopsticks and dip into hot sauces.

Salad bars incorporate multicultural fare—noodles, pasta salad, pita chips, tortilla strips—into refreshing layers of carbohydrates with raw vegetables and fruit. Slow Food menus feature chewy noodles along with tacos and vegetable wraps as methods of preserving world food heritage. An intriguing addition to cuisine, Penang noodle salad begins with chickpea noodles dry-fried in chili flakes and grated coconut before flavoring with curry powder. Condiments include Burmese fried garlic, Cambodian fish sauce, Chinese cabbage and pickled radish, Filipino annatto oil, Indian garam masala, Japanese green tea powder, Korean *kimchi* (fermented vegetables) and sesame salt, and Sambal chilies and lime.

See also: Customs, Food; Dye, Food; Exotic Food Clubs; Fusion Cuisine; Japanese Diet and Cuisine; Language, Food; Russian Diet and Cuisine; Tofu; Yeast.

Further Reading

Boi, Lee Geok. *Classic Asian Noodles.* Singapore: Marshall Cavendish, 2007.

Hite, Eric. *Everybody Loves Ramen: Recipes, Stories, Games, and Fun Facts About the Noodles You Love.* Kansas City, MO: Andrews McMeel, 2012.

Owens, Gavin, ed. *Cereals Processing Technology.* Boca Raton, FL: CRC, 2001.

Scicolone, Michele. *Pasta, Noodles, and Dumplings.* New York: Simon & Schuster, 2005.

North African Diet and Cuisine

Originating between desert and sea, the cookery of Algeria, Egypt, Libya, Morocco, and Tunisia elevated the sensual pleasures of eating. Ingredients thrived on the continent's north shore. Berber growers cultivated wheat from 30,000 B.C.E. Dates flourished in Egyptian gardens as early as 4000 B.C.E., Cretan olives after 3000 B.C.E., and almonds around 1325 B.C.E.

After 1000 B.C.E., Phoenician seafarers augmented the northeast African peasant triad of beer, bread, and onions with *merguez,* a spiced sausage based on mutton or goat meat, *asida* (buttered wheat custard), seafood, and porridge made from barley, bulgur wheat, and semolina, a coarse meal ground from durum wheat. By 200 B.C.E., the North African elite dined Greek style with shallow dishes and handled drinking bowls. Roman occupation after 146 B.C.E. introduced figs, pomegranates, artichokes, and truffles and deeper bowls for pulses. Engineers set up the technology for pressing olives into olive oil and brewing barley into beer, a specialty at Cyrene, a Greek colony in Libya. In Algeria, local vineyards supplied Roman wineries.

Berber nomads developed couscous, a soft carbohydrate served with ewe's milk that blended with meat offal, roast quail, and vegetables. By shaping clay into the conical *tagine* and heating it over an olive wood fire, desert wanderers developed a slow-braised stewing technique for lamb, pigeons, rabbit, and meatballs that flourished in Morocco. The flavoring of the mix with pome fruit, raisins, plums, melons, and quince and a sweet-sour emulsion of honey and lemon pulp enhanced aromas and flavors. Hibiscus, Koshary, or mint tea or tamarind juice rounded out the evening with a bracing taste that settled the stomach for sleep.

To tagine cookery, in the 600s, Arab traders introduced Indian and Malaysian flavorings—cloves, ginger, saffron, nutmeg, cinnamon, turmeric, paprika, and mace. From a trove of new flavors, the developing Islamic culture evolved complex combinations of *ras el hanout,* a spice blend made from cardamom, mallow, dill, pepper, anise, cumin, caraway, nutmeg, fenugreek, orrisroot, and dried roses. The flavorings boosted the overnight baking of stew in urns, a one-pot meal shared by extended families. Ottoman pastry chefs demonstrated methods of combining wheat flour, honey, nuts, and spices into baklava and dessert pancakes topped with yogurt.

Spanish discoveries in the 1500s united Mediterranean Rim cuisine with corn, zucchini, tomatoes, chili peppers, vanilla, peanuts, and potatoes from Mexico and Peru. With *khubz* (flatbread) and puffy pita bread, North Africans initiated the shaping of flat cakes into utensils for scooping tahini (sesame) sauces, wrapping falafel (chickpea patties), and sliding kebabs off skewers. Greek stuffed grape leaves added another dimension to finger food that enfolded juicy tomato and onion sauce and rice in a handy sleeve.

Tagine innovations extended to the tenderizing of quail and pigeon, fish, egg mixtures, and dried chickpeas with the condensation that trickled down the steepled lid. North African chefs evolved unique herbal blends unknown in Cyprus and Greece, notably smoky *harissa,* a mix of chili peppers, coriander, cayenne, caraway, olive oil, and garlic. By rubbing haunches of roasted meat and eggplant with the blend, Tunisians individualized their

Moroccan tagines are long-simmering stews—this one made with chicken, prunes, tomatoes, and seasonings—named for the clay vessel in which they are cooked. The conical cover directs condensation downward; the round base becomes a serving dish. *(Larry Crowe/Associated Press)*

cuisine from that of Egypt and Morocco. An additional touch, the thickening of puddings with mastic changed custard texture into a chewy dessert.

Colonialism by French and Italians imparted touches of European elegance, such as breakfast omelets, ratatouille, nougat, rice pudding, wine, yeast breads, fava bean snacks, and poached saltwater fish. The Moorish occupation of Iberia added gazpacho to Algerian soups, salads of oranges and fennel, and *tabil* (ground coriander and caraway) for seasoning veal and game.

See also: Egyptian Diet and Cuisine, Ancient; Heritage Foods; Ibn Battuta; Idiocuisine; National Dishes; Olives and Olive Oil; Trading Vessels.

Further Reading

Benayoun, Aline. *Casablanca Cuisine: French North African Cooking.* London: Serif, 2000.
Davies, Ethel, Maria Randell, and Malcolm Barnes. *North Africa: The Roman Coast.* Guilford, CT: Globe Pequot, 2009.
Heine, Peter. *Food Culture in the Near East, Middle East, and North Africa.* Westport, CT: Greenwood, 2004.

North American Diet and Cuisine

The initial settlement of British, French, and Dutch pioneers in Canada, the Maritimes, and New England introduced newcomers to an unfamiliar milieu. From the colonial era, continental cuisine made use of unique ingredients—maple sugar and syrup, cranberries, persimmons, and hickory nuts as well as abalone and prairie chicken. Kitchen herb beds grew mint, chives, wild celery, and lavender for flavoring succotash, pheasant, catfish, lobster, clam chowder, oysters, and bream. The woods rewarded children's expeditions with bird eggs, mushrooms, fiddlehead ferns, and wild onions. They eagerly crushed and seeded saskatoon berries, rose hips, and muscadines for jam and fruit leather.

Dogtrot cabins centered meal preparation and preservation at a stone fireplace on one side of a central hallway. Above the hearth, leather breeches, beans, and squash or pumpkin rounds dried for winter one-pot meals flavored with bacon. In the domestic area, the housewife churned cow's milk, rolled butter, pulverized maple sugar, boiled sweet corn and crabs, and secured canned turnips, carrots, and berries in chimney cupboards that kept garden goods from freezing in winter. Cabbage chilled in the springhouse. Mounted pegs held drying dill and rosemary for pickling cucumbers and beef.

Gendered training readied girls for shelling corn for pone, pouring griddle cakes, and mortaring lard with sage and bay leaves for frying trout and venison. Kitchen amenities included a tin sausage stuffer for preserving pork, an osier basket for draining cottage cheese, jugs for poaching hare, and a cheese ditch, a spouted trough on legs for paddling cheese curds and draining whey. Cooks sped the roasting of turkey, pheasant, and quail by spitting carcasses in a tin reflector and seasoning with imported mace, pepper, nutmeg, and an onion studded with cloves. Affluent households preferred biscuits and milk gravy for breakfast. For pudding, the cook mixed flour, sugar, dried peaches or apples, raisins, and nutmeg and boiled the dough in a cloth bag.

Young men learned cider making, grain reaping, hunting, fishing, and trapping, a source of crabs, lobsters, rabbits, opossums, squirrels, snipe, and groundhogs. In Montreal and Halifax, lads sliced caribou and sockeye salmon into strips for jerky, salted cod, and hung pork chines for smoked meat. Grist milling, another man's job, produced the flour and meal for colonial oatmeal cookies, corn bread, and cornmeal mush. Men chopped hardwoods to stoke the community beehive oven, which produced the baked beans, rye loaves, spoonbread, muffins, apple pie, and pones of a diet heavy in carbohydrates.

Integral to North American diet and cuisine, the exploration of western territories, Alaska, and the Hawaiian Islands enlarged staples with Indian hominy, buffalo, wild rice, bear, seal, pineapple, salmon, passion fruit, candlefish, nene, and elk. The importation of African slaves added okra, black-eyed peas, Brunswick stew, and collard greens. Black farmers grew peppers for barbecue sauce, shelled peanuts for pocket snacks, raised hogs for sausage and brains, and kept chickens for eggs. Lard and fat meat seasoned such soul food as fried chicken, frog's legs, poke greens, pork rinds, and hoppin' John. Cajuns turned pecans into ingredients for pies and pralines, sliced cold cuts for poor boys, and added *filé* powder (ground sassafras) to jambalaya, a one-dish rice-and-meat meal.

The American melting pot layered outback recipes with new takes on cooking and foodways. From Germany came lager, bratwurst, kaiser rolls, stollen, and kuchen; from Ireland, white potatoes, bannocks, and whiskey. Jewish cooks turned potatoes into latkes and cucumbers into dill pickles. Scots cattle ranchers bred sturdy herds on the frontier. Nordic immigrants spread holiday tables with lutefisk and berry jams.

After 1798, a resurgence of admiration for French revolutionaries restored respect for egg dishes, ices, beignets, Quebec taffy, bûche de Noël (Yule log), and vanilla custards. Florida citrus groves yielded fruit for breakfast and snacks. Pennsylvania mining communities and logging camps around the Great Lakes amalgamated the influence of Scandinavians, Pole, Italians, Slavs, and Russians into an all-American taste for pastrami, horseradish, corned beef, gin, sauerkraut, deep-dish pizza, pretzels, cole slaw, hot dogs, gyros, pierogis, and pickled herring.

The combined juxtaposition of East with West in World War II, the Korean War, the Vietnam War, and the Iraq and Afghanistan wars widened American awareness of foreign cuisines. Urban restaurants offered French wines with coq au vin. Mom and Pop café menus featured *kimchi,* pad thai, *satay,* spring rolls, and fish sauce. Into the twenty-first century, soldiers returning from Afghanistan and Iraq retained a fondness for flatbread and pilaf.

See also: African Slave Diet; Amerindian Diet; Beef; Buffalo; Cajun Diet and Cuisine; Cod; Columbus, Christopher; Fast Food; Immigrant Diet and Cuisine; McDonald's; Pennsylvania Dutch Diet and Cuisine; Pork; Soul Food; Tex-Mex Diet and Cuisine; Verrazzano, Giovanni da.

Further Reading

Alexander, Leslie M., and Walter C. Rucker, eds. *Encyclopedia of African American History.* Santa Barbara, CA: ABC-Clio, 2010.

Beard, James. *Beard on Food: The Best Recipes and Kitchen Wisdom from the Dean of American Cooking.* Ed. José Wilson. New York: Bloomsbury, 2007.

Dunmire, William W. *Gardens of New Spain: How Mediterranean Plants and Foods Changed America.* Austin: University of Texas Press, 2004.

Nenes, Michael F. *American Regional Cuisine.* Hoboken, NJ: John Wiley & Sons, 2007.

North Borneo Company

A chartered Malaysian trading firm from the early 1880s to the end of World War II, the British North Borneo Company Provisional Association, Ltd., developed into both colonial governor and trading syndicate. Profiteers hoped to replicate the successes of British imperialism in Africa and India by specializing in such culinary exotica as dried cuttlefish for wok frying and bird's nests for Chinese soup. Under the aegis of the British Empire, the venture, chaired by Alfred Bent, went into business in August 1881 in Sabah and exploited trade relations with China.

After obtaining a charter from Queen Victoria on November 1, the firm headquartered at Pulau Gaya and maintained an arsenal at Kudat to add military muscle to the warehousing and sale of prime goods. By replacing counterfeiting, opium dealing, piracy, slavery, smuggling, and tribal anarchy with sound fiscal management, exporters promoted trade in coffee, cuttlefish, oysters and skates, palm and vegetable oil, and pepper as well as in cutch dye, rattan, rubber, timber, tin, and tobacco. Company balance sheets omitted a sizable investment in local gambling and opium, a popular recreation among Chinese and Muslims that bolstered struggling commerce in food.

Officially, the North Borneo syndicate nurtured trade in standard jungle goods from Mantanani Island, the Padas district, and the Putatan River. Agents recruited indentured field labor from Java and Hong Kong and encouraged immigration of Cantonese and Hakkas, who agreed on condition of their continued access to opium. British engineers began mapping rail routes through jungle and swamplands and erecting lighthouses. On the way to buyers in Bengal, Canton, Macao, Manila, and Singapore, cargoes passed through company ports in Chinese, English, and company vessels.

By 1887, exports increased by 336 percent, from $159,000 to $535,000 annually. In 1888 and 1889, sales flourished in local produce: bird's nests (for soup), dried sea cucumber, gutta-percha wood, pearls, pepper, rice, and sago. The price of swiftlet nests, retrieved from seaside cliffs and caves between February and May, remained stable, offering a huge profit for the birds' gluey saliva. Hong Kong diners consumed 60 percent of the world's supply of nests, dubbed "the caviar of the East" and "white gold."

The territory of the North Borneo Company increased in 1889 with the addition of the crown colony of Labuan to the British protectorate. Brisk sales in beeswax, camphor, guano fertilizer, gum resin for lacquers and paints, mother-of-pearl and tortoise shells, and sponges paralleled profitable food exports of agar seaweed gelatin, bananas, cocoa, keema clams, nipa palm fruit, and sugar. One exotic commodity, green, hawksbill, and leatherback turtle eggs, considered an aphrodisiac and blood tonic, required careful handling. Diners boiled them slightly, then made an opening in the shell and sucked out the gelatinous contents. Food entrepreneurs also hoped to cultivate and exploit betel nut, cassava, citronella grass, copra, mango, and sweet potatoes and to advance the food trade with Australia and the Pacific Rim.

The Japanese military occupation of Borneo from December 13, 1941, to August 1, 1945, resulted in the destruction of plantations and docks and in violence against immigrant Chinese laborers. Losses bankrupted the North Borneo Company in 1946.

Further Reading

Andaya, Barbara Watson, and Leonard Y. Andaya. *A History of Malaysia.* Honolulu: University of Hawaii Press, 2001.

Black, Ian. *A Gambling Style of Government: The Establishment of the Chartered Company's Rule in Sabah, 1878–1915.* Oxford, UK: Oxford University Press, 1983.

Horstmann, Alexander, and Reed L. Wadley. *Centering the Margin: Agency and Narrative in Southeast Asian Borderlands.* Oxford, UK: Berghahn, 2009.

Tregonning, Kennedy Gordon. *Under Chartered Company Rule (North Borneo, 1881–1946).* New York: Oxford University Press, 1958.

Nouvelle Cuisine

A shift in French cookery from rich, embellished show-pieces to simpler fare using less flour and fat earned the name *nouvelle cuisine* (new cookery), a much ballyhooed fashion of the 1960s and 1970s.

Classic French style, which dominated much of the world's menus and intimidated lesser cooks, carried the name *haute cuisine française* (high French cookery) both as a description of its ambitions and of the heaped entrées that adorned platters and banquet centerpieces. Originated in the royal kitchens of Louis XIV after 1643 for his marathon banquets at the Palais de Versailles outside Paris, this complex food preparation idealized rich marinades and flambé saucing. Event managers aimed for elegant presentation and table staging *à la française* (in the French style) for public display and carving and plating by liveried waiters.

Food Fight

Exemplified in the writings and work of chef Auguste Escoffier during the belle epoque, haute cuisine achieved a top-heavy grandeur and high drama. Amid feather and flower garnishes, flavor and nutrition received perfunctory attention.

Prefaced in the 1930s by the radio broadcasts of nutritionist-chef Édouard de Pomiane, pared-down style gained credence during the rationing and austerity of World War II. Nouvelle cuisine facilitated a revolt against the complicated celebrity fare of cookbook mavens and television chefs. The trend gained cachet by targeting the slim, adventurous esthete, the jet-setter who sampled exotica in remote global settings.

Around 1960, food critics Henri Gault and his colleague Christian Millau, authors of a series of travel guides, revived the term *nouvelle cuisine* from the writings of Vincent La Chapelle, chief cook to the Earl of Chesterfield and the Prince of Orange, who pioneered a scaled-down gastronomy in *Cuisine Moderne (Modern Cookery, 1733)*. Gault and Millau marveled at the creativity of French chef Paul Bocuse, the "Pope of Nouvelle Cuisine," and his imitators, Alain Chapel, Michel Guérard, Paul Haeberlin, Jean and Pierre Troisgros, and Roger Verge. Their unconventional free-form cookery, which began in 1959, renounced French formalism. Designer recipes and kitchen techniques called for less starch in thickeners and binders in favor of mild, light-textured fruit and vegetable purées.

Chef as Artist

Serving sensual arrangements of foods in unusual combinations required a larger plate, which framed a small quantity of ingredients that the cook posed at center like a work of art. In place of massive servings, these scaled-down groupings of stir fries, sautéed vegetables, pasta, and ragouts drew the eye to clever twists of mesclun, miniature ears of corn, slices of kiwi and mango, slivered almonds, sushi, and raspberry sauce. Herb- and fruit-enhanced vinegars, tasty stock, and pot liquor redolent with peppercorns and the savor of the main course greeted the eyes, nose, and palate. Media food writers and television chefs tempted the enterprising cook with regional specialties, such as Southern grits and shrimp, Greek goat cheese soufflé, Southwestern salads with piki corn chips, and native American squash blossoms stuffed with rice and piñon nuts.

Redesigned meals liberated menus from affectation. Novel recipes bore little resemblance to historic feasts and excesses, such as roast boar on a platter, the disguise of a chicken breast under Mornay sauce. The credo of the new gastronomy appeared in "Vive la Nouvelle Cuisine Française," the cover story of *Nouveau Guide Gault-Millau* magazine for October 1973. The text promoted daily selection of ingredients requiring less refrigeration and stove time and light saucing with reductions rather than traditional cream and roux (fried flour). Professional cooks favored more limited menus that changed frequently to reflect seasonal ingredients.

In a period of renewal, professionals and home cooks, particularly in Britain, France, and the United States, abandoned food snobbery. For guidance, they turned to the recipes and suggestions of Bocuse's two classics—*La Cuisine du Marché* (*The Cuisine of the Market*, 1976) and *La Journée du Cuisinier* (*The Chef's Day*, 1980). Homemakers and weekend cooks found the new cookbooks stimulating rather than daunting and the minimalist recipes rejuvenating rather than heavy and indigestible. Cooking took less effort because it used advanced technology and electronic implements rather than mallet and mortar and pestle. Dishes introduced pure juices and organic foods free of pesticides. Bocuse and his enterprising followers evolved into a rebel breed of kitchen artists and earned for Bocuse the title "Chef of the Century."

The deconstruction of extravagant *cuisine moderne* (modern cookery) reached a peak of popularity in the 1970s, the heyday of weekly television kitchen star Raymond Oliver, a judge at the Paris Wine Tasting of 1976. Chic new-wave cooking schools touted just-picked local asparagus and vacuum-packed scallops cleverly arranged and moderately enhanced by subtle citrus zest and geometric stacks and mazes. A multinational eclecticism and interest in healthful eating reduced bulk, calories, refined sugar and starch, and salt by stressing color, texture, and savor of native greens, fish, and poultry. For example, in Caribbean tourist meccas, cooked green bananas with chickpeas and kidney beans added variety and mouthfeel to salads. American steak houses offered a choice of wild rice, baby carrots and sugar snap peas, or baked sweet potatoes in place of the humdrum Idaho potato.

The emergence of innovative microwave and convection ovens and heavy-motored food processors meshed with advances in Japanese cookery, a propitious marriage of two styles of delicate cookery that rejected overlayering with sauce. Japanese chefs elevated in importance fine mousses and puréed fruits and vegetables as bases for revamped dishes.

The World's Table

More gentrified than cuisine moderne, nouvelle cuisine philosophy embraced multiculturalism. A surge of market consciousness shed political posturing and military superiority in favor of the wonder and enjoyment of the world's trade goods and remote wineries. Critic Gault admired a generation of chefs who ventured into professional kitchens that eschewed the structure and dogma of old cuisine. Food experts avoided pretense and media puffery and networked out of mutual admiration. In "The Best of" guides to Beverly Hills, Chicago, Hawaii, Las Vegas, London, Los Angeles, New York, Paris, Provence, San Francisco, and Tuscany, culinary writer André Gayot directed gourmands to meals with flair.

From long experience assessing the world's kitchens and tables, Gault remained wary of the faults of new style, especially egotism, lapses in basic sanitation and technique, and loss of respect for traditional ingredients and regional favorites. He warned of rootlessness and fads and ridiculed tiny portions, undercooking, foodstuffs as decoration, and unpalatable blends of sugar and salt with strong spices. As early as 1960, classic food writer Elizabeth David expressed a similar skepticism of bizarre menus and flamboyant plating.

After Bocuse traduced the movement and returned to tradition in the 1980s, nouvelle cuisine lost some of its mannered menus, yet retained appearance, balance, quality nutrition, and infinite variety. For example, at the Papiamento Restaurant on Aruba, owner Eduardo Ellis advertised home-raised herbs, papaya hot sauce, and chicken and shrimp kebabs cooked on the traditional island coalpot. Wolfgang Puck, an Austrian food whiz and author of *Modern French Cooking for the American Kitchen* (1980), introduced the caviar and salmon pizza at Spago, his Beverly Hills landmark. The core beliefs of French radical cookery remained vigorous in fusion cuisine, Third World diets, Tex-Mex, culinary tourism, and the local, artisanal, and health food movements.

See also: Beard, James; Child, Julia; French Diet and Cuisine; Japanese Diet and Cuisine; Kebabs; Restaurants; Taillevent.

Further Reading

Aulicino, Armand. *The Nouvelle Cuisine Cookbook: The Complete International Guide to the World of Nouvelle Cuisine.* New York: Grosset & Dunlap, 1976.

Troisgros, Jean, and Pierre Troisgros. *The Nouvelle Cuisine of Jean and Pierre Troisgros.* New York: William Morrow, 1978.

Urvater, Michele, and David Liederman. *Cooking the Nouvelle Cuisine in America.* New York: Workman, 1979.

Nutrition

Nutrition entered human concern in early Indian, Chinese, and Middle Eastern scriptures, which characterized what types of food strengthened the body and protected it from illness. The book of Leviticus (1440 B.C.E.), the Chinese *Zhouli* (*Chou-li, Rites of Chou*, compiled ca. 1116 B.C.E.), and the Indian Ayurveda (after 3000 B.C.E.) contain injunctions about selecting food and drink, hygienic storing and cooking, and food combinations to eat at a single sitting. Like the doctor or herbalist, the cook had to balance cold with hot, sweet with sour, and animal products with herbs, vegetables, grain, and fruit to avoid nutritional cancellations. The devout avoided banned items, as with wine and pig flesh, both forbidden by Koranic injunctions.

Other cultures followed their own concerns for right diet, such as the Hua of Papua, New Guinea, who stressed that ash should be removed from foods cooked in embers. Nigerians limited fruit by gender, thus denying males citrus fruit, mango, and papaya, which natives considered feminine food. Tanganyikans forbade eggs in the female diet to prevent stillbirths and twinning. In West Africa, meat was a privilege of males. Wives and daughters ate only small bits of the daily meat purchase. A similar custom in India diverted all fresh milk to boys, depriving girls of calcium and vitamin D.

Lack of nutrients in the diet pervades human history in periods of harsh weather and drought as well as during famines, pestilence, and sieges. One example from the journal of teenage writer Zlata Filipovic, titled *Zlata's Diary* (1994), records the hardships of Bosnia in 1993 during the ethnic cleansing of Muslims from Sarajevo. Reserving limited fuel for cooking, her family ate humanitarian relief packets containing tasteless white feta cheese and black market canned meat sold at outrageous prices, but little bread and produce and no fresh milk to balance intake.

Forensic studies of such meager diets in human coprolites, mummies, and skeletal and tooth remains attest to both disease and deficiencies as causes of death or contributors to crippled bodies and impaired lives. During fluctuations in the Nile's overflow in ancient Egypt, slaves were the first to succumb to a grain shortfall. The cereal-rich diet of the early Greeks threatened social stability because of periodic grain shortages. In 328 B.C.E., one such dearth forced authorities to distribute free barley to householders to prevent starvation and rebellion.

To broaden nutritional sources, early peoples ate unpalatable, unappealing, or taboo foods, even human flesh. Over long periods, the Chinese stored eggs, which developed into a national delicacy. Eskimo families, who enjoyed green vegetables during a limited period annually, traditionally ate moss and other plant material extracted from the craws of birds or stomachs of mammals. The Maori, who faced erratic supplies of foodstuffs, lined urns with ferns and stored corn that degenerated into *kanga pirau,* a foul-smelling residue. In the Caribbean, galley cooks discovered that they could keep sea turtles alive on board as a source of nutrition in sailors suffering scurvy, a deficiency of ascorbic acid.

Wellness Awareness

During the late Middle Ages, medical experts recognized the result of an inadequate or unbalanced diet, especially among the lower class and slaves. According to Abd al-Latif al-Baghdadi, an early-thirteenth-century Arab physician visiting Egypt during a famine, mothers who fed children only chickpeas and white bread caused bone and tooth malformation, dwarfism, and sickness.

The Renaissance increased awareness of the effects of food choices on wellness. The sixteenth-century Italian nutritionist Alessandro Trajano Petronio, author of *Del Viver delli Romani et di Conservar la Sanita Libri Cinque (Five Books on Roman Food and on Preserving Health,* ca. 1585), recommended to plebeian cooks a regimen of health foods, namely, lupines, sprouts, vetch, wild cherries, and cattails.

The latter called for boiling, frying, and dressing in garlic sauce.

Nutritional guides proliferated during the seventeenth century. To settlers of North America, reformer and moralist William Vaughan penned *Directions for Health Both Naturall and Artificial* (1617). When he immigrated to Newfoundland in the 1620s, he inveighed against alcohol, which he denounced for deforming fetuses. His contemporary, Salvatore Massonio, author of *Archidipno: Overo dell'Insalata e dell'Uso di Essa (The Best Banquet: The Salad and Its Uses,* 1627), advised cooks to serve fresh salads and dress them with herbs, vinaigrette, and salt. He promoted kitchen gardening by advocating the eating of crocus and nasturtiums. Later in the century, François Massialot, author of *Le Cuisinier Royal et Bourgeois (The Royal and Middle-Class Cook,* 1693) lauded the New World turkey and provided a recipe for stuffing and instructions on roasting and garnishing the protein-rich bird.

Malnutrition in the Western Hemisphere flourished amid racism, slavery, and genocide. In an autobiography written in 1912 about Washington State Salish life, Mourning Dove, the pseudonym of Christine Quintasket, reported on the annual hunger that struck native families in February. While succoring the poor and welcoming neighbors, her family watched their parfleches (storage envelopes) flatten. Her mother began a drastic rationing of food: She served meals only when necessary and allotted tiny amounts to herself while she fed her children. Mourning Dove grew bitter at the Native American injunction that adults eat first, protesting the bone and gristle left for children to gnaw.

A popularizer of the faddish term *nutrition,* U.S. President James Garfield introduced a kitchen routine that yielded well-cooked, healthful dishes, milk, coffee, and pennyroyal and catnip tea. A learned man and voracious reader, he and his wife, Lucretia Rudolph Garfield, reared seven children on wholesome bounty. The White House bent toward a well-balanced diet came to an end with the inauguration of epicure Chester A. Arthur in 1881. Only months after his return to private life, Arthur died of Bright's disease resulting from a lack of vitamin D. One critic blamed his rapid decline on inadequate exercise and a diet dominated by terrapin and fine wines.

Nutrition as Science

The populist spirit and zeal for reform in the 1800s and early 1900s produced sensible as well as bizarre regimens for upgrading nutrition. A leader of domestic science, Wilbur Olin Atwater, an agricultural chemist at Wesleyan University, outlined a diet based on the scientific analysis of foods. At Yale University, he raised American standards of agricultural chemistry and quantified the heat produced by the body's oxidation of sustenance. From his findings, Atwater charted the caloric value of foods and made world studies of how nations profit from labor maintained by a healthful diet. His conclusions supported German studies of nutrition and metabolism and remain the standard for calorimetry. His summation of the American diet and his food composition tables, distributed in 1895 from the U.S. Department of Agriculture (USDA), formed the bases of scientific food selection and levels of nutrition used at the Boston Cooking School, cook Fannie Farmer's pioneering effort in training poor housewives to buy the most nutritious foods that their families could afford.

Guilt-producing media ads tapped the homemaker's growing unease about family nutrition and suggested techniques and products to improve diet, including canned milk and bananas, a new commodity on the global market. Katharine A. Fisher, director of the Good Housekeeping Institute, issued articles directing homemakers on the importance of expending cash and energy preparing menus preplanned by nutritionists. In the March 1925 issue of *Good Housekeeping,* Evangeline Downey Tector presented a compelling argument for body-building food to supplement children's diet. Her upbeat tone and cheery attitude toward the mother's role in strengthening the family allied with simple photos of the best foods for health, including bread, cereal, dried and fresh fruit, eggs, peas, and spinach.

Women's magazines also distorted the nutritional picture with disinformation and unsubstantiated claims. In 1926, advertising by the Kitchen Craft Company of West Bend, Wisconsin, touted a waterless multistage cooker, a latch-lidded kettle holding numerous small dishes of food, as the answer to mothers seeking to preserve vitamins and minerals in entrées. In addition to citing dietitian Milo Hastings as a promoter of the device, the company guaranteed flavorful, healthful meals. The article concluded with a twist in logic—a claim that the cooker was essential to household fitness.

Nutrition as Entitlement

For those lacking the resources to keep their families adequately fed, the responsibility fell to governments and charities. During the Australian Depression of 1929, when unemployment put families on the edge of starvation, individuals lined up for handouts from the Benevolent Society. Volunteers supplied bread, condensed milk, fruit jam, syrup, and tinned meat at depression food shelters throughout New South Wales. As the Depression worsened, the society handed out food coupons at labor offices and police stations. By 1931, the governor-general volunteered the state as a dispenser of unemployment relief.

During better times late in the 1930s, mounting concern over vitamins and minerals sent meal planners to women's magazines for data on how to supplement the diet with fish. As explained by Walter Eddy, director of the Good Housekeeping Bureau of Foods, Sanitation, and Health, before the addition of iodine to salt, seafood was the best source of iodine to prevent goiter. In a magazine article specifying goitrous and nongoitrous ar-

eas of the United States, he compiled a chart of iodine-rich fish to help the home cook with selection. At the top of the chart, lobster contained 11,590 parts per billion (ppb) of iodine and clams 6,200 ppb, contrasting mackerel at 330 ppb at the bottom of the list.

During World War II, commercial rice processors began parboiling rice to produce a nutritious and stable food for Allied soldiers. The method preserved nutrients that milling would have wasted. By maintaining niacin and vitamins B1, B3, and B12, the military prevented beriberi and pellagra, both deficiency diseases that sap soldiers of efficiency and strength. A bonus from the parboiling process was a lengthened shelf life for rice, which hardened and resisted moisture damage during storage in tropical military commissaries.

In the post–World War II era, hunger grew rampant worldwide. In a press release dated February 6, 1946, President Harry S. Truman encouraged Americans not to grumble if they did not find grocery shelves stocked with the bread, meat, cheese and other dairy products, and salad dressings they preferred. He exhorted complainers to accept inconveniences as a small price for saving lives and mitigating suffering in liberated countries. The president declared stable nutrition a firm basis for peace. On June 4, 1946, he signed the National School Lunch Act, which supplied cafeterias with commodity foods, feeding the undernourished while guaranteeing farmers a venue for their goods.

In defeat, the Japanese faced national hunger. In May 1946, food allotments in Tokyo averaged half of official ration allowances. The resulting daily consumption reached only about 520 calories per person, leaving the Japanese to forage for wild food. Japanese dieticians worried about effects on health after rice consumption fell to 66.6 percent its previous level. Another deterrent to wellness, grain-polishing machines stripped the husk and germ to create a *kaku-mai* (whitened rice). The loss of the germ destroyed the layer rich in vitamin B1 and increased the threat of beriberi and heart and nerve atrophy. To rescue a generation from irreversible damage, the Japanese government began a propaganda campaign on the value of unrefined rice or blends of rice and barley.

Denis Parsons Burkitt, an Anglo-Irish surgeon and medical missionary, asked similar questions about the typically bland, over-refined Western diet. From a study of appendicitis, colitis, colon cancer, constipation, diverticulitis, gallstones, heart disease, hemorrhoids, hiatal hernia, and varicose veins in industrialized countries during the late 1960s, Burkitt evolved a theory that dietary fiber combats diseases peculiar to nations where food comes to the table devoid of fruit peels, husks, seed coats, and whole grains. Against the food habits of an overweight, white-bread world, he lectured on the selection and preparation of foods rich in unabsorbable roughage and published 300 articles and a book, *Western Diseases: Their Dietary Prevention and Reversibility* (1994). His impe-

Basic Nutrients and Consequences of Intake Deficiency

Basic Nutrient	Health Benefits	Consequences of Intake Deficiency
calcium	bolsters nerve and muscle tissue, builds bones and teeth	osteoporosis, rickets
carbohydrates	energizes	malaise
chromium	balances weight, enhances metabolism, tones muscles	glucose intolerance, muscle loss
copper	pigments hair and skin, strengthens blood and nerves	anemia, weakened bones
fats	energizes	anemia, fat deposits of the liver, impaired healing, reduced platelet count, scaly dermatitis
fiber (hemicellulose)	aids digestion	colitis, constipation, hemorrhoids
fluoride	strengthens bones and teeth	dental caries
folic acid (foliacin)	aids digestion, forms red blood cells	anemia, birth defects, bleeding gums, diarrhea, insomnia, stunted growth
iodine	helps thyroid gland regulate energy	cretinism, goiter
iron	allows blood to carry oxygen	anemia, breathlessness, fatigue, headache, weakness
magnesium	aids muscle and nerve activity, energizes, strengthens bones	confusion, loss of appetite, muscle cramp, nausea
phosphorus	bolsters nerve and muscle tissue, builds bones and teeth	anorexia, malaise, skeletal pain, weakness
potassium	balances fluids, transmits nerve impulses	impaired peristalsis, loss of appetite, malaise, nausea, unusual behavior, weakness
protein	builds cells	kwashiorkor, marasmus
selenium	activates enzymes, acts as an antioxidant	cardiopathy or weak heart muscles, muscle pain
sodium	balances body fluids	diarrhea, excessive urination, headache, muscle cramp, vomiting, weakness
vitamin A (retinol)	builds resistance to infection, prevents night blindness	deformed cornea, mucosal atrophy, night blindness, weak tooth enamel
vitamin B1 (thiamine)	aids normal growth, digestion, and memory	cardiomyopathy, constipation, encephalopathy, fatigue, indigestion, loss of appetite, nervousness, neuropathy, poor memory
vitamin B2 (riboflavin)	promotes digestion and growth	cracked lips, dizziness, eyestrain, inflamed tongue, light sensitivity, retarded growth, scaly skin
vitamin B3 (niacin)	aids appetite and memory	depression, diarrhea, impaired memory, loss of appetite, skin pellagra
vitamin B6 (pyridoxine)	energizes, aids digestion	confusion, depression, diarrhea, fatigue, infantile convulsion, irritability, rash
vitamin B12	aids memory and red blood cell formation, energizes	beriberi, indigestion, cardiac damage, anemia, paralysis, numbness, pellagra
vitamin C (ascorbic acid)	promotes oxidation and healthy blood vessels, bones, and teeth	bleeding gums, bruising, fatigue, scurvy
vitamin D (caciferol)	boosts intestinal absorption, develops teeth and skeleton	bowlegs, kidney failure, osteoporosis, rickets, skeletal malformation, softened skull
vitamin E (tocopherol)	acts as an antioxidant, bolsters reproductive system	anemia, low birth weight, muscular atrophy, nerve deterioration, poor fat absorption, reproductive failure
vitamin H (biotin)	aids metabolism	toxicity
vitamin K (phylloquinone)	enables blood to clot	hemorrhage, impaired healing
zinc	balances insulin, boosts immune system, promotes healing	anemia, female infertility, hair loss, loss of taste, slow healing, stunted growth

tus toward supplying pantries with bran cereal, fruit, nuts, wheat germ, whole wheat breads, and vegetable sources of roughage revived interest in Stone Age eating habits.

Standards

In 1993, the U.S. Food and Drug Administration further assisted home cooks in selecting nourishing foods by issuing guidelines for mandatory nutritional labeling on all edibles. As of May 1994, labels had to follow a model that listed serving size, servings per container, calories, calories from fat, total fat, saturated fat, cholesterol, sodium, carbohydrates, dietary fiber, sugars, and protein. In addition, manufacturers had to quantify vitamin and mineral content in terms that the consumer could understand. Amounts appeared in grams or milligrams and by percentage.

In February 2001, after learning that Philadelphia was America's fattest city, Chef Joseph Shilling, director of the school of culinary arts at the Art Institute of Philadelphia launched a campaign to improve food selection among urbanites. The city's fast-food restaurants and street-vended pretzels and cheese steaks produced an obesity rate of 29 percent. Shilling began educating cooks on healthful menu items, revamping recipes to decrease fat content, and instructing waiters to point out wise choices to diners. He also recommended portion reduction and an increase in fruit and vegetable consumption.

Raising Sustenance Levels

To bolster diets farther south without using pills or capsules, after 1960, the Institute of Nutrition of Central America and Panama (INCAP) supplied cooks with Incaparina, a high-protein flour made from cottonseed, corn, and sorghum and containing yeast, calcium carbonate, and vitamin A. Similar to the groundnut flour that cooks in India emulsify in water, the powder supplemented baking without altering texture, taste, or appearance. In the Philippines, school lunch providers baked Nutribuns, a low-cost, enriched biscuit that furnished local children with one day's nutrients. The Agency for International Development contracted with American food processors to extend nutrition in foodstuffs among have-not nations:

- California Packing manufactured a protein drink for East Africans' tables.

- Coca-Cola marketed a soy milk product in Brazil.

- Dorr-Oliver devised a cottonseed product to enrich the diet in India.

- General Mills supplied Pakistan with a cottonseed-soy food.

- International Milling enhanced nutrients in wheat foods for Tunisia.

- Krauss Milling fortified corn-based foods for Brazil.

- Monsanto produced Puma, a banana-flavored soya product sold in Guyana.

- Pillsbury supplied Frescavida, a protein beverage served in El Salvador.

- Swift dispatched a soy milk product to Brazilians and a protein drink to India.

In 2001, Walter Willett, chair of the department of nutrition at Harvard School of Public Health, published *Eat, Drink, and Be Healthy: The Harvard Medical School Guide to Healthy Eating,* which overturned the proportions of food advised since 1992 by the USDA, an agency he charged with promoting agriculture at the expense of public health. Willett denounced data advising homemakers to serve six to 11 portions of bread, cereal, pasta, and rice daily, blaming a heavy carbohydrate diet for causing diabetes, obesity, and early death. To spare waistlines at a time when 61 percent of Americas weighed too much, Willett called for a reduced emphasis on red meat, whole milk, and margarine and championed beans, nuts, and oils from canola, corn, olives, peanuts, soy, and sunflowers. Citing studies of health professionals, his advice to cooks stressed more fruit, vegetables, eggs, fish, and poultry.

In June 2011, the USDA issued MyPlate, the second update of the food pyramid, a pictorial guide to healthful consumption. In place of a triangular arrangement, the logo took the shape of a plate roughly divided into

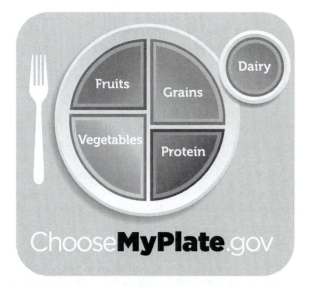

The U.S. Department of Agriculture released a new healthy eating guide, called "My Plate," in 2011. Replacing the more complex pyramid diagram, "My Plate" depicts the five major food groups in healthful proportions (with additional recommendations). *(Agriculture Department/Associated Press)*

quadrants featuring grains, fruit, protein, and vegetables and a cup containing dairy products. A list of recommendations boosted citizen awareness of the value of fruits and vegetables and the benefits of eating whole grains and lean protein and drinking skim milk. Key to the simplified chart are suggestions to eat less and to choose water over sugared beverages.

See also: Coprolites; Durante, Castor; Famine; Liebig, Justus von; Medieval Diet and Cuisine; Paleolithic Diet; Pickling; Poultry; Rumford, Count; Seaman's Diet and Cuisine; Snack Food; Trans Fat; Voegtlin, Walter L.

Further Reading

Caballero, Benjamin, Lindsay Allen, and Andrew Prentice, eds. *Encyclopedia of Human Nutrition.* Boston: Elsevier, 2005.

Gratzer, Walter Bruno. *Terrors of the Table: The Curious History of Nutrition.* New York: Oxford University Press, 2005.

Neuman, William. "Nutrition Plate Unveiled, Replacing Food Pyramid." *The New York Times,* June 2, 2011.

Steckel, Richard H., and Jerome Carl Rose, eds. *The Backbone of History: Health and Nutrition in the Western Hemisphere.* New York: Cambridge University Press, 2002.

Whitney, Eleanor Noss, and Sharon Rady Rolfes. *Understanding Nutrition.* Belmont, CA: Thomson Higher Education, 2008.

Nuts and Seeds

Consumers from cave dwellers to vegans and raw foodists have looked to nuts and seeds for convenient sources of energy, oil, and protein. Shell fruits earn their place in the human diet for their antioxidants, minerals, omega-3 and -6 fatty acids, and vitamins B1, B2, B3, and E. They satisfy hunger and vary the food intake of patients suffering from diabetes, heart disease, high cholesterol, immune deficiency, and premature aging.

High fiber makes nuts easy to digest. For their mouthfeel and energy boost, they contribute to the appeal of salads, sauces, soft drinks, and syrups and to Pakistani curry, filbert (or hazelnut) butter, pistachio halvah, Waldorf salad, and Thai cashew chicken, all recipes requiring bulk. The confection industry relies on nuts for taste and crunch, a factor in the production of almond amaretti, baklava, Chinese moon cakes, granola, Israeli coated peanuts, peanut brittle, and pralines.

History

From 778,000 B.C.E. on the shores of Lake Hula, Israel, hominins used anvils and stone hammers to crack shells and extract the kernels from acorns, almonds, pistachios, and water chestnuts. East Asians from Siberia south to Korea, Japan, and India cultivated the foxnut, the seedpod of a water lily. Indian cooks cooked the pods in porridge and stir-fried them in oil until they popped. From 14,000 B.C.E., Japanese foragers soaked acorn kernels in ponds to leach out bitter tannins and release sweetness.

Additional historic evidence of nuts as food occurred in the British Isles in 7000 B.C.E., when hazelnuts provided a major source of protein to vegetarian clans. The peanut nourished Peruvians as early as 5600 B.C.E.; in 5000 B.C.E., the mongongo nut yielded a dietary staple for San Bushmen of the Kalahari. From 4000 B.C.E., northeastern Chinese propagated the sweet chestnut, which orchardists advanced to 300 cultivars. The Bedouin of Libya and Egypt collected seeds from the wild gourd to make bread. In 1325 B.C.E., burial parties interred Egypt's king Tutankhamen with stores of Turkish almonds to delight him in the afterlife.

Nuts and seeds have fed Australian Aborigines, forest Indians, nomads, Polynesian and Portuguese sailors, polar explorers, and armies on the march with a handy power snack. Assyrians treasured sesame seeds as a sacred food. Travel writers Marco Polo and Ibn Battuta found contented mealtime chewing of betel nuts in China and India. Persians cultivated the pistachio in desert soil high in saline; British and Scottish beech hedges produced fragrant mast for smoking beer and cheese. Along the Amazon and Orinoco valleys, Bolivians and Guianans gathered Brazil nuts in the wild, revealing clusters of 8 to 24 kernels in one large fruit.

Ancient Greeks stockpiled nuts and seeds as siege food and relied on beechnuts to feed victims of sieges. Romans tossed almonds and coins at weddings as symbols of fertility and prosperity. Greeks and Iberians developed recipes for acorn flour, which also became a dietary staple for the California Miwok. To protect them from squirrels and worm infestation, the Miwok cached acorns in baskets, much like the Cherokee and Creek stored hickory nuts. To ready acorns for use in bread and porridge, cooks ground kernels into flour and leached out tannins through sand colanders.

In the Middle Ages, Silesians preferred beechnut puree instead of butter from dairy animals. Nuts took prominence on the church calendar with the *marron glacé* (candied chestnut) served in France at Christmas and roasted chestnuts honoring the feast days of Saint Martin and Saint Simon. Under the medieval system of commerce, public sale of milk met with strong buyer skepticism. A safer street purchase, almond or walnut butters and liquids, the run off of grinding, remained fresh over a longer period.

Nuts remained stable food crops in the Renaissance, when cookery became more complex and extravagant. French pastry shelves added almonds to macaroons and marzipan. In 1600, Portuguese sailors transported the peanut from Brazil to Africa. Unlike corn and sorghum, peanuts flourished in poor soil, while serving as a nitrogen fixer, and became a sustainable crop.

In the nineteenth century, an inventive vegetarian in Battle Creek, Michigan, Almeda West Lambert, found ways of replacing animal protein with nuts. In *The Guide for Nut Cookery* (1899), she proposed blends of nut butter and meal with bread crumbs, eggs, herbs, and spices to imitate fish and turkey. Her concoction, which she dubbed "nutmeato," remained viable for three decades, along with "nutgrano," a blend of ground kernels with grains. One recipe for cereal and peanut coffee began with the roasting of ground peanuts with cornmeal, malt, and wheat bran.

In World Cuisine

Nuts and seeds remain big business in the world food trade, from Georgia pecans to Australian macadamias. African growers readily sell peanuts to the poor for flour, porridge, soup, and salted snacks. In Burkina Faso, Cameroon, Congo, Mali, Zambia, and Zimbabwe, consumers look to the farinaceous Bambara groundnut for a cash crop, daily sustenance, and a solution to chronic malnutrition. Malian and Nigerian women enrich their families by selling peanut pancakes and roasted nuts on the street.

Because nuts can disable the body's immune system, concern for lethal allergies reduces the availability of nuts in public venues. School cafeterias formulate rules to protect the vulnerable from accidentally ingesting nut products. Food manufacturers voluntarily label to advertise nut-free recipes and to warn of nuts in processed products. And the problem of food reactions has proved thorny for the transportation industry. In June 2011, Air Canada banned nut products from catered meals and snacks, a ruling that inconvenienced the vegans and raw foodists who rely on nuts and seeds for protein. Irish food regulators have taken a stand against overlabeling by informing consumers that too many warnings reduced the number of food choices for people with allergies.

See also: Allergies, Food; Caching; Ibn Battuta; Medieval Diet and Cuisine; Nomad Diet and Cuisine; Wild Food.

Further Reading

Griffith, Linda, and Fred Griffith. *Nuts: Recipes from Around the World That Feature Nature's Perfect Ingredient.* New York: St. Martin's, 2003.

Laskin, Avner, and Danya Weiner. *Nuts: More Than 75 Delicious & Healthy Recipes.* New York: Sterling, 2008.

Rosengarten, Frederic. *The Book of Edible Nuts.* Mineola, NY: Dover, 2004.

Obesity

A preventable condition triggering arthritis, cancer, diabetes, kidney and liver disease, reflux, and sleep apnea, obesity refers to the accumulation of excess body fat of 20 percent or more. Overeating is the chief cause. A preference for energy-dense convenience foods from drive-throughs and vending machines depletes the diet of fiber and water while imposing a regimen of fat, salt, and sugar. The chronic increase in body mass taxes the muscles and skeleton, requiring undue expenditure of energy to function. A general malaise from inactivity exacerbates back pain and gout and generates congestive heart failure, hypertension, and varicose veins.

Around 23,000 B.C.E., Stone Age civilizations extolled the voluptuous female figure as a symbol of satiety and fertility. Mother divinities from Anatolia, Mesopotamia, and the pre-Columbian Americas honored the corpulent female as an emblem of stored nutrients and longevity for the clan. In sub-Saharan Africa, Mauritanian, Nigerian, Tanzanian, Ugandan, and Zimbabwean grooms rejected slim women as brides until potential brides entered a period of weight gain from pampering and selective eating.

After the fifth century B.C.E., Arab, Chinese, Egyptian, Greek, and Indian medical experts identified obesity as a harbinger of decreased fertility, catastrophic illness, and sudden death. Greek and Roman stage comedy ridiculed Obesus, the roly-poly stereotype, as a glutton, a figure stigmatized by the Seven Deadly Sins of Christian dogma. Despite satire and sermons, caloric intake increased during the Renaissance. As a sign of military preparedness, the Industrial Revolution made available the food to fatten up Europe's armies and prevent another debacle as devastating as the Napoleonic Wars.

Lifestyles became less strenuous in the late 1800s with the introduction of steam engines, which boosted the production and transportation of such processed food as Indian curries and pudding mixes. German chemist Wilhelm Normann's invention of trans fats—hydrogenated lard and margarine—in 1902 stabilized food for distribution and storage on warehouse shelves.

At the end of World War II, American influence on world diet precipitated overall increases in height and weight. For families, obesity precipitated hard labor, thrombosis, and stroke in pregnant women and, in their offspring, birth defects, and neonatal problems, including stillbirths. In the 1950s–1970s, corpulent adults chose bariatric stomach stapling and gastroplasty, a costly re-engineering of the alimentary canal that permanently limited food intake.

Obesity worsened in the late twentieth century because of higher daily caloric intake, notably among Nazi death camp returnees, urbanized Pima of Arizona and Mexico, and Third World survivors of child starvation. Computers and video games replaced televisions as causes of a sedentary lifestyle. Legislative incentives to American agribusiness in the 1970s decreased the cost of corn, rice, soy, and wheat in comparison with the price of fresh produce. By 2011, U.S. Department of Agriculture investment in commodity crops reached $25 billion annually. Thus, empty calories cost less, tempting the poor to spend food dollars on beer, carbohydrates, and junk food. The problem extended to the school lunch program, which subsidized cafeterias for purchasing fried potatoes and pizza rather than broccoli, juices, and salad greens.

As opposed to the food consumption in developed countries, sub-Saharan Africans maintained the lowest levels of fat from an average diet of 2,176 calories per day. In contrast, the United States supplied 3,654 calories to the daily intake, much of it from energy-dense fat, fructose, and sucrose in take-out foods. The alarming spurt in average body weight influenced food producers to market such low-caloric foods as diet cola, fat-free milk, rice cakes, Ry-Krisp, and Slim-Fast protein shakes, a regimen for eating to lose weight. One herbal drug known as fen-phen, a combination of the stimulant ephedra and the mood-elevating herb Saint-John's-wort, attempted to trick the body into dieting by raising the level of chemical serotonin in the brain, thus creating the illusion of contentment.

In this same period, portion size burgeoned in restaurant servings, microwave dinners, and packaged goods, resulting in the "super-size" syndrome. Media advertising featured the high-fat, high-sugar meal as the American way. Binge eating and overconsumption of carbohydrates from sweet beverages, fast foods, and potato chips increased the trend to fat Americans, particularly low-income women in unskilled jobs. Other causes—alcoholism, antidepressants, antismoking drugs, and steroids—contributed more weight and more stress, a source of nervous eating.

Authorities became concerned for children and teens, whose body fat accumulation threatened overall health and longevity. In the 2010s, First Lady Michelle Obama set an example of exercising, growing a White House garden, and eating wholesome meals. By 2011, obesity reached 30 percent and above in Alabama, Arkansas, Kentucky, Louisiana, Michigan, Mississippi, Missouri, Oklahoma, South Carolina, Tennessee, Texas, and West Virginia, largely from an average intake of 200 unburned calories per day. Over a span of 15 years, meanwhile, native Hawaiians doubled their rate of overweight. Black adults topped the scale at 40 percent obese, followed by Hispanics at 35 percent.

According to the World Health Organization, as of 2011, more than 2.6 million people worldwide died annually from poor diet and sedentary habits. Overweight affected nearly half of all Malaysians and Qataris, more than one third of Kuwaitis, one fourth of Canadian children, and 20 percent of the world's total population. According to the U.S. Centers for Disease Control, obesity, which plagues 29.1 percent of adult Americans, drained the country of dollars for medical care. Role models in Japan and South Korea average only 3.2 percent overweight, giving evidence that East Asian diet protects consumers from a leading preventable cause of death. While theater and media ads hyped new sources of empty calories, health initiatives by the National Heart, Lung, and Blood Institute; the National Institutes of Health; and the World Health Organization published practical nutritional advice on attaining ideal weight.

See also: Athenaeus; Fast Food; Herbs; Nutrition; Scandinavian Diet and Cuisine; Trans Fat; Voegtlin, Walter L.

Further Reading

Fairburn, Christopher G., and Kelly D. Brownell, eds. *Eating Disorders and Obesity: A Comprehensive Handbook.* New York: Guilford, 2002.

Gilman, Sander L. *Fat: A Cultural History of Obesity.* Malden, MA: Polity, 2008.

Hicks, Terry Allan. *Obesity.* New York: Marshall Cavendish Benchmark, 2009.

Kopelman, Peter F., and Ian D. Caterson. *Clinical Obesity in Adults and Children.* New York: Wiley-Blackwell, 2005.

Oils

As a cooking medium, liquid cooking fats moisturize the tissues of edibles with a nutrient essential to braising, frying, and sautéing. Animal muscle meat—anchovies, bacon, beef roast, cod, ham, mutton, salmon, sardines—exude natural lipids that even browning and heighten natural flavors. Vegetable fats from almond, argan, avocado, canola, corn, and rice and the seeds of butternut squash, citrus fruit, cotton, flax, grapes, pumpkins, and rapeseed offer a range of stability and taste for kitchen use. Additional flavor derives from the nut oils of cashews, hazelnuts, pecans, pistachios, and walnuts. When permeated with citrus peel, garlic, herbs, and peppers, specialty oils heighten taste without adding extraneous bulk.

Historically, oils figure in all cuisines, particularly the expression of macadamia nut oil by Australian Aborigines and tropical cookery with calabash seed oil, which began after 6000 B.C.E. For some 5,500 years, the Mediterranean diet has showcased olive oil, first commercialized in 3500 B.C.E. by the Minoans of Crete. Egyptians, Greeks, and Romans valued black seed (*Nigella sativa*) as a curative oil used in bread and cake. In 3000 B.C.E., when Africans in the rain forests from Angola to Senegal were commercializing palm oil for the frying of yams, Egyptians stowed the emollient in a tomb at Abydos as a grave gift for the afterlife. During the same period, Egyptian consumers depended on caravan loads of olive oil from Palestine and Syria.

While flaxseed and safflower oil dominated Middle Eastern cookery in 2500 B.C.E., residents of Harappa in the Indus Valley relied on sesame oil for baking, a primary cooking fat that spread over Asia and Africa. In 2100 B.C.E., the Mexica began growing sunflowers for oilseeds, an agrarian advance that spread north to Arizona Indians by 800 B.C.E. To the south, Peruvians domesticated the peanut as an oil source before 2000 B.C.E.

Soybeans entered the lipid market in northern China in 1000 B.C.E., the same time that Greek olive growers were capitalizing on the food oil trade. Within the millennium, olive farming was flourishing in Magna Graecia, Sicily, North Africa, and Provence as far north as the Helvetian Alps. The Romans dominated the olive trade, including fruit cured in oil and *chrism* (holy oil) revered in Jewish and Christian ritual for anointing priests.

National Cuisines

From the first century C.E., cooks in India expressed cooking fats from the oilseed turnip; brushed bread with ghee, a clarified butter oil; and boosted the pungency of fritters by frying them in mustard oil. Chinese and Japanese cooks valued tea seed oil for dressing and sauces and for low-fat stir-frying. Middle Easterners added flour and sesame seed paste to olive oil to produce hummus but sprinkled the oil lightly on foods because of the high cost of importing it by camel caravan. Muslim cooks relied on sesame oil, which also served as a condiment smeared on whole fish for roasting as a kebab and for the frying of samosas (turnovers).

West Africans turned the shea nut and egusi melon and watermelon to use as sources of cooking oils, all high in nutrition and protection from dietary cholesterol. In the 1400s, provisioners across the Levant and North Africa supplied caravans and cargo vessels with palm oil for cooking. In Russia, cooks replaced butter and lard during Lent with pine nut oil, which they added to bread dough as a preservative.

Among Aleutian Yupik, Makah, and Nootka of Vancouver Island, and the Dorset of Labrador and northern Quebec, the rendering of blubber from harp seals and stranded whales resulted in a multiuse oil for cooking, moistening dried caribou and halibut, and soaking bones for burning in stoves. Lipids preserved berries and, when mixed with snow, turned them into ice cream flavorings. As far south as Baja, Pacific Indians valued eulachon, salmon, and animal fats as a domestic flavoring or dressing for foods. Tlingit and Tsimshian exploited oil sources as a marketable item, which they sold at trade fairs.

Industry

After French brewer Nicolas Appert introduced vacuum canning in 1809, canneries packed tinned salmon in oil as a preservative and tenderizing agent. On the Upper Guinea shores in the 1830s, the French controlled the peanut oil industry and the English dominated palm oil trade. Hong Kong seized the advantage in the 1850s by profiteering on coconut oil brought from Southeast Asia to China and on return trade in peanut oil. In the 1860s, coconut oil from India, Indonesia, Malaysia, Mexico, the Pacific Islands, and Sri Lanka monopolized food oil marketing until palm and soybean extracts toppled sales. Near the end of the century, Russian food processors hybridized sunflowers to produce 50 percent more oil and turned their crops into Europe's more valued seed oil.

Peanut oil became a political advantage during the American Civil War, when Southern householders replaced lard in pastries and olive oil in dressings with the regional product. After the invention of hydrogenation in 1902, Africa, China, and India profited from the peanut oil boom, which foundered during World War I, curbing the world supply of margarine. Argentina experienced a similar food shortfall in 1936 during the Spanish Civil War, when farmers began growing sunflowers to yield enough oil to replace embargoed olive oil in traditional recipes.

A subsequent shortage of coconut oil during World War II forced Malayans to shop on the black market for coconut oil, which they used for cooking and lighting in lamps. The American margarine industry adapted to peanut oil as a substitute. Farmers sowed safflowers as a commercial experiment with a cooking oil that slowed digestion and promoted nutrient assimilation. In 1942, when World War II rationing limited the availability of butter, lard, and salad oils, homemakers accepted peanut oil, which remained free of government control. As a replacement for butter, margarine, and shortening, home cooks began using cooking oil in cakes and muffins in the 1950s. By the 1960s, the health food movement embraced peanut oil for its nutritional benefits in frying, processed foods, and salad dressing. Simultaneously, Canada joined China and India in commercializing rapeseed oil for use in cooking.

In 1961, Chicago investors Arthur E. Meyerhoff and Leon R. Rubin invented Pam, a gluten- and lactose-free cooking spray that maintained the qualities of cooking oil in light, low-calorie applications. The popular lubricant coated grills, molds, and sauté pans and eased the assembly of blender and food processor parts. Demand for Pam and its imitators resulted in specialty sprays flavored with butter, canola, garlic, lemon, and olive oil for crisping potato and poultry skins. An offshoot permeated with flour created a nonstick surface on bakeware.

Today, energy experts comb the world for biofuel substitutes for dwindling petroleum. Among these are oils extracted from the coyote melon (*Cucurbita palmata*) and jojoba of the American Southwest and Mexico and the shea nut cultivated by the Banda of central Africa as well as waste vegetable oil from fast-food restaurants and food-processing factories. As a food source, vegetable oil constitutes a profitable food industry worldwide, notably the oyster nut (*Telfairia occidentalis*) in Mozambique and Tanzania, samphire (*Salicornia europaea*) in Pakistan, coconut oil on the Philippine island of Samar, and palm oil from the Caribbean and Kenya. Malaysia exports 70 percent of global palm oil, followed by production in the Ivory Coast, New Guinea, the Philippines, the Solomon Islands, and Thailand.

See also: Cod; Fish and Fishing; Lapérouse, Jean François Galaup; Nuts and Seeds; Olives and Olive Oil; Trans Fat; Whaling.

Further Reading

Freedman, Paul H. *Food: The History of Taste.* Berkeley: University of California Press, 2007.

Pellechia, Thomas. *Garlic, Wine, and Olive Oil: Historical Anecdotes and Recipes.* Santa Barbara, CA: Capra, 2000.

Preedy, Victor R., Ronald R. Watson, and Vinood B. Patel. *Nuts and Seeds in Health and Disease Prevention.* Boston: Academic Press, 2011.

Olives and Olive Oil

A nutritional foundation in Europe, Africa, and middle and central Asia, the olive tree produces both fruit and oil as well as leaves for tea. A compact, long-lived evergreen native to Crete, Cyprus, Israel, Lebanon, and Syria since before 5000 B.C.E., the feral olive (*Olea europaea communis*) is the oldest in world agriculture, followed by the date palm, fig bush, and wine grape. The olive tree can survive for 3,000 years, even on the least arable land in drought conditions across Algeria, Ethiopia, Kenya, Morocco, Tunisia, and Uganda. It begins bearing in its fifteenth year, reaches a height of yield in the fortieth year, and slows productivity after 140 years.

Greek workers harvest olives by shaking the tree boughs and collecting the fallen fruit, typically in midwinter. Olives and olive oil, held sacred in ancient Greece, remain essential to the cuisine and economy of the eastern Mediterranean. *(Bastian Parschau/Getty Images)*

For millennia, the olive has provided growers with cooking and lamp oil, food preservatives, ritual oil, soap, unguent, and wood. The Minoans profited from the olive trade as early as 3500 B.C.E. Archaeologists attest to the centrality of olive oil to Cretan and Turkish daily life by the number of storage amphorae, decantation basins, and milling stones that survive from prehistory. So sacred were olive groves in Attica that the Athenians passed laws forbidding the hewing of olive trees under pain of death or exile.

The tree appears so frequently in frescos, funerary art, classical literature, and scripture that it attests to its own prominence in Middle Eastern diet and cuisine. Baskets of olives and urns of oil accompanied the Egyptian dead to their tombs. By 2000 B.C.E., oil from Syria was worth five times its weight in wine. Hippocrates and later healers chose olive oil as an aphrodisiac, a protection of the stomach from alcoholic excesses, and a curative for burns, dandruff, dry hair and skin, earache, and muscle ache.

Mediterranean Staple

A sacred dietary staple rounding out a triad with bread and wine, olives symbolized the elements of the settled life—bounty, peace, and wellness. In the prophet Isaiah's visions of a Hebrew savior, he foresaw the birth of Christ as a branch sprung from the root of Jesse and house of David, the parent tree. During King David's reign (ca. 1000–970 B.C.E.), he posted security guards around his olive groves and warehouses.

The mechanical press, invented around 1000 B.C.E., raised profits for Iberian and Phoenician growers, who touted their terroir for distinct flavor, quality, and viscosity of oil. Unguent and olive branches took prominence in religious anointings in the Bible and Koran, for cleansing newborns, at gravesites for bathing and mummifying the dead, and, from 776 B.C.E., at Olympic contests and Panathenaic Games. Parents honored the birth of a child by planting an olive tree, a symbol of longevity for the family and its progeny.

Commercial propagation in Greece after 700 B.C.E. involved pruning, manuring, rooting suckers, and grafting cultured stock to the wild olive tree. Where conquest took soldiers, the olive accompanied them—as far west as Iberia and east to India and Pakistan. Bountiful crops enriched growers on Chios and Melos. Commercial olive growing supported farmers in Crete, Greece, and Israel and developed fans in England, France, Germany, Romania, and Russia for the large Greek kalamata, the longish green French Picholine, and the greenish-purple

Manzanilla de Jaén from Spain. Pressing and pickling in brine or lye began in late fall. Shippers sealed both fruit and oil in amphorae for trade around the Mediterranean.

Through the Ages

The Greeks and Romans turned olives into a food industry by associating the oil with refined dining. Snobbish diners maintained that only barbarians preferred oil from animal sources. Merchants touted olive oils scented with celery, cress, fennel, juniper, mint, sage, and sesame. The Persian leader Xerxes's attack on Athens in 480 B.C.E. concluded with the burning of the olive grove on the Acropolis, a symbolic gesture of contempt for Greek power and superiority.

Colonizers spread cultivation to Massilia in southern France and Tunisia, where Romans hoped to tame the Berbers by making them arboriculturists. Shippers designed vessels solely for transporting oil. As an act of dominance in Palestine, during the Emperor Titus's assault on Jerusalem in 70 C.E., he ordered Roman legionaries to fell the trees. A half century later, the Emperor Hadrian's mint sculpted a gold aureus coin with the olive branch in the hand of the goddess Pax (peace). A subsequent silver denarius from around 134 C.E. pictured the olive branch in the hand of Hispania.

Because crushing olives for oil required cool temperatures, the first fruit processors set up presses in caves and basements. In the early Middle Ages, the invention of the screw press simplified a labor-intensive job. The shaft settled on top of mash sacks, from which oil trickled into a catch basin. Under Moorish influence after 711 C.E., the province of Spain enhanced the olive trade by grafting Arabian varieties to Iberian stock, which includes 250 olive species. Despite the high price of imported products, cookbooks to the end of the Renaissance proclaimed olive oil superior to butter and lard in cuisine for its subtle flavor and blendability.

In the New World, Franciscan and Jesuit fathers planted mission banana trees and olive groves in Alta and Baja California in the mid-1700s and, by 1795, established stone mills and screw presses to obtain oil. Commercially, Argentina, Arizona, Chile, Mexico, and Peru tapped small markets for oil and fruit. In the early nineteenth century, Oceania acquired olives from Australia and New Zealand, where growers planted stock from Brazil, France, and Sicily.

A global demand arose in the late 1800s, when cookbooks elevated olive oil over pork lard. In 1896, immigrant growers Carlo, Ferdinando, and Raffaele Costa left Genoa for Cape Town, South Africa, and joined the exploitation of the olive for food and oil. Carlo Costa advanced to Zimbabwe to launch his own groves. During the Spanish Civil War, bread, oil, and olives sustained the citizenry throughout food shortages.

Health Effects

In the 1960s, the Spanish government promoted exports of olive oil in exchange for American soy products. The effort coincided with health research that acclaimed olive oil as the most digestible of edible fats. American and European advisories revealed the value of olive oil to the cardiovascular system, generating enthusiasm for new orchards and their yield.

The survival of ancient orchards has figured in contemporary international conflict, notably the Israeli bulldozing of trees in Palestine from 1998 to the early 2000s. In an effort to rob the Spanish of their historical role in olive cultivation, some Italian entrepreneurs have imported cheap oil, herbed oil, and olives stuffed with anchovies or red peppers and labeled them in Italian, implying to consumers that the best grades came from Italy. Until the European Union reenforced labeling laws in 2007, many cheaper grades concealed the fraudulent addition of cotton, hazelnut, palm, sesame, and sunflower oils.

Currently, Spain grows more than 300 million olive trees, 70 percent of them in Jaén, Andalusia. That nation markets more than one-third of the world's 18.5 million tons (16.8 million metric tons) of olives. Since the late 1990s, in hope of developing more orchards to meet culinary demand, Indians, Japanese, Malaysians, Pakistani, and Sri Lankans have introduced their own varieties.

Wherever olives grow, from November to March, whole families carpet orchards with tarps and shake or beat trees to knock fruit to the ground. Dishes of olives are standard bar food in Spain and around the Mediterranean and a common ingredient in gourmet recipes for marinade, pasta, pizza, salad, salsa, and tapenade and dip. In Sicily, olive oil tastings and snack dishes of caponata retain the classic glory of the fruit. Engineers anticipate that the waste from olive presses will be a future source of electric power.

See also: Finger Food; Greek Diet and Cuisine, Ancient; Mediterranean Diet and Cuisine; Roman Diet and Cuisine, Ancient; Sicilian Diet and Cuisine.

Further Reading

Mariani, John F. *How Italian Food Conquered the World.* Foreword by Lidia Bastianich. New York: Palgrave Macmillan, 2011.

Mueller, Tom. *Extra Virginity: The Sublime and Scandalous World of Olive Oil.* New York: W.W. Norton, 2011.

Sibbett, G. Steven, Louise Ferguson, Joann L. Coviello, and Margaret Lindstrand. *Olive Production Manual.* Oakland: University of California, Agriculture and Natural Resources, 2005.

Taylor, Judith M. *The Olive in California: History of an Immigrant.* Berkeley, CA: Ten Speed, 2000.

Vossen, Paul. "Olive Oil: History, Production, and Characteristics of the World's Classic Oils." *Horticultural Science* 42:5 (August 2007): 1093–1100.

Organic Foods

As near as possible to its original form, organic produce comes to market in a pure state without additives and dyes, chemical fertilizer, genetic modification, irradiation, and toxins. British philosopher Christopher James Northbourne elevated organic agriculture in his book *Look to the Land* (1940), which championed environmental sustainability. The text claimed that society's ills have stemmed from the abandonment of traditional farming for capital-intensive investment agriculture. His complaints included harm to the unborn and infants, whose undeveloped immune systems leave them vulnerable to the fungicides and insecticides linked to birth defects, cancer, miscarriage, and Parkinson's disease.

Since the 1940s, dietary purists have lauded Northbourne's concept of "life chemistry" by ridding edibles of the residue of industrial farming and processing that began in the twentieth century, namely arsenic and cadmium in chicken, dye on oranges, and Alar and wax on apples. Media advertisement of organic goods aided small farms in converting from inorganic monoculture to a profitable system devoid of agrochemicals. Agroforesters and smallholders shaped the human diet by marketing varied foodstuffs, notably, the pears, tomatoes, and heritage greens and poultry that chefs applaud on their menus.

J.I. Rodale, Organic Crusader

Primarily through his own publications, American eccentric Jerome Irving Rodale (1898–1971) became the prophet of purity to home gardeners. While living on an abandoned farm in Emmaus, Pennsylvania, during the Great Depression, he agitated against fertilizer and food additives, pesticides, refined flour and sugar, processed foods, fluoridated water, and tobacco. At his experimental farm, he grew orchards and vegetables that proved his theories about the value of natural goodness from the home garden.

As editor of Rodale Press and publisher of the magazines *Prevention* and *Organic Farming and Gardening,* Rodale harangued the home gardener to return to a pure source of nourishment from the earth, kept loamy and friable with mulch and earthworms. For loosening hardpan soil, he suggested ways of turning kitchen waste, grass clippings, and leaves into humus. He popularized the term *organic food* among disciples who grew their own fruits and vegetables in tidy kitchen gardens. For his quirky blend of science and opinion, *Newsweek* dubbed him the "Don Quixote of the compost heap."

From Rodale's one-man pulpit, streams of propaganda warned that the chemical pesticide dichlorodiphenyltrichloroethane (DDT) and industrial effluent threatened survival on Earth. His ideas on ecology inspired the Boy Scouts and 4-H groups committed to rescuing food from adulteration. He founded the nonprofit Soil and Health Institute, which battled cyclamates, phosphate detergent, and monosodium glutamate. As though preaching a nutritional gospel, his trademark text *How to Grow Vegetables & Fruits by the Organic Method* (1961) advised on seed selection, natural methods of propagation, and harvesting and storage of perishables.

Late Twentieth and Early Twenty-First Centuries

Among the benefits of organic farming and gardening with natural manures, healthier soil has maintained moisture and boosted harvests during the droughts that have

Farmer and publisher J.I. Rodale of Emmaus, Pennsylvania, pioneered sustainable agriculture and popularized the term *organic* for foods grown without pesticides. He also founded such popular magazines as *Organic Gardening* and *Prevention*. (Co Rentmeester/Time Life Pictures/Getty Images)

beset Ethiopia and Sudan. The heritage methods of tillage and local food distribution allegedly improve well-being for consumers and farm laborers while cutting soil erosion, cleanup of hazardous waste and polluted aquifers, and the energy costs of growing and harvesting corn, soybeans, and wheat.

In Cuba, residents have offset the loss of privatized urban farming by supporting *organoponicos,* small town gardens. Hunger and child mortality have declined owing to the availability of cabbage, chard, chives, cucumbers, eggplant, garlic, lettuce, mint, onions, and parsley from raised beds on hotel roofs and small plots allocated by the city of Havana. A resurgence of the Cuban "grandmother's wisdom" from the older generation has revived ancient oral advice, such as the handling of plow oxen and the chopping of sugarcane waste into mulch and biofertilizer. To combat infestations in sweet potato fields, controllers began baiting banana stems with honey to lure the ants that kill borers. By the late 1990s, Cuba, a land too poor to adopt intensive agrarianism, was a leader in the marketing of organic citrus fruit and juices and in the growing of herbs for medicinal teas.

In January 2001, Dole Food Company, the world's largest fruit and vegetable seller, entered organic marketing by distributing bananas grown without bioengineering or chemical enhancements. The firm's advance into a limited specialties market coincided with issuance of the first national organic food standards by the United States Department of Agriculture (USDA), which regulates produce nationwide, beginning in August 2002. Researchers noted that although some consumers believed organic food tasted better and was more nutritional and safer, taste tests did not support their loyalty. Rather, blind tests confirmed that 10 percent of consumers willingly paid up to 14 percent more for edibles that they could not recognize as better tasting or higher in quality.

The USDA regulations for 100 percent organic foods forbade treating cropland or foodstuffs with antibiotics, chemical fertilizer, growth hormone, inorganic pesticide, irradiation, or sewage and outlawed genetic engineering. The "organic" label indicated at least 95 percent organic ingredients, and "made with organic ingredients," required 70 percent pure food. The regulations applied to fish, honey, mushrooms, and seafood. To reduce allergic reactions to eggs, milk, nuts, shellfish, soy, and wheat, food labelers dropped unfamiliar terms—*albumin* and *casein*—in favor of the clearer designations of *eggs* and *milk.* Stringent coding encouraged Earthbound Farms, the largest grower of organic salad greens, to introduce pure ingredients in baby food, which, in 2011, included kale.

A deterrent to traditional methods, the suppression of industrial techniques in the European Union and the Western Hemisphere bodes ill for risk management on artisanal farms. For the global food yield, holistic farming may not sustain future growth in the human population. In addition to more weeds, organic fields have higher levels of contamination from *Escherichia coli* (*E. coli*) and salmonella bacteria contained in manure, a source of sickness and death during such outbreaks as the vegetable-borne illness that struck 1,500 Germans and killed 16 in summer 2011. Rumors destroyed the public's confidence in Spanish cucumbers, lettuce, and tomatoes from organic farms until July 22, when researchers at the European Food Safety Authority traced the infection to fenugreek sprouts from Egypt.

See also: Aquaponics; Baby Food and Infant Feeding; Fungi; Honey; Raw Cuisine; Vegetarianism.

Further Reading

Duram, Leslie A., ed. *Encyclopedia of Organic, Sustainable, and Local Food.* Santa Barbara, CA: ABC-Clio, 2010.

———. Good Growing: *Why Organic Farming Works.* Lincoln: University of Nebraska Press, 2005.

Willer, Helga, and Minou Yussefi-Menzler. *The World of Organic Agriculture: Statistics and Emerging Trends 2008.* Sterling, VA: Earthscan, 2008.

Wright, Julia. *Sustainable Agriculture and Food Security in an Era of Oil Scarcity.* Sterling, VA: Earthscan, 2009.

Packaging

The packaging of goods for transport and sale enables food producers to secure perishables from delivery to market to domestic use. From 18,000 B.C.E., the earliest packing in animal organs, bamboo tubes, banana leaves, coconut shells, gourds, hollow logs, and parfleches (skin envelopes) involved found objects suited to wet and dry packing. Around the second century B.C.E., wrappings advanced to flexible containers—mulberry bark, linen sacks, resin-lined wineskins, and woven baskets. Unlike bronze vessels, wooden crates, and the earthenware amphorae of 6000 B.C.E., flexible casings weighed less and reduced transport costs but could not ensure the freshness and quality of edibles as well as sealing in bottles and crocks, mass-produced after 1500 B.C.E.

In this same period, Egyptian manufacturers industrialized glass urns, inert containers molded from melted limestone, sand, silica, and soda. Phoenician and Syrian crafters contributed pipe-blown glass around 500 B.C.E., producing the first round bottles. From 100 B.C.E., Egyptian and Phoenician coopering paralleled the growth of the mustard, olive oil, and salt fish industries. For vinegar and wine, convex oak barrels became both containers and aging media for imparting wood tannins to the liquid.

For dry commodities, Egyptians, Greeks, and Romans became the first to recycle used papyrus into food coverings. Asians followed in 105 C.E., when Cai Lun (Ts'ai Lun), an official of the Han dynasty, invented pulp paper to replace strips of bamboo and cloth. In 751, Arabs seized Chinese papermakers at Samarkand, in Uzbekistan, and set up paper factories in Baghdad, Bambyce, and Damascus. A Persian tourist, Nasiri Khosrau, in 1035 remarked on Cairo spice and vegetable dealers wrapping purchases in individual sheets made from recycled linen mummy wrappings. By 1665, the invention of rag-content blue paper provided a wrapping for cone sugar that doubled as a source of bluing and household dye.

Bags and Cans

After the late 1700s, European roll-stock paper reduced the cost of disposable grocery packaging. European merchants hand-glued bags for holding seeds, twisted sheets into cones and rectangles to carry candies and shrimps, and tied brown butcher paper or scraps of worn sails with rough twine to secure bulk bundles of bread and salt meat. Edam and Gouda cheeses received a wax outer coating, another form of packaging that housekeepers reused, melting it into candles. For liquids, such as ale or milk from saloons and dairies, purchasers brought their own lidded tins carried by wire bails.

After French inventor Nicolas Appert perfected preservation in heat-sterilized bottles and jars in 1809, canning advanced rapidly in Europe and the United States. The technology suited the marketing of fine brandies and whiskies, condensed milk, maple and vanilla cake flavorings, and pickles as well as locally filled soda water from gold rush towns in California and Nevada. To ensure the purity of oysters, peas and carrots, sliced peaches, and tuna with a vacuum seal, tin-plated iron and steel cans required tedious soldering at the rate of 60 cans per day. For butter cookies and mints, bakers and confectioners in the 1830s designed pleated doily cups and lidded tins to protect contents from external impact during transport. The addition of painted scenes and seasonal greetings made the tins collectible and reusable as gift and pantry containers.

At dry goods stores, consumers carried their baking needs home in commercial paper bags after 1844, when cellulose sacking reduced the cost of cotton flour and rice bags. The addition of a gusset to sacks in the 1870s produced the stand-alone design, which left both hands free for filling with dried beans and raisins. Entrepreneurs designed unique glass containers, such as the jars that held Smith Brothers cough drops in 1866. After 1889, automation simplified the hand-blown shaping of glass to protect the aroma and taste of coffee beans, olives, sake, and seltzer water.

In Brooklyn, New York, in 1890, printer Robert Gair marketed the first folding paperboard carton, which the National Biscuit Company adopted as animal cracker and biscuit containers. Paper manufacturers perfected the pulping of cotton, flax, hemp, straw, wastepaper, and wood for low-cost disposable wrappings, which they printed with colored drawings and logos, for example, the familiar Quaker on that brand of rolled oats. Factories began marketing wax- and wire-capped reusable bottles to hold carbonated drinks and milk, paper cartons for cereals and grains, and corrugated fiberboard barriers and boxes that shielded such breakables as baby food jars, hot pepper sauce, and vinegar bottles from vibration and shock.

After standardization of food contents and purity under the Pure Food and Drug Act of 1906, U.S. consumers felt safer purchasing packaged goods. They bought juice and cooking oil in sterile bottles, onions and potatoes in mesh bags, and jugs sealed with Bakelite, a wood flour resin invented in Belgium by chemist Leo Baekeland, the "Father of Modern Plastics." In 1910, cardboard boxes began replacing wooden crates for lightweight, but stable shipping of fruitcakes and shortbread. Within decades, grocers sold bananas and eggs from molded paper containers and loose peppers and tomatoes wrapped in cellophane, a regenerated cellulose barrier wrap refined in 1912 by Swiss chemical engineer Jacques E. Brandenberger.

Sealant breakthroughs distinguished processed foods, such as foil-wrapped chocolates and Tex-Mex burritos. Whitman's Sampler, the first edible sold in cellophane, enjoyed a long shelf life free of bacteria, odors, and water. In 1913, Life Savers and Wrigley's chewing gum came to market in aluminum foil sleeves. In 1914, cereal giant Will Keith Kellogg applied Waxtite to boxes of corn flakes baked in Battle Creek, Michigan. Milk was available from gable top waxed cartons in 1935.

Weight reduction dominated innovation. During World War II, the use of aluminum foil containers further reduced shipping weights of dinner rolls and frozen pies. In the late 1940s, Dole introduced an aseptic canning system that canned low-acid apricots and pears in laminated cans. The addition of Styrofoam cushioning in the 1950s ensured the safe shipping of grapefruit and oranges and protected sliced beef and pork in trays.

Pull-top cans of ready-to-eat meats and soups reached the market after inventor Mikola Kondakow made the first pull tab in Thunder Bay, Ontario, in 1956, three years before the engineering of the aluminum can. High-gloss advertisements drew shoppers to brand names. Royal Crown set R.C. Cola apart from competitors in 1964 with the first ring-pull can. Airlines and fast-food restaurants offered disposable packet portions of jelly, ketchup, and mayonnaise.

Industrialized Packaging

In the 1950s, aseptic, temperature-controlled filling of hermetic containers, shrink wrapping, and conveyor belts limited the number of contacts between edibles and human hands. Aluminum, molded pulp, and plastic blister packaging in the 1960s reduced the weight of canned goods for self-service shopping. Attractive hygienic wrappings promoted shelf appeal in grocery items, such as the individual yogurt servings in polystyrene cups. Activated charcoal and silica gel desiccants protected snack chips from moisture; plastic shopping bags suited mass consumption and reuse. In 1969, fruit growers began waxing Washington State Delicious apples, a transparent surfacing that eventually passed to packagers of green peppers, smooth melons, eggplant, citrus fruit, cucumbers, and

squash as a shield of freshness and moisture, protection from bruising, and enhancement of appearance and salability.

The moon landing on July 20, 1969, testified to the convenience and durability of packaged deep-frozen pizza and ready-made meals for lengthy transport. Open-resistant lids and seals kept children safe from choking hazards, such as cashew nuts and hot dogs; tamper-proof security seals such as shrink neckbands guaranteed portion size and purity in feta cheese and soy sauce. After 1973, Nesquik came to the shelf in a rectangular composite can printed on all four sides with ingredients and recipes. The packaging of cola drinks and hot-fill jams in transparent polyethylene terephthalate (PET) further reduced the weight of rigid, impact-safe containers.

By the mid-1970s, the green movement resulted in minimal wrapping, such as the postharvest bagging of limes and yams. Individualized labeling included suggestions for disposal or reuse. City planners provided boxes, color-coded bags, and wheeled bins to facilitate curbside collection. Civic centers recycled aluminum and steel cans, cardboard, glass, paper, and polystyrene to turn scrap into usable raw materials. In 1986, Coca-Cola announced the first refillable PET drink bottles, a boon to urban landfills choked with fast-food litter.

Because of the information revolution of the 1980s, labeling featured low-calorie, no-cholesterol, and salt-free formulations to lure health-minded consumers. By 1981, U.S. supermarkets installed 10,000 scanning devices. Scanner tills rapidly computed costs while documenting buyer age, gender, and preferences for pantry staples and luxury items. In the 1990s, unitized cases transported by robot reduced the cost and damage of handling in global favorites, such as mineral water from Perrier, France. On February 4, 2002, Cargill-Dow of Minneapolis introduced bioplastic deli trays from biodegradable corn and sugarcane rather than petroleum.

As the Internet and liberalization of national trade barriers enhanced global food sales, companies reversed earlier standards to supply labels lettered to suit the needs of consumers with impaired sight and boxing that disabled fingers can open. Border inspections protected buyers from adulterated goods. The trackable labeling and barcoding of "intelligent packaging" provided date and place of origination, a valuable tool for the Centers for Disease Control in tracing sources of *Escherichia coli* (*E. coli*) and salmonella found on frozen foods, meats, produce, and processed seafood.

A more anticipatory technology, "active packaging" contains ethanol emitters to flag stale baked goods and fish, a control promoted by Australian and Japanese consumers. Double-walled temperature-control wraps guard the freshness of beverages, meats, and ready-to-eat meals. Carbon dioxide and oxygen scavengers check changes in coffee, nuts, and snacks and indicate spoilage with darkening in colored tape. Preservative releasers emit antioxidants to extend the shelf life of bread, cereal, cheese, snacks, and vegetables. Additional safeguards derive from moisture absorbers in sandwiches and odor absorbers in dairy products and fruit juices.

See also: Bamboo; Canning; Caravans; Clipper Ships; Freeze-Drying; Soft Drinks and Juices.

Further Reading

Han, Jung H. *Innovations in Food Packaging.* San Diego, CA: Elsevier, 2005.

Kerry, Joseph, and Paul Butler. *Smart Packaging Technologies for Fast Moving Consumer Goods.* Hoboken, NJ: John Wiley & Sons, 2008.

Morris, Scott A. *Food and Package Engineering.* Ames, IA: Wiley-Blackwell, 2011.

Wilson, Charles L., ed. *Intelligent and Active Packaging for Fruits and Vegetables.* Boca Raton, FL: CRC, 2007.

Paleolithic Diet

A nutritional plan of preagricultural foragers of 200,000 B.C.E., the Paleolithic diet centered on the fiber and nutrients of fruits and berries, mushrooms, root crops, green leafy vegetables, tree nuts, seeds, eggs, insects, herbs and spices, raw honey, seaweed, and seafood. The low-fat meat of game mammals—bear, caribou, elk, ibex, moose, reindeer—and of fowl—ducks, geese, ptarmigan, seagulls, waterbirds—produced some two-thirds of daily consumption, which contributed to the development and support of a large brain. To make skinning and slicing easier, central Africans produced serrated or notched knives for cutting pieces into mouth-size chunks for eating raw. The highly carnivorous Eskimo collected berries, mushrooms, tubers, and willow leaves as condiments to relieve the tedium of meals of beluga and bowhead whales, seals, and walruses. The Ohalo II dwellers in Israel's Rift Valley supplemented meat with grass seed; the Netiv Hagdud on the West Bank added wild barley, beans, and nuts to the Paleo diet. Similar alterations to heavy protein consumption at Jerf el-Ahmer and Mureybet, Syria, included wild barley and rye.

About 10,500 B.C.E. at Nevali Cori, Turkey, inhabitants began the revolutionary transition to domesticated einkorn, a hulled wheat. The innovations of Neolithic, or New Stone Age, humankind around 8000 B.C.E. shifted emphasis from meat to cooked beans, manioc, peanuts, potatoes, and grains—barley, corn, millet, oats, rice, sorghum, and wheat, the bases of bread, flour, noodles, and pasta. Easily stored and transported, these high-calorie foods reduced the fiber of the preagrarian diet while scaling back body height and bulk and boosting energy. In this same period, residents of central Texas lined earth ovens with rock to bake

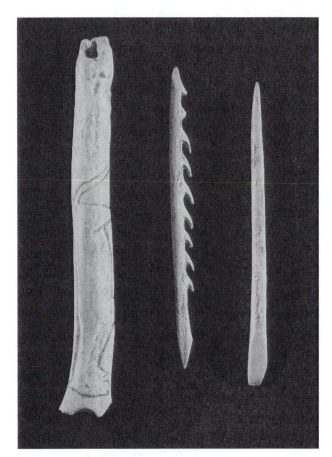

Hunter-gatherers from the Upper Paleolithic (Late Stone Age, 40,000 to 10,000 years ago) in France carved these bone tools for hunting and fishing. The end of that era marked the transition to domestic agriculture. *(Dea/A. Dagli Orti/De Agostini/Getty Images)*

camas bulbs. In the Chihuahua Desert on the Tex-Mex border, around 7500 B.C.E., Paleo-Indians appear to have pit-baked agave, sotol, and wild onion, the triad of their diet. Contributing to post-Paleolithic ills, communities settled on farmland, became more sedentary, and consumed quantities of domesticated meat, grain, cheese, and milk. Their highly organized communities easily bested hunter-gatherers, who flourished in the arctic, deserts, and remote jungles.

Coprolitic study gives a clear view of prehistoric diet in southwestern Texas around 7000 B.C.E. Sampled at Comstock in Val Verde County, Paleo-Indian feces attest to a diet that was 75 percent carbohydrate. In addition to fat and protein from birds, caterpillars, clams, deer, eggs, grasshoppers, lizards, mice, rabbits, and rats, Paleo-Indians chose fibrous local flora. Enriching the foragers with substantial plant nutrition were acorns, agave, berries, biscuit root, cacti, grapes, mesquite, pecans, persimmons, sunflower seeds, and walnuts. Anthropological details describe cookery as clay pot cuisine eaten from gourd bowls with wooden spoons. Forensic study of skeletal remains proves that the varied diet left diners healthy, trim, and almost parasite free.

In 1975, Seattle gastroenterologist Walter Lyle Voegtlin, author of *The Stone Age Diet* (1975), promoted caveman fare as the ideal sustenance for human health and vigor. In 1982, Loren Cordain, a professor of health and exercise science at Colorado State University, popularized the Paleo diet. Influenced by physician Stanley Boyd Eaton and Melvin J. Konner, an anthropologist and neurologist at Emory University, the authors of the treatise *Paleolithic Nutrition* (1985), Cordain increased the endurance of athletes with a prehistoric diet. Stripping the daily intake of alcoholic and caffeinated beverages, dairy foods, carbohydrates, sodium, processed oil, salt, food additives and preservatives, manufactured vitamins, and refined sugar, he proposed an evolutionary diet to rid humans of chronic afflictions—acne, alcoholism, allergies, arthritis, asthma, autoimmune disease, cancer, depression, diabetes, emphysema, gout, heart disease, high blood pressure, kidney stones, migraines, obesity, osteoporosis, schizophrenia, stroke, and tooth decay. A trendy Stone Age or "Garden of Eden" diet of meat, fish, and raw or cooked fruits and vegetables gained respect for its promotion of wellness, athletic performance, mental acuity, and longevity.

Critiques of the primal or ancestral diet vary, from evidence in cave paintings and forensic research to extremes of speculation. From studies of New Guineans on the island of Kitava, nutritionists have pondered the value of bone marrow, brain tissue, and organ meats along with tubers and root crops—beets, carrots, celeriac, parsnips, rutabagas, salsify, sweet potatoes, turnips, and yams—to a health regimen that naturally suppresses hypoglycemia and diabetes. Experts value almonds and walnuts for adding copper, iodine, iron, selenium, and zinc to brain development and function. Other specialists refute hasty claims of long and healthy lives from restricted diet, because Paleolithic nomads did not live long enough to develop the so-called "diseases of affluence." The reversion to spring water lacking chlorine and fluoride raised questions of sanitation and threats to bone and tooth resilience as well as the waste generated by plastic water bottles. Economists note that a global adherence to the caveman diet would endanger populations that depend on grain-rich fare and grass-fed herds. The inclusion of such exotic foodstuffs as coconut water likewise would place a hardship on countries north of the tropics.

See also: Agribusiness; Hunter-Gatherers; Pemmican; Voegtlin, Walter L.

Further Reading

Bryant, Vaughn M., Jr. "Slim, Trim, and Paleo-Indian: Why Our Diets Are Killing Us." In *Primitive Technology II: Ancestral Skills,* ed. David Wescott. Salt Lake City, UT: Gibbs Smith, 2001.

De Vany, Arthur. *The New Evolution Diet: What Our Paleolithic Ancestors Can Teach Us About Weight Loss, Fitness, and Aging.* Emmaus, PA: Rodale, 2011.

Speth, John D. *The Paleoanthropology and Archaeology of Big-Game Hunting: Protein, Fat, or Politics?* New York: Springer, 2010.

Ungar, Peter S., ed. *Evolution of the Human Diet: The Known, the Unknown, and the Unknowable.* New York: Oxford University Press, 2006.

Voegtlin, Walter Lyle. *The Stone Age Diet: Based on In-depth Studies of Human Ecology and the Diet of Man.* New York: Vantage, 1975.

Pan-European Diet and Cuisine

The Continental cuisine of Europe, called Western cuisine, distinguishes itself from Asian menus in the high proportion of dairy and meat items to carbohydrates, fruits, and vegetables. During the Middle Ages, cereals in the form of frumenty or fermenty (cracked wheat boiled in milk), gruel, and porridge dominated meals for the millennium, with beans, peas, and turnips playing a lesser role in period open-hearth cookery. Those who could afford meat favored cod, herring, pork, and poultry over beef, the most expensive. Middle Eastern intellectual exchange during the Crusades encouraged spicing as an alternative to ancient forms of food preservation by air-drying, brining, brewing, fermenting, pickling, salting, and smoking.

In the 1300s, barley, oat, rye, and wheat breads formed a literal basis for dishes as trenchers on which servers ladled stews. Cooks varied predictable tastes and textures with sweet-and-sour alternatives produced by blending honey and sugar with verjuice from unripe grapes or crab apples and vinegar. Thickening with bread crumbs and ground chestnuts gave place to a more delicate texturizing with almond flour, milk, and paste. Apprentices studied methods firsthand and memorized portions. Church control enforced fast days as a means of controlling gluttony, one of the seven deadly sins. Sumptuary laws restricted the lower classes from emulating the table excesses of nobles and Benedictine monks, the best fed of Europe's monastics.

The Renaissance produced experimentation in pastries and pies and kitchen notation, the forerunner of the modern recipe. Professional food service at cookshops and roadside inns fed travelers on fritters, pasties (meat pies), rotisserie mutton and pork, soups, and turnovers. Pubs offered ale, cider, perry, and wine and a cold snack later dubbed the "plowman's lunch," a serving of boiled egg, bread, cheese, onion, pickle spear, and sausage. In contrast, aristocrats expected meat service of geese, peafowl, rabbit, quail, songbirds, and swans. Carvers made a display of slicing and plating bites from whole stuffed carp and lampreys. Sommeliers served appropriate wines, an introit to Europe's famed table vintages.

The Columbian Exchange increased pantry choices to include coffee, tea, and hot chocolate, flavored with sugar and vanilla. Bland recipes took on a New World sparkle from the addition of chili peppers, cocoa, corn, kidney and lima beans, potatoes, sweet potatoes, and tomatoes. Prosperity from the import-export food trade encouraged mealtime escapes from Mediterranean pasta and German and Slavic dumplings with the latest in potato and rice dishes. As cash flow allowed, consumption of imported brandies, meat, and olive oil increased in Great Britain, as did the social consumption of tea with biscuits and marmalade, an upgrade of the classic Roman *defrutum.*

The formation of food guilds promoted cooking specialties in confections, distilled beverages, pastry, meats, and saucing as well as cookbooks designed for the professional caterer. The kitchen wizardry of Florentine chefs imported to France in 1533 by Catherine de' Médici for her marriage to Henry II kindled a burst of innovation with aspic, broths, choux pastry, fruit ices, gratins, and vegetable arrays of artichokes and cardoons. Master cook Bartolomeo Scappi, the chef to popes Pius IV and Pius V, captured the flair of Italian cuisine in *Opera dell'Arte del Cucinare* (*Culinary Works of Art,* 1570), a compilation of 1,000 recipes for caviar, foie gras (goose liver), kidney fat pastries, Parmesan cheese, precise cuts of calf's head and ox tongue, and soused (brined) perch, rays, and sturgeon. Translations of Scappi's cookbook inspired alternatives to the salt-fish cuisines of Holland and Iberia.

Additional cooking guides—Marx Rumpolt's 2,000 recipes in *Ein New Kochbuch* (*The New Cookbook,* ca. 1581) and gentleman farmer Hugh Platt's *Delightes for Ladies* (1600)—outlined emerging national cuisines. Rumpolt spoke from experience of the balancing of entrées at banquets; Platt described hands-on kitchen experiments in candying and conserves and championed imported French wines for quality. Refined dining reached a height with the issuance of chef François Pierre La Varenne's *Cuisinier François* (1651), a tribute to *haut goût* (full flavor), and food writer François Massialot's *Le Cuisinier Royal et Bourgeois* (*The Royal and Middle-Class Cook,* 1693), which simplified the roasting of turkeys, a fad food imported from North America.

The shift toward simple preparation of fresh produce in the modern era produced a general term—*Mediterranean diet*—to describe the pervasive southern European consumption of seafood, whole grains, legumes, and salads dressed with lemon juice and olive oil. Middle Eastern elements—falafel, garlic, grilled fish and mutton, hummus, and pita bread—complement the Portuguese addition of *feijoada* (beef or pork stew) and Majorcan paella, a rice-based mélange of fresh vegetables, clams and mussels, and ham. Ethnic heritage dishes—Albanian cucumber and yogurt soup, Macedonian skillet beans, Maltese stuffed artichokes, and Sicilian manicotti—maintain the health benefits of regional dishes.

Central European contributions to Continental menus feature indigenous eggs, meat, and vegetables in Armenian string cheese, Serbian lamb soup, and the Slovenian *fritaja* (omelette), made with garlic sprouts and wild asparagus. Russian *solyanka* (cabbage and pickle soup), Georgian *lobio* (spiced beans), Slovak potato dumplings, and Bulgarian spicy salami epitomize the earthy fragrance and richness of the regional diet. Heavier meals to the north—Czech fried potato cakes, German sauerbraten, Polish kielbasa, and Slavic pierogi (boiled dumplings)—break the Mediterranean pattern of light meat servings with heartier blends of meat with carbohydrates.

Northern Europe maintains a distinct presence in Continental fare, from Estonian black bread and rhubarb pie to Sami fried reindeer with mountain sorrel stew. The British Isles produce flavorful combination dishes, including English fish and chips, Irish Celtic steak with egg mayonnaise, Scots finnan haddie (smoked haddock) poached in milk, and Welsh faggots (meatballs) and leek soup. Like Russian and German menus, Scandinavian cookery favors strength of aroma and taste, the memorable elements of Danish red sausage, Finnish lingonberry jam, Norwegian gravlax (cured salmon), and the Swedish smorgasbord and vodka cocktails.

See also: Medieval Diet and Cuisine; Mediterranean Diet and Cuisine; Pastry; Wine.

Further Reading

Albala, Ken. *Food in Early Modern Europe.* Westport, CT: Greenwood, 2003.

Fitzpatrick, Joan, ed. *Renaissance Food from Rabelais to Shakespeare: Culinary Readings and Culinary Histories.* Burlington, VT: Ashgate, 2010.

Freedman, Paul H. *Food: The History of Taste.* Berkeley: University of California Press, 2007.

MacVeigh, Jeremy. *International Cuisine.* Clifton Park, NY: Delmar Cengage Learning, 2009.

Pasta

A popular form of grain worldwide, pasta offers 350 shapes and a variety of applications for cheese, meat, sauced, and sweetened dishes. A national staple in Italy, dried and fresh pipes, strands, and swirls made from hard durum semolina, eggs or egg yolks, salt, and water contribute protein to the diet. A classic food description from the Greek *pasta* (barley porridge), shaped pasta appears to have begun in Etruscan Italy after 750 B.C.E. as a wide noodle that cooks flattened with a rolling pin and sliced with a cutter. The term *lagana* appears in *Sermones* (*Satires,* ca. 30 B.C.E.) of the Roman poet Horace, who referred to a common supper of sheets of fried dough similar to the lasagna noodle, a pasta featured in simple baked dishes.

Additional mention a century later by the Greek healer Galen and by rabbis in the Jerusalem Talmud (ca. 350 C.E.) precedes a more detailed description of Arab travel food in the 400s and by Libyan soldiers in the 690s during the forced conversion of North Africa to Islam. Recipes from the eighth century featured the Arab preparation of macaroni in saffron-dyed chicken soup and listed the addition of cinnamon and raisins to noodles mass-produced in Palermo, Sicily. In the early 900s Jewish doctor Isho bar Ali, a Syriac lexicographer working in a Baghdad convent, characterized the extruding of semolina *atriya* (strings) for drying. After 1090, Arab cookbooks listed 80 recipes for triangular *sambusa* (ravioli or meat pockets).

In 1154, Arab travel writer Muhammad al-Idrisi described the pasta industry that flourished in Trabia, Sicily, and Sardinia, a producer of free-threshing durum wheat. Exporters in Genoa and Pisa bore shipments to Calabria and over Europe and the Middle East, where suppliers bought pasta to supply camel caravans and ship crews. Upon the return of Venetian merchant Marco Polo from China in 1295, he brought a similar product, rice wonton wraps for dumplings, which reminded him of the pasta of home. Culinary historians surmise that Italians invented the table fork around 1300 as a means of handling hot, slippery servings.

Pasta Culture

The anonymous *Libro de Coquino* (*Book of the Cook*, ca. 1300) described the filling of ravioli with small meatballs and the sealing of edges for frying in oil and serving with honey, a vast difference from saucing after the discovery of the tomato in the sixteenth century. At Leonessa on Fat Thursday preceding Good Friday, *pencarelli* (long, thin spaghetti) marked the arrival of Lent; in Vulture, in south-central Italy, cooks honored Ascension Day, the fortieth day after Easter, with *tagliolini* (noodles) simmered in chicken broth. At Orvieto, north of Rome, Christmas Eve macaroni came to the table with honey and walnuts. The Abruzzi welcomed December 26 with *volarelle* (squares with scalloped edges) in broth with cardoons; at Romagna, outside Bologna, Christmas demanded the filling of *cappelletti* (little hats) with ricotta cheese. Other communities celebrated the Yuletide and Easter with *tagliatelle* (ribbons).

On the cusp of the Italian Renaissance, mechanization in Naples in the 1300s simplified the varied pasta extrusions of semolina stomped by laborers' feet. Throughout Campania, the Sarno River powered small wooden mills that passed dough through interchangeable bronze or nickel dies, a time-saver over homemade technology using knitting needles, reeds, and umbrella spokes. At urban spaghetterias, shapes such as *gemelli* (twins), *radiatore* (wheels), and *stelline* (little stars) held the flavor of sauced dishes and the dressings in pasta salads. Meanwhile, peasant women continued to shape by hand the more complicated *farfalline* (little butterflies) and *orecchiette* (little ears). By lowering costs, dealers targeted the average consumer, who turned pasta into the national dish of Italy.

Other shapes received professional discussion, especially ravioli. In *Libro de Arte Coquinaria* (*Book of the Cook's Art,* 1465), Maestro Martino de Rossi, a chef under Pope Paul II, summarized how to curl Sicilian *pasta pertusata* (macaroni) on iron rods and make Roman fettuccine by folding dough over a stick for cutting into ribbons. Martino boiled the fresh lengths for two hours. His enthusiasm for pasta created an urban demand for the dried commercial fad food. Around 1490, Neapolitans satisfied their customers by importing Sicilian pasta to serve with butter and cheese.

Haute Cuisine

Stuffed pasta epitomized the sophisticated recipes of high Renaissance cuisine. On December 12, 1549, master chef Scappi served the small meat pies in broth at a conclave for Vatican cardinals following the death of Pope Paul III. Scappi's original pasta recipes called for lasagna noodles for wrapping capons, ducks, and geese and for serving light pasta in broth as invalid meals.

By the seventeenth century, Parmesan cheese–topped pasta became a standard side dish for the Neapolitan elite but a whole meal for the lucky Italian peasant who could afford it. Florentine author Giovanni Del Turco's *Epulario e Segreti Vari* (*The Italian Banquet and Various Secrets,* 1602–1636) cut the boiling time for pasta to minutes to produce an *al dente* (firm) consistency and lessen work for the home cook. Throughout Liguria, mills at Imperia, San Remo, and Savona hurried to keep pace with demand for pasta. By the 1700s, Naples led the world in open-air pasta factories.

In 1790, Roman chef Francesco Leonardi's *L'Apicio Moderno* (*The Modern Apicius*) featured the fusion of European pasta with cheese and New World tomato sauce, a dramatic moment in culinary history. By the early 1800s, baked lasagna earned favor with nobility at the court of Naples. In 1855, Sardinian die makers patented more sophisticated pasta machines from engineering derived from the Industrial Revolution. In 1860, liberator Giuseppe Garibaldi predicted that the popular dish would unify Italy into a modern nation. By 1891, a Palermo catalog, *Esposizione Nazionale Illustra di Palermo 1891–1892* (*The National Illustrated Exposition of Palermo*), offered more than 100 pasta shapes. In 1934 at Uzwil, Swiss brothers Hanspeter and René Bühler invented the piston-driven metal worm for continuous macaroni extrusion.

Currently, Italians select a pasta dish for the first course of the meal, whether *pastina* (tiny shapes) in broth or *pasta ripiena* (stuffed pasta) baked in sauce. Natives consume 60 pounds (27 kilograms) of pasta annually, an amount three times that of Americans. Versions gained popularity worldwide—in China served with sausage, in India spiced with cumin and turmeric, and in the Philippines topped with banana ketchup and hot dog slices. Sicilians prefer a winter dish that tops linguine with tuna and cracker crumbs. In Mexico, cooks add spaghetti to soup; farther south, in Argentina and Brazil, immigrants from Italy preserve original recipes for gnocchi (potato dumplings) and ravioli.

See also: Israeli Diet and Cuisine; Italian Diet and Cuisine; Mediterranean Diet and Cuisine; Sicilian Diet and Cuisine; Yeast.

Further Reading

Capatti, Alberto, and Massimo Montanari. *Italian Cuisine: A Cultural History.* Trans. Aine O'Healy. New York: Columbia University Press, 2003.

De Vita, Oretta Zanini. *Encyclopedia of Pasta.* Berkeley: University of California Press, 2009.

Scicolone, Michele. *Pasta, Noodles, and Dumplings.* New York: Simon & Schuster, 2005.

Serventi, Silvano, and Françoise Sabban. *Pasta: The Story of a Universal Food.* New York: Columbia University Press, 2002.

Pastry

Tender baked goods made from soft, low-gluten dough, pastry employs grains and emollients to produce a crumbly or flaky texture. The Egyptians, Greeks, Phoenicians, and Romans developed phyllo dough for multilayered confections filled with cream, fruit, honey, and nuts. Egyptian bakers from 3000 B.C.E. filled their cakes with almonds, dates, honey, pine nuts and walnuts, and poppy and sesame seeds. After 1186 B.C.E. under Ramses III, the devout annually sacrificed 9,000 cakes to souls in the afterlife.

In the first century C.E., Chrysippus of Tyana, Cappadocia, compiled Greek pastry recipes in *Treatise on Baking,* a cookbook now lost. According to Apicius, a respected gourmand from the same era, Roman cooks deep-fried fruit fritters, the forerunner of beignets (fried dough). Specialists made *crustuli* (cookies) from nut flour, stacked wedding cakes, and shaped pastries into crescents in honor of Luna, the moon goddess. Chinese bakers made traditional moon cakes and *zong* by filling sticky rice with jujubes or sweet bean paste and wrapping the dumpling in bamboo leaves for steaming.

Parallel with advances in oven building after 1000, medieval pastry makers improved on classic recipes. They replaced oil with butter and lard and glazed custard and fruit surfaces with egg yolk. Middle Eastern pastry flourished in the late eleventh century, when it impressed crusaders with its crunch and layered sweetness. An Eastern European favorite, the Polish *paczki* (jelly doughnut) marked the Thursday before Easter as a special day, when cooks used up pantry stock to prevent the family from violating the strictures of Lent. For Epiphany, the Dutch created the *oliebol,* a deep-fried dumpling and forerunner of doughnuts. In the 1200s, Austrian pastry specialists made *kipferls,* crescents filled with fruit or nuts.

In 1303, the word *pie* appeared in literature as a popular recipe for fruit blends and mincemeat. The Chinese commented in 1330 on *gullach,* a Ramadan specialty similar in its layering to baklava. The light, flaky dessert, featuring honey and nuts, reputedly received refinement under Turkish cooks at the Topkapi Palace in Istanbul after 1465.

In 1404, brioche (sweet egg bread) first appeared on record as a spiced bun or cake of Norman origin served at communion as "blessed bread." Italians made the first nougat at Cremona early in the 1400s, contemporaneous with the creation of Venetian marzipan and almond and honey *turrón* (nougat bars) in Sexona, Spain. In the early 1500s, Portuguese voyagers returned from China with a star-shaped technology for extruding dough into churros, a Hispanic breakfast treat served with *café con leche* (milky coffee) or hot chocolate.

Throughout the Christian realm, bakers and confectioners connected sweet treats with salvation. At Advent, Christmas, Epiphany, and Easter, they filled their showcases with gilded and sugared cookies shaped like fish and tarts and marked with religious acronyms and symbols. The Catholic Church dispatched pastry makers from French convents to the colonies to raise funds by selling chocolate cookies, *feuillantines* (flaky blocks), fritters, and *oublies* (waffles).

Baked Delicacies

When Catherine de' Médici moved from Florence to France in 1533 to marry Henry II, she brought pastry artists who designed the almond and *chantilly* (whipped cream) stuffed *frangipane* and the *macaron,* a cookie sandwich made from almond flour and filled with buttercream. Chef Nicolò della Pigna refined *pastillage,* the creation of architectural pastry centerpieces from sugar flowers and gum paste figures. Panterelli, the new queen's head chef, created the first egg-based choux pastry in 1540. The recipe set a standard for light, flaky desserts and treats, a contrast to the dense blends of chocolate, kirsch (cherry brandy), sour cherries, and whipped cream in the late sixteenth century for Black Forest cake, named for Schwarzwald, Germany.

With imported chocolate and cane sugar, seventeenth-century European bakers created unique traditions for service with coffee and tea, notably, the Austrian linzer torte, the world's oldest extant recipe. Innovations included French baker Cyprien Ragueneau's almond tartlets and marzipan cakes in 1638, cookbook author François Pierre La Varenne's *mille-feuille* (thousand leaf) of 1651, and croissants (buttery yeast rolls), created in 1686 in Budapest to replicate the crescent on the Ottoman banner. In 1653, the founding of the Lebküchler guild in Nuremberg recognized professional German pastry makers. American colonists made pastry of unique ingredients—blueberries for cobbler, corn and molasses for popcorn balls, pecans for pie and pralines, persimmons for pudding, and pumpkin and sweet potatoes for pies.

In the eighteenth-century, cooks created the Austrian apple strudel, the cinnamon and egg tart made in Portuguese convents, and the delicate French petit four for crisping in coal ovens. In 1740, the Polish king Stanislas Leszczynski brought to France *baba au rhum,* a Slavic cake soaked in alcohol; chef Jean Avice, Talleyrand's Parisian caterer, added his own touch in 1760 with toasted choux, which he filled with cream. Marie Antoinette broadened the French flair for treats in 1770 by introducing the Hungarian croissant and Viennese pastry.

In 1815, the published techniques of master pastry chef Marie-Antoine Carême, called the "Palladio of Pâtisserie," promoted *babas,* marzipan, meringues, *pastilles* (lozenges), profiteroles (cream puffs), spun sugar, and tarts as a culinary art. He earned fame for his almond *croquants* (crisps) and the *crustade des peches* (peach pie) he designed for the coronation of the Emperor Napoleon. Carême's primary work, the *pièce montée* (mounted display), consisted of an architectural fountain, pyramid, ruin, ship, or temple of choux pastries glued with gum arabic and mastic. He topped the edible extraordinaire with caramel, chocolate, and sugared almonds and enlaced it with sugary ribbons and threads. During the same era, German chocolatiers refined the Sacher torte and pastries painted with cocoa powder.

Business

During the Industrial Revolution, pastry graduated from art to entrepreneurial skill. After publisher August Zang opened a bakery in 1838 in Vienna, he initiated use of the steam oven, which preserved the taste of baked pastry. The Viennese dominated puff pastry, a buttery, paper-thin basis that Italians called *pasta sfogliata* (folded pasta). The *crème pâtissière* (custard) filling emphasized the flavors of cream and eggs with confectioner's sugar, lemon, and vanilla. Austrians assembled the rich delights of the Continental breakfast—*chausson aux pommes* (apple turnover) and *pain au chocolat* (chocolate bread) and *pain aux raisins* (raisin bread).

Danish pastry got its start in 1850, when a strike of bakers and confectioners required the hiring of the part-time labor of French outsiders. American restaurants adopted French specialties in 1851 with the introduction of the cream puff. The éclair appeared on menus in the 1860s and in *The Royal Book of Pastry and Confectionary* (1873), by Paris food writer Jules Gauffé.

Late-nineteenth-century industrialization brought mechanized mixing and kneading to commercial baking. Speed enabled bakeshops to relieve the householder of daily chores. Emulsifiers and stabilizers lengthened shelf life of goods untouched by human hands until the 1970s, when artisanal bakeries revived waning appetites for cheese straws, crullers, and fruit turnovers. Supermarkets added artisanal pastry shops for made-to-order birthday cakes and holiday tarts.

See also: Carême, Marie-Antoine; French Diet and Cuisine; Haute Cuisine; Ice Cream; Yeast.

Further Reading

Krondl, Michael. *Sweet Invention: A History of Dessert.* Chicago: Chicago Review Press, 2011.

Rinsky, Glenn, and Laura Halpin Rinsky. *The Pastry Chef's Companion.* Hoboken, NJ: John Wiley & Sons, 2009.

Sarramon, Christian, and Carmella Abramowitz-Moreau. *Paris Patisseries: History, Shops, Recipes.* Paris: Flammarion, 2010.

Stamm, Mitch. *The Pastry Chef's Apprentice.* Beverly, MA: Quarry, 2011.

Suas, Michel. *Advanced Bread and Pastry.* Detroit, MI: Delmar Cengage Learning, 2009.

Paula Marín, Francisco de (1774–1837)

Spanish horticulturist Francisco de Paula Marín broadened the range of fruits and vegetables grown for sale in the Hawaiian Islands.

A native of Jerez de la Frontera northeast of Cádiz, Andalucia, Marín went to sea at age 15 with the Alessandro Malaspina expedition from Vancouver, British Columbia, to Nootka, Alaska. In December 1794, he deserted the Spanish navy and sailed to Hawaii on an American vessel, the *Lady Washington.* At age 20, he joined the staff of King Kamehameha I as accountant, diplomat, translator, and ordnance expert.

In 1811, with acreage at Honolulu, Marín—known as Manini or Marini—built a home for his growing family of five wives and 23 children. In addition to teaching local builders to make adobe, he tested soil and planted experimental gardens of asparagus, bananas, barley, beans, cabbage, carrots, celery, corn, garlic, greens, horseradish, lettuce, melons, onions, rice, tomatoes, turnips, and wheat. From Peru, he imported healing herbs to treat dysentery and influenza and to combat the unidentified fevers that generated a child mortality rate of 50 percent. He operated a livery stable and served the king as royal physician. At Marín's boardinghouse and tavern, foreign merchant captains and whalers gathered. From their gifts of seeds and roots from California, Central and South America, and the West Indies, he became Hawaii's first commercial farmer and the first to recycle food by-products into such commodities as beer, candles, and soap.

Navigators and privateers brought Marín cattle, goats, horses, poultry, and sheep, which he raised on Ford Island in Pearl Harbor. In 1813, he planted the region's first lemons, oranges, and pineapples and two more firsts, cotton and the Tahitian mango. His first coffee plantation failed in 1817, but he harvested the first oranges two years later. An 80-foot (24-meter) mango tree became a Honolulu landmark. He introduced grapes from mission vineyards in Santa Barbara, California, and made the first peach brandy and wine. Marín also made beer and grew sugarcane for rum, and by the 1820s, his distilleries manufactured beverages for sale. During his service to Kamehameha II, food taboos ended for women, allowing them to eat the same menu as males. For Marín's contributions to the islands, he earned a captaincy in the Hawaiian army.

In 1825, Marín hired English agriculture instructor John Wilkinson and added to his fields arabica coffee plants procured from Brazil by Scots botanist James Macrae. Marín imported from England apple, cherry, custard apple, peach, plum, and nectarine trees. His suppliers donated Guatemalan cocoa, Mexican avocado and chilies, Tahitian breadfruit, and citrus, guava, myrtle, and sassafras plants from Rio de Janeiro. He shipped mangoes and pineapples to California and stocked ships' larders with his products—butter, castor oil, cigars, coconut oil, hay, *kukui* skin oil, lemon syrup, lime, molasses, pickles, plant stock, poi, pond fish, rose bushes, salt, soap, and sugar.

In Marín's late fifties, Hiram Bingham, a puritanical missionary from Vermont, agitated for restrictions on the sale of Marín's alcoholic beverages and for the banning of grog shops. Marín's introduction of cotton succeeded in 1835 with the completion of a cloth mill at Kailua. In 1837, he planted the islands' first macadamia tree. German botanists and Russian horticulturists visiting his gardens and parcel in the Pauoa Valley in northeastern Oahu admired the adaptation of food plants from many sources, including the avocado, olive, papaya, prickly pear, and tamarind. Altogether, Marín introduced 65 edible species to Hawaii.

See also: Beer; Maritime Trade Routes.

Further Reading

Gast, Ross H. *Don Francisco De Paula Marin, a Biography: The Letters and Journals of Francisco De Paula Marin.* Ed. Agnes C. Conrad. Honolulu: University of Hawaii Press, 2002.

Lee, Blanche Kaualua Lolokukalani. *The Unforgettable Spaniard: Hawaii's First Western Farmer.* 2nd ed. Pittsburgh: RoseDog, 2004.

Pemmican

A trade item of the Canadian Assiniboin and Métis peoples, pemmican earned the name "bread of the wilderness" for its value to expeditioners. In the Canadian Northwest, the preserved food derived its name from the Cree *pimikian*. It provided a lightweight, nutritious, and easily transported snack and trail food for the region's *coureurs de bois* (woods runners), traders, and explorers.

For thousands of years, Plains Indians extended the use of buffalo meat by preserving it in pemmican and storing it in sacks as survival rations. Eskimos survived for centuries on the all-meat diet, which they based on the flesh of musk ox, seal, and bear. Spanish conquistador Francisco de Coronado made the first historic reference to pemmican in 1541 during his New Mexican expedition, which encountered the forerunner of Southwestern chili on the route between New Mexico and the Texas Panhandle.

To the north, the Assiniboin of Pembina, North Dakota, developed the pemmican industry to its height. After the arrival of the French in 1640, Catholic priests who converted the Dakota Indians substituted pemmican for scarce communion bread. Native buffalo hunters taught Euro-Canadians the right time to stalk herds, the difference in meat from bull and cow, and the selection of the choice meat from hump and rump for preservation. By trading condensed meat rations for clay pipes, glass beads, horses, tobacco, and tools, natives enabled fur traders and mountaineers to survive in the Canadian West and Arctic regions.

Pemmican production united matriarchal societies into effective manufacturers. Made by women, pemmican required labor-intensive boning and slicing of buffalo, deer, elk, moose, or wild sheep meat into strips for fire or sun drying over willow. For a 90-pound (41-kilogram) bag of pemmican, preparers required two buffalo cows. They pulverized the dried meat into powder with a wooden mallet or shredded it into flakes with a flail or between stone pestle and mortar. The women seasoned the condensed jerky with hot buffalo tallow from the hump or rump or with marrow fat, which men extracted by cracking the bones and boiling them in water. A high-grade mix, called fine pemmican, involved using fat only from the buffalo udder. For seed pemmican, women flavored the mix with ground blueberries, buffalo berries, chokecherries, cranberries, prairie pear, or saskatoons as well as wild onions. The Blackfoot of Saskatchewan preferred to flavor meat with mint leaves, a powerful digestive aid. The Sioux produced a meatless version made from parched corn.

In western Alaska, Eskimo preparers of *agutak* whipped fat from caribou, seal, or walrus into a froth for blending with salmon or caribou meat, moose or raindeer tallow, roots, sugar, and fruit, such as blueberries, cranberries, crowberries, or salmonberries. Farther west at Kamchatka, Russia, the Chukchi, nomadic hunter-gatherers, followed a similar recipe, combining dried or flaked fish, roe, reindeer or seal fat, and bilberries.

Meat Preservation

Preservation simplified storage and haulage by reducing watery content. For cooling, hardening, and distribution,

Sioux women made pemmican by pounding venison, berries, seeds, and fat in a mortar and shaping the mixture into small patties. Native peoples preferred local sources of fat and protein to flavor such high-energy, easy-to-transport survival foods. *(Marilyn Angel Wynn/ Getty Images)*

pemmican makers stitched the finished product into buffalo parfleches (hide bags) with a sinew and walked over each to squeeze out air pockets. Users tied pemmican by thongs onto pack animals or stored slabs in a ground cache or under a riverbank as an insurance of emergency food during winter or under siege. Plains Indians distributed pemmican as gifts to relatives; young Hidatsa males gave slabs of pemmican to likely mates as engagement presents. Arctic aborigines fed the trail mix to their sled dogs. Tundra trekkers ate the high-energy product raw while on the move, floured and fried it in oil like steak, cooked it with flour into *hoosh* or *rubbaboo* (stew), or broiled it with wild parsnips over campfires. They also could layer pemmican in caches on rock beds to preserve it for as long as 30 years.

The Algonquin recipe for pemmican consisted of half protein, for sustaining muscles and organs, and half fat, for energy. The Lewis and Clark expedition received stores of pemmican from the Mandan and recorded their first taste of pemmican cakes on September 26, 1804, when the Teton Sioux served it with dog meat and ground camas tubers near Fort Pierre, South Dakota. Robert Michael Ballantyne, a Hudson's Bay Company clerk at the Red River Settlement, preserved details of pemmican making in his books on frontier life. In 1840, the annual Canadian Métis buffalo hunt on the Red River filled 1,000 big-wheeled oxcarts with 500 tons (450 metric tons) of pemmican. Because grass-fed stock and the addition of dried berries prevented scurvy, which weakens connective tissue from too little ascorbic acid in the diet, traders sold large amounts every year to boatmen of the Hudson's Bay Company. European settlers and soldiers augmented the Plains Indian recipe with beef jerky and suet and more berries, cherries, cur-

rants, and raisins to enhance the gamy flavor and increase saliva.

Pemmican as an Industry

Explorers relied on pemmican for trade gifts with Indians and as lightweight rations, which the British Royal Navy adopted as its primary sledging ration for polar exploration. Condensed meat contributed to the success of international explorers. A significant advantage of a pemmican-based diet, the reduction of bowel movements to once weekly reduced the risk of frostbite to exposed skin.

For packing condensed meat, John Richardson, a seeker of the Northwest Passage in 1825, made pemmican on a brewer's malting equipment. The Burke and Wills expedition of April 1861, on a north-south route across Australia, relied on pemmican as pack food or overland "sledging rations." Robert E. Peary, discoverer of the North Pole in 1909, valued pemmican as the sine qua non of survival food for its palatability and instant use; for a sled team, he recommended Bovril pemmican, a dog food marketed by Bovril Ltd. of London. For the arduous trek to the Arctic Circle, Peary carried only condensed milk, hardtack, pemmican, and tea. That same year, Ernest Shackleton boosted body heat among trekkers by purchasing Danish pemmican from Beauvais of Copenhagen, a canner of tinned meat, soup, and vegetables. Shackleton augmented the meat stash with glydin (processed protein), oatmeal, and sugar and ate it with hot cocoa to maintain energy levels on his route to McMurdo Sound, Antarctica. For traversing Greenland in 1924, Knud Rasmussen added rice and vegetables to the condensed meat supply. From 1924 to 1925, Arctic adventurer Vilhjalmur Stefansson lived a full year on pemmican as a test of the Inuit all-meat diet.

Adaptations

In American, Australian, Canadian, Danish, Dutch, English, French, and Norwegian factories, the twentieth-century manufacturers tinkered with the nutritional makeup of Paleo-Indian condensed pemmican with the addition of dog meat, horse meat, sugar, and chocolate. To protect meat supplies from spoilage during Richard Byrd's Antarctic exploration in 1929, Dr. Dana Coman of Johns Hopkins Medical School formulated a new recipe for pemmican in collaboration with Armour and Company. The mixture included soy flour and brewer's yeast and ginger, pepper, and thyme as flavorings. In preparation for the Oxford University expedition to the far north Spitsbergen Island in 1934, Dr. Sylvester Solomon Zilva of the Lister Institute in London advocated bolstering pemmican with vitamin C as a deterrent to scurvy. Diners dubbed the resulting recipe Potage Antiscorbutique, the forerunner of K ration or Meal, Ready-to-Eat (MRE).

During World War II, the German and U.S. militaries experimented with pemmican as survival food, following the example of the British army, which had purchased pemmican from the Dutch and distributed it during the Second Boer War (1899–1902). U.S. nutritionists rejected the gamy flavor and questionable nutrition of condensed meat. To improve flavor, in the mid-1940s, biochemist Robert S. Harris, at the nutrition laboratory of Massachusetts Institute of Technology, experimented with supplements of beef liver, peanut butter, coconut oil, powdered milk, vigex (a mix of energizing herbs), calcium, and glutamic acid, a flavor enhancer. In 1956, for a British

Recipe: European Pemmican

Chop or grind a pound of dry beef jerky to a powder. Grind separately a cup of blueberries, cranberries, currants, figs, raisins, or dried apples, apricots, or cherries. Mix the meat with the fruit. (Optional: Add honey, sunflower or other seeds, and/or unsalted nuts.) Cut a pound of beef suet into chunks and melt over a low fire. Filter and cool the tawny-colored liquid until it turns white. Reheat the beef-and-fruit mixture and pour the liquid fat over it. As it cools, mold into bars or blocks and wrap in waxed paper or zip into plastic bags.

A half pound of pemmican per day supplies the adult dietary need of 1,500 calories. For grueling exertion, such as portaging, snowshoeing, or mountain climbing, the daily average increases to 3/4 of a pound or 1 pound per day.

expedition to the Ross Sea, Cadbury, a food manufacturer in Dunedin, New Zealand, produced pemmican for sled dogs from dehydrated meat, meal, whole wheat and wheat germ, tallow, treacle, and cod liver oil. In the first decade of the twenty-first century, vegetarians proposed a meatless pemmican recipe consisting of equal parts peanuts and hickory nuts, cornmeal, pumpkin or squash, maple syrup or honey, raisins, and dried apples.

See also: Biscuit; Hudson's Bay Company; Industrial Food Processing; Religion and Food.

Further Reading

Duncan, Dorothy. *Canadians at Table: Food, Fellowship, and Folklore: A Culinary History of Canada.* Toronto: Dundurn, 2006.

Keoke, Emory Dean, and Kay Marie Porterfield. *American Indian Contributions to the World: 15,000 Years of Inventions and Innovations.* New York: Checkmark, 2003.

Roy, Suman, and Brooke Ali. *From Pemmican to Poutine: A Journey Through Canada's Culinary History.* Toronto: Key, 2010.

Pennsylvania Dutch Diet and Cuisine

Pennsylvania Dutch cuisine of the central and southeastern sectors of the state expresses the unpretentious, robust diet of Huguenot, Jewish, and Mennonite Rhinelanders. Emerging from an agrarian culture of Deutsch, or German, immigrants fleeing religious persecution in Alsace and the Palatinate, "plain" people made up one-third of the state's population as early as 1683. As befits a folk culture, they ate from the land. Cooks bought little at grocery stores beyond coffee, pepper, salt, and sugar. They gathered mint and pennyroyal to dry for tea and chickweed for pie; they made their own baking powder and reduced horseradish and mustard into table condiments to serve with fresh shad and oyster stew.

A modest addition to North American cookery, Pennsylvania Dutch food nourished citizens at turning points in history. During the winter of 1777–1778, the Dutch *schnitz* pie, made from dried apples, solaced hungry Continental soldiers for breakfast at Valley Forge. Peasant open-hearth cookery in copper cauldrons and food preservation in jars appeared in print in 1848 in America's first ethnic cookbook, *Die Geschickte Hausfrau* (*The Housewife's Tale*), a collection of high-calorie dishes acquired by a recipe pirate, Gustav Sigismund Peters. To suit the language of 40 percent of the regional populace, he wrote in German, the language that isolated the newcomers from their English neighbors.

During the Civil War, rural table customs earned local people the name "Sauerkraut Yankees," a reference to their taste for savory meals. Legacy recipes, originally inscribed in the Pennsylfaanisch dialect, make use of such homemade foods as cassia-spiced pickles and ham

Recipe: Wilted Lettuce

Pick and wash fresh lettuce and salad greens. Break into bite-size pieces. Snip bacon into 1/2-inch pieces and fry to a crisp. Remove the bacon, reheat the drippings, and add an equal amount of tarragon vinegar. Return bacon to the pan and pour the dressing over the greens.

with schnitz (dried apples) and dumplings. To the elongation of table talk, hosts removed crullers, *fastnachts* (doughnuts), and *lebkuchen* from outdoor brick ovens and shared their sweets for dunking in hot black coffee.

On self-sustaining farms, traditional cooks focus on humble substances as handy as molasses and dandelion greens. Ingenuity transforms the ordinary into a filling comfort food as common as shoofly pie with elderberry wine and walnut mooschi (candy) and as winter hearty as *kubelis,* a casserole of bacon, onions, and potatoes. Kitchen crews dole out ingredients in pinches and dabs rather than standard measures for such traditional foods as corn pie for harvesters and sausage gravy, a breakfast staple thickened with spelt flour. Examples of food recycling range from scrapple (pork scraps in corn mush) and stuffed hog maw (pig stomach) to chow-chow, an end-of-the-garden relish that housekeepers can in early fall from odds and ends of the vegetable patch. By balancing sour with sweet, cooks enhance the flavors of community favorites, such as a dinner of pork shoulder and sauerkraut served with biscuits and apple or grape butter. For toddlers and the sick, servings of buttermilk corn bread and baked custard turn dietetic meals into savory treats.

Following the "seven sweets and seven sours" principle, Pennsylvania Dutch cooks retain the customs of Hungarian, Jewish, and Scandic cuisine. Their cookbooks delight the senses with foods that present interesting textures and colors, along with the vivid aromas and tastes found in *hasenpfeffer* (rabbit stew), rhubarb crumb pie, birch or lager beer, and cup cheese (a soft, spreadable cheese). Traditional preparers apply a hands-on method of crumbling rivvels (stringy dumplings) into chicken stock for soup and drizzling batter through a funnel for a fried *drechter kuche* (dough cake). To ensure a supply of workable ingredients, householders value root crops, dried corn, buckwheat, sour cream, and vinegar.

A unique population, the Amish contingent of Pennsylvania Dutch consists of some 16,000 living in Lancaster County and preserving the culture of Swiss Anabaptists. After settling on farms, they turned staples—eggs and poultry, apples, corn and potatoes, wheat and barley—into appealing dishes for *Nachtesse* (night eating). Central to kitchen work, the preparation of fresh chowders, creamed cabbage, and spiced lemonade replicates food peeling, chopping, and grating that date back to the European practice of making the most out of edibles. Girls learn to turn apples into cider and jelly, fresh roasting ears into dried corn, and milk into *schmierkase,* a light cottage cheese.

Family gatherings for school holidays or a wedding involve preparation of favorites, such as snow cream, raisin pie, and pickled green tomatoes. To maximize flavor, cooks fry in butter or leaf lard, sandwich meat between slices of pumpernickel and rye bread, and top coleslaw and leaf greens with hot savory bacon dressings. Baskets and platters of food tempt diners with the shapes of potato croquettes and pig's knuckle dumplings and the aroma of roast duck. Amish food markets specialize in Lebanon bologna and whoopie pies, traditional fare that holds a unique spot in ethnic American cuisine.

See also: Appetizers and Hors d'Oeuvres; Breakfast; Noodles; Pickling.

Further Reading

Kittler, Pamela Goyan, and Kathryn Sucher. *Food and Culture.* Belmont, CA: Wadsworth/Thomson Learning, 2004.

Richman, Irwin. *The Pennsylvania Dutch Company.* Charleston, SC: Arcadia, 2004.

Weaver, William Woys. *Country Scrapple: An American Tradition.* Mechanicsburg, PA: Stackpole, 2003.

———. *Pennsylvania Trail of History Cookbook.* Mechanicsburg, PA: Stackpole, 2004.

———. "The Water Gate Inn: Pennsylvania Dutch Cuisine Goes Mainstream." *Gastronomica* 9:3 (Summer 2009): 25–31.

Peppers

The *Capsicum* and *Piper* pepper families impart zip and heat to a broad range of world cuisines, allegedly adding years to life and sexual potency. The *Capsicum* pepper originated in Bolivia in the Amazon River basin around 7500 B.C.E., producing some 25 species. Peruvians domesticated the habañero chili after 6500 B.C.E. and added its blossomy fragrance and lemony taste to mescal, an alcoholic drink later distilled from agave in Oaxaca, Mexico. By 4000 B.C.E., kitchen gardens in Ecuador featured *Capsicum* pepper patches as sources of food, aphrodisiacs, and antifungal, antimicrobial, and antivermin agents.

Mesoamericans discovered that *Capsicum* peppers produce capsaicin, an alkaloid that stimulates appetite and digestion by increasing the flow of gastric juices. The hottest flavors emerged from the habañero, Naga, and Scotch bonnet, which, on the Scoville scale, ranks 300,000 times hotter than the bell pepper. Cooks dried pods with smoke or sunlight, turning the jalapeño into chipotles for grinding into a musky paste to enliven braised meat, chocolate beverages, soups, and stews. Poblanos, either roasted, sliced, or dried as anchos, added flavor to finger foods and garnishes and to *mole poblano* (pepper sauce) and stuffings for poultry.

Misidentified as black pepper by Christopher Columbus on his first voyage to the New World in 1492, the bell pepper or chili pepper (*Capsicum annuum*) originated in Mexico and Panama. The species that Columbus sampled in Hispaniola contributed a crisp bite to salads and finger foods and intense tang to paprika, the powdered form of chili. By 1493, he had already plotted how to export 50 shiploads of sweet peppers annually to Spain.

Mouthfeel and sweetness varied according to terroir, the combination of weather and topographical growing conditions, which ranged from eastern Asia to Ghana, Holland, and Romania. Basque cooks became the first Europeans to develop a fiery cuisine based on dried and pickled peppers and to sell peppers to Africa, the Levant, and the Far East. Spaniards developed the red *choricero* variety at Vizcaya for use in chorizo sausage. Hungarians turned paprika pepper into their national table condiment, particularly for flavoring cracked wheat, fried onions, eggplants, and meat stew.

Black Pepper

Unlike *Capsicum* stock, *Piper* has a shorter history, beginning on the Malabar coast of India around 2000 B.C.E. and becoming the world's most popular spice. Egyptians valued pepper as early as 1550 B.C.E. After 1000 B.C.E., pepper vines became a standard addition of home gardens and the least expensive flavoring at farmer's markets. By the 800s B.C.E., Arabs were dispensing *Piper cubeba* (bitter pepper) as a treatment for infertility and an antidote to poisoning and introducing pepper to European cooks. Arab traders guarded the secret of where and how they acquired peppercorns for sale.

Both the Greeks and Romans valued *Piper longum* (long pepper) and *Piper nigrum* (black pepper). Shipments traveled from India inland by caravan from the Arabian Sea over the Silk Road and by ship from the Red Sea and barge from Alexandria across the Mediterranean Sea. The lengthy journey from Baghdad through Constantinople and Venice increased the cost of pepper, which, throughout the Crusades, remained higher in value than gold. Profits benefited China and elevated Venetian markets to one of the world's more lucrative trading centers.

In the 1500s, the Portuguese diminished the control of southern India on the pepper trade. Navigators transplanted Indian pepper vines to Java, Madagascar, and Malaysia, favoring the mildly fragrant Lampong black and fruity Sarawak black over the bolder Tellicherry black from southern India. European demand for black pepper inspired the voyages of discovery that preceded Portuguese colonies.

After 1602, the Dutch East India Company monopolized commerce in black pepper for 167 years. The harvesting of black pepper from Goa focused on land planted in areca nut, betel palm, or mango trees on which pepper vines grew. During the three-year wait for a first harvest, workers stitched hemp sacks. Pepper berries required a month's drying period before packing and warehousing for sale. Indian aficionados turned pepper oil into a massage emollient for Ayurvedic healing. By 1629, wealthy American colonists imported black pepper for table use. In 1750, the French East India Company transplanted Javanese pepper vines to Mauritius, Réunion, and the Seychelles.

In 1769, Danish, English, and French traders seized control of Dutch spice routes and sparked a rush of investment in the pepper market. The British East India Company imported so many peppercorns to Europe that the price fell to an amount that ordinary citizens could afford. From that time, pepper held second place to salt as the most common food seasoning.

Use in Recipes

Capsicum and *Piper* peppers made vast changes in Asian cuisines, alarming Buddhists with the inflammation of human passions. Black pepper gave Chinese beverages and sauces a pungency and lasting aftertaste. In the late 1600s, the transport from South America of hot chili peppers, either whole or in flaked or powdered form, introduced the basis for Szechuan cuisine. Guinea peppers (cayenne), either plain or added to a vinegar sauce, topped the surface of fish and meat with a spicy flavor. Seventeenth-century naturopath Nicholas Culpeper summarized numerous uses for cayenne for treating colds, coughs, stings, tremors, and tumors.

From Bantam (now Banten), Malaysia and the Indian subcontinent acquired the extra-hot long pepper, a staple of Indonesian gastronomy and of Indian curries and vegetable pickling. Bhutanese recipes flavored cheese with chili peppers. Filipino cooks valued pepper plant leaves as greens and flavorings for chicken soup. Koreans fermented the leaves in *kimchi* (pickled vegetables). Thai pepper processors dried green pods for their fresh, vivid taste and bottled chili sauce blended with garlic, salt, sugar, and vinegar for seafood dips and saucing spring rolls.

Americans made their own discoveries about peppered dishes, including chili con carne, jalapeño poppers, and pork sausage, as well as patent medicines such as Stanley's snake oil. With red pepper flakes, an inexpensive substitute for black pepper, pioneering cooks turned out Cajun jambalaya, chowchow, Jamaican pepper pot, ketchup, okra and pepper pickles, sauces, and sawmill gravy (white milk gravy). Later experiments resulted in distinctive recipes exhibiting immigrant specialties, such as adobo rub for beef and chicken, Creole bouillabaisse (fish stew), Cuban sandwiches, salt-and-pepper catfish, Szechuan bean sauce, shaker blends for topping pizza, and hot sauces.

See also: New World Commodities; Szechuan Diet and Cuisine; Tex-Mex Diet and Cuisine; Trading Vessels.

Further Reading

Janer, Zilkia. *Latino Food Culture*. Westport, CT: Greenwood, 2008.

Phillips, James Duncan. *Pepper and Pirates: Adventures in the Sumatra Pepper Trade of Salem*. Boston: Houghton Mifflin, 1949.

Prange, Sebastian R. "Where the Pepper Grows." *Saudi Aramco World* 59:1 (January/February 2008): 10–17.

Ravindran, P.N., ed. *Black Pepper: Piper Nigrum*. Amsterdam, Netherlands: Overseas, 2000.

Persian Diet and Cuisine

Arising from central Asia north of the Fertile Crescent in 2000 B.C.E., Persians developed a colorful culture based on a profusion of foods adapted and refined from other lands. Beginning with the Medes in 1000 B.C.E. and advancing to the Achaemenid Empire in 550 B.C.E., Persia grew into the largest and most hospitable empire of the ancient world. The Achaemenid kings observed the classical world's respect for the host-guest relationship. Agronomists imported Babylonian sesame, Anatolian fruit trees, Syrian pistachios, and alfalfa seeds from the

A medieval illustration from the *Shahnameh* (*Book of Kings,* ca. 1010), the national epic poem of Iran, depicts the Golden Age of Paradise. Men and beasts enjoy the fruits of the earth—a metaphor for the rich abundance of foods in classical Persian culture. *(UniversalImagesGroup/Getty Images)*

Mediterranean and watered them with underground irrigation systems. Careful governmental control and stockpiling prevented the famines that beset other Asian lands. Except for irrigation failures, food prices remained stable.

Around 870 B.C.E., King Ashurnasirpal held a ten-day festival at Nirum and invited 47,074 Assyrians for a display of imaginative, plentiful cookery. The purchase of Indian rice inspired meticulous soaking and steaming to produce separate aromatic grains. Under Judaic law, the people avoided Egyptian luxuries, favored Persian eggplant and spinach, and ate no waterfowl and only those animals named in the Torah. For freshness and taste, hosts offered platters of plain herbs, mixing chives, cilantro, and cress with dill, mint, radishes, scallions, and tarragon. From the legend of Esther's feast for King Xerxes I, Jews derived the feast of Purim.

Around 430 B.C.E., Herodotus's *Histories* reported the simplicity of Persian sacrificial meals as contrasted with court pomp. Herodotus noted that Darius the Great kept a phalanx of food researchers who combed the outside world for rare and different taste sensations, such as garlic from Cyprus. Xerxes, Darius's son, expected such grandeur at meals that when he visited other cities, he left them in ruins. For a royal birthday, chefs roasted whole camels, donkeys, horses, and oxen. Interspersed between entrées, they served desserts. Guests, who drank themselves into a stupor, showed fondness for foreign customs, particularly forms of pleasure.

Celebrating Food

At the height of the Persian Empire, stewards employed confectioners, cupbearers, and sommeliers to carry entrées and sherry to the table of Darius. At Persepolis, grand processions accompanied platters of ostrich breast and roast camel. Cooks spread colorful feasts of tasty, nutritionally balanced dishes heady with aroma and served with flatbreads. Persian kitchens, equipped with mortar and pestle and soup cauldrons, introduced basil and coriander, almond and pistachio sweets, sweet and sour sauce, pomegranate juice, and kebabs. They flavored eclectic rice recipes featuring cinnamon, garlic, lemon and lime, nuts, onions, parsley, pomegranate seeds, raisins and prune, and saffron. According to astronomer Berossus, a priest of Bel Marduk who compiled the *Babyloniaca* (*History of Babylonia,* ca. 290 B.C.E.), God blessed the Tigris and Euphrates region with abundant foodstuffs as a sign of his blessing.

Subsequent expansion augmented Persian cuisine in the third century C.E. with chicken, cucumbers, peacocks, sugar, and walnuts. Caravans introduced Chinese tea, apricots, peaches, and rhubarb to be served on gold and silver plate. Wine from gold carafes filled the king's rhytons, horned cups with animal-shaped bases shared with the royal cup-companions. The Sassanians of the third to the seventh centuries favored intense flavors,

Recipe: Cold Stuffed Dolma

Steam 1 cup of basmati rice. Simmer with three chopped tomatoes, one chopped onion, and 2 tablespoons each of snipped mint and parsley. Flavor with a pinch each of allspice, cinnamon, pepper, and salt. Place 1/2 pound of fresh grape leaves in a bowl and blanch with boiling water. Spread the leaves flat, with the vein side up. Stir two chopped tomatoes into the rice mixture. Roll 1 tablespoon of mixture in each leaf, with the stem end pointed to the middle. Squeeze out any excess juice. Chill and serve with a topping of raisins and a dollop of yogurt.

including ox meat cooked in beef bouillion and rabbit ragout. The chefs of King Khosrow I served succulent stews with cold soups, candied lozenges, apple and quince jelly, sherbet, and nut pastries. Blending produced unique combinations of coconut with pistachio, infant lambs stuffed with dates and raisins, parsley soup with green plums, lamb hearts in cinnamon, and dates with peaches and nuts. Queen Pourandokht instructed her chef to serve *borani,* vegetables in yogurt. King Khosrow II and Queen Shirin carried triumph to excess in Alexandria, Antioch, Damascus, and Jerusalem and lavished huge sums on date puree, jellied rice, mutton with pomegranate sauce, rice pudding, spit-roasted hen fed on hemp seed, and stuffed grape leaves. For the poor, the queen, a native of Armenia, commanded charity serving of *harissa,* a wheat porridge flavored with fat and sugar.

An End to Excess

In 656, Arab invasions ended the hedonism of the Sassanid Empire and replaced it with Bedouin pastoral diet—barley gruel, game, milk, mutton, onions, palm hearts, and wild berries. Opulence and spicing disappeared from recipes, as Arab traders transported luxury goods to Italian markets for profit. Zoroastrian harmony of opposites in cookery, such as mint and vinegar sauce on lamb, gave way to less refined Islamic culture. (After Arabs completed a hasty meal standing up, they licked their fingers in the manner of the prophet Muhammad.) With the rise of the Abbasid dynasty, the Islamic Golden Age, Arab recipes adapted to sophisticated Persian tastes and aromatics. Cosmopolitan cuisine at Baghdad, the center of the Abbasid culture, revived classical cuisine. Cooks added dates and figs to lamb dishes and heightened visual appeal with saffron and turmeric. To basic flavorings—coriander, mint, parsley, and sesame—chefs added lavender, mallow, purslane, rosebuds, rue, tarragon, and thyme. Under the influence of Harun-al-Rashid in 786, subtle cuisine became a Persian art form praised by caliphs, poets, princes, and

scholars. The creation of inspired stuffed vegetables and tiny pies and praise anthems sung by revelers raised the banquet to the height of celebration and sensuality. Connoisseurs issued handbooks of table pleasures. Specialists advised on regulating human moods and physical constitution with dietetics, which recommended blends of lentils with spinach to strengthen the sick. The elegant bounty of Persian cuisine influenced cookery in India and Turkey and spread flavored pilaus to the royal courts of medieval Europe.

In 1226, Baghdad cookbook compiler Mohammad ibn al-Hasan proclaimed gastronomy the height of the noble life. Meals begin with the host's proclamation, "Bismillah" (in the name of God), followed by silent eating. The king of Persian entrées, *narinj pilau,* is a rice dish flavored with almonds, orange peel, spices, and sugar. Diners sat cross-legged on an ox hide or cloth, receiving Caspian caviar or feta cheese served on flatbread and picking apart a roast partridge, quail, or fat-tailed sheep with the fingers. More difficult, the scooping of stuffed gourds with the right hand and rolling it into a ball demanded that no morsel fall to the cloth. Meals concluded with heaps of seasonal fruits and melons. Servants prepared sherbet, a cooling blend of lemon, orange, or pomegranate juice or willow flowers poured into a decanter with water and lump sugar topped with ice or snow. Fruit became so essential to thirst quenching that women and children carried fruit baskets to the public bath and gorged on grapes, oranges, peaches, and pomegranates and sips of rosewater. For health, families dined daily on melons and cow, goat, or sheep milk yogurt.

All levels of society thrived on fresh staples and ate by moonlight on their housetops, chatting across the way with neighbors. In winter, they put a carpet over the oven and sat at the edge to enjoy warmth and hot food. Servants fed on the master's leftovers. The poorest muleteer or nomad dined only a few times of the year on meat and subsisted primarily on barley or rye bread, cheese, and dates with occasional curds, hard-cooked eggs, and soup for a treat. Urban peasants lived on similar fare augmented with apricots, cucumbers, grapes, lettuce, and onions. For breakfast, they added molasses to clabbered milk. To preserve milk solids, they boiled butter and decanted the oil into clay pitchers, where it remained fresh for up to two years. Bazaar dining consisted of slices of whole roasted sheep and mutton, onion kebabs, and pickled cauliflower and cucumber sticks wrapped in bread. With the Mongol capture of Baghdad in 1258, religious puritanism supplanted Abbasid brilliance. The poet Shams Hafiz shamed his host Ali Agha Isfahani for serving excesses of food, which Shams considered an embarrassment of wealth.

See also: Athenaeus; Breakfast; Fertile Crescent Diet and Food Trade; Nuts and Seeds; Soft Drinks and Juices; Trade Routes.

Further Reading

Batmanglij, Najmieh. *A Taste of Persia: An Introduction to Persian Cooking.* London: I.B. Tauris, 2007.

———. *Food of Life: Ancient Persian and Modern Iranian Cooking and Ceremonies.* 4th ed. Washington, DC: Mage, 2011.

Ghanoonparvar, M.R. *Persian Cuisine: Traditional, Regional, and Modern Foods.* Costa Mesa, CA: Mazda, 2006.

Peyote

The Native American Church, the largest Indian religious constituency, reveres the sacramental consumption of powdered mescal, peyote tea, or fresh peyote buttons, a bitter, non-habit-forming alkaloid. The spongy, spineless knob of the *Lophophora williamsii*, a gray-blue-green hallucinogen of the cactus family indigenous to the Pacific coast of Mexico and the Lower Pecos region of Texas, gained sacred status from around 8500 B.C.E. and flourished among the Lipan Apache and Tonkawa. Peyoteros (suppliers) made pilgrimages into the Chihuahua Desert to collect the cactus. Users consumed from four to twelve buttons, either fresh or dried for steeping into a tea.

European proselytizers targeted peyote consumption as sacrilege. In 1521, Catholic missionaries outlawed the eating of hallucinogenic mushrooms and peyote. According to Spanish chronicler and Franciscan friar Bernardino de Sahagún in 1560, the Aztec, Chichimeca, Huichol, Mexica, and Navajo, the plains tribes of the Rio Grande basin, and the Tarahumara of central Mexico continued to chew peyote buttons as part of pagan ritual. Into the mid-eighteenth century, Catholic priests condemned the use of peyote by prophets for divination.

In the 1850s, the near extinction of the buffalo and genocidal forays by the U.S. cavalry spread despair among the Apache, Caddo, Comanche, Kiowa, Shoshone, and Toltec. Shamans sought the holy herb and disseminated cultic ceremonies west to the Ute and north into the Canadian plains. Because of the rapid growth of peyotism, Congress in 1918 outlawed the cult. To secure constitutional rights to traditional folk worship, priests incorporated the Native American Church. In 1923, the outlawing of peyotism in Montana resulted in arrests of worshippers for eating a hallowed controlled substance.

After resettlement in Indian Territory (Oklahoma), the Kickapoo, Kiowa, Shawnee, and Wichita popularized religious peyote ingestion, which engendered euphoria and the illusion of timelessness for a 10- to 12-hour period. The most powerful plant in native herbalism, peyote offered users a substitute to debauchery from alcohol and marijuana.

Currently, some 400,000 Native American Church members value the cactus as a source of introspection; healers recognize the worth of peyote to heal infection and to relieve pain and the effects of asthma. Accompanying the holy cactus meals, priests heal the sick and conduct seances and visions while celebrants chant and dance to all-night drumming. The ritual inspires reverence for the Mother Earth and the harmony of human life with nature. Lakota midwives prescribe peyote for parturient women during labor. In some states, Christian proselytizing and antidrug laws contravene claims of religious freedom to ingest the psychotropic mescaline in peyote.

See also: Wild Food.

Further Reading

Epps, Garrett. *Peyote vs. the State: Religious Freedom on Trial.* Norman: University of Oklahoma Press, 2009.

Fisher, Louis. *Congressional Protection of Religious Liberty.* New York: Novinka, 2003.

Maroukis, Thomas Constantine. *Peyote and the Yankton Sioux: The Life and Times of Sam Necklace.* Norman: University of Oklahoma Press, 2005.

———. *The Peyote Road: Religious Freedom and the Native American Church.* Norman: University of Oklahoma Press, 2010.

Olive, M. Foster. *Peyote and Mescaline.* New York: Chelsea House, 2007.

Phoenician Diet and Cuisine

A Semitic merchant culture from 1200 to 333 B.C.E. at Byblos, Sidon, and Tyre in present-day Lebanon, the Phoenicians, known in the Bible as Canaanites, enjoyed a varied diet from imported livestock and trade goods. To supplement their narrow strip of arable land, they depended upon the first navigator-trader relationship with the Far East. From Greece and Egypt, their commercial vessels carried bags of grain and sea salt, chests of saffron, and amphorae—two-handled jugs that ended in a knob for ease of pouring—of olives, olive oil, and wine.

In a string of city-states, working-class Phoenicians tended toward informal meals of finger food. Hearty cuts of garlic-flavored goat and lamb accompanied slices of

Recipe: Cucumbers in Yogurt

Peel and dice four large cucumbers, and mix them into 1 cup of plain yogurt and 1 cup of sour cream. Add 1 tablespoon of fresh chopped mint, 1 teaspoon of sea salt, a sprinkle of dried dill, a few drops of tarragon vinegar, and one minced garlic clove. Chill and serve with pita triangles as a side dish to grilled fish or lamb kebabs.

dried bream and mullet, cheese, honeyed bread, and melons and berries, all of which suited the limited galleys and tableware of trading coasters. For seafarers, almonds, chestnuts, hazelnuts, pistachios, and walnuts served as pocket snacks.

Fish, mutton, poultry, and snails served the needs of ordinary citizens. Fed sophisticated dishes by Cadmos, the chef of King Agenor of Sidon around 2000 B.C.E., aristocrats demanded excellent fare served on distinctive faience and red slip pottery. They afforded pantry exotica from Egypt, Greece, Mesopotamia, Sardinia, Sicily, and the Atlantic coast of Spain with the profits of the purple dye they made from the *Murex brandaris,* a tidal sea snail. At natural salt pans, they preserved sturgeon and tuna as well as moray eels. From fish parts and entrails, food processors fermented *garum,* a sauce used as a condiment and popular trade item. The wealthy enjoyed game and the occasional dolphin served with cardoons from Cartagena, Spain.

Until Alexander the Great killed 10,000 Tyrians and sold 30,000 into slavery in 332 B.C.E., the famed Phoenician navigators developed a service economy that bought and sold barley and wheat from Palestine and Syria. The Romans identified *puls punica* (Phoenician cereal) as a boiled porridge stabilized with chicken or ostrich eggs and flavored with cheese and honey. Daily dinners based on dairy products with *punicum* (flatcake) paired with olives, a Mediterranean staple. Phoenicians also favored beer with bread and pulses blended from broad beans, chickpeas, lentils, and peas.

As farmers, Phoenicians excelled at orchardry and vegetable gardens. Until overpopulation sapped their food supply, they stocked rows with artichokes and cabbages and sowed corn, cucumbers, and herbs. In addition to grapes and raisins, they produced delectable dates and figs, which they used as fresh or dried sweeteners, an alternative to costly honey.

In a 28-book treatise in Punic, Mago the Carthaginian, the "Father of Husbandry," summarized regional winemaking, beekeeping, and the harvesting of fen sedges and wetland reeds and rushes. He described the preservation of fresh pomegranates by parboiling and drying or by coating in clay. Another method involved packing the succulent globes in sawdust in a clay pot and sealing it for later use. Phoenician wine gained respect in Carthage as a part of religious ritual. As a burial ritual, mourners placed plates of food and jugs of wine beside the funerary urns of the dead.

See also: Fish and Fishing; Maritime Trade Routes; North African Diet and Cuisine; Trading Vessels; Yeast.

Further Reading

Aubet, Maria Eugenia. *The Phoenicians and the West: Politics, Colonies, and Trade.* Trans. Mary Turton. Cambridge, UK: Cambridge University Press, 2001.

Bierline, Marilyn R., and Seymour Gitin. *The Phoenicians in Spain: An Archaeological Review of the Eighth–Sixth Centuries* B.C.E. Winona Lake, IN: Eisenbrauns, 2002.

Kaufman, Asher. *Reviving Phoenicia: The Search for Identity in Lebanon.* London: I.B. Tauris, 2004.

Moscati, Sabatino. *The Phoenicians.* New York: I.B. Tauris, 2001.

Schneller, Thomas. *Poultry: Identification, Fabrication, Utilization.* Clifton Park, NY: Delmar, 2010.

Physic Gardening

The physic garden, an herb bed producing medicinal plants for healers and druggists, offers edible flora for aromatherapy, fumigation, nutrition, disease prevention, and restorative teas. Historians date the earliest garden to Karnak in central Egypt in 1400 B.C.E., when priests cultivated aloe, myrrh, and opium poppies alongside a kitchen bed. St. Anthony introduced medicinal gardening at Faiyum in northern Egypt in 305 C.E. as a source of culinary herbs and "simples."

Most plant knowledge preceding the Middle Ages remained anecdotal, transferred from one apothecary to another during apprenticeship. Gradually, texts such as Hildegard of Bingen's *Physica* (*Medicines,* ca. 1152) and Albert the Great's *De vegetabilibus* (*On vegetables,* 1259) codified the role of biodiversity in medical treatment. The basis for kitchen economy and the chemical analysis of food substances, plant research offered solutions to appetite stimulation in invalids and to hospital diets for surgical patients.

In the tradition of Greek and Roman herbaries, medieval monasteries, such as the ninth-century Benedictine *herbularium* (healing garden) at St. Gall in Switzerland and the twelfth-century Cistercian garden at Grey Abbey, Ireland, cultivated infirmary herb beds to provide medicines and nutrients. Infirmarians preferred gentle curatives, such as disinfectant rue and bitters from lovage leaves and yarrow tea for the sick and infirm. Outside sacred precincts, monks scoured meadows and hedgerows for endive, leeks, pennyroyal, rocket (arugula), sweet clover, and wild onions and parsnips, common ingredients in meatless broth.

Renaissance universities institutionalized physic gardening, beginning in Pisa in 1543 and in Florence in 1545. At Padua, lecturer Luca Ghini invented the herbarium, a catalog of dried plant specimens. In 1587, the town of Leiden, Holland, founded a teaching garden for use by medical students at the University of Leiden. With donations from the Dutch East India Company, Flemish botanist Carolus Clusius expanded the original plot to 1,000 plant specimens, some sent from Dutch trading centers in Japan. A Chinese original, the *Ginkgo biloba* tree produced nuts used in pudding and Buddha's delight, a vegetarian mélange favored by Buddhist monks for alimentary canal purification.

England began isolating beneficial plants at Oxford University in 1621. Five years later, Louis XIII founded the Jardin Royal des Plantes Médicinales in Paris. Scotland followed in 1670 with the Edinburgh botanic garden, an array of 15,000 plants encompassing algae, ferns, and fungi for the instruction of apprentice apothecaries and surgeons. The importation of curiosities from world voyages gave rise to speculation about the healing and dietary properties of breadfruit, cassava, castor oil, and quinine (extracted from the bark of the cinchona tree).

In 1673, the 4-acre (1.6-hectare) Chelsea Physic Garden in London applied to healing the botanic skills of the Worshipful Society of Apothecaries. In 1682, members established a seed exchange with the Leiden Botanical Garden in the Netherlands that extended pharmaceutical knowledge of alpine plants and nutritional herbs. Gardeners developed world medicine beds featuring stock valued in Ayurvedic and Maori medicine, among Native American shamans, and as curatives in China, northern Europe, and South Africa. Labeling differentiated plant parts relevant to the treatment of cancer, eye disease, parasitology, and psychiatry.

In 1722, Scots botanist Philip Miller, the chief gardener and author of *The Gardeners Dictionary* (1741), increased the range of known therapeutic and nutritive plants from varied climates. He cataloged barrels of evergreen stock dispatched by naturalist John Bartram from Pennsylvania. Each year, the Chelsea Physic Garden presented the Royal Society with 50 curative herbs from 2,000 plants. The stock supplied garden curator Isaac Rand with remedies for his *Index Plantarum Officinalium* (1730).

Scots illustrator Elizabeth Blackwell settled at Swan Walk near the Chelsea garden to draw 500 specimens for *A Curious Herbal* (1737–1739), a valuable medical text. Her hand-painted copper plates featured the cantaloupe, chamomile, coffee, cucumber, and sassafras, an American Indian staple cooked in gumbo, used to flavor root beer, and steeped as a tea. Her edibles showcased the physic garden's stock of catnip, chicory, medlars, olive trees, pomegranates, saffron, and tea. She depicted figs for syrups, grapes and hot peppers to whet appetite, quince for jelly, radishes to cure scurvy, Saint-John's-wort as an additive to wine, and dandelion, nettles, rosemary, and tomatoes, common salad and stew ingredients.

Other physic gardens, such as the *jardin potager* (soup garden) at Cowbridge, Wales, and beds of simples at the University of British Columbia, illustrate the close connection between plant science and food. Gardeners placed *materia medica* at hand for application to disease. At Pennsylvania Hospital, North America's first colonial hospital, the indigenous plantings begun in 1774 attest to the orderly arrangements of gardener Adam Kuhn, the school's first professor of botanic pharmaceuticals and director of vegetable and diet research.

See also: Curative Foods; Herbs; Manioc; Medieval Diet and Cuisine.

Further Reading

Elliott, Charles. *The Potting-Shed Papers: On Gardens, Gardeners, and Garden History.* Guilford, CT: Lyons, 2002.

Lock, Stephen, John M. Last, and George Dunea. *The Oxford Illustrated Companion to Medicine.* New York: Oxford University Press, 2001.

Rose, Sarah. *For All the Tea in China: How England Stole the World's Favorite Drink and Changed History.* New York: Viking, 2010.

Sumner, Judith. *The Natural History of Medicinal Plants.* Portland, OR: Timber, 2000.

Taylor, Patrick. *The Oxford Companion to the Garden.* Oxford, UK: Oxford University Press, 2006.

Pickling

A food conservation method dating to Mesopotamia in 2400 B.C.E., pickling in brine prevents spoilage by replacing natural liquids with preservatives. Whether hot, salty, spicy, sweet, or vinegary, the solution excludes oxygen while producing an acid marinade that sours by lacto-fermentation. From early time, pickling made available such seasonal vegetables as cucumbers and cauliflower for long sea voyages and lemons and peaches for nomadic journeys.

Pickles accompanied Roman legionaries into Gaul in 58 B.C.E. and Napoleon's forces in France and Belgium in 1809 and protected pioneers from scurvy along the

The mason jar, which features see-through glass strong enough to withstand boiling and a lid that seals the contents in a vacuum, revolutionized home canning and pickling after its invention in 1858. *(MCT/Getty Images)*

Oregon Trail in the mid-1800s. In lieu of a varied menu, cooks valued pickles for their color and their aid to appetite and digestion. Dieticians recognized that pickling increases B vitamin content.

The development of condiment recipes parallels the global food exchange that followed early sea ventures. In 900 C.E., the transfer of dill seed from Sumatra to Western Europe introduced a distinct pickle taste. Allspice, asafetida, caraway, cumin, and turmeric contributed unmistakable aromas and bite to otherwise bland vegetable condiments. Christopher Columbus introduced the European pickled cucumber in 1494 in Haiti, where he planted the first seeds.

In the 1500s, Dutch merchants in the Hudson River valley supported New York's commercial picklers, an outgrowth of colonial preferences for piquant flavor and crunch. Colonial housekeepers treasured recipes that allotted the bay leaf, ginger, horseradish, mace, and nutmeg to pickling crocks. To save money, picklers replaced costly sugar with small amounts of herbs and spices.

Pickling targeted perishables in traditional cuisine—beets in Romania, bitter melons in Thailand, cabbage in Korea, capers in France, chili peppers in Mexico, eggplant and garlic in Greece, mushrooms in Britain, olives in Spain, radishes in China, and turnips in Japan. Fruits, too, adapted well to marinade, such as lemons in Israel and mangos in India. Picklers also brined sources of protein, including almonds in Turkey, butter in Scotland, cod in France, eels and walnuts in England, eggs in Pennsylvania Dutch territory, herring in Scandinavia, river snails and shark in China, seabirds in Iceland, and whale among the Inuit. Italy created a unique blend of carrot, cauliflower, onion, and pimiento pepper for *giardinera,* a colorful mix for serving with antipasti and meat dishes.

The mechanics of pickling offered three methods—fermented, fresh pack, and heat pack, or pasteurized. See-through jars improved processing in 1858, when Philadelphia tinsmith John Landis Mason patented thick glass strong enough to withstand the boiling that rids foods of bacteria. The use of pure pickling salt created a niche market for salt makers.

Cooks held lids in place with wire bails or galvanized metal screw-on caps until 1881, when Indiana inventor Alfred Louis Bernardin designed a canning jar lid suited to high-acid foods. At the domestic tents at county and state fairs, the bright colors and shapes of green tomatoes, okra, and watermelon rind pickle generated interest in canning displays.

In 1893, at the height of North America's pickle mania, Henry J. Heinz featured 57 pickle varieties. That same year, William Moore and food processors in St. Charles, Illinois, formed the Pickle Packers International. Independent German, Italian, and Polish street vendors pushed barrows through urban ghettos and dipped gherkins and dill pickles from stone crocks for use in potato salad and pastrami sandwiches. At baseball games, the purchase of a hot dog with mustard and pickle relish contributed to the American flavor of the sport.

See also: Salt; Sausage; Scandinavian Diet and Cuisine; Tudor Diet and Cuisine; Vinegar.

Further Reading

Hutkins, Robert Wayne. *Microbiology and Technology of Fermented Foods.* Chicago: IFT, 2006.

Snodgrass, Mary Ellen. *Encyclopedia of Kitchen History.* New York: Fitzroy Dearborn, 2004.

Sumner, Judith. *American Household Botany: A History of Useful Plants, 1620–1900.* Portland, OR: Timber, 2004.

Walker, Juliet E.K. *The History of Black Business in America: Capitalism, Race, Entrepreneurship.* Chapel Hill: University of North Carolina Press, 2009.

Pit Cookery

Pit cookery dates to pragmatic solutions to problems with open-flame heating methods. Before the crafting of earthen cook pots, the simplest human settlements developed around earth ovens, evidence of hunter-gatherer ingenuity for baking bread or smoking and steaming vegetables and meat. The use of a confined heat source reduced the need for fuel and freed the cook from shielding foods from burning or drying out. Pit cookery encouraged sophisticated flavoring and allowed the cook to roast more than one food for a meal. Because of the control that sealed earth craters afforded women, they remained free to tend their children and pursue crafts.

Moroccans and the Tuareg of the Sahara Desert as well as the Pintubi of Australia and the New England Penobscot applied pit hearth cookery to the logistics of feeding an army or to the needs of a celebration or ritual dinner, such as a clambake or a kangaroo hunt. The communal style of pit cooking incorporated whole villages in digging a pit, selecting stones, and gathering firewood and succulent plants for layering.

As applied by the Cochise culture of Arizona in 8,000 B.C.E. and the Basket Maker peoples of the Rio Grande in 7000 B.C.E., a steaming crater symbolized the cooking of

Recipe: Olive Spread

Rinse and drain a 16-ounce jar of *giardinera.* Coarsely chop in a food processor and set aside. Coarsely chop 1 cup of mixed green, black, and kalamata olives with 1 cup of celery. Blend into the giardinera. Flavor with the juice of one Meyer lemon and 1 teaspoon of dill weed. Serve cold with crackers and pita triangles.

game and agave close to the heart of Mother Earth. To retain flavor, diggers of the pit removed soil about three times the mass of the food and lined the hole with dry flat stones before lighting slow-burning hardwood. After the stones heated with coals filling half the crater, cooks tamped sand over the embers and sealed boned meat in moist camas bulbs, cactus pads, dandelion greens, seaweed, or watercress to prevent burning.

The last stage involved moistening the greens and sealing the top with bark slabs and earth to slow the cooking process to six to eight hours. Whole pigs or venison slabs or, among the Inca of Chile and Peru, a whole llama, took up to 12 hours. In contrast, at Ballyvourney in southern Ireland, the roasting of deer or mutton in a damp peat trough around 5000 B.C.E. took only four hours.

From the Bedouin of Egypt and Arabia, pit cookery advanced among the Persians and passed to Afghans and the Harappans of India around 3000 B.C.E. In marginal territory offering few combustibles, the method retained steam with little fuel to tenderize game birds and haunches of meat. To incorporate bread with the meal, cooks placed the meat in a tandoor pot to be sauced with yogurt and sealed with chapati dough. For flavoring, they ground cardamom, chilies, clove, coriander, garlic, ginger, lime juice, mint, onions, and peppercorns into a paste and slathered it over the meat. In a simpler tradition in Sardinia, pit roasters preferred myrtle wood for flavoring pork.

By shielding hot coals in a depression in the ground or among rocks, cooks in rural India slowed the burning of combustibles to retain natural juices. Attendants increased the flame by blowing into a reed or tube to maintain the temperature for adequate roasting. Because the in-earth cuisine gave off no visible smoke, sheep rustlers in Crete could hide their thievery from herders.

Across the Western Hemisphere, reusable earth ovens layered with leaves or seaweed contributed a smoky savor to slow-roasted meats and shellfish. In Peru, the addition of cassava, roasting ears, sweet potatoes, or tamales rounded out *pachamanca,* an Inca specialty dominated by guinea pig, pork, or poultry. Around 1580 B.C.E., the aborigines of Marble Range, British Columbia, created a unique earth oven for roasting balsam roots, lily bulbs, and nuts under layers of sword fern and salal, a curative plant known for easing fever and swelling. Among the Paiute of the North American plains, communal rabbit drives resulted in large amounts of meat for pit roasting.

American pit cookery adapted brisket and venison to the barbecue pit for simmering over charcoal or a mesquite fire. In the 1600s among the *boucaniers* (French pirates) of the Mississippi River delta, a rough life of thieving and hiding in Louisiana wetlands required ingenuity in cuisine. To conceal their hideouts, they pit-cooked fish and the meat of alligators and wild boar in steamy holes heated with fruitwood or hickory. To flavor their dinner, they added fruit and spice.

See also: Amerindian Diet; Barbecue; Grilling; Luau; Manioc; Polynesian Diet and Cuisine.

Further Reading

Civitello, Linda. *Cuisine and Culture: A History of Food and People.* 3rd ed. Hoboken, NJ: John Wiley & Sons, 2011.

Prentiss, William C., and Ian Kujit, eds. *Complex Hunter-Gatherers: Evolution and Organization of Prehistoric Communities on the Plateau of Northwestern North America.* Salt Lake City: University of Utah Press, 2004.

Pritzker, Barry. *A Native American Encyclopedia: History, Culture, and Peoples.* New York: Oxford University Press, 2000.

Rumble, Victoria R. *Soup Through the Ages: A Culinary History with Period Recipes.* Jefferson, NC: McFarland, 2009.

Plant Disease and Prevention

More than 50,000 plant diseases pose an ongoing threat to crop quality and food security, especially in countries such as Ethiopia and Sudan that rely on a few staples. Fungi cause 85 percent of loss to agriculture by absorbing nutrients and permeating growth layers with tubular filaments. More than 85 countries battle *Magnaporthe grisea* (leaf blast) to preserve rice, a principal food crop. In Kenya and Uganda, Pucciniales (stem rusts) can overtake stands of wheat, much as wind-borne soybean rust attacks fields in Australia and South America, coffee rust destroys coffee plants in Sri Lanka, and guava rust reduces yields in Brazil and Hawaii.

The range of plant disease creates an ever-changing variety of challenges to agronomy. Disasters emerge from black root rot in Egyptian cotton, damping off on sprouted seeds in Japanese greenhouses, water-borne *Erwinia carotovora* (soft rot) on onions and potatoes, *Botrytis* (gray mold) in California kiwi groves, canker in butternut trees in Iowa and rapeseed in China, verticillium in New England maple groves and French sunflowers, and nematodes and fusarium wilt, which cause root knot and brown leaves in southeastern American tomato and zucchini plants.

The most serious infestation involves disease in perennial plants, particularly sugarcane smut in South Africa and southwestern Asia and leaf curl in Georgia peaches. The loss of a perennial crop requires the sterilization and replanting of an entire field or orchard. Control of the world's 1 million insects suppresses the spread of brown rot in cherry and plum orchards by flies, fire blight in pear trees by honeybees, and soft rot fungi in blackberries by curculio weevils.

Plant Pathology History

Blight figures in the early agricultural history of Babylonians, Hebrews, and Indians, as recounted in the books of Deuteronomy around 2000 B.C.E., Rig-Veda (ca. 1200 B.C.E.), and Amos (750 B.C.E.). The writings of Homer in 850 B.C.E. and of Cleidemus, Aristotle, and Theophrastus, the "Father of Botany," from the fourth century B.C.E. indicated serious concern for crop failures and dependence on sulfur for combating plant disease in figs, grapes, and olives, major export crops in the eastern Mediterranean. In Sicily, Theocritus, a third-century B.C.E. pastoralist, recommended the use of ground olive pits as a rust preventative. Still prevalent in the Roman Empire in 66 and 188 C.E., rust in cereal crops and legumes precipitated periods of hunger. To ensure food supplies for a growing population, government officials courted Egyptian grain exporters.

In Guangdong Province, Hsi Han's *Nan Fang Tshao Mu Chuang* (*A Prospect of Plants and Trees of the Southern Regions,* 304), China's earliest botanic encyclopedia, suggested disease prevention methods for banana and banyan trees, melons, and millet, including the placement of bags of ants in citrus trees to attack pathogens. Asian farmers perfected systems of companion planting, such as planting nitrogen-fixing mosquito ferns in rice paddies to control disease and increase harvests.

Native Americans planted corn near wild grasses that shed disease-resistant pollens. Growers spaced beans around corn hills to fix nitrogen in the soil and enhance the strength of corn stalks. Growing squash around these vegetables protected the root systems from sunlight and prevented wilt. The interaction of beans, corn, and squash against pathogens created an agricultural triad known as the "three sisters."

Scientific observations raised questions about infection, such as the concern of Connecticut growers in the early 1700s that wheat rust seemed worse near barberry bushes. In 1729, Italian botanist Pier Antonio Micheli identified 900 fungi and reported on their effects on melons. Specific chemical deterrents to disease evolved from the research of plant specialists, notably French mycologist Matthieu du Tillet, who, in 1755, discovered the efficacy of copper sulfate in destroying wheat smut. In 1808, Karl Asmund Rudolphi, a Swedish botanist, identified the nematodes that caused cysts in beets, corn, potatoes, soybeans, and tomatoes. The fight against root fungus received theoretical assistance in 1815 from Swiss botanist Augustin Pyramus de Candolle, who coined the term *Nature's war* to describe the attack of one organism on another.

In 1841, English plant pathologist Miles Joseph Berkeley summarized the cause of fungus in cabbage, coffee, hops, onions, pears, and wheat. His overview proved prophetic of the Highlands and Irish Potato Famine of 1845–1852. Fungal spores from guano imported from Peru spread over northwestern Europe, subjecting Belgian, Flemish, Irish, Prussian, and Scots crofters to a devastating plant blight and resultant starvation and declines in population. In 1861, German microbiologist Anton de Bary, the "Father of Plant Pathology," advanced theories of plant susceptibility to disease, which he applied to potato blight and wheat rust.

Aggressive pathogens erupted in the mid- to late 1800s, when coffee rust destroyed Ceylon's plantations, which growers replaced with tea. In Languedoc, France, from 1858 to 1875, downy mildew imported on grape cuttings from North America stripped 40 percent of vineyards of their leaves. French botanist Alexis Millardet's application of Bordeaux mixture, a blend of copper sulfate and slaked lime, and the grafting of Assyrtiko rootstock imported from the islands of Paros and Santorini rescued French vintners following a total loss of 10 billion francs.

In 1888, California citrus growers overcame scale after Charles Valentine Riley, the grasshopper specialist for the U.S. Entomological Commission, imported vedalia beetles from New Zealand as a green pesticide. In 1898, Dutch microbiologist Martinus Beijerinck tackled the causes of destruction of squash and walnuts. He theorized that mosaic and ring spot developed from a virus, a microbe smaller than bacteria. His work explained the role of unsanitary tools in the spread of leaf mosaic in apple orchards and Bidens mottle virus, which distorted the leaves of endive, lettuce, and peppers.

By the end of the nineteenth century, college curricula featured plant pathology as a preparation for careers in agronomy, a crucial profession to developing nations. Widespread crop failure assailed populations at a time when food security was tenuous. In Cameroon, South Africa, and Zimbabwe in 1903, an ergot fungus, *Claviceps africana,* infected sorghum and decimated the seed yield. A three-year famine resulted after beetles, flies, and wasps fed on the sweet secretion and spread the fungus to healthy fields.

In the United States, the Smith-Lever Act of 1914 set up the Cooperative Extension Service of the Department of Agriculture to educate farmers in plant pest identification, prevention, and eradication. Field agents introduced pesticides to communities and taught appropriate dilution rates. Passage of the Food and Environment Protection Act of 1985 enforced the correct storage and application of disease suppressants for the stated purpose, such as shielding preemergent crops. Trade restrictions on imported crops prevented exotic pathogens such as fire blight in pome fruit and potato wart from spreading to virgin soil.

Pesticides

Low-toxicity organic pesticides shield plants from invasive microbes. For example, jojoba oil and cow's milk both control mildew on grapes, and cinnamaldehyde from cinnamon bark and eugenol from cloves both kill wood decay in apple orchards and banana and mango trees. In the 1920s, Sydney research chemist Arthur de Ramon Penfold promoted the use of tea tree oil (*Melaleuca alternifolia*), a native Australian biocide found effective on microbial biofilm, the slime communities that invade grapes, peppers, and tomatoes.

Neem oil (*Azadirachta indica*), a biodegradable deterrent pressed from the fruit and seeds of a common evergreen in India, kills the eggs of ants, beet armyworms, cabbage worms, and mushroom flies. The oil also destroys tuber-eating nematodes that distort the roots of carrots and form cysts in cactus, potatoes, and soybeans. Farmers value neem oil spray for suppressing apple and citrus canker, powdery mildew on cucumbers and grapes, and rust on wheat.

Pesticide production burgeoned in the 1940s with the development of fungicides and, a decade later, with nematicides. However, advances did not aid individual growers fast enough to spare Bengal a blight of brown spot on rice in 1942, prevent crown rust in Victoria oats on the North American plains in 1945, or stop wheat rust in Madhya, India, in 1946–1947. The 1960s brought Japanese chemist Yoshiharu Doi's identification of mycoplasmas, a plant crippler that leafhoppers spread in cotton, rice, and sugarcane. Scientists contributed fertilizers to halt stunting, edema (corky scab), and dwarfism from polluted air and soil, waterlogging, and weather stress from temperature extremes and wind.

More toxic pesticides required special handling to prevent human ingestion in toxic amounts. One example, diazinon, which Ciba-Geigy first marketed for home gardens in 1952, came under increased surveillance until the U.S. Department of Agriculture outlawed its sale in 2004. In 1962, American biologist Rachel Carson's *Silent Spring* blamed dichlorodiphenyltrichloroethane (DDT) for killing birds, a main line of defense against insect vectors of disease. Another pesticide, vinclozolin, a general fungicide that BASF formulated in 1981, raised so many questions about cancer generation that, in 2004, the company restricted application of vinclozolin to *Brassica napus,* the source of canola oil. In 2011, the Endocrine Society pressed for more study of the fungicide's effects on the human hormone system.

Disease Prevention

Historically, natural pest control has succeeded worldwide, such as the plowing of eggshells and human hair into soil to increase plant sustainability. Organic chemicals— Bordeaux mixture, copper, fungicidal soap—destroy pests. Weather forecasting and satellite monitoring warn planters of unfavorable conditions, particularly too heavy or too light rainfall to grow oats or winter wheat. Such natural predators as wasps consume the whiteflies that spread sooty mold.

Soil preparation encourages healthy crops, such as plowing diatomaceous earth in vegetable fields to forestall nematodes and the inoculation of beet, corn, cotton, potato, soybean, tomato, and wheat seeds with chitosan, a product extracted from shrimp shells, to boost plant immunity to fungi. Aeration and drainage prevent soggy fields, which perpetuate club root.

As ecologists whittled down the number of pesticides safe for food crops, from the 1990s, they formulated more natural methods of warding off disease via molecular breeding of certified disease-resistant cultivars and plantings of Indian mustard to thwart nematodes. Growers developed regimens of buying pure seed, applying systemic paldoxins (fungicides) to rows, rotating crops to deprive pathogens of hosts, sterilizing tools, spraying sooty mold with detergent or chamomile tea, and quarantining infected plantings. The application of compost and organic manure controls antagonistic pathogens; the injection of steam into soil sterilizes it by killing microbes. Paired plantings promote natural protection, for example, chives and garlic among leaf vegetables, horseradish with potatoes, sage with cabbage, and marigolds to prevent root knot in cereal crops, eggplant, and lettuce.

A dusting of sulfur reduces botrytis in strawberries and scab on apricots and melons; iron sulfate saves Hawaiian pineapples from chlorosis (yellowing). In southern California vineyards, sulfites halt Pierce's disease caused by *Xylella* bacteria. Underground and drip-line irrigation systems prevent watering from enhancing humid conditions that feed fungi. An end-of-harvest removal and burning of plant gall and insect casings circumvent the life cycle of beetle stem invaders and flying leafhoppers that spread such fungi as ergot on rye and chlorosis in the coconut palms of Florida, Jamaica, Mexico, Tanzania, and Texas.

See also: Agriculture; Famine; Hanna, Gordie C.; Monoculture.

Further Reading

Agrios, G.N. *Plant Pathology.* 5th ed. San Diego, CA: Academic Press, 2005.

Mann, Charles C. *1493: Uncovering the New World Columbus Created.* New York: Random House, 2011.

Simberloff, Daniel, and Marcel Rejmánek. *Encyclopedia of Biological Invasions.* Berkeley: University of California Press, 2011.

Vivian, John. "The Three Sisters." *Mother Earth News* 184 (February/March 2001): 50–54.

Pliny the Elder (23–79 C.E.)

Imperial Rome's prize encyclopedist, Caius Plinius Secundus (Pliny the Elder), included cookery, curatives, and pure food in his scientific research.

A native of Como, in northern Italy, Pliny enjoyed the privilege of equestrian rank, which afforded him a broad education in history, law, literature, and the sciences. During the reign of the Emperor Vespasian (69–79 C.E.), Pliny achieved promotions to infantry commander, cavalry and naval prefect, and procurator of Africa, Belgica, and southeastern Gaul. While indulging his intellectual curiosity, he compiled the 37-book *Historia Naturae* (*Natural History*, ca. 77 C.E.), a life's work. He mentored his sister Plinia's son, Pliny the Younger, and tried to shelter the boy and his mother during the eruption of Vesuvius on August 25, 79 C.E. Answering a call to aid friends attempting to escape by galleys at Stabiae, Pliny began overseeing their boarding. Because of asthma and obesity, he died suddenly on the beach of respiratory failure, leaving unedited the last 27 books of his nature compendium.

The breadth of knowledge in Pliny's writings suggests a man devoted to basic facts as well as curiosities gleaned from 2,000 books in Greek and Latin by 400 authorities. Pliny covered oddities—the eating of vipers in India—as well as agricultural myth—the goddess Ceres's teachings on grinding grain for bread making. His interest in health encompassed superstitions and practical medicine, for example, causes of kidney stones and the morning sickness of parturient women. He wrote on ordinary commodities, namely, balsam, cinnamon, ginger, honey, myrrh, pepper, shallots, and sugar and perused agrarian pursuits, such as fish and oyster farming and shipping.

Polymath

Pliny's in-depth reading preceded a warehousing of information. In books 18–28, his encyclopedia surveyed agriculture, naming grains, herbs, and vegetable crops and describing in detail the technology of Roman watermills that ground barley and wheat. On common cures, Pliny cited a recipe for stewed frog, a folk treatment for cough and ophthalmia. Comments on cuisine lauded pork shoulder above all meats for flavor and praised a Roman delicacy, goose liver soaked in honey and milk. Other poultry uses specified roasted webbed feet, cockscombs for stew, and the recycling of goose down for pillows.

In his study of cuisine, Pliny maintained objectivity, even toward the intrusive perversions of Parthian cookery on Roman foodways. As an empiricist, he rejected the analysis of dreams after a heavy meal as spurious but recognized that foods could cause disease. He extolled unborn and infant rabbits as delicacies and thanked nature for making the animals so prolific. Of the luxuries that threatened Roman values, he demeaned "Armenian plums" (apricots) as rich men's food and specified chervil as an aphrodisiac and stork as an unrivaled entrée. His egalitarian principles, a holdover from Republican Rome, required that servers present all diners the same fare.

Pliny excelled at minutiae. He identified the first farmers to fatten peacocks, pullets, and thrushes for the table. His advice on foodstuffs explained why crayfish should be boiled alive and why wise cooks limited the presentation of oysters to the nine months between August and April. Of fish for the table, he identified 1,000 species. He recommended mullet, rockfish, scarus, sturgeon, and wolffish and singled out the anchovy that cookbook compiler Apicius pickled in *garum* (fish sauce) as Rome's most expensive condiment. Because of the centrality of fish in the Roman kitchen, Pliny complained of the price of fine seafood, which could cost as much as an enslaved cook.

Food Preferences

Pliny's practicality informed Roman cooks on the best viands for the menu. His text specified almonds from Thasos, Belgian geese, damsons from Damascus, green carobs, parsley stalks and seeds, and powdered bees. From his own experience, Pliny recommended berries for breath sweetening. His evaluation of food and emotion typified lentils as a moderator of temper. He suggested methods of keeping hearth fires lit and the capping of a pestle with iron to ease the work of crushing and pounding. His recipes described rocket (arugula) pureed in honey and water and a dish of asphodel bulbs ground in a mortar with figs, oil, and salt. For the tastiest asparagus, he advised growing spears in heavily manured soil; for the strongest onions, he chose red varieties from Africa over white bulbs from Gaul. Beans he rejected entirely for their smell and for causing gut distention and flatulence.

Despite his scientific bent, chauvinism permeated Pliny's writings, which maintained the superiority of Italy for food production and offshore fishing. Pliny admired the mild, sunny climate and well-watered pastures for generating the sweetest endive, Calabrian grapes, leeks, and olives. He bought only Tarantine salt and specified the Piedmont for producing *secale* (rye), a famine food and eventual supplanter of spelt. He valued cow's milk for cheese more than for butter, a barbarian food, and fish heads over the rest of piscine meat. Orchardists followed his advice on picking apples on dry days, avoiding windfalls, and storing unbruised fruit in a cool, dry bin. To raise the best figs, he proposed growing domestic stock alongside wild fig bushes, an early method of hybridizing fruit.

Some of Pliny's entries contain necessary alerts. His instructions for vineyards outlined meticulous details of planting and pruning, which ensured quality vintage in Opimian wine. Of *perpotatio* (wine parties), Pliny warned of licentious behavior caused by drunkenness, especially where married women dined alongside their husbands in full view of lustful rivals. He valued all types of parsnips and turnip greens and described the tinting of plain white turnips with harmless purple food dye and five other colors. In one of the first consumer reports from the ancient world, he warned that unscrupulous dealers adulterated other foods—balsam and myrrh with gum, bread with chalk, livestock fodder with weeds, olive oil and wine with unwholesome additives, and pepper with juniper berries. For these infractions of buyer trust, the polluters risked banishment or enslavement in the mines.

See also: Adulterated Food; Apicius; Poisonous Foods; Roman Diet and Cuisine, Ancient; Shellfish.

Further Reading

Carey, Sorcha. *Pliny's Catalogue of Culture: Art and Empire in the Natural History.* New York: Oxford University Press, 2006.

Murphy, Trevor Morgan. *Pliny the Elder's Natural History: The Empire in the Encyclopedia.* New York: Oxford University Press, 2004.

Poisonous Foods

The sampling of unknown mushrooms, nuts, plants, and toxic fish and meat caused the world's first food poisoning. Seemingly harmless substances, such as almonds, castor beans, and elderberries, can produce skin rash, burning or swelling tongue and lips, stomach and intestinal upset, gasping, seizure, and sudden death. An unusual conveyance of toxins, red tide, an algae bloom producing a neurotoxin, can contaminate oysters and generate a gaseous irritant especially harmful to people with asthma. More dramatic suffering occurs when people consume quail that feed on hemlock seeds, which cause creeping paralysis that stops the heart.

Nicander of Colophon, an Ionian botanist and priest of Apollo, became the first scientist to issue a list of death-dealing substances. The focus of *Alexipharmaca* (*Antidotes,* ca. 140 B.C.E.), which Nicander based on the research of third-century B.C.E. toxicologist Apollodorus of Alexandria, warned of the effects of henbane and thorn apple (datura). More poet than botanist, Nicander laced his verse claxon with victims of hemlock poisoning crawling the streets, gagging, arteries contracting, and eyes rolling. He sensationalized how the eating of a greenish toad caused heartburn and terminal hiccups that convulsed the victim to death.

Dangerous Dining

In the Western Hemisphere, examples of noxious foods come from substances as common as agave, dal, kidney beans, peach seeds, pokeweed greens, potato peelings, and raw carp. Manioc, a source of hydrogen cyanide, requires grating and soaking to leach out toxic cyanides; similarly, acorns need a lengthy rinsing to remove bitter tannin before Korean cooks can extract acorn starch for cakes and noodles.

Slower poisonings result from vitamin B1 depletion from nardoo root (*Marsilea drummondii*), an Australian water fern, and from the nitrosamines in smoked foods and mercury in fish, both potentially lethal to humans. Another slow-acting toxin derives from water passed through lead plumbing and from acid foods cooked in vessels soldered with lead. The deaths of 163 Nigerians in early summer 2010 resulted from lead-laced water in the gold-mining region of Zamfara.

In the Caribbean, consumption of reef fish contaminated with ciguatera produces hallucination and a shambling gait. Servings of ackee fruit (*Blighia sapida*) require judgment about ripeness: underripe or overripe fruit can kill from the effects of alkaloids. Similarly, botulism from *Clostridium botulinum,* a bacterial toxin found in honey and contaminated canned goods, paralyzes the face and respiratory system.

Another lethal comestible, toxic mushrooms may look as harmless as edible varieties—for instance, the deadly amanita and the harmless puffball. Folklore classifies the killer mushroom as a "toadstool," a Middle English rural belief that toads secrete poison. The Roman Empress Agrippina reputedly murdered the Emperor Claudius in 54 C.E. by feeding him the edible *Amanita caesarea* blended with *Amanita phalloides* (death cap mushrooms). Another victim, Holy Roman Emperor Charles VI died in Vienna after eating amanitas on October 20, 1740.

In Asia and the Pacific, the availability of poisonous nettles and nuts endangered Allied soldiers during World War II. The U.S. War Department issued an illustrated guide to foraging, *Emergency Food Plants and Poisonous Plants of the Islands of the Pacific* (1943). The text advised watching monkeys and eating the native fruits that the primates ate.

Food fads intrigue the adventurous to risk the processing of poisonous food for hazardous cuisine, including the angelfish, basket shell snail, blue-ringed octopus, floral egg crab, and purple fluorescent frog. In Japan, consumption of parts of the fugu (a poisonous type of puffer fish or blowfish) bearing tetrodotoxin can kill instantly. In one instance, fugu livers killed kabuki actor Bando Mitsugoro in Kyoto in 1975. To prevent diner collapse, officials require licensing of chefs who fry or grill fugu or use it in hot pots and sashimi. By law, the imperial chef may not serve fugu to the Japanese emperor.

Deadly Fungus

A fungal contaminant of grain, ergot has a lengthy history, as demonstrated by tablets from the Fertile Crescent and in the writings of ancient Greek physicians Galen and Hippocrates, the ancient Greek and Roman scientists Theophrastus and Pliny, and tenth-century Persian healer Muwaffak. The poison, lysergic acid, convulses the limbs and causes them to rot. Spread by insects seeking the honey drops from infected grains, the growth of ergot fungus caused Romans to remove diseased grains from the threshing floor to circumvent the poisonous bread that had weakened Caesar's troops at the Siege of Marseilles from March to September 49 B.C.E.

In 943 C.E., the growth of sweet, black *Claviceps purpurea* fungus on rye killed 40,000 people in Limoges, France. The malady, later dubbed *ignis sacer* or Saint Anthony's Fire, spread over Germany and Spain, causing hallucinations and mad outbursts as well as gangrene. The epidemic remained puzzling until 1557, when German herbalist Adam Lonicer of Marburg informed people about the dangers of ergot-contaminated rye bread and flour. The fungus remained virulent in the twenty-first century, when it infested barley in Addis Ababa, Ethiopia, in summer 2001.

Food Testing and Tasting

Because of the fear of harmful food, royalty and dignitaries under threat have traditionally employed animal and human tasters, a role graphically illustrated in the film *Cleopatra* (1963) and the television series *Rome* (2005–2007). As a precaution against assassination attempts, the taster sampled servings of the dishes or dipped bread into their juices to determine wholesomeness. Upon confirming meal safety, the taster covered the dishes, which the pantler and pages carried to the dining table.

Food-tasting protocol derives from centuries-old regimens. For wines, in the Middle Ages, the royal diner kept a slice of supposed unicorn horn (actually from a narwhal) attached to a cup for testing beverages and pieces of table bread. The valet carried water used for hand washing to the porter's buffet to pour it over the horn and watch for any change of color, indicating poison. The unicorn horn, they maintained, was the only sure means of assaying the quality of each serving. The hall usher tested the royal napkin in front of the pantry porter by kissing it to prove it pure and safe. In India, rulers relied on citron, a citrus fruit deemed effective as an antidote to all poisonous food.

See also: Adulterated Food; Coprolites; Manioc; Wild Food.

Further Reading

Brüssow, Harald. *The Quest for Food: A Natural History of Eating.* New York: Springer, 2007.

Fernández-Armesto, Felipe. *Near a Thousand Tables: A History of Food.* New York: Simon & Schuster, 2002.

Houston, Lynn Marie. *Food Culture in the Caribbean.* Westport, CT: Greenwood, 2005.

Satin, Morton. *Food Alert! The Ultimate Sourcebook for Food Safety.* New York: Facts on File, 2008.

Stuart, David C. *Dangerous Garden: The Quest for Plants to Change Our Lives.* Cambridge, MA: Harvard University Press, 2004.

Polo, Marco (ca. 1254–1324)

In *The Travels of Marco Polo* (ca. 1300), a pro-Christian memoir rich with cultural and historical details, Venetian merchant and explorer Marco Polo provided details of life—and food—in the Middle East, central Asia, China, Indonesia, the Indian subcontinent, and Byzantium.

Marco Polo came of age in a vast trading hub on the Adriatic Sea, where warehouses stocked clove, ginger, nutmeg, pepper, and saffron. At age 15, he fell under the spell of journey stories of his father, Niccolò Polo, and Niccolò's brother Maffeo Polo, traders in luxury goods who had visited Constantinople and the Mongol Empire. They had met Kublai Khan, the first Yuan emperor and grandson of Genghis Khan, the universal ruler of Tartars (Mongols). In fall 1271, the Polo trio—father, son, and uncle—set sail for Acre, Israel, on a 24-year journey to Asia covering 24,000 miles (38,600 kilometers). By camel train, they proceeded to Hormuz, on the Arabian Sea, but found no dependable ship bound for Cathay (China), the world's largest empire.

Traveling the Silk Road, which Maffeo and Niccolò knew from past journeys, the Venetians spent 42 months on the land route to East Asia. They witnessed unusual cuisine, such as the all-meat diet of Turkish cattlemen. From Armenia into Iran, the merchants observed brisk trade in fruit and vegetables and Persian tableware made of ceramics and metals. At inns, they entered paved courtyards fragrant with stew simmering over fires. The focus on herding horses and sheep in the grasslands of Afghanistan presented table fare rich in koumiss (mare's or camel's milk) and a range of meats, including the flesh of rabbits, which Afghans captured via falconry. In the Taklimakan Desert, by contrast to lush mountain passes, the Polos found no rest stops or food in the wild until they reached the Badakhshan Mountains in northeastern Afghanistan.

For provisions, they packed a month's supply for themselves and their mounts. At various points, the greenish water tasted either bitter or brackish. Marco Polo fell ill from the unpalatable fare and rested for a year in the mountains before setting out once more over the Oxus River into the Pamir Mountains of Tajikistan. During a 12-day march at an altitude of 20,000 feet (6,100 meters), because of the thin atmosphere, the men failed to kindle fires to cook their meals.

The Khan's China

Accommodations and dining for the trio improved in 1275. The approach to the winter palace in Dadu (Beijing) offered travel stops and inns as well as street snacks at stalls and hot shops. The local diet favored millet and included herbal medicines, turmeric, and sake, a powerful alcoholic drink fermented like beer from rice. A mingling of world cuisines appeared in stocks of cinnamon bark, rhubarb, and tea. At Shandu (Xanadu) in Inner Mongolia, the location of the bamboo and marble summer palaces of 60-year-old Kublai Khan, Marco Polo presented letters of introduction from Pope Gregory X and a gift of sacred oil from Christ's holy sepulcher in Jerusalem. The khan was so pleased that he hosted festivals and banquets to honor his Venetian guests.

In the new Mongolian city of Khanbaliq, begun in 1272, the khan's winter court staggered the Polos with its adornments of hall and chambers. The population within the palace walls rose so high that the royal kitchen served more than 6,000 at each meal. Among serving pieces, chefs featured multistage platters for coordinating entrées with sauces and toppings. Wait staff used gold ladles to transfer entrées from lacquer bowls to plates. The khan himself supped on the milk of albino herds. To shield the khan's servings from the exhalations of servants' mouths and nostrils and from the odor of their bodies, servers wrapped their lower faces in silk veils and knelt on the floor.

Mongolian Cuisine

Marco Polo cited popular recipes of nomadic Mongolian hunter-gatherers. Lacking chickens, pigs, and fresh vegetables, they relied heavily on dairy products of ewes and mares. He described fermented milk as an unassuming drink that left him feeling fully nourished. In the field, Mongol warriors ate their rations raw or cooked in earthen pots heated over fires of cow or horse dung. In lieu of cookware, they emptied the belly of their kill and boiled meat inside in water over the fire. When the dinner was ready, Mongols ate the meat, broth, and animal stomach container. In summer, they varied their meat diet with apples, cherries, hazelnuts, juniper berries, leeks, and onions.

Directions for curative and strengthening foods from the era tied the "Five Flavors" to the "Five Viscera." By balancing nutrition, individuals could promote *qi* (body energy) and ward off illness or organic distress in specific areas of the body and spirit:

Food	Protected Area
barley soup	spleen, stomach, and intestines
bear soup	feet and joints
bottle gourd and mutton soup	bladder, kidneys, and pancreas
dog meat	vascular system
horse heart	spirit
horse meat	bones and stamina
horse stomach and intestines	general well-being
sheep's heart with saffron	heart and spirit
wild camel meat	skin

Recipe: Mongolian Cauldron Stew

In a large kettle, combine mutton (originally wild Bactrian camel hump) with sheep's fat, haunches, lungs, stomach, tail, or tongue. Season with goose fat. For flavoring, boil the mix with black pepper, cardamom or cinnamon, fenugreek seed, saffron, and turmeric. Serve the stew with bottle gourd, cheese, or chickpeas.

On a hard gallop that made meals difficult, Tartar riders sucked blood from nicks in the veins of their mounts. They reduced mare's milk to a paste first boiled, then dried in the sun. Indoors, cooks favored noodles or macaroni combined with eggs, mushrooms, mutton, sheep intestines, and sprouted ginger. They served the mix in clear broth flavored with pepper, salt, and vinegar. For Russian olive soup, a chopped leg of mutton or sliced sheep torso acquired subtle flavoring from cardamom, Chinese cabbage or nettles, and Russian olives. Another meal, butter skin *yuqba,* began with minced mutton and sheep's tail and tallow. The addition of mandarin orange peel, sprouted ginger, salt, and spices preceded the coating of skin in rice and wheat flour and vegetable oil. Marco Polo also admired the black meat of Fujian poultry, the variety of fruit and vegetables, and the availability of conserves and sugar, which sweetened cups of tea.

More Journeys and Observations

As a court guest under semiofficial house arrest, Marco Polo accepted inspection embassies to Yunnan, Sichuan, Fujien, Tibet, and Pagan and, in 1282, as far south as Burma. The provincials of Yunnan ate dogs and "brute beasts and animals of every kind," which the Venetian rejected as disgusting. He observed the wealth in salt mining and the transport of salt cakes and ginger along the Yalu and Yangtze rivers. In place of metal coins, diners spent whole salt disks and used broken pieces to flavor their food. At Mien, he marveled at the assortment of great beasts—elephants, oxen, and deer. Because of his proficiency in four languages—probably Chinese, Mongolian, Persian, and Uighur—Marco Polo crossed borders with a gold passport and served the khan well as a legate. He governed Yangchou for three years but predicted that the Mongol rule—and the welcome to Venetians—would weaken. In winter 1291–1292, after 17 years at the khan's court, the three Polos departed China's southeastern coast at Zaitun to join Princess Kokijin and her Persian wedding party of 600 bound by a 14-junk flotilla to Hormuz.

At Kinsai (Hangzhou), the Polos enjoyed the luxuries of a splendid commercial center selling jewels, pearls, and spices. During a two-year voyage from Quangzhou in Southeast Asia to Sumatra, Marco Polo continued recording unusual animals, particularly unicorns, and indulging his obsession with Asian cuisine. In Java and Nicobar, he became one of the first Europeans to recognize and describe the "Pharaoh's nut" (coconut), which he helped to popularize into a fad as a basis for sweets and beverages. On observation of table customs, he stated that Javanese diners ate five times the rations consumed by Venetians. He commented on the importance of sago at Fansur in northern Sumatra for the making of lasagna and provisioned his entourage with enough sago flour to take some home to Venice. On the way through Ceylon and Malabar, India, he spoke of the centrality of tamarind as a medical purgative and pantry staple, which he introduced to Europeans.

Marco Polo's musings on local custom included the importance of proprieties to daily affairs and religious ritual. He commented, for example, on the different valuation of right and left hands. Because Buddhists and Hindus reserved the left hand for wiping and cleansing the ears, nostrils, and anus, they observed a taboo requiring that only the right hand touch table implements and food. Buddhist festivals at Malabar required strict preparation of meat dishes for idols. The women who served waited a suitable length of time for the god to eat, then removed the uneaten portions and treated themselves to the divine repast. At Lar (Gujarat), where farmers excelled at raising ginger and pepper, he counted 20,000 dancing girls singing and offering flowers and food to Buddha. In reference to human longevity and wellness, he lauded yogis for abstinence from impure food and for cooking and eating only wholesome meals of bland semolina or bran, rice, milk, and water. Their self-discipline included several annual fasts, a regimen that Marco Polo characterized as the world's hardest lifestyle.

From the Arabian Sea, the trio reached Aden, where the diet for horses centered on dried fish and for people on jujubes. The Polos sped overland from the Persian Gulf to Iran, to Trebizond on the Black Sea, and through the Bosporus to Constantinople (Istanbul). An intercontinental crossroads, ruled by Mamluks, the city prospered from the sale of enamelware, incense, leather, and spices from India. The final sea leg of the journey returned the three travelers to tasteless meals aboard ship, where the dark mess area stank of rotting food and toilet waste, worsened by bouts of human seasickness. Ship's cooks contended with invasions of cockroaches, lice, and rats.

Arriving home in 1295 during the second Venetian war with Genoa, Marco Polo was seized on board a galley and lodged in a cell as a political prisoner. He spent four years dictating his travelogue to a fellow prisoner, romance writer Rustichello da Pisa, under the title *Il Milione* (*The Million,* ca. 1300). Marco Polo's fanciful memoirs became one of the most popular works of the late Middle Ages. After marriage and a career in merchandising, he died around age 70 on January 9, 1324. His adventures generated great interest in the East Asian diet and spurred Christopher Columbus to route his vessels by sea west to the Spice Islands.

See also: Medieval Diet and Cuisine; Pasta; Poultry; Silk Road.

Further Reading

Akbari, Suzanne Conklin, Amilcare A. Iannucci, and John Tulk, eds. *Marco Polo and the Encounter of East and West.* Toronto: University of Toronto Press, 2008.

Belliveau, Denis, and Francis O'Donnell. *In the Footsteps of Marco Polo.* Lanham, MD: Rowman & Littlefield, 2008.

Bergreen, Laurence. *Marco Polo: From Venice to Xanadu.* New York: Random House, 2007.

Edwards, Mike. "The Adventures of Marco Polo." *National Geographic* 199:5 (May 2001): 2–31; 199:6 (June 2001): 20–45; 199:7 (July 2001): 26–47.

Polynesian Diet and Cuisine

Lacking cereals and domesticated animals, the traditional Polynesian diet is a testimonial to tropical whole foods served succulent and sweet. Tikopia islanders became so attuned to food sources that they determined time spans by the ripening of tropical fruits and vegetation and by eel and fish runs. Tahitians used food gifts to keep ancestors close to the living. Solomon Islanders lengthened the shelf life of perishable breadfruit by fermenting them in pits and roasting or steaming them in *umus* (earth ovens). Balls of breadfruit paste sustained natives through September and October, the stormy season. For trade with passing ships, they reserved the meat of dolphins, pigs, sharks, and turtles.

For hunter-gatherers at Tongareva, lagoons offered the safest and most reliable source of fish and shade palms as well as algae, lichen, moss, and seaweed. A stronger agrarian tradition of dry and irrigated crops and tree fruit fed the people of Anuta, Easter, Marquesas, and Pitcairn islands, where marine resources were scarce. By the arrival of the sweet potato from South America to Hawaii and Rapa Nui, around 1000 C.E., the addition of a pantry staple and trade item eased the strain of protecting wild plants from the whims of Pacific weather.

On the 12,000 islands that dotted a stretch of 9,000 miles (14,500 kilometers) across the Pacific, Melanesians, Micronesians, and Polynesians participated in a gendered food collection. Men loaded coconut clusters and plantain bunches on notched sticks, while women gathered shrimp and kava root into frond baskets and pandanus bags. Fish species varied with the availability of fresh water streams, which numbered 15 on Tahiti and 111 in New Guinea. For famine food, villages relied on almonds, fern, Malay apples, sago, and kudzu or turmeric root, which also served as a common dyestuff.

Carbohydrate-Rich Diet

Dominating Oceania's cuisine, starchy vegetables such as the Maori fern root required pounding by stone pestle. The earliest meals developed variety by incorporating fruit bats, iguanas, and seabirds along with grouper, jacks, parrotfish, tangs, and turtles. Wrapped in pandanus or ti bundles, macerated bulbs and tubers shared space in earth ovens with roasted ahi and swordfish, steamed mollusks and octopi, and coconut puddings contained in coconut shells.

Families bred birds, the flightless nene in Hawaii and the moa in New Zealand, both of which eventually became extinct from overconsumption. Bamboo splits served as cutting tools and tubes for cooking vegetables over hot coals alongside spitted dogs. The first kitchen tools cracked bones, peeled breadfruit, and grated tubers. Cooks strained liquids through bark cloth. More specialized equipment

A nutritious, high-fiber starch of the Polynesian islands, *poi* is prepared by pounding cooked taro corms (roots) and mixing the paste with water until it reaches a thick, smooth consistency. Hawaiians and other Polynesian natives considered the dish sacred. *(Sean Thompson/ Associated Press)*

hooked or trapped fish in stone weirs, netted pigeons, or snared doves to eat with breadfruit and taro.

From prehistory, Hawaiian food developed into a fusion cuisine enriched by foods from Africa, Asia, Australia, Europe, and the Americas. Marquesans added breadfruit to the typical menu; Tahitians contributed baked bananas and coconuts. On Tonga, from around 1000 B.C.E., cooks used spears for fishing and pottery jars for boiling the meat in herbed water. For ritual sea voyages by double-hulled canoe or outrigger back to Tahiti, mariners ate fresh supplies—bananas, candlenuts, coconut, and sugarcane—and netted or trolled for fresh tuna and snapper before relying on "canoe foods," dried coconut pulp or fermented breadfruit.

Celebratory dishes displayed the island chefs' imaginative use of local meats and produce. The Polynesian mythographer David Kalakaua, Hawaii's king from 1874 to 1891, compiled *The Legends and Myths of Hawaii: The Fables and Folklore of a Strange People* (1888), which included pagan foodways. He preserved such events as the five-day luau, a mythic feast of the bride Lono and the Tahitian chief Laa's marriage and feast. The nuptials for three couples concluded with an evening feast for 1,000 guests. Food service accompanied hula exhibitions and *mele-inoas* (postwedding songs). Indulgence in kava (*Piper methysticum*) reduced many guests to days of recuperation.

By 1600 C.E., Polynesians inhabited Pacific lands from Easter Island and Hawaii to New Zealand. After the arrival of Captain James Cook in 1778, the Hawaiian diet included goats, melons, onions, pumpkins, and wild boar, the focus of the luau. In the 1800s, cattle ranching shifted entrées once more toward beef and broiled beef jerky. Most of the warmer islands developed kava into the national narcotic drink, which Christian missionaries began eradicating after 1822. Undeterred by New England Puritans, Kamehameha III in 1847 hosted 10,000 guests to a feast of oxen and pork, cabbage and onions, and citrus fruit and pineapples.

Specialized Cuisine

Traditional Hawaiian cuisine features *poi,* a nutritious fermented paste of the taro corm that contributes to wellness. Because of its digestibility and fiber content, poi nourishes weak infants and strengthens athletes. The consumption of poi in the 1980s resulted from a popular low-fat regimen, the Wai'anae Diet, a source of energy and stamina. To a bland entrée, Hawaiian chefs add chicken, crab, limpet, and squid and side dishes of arrowroot, bananas, berries, fern, pickled seaweed, sea salt, and yams.

On Samoa, food gifts indicate camaraderie and friendship, a token of affection to a potential bride, or a dowry. Cooks build menus around boiled taro or rice steamed in coconut milk. Chicken and mahimahi come to the table broiled and seasoned with lemon rather than fried in oil. Dishes of breadfruit, crayfish, green bananas and papayas, seaweed, and taro leaves in coconut cream

Recipe: Tahitian Vanilla Custard

Heat 2 cups of cream with one whole vanilla bean. Remove the bean and whisk in eight egg yolks, 1 cup of sugar, and one pinch of salt. Cool and add 1 quart of coconut cream and one egg. Bake at 325 degrees Fahrenheit in a bain-marie for one-half hour. Top with 1 cup of confectioners' sugar and 1 teaspoon of vanilla extract. Broil or brown with a chef's torch until the sugar melts and forms a crust.

accompany the starchy entrée. Because of Samoan lactose intolerance, beverages range from cocoa to lemon grass or orange leaf tea but do not include milk. Snacks consist of pineapple and macadamia nuts.

Tahitian finger food resembles Samoan dishes. Like Hawaiians, Tahitians in the eighteenth and nineteenth centuries eagerly imported provisions from passing ships. From French mariners, they gained cabbage and chervil; from Chile and Peru, potatoes and white beans. To recipes for steamed rice, goat meat, and yams, cooks added mangoes, oranges, pomelos, tamarind, and guava, a South African fruit that Captain William Bligh introduced when the *Bounty* anchored at Matavai Bay in 1787. For traditional meals, fafa (taro leaves) accompanied *poisson cru,* lagoon and ocean fish marinated raw in lime juice. Native vanilla added fragrance and sweetness to custard and pastry as well as cash from horticultural exports.

Throughout Oceania, the influx of Europeans in the 1800s and of Allied and Japanese troops during World War II forever altered the Polynesian diet through ecological exchange. The introduction of fatty meats, such as Spam and potted ham, upended proportions of carbohydrates to protein and encouraged cardiovascular disease, diabetes, and obesity. To traditional snacks of cycad nuts on Guam, Dyer's figs on Tuvalu, Indian almonds in Papua New Guinea, mangrove fruit on Fiji and Yap, pawpaw on Kiribati in the Gilbert Islands, and Tahitian chestnuts, throughout Melanesia, candy, chips, colas, peanuts, and processed cheeses have introduced the nutritional anomalies of the industrialized world.

See also: Cook, James; Luau; Paula Marín, Francisco de; Pit Cookery; Seaweed; Shellfish; Taro.

Further Reading

Gillespie, Rosemary G., and D.A. Clague. *Encyclopedia of Islands.* Berkeley: University of California Press, 2009.

Haden, Roger. *Food Culture in the Pacific Islands.* Santa Barbara, CA: Greenwood, 2009.

Lorey, David E. *Global Environmental Challenges of the Twenty-First Century: Resources, Consumption, and Sustainable Solutions.* Wilmington, DE: SR, 2003.

Newell, Jennifer. *Trading Nature: Tahitians, Europeans, and Ecological Exchange.* Honolulu: University of Hawaii Press, 2010.

Oliver, Douglas L. *Polynesia in Early Historic Times.* Honolulu, HI: Bess, 2002.

Pork

A source of meat since 8000 B.C.E., swine are humankind's oldest livestock, predating the cultivation of barley and wheat. Domesticated from the wild boar (*Sus scrofa*) in western China and the Middle East, swine produced meat for farmers in Algeria, Egypt, Greece, Iraq, Palestine, the Sahara, and Turkey. Pork production flourished in China in 4300 B.C.E. and reached a height of sophistication between 2200 and 1100 B.C.E.

Cantonese gourmands paid the highest prices for thin-skinned animals and served roast pig ears with strong black tea. Home cooks preferred cooking ham on the shank for flavoring the stockpot, ribs for barbecue, salt pork for seasoning bok choy or mustard greens, and pig's feet and skin for milk soup. They stir-fried intestines with vegetables, pounded meat for pork buns, and ground fat and tendons for meatballs. Chinese chefs simmered pork with chicken and duck in wine sauce in a clay crock for a fragrant one-pot meal. For *lap cheong* (sausage), they blended pork liver and ham or sliced bacon with duck liver. A Chinese recipe from 500 B.C.E. lists dates as the appropriate stuffing for suckling pig, which cooks swathed in straw and roasted in a pit.

Europe

Swineherding passed to Europe in 4000 B.C.E. Forest dwellers diversified their diet of birds, fish, small game, and venison by adding pork, a savory seasoning for boiled turnips and greens. Communities that ate pork cooked below 145 degrees Fahrenheit (63 degrees Celsius) risked infestation with hookworm, pinworm, roundworm, and tapeworm.

In the late second century B.C.E., Athenaeus, a Greek food writer living in Egypt, equated a pork dinner with the good life. Greek cooks served pork with lentils; Romans placed corned pork on the plate with fava beans. Roman *suarii* (hog butchers) and Gallic swine farmers dry-rubbed raw pork with aromatic condiments and salt and flavored their products with garlic, herbs, and onions. Apicius, a Roman gourmand from the first century C.E., wrote instructions for skewering a sow's udder and for stuffing a piglet with birds, dates, sausage, and snails.

The pig enriched farmers by farrowing three times a year at the rate of 10 to 12 piglets per litter. The anonymous *Le Ménagier de Paris* (*The Goodman of Paris,* 1393) declared that the city's pork butchers sold 30,794 pigs annually. Fed on acorns, apples, beechnuts, berries, chestnuts, hazelnuts, hawthorns, and rodents, pigs assisted farmers by locating truffles and unearthing grubs and roots, thus aerating soil. Iberian pork, called *jamón iberico,* gained fame for delicacy and flavor generated by feral pigs feeding in oak forests.

Because pigs thrived in small pens and ate most animal and vegetable refuse, they surpassed cattle in food economy and popularity, especially in Asia. Families kept sties as an assurance of food in the event of crop failures and as symbols of household well-being. Slaughter of a young pig produced up to 240 pounds (110 kilograms) of meat for curing into bacon and ham.

The pig sticker, a traveling specialist, organized communities for the rapid conversion of carcasses to bristle for brushes, fat for lard, and meat for varied purposes. Meat preservation consisted of air-drying, brining, salting, smoking, or sugaring chines or a combination of methods, such as the curing and casing of Scotch ham, the smoking of dry-rubbed Westphalian ham over a beech or juniper fire, and the air-drying, salting, and seasoning of Italian prosciutto. Cooks esteemed the delicate flavor of organ meats, particularly kidneys, liver, and sweetbreads, a common name for the pancreas and thyroid glands. With a brass wire threaded with linen, preparers turned pig intestines and soaked them in readiness for stuffing with sausage mix, blended with beef, cumin, mushrooms, myrtle leaves, nuts, olives, paprika, peppercorns, sage, or salt, and for brushing the outside with ashes, gelatin, or pepper before drying or smoking.

In the Middle Ages, swineherds occupied the lowest social rung because of the pig's affinity for latrines and swiddens, but pork-houses provided respectable employment for meat cutters, salt dealers, and coopers. Institutions kept pigs to consume the by-products of grain and oil mills. Abbeys, hospitals, and villages slopped hogs with their garbage, sewage, surgical waste, and surplus crops.

In the 1400s, French *charcutiers* (pork cutters) formed guilds governing the preparation and sale of bacon, brawn or souse, confit, *galantine,* ham, lard, pâté, ribs, rillettes, salami, sausage, terrine, and trotters. The collection of apples and the slaughtering of hogs in late fall paired the fruit and meat in recipes, including roast pork with applesauce and pork tenderloin with steamed apples in cinnamon and honey. For simpler meals, mustard accompanied ham slices.

After Catholic forces reconquered Iberia from Muslims in 1492, religious zealots used pork consumption as a test of faith to identify Moriscos and Jews of suspicious lineage and faked conversions to Christianity. At the request of Queen Isabella of Castile, eight of the animals accompanied Christopher Columbus in 1493 on his journey to Cuba.

New World

After Spanish explorer Francisco Pizarro brought Panamanian black pigs to Peru in 1532, cooks added frying in lard to their kitchen techniques. Conquistador and explorer Hernando de Soto imported tusked swine from Extremadura, Spain, to Tampa, Florida, in 1539. Within three years, he propagated a herd of 700 by letting his animals scavenge for clams, corn, frogs, hickory nuts, lizards, pecans, snakes, tubers, and worms. Subsequent New World introductions by Hernán de Cortés to New Mexico in 1600 and to Jamestown, Virginia, by Walter Raleigh in 1607 continued the spread of swine among American livestock.

Within a half century, the proliferation of livestock in colonial New York, Pennsylvania, and Virginia required statutes limiting the free range of pigs. By 1662 in Connecticut, Maine, Massachusetts, and Rhode Island, cured pork sold at 2.5 cents per pound, 66.7 percent higher than cured beef, which cost 1.5 cents per pound. Farmers relied on barrels of pickled pork as trade items for cotton, salt, and sugar from Barbados, Bermuda, and Jamaica. Seagoing provisioners bargained for pork to feed sailors.

Country curing began with the stall feeding of hogs on acorns, corn, fruit, and peanuts. Some curing methods required the hanging of hams for one to seven years, injecting it with brine and saltpeter (potassium nitrate), pickling the meat in molasses or sugar, or soaking of chines in court bouillon and red wine. Home preparers soaked intestines in vinegar and hot brine and incorporated cornmeal into liver mush and blood, brains, and lungs into meat pudding and sausage. Pork remained a dietary staple among Native Americans and on the North American frontier because of its ease of packing and transport. Barrels of salt pork supplied lumber, mining, and rail camps as well as provisioners for wagon trains.

Industrial Meatpacking

Before the American Civil War, Cincinnati, Ohio, became the nation's "Porkopolis" because of the availability of canal and river transport for meat. In 1848, the city butchered 35,000 hogs. Chicago meatpacker Philip Danforth Armour revolutionized the pork business by shipping live hogs to the Union Stock Yard & Transit Company for processing. By 1860, Chicago's abattoirs outpaced Cincinnati's by bleeding, shaving, scraping, scalding, gutting, quartering, and sectioning 250,000 hogs. The operation became ten times busier in December than in July, before pigs began gaining winter weight.

During the Civil War, commercial pork supplied both armies with meat, some of it from wild razorbacks. Northern provisioners used fruitwood for smoking; rebel meat sellers preferred hickory and pecan wood. The Union raids of Southern smokehouses stripped families of their chief source of red meat for cooking with beans and cabbage. The closure of the Mississippi River to barge and ship travel advanced Chicago stockyards over the packing houses in Cincinnati.

After 1883, railcars refrigerated with compressed ammonia brought pork to packing operations in Kansas City, Kansas; Omaha, Nebraska; Peoria, Illinois; St. Joseph, Missouri; and Sioux City, Iowa, for distribution nationwide. In 1919, Chicago continued to reign as pork capital by employing 30,000 meat cutters to process 19 million hogs. Refrigerated trucks began relieving the pork-packing business of its reliance on rail lines.

Bacon, ham, and sausage took prime positions as breakfast foods. Oleomargarine, made from waste pork fat, competed with butter at half the price. Soul food menus featured barbecued spareribs and chitterlings for the table and pork crackling snacks to delight children. Corn growers in the Midwest profited from demands for feedlot supplies, thus linking the Hog Belt with the Corn Belt.

Industrial pork production increased the accessibility of meat in grocery stores. George A. Hormel's company engineered the first canned ham in 1926 by pressing pieces into a form and filling in gaps with gelatin. The Great Depression increased the popularity of the pork frankfurter. In 1937, Hormel added spiced ham to the market as Spam, a ground convenience food made from economy cuts.

Meat handlers prevented the transfer of pathogens to consumers by feeding no raw garbage or wild game to swine and by irradiating meat to sterilize parasites. In the 1990s, a trend toward low-fat meats spurred breeders to produce leaner animals. Efficient husbandry and injections of antibiotics and growth hormones in piglets made the United States competitive with pork producers in Canada and Denmark.

By 2002, developing countries increased their consumption of pork by 66.7 percent from 1970 rates. The United Nations predicted the meat trend would continue to grow because pigs convert grain to meat more efficiently than cattle and poultry. While U.S. pork consumption remained stable at 47 pounds (21 kilograms) per capita between 2002 and 2007, meat distributors experienced a doubling of pork exports.

As of early 2012, 38 percent of meat consumed globally consists of pork and pork products, which are rich in phosphorus, potassium, and thiamin. Just as baked ham anchors the Easter meals of American Christians and pork sausage stars during celebrations of the Chinese Lunar New Year, so pork roast and suckling pig figure in holiday feasts in Austria, Denmark, and New Guinea. Hungarian and Slovakian food festivals feature blood and liver sausage, much as British pubs advertise mince pie and Jamaica hypes jerked pork to islanders and tourists.

See also: Animal Husbandry; Halal; Kosher Food; Szechuan Diet and Cuisine; Taboos, Food.

Further Reading

Aidells, Bruce, and Lisa Weiss. *Bruce Aidells's Complete Book of Pork.* New York: HarperCollins, 2004.

D'Eramo, Marco. *The Pig and the Skyscraper: Chicago, a History of Our Future.* Trans. Graeme Thomson. New York: Verso, 2002.

Malcolmson, Robert W., and Stephanos Mastoris. *The English Pig: A History.* New York: Continuum, 2001.

Portuguese Diet and Cuisine

Like other European foodways, Portuguese cookery blends native Iberian staples with the robust aromas and savor of spices from the nation's former colonies. Rabbits and wild greens—asparagus, fennel, and sorrel—flourish in the countryside. Such specialties as Madeira bananas, Azores fish stew, Moorish baby clams in tomato sauce, mountain herb cheeses, and Minho yeast corn bread mark the preferences of small areas.

Because of the use of egg white in stucco church construction and the starching of nuns' habits, throughout the Middle Ages, convents converted thousands of surplus egg yolks into confections. Sisters fashioned intricate egg sweets, custards in pasta that they dusted with cinnamon sugar and drizzled with burnt-sugar syrup or lemon. Income from the sale of erotically named "nuns' sighs" and "maidens' bellies," some in provocative shapes of breasts and navels, funded the convents while providing an outlet for romantic fantasies among the celibate.

Historically, native cooks focused on meat-heavy menus favoring beef and smoked ham as well as shellfish. Side dishes of *caldo verde* (cabbage or kale and potato soup) and earthy "dry soups" enhanced the reputation of Portuguese recipes for hearty goodness. Moorish influence added almond and Algarve fig sweets, lemon beverages, and egg custards. During the Crusades, the Knights Templars occupied Tomar north of Lisbon from 1160 to the 1550s and

Recipe: Portuguese Gazpacho

Puree eight plum tomatoes, three 2-inch cucumbers, two large bell peppers, and one red onion. Flavor with 1/4 cup each of tarragon vinegar and light olive oil, 2 tablespoons of lemon juice, one minced garlic clove, one chopped sprig each of oregano and parsley, and sea salt and coarsely ground pepper to taste. Stir in 1 cup of seasoned bread crumbs. Add 1 quart of ice and chill overnight. Garnish with thin cucumber slices and tiny shrimp.

contributed to local cuisine the nutty, smoky savor of sheep cheese.

Portuguese ships became the conduit of cultural enrichment. During the religious persecutions of the eleventh and twelfth centuries, roasted pig fattened on chestnuts tested the faith of Sephardic Jews who pretended to convert to Catholicism by eating nonkosher foods. In the 1380s, according to historian Fernao Lopes, Lisbon chefs imported a Castilian specialty, tripe with white beans, a national dish. In his *Cancioneiro* (*Songbook,* 1516), Renaissance troubadour Garcia de Resende, an aide to King João II, described the centrality of grand meat dishes at court. For one example of royal excess, the palace staff roasted an ox and served it encircled with poultry. Provincial one-dish *cozido* incorporated cured pork and beef with cabbage, carrots, and turnips for ladling over rice.

Portugal established its diet in the European age of discovery, which its navigators launched in the early 1400s with the development of the caravel. After 1500, while destroying the food monopolies of the Arabs, Italians, and Turks, Portuguese traders contributed to an era of global species exchange. They made sweet oranges from India the basis of Iberian marmalade, first mentioned in 1521. The importation of coriander, curry, and ginger set native cuisine apart from the rest of Iberia with its bold flavors.

Portuguese travelogue writer Duarte Barbosa, who sailed with navigators Pedro Alvares Cabral and Ferdinand Magellan from 1500 to 1521, observed the value of trading vessels to world culinary exchange. Through the Mozambique Company and the Portuguese East India Company, markets acquired coriander from West Africa, cashews and peanuts from East Africa, and two spices, cinnamon from Ceylon and Indonesian pepper. Extend-

ing sea routes introduced mariners to coffee from Brazil and Timor, Japanese sugar, and the tea of Macau.

The Portuguese brought Iberian cookery to its enclaves in Angola; Goa, India; Sierra Leone; and the Caribbean and to trader ports in Canton, China; Nagasaki, Japan; Sao Paulo, Brazil; and the Strait of Malacca. Elements of the Mediterranean diet—anchovies, cheese, garlic, olives and olive oil, onions, and wine vinegar—contributed to Portuguese dishes based on the Atlantic cod, sardine, and tuna industry. Dramatic entrées featured clams, dried rays, eels, lobster, periwinkles (snails), prawns, sausages, and scallops. Side dishes of fried meat tarts, pickled cauliflower, and candied fruit displayed the Portuguese attention to texture and flavor, even in small servings.

See also: Abreu, António de, and Francisco Serrao; Gama, Vasco da; Indonesian Diet and Cuisine; Mozambique Company; Portuguese East India Company; Trading Vessels.

Further Reading

Cheung, Sidney C.H., and Tan Chee-Beng, eds. *Food and Food-ways in Asia: Resource, Tradition, and Cooking.* New York: Routledge, 2007.

Fraser, Evan D.G., and Andrew Rimas. *Empires of Food: Feast, Famine, and the Rise and Fall of Civilizations.* New York: Simon & Schuster, 2010.

Hutton, Wendy. *The Food of Love: Four Centuries of East-West Cuisine.* Singapore: Marshall Cavendish, 2007.

Kijac, Maria Baez. *The South American Table: The Flavor and Soul of Authentic Home Cooking from Patagonia to Rio de Janeiro.* Boston: Harvard Common, 2003.

Leite, David. *The New Portuguese Table: Exciting Flavors from Europe's Western Coast.* New York: Clarkson Potter, 2009.

Bacalhau, dried salted cod, is the unofficial national dish of Portugal. The preparation dates to the time before refrigerators, as a means of preservation. The Portuguese boast that there is a different bacalhau recipe for every day of the year—and more. *(Paul Bernhardt/Getty Images)*

Portuguese East India Company

For five years (1628–1633), the Portuguese East India Company (*Companhia do commércio da Índia*) monopolized commerce in India's food products but foundered against overwhelming economic and political odds.

The chartered forerunner began in 1499 with Vasco da Gama's voyage to the Indian subcontinent and the foundation of the Casa da India (House of India) at Cananor. A factor oversaw warehousing of coconuts, dried fish, honey, oil, rice, and sugar and dismayed Muslim traders by ending their monopoly in pepper and drugs. Before da Gama died of malaria at Goa on December 24, 1524, he established a Portuguese cinnamon monopoly with Ceylon, a promising foothold in the burgeoning European spice market.

From 1560 to 1570, with mismanagement plaguing the venture, King Sebastian I opened commerce to private Portuguese traders. In August 1578, his successor, Henry I, substituted an open monopoly for yearlong contracts. To combat mounting competition by the English East India Company (EEIC), Portugal's economic advisers reorganized the trading system. Under Philip I, the Crown failed to ally with Venetian spice dealers. In 1597, King Philip revived the original monopoly arrangement. Closer scrutiny of the market from 1605 to 1614 failed to produce anticipated revenues. Sailors' complaints of inadequate biscuit, dried fish, olive oil, rice, salt meat, and wine revealed malfeasance of contract provisioners. Impure meat and lack of fresh fruits and vegetables and potable water increased losses of crew to disease.

Under a proposal published by Duarte Gomes Solis in 1628, the Portuguese East India Company aggressively vied with the EEIC and the Dutch using private rather than royal capital. Superintended by Jorge Mascarenhas, Lisbon's mayor, the new stock venture, formed by Philip III, entered its first decade of trade, which included outgoing cargo of alum, cochineal food dye, saffron, and vermilion. Formally incorporated at Madrid in August 1628, the company began collecting customs under royal charter. By cornering trade in Ceylonese cinnamon bark, coral, cowrie shells, indigo, and Malaysian pepper and by pilfering food from the holds of captured Dutch and English merchantmen, the firm prospered at shipping and allowed European dealers to control spice distribution.

The Portuguese enterprise enjoyed low overhead from the peeling and packing of wild cinnamon bark, but it never broke the Dutch control of cloves, mace, and nutmeg. Although pepper profits reached 143 percent for the cargo of the *Santíssimo Sacramento* in 1630 and 153 percent for the *Bom Jesus de Monte Calvario* in 1631, ocean currents and winds took their toll on the original fleet of 15 *naos* (carracks), returning only seven from Goa to Lis-

bon. In 1632, the monopoly of coir rope from the Maldives, south of India, increased potential for profit, but it could not generate enough cash flow to counter the rise in Indian pepper prices by 40 percent. Retaliation by the English and Dutch, as well as the Dutch blockade of the Malacca Strait, quickly redirected the spice trade away from Portugal. High overhead from military expenses and a falling pepper market in Lisbon compromised profits to the breaking point. Lacking the naval strength to oust rivals, the Portuguese East India Company disbanded in April 1633.

See also: British East India Company; Gama, Vasco da.

Further Reading

Ames, Glenn Joseph. *Vasco da Gama: Renaissance Crusader.* New York: Pearson/Longman, 2005.

Bethencourt, Francisco, and Diogo Ramada Curto. *Portuguese Oceanic Expansion, 1400–1800.* New York: Cambridge University Press, 2007.

Disney, A.R. "The First Portuguese India Company, 1628–33." *Economic History Review* 30:2 (1977): 242–258.

Potatoes

A prolific starchy tuber, the white potato (*Solanum tuberosum*) joins corn, rice, and wheat in supplying the world with carbohydrates. Growing wild from 11,000 B.C.E., the cultivated potato evolved in western South America after 8000 B.C.E. Natural selection among wild hybrids in Altiplano, the upper elevation of the Andes Mountains, generated more than 3,000 cultivars, which Quechua speakers called *papas*.

The Peruvian Inca at Machu Picchu cultivated dozens of potato varieties within a single plot, a method that reduced the crop failures of monocropping. Because their cultivars were susceptible to storage rot, Bolivian and Peruvian growers freeze-dried tubers under low air pressure at altitudes reaching 10,000–15,000 feet (3,000–4,600 meters). After moisture evaporated, the tubers shrank into light, brittle *chuño*, which remained edible for a decade. Inca cooks reconstituted the wrinkled pantry stock with broth or water.

Domesticated in Bolivia, Ecuador, and Peru, potatoes traveled to coastal tribes, the Haida, Salish, and Tsimshian. When Christopher Columbus first encountered potatoes in Cuba on October 28, 1492, he compared the flavor to chestnuts. Throughout the Caribbean, potatoes impressed Spanish explorers with their addition of an antiscorbutic to staple carbohydrates. Return voyages after 1537 by privateer Francis Drake and historian Thomas Harriot brought the tubers to England, Holland, and Spain. In 1588, Walter Raleigh grew potatoes in his garden outside Cork, Ireland.

THE EVICTION

An Irish cartoon from the 1840s dramatizes the eviction of a tenant farmer for failure to pay rent. A blight on potato crops caused the death or displacement of millions of Irish, up to one third of whom depended on the potato for sustenance. *(Buyenlarge/Getty Images)*

In new terroir, the potato developed hybrids, increasing the total to 5,000 cultivars. More growers claimed the tuber in the Canary Islands in 1567 and in subsequent colonies of Kenya, Rwanda, and Uganda. By 1600, enthusiasts spread potato cultivation to Austria, Belgium, China, France, Germany, Indonesia, and the Philippines. Sailors continued the dissemination of seed potatoes to Port Royal, Nova Scotia, where gardeners cultivated them in 1623. Scots-Irish immigrants brought potatoes on their 1719 voyage to New Hampshire, where farmers valued the tubers as hog food.

From the British Isles to Italy, potatoes were reserved for feeding convicts, livestock, slaves, and soldiers and for nourishing hospital patients suffering from consumption, measles, and scurvy. In Kolberg, Prussia, in 1744, Frederick the Great recognized potatoes as a culinary backup. For 30 years, Frederick coaxed farmers into planting free seed potatoes and distributed cultivation and harvesting manuals. An underground crop raised in France, Holland, and Prussia to prevent food shortages, it

survived the advance of mounted cavalry through grain fields and vineyards.

Contributing to advertisement of the potato, French nutritionist Antoine-Augustin Parmentier returned from imprisonment in Prussia during the Seven Years' War with a scientific zeal for potatoes as famine food. In 1773, he proposed potato meals to cure dysentery. By 1785, a potato fad increased enthusiasm for the new kitchen garden crop in France, the Low Countries, and Russia, where Catherine the Great ordered the planting of seed potatoes. Pragmatists admired the tuber above the turnip for providing an easily harvested food that cost less than rye and came to table more easily than bread made from milled grain.

Chefs honored Parmentier's campaign by concocting potato hash and shepherd's pie, a one-dish meal of mashed potatoes, ground meat, butter, garlic, onions, and seasonings. The satisfying staple sustained workers during the Industrial Revolution, when cooks in Liverpool, London, and Manchester baked, boiled, fried, and roasted potatoes, steamed and cubed them for salads, and grated them into curry, pudding, and soup. The tuber altered forever the Jewish diet, which had previously favored the egg noodle as a culinary starch. Potatoes bolstered meals of buttermilk and herring, an ethnic cuisine that Jewish immigrants brought to the Americas. Potato crops flourished in the Monticello gardens of U.S. President Thomas Jefferson and in Colorado, Idaho, Maine, New Brunswick, Oregon, Prince Edward Island, and Washington.

In the late 1700s, while Poles revolutionized vodka by distilling it from potatoes, Norwegians made aquavit from the same source. The rural Irish applied the tuber to runs of *poitín*, a potent moonshine. Ireland experienced a population explosion from weekday meals of milk and lumper potatoes, relieved on Sundays by greens with bacon or oat gruel. The Irish reliance on 12 pounds (5.4 kilograms) per person per week turned the Irish Potato Famine of 1845–1852 into a mass catastrophe of rapid depletion of body mass and malnutrition that reduced the population by 56 percent.

After a two-year process of selection, American agronomist Luther Burbank developed a rare seedpod into the russet Burbank potato, a white-fleshed tuber and forerunner of the Idaho russet. He sold rights to his hearty cultivar in 1874 for $150. His hybrid relieved the Irish of future famines by combatting *Phytophthora infestans* (potato blight). The problem remained puzzling until French agronomist Alexis Millardet formulated an effective fungicide in 1883. Meanwhile, displacement of the Irish and Scots altered the Australian and North American population and cuisine through immigration of 1.5 million potato eaters to more promising locales.

In the late 1980s, China and India pursued potato production, rivaling the Americas and Europe in mass harvests. In 2007, American hybridizers supplied fast-food chains with a more fibrous tuber for French fries and potato chips. In 2008, formulation of a copper fungicide increased the acceptability of sprays on organic potato fields. Genetic modification by BASF and Monsanto bred cultivars resistant to potato beetles and immune to common fungi. Scientists intended to apply sturdier cultivars to stemming hunger in developing nations.

See also: Famine; Freeze-Drying; Jiménez de Quesada, Gonzalo; Inca Diet and Cuisine; Monoculture; New World Commodities; Plant Disease and Prevention; Scandinavian Diet and Cuisine; South American Diet and Cuisine.

Further Reading

Chapman, Jeff. "The Impact of the Potato." *History* 1:6 (December/January 2000), 41–44.

Mann, Charles C. *1493: Uncovering the New World Columbus Created.* New York: Random House, 2011.

Reader, John. *Potato: A History of the Propitious Esculent.* New Haven, CT: Yale University Press, 2009.

Poultry

The world's second-most-common food after pigs, avifauna provides eggs, meat, and oil as sustenance and feathers and leather for costumes and furniture. Hunting-and-gathering societies of the Olduvai Gorge in Tanzania as early as 60,000 B.C.E. and of the Paleo-Indian Paisley Caves of Oregon after 12,300 B.C.E. dispatched women and children to search for birds and eggs. Before 7500 B.C.E., Malaysian, north Indian, Thai, and Vietnamese domesticators chose to breed in captivity the red jungle fowl, ancestor of the common chicken (*Gallus domesticus*). Cross-breeding with the Ceylon, Java, and Jungle Grey chickens introduced poultry husbandry into Asian livestock skills as far southeast as Sumatra. Coop keepers discovered that removal of eggs from nests induced hens to continue to produce fresh eggs.

Through observation, Egyptian poulterers timed the natural fattening of wild cranes, ducks, and geese for migration. The household of the Pharaoh Ti around 2500 B.C.E. devised a system of force-feeding birds through funnels and massaging the throats to produce artificially engorged livers. At peak time, cooks slaughtered birds to obtain the fatty liver, the forerunner of French foie gras, a luxury smoked pâté. From Egyptian cookery, consumption of birds and eggs influenced North African cuisine as far west as Morocco, but central Africans revered poultry too much for divination and religion to slaughter birds for food.

After 2000 B.C.E., Northeastern Indians and Malaysians bred the deep-breasted Brahmaputra chicken, the largest hybrid, known as *Gallus giganteus.* Compared with the smaller bantam, the hardy Brahmaputra ate sparingly, yet it weighed about 13 pounds (5.9 kilograms), or more than ten times that of the Javanese bantam. The Brahmaputra laid a 4.25-ounce (120-gram) egg, 33.3 percent larger than the average hen egg, and continued laying in winter when other breeds stopped.

Recipes from state dinners in Assyria and Elam beginning around 1900 B.C.E. summarized cauldron preparation of partridge and pigeon. By 1520 B.C.E., Chinese and eastern Indian breeders produced for the table the Cochin chicken, which attained a weight of 8 pounds (3.6 kilograms). Chinese poulterers developed sophisticated methods of preserving and shipping eggs to Formosa, Korea, Manchuria, and Mongolia. Vietnamese consumers allowed fertilized eggs to develop and ate the unborn chicks, also a favorite of Filipinos. Chinese cooks simmered Cochin carcasses to make stock and preserved century eggs by salting alkaline clay, mixing it with rice husks, and molding it around the shells. In contrast to the Asian relish of poultry and eggs, Javanese and Tibetan Buddhists and Indian Hindus denounced avifauna as food because the birds devoured excrement and worms.

From 1400 B.C.E., Egyptians and Sumerians stocked hen yards and valued ostrich and pelican eggs as temple gifts. Greeks admired Egyptian poultry technicians, who designed a clay brick incubator to increase the size of flocks. Historians surmise that Egyptian provisioners fed chickens and eggs to the builders of the pyramids much as the Chinese raised flocks as food for workers on the Great Wall of China.

Greek writers detailed bird life more as a curiosity of nature than as a source of food. In the *Iliad* (ca. 850 B.C.E.), Homer pictured geese and swans as models of aquatic avifauna. The Greeks preferred the China goose for rich meat and raised quail for their tiny eggs, a table delicacy. Chariades of Athens added a white omelet to the traditional Greek *thríon*, fig leaves stuffed with bacon, cheese, eggs, and milk. For tender meat, Greek importers bought the heavy Rhodian chickens of Delos, Medea, and Persia. According to Greco-Syracusan poet Archestratus's *Hedypatheia* (*Life of Luxury*, ca. 350 B.C.E.), Greeks emulated the Egyptian method of fattening goose livers, which Archestratus prized as the bird's soul.

In western Asia, Syrian author ibn Sayyar al-Warraq of Baghdad summarized the Abbasid preferences for bird pies and stuffed and roasted fowl. Babylonians raised chickens for meat as early as 600 B.C.E. and welcomed the first eggs of spring, a forerunner of the Easter egg. Eastern Europeans received the gamecock and pheasant from Persia and the peafowl from India around 500 B.C.E. Skillful husbandry in temperate zones tamed the greylag goose (*Anser ferus*) into the barnyard goose, which poulterers crossbred with domestic species.

Specialties for the Table

During the Roman Empire, poultry keepers fattened hens on milk, raisins, or bread soaked in wine. Chefs chose eggs of the compact, short-legged Dorking hen (*Gallus pentadactylus*) as a first course. For entrées for feasts, preparers dramatized the goose, pheasant, and swan by decking the roast birds in their original feathers and stuffing them with songbirds. Legionaries introduced the Dorking chicken to Gallic and British Celts for eggs and meat, as well as the Pakistani Asil for cockfighting, perhaps the world's oldest spectator sport, dating to 1280 B.C.E.

Throughout the Middle Ages, the castration of roosters produced plump capons, a common banquet feature. The English and Norwegians developed dishes from gull eggs; Africans preferred guinea eggs, which the birds produced from May until summer's end. Upon returning from China in 1300, Venetian traveler Marco Polo reported that courtship rituals featured Mandarin duck soup. The Dutch and Iberians bred the Hamburg fowl and the glossy black Spanish chicken, a layer of 4.5-ounce (128-gram) eggs. Norman-French food master Taillevent's *Le Viandier* (*The Provisioner*, ca. 1375) praised herbed chicken broth, an eventual basis for early-nineteenth-century French haute cuisine. The anonymous *Le Ménagier*

de Paris (*The Goodman of Paris*, 1393) advised on adding eggs to the invalid's diet.

The Western Hemisphere produced unique poultry strains in the Muscovy duck of Brazil, the Argentine rhea, the Chilean Araucana chicken, and the wild turkey (*Meleagris gallopavo*), which ranged from its origins in Mexico to Canada. In the 12-book *Historia General de las Cosas de Nueva España* (*General History of the Things of New Spain*, 1540–1569), ethnographer Bernardino de Sahagún reported on the turkey, the only domesticated poultry in Mexico. At the Tepeyac market, he found vendors selling 1,600 turkeys a day.

In 1500, Spanish explorer Vicente Yáñez Pinzón introduced Iberian chickens to Brazil. To the upkeep of Henry VII's household, gamekeepers contributed geese, larks, pigeons, partridges, snipe, and woodcocks. After sailing to the New World with Sebastian Cabot in 1516, voyager William Strickland brought the New World turkey home to England, where chefs gilded the skin before presentation. In 1540, the French obtained from Guiana the Muscovy duck, a tender, full-flavored table bird best eaten in its prime.

During meat shortages, Europeans kept poultry yards of chickens, ducks, and geese and hunted coastal puffins, which Christians authorized for the meatless meals of Lent. The laboring class sold eggs and hens as a source of cash. The Aylesbury duck rewarded British keepers with 300 eggs per year in exchange for modest amounts of grain.

French gourmands raised the Rouen duck for its kidneys for pies and for its succulent meat, the result of feeding roasters on horseflesh. Less discriminating diners ranked the Dreux at the top of the chicken market, followed by the Houdan and the Nogent le Roi. Cooks boiled down the feet, head, and neck for chicken jelly and sauce. Mestre Robert (or Rupert de Nola), author of *El Llibre del Coch* (*The Cook's Book*, 1520), a Catalan culinary guide, trusted stews of spiced chicken to revive the sickest patient. In the 1600s, French egg fanciers developed the citrus curd by scrambling eggs with lemon or orange juice.

European immigrants brought to America the Brahmaputra, Cochin, Crevecoeur, and Leghorn chickens, breeds that ensured profitability for the hen yard as well as good gaming for cockfighting. Poulterers ranked the Leghorn tops for eggs and health, and Brahmaputras best for raising chicks for meat. To soften the muscles, coop keepers penned the birds for weeks of fattening on carrots, corn, and pumpkin. The addition of milk and oats to the feed ensured juice in the meat. In 1634, a report on the cuisine of Jamestown, Virginia, noted the availability of capons, geese, stewing hens, and turkeys. Around the Chesapeake Bay, Indians traded stray chickens and turkeys for cooking pots and rifles.

Hen yards relieved some of the problems with food storage in colonial anticipation of hard times. On plantations in the American South, the Caribbean, and South America, slave dealers profited from selling Africans who had experience in raising guinea fowl. Slaves increased personal wealth by keeping poultry at their cabins and bartering eggs and meat for clothing and medicine. For meals at Mount Vernon, Virginia, Martha Custis Washington's *Book of Cookery* (1749) described how to make chicken pie and olio pie, a catchall of fowl, rabbit, artichokes, potatoes, citrus fruit, and dates. In Australia, Aborigines snared albatross and muttonbirds and robbed their nests of eggs. After 1788, English colonists domesticated the black swan, emu, and ostrich, the world's largest bird and a survival food stuffed and roasted at the fireside.

In 1850, the first Brahmaputras arrived in New York. New chicken breeds emerged, making favorites of the Dominique, Rhode Island Red, and Wyandotte. By 1860, importers from the Ukraine brought the Sebastapol goose, a plump bird averaging 12 pounds (5.4 kilograms). American flock keepers boosted the weight by 30 percent through interbreeding with German Embden geese. During the Civil War, Southern women replaced roasted Dorking, Leghorn, and Scotch Grey chickens with songbird pies from blackbirds, chickadees, or robins snared in their yards. By 1880, poultry keeping emerged as an official division in husbandry science.

Industry

American poulterers—usually women—gathered eggs daily. During periods of low demand, they coated shells with butter, paraffin, varnish, or vaseline and bedded them on dry bran or salt to prevent evaporation. Others stored eggs in a crock filled with lime water or glasswater, a silica gel formed from melting sand with alkali. When prices rose in winter for eggnog and Christmas custards, hen yards became three times more profitable than in spring.

In the 1880s, Jewish immigrants to Petaluma, California, turned the region into "the egg basket of the world" for the sale of 100 million eggs annually to Alaska, New York, and the Pacific Coast. Cooks invented egg drop soup, dumplings, poached unlaid eggs, mayonnaise, and egg salad, a combination of chopped salted onions and hard-boiled eggs. Kosher cooks experimented with poultry recipes, especially noodle soups. Ashkenazim raised the hen to the height of importance in Jewish cookery, particularly for Sabbath dinner.

Cold storage evened out the seasonal egg business by proving to consumers that refrigerated winter eggs taste as fresh as spring stock. To boost business, promoters in 1915 dropped prices on the spring glut of eggs by half, from 60 cents to 30 cents per dozen. A decade later, the U.S. Department of Agriculture replaced the dating of stock with national egg standards, which graded the size of the air cell in each shell.

Poulterers further lessened the seasonality of the egg business in the 1920s by breeding hens that laid eggs year-round. Farmers tricked chickens by raising them in heated coops under electric lights and by feeding them scientific formulations that increased off-season yield. Treatment with antibiotics reduced disease. By 1946, annual egg production had risen by 67 percent. In the aftermath of World War II, American nutritionists encouraged Europeans to eat more eggs and poultry meat to restore the malnourished to health. Julia Child's *Mastering the Art of French Cooking* (1961) reinstated glamour to poultry by educating Americans on stuffing and trussing a bird for roasting.

Today, growers of chickens, doves, ducks, geese, guineas, pheasants, pigeons, quail, and turkeys favor the chest and leg meat, the muscles developed by locomotion. Cooks value the meat and eggs as cuisine mainstays for buffalo wings, chicken nuggets, omelets, and toppings for salads and tacos. American poulterers raise some 100 strains of chickens; the English and French prefer the Brahmaputra. The golden pheasant remains a prize dish in China, Mongolia, and the Taurus Mountain region. The Chinese, who raise nearly 4 billion chickens per year, enjoy the tea egg, an aromatic treat flavored with cinnamon, clove, fennel, pepper, soy sauce, star anise, and tea leaves. Other egg treats include the batter-fried chicken or quail egg, brined duck egg, soy egg, and spiced iron egg. From street vendors, Cambodian, Filipino, and Vietnamese diners buy fertilized duck embryos as snacks, appetizers, and aphrodisiacs.

See also: Agribusiness; Animal Husbandry; Cussy, Louis, Marquis de; Polynesian Diet and Cuisine; Tudor Diet and Cuisine.

Further Reading

Nelson, Melissa. *The Complete Guide to Poultry Breeds.* Ocala, FL: Atlantic, 2011.

Smith, Andrew F. *The Turkey: An American Story.* Urbana: University of Illinois Press, 2006.

Squier, Susan Merrill. *Poultry Science, Chicken Culture: A Partial Alphabet.* New Brunswick, NJ: Rutgers University Press, 2011.

Recipe: Kosher Chicken Soup

Slaughter and pluck a plump hen. Soak it in cold salted water to leach out the blood. Coat the carcass in kosher salt and drain it for an hour on a tilted board. Rinse in three changes of cold water. In a large soup pot, cover the bird in water and add root vegetables—carrots, onions, parsnips, potatoes, rutabagas, turnips. Slow-cook for several hours to surround the flesh with a thick broth.

Williams-Forson, Psyche A. *Building Houses out of Chicken Legs: Black Women, Food, and Power.* Chapel Hill: University of North Carolina Press, 2006.

Preservation, Food

See Caching; Canning; Curing; Dried Food; Freeze-Drying; Pickling; Refrigeration; Smoked Food; Storage, Food

Processed Foods

See Industrial Food Processing

Prohibition

The control of intoxicating drinks is an old crusade. After 650 C.E., the Koran equated drinking with gambling, both satanic ploys in the view of Muslims. Historical records from China and Japan report priests and royals hoarding distilled drinks for themselves or for holy ritual. In 1529, Charles V of Spain issued a ban on Aztec tequila, which Indians had fermented from cactus for centuries. His controls failed, just as Asian secrecy lost out to bootlegging and discreetly published home distilling guides. In the British navy in 1740, Admiral Edward Vernon ordered the watering of grog and cut sailors' daily allotment to stem drunkenness on watch.

In North America, where the decades-old temperance movement finally led to outright prohibition from 1920 to 1933, drinking had supported diverse activities. From colonial times, cider and ale served both rich and poor as a form of recreation and a stimulus to group involvement. Taverns provided convenient locales for political and public gatherings, as they did for the Sons of Liberty, a secret anticolonial brotherhood. The cultural and religious mores of immigrant French, Germans, Irish, Italians, Jews, and Poles called for the generous distribution of brandy, beer, and rum, often as additives to sauces and fruitcakes. Religious services, including the Christian Eucharist and the Jewish wedding ceremony and *bris* (ritual circumcision), involved the ritual sipping of wine. Saloons lured patrons with free lunch. Jails bulged with weekend traffic from public drunks and fistfights. After 1832, German immigration made Cincinnati, Ohio, the capital of oompah bands and Teutonic beer steins. Honeymooners flocked to *Bierstuben* (beer halls) and restaurants. Tavern owners put on a conservative front and bolstered their investments by running for city council, constable, or mayor.

Crusading "Drys"

As women's groups grew more vocal in defense of civic decency and family, city accountants pondered in private the effect of prohibition on tax receipts from business lunches and men's lodges. Tourist centers feared that the loss of liquor licenses would scare off investors in restaurants and hotels. To save their jobs, barkeeps and waiters in 1891 formed the Hotel and Restaurant Employees' International Alliance and the Bartenders' International League of America.

Beginning in the late nineteenth century, Protestant prohibitionists and the Anti-Saloon League, founded in 1893 in Ohio, amplified political pressures to end public drunkenness and squalid taverns. Crusaders succeeded in closing watering holes but failed to stop them from opening in new locations. Restaurateurs, who earned 35 percent of their profits from alcohol, protested controls, which would lower profits to only 15 percent of sales from food and nonalcoholic beverage service. Owners of sports complexes, backed by brewers and coopers, protested the loss of beer franchises.

The antiliquor drive failed in New Zealand in 1911 but proved effective on Prince Edward Island in 1907, in Russia and Iceland in 1914 and 1915, and in Norway in 1916. The growing revolt against saloons reached Finland and Hungary in 1919. Some U.S. counties managed to vote "dry," forcing diners and tipplers to patronize inns across the county line. Prohibition gained momentum after the 1917 declaration of war against Germany. Ostensibly to redirect grain to military use, the War Prohibition Act of November 1918 halted the production and sale of beer, liquor, and wine until demobilization.

Volstead Act

The National Prohibition Act, or Volstead Act, passed by Congress on October 28, 1919, as the enabling legislation of the Eighteenth Amendment to the U.S. Constitution, prohibited the manufacture, transport, and sale of any beverage containing more than 0.5 percent alcohol. Although wine, brandy, and moonshine whiskey headed the list of home restoratives for a variety of illnesses, dry pressure groups such as the Woman's Christian Temperance Union (WCTU) cheered the defeat of "demon rum" and the attendant corruption from brothels and gambling.

On January 15, 1920, during Warren G. Harding's successful run as Republican and dry candidate for the U.S. presidency, New Hampshire cast the thirty-sixth and final vote needed to pass the law. Intended to lessen rowdyism, spousal abuse, underage drinking, and child neglect, the squelching of strong drink in reality aroused fierce libertarianism, even among drys. Restricted entertainment ushered in the Roaring Twenties, an era known for the buying and consumption of illegal bathtub gin and flavored wood alcohol.

The ban failed to halt illicit hooch from stills around the nation, particularly in crime-plagued Chicago. Runners made hauls across the Canadian and Mexican borders and turned small investments into millions by smuggling booze from rum factories in Antigua, Bermuda, Cuba,

Jamaica, and the Bahamas. Aficionados of speakeasies (places selling illegal alcohol) made dinner reservations under "John Smith."

Alcohol and Crime

Because of ethnic culinary demands, much of the nation ignored or refused to comply with Prohibition, which suppressed a vast enterprise. In the hard-pressed Appalachians, mountaineers and farmers turned corn into "squeezins," affectionately known as "ole tanglefoot." Their under-the-table business caused Treasury Department agents, or T-men, to seize some 670,000 amateur operations and establishments. Raids recouped national excise taxes and protected the unwary from lead-laced brews filtered through car radiators.

In addition to producing alcohol for home use, freelance distillers and distributors supplied speakeasies and strings of fake drugstores, which sold alcohol as a prescription drug. Within a decade, federal officials had collared more than a half million violators. Assistant U.S. Attorney General Mabel Walker Willebrandt sent scofflaws to prison but did little to halt the bootlegging trade.

The glamour of home distilling "sugar moon" and "tarantula juice," racketeering, rum running, and hauling "white lightning" increased violence from organized crime, raids, and drunk driving. Treasury agent Eliot Ness and his Untouchables earned a reputation for diligence in trailing brewers and haulers to their lairs for highly publicized raids.

Not all of legally mandated sobriety turned tawdry and crime ridden. At Washington Island on Lake Michigan, Danish immigrant Tom Nelson introduced Angostura Bitters, a flavoring invented in Trinidad in 1824 for treating digestive upset and seasickness and for use in cocktails and Caribbean dishes. With the digestive, Nelson perpetrated a legal dodge certified by a pharmaceutical license and handwritten prescriptions.

End of an Era

For professional food service, the Prohibition experiment tolled a death knell for the elegant catering and *table d'hote* dining in fine establishments that had flourished since 1890, the dawn of the Gilded Age. Loss of fine wines substantially reduced the demand for table service; more people stayed home and served wine and liquor from private stock at cocktail parties.

When the era came to a close, the family-centered cafeteria and diner dominated the restaurant scene. On the up side, Prohibition boosted the sale of soft drinks, cooking wines, and flavored brandies and promoted club luncheons and the opening of tearooms, a popular kitchen business for women. For public personalities who had once made grand entrances at New York's Waldorf-Astoria Hotel, being seen required a new thrill, the supper club, child of the speakeasy.

Gradually, the power of the fundamentalist middle class and the solidarity of anti-immigrant and anti-Catholic factions lost cohesion. By 1929, nearly 81 percent of the nation wanted the law repealed or modified. Under the presidency of Herbert Hoover and the rise of the Democratic repeal platform, Prohibition ended on December 5, 1933. Utah became the thirty-sixth state to ratify the Twenty-First Amendment, which overturned the Eighteenth.

See also: Alcoholic Beverages; Beer; Religion and Food; Taboos, Food; Whiskey; Wine.

Further Reading

Beyer, Mark. *Temperance and Prohibition: The Movement to Pass Anti-Liquor Laws in America.* New York: Rosen, 2006.

Kyvig, David E. *Repealing National Prohibition.* Kent, OH: Kent State University Press, 2000.

Okrent, Daniel. *Last Call: The Rise and Fall of Prohibition.* New York: Simon & Schuster, 2010.

Peck, Garrett. *The Prohibition Hangover: Alcohol in America from Demon Rum to Cult Cabernet.* New Brunswick, NJ: Rutgers University Press, 2009.

Slavicek, Louise Chipley. *The Prohibition Era: Temperance in the United States.* New York: Chelsea House, 2009.

Proust, Joseph-Louis (1754–1826)

One of the founders of analytical chemistry, Joseph-Louis Proust identified glucose as the sweetener in grapes and honey.

Born in Angers, France, Proust learned about the elements at an Oratorian college and in the shop of his father, an apothecary. At age 22, he lectured at the royal palace and served at Salpetrière Hospital in Paris as pharmacist. While he taught chemistry in Salamanca and Segovia, Spain, he published a hypothesis that substances in binary combinations join in fixed and definite proportions by weight. In addition to his studies of bronze and gunpowder, he took an interest in nutritional chemistry and, funded by Charles IV, established one of Europe's most advanced research laboratories.

Proust made his discoveries about food sugar during the chemical revolution that followed the English and French food riots around 1789. While teaching in Madrid in 1799, he noted the presence of three types of saccharine juices in vegetables—fructose, glucose, and sucrose—and demonstrated to his students the chemical makeup of glucose. After purifying sugar syrups through charcoal filters, he isolated four amino acids, elements of protein—leucine in cheese and mannitol in manna and mushrooms, also gliadin in wheat and hordein in barley. He theorized that manufacturers could synthesize nutritional supplements. His discovery offered a cheaper source of sugar than the sweetener crystallized from West Indian cane.

Proust's research provided practical solutions to a European food crisis. In 1809, he isolated sorbitol, a sweetener found in algae, apples, berries, cherries, molasses, peaches, pears, plums, and seaweed. As a sugar shortage destabilized food prices during the British blockade of cane sugar imports from the West Indies, Napoleon Bonaparte offered 100,000 francs to the chemist who could produce sugar from indigenous flora. In 1810, Proust won the purse by extracting dextrose from grapes. His analysis of major nutrients enabled physicians to calculate energy metabolism. For his contributions to science, he earned membership in the French Academy of Sciences, a Legion of Honor, and a royal pension.

Further Reading

Hunter, Beatrice Trum. *The Sweetener Trap & How to Avoid It.* Laguna Beach, CA: Basic Health, 2010.

Hunter, Graeme K. *Vital Forces: The Discovery of the Molecular Basis of Life.* San Diego, CA: Academic Press, 2000.

McArdle, William D., Frank L. Katch, and Victor L. Katch. *Exercise Physiology: Nutrition, Energy, and Human Performance.* Baltimore: Lippincott Williams & Wilkins, 2010.

Oakes, Elizabeth H. *Encyclopedia of World Scientists.* New York: Facts on File, 2007.

Young, Robyn V., and Suzanne Sessine. *World of Chemistry.* Detroit, MI: Gale Group, 2000.

Pulses

Until the refinement of barley and advent of wheat oven breads about 10,000 years ago, pulse, a lysine-rich paste or porridge of legumes, sustained much of the Mediterranean world and the Middle East. The name *bean* derives from the *baiana* (fava bean) of Baiae in coastal Campania in southwestern Italy. Currently, beans, lentils, and peas dominate peasant agriculture and supply 8 percent of the world's protein, usually in one-pot meals.

Neolithic Syrians plucked wild lentils as early as 12,000 B.C.E., Greek agriculture incorporated lentils before 6000 B.C.E., and farmers in southern Italy, Spain, and Thessaly began cultivating them around 3000 B.C.E. Ancient Jews reserved boiled lentils with eggs for periods of mourning. Broad beans appear to have emerged as wild food in Afghanistan and the Himalayan hill country. Fava bean gardening passed from Egypt north to northern Italy and Gaul and east to Troy and Syria-Palestine, where Muslims incorporated pulses into Ramadan dishes.

Cuisine

Because pulses lack complete protein for sustenance, they entered culinary history among the Anasazi and Aztec in combination with corn. A parallel yoking of staples occurred in ancient Persia and eastern Asia with meat, rice, and sweet-and-sour sauces, such as Persian *polow* and Laotian tofu salad. Early gatherers in the dry areas of Pakistan and Guatemala spread fresh beans and peas in the sun to air-dry, a preservation method that retained fat and protein content while preventing mold.

In the post-Homeric era (after the eighth century B.C.E.) in Egypt and Greece, the more expensive processed peas, either split or skinned, suited boiling and roasting with salt. Split peas accompanied fish and lamb dishes, such as red lentil soup with grilled sea bream. The more sophisticated diner ate bean pods raw or sautéed in oil. The Egyptians turned one pulse, the carob bean, into a sweet drink. Spartans preferred black-eyed peas with figs for dessert.

When social distinctions lowered the prestige of legumes, only the poor in classical Greece served them in *etnos* (bean soup) dressed with vinegar and baked bread from bean meal. Virgil's *Georgics* (29 B.C.E.) lists kidney beans with vetch as "lowly" crops. Similarly judgmental, Trojans grew vetch only for famine supplies and animal fodder.

Priests fed Rome's sacred geese on pulse and employed bean gruel in sacrifices; mothers weaned their children on legume pap. Jokesters teased bean eaters about possible flatulence, a social embarrassment. To prevent intestinal fermentation, cooks grilled or roasted beans, baked them with onions into a casserole, or employed anise, coriander, and cumin seed as natural carminatives.

Health Effects

Classical writings connected the consumption of legumes with sensible diet. Table maxims about moderation warned of gluttony and wine guzzling and encouraged consumption of cheese, fish, and a gruel of beans, lentils, or peas along with whole-grain bread, pork fat, and fresh and dried fruit. In the treatise *De Alimentorum Facultatibus* (*On the Powers of Foods,* 175 C.E.), the physician Galen of Pergamum respected the chickpea for exciting the libido and breaking up kidney stones. He recommended serving earthy lupine seeds with a tart sauce, such as bulbs or sumac and vinegar.

In the late fourth century B.C.E., encyclopedist Theophrastus of Lesbos, the "Father of Botany," indicated the centrality of legumes to the Mediterranean diet. He evaluated pulses made from fava beans and lentils, which he considered "heavy" for the body to assimilate. He identified chickpeas and lupines as plants historically stockpiled as famine food and described the nitrogen process by which legumes enrich soil.

Apicius, a Roman cook around 40 C.E., advised cleaning and soaking legumes as a means of tenderizing the thiamine-rich outer coat. He touted the blending of eight leafy greens with three types of pulses and barley for a vegetable *tisana* (pottage), a digestible ragout high in fiber and protein. The stew parallels the ingredients of a Moroccan *harira,* as both generate aroma from coriander and onions. In Renaissance Venice, a similar blend of beans, pork, and flavorings with a generous topping of cheese and lard made the filling of *torta de faxolli freschi,* a crusty bean pie.

A Versatile Staple

Beans and peas took their place in culinary history in unique forms, such as the eastern Mediterranean fried chickpea ball, Venezuelan tonka beans fermented in rum, Australian bush tucker bean cakes, and the Genoan chickpea crepe. In his memoir *Travels of a Philosopher; or, Observations on the Manners and Arts of Various Nations in Africa and Asia* (1770), Pierre Poivre, a French botanist and biopirate, acknowledged the vegetarianism of Hindus of Malabar, India. He approved an abstemious diet based on butter, fruit, and grain and pulses but nothing that enjoyed an animal life.

On the American frontier, pulses acquired their own culinary lore in chuck wagons, log cabins, and sod huts. As a prevention of scurvy, green beans became popular provisions for sailing crews and prison labor camps. Among rural Southerners, the lengthy cooking of black-eyed peas or pinto beans in fatback, the fatty outer skin of the pig, produced a rich pot liquor in which to sop corn bread or biscuits. Families used the pot liquor as an all-around curative for anemia and coughs.

Lebanon and Syria, both influenced by Ottoman Turk cookery, valued pulses and bulgur, or cracked wheat. In India, sweets made of chickpeas or lentils, seeds, and dairy products produced *halva,* a dense confection suited to hospitality and dinner parties. In Iran, sour pulse soups got their savor from herbs. In Britain and Luxembourg, ham and pea soup bolstered limited menus during the rationing of World War II.

In World Kitchens

Pulses retain their importance to contemporary global cookery. In sub-Saharan Africa, the collection of pigeon peas and winged beans in the wild provides both porridge material and green pods as a vegetable. Less dependable, the adzuki bean grows slowly and withers from frost. Intercropped with rice, rapeseed, or millet, legumes offer sources of plant oil and meat substitutes and pair well with rice and with buckwheat and teff flour pancakes.

The chickpea and split pea, two affordable pulses in Eritrea, Ethiopia, and Sudan, contain less protein than other legumes but suit infant and invalid needs for their digestibility, especially in mush. Unlike the poor of Bangladesh, consumers in Kenya, Malawi, Tanzania, Uganda, and Zimbabwe rarely incorporate the chickpea in their native cuisine. In India, chickpea snacks satisfy while bolstering nutrition. In central and western India, the drought-resistant moth bean generates sweet sprouts for salad and pairs well with pearl millet and sorghum.

Pulses, such as the lima bean of Madagascar and the United States and the tepary bean grown in Mexico, make excellent meal extenders. Growers produce dense populations, especially in the case of pole beans, sugar snap peas, and climbing scarlet runner beans. Legumes also store well as mature seeds and ward off weevils. Most species suit varied recipes, such as the mix of mung beans or soybeans with foxtail millet or noodles in China. Southeast Asians add soybean sprouts, both fresh and fermented, to salads and sell their crops commercially for the production of soy cheese, curd, milk, sauce, and tofu.

Cooks in the Caribbean prefer legumes in the immature stage, particularly haricot verts and pickled pigeon peas. In Bulgaria and other parts of southeastern Europe, broad beans, dumplings, and cabbage accompany poultry and pork. To facilitate the breakdown in the stomach of the outer legume coat, cooks parboil and rinse or add a pinch of baking soda to the boiling water.

Legumes provide valuable sustenance to the marginally arable fringe of the Sahara Desert. In Botswana, Burkina Faso, Mali, and Nigeria, the Bambara groundnut boosts crop income for smallholders because of its stable price in farmer's markets. Nutritionists with the International Bambara Groundnut Network have hopes of exploiting the peanut as a canned staple and a rescue food for "hungry times."

See also: Agriculture; Cereal; Italian Diet and Cuisine; Roman Diet and Cuisine, Ancient; Sicilian Diet and Cuisine.

Further Reading
Albala, Ken. *Beans: A History.* New York: Berg, 2007.
Board on Science and Technology for International Development, National Research Council. *Lost Crops of Africa.* Vol. 2, *Vegetables.* Washington, DC: National Academy Press, 2006.
Dalby, Andrew. *Food in the Ancient World from A to Z.* London: Routledge, 2003.
Prance, Ghillean T., and Mark Nesbitt. *The Cultural History of Plants.* New York: Taylor & Francis, 2005.
Shurtleff, William, and Akiko Aoyagi. *History of Soybeans and Soyfoods in Canada (1831–2010).* Lafayette, CA: Soyinfo Center, 2010.

Randolph, Mary (1762–1828)

Renowned author Mary "Molly" Randolph compiled America's first cookbook, a guide to enhance regional Tidewater cuisine called *The Virginia House-Wife* (1824).

Born to Anne Cary and Thomas Mann Randolph on August 9, 1762, Randolph grew up on the plantation of her maternal grandparents at Ampthill, Virginia. In addition to tutoring, she learned household skills, including the supervision of food preservation and slaves. After marrying a cousin, David Meade Randolph, at age 18, she settled on the James River on a 750-acre (300-hectare) plantation at Presque Isle, northeast of Hopewell, and reared their nine children.

Randolph's eclectic sources illustrate the evolving nature of regional cuisine. She drew heavily on Englishwoman Maria Rundell's *New System of Domestic Cookery* (1807). In her own education, Randolph came in contact with French-educated chefs at Monticello, home of her kinsman Thomas Jefferson. She seemed unaware that "gazpacho" was Spanish, "dough-nuts" were German, clotted cream came from England, polenta originated in Italy, and eggplant and field peas derived from the diet of black slaves.

After a move to Richmond, Randolph acquired a reputation for cookery and entertaining prestigious families. In 1800, the family lost its position in society after President Thomas Jefferson fired David Randolph from his post as federal marshal. Mary Randolph opened a genteel boardinghouse, which admirers dubbed "the Queen." In retirement in Washington, D.C., she collected housekeeping advice and recipes in *The Virginia House-Wife; or, Methodical Cook,* a concise review of unfussy colonial and postcolonial tastes.

Randolph's collection featured the Southern specialties that anchored regional cuisine. Her list included the first published mention of "gumbs" (later, "gumbo"). She recorded recipes for baked ham and roasted game, corn bread and hominy, sweet potato pudding, turnip greens with bacon, and hot breads and hush puppies, antebellum table fare based on local produce. She recommended cinnamon and brandy as flavorings and introduced macaroni and vanilla to Virginia cookery. The range of entrées included organ meats and eel, plus forcemeat, field peas, fried oysters, and rice waffles, the economical choices for straitened circumstances. She also outlined a method of hang-drying a calf stomach as a source of rennet.

Because Randolph supervised slave kitchen help, she made light of a half hour's beating of biscuits with a pestle. Her respect for side dishes appeared in recipes for Jerusalem artichokes and salsify and for "Tomatoe & Ochre Soup," a dish with West African origins that emerged in the Caribbean as callaloo. For dessert, she favored puddings and fritters as well as cold creams and jellies. Her dessert collection was the first American anthology to feature ice cream and sherbet. True to her sense of order, she concluded sections on pickling and cordials with directions for making soap and starch along with silver polish and stove blacking.

See also: Cookbooks; Ice Cream; Ketchup.

Further Reading

Fowler, Damon Lee. *Classical Southern Cooking.* Layton, UT: Gibbs Smith, 2008.

Harris, Jessica B. *High on the Hog: A Culinary Journey from Africa to America.* New York: Bloomsbury, 2011.

Hess, John L., and Karen Hess. *The Taste of America.* Urbana: University of Illinois Press, 2000.

Tucker, Susan. *New Orleans Cuisine: Fourteen Signature Dishes and Their Histories.* Foreword by S. Frederick Starr. Jackson: University Press of Mississippi, 2009.

Rationing

The allotment of foods during wars and national emergencies is a pattern that has affected much of culinary history and human diet. Systematized rationing reached new levels during the global conflicts of the twentieth century.

World War I

In January 1915, six months into World War I, Germany's Bread Supply Office began rationing baked goods in Berlin. The stress of making the system work fell on bakers, who kept flour inventories for government perusal. Throughout tenements and bakeshops, where people spent 12 percent of their income, commerce via paper coupons distributed weekly compromised social harmony and consumer cooperation.

Theft of ration cards from food commission offices increased during winter 1916–1917. To enforce codes and restrictions, officials raised fines and jail sentences and guarded coupons as though they were cash. Retaliation against black marketers alienated consumers, primarily women. Shortfalls seriously undermined the war effort as Germans began to think like hungry individuals rather than as patriots. Some acquired permanent digestive ills ranging from dyspepsia to ulcers.

The home kitchen became a battleground as women helped noncombatants endure by wise provisioning and skilled cookery adapted to the nation's needs. From 1914 to 1918, some 200 wartime cookbooks from various associations aided German and Austrian women in their work. Compiled by food writers and domestic science teachers, they bore similar titles—Hedwig Heyl's *Little Wartime Cookbook* (1914), Anna Larisch's *160 Recipes for Wartime* (1915), Josephine Nagel's *The New War-Cook* (ca. 1915), Maria Schneider's *The Rhineland Cook in Wartime* (1915), Louise Holle's *Practical War Cookbook* (1916), and Mary Hahn's *War Cookbook* (1916).

These works bore statements intended to alter cultural foodways to suit the supplies at hand. Women learned to substitute turnips for meat and to enhance menus with more skim milk and cereals, especially barley, buckwheat, corn, groats (hulled grains), millet, and oats. To keep children from starving, families made the most of butcher bones and black bread and extracted personal favors from neighborhood grocers where possible. Even older consumers and the disabled stood in breadlines stretching for miles. Shoppers besieged bakeshops, where bakers cut wheat flour with barley, oats, and rye to stretch supplies. Food riots were common, but strictly censored mail kept the news from men at the front.

At the war's outbreak, the German Navy inflicted a submarine blockade on Britain, an island dependent on imports. During winter 1916, U-boats destroyed convoys carrying 300,000 tons (270,000 metric tons) of food per month. By March 1916, the total rose to 507,000 tons (460,000 metric tons). British families suffered from shortages of meat, potatoes, and sugar. To survive, Britain upped food production, succeeding at its maximum wheat harvest. By winter 1917, however, fear gripped Britons and fueled panic buying and hoarding. In January 1918, the Ministry of Food reduced consumption by rationing sugar, followed by fresh meat.

In the United States, the American Dietetic Association got its start in 1917 in part from the need for food conservation. To ensure economy in hospital kitchens, staff and student nurses weighed each day's garbage and adjusted portions to reduce waste. Nutritionist Mary Swartz Rose, deputy director of New York's Bureau of Food Conservation and the author of *Everyday Foods in Wartime* (1918), informed homemakers how to economize on pantry supplies. The U.S. Food Administration legiti-

mized domestic science as part of the chain of command enforcing stern measures. Government spokesman Herbert Hoover expressed his enthusiasm for thrift in the slogan "Food Will Win the War!"

World War II

Preceding World War II, German officials encouraged housewives to save on food and charcoal and to cook one-dish meals. To even out goods in short supply, the food commission rationed fats, meat, and sugar. In September 1939, the bureaucracy distributed to each civilian monthly perforated ration cards to separate at the time of purchase. Only those with physically demanding jobs received extra compensation. For a decade, potatoes and root vegetables were available but butter, chocolates, and whipped cream were unthinkable indulgences. When imports dwindled, cooks served roasted grain beverages in place of coffee. Cafés had no bananas or Coca-Cola to sell.

As Nazism increased persecution in Warsaw in 1939, anti-Semitic Poles burned ghetto markets, which laws had closed. Farmers grew anxious to sell perishables. Against the tide of hatred that limited Jewish commerce, vendors took their goods to the streets. Jewish housewives crowded into outdoor stalls to buy supplies threatened by increasing anti-Semitic sentiment. By 1942, the situation had declined to desperation for the hungry. Firing squads executed food vendors who sold illegally to Jews.

Facing more dire situations were the thousands of displaced persons and camp internees. In September 1941, memoirist Esther Rudomin Hautzig, at age nine, endured the hardships of a deportee living in a prison commune on the Russian steppes far from her home in Vilna, Poland. In a memoir, *The Endlesse Steppe* (1968), she recalled the early arrival of cold weather and desolation at the distribution of bread and a small allotment of *brinza,* a sheep cheese stored in barrels of saltwater. Because deportation had begun after the planting season, the family had vegetable stores. To supplement the meager allotment, she gleaned tiny green potatoes that growers had left behind.

When the siege reached its height in April 1943, a dearth of staples limited home cooking. The rich hoarded goods, but poor families lacked the cash to stock up for hard times. Housewives cooked unpeeled root vegetables to preserve every scrap of nourishment. Eventually, shoppers found no food for sale. Temporarily, Nazis distributed free bread. Relatives sent food parcels through the mail, which post office workers pilfered.

Throughout Europe, homemakers, professional cooks, and the military mess hall scrimped on nutrition. Of shortages and hunger, Soviet Premier Nikita Khrushchev declared that the Russian army would have gone hungry if it had not been for Spam, a canned chopped-meat product requiring no refrigeration. The J.C. Hormel Company in Minnesota had begun exporting Spam in 1937 under an acronym for "shoulder of pork and ham."

In Japan, desperate shoppers joined queues without knowing what they were waiting for. While taxation rose 150 percent to diminish citizen spending power, normal consumption of rice dropped by one-quarter. A distribution system monitored the quotas on farms. To prevent neighborhood dissension, individuals said little about grocery purchases. Those with food boiled it rather than broiling it, to keep aromas within the kitchen. The government control of rice remained in effect until 1995.

In England, officials assigned 40,000 conscientious objectors to work in agriculture and launched Food Defence Plans to protect warehouses and bond stores against bombing. Staff issued ration books color-coded by the receiver's age and required consumers to register with a grocer. To increase social cohesion and quell panic, posters urged "Serve to Save" and "Your Country Needs You." In addition to promotion of food distribution, families surrendered pots and pans for recycling as munitions.

For more than 14 years, from January 1940 to July 1954, British cooks learned methods of replacing in recipes such ingredients as bacon, bananas, canned fish, cheese, eggs, grapes, ham, jam, lemons, onions, pepper, and sugar and of feeding their households on whatever the market provided. They subsisted on a seriously restricted weekly allotment:

- One egg
- 2 ounces of tea
- 4 ounces each of bacon, ham, and butter
- 3 pints of canned milk
- 8 ounces of jam, marmalade, syrup, or treacle
- 8 ounces of cheese, which shrank to 1 ounce by May 1941
- 12 ounces of sugar, cut to 8 ounces after Christmas 1940
- 16 ounces of other meat

A complicated point system supervised the sale of biscuits, canned goods, dried fruit, jam, and rice, but butcher shops could sell unrestricted amounts of bones, sausage, and offal, consisting of brains, gizzards, hearts, kidneys, and livers. Hunters and trappers supplemented kitchen stocks with rook (crow) and squirrel.

Beginning in 1940, Frederick James Woolton of Liverpool, the Bitish minister of food, forced farmers to slaughter dairy herds to free pastures for growing grain and vegetables. The move produced an immediate milk shortage. Advertisements lauded high-energy foods and protective substances, especially oatmeal and cod liver oil. The ministry organized Kitchen Front exhibitions at

Harrods department store and investigated bartering and black market systems. For those sellers who violated regulations, the ministry confiscated goods and fined them £100 or sentenced them to three months in prison.

The ministry created a meatless recipe dubbed Woolton pie, an unappetizing pastry consisting of carrots, onions, cauliflower, and swedes (rutabagas) baked in a crust and topped with mashed potatoes. Staff also pushed carrot marmalade, toffee carrots, and carrolade, a nourishing beverage made from carrot and swede juice. The military experimented with high-carotene carrots and synthetic carotene to rid pilots of night blindness. Producers of margarine bolstered its questionable nutrition with artificial vitamins A and D.

Shortages and Substitutions

The spread of combat throughout Europe created shortages in coconut and olive oil, sage from Greece and Yugoslavia, French thyme, Hungarian paprika, saffron from Spain, and, in the last two years of World War II, Indian peppercorns. An advanced form of dehydration—producing what *Popular Mechanics* touted as "mummy food"—helped simplify food packaging and distribution by removing water to make the stock lighter and easier to pack in duffel bags. In *House Beautiful*, Clementine Paddleford's "What War Has Done to Life in the Kitchen" declared that egg yolk, fruit, milk, soup, and entire dinners came to the kitchen dried. With the era's forced cheer, she quipped, "Slip the grocery assortment in your pocketbook and be your own delivery boy."

Families began making substitutions—sunflower and corn oil for olive oil and butter and corn syrup, honey, and molasses for sugar. Jews and Muslims traded bacon and meat allotments for more cheese and vegetable oil. Clarence Birdseye, inventor of frozen foods, suggested the replacement of scarce livestock meats with lynx, muskrat, prairie dog, seal, and squirrel. To ensure adequate intake of vitamins and minerals, a spokesperson for Women in National Service urged homemakers in the October 1943 issue of *Ladies' Home Journal* to bake with enriched or whole-wheat flour. A simpler end avoidance of rationing was the purchase of store-bought breads, cakes, and pastries.

The Royal Horticultural Society publication *The Vegetable Garden Displayed* (1941) and Constance Spry's *Come into the Garden, Cook* (1942) recorded "Dig for Victory" efforts to replant lawns and rose beds with kitchen gardens. Food writers based their recipes on make-do—salmon custard, baked pig's cheek, tripe and onions, and desserts improvised from prunes and rice. In Ireland, cooks baked soda bread and mashed parsnips with bananas and pineapples for flavoring. Leaflets urged heating only enough water necessary for tea and using oven heat and steam to cook several dishes at one time.

Aiding British civilians from 1942 into the postwar period, Marguerite Patten, a food consultant for the

Ministry of Food, broadcast five-minute radio segments of "The Kitchen Front." To help a nation of meat eaters adapt, she informed struggling consumers on stretching limited supplies, such as tuna, whale meat paté, mock crab made from sour milk, and an oily barracuda called "snoek." She helped the average cook incorporate brown bananas, fatty-tasting corned beef from Argentina and New Zealand, pilchards and Canadian salmon, and powdered eggs.

The worst times were the dead of winter, when grocers had less produce available to tempt consumers and when school lunchroom staff was reduced to frying Spam fritters. Patten created such inventive recipes as pease pudding, faggots (offal meatballs), and gingerbread with applesauce to relieve tedium, one of the psychological factors that worsened during German aerial attacks.

The tightening of belts bolstered the nation's health, in part because rationing equalized food supplies for the rich and poor. Families refined their menus with the brown Hovis loaf, husk bread, and the national loaf, a calcium-fortified whole-grain bread that replaced white bread.

Pregnant and nursing women drank a pint of milk a day. Nursing mothers and young children received oranges and orange juice, milk, and cod liver oil. In lieu of tea, older children got high-energy fruit juice, dried fruit, and chocolate. Preschoolers devoured a pound of oranges per week as well as rose hip syrup. Cartoon characters Dr. Carrot and Potato Pete encouraged the eating of healthful home meals; school lunches centered on vegetable pie and the Oslo meal, salad with bread, cheese, and milk. As a result, children flourished under a more balanced diet that reduced fat and sugar.

American Rationing

After the United States entered the fighting in December 1941, supporting the war effort formed a turning point in American diet. Worse than the privations of the Civil War, which afflicted people unevenly, the rationing and limited selection of foods during World War II affected all lives, particularly the stay-at-home mom, emblem of home and sanctity. While noncombatants reduced their consumption of meat to 125 pounds (57 kilograms) annually, soldiers increased theirs to 360 pounds (163 kilograms) and returned home heavier.

To maintain military supplies, the U.S. government restricted most commodities at some time and issued "Basic 7 Food Group" and "Recommended Daily Allowance" charts. An executive order from President Franklin D. Roosevelt in August 1941 established an emergency allotment board, the Office of Price Administration (OPA), which registered a half million dealers and 150 million consumers.

The wartime bureaucracy slowed the sugar trade in April 1942, forcing movie concessionaires to abandon candy and cola in favor of popcorn. In May, authorities

issued ration stamps in paper booklets to every citizen with the promise of "your fair share of goods made scarce by war." Immediately, families began hoarding. An underground enterprise stockpiled goods for black market sale.

In September 1942, the Food Requirements Committee initiated the assistance of women's magazines to circumvent unfair and illicit practices. *Women's Day* helped cooks alter their habits to conform to dwindling supplies. In a call for fair play, the October 1943 issue of *Ladies' Home Journal* published "Let's Face the Facts about Food," charging that buying rationed groceries from black marketeers was "like sniping our fighting men from behind." The Crosley Refrigerator Company advertised its patriotism in the February 12, 1944, issue of the *Saturday Evening Post* with an upbeat slogan: "Planning meals is the way *I* can fight."

To give sidelined noncombatants a positive role, the Office of War Information urged women to garden and preserve food and to pay legal prices and ration stamps for groceries. The University of California ranked spinach as the top crop for efficiency and nutrition, followed by carrots and onions. The slowest-growing and least productive included asparagus, watermelon, and lima beans. Cities supported home produce by rescinding anti-livestock ordinances and urging the sharing of eggs and rabbits. Families raised 40 percent of all vegetables and canned 4.1 billion jars of food, yet one-quarter of Americans experienced hunger.

Anthropologist Margaret Mead headed the Committee on Food Habits (CFH) to promote family nutrition without undue coercion or limitation. Committeeman Kurt Lewin, a noted psychologist, created methods of dispensing canned milk to children and enticing them to eat unappealing organ meats and soybeans. To lessen the insult of orders from pompous, faceless nutritionists, the CFH instituted a block plan to distribute meal-planning advice through neighborhood volunteers.

Cookbook authors made their pitch to the beleaguered homemaker. Witty food writer M.F.K. Fisher suggested ways of cooking unfamiliar parts of animals in *How to Cook a Wolf* (1942), which included a goulash of ground meat and vegetables she called "Sludge." An upbeat pamphlet from Betty Crocker called *Your Share* (1943) outlined the hobo party, a bandanna dinner served around an empty stew kettle placed over red paper flames for "roughing it" ambience. Lotta Jean Bogert's *Good Nutrition for Everybody* (1942) called wartime exigencies a time to bolster family health and happiness through efficiency and nutrition. Marjorie Mills introduced *Cooking on a Ration: Food Is Still Fun* (1943) with an assurance that cooks could continue making nourishing meals while promoting cheer and neighborliness. Susan B. Anthony II published a meatier challenge in *Out of the Kitchen—Into the War: Women's Winning Role in the Nation's Drama* (1943). The American people, who were used to a high standard of living, struggled to control kitchen excesses.

As the war advanced into the Pacific, rationing intensified. To ensure a fair share, one by one, the government added coffee, canned goods, meat, cheese and dairy products, and fish to stamp books. The added paperwork annoyed local grocers and butchers, who had to account for commodity inventories and dispersal. As wheat supplies dried up, ice cream vendors improvised a new cone-making flour from crushed, sweetened popcorn.

In 1944, singer Kate Smith praised the women who obeyed the law by canning vegetables from some 20 million Victory Gardens. George Burns and Gracie Allen's radio program lauded the housekeepers who removed tops and bottoms of tin cans, soaked off the labels, and flattened the cans. Public-spirited groups held scrap metal drives and garnered bacon grease, meat drippings, and skillet fat to make glycerine for explosives.

Part of the acceptance of frozen goods derived from wartime exigencies and labor shortages. Female defense plant workers, romanticized as Rosie the Riveter, had less time to cook from scratch. At the same time, the government rationed canned goods to reserve tin for military use.

For Japanese Americans, forcible evacuation from their homes into internment camps meant a severe disruption in ethnic diet and family-style eating. In a poignant memoir of her family's sufferings, writer Jeanne Wakatsuki Houston joined husband James D. Houston in writing *Farewell to Manzanar* (1973) three decades after her family lost everything during a miserable incarceration. The 1976 film version contrasted prewar eating at home in Ocean Park, California, with the mess hall at Manzanar, a tar paper concentration camp near Death Valley.

After the Japanese surrender in August 1945, the OPA rescinded rationing, ending controls on meat and butter on November 23, 1945. More welcome was the end of rice distribution centers, to which housewives carried backpack baskets woven tightly and frequently inspected for holes to assure the safety of each grain. Only sugar restrictions remained in effect until June 1947. The end of hard times brought a hunger for expansive cookery and varied flavors.

See also: Corn and Maize; Honey; Israeli Diet and Cuisine; Kebabs; Russian Diet and Cuisine.

Further Reading

Aoyama, Tomoko. *Reading Food in Modern Japanese Literature.* Honolulu: University of Hawaii Press, 2008.

Deutsch, Tracey. *Building a Housewife's Paradise: Gender, Politics, and American Grocery Stores in the Twentieth Century.* Chapel Hill: University of North Carolina Press, 2010.

Hayes, Joanne Lamb. *Grandma's Wartime Baking Book: World War II and the Way We Baked.* New York: St. Martin's, 2003.

Mudry, Jessica J. *Measured Meals: Nutrition in America.* Albany: State University of New York Press, 2009.

Zweiniger-Bargielowska, Ina. *Austerity in Britain: Rationing, Controls, and Consumption, 1939–1955.* Oxford, UK: Oxford University Press, 2000.

Raw Cuisine

Raw foodism, or rawism, allows the consumption of only unheated foods, primarily beans, grains, fruits, nut pastes and seeds, plant oils, land and sea vegetables, juices, and fermented or uncooked meats. The focus of eating so-called living food is the preservation of digestive enzymes and nutrients, which high temperatures denature and destroy. Stressing organic produce and unprocessed ingredients, raw food advocates eat sensual, uncomplicated dishes comprising dried and fresh fruits, legumes, nut patties, olives, sea salt, seeds, and unfiltered honey.

Uncooked meals satisfy rawists with aroma, flavor, and mouthfeel. Their selection of vegetables includes blended energy drinks, dulce and kelp, high-protein pumpkin seeds, and sprouts. In place of processed chocolate and sugary sweets, they flavor raw dark chocolate pie with agave syrup, a natural nectar extruded from cactus, and sundaes made with raw ice cream and Thai coconut.

According to legend, from 130 to 27 B.C.E., fasting and raw foodism influenced the Nazorean Essenes, the ascetic authors of the Dead Sea Scrolls who retreated to a compound at Wadi Qumran, the desert frontier near Jericho. Historically, uncooked cuisine came naturally to polar peoples, for example, the Inuit of North America or the Nenet of Siberia. In addition to berries and the seaweed and vegetation retrieved from bird stomachs, polar residents eat organ and muscle meat raw because of their lack of burnables for cook fires.

Another culture that consumes a raw diet, the Hunza of northern Afghanistan and Pakistan, produces many centenarians. Researchers credit longevity to a vigorous lifestyle and the eating of almonds, pome fruit, mulberries, onions, pomegranates, pulses, raw goat's milk, and wild plums washed down with melted snow. The contemporary holistic physician and nutritionist Gabriel Cousens refers to the action of such living foods as "youthing," the shedding of dying cells and toxins and the growth of healthy blood cells and energized tissue.

Raw cuisine research began late in the nineteenth century. In 1897, a Swiss physician named Maximilian Oskar Bircher-Benner introduced raw foodism at a Zurich sanatorium, the Bircher-Benner Clinic. In 1905, he formulated a dietetic theory of well-being through consumption of uncooked foods. In the early 1900s, Scots nutritionist Norman Wardhaugh Walker, the "Father of the Raw Food Movement" and inventor of a juicer, taught a form of rawism he called "vibrant health." Among the foods he banned were bread, pasta, rice, and sugar.

In 1936, holistic dentist Weston Andrew Price of Newburgh, Ontario, examined the teeth of the first generation of pasteurized milk drinkers. After studying the mouths of aborigines in Africa, Australia, Europe, North America, and Polynesia, he concluded that indigenous diets produced stronger jaws. In older people who lived closer to nature, he observed less malocclusion and fewer dental caries because their intake was richer in raw nutrients.

More recent nutritional theories from the National Cancer Institute and the University of Toronto approve the raw food movement for boosting gut flora with bacteria beneficial to the immune system and for ridding the diet of dyes, fats, flavorings, preservatives, and stimulants, including alcohol, caffeine, and tannins. The high antioxidant count allegedly suppresses premature aging and breast, colon, and stomach cancer.

The documentary *The Beautiful Truth* (2008) corroborates the detoxification theories of German internist Max Gerson. In 1927, Gerson charged the modern diet with poisoning the body by reducing the digestibility of foods by polluting them with additives, alcohol, pesticides, and pharmaceuticals. Adherents to Gerson's theories have included actors Woody Harrelson and Demi Moore, couturier Donna Karan, and model Carol Alt.

Followers of a raw omnivorous regimen eat more than the stereotyped meal of greens and apples. Their intake of living foods ranges from alga, unpasteurized dairy foods, distilled water, fresh eggs, and sprouted lentils to fermented, seared, and uncooked fish and red meat, including carpaccio, ceviche, and sashimi. Proponents claim that the unheated ingredients in citrus salads, gazpacho, melon sorbet, muesli, nut butter, smoothies, sun-dried tomatoes, and sushi cleanse and rejuvenate the body, producing euphoria and a sense of wellness. For clearer skin, raw foodists rely on bee pollen and goji berries, two valuable antioxidants and appetite stimulants. For libido, they choose *maca* and *suma* roots and yerba maté (holly tea) flavored with stevia, a natural herbal sweetener.

Nutritionists disagree on the principles of eating uncanned, uncooked, unfrozen, unsmoked, and unradiated foods. Critics of rawism point to amenorrhea, childlessness, dental erosion, gastroenteritis, osteoporosis, underweight, and vitamin B12 deficiency as evidence of serious flaws in the diet. In 1997, California physician Steven Bratman, an expert on alternative medicine, coined the terms *orthorexia* and *orthorexia nervosa* to identify an eating disorder in people obsessed with health food regimens and righteous dieting.

See also: Cookware; Fructarianism; Huou; Japanese Diet and Cuisine; Kitchen Gardening; Symbolism, Food; Veganism.

Further Reading

Alt, Carol, and David Roth. *Eating in the Raw*. New York: Clarkson Potter, 2004.

Boutenko, Victoria. *12 Steps to Raw Foods: How to End Your Dependency on Cooked Food*. Berkeley, CA: North Atlantic, 2007.

Ferrara, Suzanne Alex. *The Raw Food Primer*. San Francisco: Council Oak, 2003.

Rose, Natalia. *The Raw Food Detox Diet*. New York: HarperCollins, 2006.

Russo, Ruthann. *The Raw Food Lifestyle: The Philosophy and Nutrition Behind Raw and Live Foods*. Berkeley, CA: North Atlantic, 2009.

Refrigeration

Technological advances in refrigeration replaced tedious brining, drying, fermentation, pickling, salting, and smoking with a method of preserving fresh goods without altering taste or texture. Prehistoric hunters stored fish and game in caves, pools of meltwater, snowbanks, springhouses, or underground caches. In India after 3000 B.C.E. and in Egypt and Persia from 2500 B.C.E., householders used evaporation from clay jars as a means of lowering the temperatures of cooked foods and wine.

The Nigerian pot-in-pot chiller, or *zeer* pot, required the lining of a porous outer container with damp sand and a covering of a ceramic lid or cloth. As fluid evaporated, the outer layer drew latent heat from the inner pot. The method reduced spoilage in eggplant and tomatoes, increased culinary quality and variety of carrots and okra, and gave growers a longer window of commercial profit from greens, meat, peppers, and sorghum.

Around 1175 B.C.E., Chinese storage methods required the harvesting of ice for long-term chilling. In Greece, Rome, and the Middle East, food preservers lined icehouses and storage pits with grass, logs, and straw before packing snow on the bottom and placing perishables on top. In 765 C.E., the Abbasid Caliph Muhammad ibn Mansur al-Mahdi turned snow into a means of chilling food during caravan transport over the Arabian Desert from Mecca to Baghdad. For a coolant, he collected snow for packing it around his goods.

Refrigerants remained primitive until the 1600s, when French chemists added saltpeter (sodium nitrate) to coolants to harden water into ice. The popularity of iced beverages and desserts supplied a new dimension to culinary service. World demand for chemical refrigerants gave Chilean and Peruvian shippers a source of profit in the food business.

The First Refrigerators

In 1748 at the University of Glasgow, Scots agronomist William Cullen experimented with the boiling of diethyl ether, which, when boiled, absorbed ambient heat, thus dropping the temperature. Cullen applied the concept to an artificial refrigerated environment, which he demonstrated to the public. The widely acknowledged father of refrigeration, Oliver Evans, an engineer from

Newport, Delaware, invented a refrigerator in 1805 by applying vapor compression to an enclosed space. As a pragmatic example of the value of technological chilling, German immigrants to North America introduced lager, a brew cooled during processing for year-round availability and consistency.

On August 14, 1834, mechanical engineer Jacob Perkins of Newburyport, Massachusetts, patented a refrigerator that cooled fluids and made ice by means of a crank-operated compressor. On May 6, 1851, physician John Gorrie of Apalachicola, Florida, actualized the theory of refrigeration into a commercial machine containing radiating coils to channel compressed gas. He mounted his device in patient rooms to cool the air, chill beverages, and help suppress fevers from tropical malaria and yellow fever. Two years later in Cleveland, Ohio, entrepreneur Alexander Catlin Twining patented commercial chillers that made 83 pounds (38 kilograms) of ice per hour.

Technology Advances

Advances altered the awkward early systems into dependable means of preserving foods. In Geelong, Australia, Scots inventor James Harrison applied the vapor-compression refrigeration concept at abattoirs, bakeries, breweries, confectioners, and pasta shops in the 1850s. He intended the device to boost Australia's advantage against the U.S. meatpacking monopoly by generating 275 pounds (125 kilograms) of ice per hour. The first delivery of chilled beef to England failed, thus confirming consumer skepticism about the edibility and purity of refrigerated meats.

With urban growth came a higher demand for fresh fruit, meat, milk, and vegetables, the beginnings of a nutritional revolution in industrialized countries. Geography no longer prevented Kansans from eating oysters or Quebec grocers from selling strawberries. In Moislains, France, in 1859, engineer Ferdinand Pierre Edouard Carré's ammonia-based absorbent refrigerant set a model of low temperatures for industrial chilling. His model produced 440 pounds (200 kilograms) of ice per hour. Carré demonstrated the device at the Universal London Exhibition in 1862 as the future of long-distance transport of frozen foods.

Ironically, refrigeration was becoming the norm in North America while ice remained a rarity in Europe. During the American Civil War, privateers met the South's need for ice by smuggling a Carré model through the coastal blockade to San Antonio, Texas, where food shipper Daniel Livingston Holden made clear ice from distilled water. Meanwhile, the English preferred their beer warm; European cooks continued to shop daily for fresh fish, grapes, meat, and salad makings. Italians demonized ice as a deterrent to appetite and gastric health. And the French suspected cold storage as a means of hiding deterioration in old stock.

By the late 1860s, rapid ice production simplified transport of berries, butter, milk, and seafood in refrigerated railcars, invented in Detroit by John B. Sutherland. The first shipload of frozen beef reached New Orleans from Texas in 1868 and appeared on the menu at the St. Charles Hotel. In 1870 at Samuel Liebmann's Sons Brewing Company in Brooklyn, New York, mechanical refrigeration turned yeast-fermentation brewing into a controllable science. A year later, Daniel Livingston Holden launched the first refrigerated abattoir at Fulton, Texas, the model of a technologically advanced industry.

Commercial refrigeration replaced reliance on polluted ice from ponds with a clean, year-round source of chilling and freezing. In 1873, the first rail shipment of Texas beef reached New York simultaneously with the opening of the nation's first ice plant at Jefferson, Texas. More commercial ice factories operated at Austin and San Antonio, Atlanta, Chicago, and Pittsburgh, reaching a total of 766 across the nation by 1900.

Simultaneously, during the 1890s gold rush in Coolgardie, Australia, contractor Arthur Patrick McCormick invented the Coolgardie safe, a primitive evaporation system. His chamber lowered temperatures from the placement of a hemp sack in a tray of water and the evaporation generated by breezes. The absorption of heat from cooling foods enabled outback campers to enjoy chilled perishables.

Industrial Refrigeration

By 1913, Frederick W. Wolf, Jr., a Chicago engineer, adapted a home icebox, the Domelre (*DOMestic ELectric REfrigerator*), to electric power. He sold the machine, with a flexible ice cube tray, for $900. Leading Chicago meatpackers—Armour, Cudahy, and Swift—adopted cold storage chilled by liquid air, a system that Carl von Linde devised in Munich, Germany, in 1895. The reliable cooling system replaced seasonal livestock shipping and slaughter with year-round production of higher-quality beef, a boon to butcher shops, grocers, hotels, and restaurants. Growers claimed territories—California grapes and lettuce, Florida orange juice, Georgia peaches, Idaho potatoes, North Carolina eggs and pork, Washington State cherries and red Delicious apples, Wisconsin cheese—by supporting rail distribution centers, which carried fresh goods throughout the Western Hemisphere.

In the 1920s, a vitamin craze elevated the value of freshness to eggs, fish, fruit, and meat, a principle ballyhooed in *Ladies' Home Journal* within months after the Spanish influenza scare. To replace toxic anhydrous ammonia, chloromethane, methyl chloride, methyl formate, propane, and sulfur dioxide, Frigidaire compounded Freon, a nonflammable, nontoxic synthetic chlorofluorocarbon (CFC), developed by chemical engineer Thomas Midgley, Jr., of Beaver Falls, Pennsylvania. The shift from dangerous refrigerants proved a selling point to the manufacture of home food coolers and freezers.

The first icebox dealers advertised wood cabinets lined with tin or zinc over layers of sawdust, seaweed, or wood shavings for insulation. A 1922 Kelvinator model contained an ice cube tray; the frost-free heating coil received a patent in 1927. The appliance industry quickly put delivery of ice out of business by mass-producing the ice-making system. Ice makers fought back by claiming to keep fruits crisp, meat moist, and vegetables packed with vitamins. Electric companies answered that ice rises and falls in temperature, keeping citrus fruit, cream, and melons in a state of flux. Aggressive appliance ads and complementary recipe booklets touted aspic and salad molds and a luncheon supply of capers, lettuce, pimiento, and olives as an inducement to children's finicky appetites.

At decade's end, with the American diet tilting from grain and red meat to dairy products, fruit, and green vegetables, Postum, the parent company of General Foods, began marketing quick-frozen cherries, fish fillets, meat, oysters, peas, and spinach. The manufacturer chose the cold brine method refined by Clarence Frank Birdseye of Gloucester, Massachusetts, in 1922 for freezing goods at the harvest site. With assistance from the Inuit, Birdseye applied ancient chilling methods to a portable subzero conveyor belt and packaging pressed between icy metal plates. Postum's marketing required the invention of a freezer cabinet to display frozen foods in grocery stores. In 1934, markets began stocking their freezer cases, which enabled housewives to buy fresher foods to keep on hand at home at temperatures from –18 to –35 degrees Fahrenheit (–28 to –37 degrees Celsius).

After World War II, rising home incomes and rural electrification increased business in home refrigerator-freezer models and in commercial refrigerators and ice plants that make dry ice and crushed ice for caterers and shippers. Refrigerators preserved fresh goods in bakeries, hospitals, inns, pubs, raw bars, restaurants, and soda fountains. In 1949, mechanic Frederick McKinley Jones mounted a chiller on the first refrigerated truck, a more direct transporter of such perishables as blueberries and scallops. The invention required a trailer insulated to sustain dry ice and ventilated to exhaust heat. The ease of delivering fresh produce to local markets or through the mail introduced consumers to world foods as delicate as acai berries and sashimi.

The 1950s confirmed the shift of American tastes toward frozen and refrigerated items. In Peoria, Illinois, in 1954, C.A. Swanson & Sons designer Gerry Thomas engineered the first TV meal, a covered, three-stage dinner for one. A year later, Campbell's Soup bought the Swanson line and augmented frozen inventory to 65 dinners. Two more purchases—Coca-Cola's acquisition of Minute Maid and the H.J. Heinz takeover of Ore-Ida—ensured the availability of popular breakfast juices and frozen french fries.

The discovery of CFCs, still commonly used as refrigerants, in the Earth's atmosphere in 1973 precipitated scientific study of potential damage to ozone in the stratosphere. In 1990, the investigation of an ozone hole over Antarctica increased concerns for the planet's protective mantle. An international treaty, the Montreal Protocol on Substances That Deplete the Ozone Layer, signed by 197 states on September 16, 2009, plans the phaseout of CFCs by 2015 and a recovery of the ozone layer by 2050.

See also: Asian Food Trade; Freeze-Drying; Ice; Marshall, Agnes; Rationing; Trade Routes.

Further Reading

Dincer, Ibrahim, and Mehmet Kanoglu. *Refrigeration Systems and Applications.* Hoboken, NJ: John Wiley & Sons, 2010.

Freidberg, Susanne. *Fresh: A Perishable History.* Cambridge, MA: Belknap Press, 2009.

Krasner-Khait, Barbara. "The Impact of Refrigeration." *History* 1:3 (February/March 2000): 41–44.

Regional Cuisine

Regional specialities—the paella of Majorca, black *mole* (sauce) of Oaxaca, corn smut and *nopales* (cactus paddles) of the Comanche and Hopi, noodle soups of Vietnam, and grasshopper and butterfly larva tacos among the Aztec of Mexico City—survive as a testimonial of cooking methods, local beliefs and customs, and the availability of regional foodstuffs. Supply settles practical matters of how and where to find staples, such as pineapple in Hawaii and pecans in the Carolinas. Patagonia, on the southern tip of South America, has access to Antarctic krill and king crab, two contributors to an ample seafood diet. Similarly, the availability of conch and rock lobster influences the seafood menus of the Caribbean much as mussels and sea pie dominate the restaurant offerings in Halifax, Nova Scotia.

Topography and religion impact the gastronomy of specific areas. In central Africa, rampant disease among herds prevents the consumption of milk and cookery with dairy products. Because Hindus revere the cow, regional Indian and Nepalese fare forbids beef dishes and focuses on vegetarian recipes. In contrast, the pastoral Masai of East Africa base their diet on meat, blood, and milk from their herds of cattle. They flavor baby food, beans, corn, and porridge with butter, an essential fat in their recipes.

Historic encounters between peoples alter agriculture and the demand for imported goods, such as cocoa and coconuts. Medieval trade between sub-Saharan Africa and southern Asia permeated age-old African meat dishes with vegetarian curry spices and rice. The two regional agricultures swapped the African mango for the Indian tamarind, generating new possibilities for traditional dishes on two continents.

Similarly, the Muslim conquest of North Africa during the eighth century C.E. introduced Algeria, Egypt, Libya, and Morocco to chickpeas, pilafs, and shish kebab. When Moors from Morocco pressed north into Iberia in 711, they added almonds, aniseed, coriander, eggplant, oranges, and rice to regional agriculture. These ingredients, tinged with Berber accents, boosted area cuisine to include savory and sweet cakes and nougats and the sharing of paella from a communal pot. On their expulsion from Granada in 1492, the Moors took with them an appreciation for fennel and lavender as flavorings and aromatics and the fresh ingredients of Andalusian pepper soup and balsamic vinegar.

After the melding of European and Asian commodities and recipes in the 1300s, long-distance shipping spread coffee and tea worldwide and familiarized global consumers with black pepper, cinnamon, curry, nutmeg, ginger, and turmeric. Christopher Columbus's expedition to the Caribbean in 1492 jolted world cookery with new regional ingredients, introducing the Irish to potatoes, Italians to corn, Spaniards to tomato sauce, and Thai to chili and peanuts. The vegetables regionalized in the sixteenth century added to area cuisine Irish colcannon, Italian polenta, Spanish gazpacho, and Thai chili-peanut dip.

By the early 1900s, with the advent of refrigeration, regional ingredients shipped by air, rail, steamer, or truck earned global respect—for example, the acai berries of Belize, Barbadian flying fish, Costa Rican chayote, durum wheat from Italy, Swedish lutefisk, and red snapper caught off Veracruz, Mexico. Samplings of traditional dishes created diversity in dining, engendering enthusiasm for Cantonese dim sum, English cider, German sauerbraten, Indian ghee (clarified butter) and naan (flatbread), Mongolian hot pots, and Thai spring rolls. Although consumers broadened their experience with unfamiliar aromas, flavors, and textures, their regional dishes continued to flourish as comfort food and ritual servings indigenous to their foodways.

See also: Local Food Movement; Mediterranean Diet and Cuisine; Randolph, Mary.

Further Reading

Civitello, Linda. *Cuisine and Culture: A History of Food and People.* 3rd ed. Hoboken, NJ: John Wiley & Sons, 2011.

Hjalager, Anne-Mette, and Greg Richards, eds. *Tourism and Gastronomy.* New York: Routledge, 2002.

Swislocki, Mark. *Culinary Nostalgia: Regional Food Culture and the Urban Experience in Shanghai.* Stanford, CA: Stanford University Press, 2009.

Religion and Food

From prehistory, acknowledgement of the powers of nature influenced the devout to propitiate deity with food offerings. Suppliants shared meals as a token of civility and piety, such as the communal dinners the Essenes consumed at Qumran (in today's West Bank). To worshippers, sacred food, an essential of most religions, represented sustenance from nature, a divine gift. At the pan-Hellenic presentation of *theoxenia* (god welcome) at Delphi, families spread whole meals before a divinity at a sacred table as models of wholehearted thanks to the guest god. To connect sustenance with celebration, groups reserved the suckling pig for Chinese weddings and served cabbage and brisket for St. Patrick's Day, kegs of beer for Polish holidays, lamb for Easter, pancakes for Shrove Tuesday, champagne for New Year's Eve, bitter herbs and roasted eggs for the Passover seder, pumpkins for Halloween, dates on Eid al-Fitr, turkey for Thanksgiving, and eggnog and fruitcake for Christmas.

From an ascetic perspective, the Buddhists and Jains of India originated food taboos to challenge Hinduism by pioneering vegetarianism, a cuisine "innocent" of animal slaughter. Sikhs perpetuated the assault on established foodways by proscribing alcohol and tobacco. Currently, Mormons carry asceticism to greater lengths by rejecting alcohol as well as stimulants, including coffee and tea.

In Western thought, food consumption reflected the status of human mores and behavior. The Greeks treasured myths of Dionysus, the god of wine, who wandered the earth in disguise and shared meals with the humble. Both Greeks and Romans worshipped Apollo, the god of light, with bean feasts, an homage to the procreative power of humble vegetables also found among Celts at Beltane, with a fertility rite held on May Day. Roman households paused after *cena,* the evening meal, and before dessert to offer salt, wheat, and wine on the altar of the *lares* (house gods) and *penates* (pantry deities). At the house of Pansa in Pompeii, a kitchen painting features images of a hare, a boa constrictor's head, game birds, a string of fish, loaves, and an onion, illustrations of standard food sacrifices. Similarly, the devout Hindu of India observed hearth protocols calling for the casting of portions of each dish into the cooking fire along with the recitation of prayers to the gods and ancestors.

Food and Earth Gifts

In the New World, the worship styles of first peoples manifested awe at the availability of foods in nature, particularly acorns, buffalo, corn, seals, and whales. In Mesoamerica, the Maya ground cacao beans with chili, cornmeal, and honey to make *xocolatl,* a chocolate drink sipped by the elite and presented as a ritual altar gift. The Lakota valued pemmican mixed with berries as a

A Russian Orthodox priest sprinkles Easter cakes and eggs with holy water at a city near Moscow. On Holy Saturday, the devout spread a ritual table with three meats representing the Trinity and eggs symbolizing rebirth. The meal lasts until Easter Monday. *(Ivan Sekretarev/Associated Press)*

communion dish for the Horn Society, a prestigious warrior brotherhood. For the Sun Dance, participants consumed boiled buffalo tongue. Before passing the sacred pipe at the All Smoking ceremony, participants thickened blood soup with cornmeal, a somber blending of animal with grain bestowed by the Earth Mother.

Typically, thanksgiving gifts take the form of first fruits, such as the raw foods presented to Polynesian gods at Bellona in the Marshall Islands and the luau in the Hawaiian Islands. Taking an inclusive approach to gratitude, the Greek Anthesteria festival dish *panspermia,* a midwinter supper of mixed seeds, represented the mystery of germination and the magic of human nourishment. In China, traditionally, each family honored the kitchen god at the hearth mantel, where they offered sweet cakes of sticky rice shaped like lotus root and taffy molded in the form of melons. The veneration of roots and seeds propitiated good luck in the coming months from above and below ground. In more complex altar offerings, processed food could be liquid, as in a cup of milk or vintage wine; or cooked or preserved dishes, such as cake, cheese, consecrated bread, preserved or salt meat;

or sweets, such as sticky rice cake stuffed with bean paste that the Vietnamese eat to celebrate Tet, a New Year's holiday. In North Carolina in 1727, Moravians at Salem held their first love feast, a gesture to fellowship. Women distributed simple servings of hot coffee and paper-thin spice cookies, a tradition still honored throughout the Piedmont. In the past half century, the Kwanzaa table has reverted to raw foods by displaying garden fruits and vegetables, a celebration of Swahili values that evolved in the 1960s during a pan-African movement.

More controversial ritual calls for animal sacrifice, a focal observance among Santerians with the beheading of goats and roosters. In Genesis, Abraham, the Hebrew patriarch, honored Yahweh by first preparing his son Isaac for child sacrifice, then accepting the gift of a ram, interpreted by Christian theologians as a foreshadowing of God's intervention in human sorrow through Jesus's sacrifice. The Aztec outraged conquistador Hernán de Cortés by blending the blood of sacrificial adults and children in sacramental drink and food, along with hearth ash and pulverized bones as tokens of human suffering. In Palestine, by burning gifts of grain, meat from an unblemished animal, and oil with incense, the devout propitiated the gods with smoke and pleasing aromas, which rose to heaven. A welcome altar meal might procure an earthly request, such as victory in battle, success in business, or forgiveness and salvation in the afterlife.

Holy Beverages

Holy drinks took on spiritual and emotional meaning after brewers turned simple liquid into ritual intoxicants, magical sources of spiritual cleansing and regeneration. Persian Zoroastrians and the devout of Aryan India elevated to godly elixir the beverage soma, a mysterious liquid that may have derived from the stalk of *Ephedra sinica,* a species of shrub. Soma makers pressed the juice and drank it fresh at ritual events honoring the god Indra, the Hindu lord of heaven. Much of the Rigveda (Praise Stanzas, ca. 1200 B.C.E.) lauded soma as a libation prepared to revere human and animal procreation. With parallel enthusiasm, Greek imbibers revered wine-generated giddiness as an internalization of the god Dionysus, a life giver whose worship inspired the drinkers of heady cupfuls to don masks, chant dithyrambs (hymns), and create drama. In like fashion, the Khanty, seminomadic reindeer herders of the Russian tundra, prayed to the invisible beings of their tepee before tossing a mug of vodka into the cookstove. The explosion of alcohol in the chamber communicated with animistic spirits of heavenly bodies, forests, rivers, trees, and animals.

In Japan, a sacred beverage evolved after the accidental fermentation of rice before 200 B.C.E. Sake became a religious icon and a cultural symbol of welcome and conviviality. Brewers created it primarily for the emperor's table and for monks and priests to use as gifts to the *kami* (nature gods), in street processions, and in rituals performed at Shinto temples and shrines. Although it became a secular drink manufactured for sale and trade during the early 1100s, rice wine retained its centrality in folk customs, especially weddings. Bride and groom drank sake from lacquered cups as symbols of unity and the home. In addition to supplying the family table with a staple cereal, rice initiated observance of two national thanksgivings, Kan-name-sai and Nii-name-sai.

Sacramental drinks carried a similar panache in the pre-Columbian Americas. According to Franciscan historian and ethnologist Bernardino de Sahagún's encyclopedia, the 12-book *Historia General de las Cosas de Nueva España* (*General History of the Things of New Spain,* 1540–1569), native Mexicans conducted ceremonial feedings of their pagan gods with tamales and a stew of dog or poultry. Alongside plates, they burned incense in clay containers and sang and drank *pulque,* the fermented sap of the maguey plant. The drink also honored their deities and poor relatives on All Saints' Day, a syncretic feast that Mesoamericans still observe from October 31 through November 2. Farther south, tribes along the Amazon as far west as the Andes Mountains cut alkaloid tendrils for boiling or pressing to obtain *ayahuasca* (spirit vine). A hallucinogen and vermifuge, ayahuasca empowered a native sacrament, particularly for coming-of-age rituals and vision ceremonies treating addiction and depression.

Sacred Cooking

Kitchen workers have traditionally worshipped deities connected with living plants and animals that comprised major sources of food, such as the Hopi and Mandan corn gods and the service of a holy broth made from clam stock and brown kelp to esteem the Korean mother after childbirth. From early times, the Inuit of Greenland and Baffin Island interrupted their chopping and cooking of seal and whale carcasses to sing and praise the spirits of nature. To ward off evil spirits, in China, Bai villagers tossed bread with coins baked inside from the roof and smeared cock's blood on a kitchen post. The placement of a crucifix in the kitchen of a Christian home or the "eye of God" over the kitchen door in a Turkish Islamic household indicates the cook's reliance on a supreme being to nurture and protect the family. To household deities of the Shinto faith, the Japanese made regular offerings at the *Kami-dana* (altar) of steamed rice and rice balls topped with diced lotus bulb and sesame seed and coated with bean paste. Shinto temples contained their own kitchens for the ritual preparation of sweetmeats and festival foods and for meals served to pilgrims.

In perversions of sacred cooking, some worshippers slaughtered nonbelievers, who died like animals sacrificed for the altar. Roasting was a diabolical battlefield punishment for Placidas, an apocryphal second-century C.E. Roman general and captain of the imperial guard. After Placidas and his wife Tatiana converted to Christianity in the time of the Emperor Trajan, he altered his name to Eustachius, and she took the baptismal name Theopista. At a victory celebration in 118 C.E. under Hadrian, Trajan's successor, the general refused to participate in a sacrifice to Rome's gods. When his troops retaliated, they confined Eustachius, Theopista, and their sons Agapius and Theopistus in a brass bull and cooked them alive. Although he became St. Eustace, the patron of hunters, artists depicted him with a cross, stag, and oven in token of his martyrdom.

The act of cooking took on holy overtones among the ancient Inca of Cuzco, Peru. The raising of domestic meat for religious use focused on dogs. After the Spanish conquest, mestizo chronicler Garcilaso de la Vega compiled *Comentarios Reales de los Incas* (*The Royal Commentaries of the Incas,* 1609–1617), which summarized native behaviors from an aboriginal point of view. He spoke of his people's rivals, the Huanca of the Xauxa River valley at Lima, who worshipped dogs, which native cooks raised, fattened, and sacrificed at ritual feasts. In the capital city, natives honored the sun god by burning food at the temple and pouring *chicha* (corn beer) into a holy fountain. The most sacred precinct in Cuzco, the House of Chosen Women, held huge corncribs from which the emperor drew food for holiday banquets. To supply the gods' kitchen, religious authorities selected eight girls aged 13 or 14 on the basis of beauty, health, and unspotted lineage to be invested as the "Brides of the Sun." Like the Vestal Virgins who kindled the sacred hearth fires of ancient Rome, the Peruvian maidens lived in houses of the elect at the shrine at Pachacámac and studied ritual and holy bread making under chosen women, stately, virginal matrons who had once been the sun's mates before becoming priestesses. As the girls excelled, some advanced from kitchen work to become royal brides or noble housekeepers.

Fasting and Feasting

Unlike atavistic religions, Christian philosophy tended toward exoneration for human weakness through asceticism. Although the church evolved no uniform core of fasting and diet, theologians advocated vegetarianism because of an aversion to the physical implications of meat, a product of animal coition and bloodletting. In the third century C.E., the polemicist Tertullian's *De Jejunio Adversus Psychicos* (*On Fasting*) enlarged on the gospel of Mark 9:29, in which Christ states that healing power derives from prayer and fasting. In the early seventh century, St. Isidore of Seville, the "schoolmaster of the Middle Ages," imbued abstention from the table with religiosity and morality by sanctifying the ritual fast as holy self-control. Basing his dietary philosophy on the four humors, he charged red meat consumption with goading the weak to carnal lust and lechery. From his exhortation, theologians devised calendars of fasting that called for abstinence from meat at Advent, Lent, Epiphany, and Pentecost. To preface the self-abnegation of 40 days of Lent, Christians invented Carnival, a sybaritic glutton fest heightened by carnality and merriment. Late in the era, the pious abstained from eggs and meat during the entire 40 days preceding Easter. The end of this prolonged fast culminated in a blessing of eggs on Good Saturday before Easter, the beginning of the custom of dyeing Easter eggs, a symbol of regenerated life.

For Christians, the holiest ritual, the Eucharist, generates intimacy with the almighty through participation in a sacrament mimicking Jesus's last supper with his disciples. The taking of communion involves a symbolic re-creation of Jesus's pre-crucifixion meal. The Christian Eucharist employed horn vessels until 785 C.E., when the Catholic Church forbade preparers to serve ceremonial wine in horn cups to accompany holy bread. King Aelfric clarified the order in 975 by specifying wood as a less pagan material for ritual chalices. After William the Conqueror took Britain from the Anglo-Saxons in 1066, Norman lords retained the early horn drinking vessels for ritual use and reengineered them with silver mounts and feet so they would stand on an altar. The quibble reig-

nited in 1071, when priests at Winchester determined that wood committed a sacrilege by absorbing wine, which, by the principle of transubstantiation, became the blood of Christ. King Richard I further muddied the issue in 1175 by demanding that only gold and silver should convey communion wine, thus placing a burden on poorer religious communities better able to supply their altars with horn or wood containers.

Variants of communion service invested different branches of Christianity, such as temperance fundamentalists, who substituted grape juice for wine, and holistic observers of Maundy Thursday, who passed whole loaves for each partaker to pinch off one bite. After the conquest of Mexico, Spanish priests supervised the planting of wheat to provide bread for the Eucharist. While their overlords raised wheat wafers for the priestly blessing, Mexica converts continued to celebrate communion with tortillas, a syncretic token of reverence to ancient corn deities. In May 1750, at a Greek Orthodox Eucharist in Anatolia, Swedish ethnobotanist Johan Hasselquist witnessed a bishop breaking small wheat cakes and distributing pieces mixed with wine in a common chalice before the ritual washing of feet. In the late 1800s, Protestants channeled discontent with orthodox strictures by replacing the communal chalice with individual cups.

Orthodox Food Service

Medieval issues of purity questioned the readiness of both body and spirit and influenced the thoughts, words, and prayers of the pious. In Syria, Muslim women set dinner tables only in the evenings, when families mingled with friends. To accommodate night dining, men closed shops and businesses early and offered portions to beggars in obedience to Islamic injunctions to succor the poor.

In Great Britain, on a long trek of the Celtic highlands and islands, anthologist Alexander Carmichael compiled Gaelic auguries, charms, hymns, incantations, omens, prayers, and table rituals for the *Carmina Gadelica* (*Gaelic Hymns,* 1900), which his family completed after his death. Among the verses, he included a humble Scottish runic chant, "The Blessing of the Kindling." As the fire maker bent to the daily domestic ritual, she felt herself in the presence of the angels Ariel and Uriel. In otherworldly company as she began meal preparation, she emptied her spirit of negatives and served God by lighting the hearth and asking God to kindle her heart with love. Celtic peasants looked upon fire as a divine miracle that warmed the body and cooked food. The fire became an emblem of need and reminded them that they, too, needed constant mental and physical nourishment.

Other parts of the world have established a tradition of reverence to the gods through home-cooked delicacies. In Soka, Bali, throughout the process of growing food for the table, farmers propitiated Dewi Sri, the rice goddess, with gifts of eggs, grain, palm leaves, and flowers raised alongside their fields. Among the Maya of Yucatán, into the mid-twentieth century, a Chachaac ceremony called for gifts of ground corn and squash seeds from housewives to Chaac, the rain god. At the altar, gourd bowls hung from an arch or lay on beds of *chimché* leaves. Men complemented the womanly offerings by making *zacá,* a sacred drink fermented from corn and water. Among fisherfolk in Kuzaki, on Enshu Bay east of Osaka, offerings of seafood required a special preparation of the abalone catch. One ancient rite called for the excision of the circular abalone muscle in an unbroken strip. The cook sun-dried the muscle, then divided it and tied it with rice straw for home use.

See also: Afterlife and Food; Charlemagne; Cussy, Louis, Marquis de; Halal; Holiday Dishes and Festival Foods; Ibn Battuta; Kosher Food; McDonald's; Medieval Diet and Cuisine; Peyote; Polo, Marco; Pork; Poultry; Shellfish; Sicilian Diet and Cuisine; Water; Yeast.

Further Reading

Anderson, Eugene N. *Everyone Eats: Understanding Food and Culture.* New York: New York University Press, 2005.

Méndez Montoya, Angel F. *Theology of Food: Eating and the Eucharist.* Malden, MA: Wiley-Blackwell, 2009.

Sack, Daniel. *Whitebread Protestants: Food and Religion in American Culture.* New York: Palgrave Macmillan, 2001.

Whinfrey-Koepping, Elizabeth. *Food, Friends and Funerals: On Lived Religion.* Berlin: Lit Verlag, 2008.

Restaurants

The popularity of restaurant cuisine generated a distinctive strain of commercial on-premises dining that paralleled the rise of the middle class.

Cookshops flourished from ancient times, including caravanserais (inns) from 1500 B.C.E. across the Fertile Crescent, the *thermopolia* (hot food counters) of Rome, and the street vendors of Aztec Mesoamerica. From 960 C.E., Chinese teahouses encouraged a pleasant atmosphere by providing patrons with dishes of finger food and pots of tea. In the 1300s, Chungking (Chongqing) hot pots lured Chinese diners to small cafés and street stalls for a one-dish meal. Kyoto's first restaurant, the Nakamura-ro, opened in the Gion District in 1575 with a short menu—egg miso and charcoal-broiled tofu.

In the late 1600s, caterers in England and France varied ingredients by plating a single option, salmagundi, an eye-catching arrangement of eggs, fish, greens, and meat topped with dressing and spices. Similarly limited in choices, the *table d'hôte* style of food service set a time and fixed menu, a benefit to travelers and to people who ate out daily.

In 1723, Simpson's Fish Dinner House, a famed London chophouse in Beil Alley, Cheapside, charged 2 shillings each for a dependable spread of cheese, mutton, oysters, partridge, and soup, served promptly at 1 P.M. following a brief table blessing. In view of the Thames,

patrons paid one price to sit communally at a long table, share platters and covered dishes, and sip punch for 1 shilling per glass. A less filling menu at the Caffè Florian in Piazza San Marco, Venice, which opened in 1720, offered finger food and pastries to accompany coffee and tea. An elegant setting for artists and writers, the restaurant drew the patronage of Giacomo Casanova, Charles Dickens, Robert Browning, Goethe, Gertrude Stein, Richard Wagner, and Lord Byron.

Eighteenth Century

In 1765 in the heart of Paris, wine dealer A. Boulanger served bouillon and *pot-au-feu* at the first Western restaurant, a business devoted entirely to full meals. He called his brasserie a *restaurant* (restoring), a distributor of *restoratifs,* hearty meat soups. After the collapse of the Bourbon dynasty during the French Revolution in 1789, the democratized nouveau riche sought refined commercial meals rather than hire cooks and servants for in-home cuisine. Historians refer to the fad for table service as *manie des dîners* (dinner mania), a public craze for quiet assignations and such romantic entrées for two as chateaubriand, a thick cut of tenderloin in a white wine sauce. Similar establishments in Berlin, London, and New York City catered to the elite with menus typically written in French and featuring set prices.

The vogue for dining out or hiring caterers inspired chef Marie-Antoine Carême's development of gourmet dishes, sauces, and pastries for restaurants in London, Paris, and Vienna. The first food critic, Alexandre Laurent Grimod de la Reynière, issued *L'Almanach des Gourmands* (*The Food Fancier's Almanac,* 1803–1812), a survey of Paris bistros and cuisine itineraries of the city's neighborhoods. Grimod's critiques highlighted the ethos of gastronomy. He celebrated the spectacle of food presentation and the drama of dining room conduct, from oyster appetizers to veal entrées and lark-filled pastries. In evaluating the standards of the Napoleonic era, he stressed the value of good cooking, which he praised in the kitchens of Le Gacque and Madame Véry.

Europe developed Anglo-Indian eateries that specialized in chutney and curry, imports from the British Empire. The spicy fare spread to English establishments in Antigua, Barbados, Guyana, Jamaica, Tobago, and Trinidad. In France, Monte Carlo, and Switzerland, Georges Auguste Escoffier, the "Father of Modern French Cuisine," built the reputation of haute cuisine and the notoriety of the celebrity chef. Contributing to the allure of grand entrées, upscale tableware and professional wait staff enhanced the diner's enjoyment of individualized service. In 1875, the first vegetarian restaurant opened in Leipzig, Germany, featuring meatless curry and ragout.

North American Venues

In North America, stagecoach stops and oyster houses offered the first restaurant business model. From 1762, the Fraunces Tavern on Pearl Street in New York City welcomed influential patriots, notably the Sons of Liberty, General George Washington, and officers of the Continental Army. Waves of immigration in Canada and the United States introduced consumers to inexpensive idiocuisine—Japanese udon, Jamaican jerk chicken, Czech sausage, Scandinavian pickled herring, Greek spinach pie, German stollen, and Mexican churros. Delis compromised on expensive restaurant ambience by offering tables for consumers selecting salads, cheeses, and cold cuts from the counter. Cafeterias emphasized tray service from a variety of dishes ladled from steam tables.

Coastal restaurants developed specialties—lobster and crab sandwiches in Nova Scotia, clam chowder in Maine, and salt-and-pepper flounder on the coastal Carolinas. Plains inns offered cider and prairie chicken as well as the most recent game. Frontier cooks broiled and fried buffalo steaks, roasted ribs, and baked the nose and tongue. In New Orleans's French Quarter, from 1840, Antoine's specialized in bouillabaisse and lobster bisque and originated Oysters Rockefeller; Galatoire's served oyster cocktails, Crab Ravigote, and foie gras, a reminder of the city's French roots.

In Manhattan's Madison Square, Charles Ranhofer, a French chef from Saint-Denis, popularized Delmonico's Restaurant. He incorporated artichokes, avocados, eggplant, and endive into an 11-page menu and created iced and dairy treats to satisfy the tastes of the Gilded Age. His menu offered vintage wines from a cellar holding 16,000 bottles. His two-volume book *The Epicurean* (1894) surveyed an era of fine dining on capon, thrush, pike, turtle, and young rabbit.

In 1849, Norman Asing opened Macao and Woosung, the nation's first Chinese restaurant, in San Francisco's Chinatown. At an all-you-can-eat buffet, police and politicians met to discuss the volatile atmosphere caused by the California gold rush and subsequent anti-Asian unrest. The city developed an eclectic mix of restaurants, including German, Italian, Japanese, and Spanish fare. California's *Overland Review* incorporated the restaurant introduction among political commentary and literary critiques.

Delmonico's steak house in New York City, seen here at its 1903 midtown location, opened in 1837. The namesake of the Delmonico steak, it claims to be "America's first fine dining restaurant" and the first eatery to offer an à la carte menu and wine list. *(Library of Congress)*

Travelers' Eateries

During the importation of Chinese laborers to build the transcontinental railroad in the mid-1800s, Cantonese dim sum eateries sprang up along the Union Pacific track from California to Missouri. In 1868, Pullman cars replicated restaurant table service with servings of caviar, filet mignon, and champagne; at Santa Fe Railroad stops, Frederick Henry Harvey opened a chain of road food eateries called Harvey Houses, which featured a breakfast of calf's liver, beef hash, mackerel, and trout. In 1898, North American exporters on the Pacific Coast shipped fresh beef from Kansas and Texas to Hawaii, Hong Kong, and the Philippines for serving at inns and restaurants, where demand boosted ranchers' profits. During World War I, when suppliers turned their attention to military needs, New York restaurants coped with beef shortages by replacing it with fish in appetizers and stews.

In imitation of rising restaurant standards, the Venice Simplon-Orient-Express added an upscale restaurant car offering petite vegetables in butter sauce, medallions of roast beef in *bordelaise* sauce, and a cheese tray. Cruise lines profited from à la carte dining of such exotica as prime game, champagne, and flambéed desserts. Into the mid-twentieth century, Michelin Guides awarded stars to the restaurants of luxury hotels catering to travelers and gourmands, such as the Majorcan tourist retreats featuring French *rôtis* and Spanish paello.

At the other end of the economic spectrum, post–World War I diners set up kitchens in recycled trolley cars, the source of Henry Perry's Kansas City barbecue and rib eatery, an early black-owned food business. A family-minded restaurant trade favored the Howard Johnson chain, which featured clam strips and HoJo's ice cream after its debut in 1928 in Quincy, Massachusetts. During the Great Depression, restaurant managers survived by abandoning pretentious French terms on menus—*au gratin, pamplemousse, fricassée, pomme de terre, potage, ragoût*—and by offering simpler soul food specials, such as chicken pot pie and black-eyed peas and ham hock.

The end of Prohibition in 1933 returned patrons to leisurely dining in restaurants serving cocktails and wine. Poorer consumers supported neighborhood alehouses and lunchrooms and, in 1936, the first drive-through, which opened in Glendale, California. In the late 1940s, fast-food diners and steakhouses threatened the profitability of chain and owner-operated restaurants. Convenience dining on burgers and pizza replaced the relaxed consumption of multicourse meals and the savoring of after-dinner wine and mixed drinks.

Healthful Food

The local food movement, an offshoot of faddish veganism, offered chefs a year-round supply of salad greens and summer vegetables from greenhouses, a boon to the menu of the Four Seasons, one of New York City's top-rated landmarks. The baroque offerings ranged from sturgeon and wild mallard to woodcock and suckling pig. Food writer Craig Claiborne promoted dining out in the late 1950s with the restaurant reviews he composed for *The New York Times*. Contributing to the resurgence of traditional Gallic fare and to the notoriety of chef Jacques Pepin, clientele at New York's La Côte Basque and Le Pavillon dined regally on mousse de sole, sweetbreads meunière, and jellied ham. Glamorous guests—Joseph P. Kennedy, the Duchess of Windsor, and Igor Stravinsky—tended to pose in mid-meal in photo sections of society pages.

In the same era as the epicurean delights at the Forum of the Twelve Caesars in New York City, the fusion cuisine of Tex-Mex restaurants of the 1960s ventured away from traditional Mesoamerican fare by adding fajitas, nachos, and low-calorie taco salads to menus. Into the 1970s, butter and cream returned to favor after food maven Julia Child's lectures, televised kitchen demonstrations, and books generated enthusiasm for fine French dining.

At the end of the Vietnam War, Asian family-style restaurants in large cities popularized sushi, chai tea, fish sauce, Korean barbecued ribs, and pad thai. The competition and health consciousness, along with publication of Morgan Spurlock's exposé *Super Size Me* (2004), forced restaurateurs to intersperse extensive veal and pork offerings with more healthful offerings, such as mahimahi and salmon. Menus coded choices with symbols for "heart healthy," "no trans fat," "organic," and "neo soul food," a rethinking of cholesterol-burdened dishes featuring pork fat. The appeal of lighter menus wooed more stay-at-homes into the commercial food marketplace.

Total U.S. expenditures on commercial dining topped $475 billion in 2005, when chefs vied for customers by advertising innovative dishes and a relaxed atmosphere. In 2009, citizens averaged five restaurant meals per week. Mall dining, which combined with movies and shopping to draw patrons, elevated Applebee's and other chains to a global phenomenon. As of 2010, Americans spent some 53 percent of their food budget on away-from-home food.

Currently, travel and tourism undergird the success of many bistros and restaurants worldwide. Evidence of the staying power of historical cuisine survives in Nakamura-ro, which has fed patrons in Kyoto, Japan, for nearly 450 years; Venice's Caffè Florian, still in business since 1720; and the Fraunces Tavern, a New York landmark where George Washington ate pub grub. Tony urban restaurants in Algiers, Brussels, Guangzhou, Lima, Montreal, Nairobi, and Washington, D.C., offer an artisanal mélange of chapati, *koushari,* miso soup, smoked or sun-dried fish and game, wild greens and berries as side dishes, and cappuccino and espresso with beignets.

By 2012, trends toward online reservations, gift cards, longer dining room hours, and curbside pickup had boosted the American dining trade despite flat consumer spending overall. Restaurants tend to modify innovation with niches for hamburgers, vegetable beef soup, and macaroni and cheese, standard comfort foods. Television demonstrations on the Food Network encourage cooks to imitate restaurant specialties with ingredients purchased locally or from online gourmet shops selling coffee and tea, herbs, spices, and specialty foods.

See also: Cooking Schools; Fusion Cuisine; Gourmet Cuisine; McDonald's; Nouvelle Cuisine; Prohibition; Salad and Salad Bars; Shellfish; Travel Food.

Further Reading

Denker, Joel. *The World on a Plate: A Tour Through the History of America's Ethnic Cuisine.* Lincoln: University of Nebraska Press, 2007.

Freedman, Paul H. *Food: The History of Taste.* Berkeley: University of California Press, 2007.

Hjalager, Anne-Mette, and Greg Richards, eds. *Tourism and Gastronomy.* New York: Routledge, 2002.

Spang, Rebecca L. *The Invention of the Restaurant.* Cambridge, MA: Harvard University Press, 2000.

Rice

For 20 percent of the world's population, traditional rice entrées, congees (gruel), condiments, sweets, pickles, popped snacks, tonics, vinegar, beer, and wine form much of the week's menus. A wild grain appealing to hunter-gatherers around 18,000 B.C.E., rice became Asia's first cultivated crop. For centuries, domesticated stands thrived at the edges of ponds and in paddies flooded 4 inches (10 centimeters) deep, beginning in the Yangtze River region of China in 9500 B.C.E. and in Vietnam after 9000 B.C.E. Varieties in southern China's "rice region" fed the residents of Guangdong, Hunan, Fujian, Jiangxi, and other provinces.

An aquatic people first sowed the grain from 5000 B.C.E. Cooks of the Hemudu and Majiabang cultures around Hangzhou Bay in China served the high-energy grain. Rice balanced nutrition and the textures of vegetables and the meat of frogs, deer, dogs, pigs, and stuffed fowl. Easily stored and digested, the grain absorbed the flavors and aromas of herbs and spices, thus promoting gastronomic innovation.

Japanese and Koreans contoured rice paddies from 3500 B.C.E.; Thai rice plantations existed as early as 3000 B.C.E., contemporaneous with tomb art in Thebes picturing rice husking in Egypt. Defying poor soil, nematodes, and difficult climate conditions, African "black rice" (*Oryza glaberrima*) covered fields of the upper Niger River valley from 1500 B.C.E. In India, rice entered scripture in the Sanskrit text Yajurveda (1400 B.C.E.) and centered birth and death rituals as evidence of the grain's significance to longevity.

For aboriginal North Americans, wild rice (*Zizania palustris*), a separate species from the predominant *Oryza sativa,* dated into prehistory as the famine food of the Great Lakes Ojibwa. Chinese varieties of wild rice once flourished around 1050 B.C.E. in the Yangtze River basin, Manchuria, Korea, Annam, and Malaya as a grain and a stem steamed like bamboo shoots for slicing into stir-fries.

Technology and Production

Iron tools and plow animals, introduced to rice cultivation after 722 B.C.E., eased the labor-intensive rice season. In the 500s B.C.E., hydraulic engineering through dikes and gates offered control of river and canal irrigation and precipitation runoff. In Sri Lanka after 540 B.C.E., Indio-Aryan farmers introduced dryland rice farming and centered their cuisine on their crops. Grain dealers exported surplus harvests from southern Asia to the outside world. The yield multiplied in southern China after Indian and Indochinese rice varieties added new cultivars suited to flooding and saline soil. In the lowlands, such natural hybrids as deep-water, drought-resistant, semidwarf, and upland cultivars increased varieties to 40,000.

Around 200 C.E., Chinese texts described the production and use of two types of grains, dry and sticky, by the laborious method of transplanting seedlings in mucky puddles. Quick-ripening hybrids and double cropping supported the dense urban populations that developed south of the Yangtze River after 1250, about the same time that the Moors cultivated African *glaberrima* in Iberia. To ensure a productive habitat, Chinese farmers rented ducks to devour insects and weeds.

During the Renaissance, rice traveled by voyagers to the Volga River valley, Yemen, Sicily, Majorca, and Lombardy and served as the foundation of sweet desserts mixed with egg custard and fruit. The Spanish introduced rice seed in the 1520s at Veracruz, Mexico, where chefs added the grains to fish and shrimp entrées. In 1562, Portuguese navigators bought *glaberrima* seed from Arabs and female traders in Sierra Leone and spread rice culture to the Maranhão plantations of Bahia, Brazil. Marketers sold their grain in Rio de Janeiro, where cooks developed rice salads and vegetarian dishes from combinations with onion and tomatoes.

North America produced its first *sativa* cultivar, Carolina White, in 1686 after Henry Woodward of Johns Island, South Carolina, experimented with a small planting that yielded the world's finest seed. In the late 1600s, enslaved Mandinka cultivators imported from rural Gambia, Guinea, and Senegal recipes for rice and beans. The combination influenced the coconut-flavored Costa Rican dish known as *gallo pinto* (spotted rooster) and the hoppin' John of coastal South Carolina, Georgia, and Louisiana Creole cuisine. Venezuelans turned the one-pot meal into their national dish.

Recipe: Hoppin' John

In a large pot, fry four strips of bacon; crumble after frying. To the bacon and fat, add three bay leaves, 2 teaspoons of red pepper flakes, and one each of chopped green pepper and onion. Add 1 quart of water, two smoked ham hocks, and 1/4 pound of dried black beans or black-eyed peas. Bring the mixture to a boil and simmer for one hour. Add 1 cup of brown or white rice, 1/4 teaspoon of cayenne pepper, and sea salt to taste. Simmer for 30 minutes. Serve with chowchow or piccalilli.

England's rice trade relied on the Carolina crop and imports from Bengal and Madras until 1852, when the British Empire annexed Burma and its fertile paddies. More cultivars diversified U.S. rice crops in 1890 and 1899 with the introduction of the Honduras and Japanese strains. The U.S. Department of Agriculture set up experimental crop improvement programs, which spread rice cultivation to Arkansas, Louisiana, Texas, and California. In the late 1930s, farmers in Florida, Missouri, and Mississippi added stations for monitoring gene segregation and recombination. Technology improved the pearling, or polishing, of grains to create an even white product.

Feeding the World

After World War II, China devoted 25 percent of its tilled land to rice, producing 20 times the harvest of the United States. India's Andhra Pradesh region, the nation's rice bowl, expended 77 percent of cropland on paddies. While Americans devoted 38 percent of their diet to cereals and legumes and 21 percent to eggs and meat, the intake of rural Chinese rose to 88 percent grain and only 3 percent eggs and meat. Residents of Fujian Province, with the best supplies of grain, ate rice at every meal; adult males consumed up to 485 pounds (220 kilograms) each per year. In India and Indonesia, the Green Revolution of the 1940s–1970s produced "miracle rice," a semidwarf cultivar that permits three annual plantings.

Today, 95 countries around the world produce rice. While consumption has been lapsing in Japan, it is burgeoning overall from exports of Madagascar's long- and large-grain rice, from increased harvests of glutinous rice from the Mekong River valley of Vietnam, and, outside Milan, Italy, from the traditional consumption of arborio varieties, the source of risotto dishes. Thai farmers hedge the ups and downs of commodities marketing by growing jasmine rice, a high-quality fragrant grain that earns twice the profits of ordinary species. Other markets in Hong Kong, North Africa, and the Pacific islands show potential for growth in the world's rice output.

The crossbreeding of rice seeds by the International Rice Research Institute in Indonesia, Nepal, the Philippines, and Southeast Asia aims at producing a perennial cultivar that can withstand blast fungus, drought, and flooding. Success in Guinea raised the annual yield by 30 percent, a boost to nutrition and a substantial shield against famine. Hopes for New Rice for Africa (NERICA) arise from agronomist Monty Jones's propagation of a hardy, high-protein seed from common *sativa* rice and African *glaberrima* rice.

See also: Amerindian Diet; Cantonese Diet and Cuisine; Irrigation; Japanese Diet and Cuisine; Persian Diet and Cuisine; Szechuan Diet and Cuisine.

Further Reading

Carney, Judith Ann. *Black Rice: The African Origins of Rice Cultivation in the Americas.* Cambridge, MA: Harvard University Press, 2001.
Schulze, Richard. *Carolina Gold Rice.* Charleston, SC: History, 2005.
Sharma, S.D., ed. *Rice: Origin, Antiquity, and History.* Enfield, NJ: Science, 2010.
Smith, C. Wayne, and Robert Henry Dilday, eds. *Rice: Origin, History, Technology, and Production.* Hoboken, NJ: John Wiley & Sons, 2003.

Roman Diet and Cuisine, Ancient

From its rise from a pastoral culture to an international superpower, ancient Rome advanced in quality and variety of cuisine and in attention to nutrition. Systems of dietetics offered a source of health and fitness as well as a denotation of social class. While country folk kept to a daily regimen of meatless dishes of chickpeas, garlic cheeses, lentils, and vegetable soups, herders lived most of the year on stone-ground barley loaves soaked in milk or wine. Male enclaves offered the occasional wild boar's head, a center of hunting party feasts, plated and adorned with leaves and herbs. Ligurians specialized in baking flatbread, the ancestor of focaccia; Lucania, home to the poet Horace, developed game recipes and sausage making; Calabrians added grape hyacinth bulbs and lupin seeds as recipe flavorings; Lombards gained fame for crisp apples, cherries, and cole vegetables and for fermenting lake fish.

On the march, legionaries made do on barley mush, the forerunner of orzo pasta, or *farinata*, a gruel of wheat flour and water flavored with fat. They carried their own mortars and rations and took charge of the day's cooking. A cold beverage, *posca*, began with the dilution of sour wine or vinegar with water topped with a sprinkle of herbs. Combat casualties received their nourishment in barley water, a sweetened tonic.

In the homes of wealthy ancient Romans, the kitchen—depicted here in 100 C.E.—was a center of activity. Clay ovens baked wheat breads and barley cakes. Amphorae stored essential grains and liquids, as well as exotica from around the empire. *(The Granger Collection, New York)*

As Rome grew into a metropolis, city dwellers relegated more of their food preparation to others, especially laborers at the salt pits that flourished after 200 B.C.E. At outdoor markets, kitchen slaves chose the freshest supplies of artichokes, asparagus, cabbage, endive, lettuce, mint, nasturtiums, and parsley and picked over baskets of root and row crops—beets, cucumbers, elecampane, garlic, gourds, leeks, onions, parsnips, radishes, skirrets, and turnips. Busy urbanites and visitors patronized street vendors and *tavernae,* fast-food counters and wine bars. Along with gambling and prostitution, these food marts offered bowls of blood pudding, fish skins, flatbread cooked over domed clay pots, honeyed omelettes, hot offal and sausages, mulled wine, salted chickpeas and turnips, and wheat pancakes. Holiday cuisine called for the crushing of walnuts with sesame seeds and soaking this mix in honey. Savvy wives offered overeaters sips of walnut *digestivo,* a liqueur taken to settle the stomach, purge and soothe the intestinal tract, and ward off anemia. Wisely, nine days after a funeral, mourners spared the dead similar bellyaches by leaving bowls of broad beans and chickpeas at gravesites.

Dining Patterns

Daily meals began with a light *ientaculum* (breakfast) of bread, cheese, dried fruit, and olives. Multiple courses at *cena,* the main meal at midday, preceded *vesperna* (evening meal) in the city or, in the country, *merenda* (light supper), for which male and female diners convened and sat on chairs at a communal table. By the time of Julius Caesar, around 50 B.C.E., *prandium* (lunch) offered a spread of hot and cold dishes served simultaneously rather than in formal courses. For recipe preparation, chefs stocked processed condiments: *caroenum* and *sapa* (wine concentrates), *liquamen* (fermented fish sauce), and *oenogarum* (thick fish sauce blended with wine). Snacking at the public baths promoted overindulgence in food and drink, by which aristocrats gained reputations for imbibing.

A trend toward the late-afternoon cena and the *convivium* (private banquet) extended the service of many courses into the evening. Hosts dispatched slave runners with verbal invitations; guests provided their own napkins. Men, dining apart from proper matrons, relaxed barefoot at a *triclinium,* a U-shaped arrangement of tables and couches in house or garden, and extended their hands for servants to wash. Tasteful hosts offered fresh water fish from stocked ponds and kept cellars of mountain wines from Ancona and Falernian wine from Campania, a perennial favorite. Multiple tales of food poisoning linked common toxic additives—aconite, death cap mushroom, or mandragora—with killers who exploited the drunkenness of their victims.

Meals at Home and Away

The *gustatio* (salad course) consisted of eggs, lettuce, mushrooms, and radishes adorned for more sumptuous gatherings with boiled fungus, clams, jellyfish, mussels, oysters, prawns, and sea urchins. Hosts served these rich appetizers with *mulsum* (Roman sherry), a sweet aperitif made from three parts grape must reconstituted with ten parts honey. Throughout six or seven courses, contrast dominated recipes, offsetting honey and vinegar. Fern shoots and onions were favorite sources of pickles. After guests' meticulous hand dabbling in aromatic water, a fine meal concluded in two stages—with *bellaria* (dessert), usually apples, cheesecake, custard, dates, figs, grapes, honey cakes, pears, and pine nuts. From this arrangement derived the cliché for a grand meal, *ab ovis ad mala* (from eggs to apples), the Roman equivalent of "soup to nuts." The *comissatio,* a pouring of dessert wines, initiated lengthy table talk and enjoyment of music, riddles and word games, and professional reciters of verse. Public dining at a hired hall, forum (marketplace), or temple acknowledged the calendar with religious sacrifices, distribution of animal parts about the city, and communal feasting, which reached a peak of debauchery at Saturnalia, Roman Christmas.

Because of the scarcity of *deversoria* (hotels) and *hospitia* (inns), welcome into private homes placed demands on both traveler or stranger and host. Treasured mores obliged the homeowner to offer hospitality, a duty expressing the civility and refinement of the host and, by extension, of all Romans. For business and political ends, the peaceful sharing of meals and a discreet distribution of leftovers enhanced contractual arrangements and demanded reciprocity from all parties. The lessening of animosity and xenophobia accounted for the evolution of the word *hostis* (enemy) into a stranger or visitor welcomed to the table. The punctilious host offered *lautia* (washing

items) and *loca* (quarters) along with *munera* (gifts), tableware and chalices crafted from precious metals.

The head of household acquired esteem for his sharing of meals with strangers as well as dignitaries. One example, Marcus Tullius Cicero, the Republican era's master orator and statesman, opened his villa on the Palatine Hill to guests. Unlike the Greeks, who separated dining from wine consumption, Romans drank watered wine with communal meals, a means of stemming out-of-control mealtime aggression. Visitors displayed their thanks for fine dining with handclasps, wine toasts, and symbolic gifts that denoted ongoing friendship, patronage, and trade relations.

At the bottom of the plebeian class, courtesies took second place to the exigency of near starvation. Youths pilfered fruit stalls. Rioters demanded the bread dole, supplied by grain freighters from Alexandria to Ostia, Rome's warehouse and food distribution center. To reduce the number of beggars and petty criminals on the streets, the harried senatorial class continued feeding the poor.

Ostentation at the Table

Rich cosmopolites displayed their superiority by demanding gastronomical specialities, such as Asian aromatics and dyes for entrées. Extremes of cuisine included roasted peacocks served in their feathers and cage-bred dormice fattened on walnuts and stuffed with pork or veal. Professional chefs consulted the era's first cookbook, *De Re Coquinaria* (*On Cookery,* ca. 35 C.E.), compiled by Marcus Gavius Apicius, a noted gourmet. In response to foolhardy lifestyles, the physicians Celsus, Galen of Pergamum, Rufus of Ephesus, Oribasius, Scribonius Largus, Asclepiades, Athenaeus, and Anthimus issued treatises on bathing and hygiene, exercise, holistic dietetics, and the therapeutic nature of balanced meals of sensible portions. In *De Alimentorum Facultatibus* (*On the Powers of Food,* ca. 175 C.E.), Galen, the Turco-Roman nutritionist and physician to the Emperor Commodus, discussed foodstuffs by category—seeds, fruit and nuts, roots, animals and animal products, honey, and wine. He recommended honey for its stable sweetness and powers of healing, whether raw or cooked.

In an era when Romans lived along the sewage-choked Tiber and clogged city runnels, many died in their 30s from fevers, sudden gut ailments, and organ failures. Galen's directives said nothing about the scarcity of soap, which, in 300 C.E., cost the equivalent of two days' wages for a city baker or miller to buy 1 pound in liquid or solid form. Galen's *De Subtiliante Dieta* (*On the Thinning Diet,* ca. 175 C.E.), a brief treatise on weight control, abandoned scientific jargon and Greek medical snobbery to acknowledge the worth of rustic Italian staples, which included chicory, lettuce, and wild herbs. For the sake of digestion, Galen contrasted baked with boiled foods in terms of palatability. To simplify the choices of

Recipe: Sweet-and-Sour Cole Slaw

Oribasius, the Greek encyclopedist and dietetic adviser to the Emperor Julian after 361 C.E., followed the advice of Cato the Elder, a promoter of cabbage in *De Agricultura* (*On Agriculture,* ca. 160 B.C.E.). For a flavorful slaw, Oribasius chopped one-quarter head of red cabbage and tossed it with one chopped stalk of rue and one bunch of shredded coriander. For 2 tablespoons of dressing, he blended equal parts honey and wine vinegar and saturated the greens with the emulsion. To finish the salad, he topped it with a sprinkling of powdered asafetida, an antiflatulant and digestive aid common to condiment and pickle recipes.

body-friendly foods, he coded each as cold or hot, dry or moist, and matched suggested regimens to the individual's age, gender, and body humors. Table maxims about moderation warned of gluttony and wine guzzling and encouraged consumption of cheese, fish, and pulses (wheat porridge) along with whole-grain bread, pork fat, and fresh and dried fruit.

The refined urbanite ridiculed barbarians, who ate with both hands from common pots and haunches on spits and observed no table etiquette. For the privileged, from around 100 B.C.E., the household *coquus* (cook) superintended artistic meal preparation—bread, fresh produce, game, meats, and seafood. Shore favorites—crustaceans, cuttlefish, mollusks, snails, tuna—cost double the price of pork. Essential to the everyday diet, salty *garum* (fish sauce) served as a standard table condiment, a contrast to the complicated saucing of nuts with herbs and the salvers of delicate *globuli* (cheese dumplings) and fish hors d'oeuvres offered at the tables of the wealthy. Moray, red barbel, and sturgeon, like present-day caviar and fugu fish, retained snob appeal.

The Roman *confarreatio* (patrician wedding) enhanced table civility by an advantageous alliance of bride and groom. An evening ritual involved the escort of the bride to the groom's home. While singers serenaded the new female head of household, the mother of the bride brandished a torch, symbol of the hearth. Gifts to the bride included a grain pan, pestle, and sieve. Prayers to Ceres, goddess of grain, and Juno, protectress of wives and pregnant women, accompanied ritual foods—a piece of honey-sesame wedding cake and a quince—representatives of wifely hospitality and fecundity. The evening concluded with a wedding dinner and the showering of nuts on the bride. The groom conferred blessing on his wife with gifts of fire and water, symbols of domestic responsibilities that traditionally belonged to women.

The Roman Sybarite

After Alexander the Great subdued Persia and Egypt in 333 B.C.E., Roman cuisine began its evolution into opulence with elements of Persian and Egyptian exotica. Improvements to waterways and canals at Milan and Ostia sped commodities and green goods to city markets and the kitchens of caterers. In place of lovage, mint, rue, and grape marinade, cooks began incorporating heavier Asian pepper and spices, notably asafetida and ginger. The Lex Fannia, legislation that Consul Caius Fannius Strabo sponsored in 161 B.C.E., regulated the amount citizens could spend on fish and meat and on the weight of silverware at table. Under Augustus, the first emperor (r. 27 B.C.E.–14 C.E.), sumptuary laws restricted extravagant banqueting and private expense for food, wine, and clothing, particularly Asian imports. Austerity represented a return to early Roman values instituted by a pastoral culture, a means of upholding

the Roman ethos that the mythographer Ovid urged in *Fasti* (*Holidays,* 8 C.E.).

Both Tiberius and Nero attempted more stringent controls on fine dining, but the emerging equestrian class ignored the statutes in their passion for glamorous dress and dining experiences. The occasional poet Catullus outlined the secret flirtations and grovelings at table; Petronius Arbiter satirized food fads of social climbers in *Trimalchio's Dinner* (ca. 65 C.E.) and joked about a wine switch from a prime Opimian to an inferior vintage. Rome's imperial land grab extended agricultural experimentation to Gaul, Germany, Hispania, and North Africa and as far north as land could produce wine grapes. To northern Gauls, officers of legions introduced carrots, celery, chickpeas, coriander, cumin, peaches, and silphium along with chickens, peacocks, pheasants, and rabbits. Armies established bimonthly food bazaars in North Africa and more frequent farmer's markets in Anatolia and Palestine.

Reciprocity made lasting changes in predictable Roman menus, producing a Hellenized fusion cuisine. Soldiers on leave brought home tales of African bushmeat, Belgian ham, Caspian caviar, Egyptian ibis and mustard, French oysters, Greek figs and wines, Lusitanian pomegranates and sweet olives, Palestinian arum root, Persian lemons and saffron, Spanish salt mackerel and wine, Syrian marjoram, and Turkish fish, and they developed a thirst for British barley beer. From Sicily, they learned the grating of goat and sheep milk cheeses over baked dishes to form a flavorful au gratin (cheese crust). Around 220 C.E., the Syrio-Roman Emperor Elagabalus spread color-themed banquets with chased silver casseroles of camel feet, crayfish forced meat, flamingo and nightingale tongues, mullet beards, ostrich brains, parrot heads, pig wombs, and raw cockscombs. He offered door prizes, invented the progressive, or house-to-house, dinner, and served embroidered napkins with joke desserts carved of clay, ivory, marble, or wax.

Famine precipitated an urban collapse. In 284 C.E., the Emperor Diocletian recognized the dangers of inflation and the desertion of farms as a subsequent threat to food markets. In Rome's declining days, in the late 300s C.E., St. Augustine condemned gluttons and sots for risking health through a disgraceful perversion of normal eating. After the collapse of taxation and the economy, food shipments ceased. Authorities banished outsiders. The siege by Visigoths in September 408 C.E. forced the city into a food panic. The reduction of the daily wheat ration from one-half to one-third precipitated the fall of the Roman Empire.

See also: Apicius; Einkorn Wheat; Emmer Wheat; Grilling; Maritime Trade Routes; Pickling; Pliny the Elder; Poultry; Pulses; Religion and Food; Sicilian Diet and Cuisine; Silk Road; Trade Routes; Trading Vessels; Vegetarianism; Vinegar; Yeast.

Further Reading

Bettoja, Jo. *In a Roman Kitchen: Timeless Recipes from the Eternal City.* Hoboken, NJ: John Wiley & Sons, 2003.

Downie, David. *Food Wine Rome: A Terroir Guide.* New York: Little Bookroom, 2009.

Faas, Patrick. *Around the Roman Table: Food and Feasting in Ancient Rome.* Trans. Shaun Whiteside. Chicago: University of Chicago Press, 2005.

Renfrew, Jane M. *Roman Cookery: Recipes & History.* London: English Heritage, 2004.

Royal Greenland Trade Department

Beginning in 1774, the Royal Greenland Trade Department (Den Kongelige Grønlandske Handel, or KGH) monopolized commerce between the Inuit and Denmark for two centuries. At the time, Greenland's nomadic Eskimo flourished at commercial open-water fishing for cod and halibut, a Scandic staple. According to research into Inuit middens, their diet veered from seafood toward fat and red meat from caribou, polar bears, and seals, their principal food.

Investors pondered commercializing the far north for 35 years. Under order of Frederick IV, the king of Denmark-Norway, in November 1719, the Danes at Bergen broached the possibility of trading in fish, oil, and seals in the Faeroe Islands and Greenland. Because rumors of savagery and cannibalism of shipwrecked crews dissuaded Danish investors from colonizing Greenland, colonial plans faltered. Under royal charter, Hans Poulsen Egede, a Norwegian Lutheran missionary-colonizer and his Danish wife, Gertrud Rasch Egede, pioneered European trade on July 3, 1721, by settling 25 religious workers at Godthaab (present-day Nuuk).

In his treatise *A Description of Greenland* (1818), Egede observed the Inuit cuisine and reported the consumption of boiled, dried, and raw meat from hares, partridges, and reindeer and of air-dried halibut and salmon roe. The Inuit sauced fish dishes with fat, scraped sealskins for tissue for pancakes, and drank only water as a beverage. During famine, they consumed catfish, discarded animal skins, partridge and reindeer intestines along with the dung, and red seaweed. The lack of cleanliness repulsed Egede, who watched families eat from dirty pots and dishes whenever they felt hungry. Men invited neighbor males to share meals; women gathered during the day while the men fished.

As whaling flourished, trading outposts along the west coast—Christianshaab, Frederikshaab, Godthaab, Jakobshavn—set the tone and style of interaction with nomadic natives. With the Danes, the Inuit exchanged fish, hides, kayaks, narwhal and walrus tusks, soapstone kettles and kitchen utensils, walrus rope, and whale blubber and bone sleds for gin, metal tools, and cookware.

Moravian missionaries extended business at their own trading stations in 1765 and established gardens outside their island hospital. In *The History of Greenland* (1767), Moravian historian David Crantz reported on native meals of seafowl and small rosefish stewed in seawater. For snacks, the Inuit chose squares of raw *mattak* (narwhal or whale skin). Outsiders found inedible their prized delicacy—semi-frozen *mikkiak,* harbor seal flippers and heads rotted under grass until the hair fell off. For salad greens, the Inuit gathered angelica (wild celery), dandelion and sedum root, scurvy grass, and sorrel. They delighted in bilberries, cranberries, and crowberries, eaten with cod livers. Radishes, turnips, and wild peas were major vegetables; wild thyme provided leaves for an aphrodisiac tea.

As the monopoly gained hold, by March 18, 1776, colonial outposts and whaling stations rejected commerce with outsiders, particularly the competitive Dutch and English whalers. Danish law banned intrusive vessels within 4 miles (6.4 kilometers) of the coast, while state vessels offloaded seal blubber for refining at headquarters in Copenhagen into high-grade oil. In its sixteenth year, the KGH broke all religious ties and established a trading fleet under Danish sovereignty. In exchange for sole mercantile connections with the interior, Danish-Norwegian merchants established a paternalism that protected first peoples and preserved their bear- and fox-hunting economy. Nonetheless, the Inuit adopted European ways, including smoking tobacco and drinking coffee and whiskey and cooking in copper and iron vessels. Encounters with Europeans introduced the Inuit to the luxuries of brown bread with butter and oatmeal.

In 1814, as a result of the Napoleonic Wars, Denmark broke ties with Norway and allowed Danish shippers Dahlén and Kall to vie for business at the Napossoq fishing station. In 1830, the fish and whale business yielded steady profits that paid colonial debts. Unswayed by European customs, the Inuit continued to revere their national dishes—walrus liver, seal ribs, and the meat of reindeer, which grew scarce from overhunting. They regarded bear and seal as caloric fuel for travelers. In *A Treatise on Food and Diet* (1845), pharmacologist Jonathan Pereira endorsed the traditional Greenlandic diet and cuisine as healthful and therapeutic in a frigid climate. He declared the basing of nutrition on fat and oil saved the aborigines from disease and early death. By 1912, commercial domination gave place to control by Grølands Styrelse (Greenland Administration). The KGH lost more autonomy in 1950 and separated from the royal company in 1990, when Greenland became self-governing.

Further Reading

Beukel, Erik, Frede P. Jensen, and Jens Elo Rytter. *Phasing Out the Colonial Status of Greenland, 1945–54: A Historical Study.* Copenhagen, Denmark: Museum Tusculanum, 2010.

Gombay, Nicole. *Making a Living: Place, Food, and Economy in an Inuit Community.* Saskatoon, Saskatchewan, Canada: Purich, 2010.

Marcus, Geoffrey Jules. *The Conquest of the North Atlantic.* Woodbridge, UK: Boydell & Brewer, 2007.

Rumford, Count (1753–1814)

An inventor and social strategist, Sir Benjamin Thompson, Count Rumford, created the science of nutrition and promoted home economics, dietetics, and sanitation as sciences.

Born on March 26, 1753 in Woburn, Massachusetts, Rumford apprenticed in commerce in his teens and educated himself in physics by attending lectures at Harvard. Wedded to heiress Sarah Walker, he advanced to major of the New Hampshire Militia and took the Tory side during the American Revolution. Because of charges of spying for the British, he abandoned his wife and daughter and left for England, where he served as under-secretary in the War Department. At age 30, he settled in Bavaria, where he received the post of major-general of the cavalry.

In his roles as humanitarian and nutritionist, Rumford declared cold and hunger the greatest enemies of humankind. He pitied the underemployed industrial class and introduced corn and potato cultivation and the use of macaroni and polenta as antidotes to slow starvation. In 1790, to feed Munich's 2,600 beggars, he established the Poor People's Institute, where he disguised potatoes by mashing them until the underclass accepted them as food. To nourish the troops of the duke of Bavaria, he experimented with boiling bones along with inexpensive cuts of meat in huge vats called "digesters."

Calculating the maximum nutrition for the least expenditure, the count formulated Rumford's Soup from barley, peas, and potatoes boiled in sour beer and served it at feeding stations three times a day with 5 ounces (142 grams) of rye bread. He declared bread rations indispensable and denounced tea as a deterrent to health and a waste of money. For "burnt soup," a substitute for coffee and tea, he roasted wheat and rye meal in butter and added pepper, salt, and vinegar. By putting the homeless to work in military factories, he provided them with meals, sanitation, and warmth. He later published the result in an essay, "Of Food and Particularly of Feeding the Poor" (1796).

Public kitchens and hospital dietetics offered vagrants *cuisine du pauvre,* a nourishing diet for the poor, as well as health care. In London, where 600,000 Irish immigrants arrived in a single year, Rumford's soup kitchens fed 60,000 daily. The concept spread to Marseilles and Paris, France, and Geneva and Lausanne, Switzerland. In Glasgow, Scotland, petitioners found relief for empty bellies in Rumford's recipes for barley broth and potato soup. Knighted by George III, he earned the title of Count Rumford in 1791 for his innovations with gunpowder, shell velocity, and signaling at sea, but not for his attempts to relieve human suffering.

In 1796, Rumford improved the draw of flues to direct smoke upward by rounding the fireplace opening, thus applying more heat to hearth cookery. One design involved a semicircle of masonry embedded with several small hearths. Cooks superintended pots set in holes over the flames. Within two months of building his prototype, 250 Londoners reconstructed the fireplace and grate according to his design, which improved coal combustion.

While experimenting with thermodynamics at the Royal Institution of Great Britain laboratory in 1799, Rumford invented a brick-and-cast iron kitchen stove that streamlined the use of coal and wood. In a demonstration of convection heating in closed-fire cookery, he roasted 112 pounds (51 kilograms) of beef with 3¢ worth of coal. He conveyed rising heat to hot water reserves and warming closets to drive dampness from linens.

Rumford relished details. He drew plans for a teakettle, stacked pans, and a double boiler suited to slow cooking. For the dining room, he devised a better Argand lamp, called the Balloon Illuminator, in 1805. Two years later, he pioneered a multichambered coffee percolator that retained the flavorful oil of coffee beans. Because his suggestions improved military uniforms and diet, he achieved membership in the Royal Swedish Academy of Sciences.

As a testimonial to domestic economics, environmental chemist Ellen Swallow Richards demonstrated the Rumford Kitchen at the World's Columbian Exposition in Chicago in 1893. Equipment derived from the count's specifications included steam and pressure cookers and the double-bottomed saucepan. For two months, kitchen manager Harriet Maria Daniell of Boston produced dishes for some 10,000 visitors that modeled maximum nutrition from ordinary ingredients. Menus included Rumford's recipes for baked apples, baked beans, brown bread, corn soup, fried potatoes, hasty pudding, pea soup, and potato salad. Sanitarians issued pamphlets on kitchen hygiene and the significance of carbohydrates, fats, and protein to the body. Sarah Wentworth extended Rumford's altruistic visions by establishing Rumford Kitchens for insane asylums.

See also: Beer.

Further Reading

Bradley, Duane. *Count Rumford.* Princeton, NJ: Van Nostrand, 1967.

Brown, Sanborn Conner. *Benjamin Thompson, Count Rumford.* Cambridge, MA: MIT Press, 1979.

———, ed. *Collected Works of Count Rumford.* Cambridge, MA: Belknap Press, 1968–1970.

Russian Diet and Cuisine

A regimen of food and beverage heavy in carbohydrates and saturated fats, the Russian diet and cuisine features cold-weather crops, grains, and pickled fish. The eighth-century Slavs set a pattern of combing forests for wild berries, currants, greens, and nuts and killing deer, rabbits, and squirrels. Agricultural products consisted primarily of milk, millet, and rye. Fall chores required drying, freezing, pickling, and smoking to make stocks last through winter.

From the 800s into the 1900s, peasants countered the effects of blizzards and harsh winds with home-grown root crops and cabbages and purchases of goat's milk, kefir (a fermented milk drink), and yogurt from farmer's markets and street kiosks. They stocked larders with carrots, dried cherries and cranberries, honey, game, and marinated apples and fish. Boiled beef and pork arrived at the table in loaves coated with aspic or calf's foot jelly. A constant in pantries was the makings of borscht (beet soup) and potato straws, two national dishes.

Traditional servings of soup favored cabbage, introduced in the 800s from Byzantine Greeks. Other ingredients—brined cucumbers, *kvass* (fermented rye), mushrooms, noodles, and sorrel and nettles—amplified both hot and cold soups, some garnished with a dollop of *smetana* (sour cream). From the steppes, Russia's bread-basket, came cereal grains—barley, millet, rye, wheat—which reached the table in black bread, blini (crepes), fritters, noodles, wraps for meat-filled *pirozhki* (dumplings), and alcoholic beverages, namely beer, kvass, and vodka. Siberian *pelmeni* (savory meat pies) gained flavor and mouthfeel from boiling in broth. Farther south, in Georgia, garlic dominated dishes. During famines garlic and hemp oil flavored grain dishes.

From the tenth century, Russian Orthodoxy generated control over feasting and fasting. With 200 days of the year given to fasts, peasants substituted mushrooms in recipes calling for forbidden dairy, eggs, and meat products. During Lent in the Middle Ages, only the privileged could afford fish pie and salt herring. Peasant celebrants made birch drinks and mead from honey to drink with sponge cake, which bakers marked with *XB,* the first two letters of "Christus" in the Cyrillic alphabet.

Gatherings centered on the home stove, a symbol of warmth and cheer. Thus, the Russian diet avoided raw foods and propitiated the almighty with prayers over fuel for the oven. According to peasant wisdom, "The stove is like the altar: We bake bread in it." The aphorism revealed the Russian reverence for bread as a sacred source of life.

European Imports

Periods of European influence, beginning in the late 1400s, introduced traditional cooks to the delicacies of Renaissance Austria, France, and Italy. During the reign of Ivan III, Italian stonemasons introduced pasta and

Recipe: Ukrainian Borscht

Chop two large beets with a tomato, a carrot, an onion, a potato, and a small cabbage wedge. Sauté vegetables in 2 tablespoons of butter. Place vegetables in 1 quart of salted beef broth with 1 tablespoon of peppercorns and a bay leaf. Boil for 20 minutes. Serve with a rounded tablespoon of sour cream and a generous sprinkling of red wine vinegar, black pepper, and dill weed.

gelato. Black tea arrived from China in the 1600s, when the Russians wholeheartedly adopted it as a national beverage.

After 1682, Czar Peter the Great promoted coffee prepared Turkish style and imported French chefs to refine menus with bechamel sauce, green leafy salads, and smoked fish and meat. Flaky pastries filled with caviar preceded wine and champagne and decadent chocolates and ice cream for dessert. From Russian influence, French table service changed from a full spread to course servings, which allowed cooks greater control of the temperature of individual dishes.

In the 1760s, Catherine the Great added new dimensions to cooking styles with goods from Japan and wine from Hungary. Her kitchen staff advanced from peasant fare to exacting recipes for Beef Stroganoff, Chicken Kiev, Madeira cake, and Veal Orloff, dishes popularized in China and Scandinavia. During this same period, she warehoused grain in Petersburg to ensure food and fodder for her subjects and maintained a watch on military rations.

Under the health-conscious Romanov czar Alexander III, palace kitchens served spartan meals expected of hunters and soldiers. In the 1860s, Lucien Olivier, manager of the Hermitage restaurant in Moscow, concocted the Olivier salad, a potato-and-mayonnaise salad containing diced boiled eggs, capers, caviar, duck, ham, peas, and pickles. Variations of the salad attained popularity in Belgium, Bulgaria, Greece, and Turkey.

The expansion of railroads alleviated some of the historic Russian fear of starvation during a hard winter. Supplies of goods also increased in 1896 after the crowning of Alexander's son, Nicholas II, the last Romanov czar. His magnanimous gesture to peasants caused a catastrophe at distribution centers, where some 3,000 died of trampling while struggling to grab food from the imperial allotment. The czar's ignorance of hunger boded ill for his dynasty and nation.

From Empire to Soviet State

Cookbook compiler Elena Burman Molokhovets preserved classic Russian menus in her household text *A Gift to*

A Soviet-era poster (1947) exhorts farmworkers: "Work hard during harvest time, and you will be rewarded with plenty of bread." Centrally planned collective farming produced disastrous declines in agricultural output, livestock, and food supply. *(The Granger Collection, New York)*

Young Housewives (1861), which by 1917 reached a print run of 295,000 copies. In the last 56 years of Romanov rule, from the emancipation of serfs in 1861 to the outset of the Bolshevik revolution in 1917, she covered the gamut of the bourgeois bride's responsibilities, from making fruit liqueurs to serve at evening tea to plating and garnishing pâté and mousse for a banquet table. The last 11 chapters list dishes suitable for fast days, including greens and aspics, buns, and compotes. Details mention keeping fish frozen in the icehouse and corking infusions of black currant leaves to keep them from exploding in the cold cellar during the winter.

Russian revolutionaries denounced Molokhovets's Gallic cuisine, tea with jam, colored Easter eggs, and wines as too gentrified and class conscious to befit godless Communist dogma. Breadlines and food shortages belied the bias of Molokhovets's recipes, which appealed to aristocratic households, with their vast pantries and hordes of servants to whip eggs for *babka* (coffee cake) and mince beef for bouillon. Exigency ruled food processing. In Bulgaria, Hungary, and Yugoslavia, pickling extended the commercial use of vegetables. Salting turned cabbage into sauerkraut; smoking made sausages a long-lived pantry meat.

During the Great Hunger of 1921, 10 million Soviet Russians starved to death, primarily in the Ural-Volga area. Frugal peasants reverted to hearty vegetable soups, dumplings, and meatballs made from organ meats and pig's knuckles, milk, and onions. Migration created a situational fusion cuisine as foodways from the world's largest nation blended into the Russian diet. From Estonia, Latvia, and Lithuania emerged a new emphasis on cream and egg dishes. Rice pilaf came from Uzbekistan, fried pies from Kazakhstan, carrot salad from Korea, anchovies from the Black Sea, and red wine from Georgia. To move foodstuffs across the great nation, international relief workers set up feeding stations at depots to strengthen railroad workers.

After collectivization in 1929, the hungry and homeless raided agricultural fields. Overfishing killed off native species, reducing a source of wild foods for remote villagers. Rationing continued until 1947; in the 1960s, public catering served inexpensive, regimented meals in government institutions and factories. Russian art and literature of the 1960s revealed a mystic longing for the sweet life, when grocers offered an array of imported cheeses, citrus fruit from the Middle East, and foreign coffees and canned goods.

Food Commerce after Communism

Currently, 10 percent of "New Russians" dominate the nation's wealth, while 70 percent of citizens live in poverty. Unstable economic conditions in the Russian Federation, formed in December 1991, exacerbate shortages. Child nutrition falters from unmonitored school lunches, and urbanites cultivate fewer home gardens. Nonetheless, Russia is the world's third-largest producer of roots and tubers, including celeriac, parsley root, and turnips. Farmers rely heavily on pesticides. Corn and rice, which first entered Russian cuisine in the 1990s, are still scarce. Produce in the Republic of Tyva in eastern Siberia costs five times the average price in Russia. On the Kamchatka Peninsula, on Russia's far northeastern border, inadequate produce during the winter months forces families to rely on meat-heavy meals from hunting and fishing.

Food insecurity allows unsanitary conditions and cross-contamination in abattoirs and seafood shops. Supermarkets cheat on weights and measures, rewrap foods, and remove date stamps. Least affordable are fiber-rich fish and fruits, which require lengthy transportation. In place of fresh foods, Russians rely on bread and potatoes. The results of an undependable food market and lax consumer laws are serious mortality patterns from alcoholism, binge eating, diabetes, malnutrition, and obesity, which afflicts one-third of the citizenry.

A reduction in breast feeding leaves children under-nourished from micronutrient deficiencies. Those infants who receive adequate nursing incur an insidious deterrent in milk containing polychlorinated biphenyls (PCBs) from environmental pollutants. Weaning at four months produces another divergence in child nutrition, as only some receive fortified infant food. Children of the poor are more likely to subsist on iron-deficient porridge and unfortified flour and milk, an impetus to frequent infections. Stunted growth is common in Uzbekistan, Azerbaijan, and the Kyrgyz Republic. Global food aid tends to reach only 5 percent of the needy.

Despite economic and political obstacles, Russian conviviality revolves around the table and pleasurable food consumption. To avoid the expense of home cooking, students and workers rely on canteens. Most breakfast menus list sausage, eggs, cheese, and *kasha* (porridge), a traditional grain dish that Prince Alexander Nevsky introduced in Novgorod in 1239. Lunches consist of egg and vinaigrette salads, smoked salmon, tongue and sausages, baked mushrooms, and fish soups. Desserts range from fruit blini and cottage cheese with jam to nut cakes and halvah, a spread made of nuts and sesame or sunflower seeds, served with beer, cognac, or fruit juice.

See also: Ice Cream; Kitchen Gardening; Lapérouse, Jean François Galaup; Malnutrition; Trade Routes; Wheat.

Further Reading

Glants, Musya, and Joyce Toomre, eds. *Food in Russian History and Culture.* Bloomington: Indiana University Press, 1997.

Mack, Glenn Randall, and Asele Surina. *Food Culture in Russia and Central Asia.* Westport, CT: Greenwood, 2005.

Oddy, Derek J., Peter J. Atkins, and Virginia Amilien. *The Rise of Obesity in Europe: A Twentieth Century Food History.* Burlington, VT: Ashgate, 2009.

Papashvily, Helen, and George Papashvily. *Russian Cooking (Foods of the World).* New York: Time-Life, 1969.

Wegren, Stephen K. *Russia's Food Policies and Globalization.* Lanham, MD: Lexington, 2005.

Salad and Salad Bars

One of the most individualized styles of food service, salads incorporate both cooked and raw ingredients from eggs, fruits, gelatins, grains, mushrooms, pasta, meats, and vegetables. Servings usually arrive cold or hot but can also be mixed—for example, killed lettuce, a Southern specialty sauced with hot bacon and vinegar dressing at the last moment before plating. Ingredients favor indigenous foods, as with the peanut sauce atop Indonesian *gado-gado,* a coddled egg in Irish egg mayonnaise, bean sprouts in Japanese *goi gia,* feta cheese in Greek salad, Arabic orange and onion salad, and fresh Dungeness crab in the Crab Louie, a San Francisco original.

Salad fits any meal—appetizer, main and side dishes, cold lunches, picnics, and desserts. Salad makers enhance fruit and vegetable fare with a variety of toppings—bacon bits, croutons, noodles, pepperoncinis, shredded cheese, sliced almonds, toasted crumbs, tortilla strips, walnuts, and whipped cream. Main-course salads assist diabetics, dieters, and calorie counters by topping cucumbers, greens, lettuce, peppers, and tomatoes with a seared meat, usually chicken breast, salmon, or sliced skirt steak. Restaurant menus code these servings with symbols for "heart healthy," "low carbs," and "high fiber."

The Classical World and Middle Ages

The earliest evidence of salad making appears in Egypt in 4500 B.C.E., when kitchen gardens featured chicory and lettuce. By 2400 B.C.E., Mesopotamians were marinating raw vegetables to preserve their flavor and crunch. In 465 B.C.E., the Persian king Artaxerxes favored watercress as a wild food accompaniment to roast meat.

The Greeks and Romans tempted the appetite with an uncomplicated dish of olives and lettuces flavored with anchovies, caraway, coriander, fennel, and garlic. For *moretum,* a bowl of crushed garden herbs honored in one of Virgil's minor idylls, Roman chefs grated cheese and crowned it with coriander, garlic, onions, parsley, rue, and spices. From the amalgam came the motto *E pluribus unum* (One out of many), a salute to the forerunner of pesto.

Pliny the Elder, Rome's first encyclopedist, declared that eating raw salads saves time and fuel for cooking. Because of the sharp taste of vinegar dressing, gour-mands debated whether salads belonged at the beginning or the end of the meal for maximum digestion. The physicians Hippocrates and Galen voted for an initial salad course to introduce high-fiber vegetables that soothed the alimentary canal and moved readily through the gut. Byzantine Greeks used the term *salad* to refer to the salting of fresh greens and the pickling of vegetables, a common preservation method in India and China. During Lent, Christian monks favored raw greens as a break from bread and water. For guests, they dressed their spare plates with nasturtiums, primroses, and violets, all gentle on the stomach and conducive to rest.

In Southeast Asia, a traditional Thai side dish, *som tam,* began with shredded green papaya and added crabs and fish or shrimp sauce to beans, tomatoes, and spondias, a crunchy tropical plum. Disparate flavorings—chili, garlic, lime, palm sugar—capped the whole with four tastes, hot, salty, sour, and sweet. Tabbouleh, a savory Levantine salad dating to the Middle Ages, contrasted a hot, dry climate with a mouth-moistening blend of chopped mint and parsley. Mixed with bulgur, cucumber, onion, and tomato, tabbouleh became a national Syrian specialty.

In the 1090s, European crusaders first encountered fresh side dishes of raw vegetables, which cooks in their home countries considered dangerous to the stomach. Soldiers returned home to spread healthful, tasty recipes incorporating wild herbs—fennel, fern, mint, parsley, rue, sage, and thyme. Huou, the chef of Kublai Khan's imperial kitchen, compiled the first recipe around 1330 C.E. for a Chinese fish salad. To marinated slivers of raw carp, the cook made a dressing from basil, chives, ginger, knotgrass, and radishes, all stimulants to digestive juices. A popular French mix, recorded in Taillevent's *The Provisioner* (ca. 1375), a sourcebook of medieval cuisine, involved blending herbs and saffron into strawberry salad. A deterrent to the late-medieval salad maker, outbreaks of cholera from contaminated water made rinsed raw ingredients risky for all diners, especially children and the elderly.

Modern Varieties and Purposes

The Renaissance chef turned salad into a mealtime attraction. After 1492, the concept of a raw greens course passed from Spain to North America. In the 1500s, Italians popularized the recycling of stale bread in a panzanella, a layering of garden vegetables, black olives, capers, and garlic over pieces of wheat bread. Late in the century, English botanist John Gerrard described in his *Herball, or Generall Historie of Plantes* (1597) the first potato salad, primarily plain ash-roasted tubers dressed with oil, salt, and vinegar. German cooks improved on cold potato salad with a hot version and added sauerkraut salad, a thrifty use of cabbage as an antiscorbutic.

Cross-cultivation of east and west yielded a major shift in cookery. William Shakespeare made an indirect salute to fresh foods in *Antony and Cleopatra* (1605), in which the Nile queen describes her youth as "my salad days" (I, v, 76). By 1608, Spanish tables in Seville featured cucumber salads incorporating tomatoes, a New World discovery. In 1627, Venetian physician Salvatore Massonio published *Archidipno: Overo dell'Insalata e dell'Uso di Essa* (*The Best Banquet: The Salad and Its Uses*), a scholarly view of the subject as food for rich and poor. The text isolated the contributions of garlic, oil, pepper, salt, and vinegar, and covered the nourishing, stimulating, and therapeutic effects of all types, from greens alone to beans and herbs topped with cold capons and pheasant meat.

In 1699, nutritionist John Evelyn, an English gardener at Sayes Court, Deptford, summarized the value of salad vegetables in *Acetaria: A Discourse of Sallets,* listing the health benefits of fennel as a sharpener of vision and praising cress for clearing the brain. Evelyn ventured from the ordinary by mentioning samphire, pennywort, and nettles. His expert opinion on the "herby-diet" (vegetarianism) altered English thinking about the dangers of raw foods to the stomach.

Interest in raw food increased. For the upscale diner in 1700, English and French restaurants popularized salmagundi, the original chef's salad. It consisted of a platter of eggs, fruit, greens, meat, nuts, salt herring, seafood, and vegetables topped with spice and a tarragon vinaigrette dressing. For eye appeal, chefs arranged ingredients by color, texture, or type and sprinkled the finished dish with a unifying dressing and citrus garnish. After the ouster of French aristocrats following the revolution of July 14, 1789, émigrés to England made chic a dish of mixed raw vegetables and flavorful dressing compounding vinegar and egg yolk with ground anchovies, caviar, meat extract, and soy.

Chefs continued concocting a host of salad possibilities, including the popular *macedoine de fruit* (fruit cocktail), a popular addition to menus in the 1790s. It preceded ambrosia, a mix of bananas, citrus fruits, coconut, and pineapple flavored with a bit of brandy or sherry. A nineteenth-century high-fiber favorite among Germans, three-bean salad featured the contrast of garbanzo beans with green beans and kidney beans in a sweet-sour sauce. Late in the 1800s, the Belgians introduced blanched endive and chicory to France; the Dutch devised coleslaw, basically chopped cabbage bound with mayonnaise and vinegar.

The emergence of home economics schools of cookery upended salad tradition by organizing chopped vegetables and greens and isolating them in molded gelatin. The end of the Gilded Age relaxed control of ingredients and introduced tuna salad and the tossed salad, a symbolic devil-may-care attitude toward raw foods. In 1906, to accommodate a sedentary lifestyle, Fannie Farmer, America's top cookbook writer, suggested mixes of chicory, cress, and cucumber as a way to keep cool. In 1916, botanist George Washington Carver advised black cooks to make salads from apples, bananas, cabbage, and celery and to dress them with peanuts, a cheap source of protein. A Yuletide highlight of the 1920s, the Candle salad assembled a banana in a pineapple ring and capped the "candle" with a maraschino cherry, a child-pleasing suggestion of flame.

On July 4, 1924, at a restaurant in Tijuana, Mexico, Italian American chef Cesare Cardini created a Prohibition era classic, the Caesar salad. He drew crowds from Hollywood south of the border to eat well, gamble, and drink legal alcohol. According to his daughter Rosa, when groceries ran low, he improvised a salad from hearts of romaine topped with grated parmesan cheese and soaked in flavorful dressing blended from egg yolk, garlic, lemon juice, and olive oil. Mixed at the table, traditionally in a large wooden bowl, the Caesar salad offered a side dish of finger food garnished with fresh curls of hard Italian cheese. The ingredients were so congenial that the International Society of Epicures of Paris named it America's greatest recipe for the past five decades. A fan of the salad, Wallis Warfield Simpson, the Duchess of Windsor, indulged in Caesar salad at her haunts in Barbados and on the French Riviera.

Similar distinctive blends contributed named salads to menus, such as green beans, olives, and anchovies in the Niçoise salad, a Provençal original; leaf-topped celery stalks and parsley sprigs served to Victorian diners; and the pâté de foie gras salad that memoirist Mary Chesnut ate in Charleston in April 1861 near the outbreak of the Civil War. The Waldorf salad, which Waldorf Astoria manager Oscar Michel Tschirky invented on March 13, 1893, captured the distinct flavors of apple cubes and celery dressed with mayonnaise. Less interesting, the heart of lettuce wedge of the 1920s offered a quarter of a head of iceberg lettuce with creamy French or Russian dressing.

In 1937, the Brown Derby in Los Angeles produced a standard California recipe, the Cobb salad, a mix of avocado, bacon, and chicken breast on raw vegetables topped with Roquefort cheese. In the 1950s, a tricolor Italian alliance in the *insalata caprese* imitated the colors of the national flag with basil leaves, mozzarella, and tomato slices. Tex-Mex restaurants of the 1960s adapted original menus with the taco salad, a layering of string beef and guacamole with cheese and salad ingredients in a fried shell.

The thrifty, health-conscious lunch bunch of the late 1960s promoted raw spinach and the pasta salad, an American reshaping of potato salad with pasta. Carryout shops and hotel restaurants offered the pasta dish as a cheap, refreshing à la carte item preferred by dieters. More popular in the Caribbean, French rice salads followed the same regimen by pairing bland cooked rice with raw vegetable bits and a savory vinaigrette.

Salad Bars

The salad bar, first advertised in 1951 in Springfield, Illinois, ushered in an acceptance of the salad as an individualized starter. To speed service and limit food handling, buffet counters offered diners assorted raw greens, sliced and chopped tomatoes and cucumbers, celery and green peppers, and regular and diet dressings. The self-serve bar held the customer's attention until the presentation of the dinner order. Bigger spreads, beginning with salad bars in Norman E. Brinker's Steak and Ale restaurants in Dallas, Texas, added toppings—bacon bits, deviled eggs, shredded cheese, croutons and crackers, taco strips, pita chips—and side servings of chili, coleslaw, potato salad, and soups.

In 1978, Shakey's Pizza Parlor, anchored in Sacramento, California, became the first chain restaurant to feature hot and cold salad counters. Restaurants in Australia and South Africa followed the North American example, which flourished in California, North America's "land of salads." Supermarkets cut into the restaurant trade by luring singles to pick-up boxes of fried chicken, submarine sandwiches, and salad counters selling individualized fare by the pound. Heading the bill of fare, designer greens mingled arugula with chicory, frisee, and mesclun and popular dressings, particularly honey mustard and chipotle vinaigrette.

Salad counters were scenes of the first and largest bioterrorist attack on the U.S. food supply. From August to September 1984, members of the Rajneeshee mystic commune in Oregon chose the poisoning of salad bars at 11 restaurants in The Dalles, Oregon, as a means of disabling local voters in a county election. The tainting of salad items and dressing with salmonella sickened 751 diners. Until health officials could locate the source of contamination, they closed local salad bars, including one at Mid-Columbia Medical Center. The attack failed to kill diners or to forestall the Oregon election.

The concept of the self-serve food bar survived public fear of terrorists and expanded to public schools, colleges, naval vessels, and nursing homes. In 2004, the Ruby Tuesday chain enlarged on the salad bar concept by offering low-carbohydrate, low-fat specials as a side dish or a full meal. The United Fresh Produce Association Foundation of Washington, D.C., initiated a crusade in 2010 to open a salad bar in every school. In Ipanema at the Brazilian Steak House in January 2011, management experimented with full service of antipasto, vegetables, and potatoes at the salad bar with only meat requiring an individual order.

See also: Jefferson, Thomas; Raw Cuisine; Russian Diet and Cuisine; Vegetarianism.

Further Reading

Albert, Jack. *What Caesar Did for My Salad: The Curious Stories Behind Our Favorite Foods.* New York: Perigee, 2011.

Peachey, Stuart. *The Book of Salads, 1580–1660.* Bristol, UK: Stuart, 1993.

Rorer, Sarah Tyson Heston. *New Salads for Dinners, Luncheons, Suppers and Receptions; With a Group of Odd Salads and Some Ceylon Salads.* 1897. Charleston, SC: Nabu, 2010.

Sackett, Lou, Wayne Gisslen, and Jaclyn Pestka. *Professional Garde Manger: A Comprehensive Guide to Cold Food Preparation.* Hoboken, NJ: John Wiley & Sons, 2011.

Shapiro, Laura. *Perfection Salad: Women and Cooking at the Turn of the Century.* New York: Farrar, Straus, and Giroux, 1986.

Salt

A crystallized mineral used as a seasoning, salt introduced world palates to food enhancement as well as a means of food preservation of dishes, from ciabatta bread to dill pickles.

Dealers who obtained sodium chloride by evaporating brine or seawater or by mining rock crystals turned such ancient towns as Cadiz, Jericho, Lagos, Tyre, and Zigong, China, into commercial meccas. Salt contributed so many minerals to animal well-being that it bolstered shore trade with inland cultures, providing the Assyrians, Egyptians, English, Ethiopians, Hebrews, Malians, Nigerians, Persians, Phoenicians, and Thais with a medium of exchange easier to use than coins. Around 2700 B.C.E., the Chinese described healing with 40 salt varieties, which they unearthed through bamboo shafts. The Greeks and Romans valued salt imported from Bavaria for use in preserving *garum,* a fermented fish sauce that permeated their diet and flavored their cuisine. Routes to salt mines and salt pans, such as the Via Salaria, a trans-Italian route from Castrum Truentinum to Rome, attested to the value of barter in mineral crystals. Around 800 C.E., the availability of salt enabled the Vikings to market Baltic cod, meeting a demand far from marine centers.

From the late Middle Ages, the salting of fish, especially to provisioners of armies, press gangs, and sailing vessels, enriched first Norway, then the Hanseatic League, which controlled the ports of Bergen, Brügge, Danzig, Falsterbo, Hamburg, London, Lübeck, Riga, and Visby and commercial centers at Göttingen, Köln, and Novgorod. In Sweden, where herders turned cattle and swine into the woods to fatten the animals on grass, nuts, and roots, the annual fall slaughter in late October required salting of butter, hams, joints, and sausages to preserve animal goods for winter and times of famine. In 1559, salt made up one-quarter of the country's imported goods. In 1526, King Gustavus Vasa established priorities for the use of annual salted foods to ensure an uninterrupted supply. In contrast, the British East India Company angered the Hindus of India by monopolizing and overcharging for salt supplies. The manipulation of table condiments resulted in riots and clashes with the redcoats from the Indian Ocean north to Bengal.

Amerindians recognized that the body could not survive without salt. In *Comentarios Reales de los Incas* (*The Royal Commentaries of the Incas,* 1609–1617), the Peruvian historian Garcilaso de la Vega described pre-death tissue breakdown in those with chronic deficiencies. Spanish explorer Hernando de Soto, on his march across the southeastern United States, found saltworks in operation in northwestern Louisiana and Arkansas. He summarized four sources of salt—brine springs, plant ash, rock salt, and sand. Dealers ranged outward from these sites as well as from the salt licks of Kentucky, Tennessee, and West Virginia to trade among tribes. These and other mineral sources on the borders of the Confederacy became battlegrounds during the American Civil War, as Union forces curtailed salt distribution to limit the amount of bacon available to rebel troops.

Cooks have turned salty foods into such national and regional specialties as Boston baked beans, Italian pancetta, Laotian fried algae, Norwegian lutefisk, and Zuñi dumplings. In the twenty-first century, artisanal salts have gained a reputation for complex flavors. Among these are Alaea clay sea salt and black lava salt from Hawaii, flake salt from Cyprus, English crystals from Maldon, pure Jurassic salt from the Himalayas and Utah, Kala Namak vegan salt from India, Murray River garnishing salt from Australia, Okinawan *masu,* pink Peruvian meat flavoring, Salish smoked salt from the Pacific Northwest, Welsh Halen Môn crystals from the Atlantic, and delicate Portuguese *flor de sal* or *fleur de sel,* a valuable Breton cash crop. The Balinese enter serene seas to collect water for evaporation in hollow palm trunks and use with coconut and lime. Barefoot Filipinos weather high heat while raking salt crystals from tiles laid over mineral-rich mud.

The Japanese hand-stir slow-cooked slurries into *nigari* (bittern), a flaky magnesium chloride that flavors infant formula and sports drinks and coagulates soy milk into tofu. Other specialists crystalize grains in molds to produce ingots similar to the pottery *briquetage* of ancient salt makers. Contributing to the taste appeal are trace amounts of 85 sea minerals, primarily, boron, calcium, iodine, iron, lithium, phosphorus, potassium, silicon, and sulfur. A negative effect of nigari is the increase in cravings for sodium chloride.

See also: Cod; Curing; Desalination; Grilling; Pickling; Pliny the Elder; Polo, Marco; Sausage; Scandinavian Diet and Cuisine; Theophrastus; Water.

Further Reading

Adshead, S.A.M. *Salt and Civilization.* New York: St. Martin's, 1992.

Bitterman, Mark. *Salted: A Manifesto on the World's Most Essential Mineral, with Recipes.* New York: Random House, 2010.

Kurlansky, Mark. *Salt: A World History.* New York: Penguin, 2002.

Standage, Tom. *An Edible History of Humanity.* New York: Walker, 2009.

Sanitation

Purity of foodstuffs and water supplies became a human issue after people began to connect domestic, farm, and commercial waste with sickness and death. After the development of agrarianism in 7000 B.C.E., families composted domestic garbage and fertilized plants with human feces. For reasons of family safety, as early as 6000 B.C.E., the Harappans of the Indus Valley directed home wastes to covered drains. The Talmud, a compilation of oral discussion of holy law compiled from 200 to 500 C.E., warned Jews of types and sources of contamination and levels of impurity. Specific taboos covered the contamination of perishables, disposal of peels and shells, and methods of cleaning and rinsing hands, dishes, utensils, ovens, and hearths to ensure sanitation.

Hygiene problems often resulted from carelessness with sewage, a source of cholera, dysentery, gastroenteritis, hepatitis A, and typhoid fever. The Romans protected their water supply with covered aqueducts and lead piping to and from public bathhouses and toilets. Unfortunately for Rome's urbanites, knowledge of the symptoms of lead poisoning lay far in the future. Because of ignorance of microbes during the Middle Ages, families tended to situate privies conveniently near sources of water. Newfound vigilance resulted during the mid-fourteenth century, when the Black Death increased concern for the safe disposal of tens of millions of corpses and the disinfection of contaminated dishes, bed linens, and towels.

In the early Renaissance kitchen, the cook commanded respect for a complex responsibility. Italian food critic Bartolomeo Platina's *De Honesta Voluptate et Valitudine* (*On Right Pleasure and Health,* 1475) summarized the qualifications of the cook, which required skill and experience. In addition to being free of disease and knowing the ins and outs of selecting and preparing foodstuffs, Platina added that kitchen staff should clean themselves of dirt and filth. Before food preparation, the cook had to purchase the highest-quality stock and keep it free of vermin during warehousing or shelving. Food managers and commercial cooks began storing staples in lidded containers and stoppered jugs.

Twentieth-Century Advances

In the Western Hemisphere, sanitation got a jolt from scandal. Author Upton Sinclair's muckraking novel *The Jungle* (1906) dramatized the foul conditions in Chicago's Union Stockyard. His exposé particularized unclean hands and cleavers used for the chopping of spoiled meat into sausage, grinding rats into potted meat, sweetening and deodorizing of soured meat pickle with soda, and treating spoiled hams with hot irons. As a result of public outrage, on June 30, 1906, President Theodore Roosevelt goaded Congress to pass the Pure Food and Drug Act to halt fraudulent labeling and interstate trafficking in inedible and adulterated foods and drugs. The law established the secretary of agriculture, then James Wilson, as a federal watchdog over samples of imported goods and the storage and cartage of edibles.

In 1927, Congress instituted the Bureau of Chemistry, forerunner of the Food and Drug Administration (FDA), the nation's oldest consumer protection agency. The efforts of Ruth de Forest Lamb, the FDA educational officer and compiler of *The American Chamber of Horrors: The Truth About Food and Drugs* (1936), advanced support for a subsequent law, the 1938 Federal Food, Drug, and Cosmetic Act, or Wiley Law. The legislation fought medical quackery, pesticide residue, food adulterants and dyes, and deliberate misbranding by replacing widely varying state regulations with a firm national standard of purity.

Meanwhile, machines increased the cleansing of kitchens and pantries, particularly ion and ozone purifiers and steam cleaners. One technological advance in reducing putrefaction in food was the creation of the electronic nose, which George H. Dodd of the University of Warwick and Krishna C. Persaud of the University of Manchester Institute of Science and Technologies pioneered in the United Kingdom in the 1980s. Aroma detection equipment used polymers to bind to vapor and isolate rotting foodstuffs in rail, truck, and seagoing containers before decay ruined a whole shipment. By loading microchips with minute dots of different polymers, a single detector could search for hundreds of malodorous amines and thiols, including sources of food poisoning.

In the United States and Britain, research into the nature of the *Escherichia coli* (*E. coli*) bacterium unmasked its full genome sequence. At the University of Wisconsin at Madison, geneticist Nicole Perna disclosed the origin of a strain that caused a February 1982 outbreak at a McDonald's restaurant in Oregon from undercooked hamburgers made from an infected cow. One idiosyncrasy of *E. coli* was its horizontal gene transfer from bacterial viruses, a sharing that promoted rapid mutation. While chairing a pan-European investigation of food-borne contamination, Geraldine Duffy, a microbiologist at Dublin's Teagasc National Food Centre, predicted that knowledge of the bacterium's makeup and methods of reproduction would make it easier to conquer.

Consumer agencies increased health warnings, resulting, in 1986, with a ban on Alar, a growth regulation spray for apples, and additional surveillance of food colorants and flavorings, notably additives to baby food. In December 1993, the *Wellness Letter* from the University of California, Berkeley, dispelled myths that Silver-Stone vessels and Teflon-coated, aluminum, cast-iron, copper, enamel, glass, and stainless steel cooking utensils jeopardize health. The text declared plastic, glass, ceramic, and earthenware vessels generally microwave safe. It warned against home microwaving of margarine tubs not identified safe for microwaving and indicated that the melting of thermoplastics leaches polyethylene terephthalate (PET) into food. The author cited research that acidic solutions cause stainless steel to exude chromium, iron, and nickel, sources of heavy metal poisoning and nickel allergy.

To aid people in Bangladesh, Brazil, Egypt, Ghana, Malawi, Namibia, Nigeria, Pakistan, Peru, South Africa, Sudan, and Thailand in avoiding water- and insect-borne malaria and enteritis from unsafe drinking sources, new disinfectant generators and small-neck storage vessels prevented contamination of potable water. From 1981 to 1990, the World Health Organization's Drinking Water Supply and Sanitation campaign increased accessibility to sanitary supplies but could not keep pace with population density and urbanization. One answer to the problem of impurities involved point-of-use disinfection with sodium and calcium hypochlorite, a practical alternative to boiling where fuel was scarce and expensive. Application of solar electrolysis cells for small-scale production of sodium hypochlorite from saltwater made clean water available in the poorest regions. Alternatives included on-site acidification with aluminum potassium sulfate, flocculation and sedimentation, generation of iodine and mixtures of oxidants, purification with copper sulfate, and sand or cloth filtration.

Modern Concerns

Late in the twentieth century, the Asian media advanced a range of sanitation concerns. Already leery of food contamination after 12 schoolchildren died of hemolytic uremic syndrome and 10,000 fell ill with diarrhea from *E. coli* between May and August 1996, Japanese shoppers panicked in June 2000 from a series of threats to safe foodstuffs. The dairy market weakened because 14,800 milk drinkers sickened from *Staphylococcus aureus* infections after consuming out-of-date Snow brand milk products recycled in Taiki, Hokkaido, as fresh yogurt and low-fat milk. More alerts surfaced to flies in canned juice, lizards in potato chips, and wormy pastry. Deputy Health Minister Yutaka Fukushima, a physician from Kyoto, declared impurities the result of apathy and sloppiness.

As consumer trust faltered, the Japan Food Hygiene Association reported recalls throughout summer 2000 of

Kikkoman tomato sauce and pasta sauce sabotaged with glass shards and Yakult Honsha fruit juice permeated with plastic bits. *Yomiuri,* Japan's largest newspaper, polled 1,983 readers and found that over half feared food poisoning for themselves and their families. Trust in factory hygiene fell to 55 percent; faith in safe drinking water sank to 46 percent. The Japanese Consumers' Cooperative Union's spokesman, Kazuya Fujiwara, attempted to restore faith in purity standards by discrediting the scare as media hysteria. Writing in the *Weekly Tokyo Keizai* magazine, Keinosuke Ono, professor of business at Keio University in Tokyo, surmised that unconscionable corporate principles permeated the food industry.

Other industrialized nations faced difficulties in maintaining purity standards. In summer 1991, *Salmonella poona* from Texas cantaloupe and tomatoes caused extensive food poisoning in 23 states, Newfoundland, Ontario, Quebec, and Saskatchewan. Importers crossed borders with impunity, spreading contamination from the Rio Grande northward and exposing kitchens to contagion from one of the continent's most polluted areas. American methods of insect control with the electric bug killer fell into disfavor in the late 1990s from studies indicating that the electrified cylinder killed beneficial insects as well as pests and exploded their bodies over people, outdoor tables, and uncovered food and drink at parks, outdoor cafés, and campsites.

Homemakers countered invisible impurities with inline water filters, spray cleanser for eggs and produce, and sterilizing dishwashers. In 1993, Dean O. Cliver and Nese O. Ak, microbiologists at the University of Wisconsin at Madison, determined that wood is a better material for cutting boards than plastic or glass. Their experiments proved that pathogens such as *E. coli,* listeria, and salmonella grew less rapidly and died quicker on wood than on knife-scored plastic cutting boards. They found glass dangerous because users may embed tiny shards in food.

Ecological disaster posed additional threats. A lethal food scare aroused Romanians northeast of Bucharest in January 2001, after 30 people from an impoverished area suffered cyanide poisoning from contaminated fish. The threat became obvious when thousands of dead fish surfaced in the Siret River after a cyanide spill at the Metadet chemical company. Health Department head Nicolae Trinca fined Metadet $800 and confiscated and burned tons of fish. Poor and unemployed peasants ignored warnings of gastritis and kidney damage by selling the tainted catch and serving it at their own tables.

Other sanitation concerns involved herd health and the edibility of animal products. In Europe, the double blow of hoof-and-mouth and mad cow (or Creutzfeld-Jakob) disease—bovine spongiform encephalopathy in beef resulting in an irreversible brain erosion—dramatically changed shopping and dining habits. The mad cow scare began in England in March 1996. Home cooking resulted in 90 deaths from brain deterioration, causing the meat market to plummet. In another incidence of public panic, French markets stopped selling beef intestines and sweetbreads (thymus glands) because of a rise from 31 incidents and two deaths from mad cow disease in 1999 to 90 infections in 2000. School cafeterias stopped serving beef from any source.

In April 2001, the United Kingdom continued battling herd infection with hoof-and-mouth as it spread unabated in northern England, Scotland, and Wales and cropped up as far away as Hong Kong. Wholesale extermination and burning of infected animals and those exposed within a 10-mile (16-kilometer) radius drained the finances of farmers and dairiers. To avoid mad cow, housewives and restaurateurs shifted traditional beef-heavy shopping patterns to chicken, fish, horsemeat, lamb, and exotica—crocodile, emu, kangaroo, ostrich, and whale. While panic spread to Germany and the Azores, beef disappeared from plates at home and in military camps and schools throughout the European Union.

Advanced Sanitation Methods

The status quo in food purity currently relies on more inspections and cautions. Conventional farmers replaced the fungicide copper sulfate with strobilurin-based sprays, synthetic fungicides that broke down readily and posed almost no danger to living things. Out of concern for the environment and human well-being, organic farmers backed rotenone, an organic pesticide extracted from custard apple, hoary pea, and jewel vine. Growers routinely sprayed it on fruits and vegetables and on lakes and ponds to kill Asian carp, a scavenger fish. Homeowners applied rotenone to eliminate pests on their pets and kill fire ants.

The World Health Organization declared rotenone hazardous and mildly toxic to mammals. Without government prompting, the makers of the pesticide voluntarily withdrew it from use on cereal crops, cranberries, and tomatoes. In 2005, the U.S. Department of Agriculture's (USDA's) National Organic Program prohibited rotenone from any foodstuff labeled "organic." In 2011, the U.S. National Institutes of Health confirmed a link between rotenone and Parkinson's disease, a neurodegenerative disorder that frequently disables farmers. Health Canada followed the United States lead in condemning the pesticide.

The issue of food irradiation with low-dose gamma rays surfaced late in the twentieth century as a major concern of food purists. Alarmists ignored the fact that the Massachusetts Institute of Technology had introduced the purification method in 1904 and applied it to U.S. Army rations in 1943. In intensive care wards, hospital cooks routinely serve irradiated food to patients with compromised immune systems. Consumers and government officials studied the development of irradiation on highly storable grains and beans and on meat and poultry to kill common insects and microbes. The technique suppressed bacteria and viruses and inhibited the sprouting of garlic, onions, and potatoes, thus extending their shelf stability. In opposition, the Organic Consumers Association in 2001 rejected any artificial sterilization out of fear for long-term dietary hazards and birth defects in the unborn. In July 2011, the USDA's Food Safety Inspection Service denied a request from the American Meat Institute to halt full disclosure to consumers of beef and poultry irradiation.

See also: Coprolites; Ice; Inspection and Safety, Food; Poisonous Foods; Pork; Rumford, Count; Water; Wine.

Further Reading

Beier, Ross C., Suresh D. Pillai, Timothy D. Philips, eds. *Preharvest and Postharvest Food Safety: Contemporary Issues and Future Directions.* Chicago: IFT, 2004.

Cramer, Michael M. *Food Plant Sanitation: Design, Maintenance, and Good Manufacturing Practices.* Boca Raton, FL: CRC, 2006.

Melosi, Martin V. *Garbage in the Cities: Refuse, Reform, and the Environment.* Pittsburgh, PA: University of Pittsburgh Press, 2005.

Rosemarin, Arno. *Pathways for Sustainable Sanitation: Achieving the Millennium Development Goals.* New York: IWA, 2008.

Rotberg, Robert I., ed. *Health and Disease in Human History.* Cambridge, MA: MIT Press, 2000.

Sauces and Saucing

The culinary application of creamy, liquid, or thick toppings or side dressings to foods embellishes moisture, taste, and visual aspects of table presentations. Ethnic specialties gain authenticity from the distinct flavor and character of a slow-simmered dressing. Examples include hoisin (sweet potato) sauce on Chinese beef, mayonnaise on Irish egg mayonnaise, mint sauce on English lamb, *pico de gallo* on Tex-Mex taco salad, plum sauce on Chinese American spring rolls, Salsa Lizano on Costa Rican tamales, *sofrito* on Cuban beans, and teriyaki (sweet soy sauce) on Japanese *yakitori* (skewered chicken, beef, or seafood).

Saucing is an ancient kitchen art that began as the preparation of gravy or marinade for direct moisturizing of spitted fish and meat. Mustard, added to curry at the Mohenjo Daro settlement in the Indus Valley as early as 4000 B.C.E., required macerating in a mortar to release piquant fragrance. Egyptian funerary art illustrated from 3000 B.C.E. the sharing of gravy by diners as an entrée dressing. Around 2800 B.C.E., Chinese cooks fermented soy sauce as a distinctive entrée base or topping.

Ancient Romans first turned saucing into a culinary art by importing *salsa verde* (green sauce) from the Near East. To vary an insipid diet of pulses, cooks upgraded the basic parsley and vinegar blend with anchovies, ca-

pers, and oil. Kitchen skill advanced to kitchen business by the processing of vats of *garum* (fish sauce) into a culinary topping, which may have been a recipe from the Phoenicians of the 700s B.C.E. or the Greeks of the 400s B.C.E. Romans applied the ready-to-eat fish pickle to casseroles, porridge, even beverages.

Garum

For up to nine months, sauce makers fermented fish blood, entrails, gills, and heads in saltwater at a ratio of one to eight to produce a protein-rich *salsamentum* (condiment). By recycling the discarded organs of anchovies, eel, mackerel, mullet, sprats, tuna, and wrasse in a mix with salt, garum makers turned a table condiment into a profitable processed food for sale to fast-food counters, the Roman army, Greek and Roman healers, and Mediterranean grocers. For flavor, preparers added celery, coriander, fennel, mint, and oregano.

After the 400s B.C.E., manufacturers processed for export a series of garum spin-offs—*allec* (fish liver paste), *hydrogarum* (diluted fish sauce), *liquamen* (pickled whole fish sauce), *meligarum* (honeyed fish sauce), *muria* (low-quality tuna garum), *oenogarum* (peppery Byzantine dressing thinned with wine), and *oxygarum* (a vinegary garum). The highest grade consisted solely of tuna blood; the most savory, of mackerel liver. Because Jews banned garum for its disgusting source, ancient sources imply that manufacturers fermented *garum castimoniale* (kosher fish sauce) that obeyed biblical proscription against fish without scales.

By 37 B.C.E., fish sauce fermentation extended to Baelo Claudia, Cartagena, Gades, Malaga, and Tarifa in south-coastal Hispania, from which port cities ships carried sealed amphorae to Chester and Londinium in Britannia. In the decade following 60 C.E., Aulus Umbricius Scaurus and his son managed a successful mackerel sauce factory in Pompeii that shipped branded goods to Spain. The best-quality garum, according to encyclopedist Pliny the Elder, cost 166 sestertii per pint, more than an army recruit earned in eight weeks. Other flavored fish sauces derived from Aila, Jordan; Correiros, Setubal, and Troia, Portugal; Cotto and Lixus, Morocco; and Leptiminus and Neapolis, Tunisia. In 212, the Emperor Caracalla levied a 2.5 percent tax on imported garum.

During the legionary occupation of North Africa, Roman cuisine also produced *epityrum* (olive relish) and *moretum,* a spread for bread made from garlic, herbs, and sea salt crushed into fresh cheese. The recipe, enhanced with basil, hard cheese, olive oil, and pine nuts, resulted in pesto, a bright green sauce that medieval Ligurians served over pasta or added to soups. The complex flavors of pesto suited recipes to the west, including Argentine, Peruvian, and Provençal sliced beef and potatoes.

Medieval Innovations

In the early Middle Ages, European chefs dressed meat and fish entrées with creamy British bread sauce and

French tartar sauce (egg and wine dressing) thickened with arrowroot, blood, butter, cornstarch, cream, eggs, mustard, potato or rice flour, or roux. *Probeat,* Latin for "Let it prove," a spiced apple and raisin dressing, enhanced roast beef. Another sauce, goose milk, involved the flavoring of goose drippings with ground almonds and coloring the mass with saffron for pouring over roast goose.

At abbey hearths, monastic cooks blended ale into egg yolk for caudell (or caudle) to pour over plum pudding and stirred fatty drippings into coulis, a thick puree of fish, fruit, herbs, or vegetables, for example, crayfish, raspberries, parsley, or turnips. In "Balade to Rosamonde" (1386), English poet Geoffrey Chaucer specified *galantyne,* a sauce made from bread crumbs and pounded galyngale, aromatic ginger root, for flavoring eels, pike, and plaice. Britons, Germans, and Scandinavians topped cold meats with creamed horseradish, a peppery, vinegary sauce that Central European Jews applied to gefilte fish.

At Hispaniola and Jamaica after 1492, Genoan navigator Christopher Columbus observed the saucing of barbecued chicken and pork with a liquid dressing that natives stirred from spice, sweetener, and tomato into vinegar. When Renaissance encyclopedist and linguist Bernardino da Sahagún, the "Father of Ethnography and Culinary History," first viewed Mexican saucing at Xochimilco, he admired the savor of sauced finger food sold in the markets and extolled the *moles* (sauces) that flavored cayman, crayfish, dog, jackrabbit, quail, and lake and sea fish. In Argentina, Brazil, Chile, Colombia, Nicaragua, Paraguay, and Uruguay, Spanish conquerors observed an inland *asado* (barbecue) basted with *chimichurri,* a garlic, lemon, onion, parsley, pepper, and salt marinade, or with a vinegary Creole sauce blended from onions and tomatoes.

Recipes

Formal recipes for sauces began appearing in cookbooks during the late Renaissance. After 1620, New England immigrants dressed boiled dinners with mustard and vinegar and made Old World bread sauce and New World cranberry sauce. Pilgrims sweetened the bright red "bounce berries" by jellying them in maple syrup. Newcomers learned the cranberry jelly recipe from the Wampanoag Indians for icing cakes and for serving on mutton, pork loin, turkey, and venison, a model for subsequent Thanksgiving celebrations. Shaker cooks at New Lebanon, New York, and Sabbathday Lake, Maine, altered the red sauce into a ketchup.

Settlers of the Amana colonies in Iowa and the Dutch villages of New York enjoyed horseradish dressings blended with hot beef stock or dried lovage and oregano. A recipe recorded by country wife Abigail Adams of Braintree, Massachusetts, called for the saucing of freshly ground horseradish with heavy cream and mustard for moistening beef brisket. In Iowa, horseradish combined with celery and mustard seed for a piccalilli dressing, which cooks preserved in stone jars. On South Carolina plantations, according to *The Receipt Book of Harriott Pinckney Horry* (1770), horseradish filled an essential part in flavoring meat. Unlike New England sauces, recipes from Texas and Virginia described a more emulsified state with the addition of butter and egg yolks.

In the 1600s, French cook Philippe de Mornay, prime minister under Henry IV, expanded white sauce into *chasseur* (brown sauce), lyonnaise (onion and vinegar marinade), Mornay (cheese sauce), and port sauce made from Madeira or ruby port. All Mornay's inventive recipes enlivened meats and green vegetables. Game and pheasants profited from a fragrant chasseur made from mushrooms and shallots in wine.

Another seventeenth-century favorite, béchamel (white roux), invented by Louis de Béchamel, head steward to Louis XIV, or by the king's chief chef and French food maven, Pierre La Varenne, flavored dried cod, a pantry staple throughout Europe. In 1651, La Varenne systemized the principles of regional fare and standardized ingredients for béchamel, a rudimentary hollandaise featuring creamery butter, and a Barbe Robert (or soubise), a blend of fried onions, mustard, verjuice, and vinegar for topping duck, eggs, fried fish, and rabbit. In Tudor England, the drizzling of such fine sauces over entrées received applause as the height of gustatory pleasure. Navigators returning from East Asia contributed an unforeseen twist in soy sauce, an East Asian puree, which the Chinese first made in 800 B.C.E. and bottled commercially in the 1690s. In 1737, the Dutch East India Company purchased 75 barrels of soy sauce at Dejima, Japan, for supplying Javanese kitchens.

Food historians date mayonnaise to June 29, 1756, when the chef of the Duke of Richelieu transformed velouté (blond sauce) by emulsifying egg with olive oil. The unidentified innovator called his creation "mahonnaise" for Mahon, Minorca. In Belgium, Germany, Holland, and Russia, regional adaptations with anchovies, capers, curry, lemon juice, paprika, pepper, sea salt, and sour cream deepened the flavor of mayonnaise for enhancing beef, crab, eggs, hake, and pork. Similarly impromptu, oyster sauce derived from an accidental reduction of oysters into a brown dressing in Guangdong, China, by café cook Lee Kam Sheung in 1888. The sauce added complex aromas and flavors to Buddha's delight, a popular rice and vegetable mélange.

In the 1890s, Georges Auguste Escoffier presented hearty dishes sauced with a distinctive béchamel or velouté. To basic dressings, he added hollandaise, a thick topping of clarified butter, egg yolk, and lemon juice, and tomato sauce for serving over asparagus. In the mid-1820s, chef Marie-Antoine Carême added baroque touches to French cuisine to harmonize rather than mask flavors. He categorized the four foundations or mother sauces as béchamel (white sauce), espagnole (brown ham sauce), hollandaise (butter sauce), and velouté.

See also: Condiments; Chutney; Dutch East India Company; Grilling; Ketchup; Mustard; Roman Diet and Cuisine, Ancient; Theophratus.

Further Reading

Johns, Pamela Sheldon. *50 Great Pasta Sauces.* Kansas City, MO: Andrews McMeel, 2006.

McGee, Harold. *On Food and Cooking: The Science and Lore of the Kitchen.* New York: Simon & Schuster, 2004.

Peterson, James. *Sauces: Classical and Contemporary Sauce Making.* Hoboken, NJ: John Wiley & Sons, 2008.

Symons, Michael. *A History of Cooks and Cooking.* Urbana: University of Illinois Press, 2000.

Sausage

A convenience food from early times, sausage combines brining, curing, drying, salting, fermenting, pickling, and smoking as methods of preserving meat for storage. Neolithic meat hunters preserved the tidbits left over from butchery by stuffing it into animal bladders, feet, intestines, and stomachs. These natural pockets held a mix of blood, kidney fat, and fish, meat, or poultry offal, including gristle and rind. The casings, scraped and defatted, absorbed spices and smoking and secured the meat mix for travel meals. Sumerian pastoralists adopted sausage making in 4000 B.C.E. as a storage method. Babylonians recorded blends of herbs and chopped meat for sausage in 1750 B.C.E.

Among ancient Asians, Celts, Germans, Greeks, Romans, and Slavs, the resulting blood pudding, bologna, frankfurters, haggis, kielbasa, and salami extended the edibility of the hunt in some of the world's oldest recipes. The Viennese produced the *wienerwurst* or Vienna sausage, the derivation of the term *wiener.* The Chinese commented on *lap cheong* sausage in 589 B.C.E., when cooks saved fatty pork, blood, and poultry liver to mix with rice wine, soy sauce, sticky rice, and vodka for boiling and steaming. Thai sausage makers relied on banana leaf wrappings as casings for meat fermented by natural microorganisms.

Romans valued savory blends of forcemeat pounded into a paste in a mortar with honey, mustard, and vinegar. They made plain sausage as an on-the-march food for armies, such as the occupation force of Verulamium, England, home of a meat-processing factory. In the late republic, a favorite, *lucanica,* from southern Italy fed soldiers and slaves on links flavored with bayberry, cumin, *liquamen* (fish sauce), parsley, pine nuts, rue, and savory. Mid-February celebrations of Lupercalia incorporated myrtle-spiced sausage into fertility rituals. To standardize taste, meat processors kept part of the previous batch, thus salvaging the natural flora of their butcher shop.

By the first century C.E., charcutiers the world over industrialized traditional home meat processing. The Roman Apicius's *De Re Coquinaria* (*On Cookery,* ca. 35 C.E.) enumerated sausages made from chicken, fish, peacock, pork, and shellfish and one variety stuffed into an animal womb. In the same era, Korean gourmands relished *soondae,* a course-ground sausage made with *kimchi,* noodles, pollock, and squid and forced into pig

German sausage makers stuff traditional *weisswurst* (white sausage)—ground veal, pork, and spices in casings. Literally thousands of German sausage varieties come in three categories: scalded, cooked, and raw. *(Heribert Proepper/Associated Press)*

intestines or drum fish air bladders. Japanese versions featured ground fish.

Medieval homemakers chopped meat and fat for bulk sausage, which they stored in clay pots and sealed with melted tallow for springhouse storage. For longer preservation, they poked shredded meat through greased funnels into thin casings, tied them into serving-sized links, and smoked them. Dutch, Germans, and Poles specialized in *bloedworst* and *blutwurst* (blood puddings), a congealed blend mixed with horse meat, bacon, or suet and thickened with barley, chestnuts, oatmeal, pine nuts, rice, or sweet potatoes. Brussels fish sausages satisfied the need for a meat-free entrée during Lent.

Thirteenth-century Andalusian and Saharan writings list the combination of animal giblets and glands with almonds, clove, pepper, and sugar. In Palermo, Sicily, in 1415, housewives bought fresh sausage from itinerant vendors hawking fresh links made from ox tongue, pig's brains and spleen, sheep's lungs, tuna, and wild boar. Italian cooks chose from a variety of flavorings—anise, cheese, cinnamon, citrus rind, clove, garlic, ginger, juniper berries, leeks, olives, pumpkin, red wine, and raisins. Antipasti featured sliced cold cuts, notably pancetta, a cured bacon rolled into a cylinder and pressed to remove air pockets.

Monks often collaborated with farmers to turn tougher, unattractive animal trimmings into economical meats. Bavarian Benedictines of Andechs, outside Munich, Germany, specialized in *weisswurst* (white sausage) and *saumagen,* a pork-and-potato blend pressed into a muscular pig's stomach and eaten with sauerkraut. In 1493, the refectory of St. Swithun's in Winchester, England, served morterells, sausage balls flavored with cinnamon, paprika, and parsley and fried in lard. During the 1500s and 1600s, imported herbs and spices, such as cardamom, coriander, allspice, and nutmeg, added new possibilities for dry forcemeat. Because dry mutton and oyster sausage required no refrigeration, it stocked the larders in ships and military kitchens.

Idiocuisine preserved the name of locales, as with Cumberland sausage in England; Lebanon bologna; Asturiana from Asturia, Spain; and salami from Salamis, Cyprus. Berliners and frankfurters from Berlin and Frankfurt, Germany, added popular export items to the country's 3,000 sausage varieties. Artisanal recipes became clan heritage and passed into the kitchens of family specialists. When immigrants moved to the Western Hemisphere in the 1700s and 1800s, they brought along wooden box grinders that reduced meat trimmings to the right viscous mass for stuffing with wooden plungers through tin nozzles into casings.

Latin American chorizo and *morcilla* differed from their Central European cousins in the addition of hot peppers and thyme and the wrapping of hot sausages in tortillas. Algerians and Moroccans air-dried *merguez,* a blend of beef and lamb flavored with chili, paprika, and sumac and stuffed into lamb intestines for serving with couscous. South Africans turned game into *boerewors,* a farmer's sausage made from chopped beef or game, seasoned with coriander and vinegar, and barbecued on a grill. Similarly, Australians ground kangaroo meat into mince for sausage. American soul food featured pork ground with salt and sage for a meaty additive to scrambled eggs and pancakes.

See also: Creole Diet and Cuisine; Heritage Foods; Idiocuisine; Pemmican; Pork; Travel Food.

Further Reading

Aidells, Bruce. *Bruce Aidells' Complete Sausage Book.* New York: Ten Speed, 2000.

Hasheider, Philip. *The Complete Book of Butchery, Smoking, Curing, and Sausage Making.* Minneapolis, MN: Voyageur, 2010.

Jones, Carol. *Sausage.* Philadelphia: Chelsea House, 2003.

Sandler, Nick, and Johnny Acton. *The Sausage Book.* Lanham, MD: National Book Network, 2011.

Scandinavian Diet and Cuisine

In Iceland, Denmark, Norway, Sweden, and Finland, Nordic pantry staples favor locally sustainable foods that grow in a harsh periarctic climate. Forests yield mushrooms for salads and reindeer for roasting. Fields of rye and fisheries processing a fresh catch produce the pickled herring on rye bread that accompanies blue-shell mussels and gravlax.

Because of severe weather and weeks of home-bound activity, Scandinavians demand tasty, interesting meals. Savory specialties—rosehip soup, blood pudding, aquavit, yogurt, rhubarb, sourdough bread, jellied eel, and cloudberry jam—derive from recipes dating to the Vikings. Condiments tend toward beet pickles, horseradish, capers, mustard, and balsamic vinegar rather than sugary ketchup or cream- and roux-based French sauces.

From early times, the aboriginal Sami based their meat consumption on reindeer. Vigorous Scandinavian hunter-gatherers embraced a high-protein diet of bear, boar, deer, elk, goat, hare, horse meat, musk ox, puffin, seal, and walrus, which they obtained with spears or bow and arrow. In anticipation of a long winter, preparers salted, air-dried, or smoked moose haunches, whole fish, and sausage. Coastal scavenging netted auk, oysters, mussels, grouse, waterfowl eggs, and whale meat. Sailors recognized the value of dulse and scurvy grass, which prevented bleeding gums and loose teeth.

Around 900 c.e., the Vikings gathered at the fire pit for two daily communal meals, eaten from wooden trenchers with spoons and knives. Kettle cookery in iron or soapstone cauldrons or animal pelts required the placement of heated rocks in the liquid, such as black soup, a blend of pig and goose blood. More delicate meats, such as lamb and seabirds, hung from the longhouse ceiling in a constantly smoky atmosphere.

Diners interspersed spitted meat, egg, and milk dishes with Arctic bramble, onions, elderberries, wild crab apples, sloes, nettles, hops, hazelnuts, and ground elder, a spring leaf vegetable and potherb. For winter rations, cooks made fresh cheese and submerged butter and mutton in sour whey. For beverages, they sipped myrtle-flavored ale, fruit wine, or mead from wooden cups and horn tankards. For travel, sailors stocked ships with salt herring, *stokkfisk* (dried cod), and lutefisk (lye-cured cod) for ready meals and trade items. The seafarers bartered their preserved fish as far from home as Baghdad in exchange for grape wine, figs, almonds, capers, mustard, fennel, and spices.

As agrarianism took hold in the colder climates, domesticated barley yielded a grain suited to steaming, fermenting into ale or beer, or grinding into flour. Norwegian women kneaded whole grain dough into *lefse*, a crepe prepared once a year for packing in barrels or sea chests and consuming with beer. To preserve ducks, geese, and herring, preparers plunged them into brine and added saltpeter as a stabilizer. Danes served pickled goose with yellow pea soup, a puree of peas, carrots, parsnips, and leeks. A favorite dressing combined horseradish with whipped cream sauce.

In the late Middle Ages, grain failures caused Scandinavians to double the amount of meat in their daily intake. Root vegetables anchored the military breakfast of egg and meat hash. Orchards produced 200 apple cultivars for baking and smoking. Cooks refined farmyard ingredients into porridge with whey or buttermilk and cured salmon, both remedies for dreary winter days. Cloudberries in liqueur and preserves treated gout and scurvy.

The introduction of new foods and kitchen methods made slow inroads onto the Scandinavian table. Sugar arrived in 1324 but influenced only the diet of the wealthy. By the 1500s, pie making augmented simpler methods of presenting meat and vegetables. The smorgasbord, a buffet of hors d'oeuvres, evolved in 1650 with a variety of flavors and textures sampled before a formal dinner or in hotels as light meals. In the late 1700s, potatoes became a focus of meat and vegetable soups and stews. French and Russian influence added crepes and blini to traditional dessert choices of fruit soup, berry mousse, and *romfromage* (rum meringue).

Currently, Nordic appetites tend toward hearty fiber foods, such as mackerel or trout chowder with oat or spelt bread, which keep Sweden's obesity rate at 10 percent. For flavoring celeriac, salsify, Icelandic moss, turnips, cauliflower, and boiled potatoes, cooks make liberal use of angelica, dill, fennel, juniper berries, parsley, and thyme. For braising meatballs to serve with brussels sprouts, cabbage, or kale, restaurateurs choose rapeseed oil, a deviation from the European preference for olive oil.

Desserts incorporate blueberries, cowberries, and lingonberries in light, creamy combinations.

With the opening of the Noma restaurant in Copenhagen, Denmark, in 2003, Western chefs took notice of the Nordic diet, a heart-healthy cuisine rich in omega-3 fatty acids, fiber, and antioxidants and low in processed foods and saturated fats. The Scandinavian preference for local, seasonal, and organic produce, such as the ingredients in fish kebabs, potato pancakes, moose tournedos, and sweet pea soup, interested ecologists and proponents of the healthful food movement. Critics of the wholesale adoption of traditional Nordic gastronomy warned that the sodium in salted foods increased the risk of stomach cancer, stroke, and elevated blood pressure.

See also: Beer; Cod; Kitchen Gardening; Pan-European Diet and Cuisine; Swedish East India Company; Wheat.

Further Reading

Buesseler, Cathryn Anne Hansen. *Scandinavian and German Family Cookery.* Madison, WI: Goblin Fern, 2005.

Ojakangas, Beatrice. *Scandinavian Cooking.* Minneapolis, MN: University of Minnesota Press, 2003.

Sinclair, Pat, and Joel Butkowski. *Scandinavian Classic Baking.* Gretna, LA: Pelican, 2011.

Seacole, Mary Jane (1805–1881)

One of history's first military dietitians, Mary Jane Grant Seacole, a Creole herbalist from Kingston, Jamaica, practiced culinary and healing arts in Central America and on the battlefields of the Crimea.

She was born to Captain James and Jane Grant, a Scots officer of the British army and a Jamaican healer. In addition to learning how to simmer fruit into jam and to pickle fruit and vegetables, she began an apprenticeship in folk medicine at age 12. Period curatives involved boiling thistle seed for diarrhea, chopping water lily root into a gut-soothing beverage, collecting fig sap for stomach ache, pressing plantain juice for internal bleeding, and steeping ginger tea and lemongrass to control malarial fever. After completing her education, she traveled to London and sold West Indian pickles and preserves.

After the death of Seacole's husband, Edwin Horatio Seacole, in 1844, she operated the British Hotel in Las Cruces, Panama, for convalescent sailors and soldiers. While studying the healing methods of Cuba, Haiti, Nassau, and Panama, the revered "yellow doctress" acquired experience treating cyclical cholera and malaria outbreaks. Her home remedies included emetics, a soothing drink of cinnamon water and "sugar of lead," mustard plasters, and massage with camphor, oil, and wine. In making and administering African and West Indian cures, she contracted cholera but recovered.

After battling yellow fever in Jamaica in 1853, Seacole studied medical techniques in Colombia, learning dietary treatments for scurvy. The next year, she volunteered for the British army nurse corps at the London War Office but received a chilly reception from the all-white staff. Adamant about serving, she booked passage on the Dutch steamer *Hollander* to Turkey. At Florence Nightingale's Barracks Hospital at Scutari, she toured the kitchen, where cooks were preparing the arrowroot pudding, broth, and soups that strengthened the wounded.

On the southern coast of Russia along the Black Sea, Seacole arrived in time to witness heavy losses among the allies. Quartered on the ammunition ship *Medora,* she began bandaging wounds, setting broken bones, and prescribing special diets for casualties whom medics carted to the pier at Balaclava for boat transport to Scutari. Like Florence Nightingale and military chef Alexis Soyer, Seacole felt traumatized by the carnage, but she continued to stuff her backpack with bread, cheese, and cold meats along with spirits and wine and the medicines she mixed in her pharmacy. She stiffened her spine against the mockery of British doctors and smuggled brown bread past Sevastopol sentries. On her portable kettle and field stove, she cooked blancmange and plum and rhubarb pudding, flavors from home. During heavy combat, she evacuated 200 patients to Scutari. Throughout, she managed a cheery countenance and kind demeanor that earned her the name "Mother Seacole."

In summer 1854, Seacole purchased the British Hotel at Spring Hill south of Balaclava and operated it as a hostel and rehabilitation center for English, French, and Sardinian patients. She baked bread, cooked fruit and root vegetables, made dumplings and stew, roasted mutton and bustards, and served claret punch and rice pudding. Simultaneously, her kitchen turned out the current jelly, egg dishes, herbal tonics, and teas needed for medical treatment. On August 16, 1855, she rode horseback to the front at the battle of Tchernaya to treat casualties in trenches. In September, she witnessed the fall of thousands at the Siege of Sevastopol, where she fought off sentries who tried to return her to safety at the guardhouse.

Throughout her service to the military, Seacole had to pay for her own supplies, some of which she imported from London pharmacy houses. Thus, the melding of an inn and buffet with nursing provided her with cash for bandages, drugs, and transportation. On earnings from catering, she operated a lab for mixing medicines, sterilized water for washing the wounded, and cooked a daily supply of hot, fragrant herbal elixirs for victims of blood loss and frostbite. While contending with cholera, diarrhea, jaundice, and pneumonia, she spoiled the weakened men with fruit jelly, sherry, soup, and sponge cake. Her military decorations included the British Crimea Medal, the French Legion of Honor, Russian and Sardinian decorations, and the Turkish Order of Medjidie, but she received no remuneration for her charity.

After the restoration of peace in the Crimea in 1856, Seacole sailed for England. Her financial state prevented an immediate return to Jamaica. Admirers reading of her courage and selflessness in *The Illustrated News, Punch,* and the London *Times* donated funds to repay her for volunteering and for financing a dietetic kitchen and dispensary. To recoup some of her losses, she wrote *Wonderful Adventures of Mrs. Seacole in Many Lands* (1857), Britain's first autobiography composed by a black female.

Much loved by allied soldiers whom she fed and tended, Seacole died of stroke and received military honors at her burial in Kensal Green, London, in May 1881. Posthumous awards include a statue at the Institute of Jamaica and the Order of Merit, awarded in 1990, and, in 2008, acclamation as the Greatest Black Briton.

See also: Mustard.

Further Reading

Rappaport, Helen. *No Place for Ladies: The Untold Story of Women in the Crimean War.* London: Aurum, 2007.

Robinson, Jane. *Mary Seacole: The Most Famous Black Woman of the Victorian Age.* New York: Carroll & Graf, 2005.

Seacole, Mary. *Wonderful Adventures of Mrs. Seacole in Many Lands.* Reprint, 1857. New York: Kaplan, 2009.

Seaman's Diet and Cuisine

From the earliest times, the menu for oceangoing crews fit the limitations of availability, price, and stowage. Ship's biscuit, or hardtack, served Egyptians, Romans, and crusaders because of its dehydrated constitution of flour and water and its lengthy survival of dampness and weevils. Bronze Age Greek sailors varied their bread diet with almonds, figs, raisins, and seeds. The crews of Chinese junks subsisted daily on 2.2 pounds (1 kilogram) of salt cod or herring and pork, 1.8 pounds (800 grams) of rice, 3.5 ounces (100 grams) of preserved cabbage, and 3.2 quarts (3 liters) of tea. The Indian sailor had less to look forward to at mealtime except plates of dal and rice topped with ghee (clarified butter).

For the French, ship life exposed the crew to filth and poor ventilation. The worst hardship, drinking water gone fetid in wood casks, required the addition of ale or spirits to kill algae. The lucky seaman caught fish or seabirds as a break from stowed supplies but still suffered the effects of limited calcium and potassium and deficiencies of vitamins A and C. Poor hygiene and limited diet left men vulnerable to typhoid and typhus, which rapidly undermined a fleet's fighting strength.

Varied Pantries

In the great era of sea exploration, ships' pursers broadened pantry lists with global stock as well as short-term fruits, milk, and vegetables. However, the common seaman's fare never compared to the menus of the officers' mess. In 1519, the invasion of Hernán de Cortés on the Aztec of Mexico required provisioning at the embarkation point in Cuba. For the voyage, the ship occupied by soldier-turned-chronicler Bernal Díaz dispensed anchovies, bacon, biscuits, cassava flour, cheese, chickpeas, onions, salt pork and fish, sardines, and wine. A downside to unpalatable cuisine, the consumption of grog (watered ale or rum) increased during lengthy voyages, precipitating alcohol abuse and alcoholism.

On voyages to Brazil, Guinea, and India in 1600, Portuguese mariners received measured amounts of biscuit, dried cod, olive oil, salt meat, vinegar, water, and wine. In addition, the ship's cook laid in stores of almonds, garlic, grain, honey, lentils, mustard, onions, prunes and raisins, salt, sardines, and sugar. They reserved the dried fruit, honey, and sugar for sailors in sickbay. Civilian passengers provided their own foodstuffs. The purpose of carefully allotted staples was the avoidance of fighting with pirates during calls to port.

During layovers for new stores of cod and meat, sailors had time to fish on their own and to barter for fresh produce and healing herbs. Before the discovery of vitamin C, concern for epidemic scurvy encouraged English captain James Lancaster to dose sailors for the East India Company each morning with three spoonfuls of lemon juice. In 1634, the Danish East India Company (*Dansk Østindisk Kompagni,* or *OK*) equipped the *St. Anna* for a run from India to Copenhagen. In addition to the usual victualing with biscuits, dried cod, and salt beef and pork, company director Willem Leyel fought ennui and scurvy with stores of barley, beans, butter, brandy, ham, horseradish, lemon juice, prunes, smoked ox tongue, and vinegar. A fellow OK shipper loaded the *Gilded Sun* with sauerkraut, a known antiscorbutic.

Under the direction of naval provisioner Samuel Pepys in 1667, the British navy provided nourishing but monotonous fare for its recruits. The official weekly allotment consisted of 7 pounds (3.2 kilograms) of biscuit, 6 cups (1.7 liters) of oatmeal, 4 pounds (1.8 kilograms) of salt beef, 2 pounds (900 grams) of salt pork, 3 cups (0.8 liters) of peas, 4 ounces (113 grams) of cheese, and 3 ounces (85 grams) of butter. Because a galley lacked both grill and oven, cookery consisted of boiling and limited desserts to boiled pudding. Sweetening came from cane sugar, dried currants, and raisins. An American sailor enjoyed some variation of the British diet with the addition of dried onion, potatoes, and turnips. For professional sailors on voyages to the Arctic regions, more than half their caloric intake came from ale, liquor, and wine.

Malnutrition

Lengthening voyages increased the incidence of scurvy, a perpetual threat from the late sixteenth to the late nineteenth century. The silent killer robbed sailors of energy and precipitated bleeding gums and painful joints. By the onset of such symptoms as convulsions, fever, and neuropathy, the illness was irreversible.

In 1620, Captain John Smith, the founder of Virginia, advised that ships' provisioners include lemon juice along with bacon, cheese, marmalade, mutton, and wine. Both the Dutch and Spanish, on voyages along the African coast, bargained with natives for lemon juice and syrup. During one voyage to Asia of the Dutch East India Company, the captain had to call to port to buy fresh produce and to hire crewmen to replace those dead of scurvy.

From 1768 to 1779, Captain James Cook lost none of the *Endeavour*'s crew to nutritional ailments. He had his men collect berries and watercress, eat sauerkraut, and make spruce beer, an antiscorbutic known to Native Americans. Ship's botanist Joseph Banks added to the regimen scurvy grass and wild celery, both herbs he believed beneficial to sailors' health and performance. Late in the eighteenth century, the addition of sauerkraut to standard galley supplies prevented large-scale scurvy.

By the mid-1800s, sailors enjoyed ale and rum as well as canned meats, a substantial break from salt beef and pork. During the American Civil War, cooks softened hardtack in water and mixed the results with molasses and pork for a dish called dandy-funck. With adequate flour, kitchen crews also turned out duff, a floury pudding sweetened with prunes or raisins and boiled in a muslin bag. Before breakfast and after dinner, ships' stewards doled out 4 ounces (118 milliliters) of grog or, during combat, whiskey. When not engaged in sea skirmishes, men could count on coffee heated over steam boilers and sweetened with black molasses. Congressional action ended the grog ration on September 1, 1862.

The Japanese made similar progress for readiness on transoceanic missions by combating the disease afflicting 40 percent of their seamen. In 1884, Surgeon-General Takaki Kanehiro, director of the Tokyo Naval Hospital, eliminated beriberi by reducing rice intake and adding bonito, cabbage, canned beef, carrots, chicken, curry, daikon, egg omelets, greens, leeks, miso soup, pickles, potatoes, sardines, saury, seaweed, tofu, and yellowtail. Most significant to the upgrade, he changed staple purchases from polished rice to the unmilled variety, which contained vitamin B1 and prevented beriberi.

In 1889, Dutch physiologist Christiaan Eijkman furthered the study of beriberi on ships and in prisons of the Dutch East Indies by linking beriberi directly to a form of malnutrition. The mysterious ailment caused cardiac problems, neuritis, and paralysis. He earned a Nobel Prize in Medicine (1929) for identifying the missing nutrient as an unknown substance in bran, the pericarpium of rice.

The Modern Navy

After 1890, reforms of naval diet in the West, Russia, and Japan altered the philosophy of nutrition management. The French compared the food value of fresh and preserved meats on board ship; the Russians focused concern on the digestibility of salt meat and pickled vegetables. Another problem for Russian recruiters, the hardiness of Finns and sailors from the maritimes raised the question of weaknesses in men from the country's interior, who did not thrive on the staple of cabbage soup with bread.

The 1910s increased medical awareness of essential vitamins. After World War II, military nutritionists determined that high-calorie dishes increased shipboard efficiency. Food quality made a difference in long-term wellness and the ability to throw off infection, especially for exhausted or injured sailors. In the 1930s, the Japanese equated supplying foodstuffs to the military with citizen patriotism.

World War II advanced concepts of naval readiness with added dairy, fruits, and vegetables to the seagoing diet. In 1942, the U.S. Navy ration included yeast and flour enriched with vitamin B1, iron, and niacin. The military also devised combat and survival rations for battle extremes, such as abandoning ship or lengthy bombardments. By 1960, installation of high-tech kitchens preceded the formulation of 1,300 recipes and upgrades to Navy cookbooks. To maximize storage, provisioners tested compressed, concentrated, dehydrated, freeze-dried, frozen, and precooked dishes. Sterilizers sanitized cookware and dishes to curtail the spread of contagion in below-deck surroundings.

Today, battleship crews meet on the fantail for cookouts and enjoy fad foods such as deli subs, fish and chips, pizza, and tacos. Mess halls extended breakfast hours and welcomed diners to a restaurant-style atmosphere and to "midrats" (midnight rations). For submarines as well as space missions, freeze-drying makes available cottage cheese, eggs, green peas, hamburgers, hotcakes, and pasta. Galley workers store additional canned food under floors in the passageways. For long undersea duty, appetizing meals rank high as morale boosters.

See also: Biscuit; Cook, James; Crackers; Gama, Vasco da; Ibn Battuta; Lapérouse, Jean François Galaup; Lind, James; Maritime Trade Routes; Polo, Marco; Pork.

Further Reading

Bredsdorff, Asta. *The Trials and Travels of Willem Leyel: An Account of the Danish East India Company in Tranquebar, 1639–48.* Copenhagen, Denmark: University of Copenhagen, 2009.

Cox, Caroline, and Ken Albala. *Opening Up North America, 1497–1800.* New York: Facts on File, 2005.

Gurney, Alan. *Below the Convergence: Voyages toward Antarctica, 1699–1839.* New York: W.W. Norton, 2007.

McCallum, Jack Edward. *Military Medicine: From Ancient Times to the 21st Century.* Santa Barbara, CA: ABC-Clio, 2007.

Seaweed

A seashore algae used to mulch plants and feed cattle and swine, seaweed also reinforces both forage diets and table cuisine. Coastal peoples worldwide value the 9,000 varieties of brown, green, purple, and red seaweed from intertidal zones for their health benefits and as a garnish and complement to national dishes. Native Tongans, who believed that sea vegetables increased longevity, used seaweed in rituals.

Like acorns, sea flora provided a dependable spring-to-fall crop for Native American foragers. Harvesters typically paddled boats to algae-infested shoals and waters and pulled up strands on grappling hooks. The Pomo of Northern California dried their haul on the beach to serve in tortillas or fry in oil. From the Pacific Northwest to British Columbia and Alaska, Haida cooks boiled seaweed with halibut as a relish.

In China in 600 B.C.E., a description of King Ding Wang's table named seaweed as a fitting herb for the elite diner. Chinese pharmacists shaped wet fronds into a poultice and turned brown strands of *Sargassum muticum* into a powder to heal respiratory ills. Cooks chose shelf-stable lengths of *kanten* (or *tengusa*) to make a savory sea gelatin or candy and to sauté in stir-fry or to replace edible bird's nests in soup.

Kombu or *kunbu* (*Saccharina japonica,* or kelp) influenced the cuisine of Australia, Canada, China, Japan, Russia, Scandinavia, South Africa, and Tasmania. From 400 C.E., the Chinese extended papermaking technology to seaweed. They dried it and stored it in strips. In powder form, they used it to make stock and thicken meat dishes, simmer with vegetables, or flavor rice with a taste similar to anchovies or caviar. At Amoy in Fukien Province, a regional pancake secured cooked filling, seaweed, bean sprouts, and hot mustard or plum sauce for wrapping into handheld snack food.

Dulse (*Palmaria palmata,* a red algae) is another common sea edible in the North Atlantic and Northwest Pacific. In Iceland in the 900s, Norse chieftains favored dulse as a summer fiber food eaten fresh or dried. Scots ate dulse boiled in milk as well as steamed or grilled. The Irish preferred it in fish dishes and oatcakes and on potatoes. Healers recommended dulse in the diet for the fluoride content that prevented dental cavities.

Aquaculture in Australia, China, France, India, Indonesia, Japan, Korea, and the Philippines turned seaweed production into a food industry. The cultivation of nori (*Prophyra bangiaceae*), a red algae, occurred by accident in the early 1600s in Shinagawa outside Tokyo, where the shogun Ieyasu Tokugawa discovered seaweed growing on the fence around his fish farm. Although only ten varieties of algae dominated harvests, the Japanese increased their collecting to 21 strains of sea vegetables, which made up 10 percent of the diet from the eighth century until recently.

By 1900, the Japanese were harvesting enough sea vegetables from their 18,000-mile (29,000-kilometer) coastline to generate a $2 million industry. The kanten variety purified sake, a native rice wine. To make seaweed fronds appeal to the public, Hokkaido processors boiled them in iron kettles filled with fresh water and green dye before drying them on bamboo racks.

Although Chinese immigrants to California began shipping *Ulva lactuca,* a low-fat, iron-rich green algae known as sea lettuce, from San Simeon Bay in 1869, mainland Chinese came late to the seaweed cultivation market. After discovering *dashi kombu* (*Laminaria japonica*) growing wild at Dairen, Manchuria, in the mid-1920s, propagators allowed the influx of spores from Hokkaido to flourish naturally. Wartime embargos in the 1940s forced the Chinese to build their own aquaculture floats. The effort spread from Shantung as far south as Kwangtung, employing 250,000 processors in growing six varieties of sea vegetables.

Methods of seeding algae simulated the planting of a field. Spores attached to ropes or in some areas growers blasted them on rocky coasts and reefs where they developed into fronds. Japanese food processors promoted the production of nori, the most abundant sea vegetable. Transported in bales and sold in sheets, it texturized soup, topped noodles, and wrapped sushi.

Today, the variety of seaweeds lends itself to numerous food needs. Since the rise of macrobiotic diets in the 1970s, Japanese restaurants have added sweet *wakame* (*Undaria pinnatifida*), a brown algae, to their tofu salads and miso soups. Australian and Tasmanian cooks blanch wakame to fry into chips or to complement the marine flavors of abalone, oysters, and steamed snapper. Dieters and vegetarians choose wakame and dulse as fat burners and blood and organ purifiers.

As a digestive aid and as a source of calcium, iodine, and magnesium, sea vegetables enhance the diet with flavor and nutrition. A fresh water alga, *spirulina* has shown promise since the early 1980s in Belarus, China, India, Mexico, Romania, Rwanda, Togo, Ukraine, and Zaire for the rescue of starving infants and children. Japanese children carry nori-wrapped rice balls to school for lunch.

Food processors sell popcorn, rice cakes, and other snack foods in seaweed flavors. Belize diners take their seaweed in a milk beverage flavored with cinnamon, nutmeg, and vanilla. Sea lettuce has value in East Asia, the British Isles, and Scandinavia as an antiscorbutic and a ruffled additive to salads. Toasted and broken into pieces, it becomes a sauce or soup component. In Hawaii, cooks

Recipe: Welsh Toasted Laver

Rinse and wipe clean six sheets of dried sea lettuce. Mix 2 tablespoons of sesame oil with a sprinkle of sea salt and coat the lettuce. Roll each sheet into a cigar shape and let rest for a few minutes. In a skillet, heat the rolled sheets separately until crisp. Chop into pieces to serve over rice or on bread with bacon and vinegar. The Irish also dress cold meat with laver, pepper, and vinegar.

use *ogonori* (*Rhodophyta gracilaria*), a red sea moss, in pickles and salads and add it to poke, a raw fish appetizer.

German beers incorporate agar, a seaweed extract in sweetening; a similar application in Holland flavors schnapps. Carrageenan (*Chondrus crispus,* or Irish moss), a red algae, and kelp (*Laminariales*) produce glutinous material for cottage cheese, diet mayonnaise, dyes, gels, snack foods, and thickeners for coffee creamers, custard, ice cream, and soy milk.

In May 2011, Greenpeace reported that the tsunami off Fukushima, Japan, raised radiation levels by 50 times. Japanese diners on regionally grown seaweed could risk cancer from radioactive cesium and iodine.

See also: Japanese Diet and Cuisine; Kitchen Gardening; Monoculture; Tudor Diet and Cuisine; Wild Food.

Further Reading

Dubin, Margaret Denise, and Sara-Larus Tolley, eds. *Seaweed, Salmon, and Manzanita Cider: A Californian Indian Feast.* Berkeley, CA: Heyday, 2008.

Maderia, Crystal. *The New Seaweed Cookbook: A Complete Guide to Discovering the Deep Flavors of the Sea.* Berkeley, CA: North Atlantic, 2007.

Vaughan, J.G., and Catherine Geissler. *The New Oxford Book of Food Plants.* New York: Oxford University Press, 2009.

Seed Trade

Local and global seed exchange averts the potential extermination or extinction of world food sources. Trading protects the availability to growers of a range of seed families and alternative seed systems. Anecdotal advice and choices avoid the restrictions of government policies, which limit mixed cropping strategies. Village-based dispersal, such as that practiced in the Kurnool district of India and women's swaps of cassava cuttings in Amazonia, shields poor farmers from agribusinesses that threaten to displace family farms and livestock and to destroy autonomous cultures and their foodways.

International efforts, such as the Royal Botanic Gardens Kew Seed Bank begun in 1974, maintain and distribute samples from a span of wild populations in lush, semiarid, and dry lands. To stimulate biodiversity and plant reserves, British ethnobotanists abide by the principles of the United Nations Conference on Environment and Development—the Earth Summit of 1992 and 2012 in Rio de Janeiro—which advocates eco-efficiency through wise use of seeds, energy, and water. The consortium gives a voice to the traditional farmer against the mounting dominance of botanical theorists and seed brokers.

In remote parts of Ethiopia, the exchange of cultivars and information suits the means of smallholders, who may negotiate in barter, cash, seeds, or economic or social obligations, such as plowing and barn repairs. At weekly markets and annual farm fairs, growers discuss methods and share potato tubers and cereal grass, corn, and peanut seed. Regional interaction sustains agricultural commerce while nurturing varietal diffusion of germplasm, the life source of each food species.

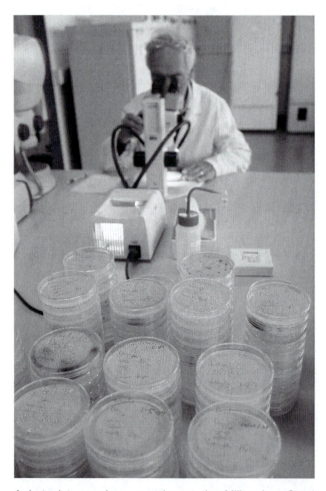

A botanist examines samples at the Millennium Seed Bank, a conservation project run by Britain's Royal Botanic Gardens, Kew. The purpose is to protect against dwindling plant diversity by preserving the seeds of wild species from around the world. *(Glyn Kirk/AFP/Getty Images)*

Unlike small-scale seed trade, wealthier, better-educated planters in Kenya profit from hybrid seed, extension services, and credit as well as up-to-date information on botanical advances in corn and grain. In contrast, Ethiopians benefit from folk networking that retains regional open-pollinated plants. One-to-one negotiation fosters goodwill and sharing during ecological disasters. A similar grassroots cooperative in Huancavelica, Peru, circulates the hundreds of native potato cultivars that form the food heritage of the Andes. In Taounate, Morocco, a parallel exchange of fava beans fosters plant strains that flourish in the North African climate and drought conditions. Such traditional swapping preserves ancestral and exotic food plants for home and community use and spurs crop evolution within a limited ecosystem.

After decades of plant engineering and the patenting of seeds in industrialized nations, growers worldwide still choose the folk seed trade over exclusive hybrid plants. The Seed Savers Exchange, a nonprofit gene bank that preserves heirloom and open-pollinated food plants, furthers diversity and the rescue of some 100,000 threatened plant species. The program began in 1975 at Heritage Farm north of Decorah, Iowa. The company states in its pledge an intent to protect consumers from genetically engineered plants out of a belief that genetic engineering threatens cultural, economic, and political welfare. On an 890-acre (360-hectare) farm, owners organize fruit tree grafts and seed swaps with the descendents of emigrants from Asia, Europe, and the Middle East. Their success with German Pink tomatoes, Koronis Purple beans, Lao eggplants, Russian pickling cucumbers, Silver Bell squash, and Turkey Craw beans furthers a camaraderie among farmers and gardeners who treasure the food plants of America's past. In addition to vegetables, Seed Savers maintains 360 grape varieties and hundreds of apple types plus tubers of horseradish, Jerusalem artichokes, potatoes, and sweet potatoes.

Other domestic and international organizations work one to one on locating obscure and endangered food sources, such as Christmas basil, Fuyu persimmons, Goji papaya, heirloom cowpeas, loquat, pawpaws, Seminole pumpkins, Surinam cherry, and wild currants. In addition to food plants, traders share herbs, such as clary sage, feverfew, gentian, and hyssop.

Adventurous gardeners obtain food sources to introduce traditional plants or new cultivars in distant locales or to shorten the growing time for bitter orange, bunching onions, cherry tomatoes, echinacea hybrids, and ghost peppers. Others seek more productive stock made possible by hard-neck garlic, medlars, rare pulses, and perennial chives, scallions, and strawberries. Internet consortia—at sites such as davesgarden.com, www.gardenweb.com, heirloomseedswap.com, seedswaps.com, wintersown.org—facilitate the dissemination of both seeds and cuttings along with suggestions from experienced growers. The Internet also has become a major marketplace for commercial seed companies around the world.

In 2008, the American Seed Trade Association (ASTA) launched a crusade to collect quality seed to protect humankind in the event of disaster. In cooperation with state and regional rescuers, ASTA investigates new technology and alerts members and the public to governmental policies affecting the distribution and development of seeds, a $12 billion business.

See also: Agribusiness; Agriculture; Heritage Foods; Hybridization; Jefferson, Thomas; Lapérouse, Jean François Galaup; Livingston, A.W.; Paula Marín, Francisco de.

Further Reading

George, Raymond A.T. *Vegetable Seed Production.* Cambridge, MA: CABI, 2009.

Kirakosyan, Ara, and Peter B. Kaufman, eds. *Recent Advances in Plant Biotechnology.* New York: Springer, 2009.

Loewer, H. Peter. *Seeds: The Definitive Guide to Growing, History, and Lore.* Portland, OR: Timber, 2005.

Tripp, Robert. *Seed Provision & Agricultural Development: The Institutions of Rural Change.* Portsmouth, NH: Heinemann, 2001.

Shellfish

A culinary highlight of coastal cuisines, fresh water and saltwater invertebrates comprise a flavorful, textured foodstuff for imaginative cookery. As early as 18,000 B.C.E., foraging for crustaceans preceded formal strategies for fishing and hunting. From age five, the children of hunter-gatherers assumed responsibility for gathering ground-level cacti, eggs, grubs, and nuts. They waded in river estuaries or tidal pools and shallows to collect edible seaweed along with cockles, cowries, crabs, crayfish, limpets, mussels, scallops, soft-shell clams, and periwinkles (sea snails).

Adults assumed the more difficult task of reef fishing with spears, diving for sea urchins, or scooping into nets and plaited baskets conches, cuttlefish, lobsters, oysters, prawns, and squid, all sources of iodine, vitamins A and B12, and high-quality protein. The early Chinese and Japanese fished or "jigged" for cuttlefish and squid at night by lantern light and dried the meat for market. Analysis of shell middens has confirmed the centrality of aquatic invertebrates as raw material for fishhooks and shell money in Oceania and as necklaces added to the grave goods of Channel Islanders.

The meat and roe provided dependable meal sources, whether stone-boiled, dried, salted, or baked in an earth oven with seaweed and ti leaves, Polynesian style. Hawaiians valued conch and crab as a curative or stimulant and the whorled exoskeletons for fashioning into trumpets. At Tanna in the New Hebrides, whelks served a similar purpose as a signal horn. In British Columbia, Indian women strung scallops on a cord to dry like apples and smoke over lodge fires.

History

Although highly perishable, seafood figured in the gastronomy of nations close enough to a shore to supply their tables with tender morsels. Religious cookbooks from Mesopotamia dating to 8000 B.C.E. exemplified local enthusiasm for refined cookery of shellfish and turtles. Because of the meticulous separation of hard-shelled invertebrates from their carapace, cooks extended small amounts of meat as ingredients in patties and stew. Healers also ground unshelled varieties into a curative plaster or salve to soothe sores.

Evidence from Abydos, Britannia, Gaul, Mycenae, and Turkey attests to the popularity of oysters, which traveled well pickled and brined in clay jars. Egyptians valued the *otaria* (ear shell), found off the estuary of Alexandria, for its delicate sweetness. Recipes from classical Greece mentioned skewered shrimp brushed with honey for roasting over embers and cuttlefish cooked with squid and sprinkled with shredded herbs. Early writings enumerated the best locations for tasty crustaceans, notably, Chalcedonian oysters, the cockles of Messina, and the periwinkles of Mitylene.

Romans not only relished crustaceans but also valued their shells ground into tooth powder and their meat as aphrodisiacs. In the first century C.E., commentary by encyclopedist Pliny the Elder identified lobster as a favorite dish, especially of legionaries stationed in Britannia. He summarized methods of whelk baiting and envied the shell fishermen of India, who harvested from the Indian Sea oysters 12 inches (30 centimeters) in diameter. His nephew, essayist Pliny the Younger, preferred the giant shrimp of Laurentum near Rome. Other sources depicted sea anemones as costly table exotica.

Later in the first century, the Roman cookbook author Apicius recommended Smyrna shrimp for grinding with celery leaves and *garum* (fermented fish sauce). Cooks shaped the mix into balls or patties. Apicius also advised on broiling and shelling lobsters and seasoning the minced meat with cumin and rue. To supply the kitchens of the Emperor Trajan late in the century, oystermen packed their quarry in snow to keep them fresh and tightly closed.

In ancient times, crabs never attained the same popularity as lobster, oysters, and snails, which both the Romans and Chinese valued as barter items, or of the razor-shell cockle, limpet, and periwinkle, sweet favorites of Athenaeus, a Greek gourmand living in Egypt in the third century C.E. As a treatment for delicate stomachs, Athenaeus recommended seasoning meat with cinnamon and pepper. To expand trade, entrepreneurs devised ways of tricking nature. Crustacean farming involved the lining of sea bottoms with pot shards. After oysters attached to the fragments, cultivators repositioned the oysters to prepared ponds.

In Byzantium, aristocrats dyed their robes with purple ink from the murex, a member of the whelk family, and chose as a table treat Black Sea zebra mussels flavored with garum. Across the Western Hemisphere, reusable earth ovens layered with leaves or seaweed contributed a smoky savor to slow-roasted crustaceans. The many choices added abundance to the Portuguese diet, which, like the cuisine of Iceland and Japan, featured more seafood than that of other nations. According to legend, the prince of Japan so prized the razor-shell cockle that he forbade fishermen to harvest them. In later centuries, New Year's celebrants claimed the Japanese *awabi* (mussel) as a symbol of the famine diet of their ancestors.

Far-flung shore peoples developed culturing ponds to enhance the shellfish industry. Mesoamericans readied tidal passages for seed by lining them with tree branches. Faeroe and Shetland Islanders farmed the scaly horse mussel as food and bait. In 1235, an Irish sailor shipwrecked in Aiguillon, France, accidentally discovered that stringing a net over the sea bottom to snare diving shore birds also attracted mussel spawn to the artificial habitat. In Normandy, growers built rafts to stabilize a variety of young crustaceans imported from Portugal.

Religious Taboos

Although Europeans relished baked *pinnae* (sea wings), cockle porridge, and cold crab and lobster sprinkled with pepper and vinegar, Muslims and Jews clung to scriptural admonitions. In the Renaissance, obedient Jews avoided crustaceans, which Leviticus 11:9–12 forbade as a form of *treif* (inedible food). Educated readers of the Torah recognized the danger from shellfish, which harbored typhoid pathogens. Muslims came to diverse opinions: Shi'ites rejected shellfish, which Sunnis considered edible. In dire situations, authorities bypassed rigid cultural taboos and allowed consumption of available seafood.

Catholic countries suffered no doubts about crustaceans. With abundant clams, lobsters, mussels, and squid from the Adriatic and Tyrrhenian shores, Italians turned shellfish into table highlights. On arrival at the French court of Henry II as a bride in 1533, Queen Catherine de' Médici contributed to her new realm the foundations of the Florentine banquet. At Chambord, her skilled chef presented herbed oysters and shellfish *insalata* (salad), a satisfying dish lacking the heavy layers of fat in the medieval ox. Moist shellfish, particularly the oyster, acquired a reputation for heightening sexual pleasure. In art, the exoskeletons of crustaceans attained symbolic worth as coded messages of desire.

Shellfishing for Sustenance and Profit

Saltwater invertebrates proved lucrative to New World settlers. In 1620, the Pilgrims of Plymouth, Massachusetts, learned from returnees at Popham colony at Sagadahoc, Maine, how to ward off starvation during dire winters. In imitation of coastal Algonquins, the English equipped fishing stations to provide enough clams and oysters to sustain a colony until spring. Thrifty colonists recycled shells as clam rakes and shovels. Dried quahogs provided trade goods for negotiations with inland tribes.

On December 13, 1621, the Wampanoag chief Massasoit led 60 to 100 tribe members to the first American Thanksgiving with gifts of five deer, turkeys, geese, ducks, eels, and shellfish. The following year, Governor William Bradford considered lobster an appropriate choice of meat to serve friends. In 1629, he purchased Tiverton, Rhode Island, for its abundant clam, mussel, and oyster beds. Within three years, the commercial possibilities of shellfish led to the "Oyster Wars" of 1632, fought over beds cultivated in the Chesapeake Bay by fishermen from Maryland and Virginia. In Connecticut and Rhode Island, oyster dredging and shucking in the 1680s foretokened a shore industry.

During the federal period, Atlantic Coast oyster houses popularized raw and fried bivalves as quick dinners for travelers and workers. The poor made do on meals of beer, bread, and oysters, much as indigent Irish reapers combed rocks for edible limpets. Hard workers earned up to $4.50 a week for filling barrels with clams. By the late 1770s, however, steady harvesting had destroyed the clam and oyster beds at Cape Cod, Massachusetts, which fishermen restocked with shellfish from Chesapeake.

Industrialization of the fishing industry brought structure to commercial shellfishing. As of October 26, 1825, the completion of the Erie Canal from the Hudson River at Albany, New York, to Lake Erie allowed the transport of fresh oysters to Ohio and canned or pickled oysters to Missouri. Thus, oyster suppers became standard celebrations in Cincinnati and St. Louis. With the spread of tuberculosis, the demand for oysters increased as iodine-rich curatives, whether fried, scalloped, or ground into sausage. Simultaneously, clam digging boosted income for Provincetown and Wellfleet, Massachusetts, and Cape May, New Jersey. In the 1840s, lobster became a staple commercial item for Connecticut and Maine fishermen, who endangered their sources by overfishing.

Commercial Cuisine

Beginning in the 1870s, commercial chilling introduced to coastal communities large-scale preservation of shellfish, a deviation from canned crab and lobster and the high-sodium content of salted fish and roe. In the late 1800s, showy table displays included ice sculptures surrounded by fish and shellfish, particularly for cruise line buffets, hotel brunches, and wedding receptions. One popular oyster recipe, *Anges à Cheval* (Angels on Horseback), involved wrapping oysters in bacon for grilling. By the 1880s, the appetite for oysters began threatening the stability of coastal beds in Europe and the United States.

As the restaurant business drew more Americans and Europeans toward flavorful menu items, ocean life continued to decline in number and quality. In 1885, the Christian Woman's Exchange of New Orleans issued *The Creole Cookery Book,* a generous list of soups and fish and shellfish dishes. Louisiana Cajun appetizers favored oyster cocktails flavored with Tabasco. Farther north in the 1890s, restaurant chefs made a table-top event of cooking Shrimp Wiggle in chafing dishes by stirring shrimp pieces into green peas and cream sauce. The post–World War II popularity of Alaskan king crab encouraged exploitation by Japanese and Russian fisheries.

Evidence of shellfish endangerment in the 1980s demanded immediate action from fishermen before species reached extinction. At a consortium of U.S. environmental experts in New Orleans in April 1995, observers evaluated habitats and identified sources of pollution and health hazards from algal blooms. Four months later, a conference in Pensacola, Florida, increased the monitoring of watersheds. From the efforts to sustain aquaculture came the Shellfish Challenge Plan to halt the failure of beds in the Gulf of Mexico.

Aquaculture and fishing has become the fastest-growing global food industry. Australia thrived on intertidal cultivation of rock oysters and the subtidal farming of mussels, oysters, and scallops, which grew on ropes or in baskets and matured rapidly from calcium-rich feedings. A similar investment in the trochus, a sea snail common to Fiji and New Zealand, focused on a hardier crustacean usually safe from attacks by crabs.

In 2002, crustaceans occupied an alarming place in the socioeconomic divide. A U.S. restaurant survey found shellfish gaining in popularity as fast-food snacks and signature menu items. About 10 percent of new specialty entrées featured shellfish. Meanwhile, among the Gitga'at Nation at Harley Bay, British Columbia, children reared on food stamps and government handouts lost contact with the age-old Pacific diet by deserting healthful shellfish for junk food.

The Future

Currently, shellfish is one of the five most common causes of food intolerance and a prime source of "red tide" toxins from algal blooms, such as the one that closed Indian Neck, Massachusetts, to fishing in June 2005. Four idiosyncratic syndromes attack the immune system with amnesia, diarrhea, nerve damage, and paralysis. Allergic

response can begin with tingling and hives and heighten to fainting and fatal shock. Infectious hepatitis, which can originate in shellfish polluted by sewage, causes jaundice, a yellowing of eyes and skin that may last for months. A source of norovirus contamination comes from the hands of seafood harvesters and sorters who unknowingly infect clams, mussels, oysters, and other filtering bivalves. Food inspectors look for adulterated decks, chopping blocks, and collection hampers as points of recontamination from raw crustaceans, which gastronomes eat at raw bars with little more flavoring than cocktail sauce and lemon juice.

Nonetheless, shellfish remains in the forefront of distinctive dishes, from Rhode Island steamed quahogs and clam chowder to Hawaiian limpets, Maryland crab cakes, Japanese sea urchin milt vinaigrette, and Malaysian nerites. Under the market name *rock lobster,* fresh water crayfish appears on menus from the Carolinas to Brazil. The demand remains so great in the Bahamas, Florida, and Louisiana that dealers import stock from Australia, Chile, New Zealand, and South Africa.

Meanwhile, industrial aquaculture from Cape Cod, Massachusetts, to the New Jersey shore has gained in intensity in recent decades. It requires either the capture of wild stock for growing in cages and tanks or domestication in marine locales, beginning with the seeding of clam, geoduck, mussel, and oyster beds. Hawaiian shellfish farms specialize in prawns. Pacific Coast suppliers in British Columbia and Washington State sell mollusks, especially live sea urchins, to the Japanese, whose domestic supplies are limited. On September 16, 2011, CBN News sponsored Operation Blessing International, a gift of 40 boats to Japanese fishermen who lost their source of income from the March 11 earthquake and tsunami. Meanwhile, researchers attempted to turn waste feathers into a filtration system to reduce toxins in Japanese shellfish.

See also: Cajun Diet and Cuisine; Chowder; Cookbooks; Disease, Food-Borne; Hunter-Gatherers; Inspection and Safety, Food; Pit Cookery; Virginia Company of Plymouth; Wild Food.

Further Reading

Brennessel, Barbara. *Good Tidings: The History and Ecology of Shellfish Farming in the Northeast.* Hanover, NH: University Press of New England, 2008.

Peterson, James. *Fish & Shellfish: The Cook's Indispensable Companion.* New York: William Morrow, 1996.

Stavely, Keith W.F., and Kathleen Fitzgerald. *America's Founding Food: The Story of New England Cooking.* Chapel Hill: University of North Carolina Press, 2004.

Whiteman, Kate. *The World Encyclopedia of Fish and Shellfish: The Definitive Guide to the Fish and Shellfish of the World.* Leicester, UK: Anness, 2012.

Sicilian Diet and Cuisine

Sicilian fare derives from the availability of fresh ingredients from land and sea—fish, olive oil, grains, fruit, rice, and vegetables. Since prehistory, Sicilians have grilled and roasted with bay leaf and oregano the region's prolific mussels, anchovies, sea urchins, swordfish, cockles, amberjack, crabs, prawns, cuttlefish, and whitebait. Short-lived wild olive trees produced fruit from 10,000 B.C.E. Around 6000 B.C.E., farmers cultivated fava beans for drying, eating raw, or adding to stews and soups, which they garnished with wild fennel.

Since 1000 B.C.E., islanders have adapted to cyclical invasions. After Corinthians founded Siracusa in 734 B.C.E., they raised goats and sheep and planted grapes, figs, hazelnuts, pomegranates, walnuts, and wheat. In the 600s B.C.E. in Messina, Greek settlers grafted wild olive trees with the verdello, a domesticated variety and source of large fruit, olive pâté, and oil for dressing greens sautéed in garlic. Residents of Magna Graecia (Sicily and southern Italy) also pickled capers, pressed and reduced syrupy grape must, and cured ham and bacon from island piggeries. The Greeks treated island wine with resin to produce retsina. Like mainland cooks, Sicilians began grilling fish, game, and lamb kebabs over charcoal foculari, slow-cooking braziers invented in Egypt.

Sicilian agriculture flourished from the creation of Greek and Roman latifundia (plantations). Traders exported thyme honey, a prime sweetener of Greek and Italian drinks and sponge cake, and shipped abundant soft wheat and flour east. In the fifth century B.C.E., Sicily joined Enotria Tellus (land of wine), a vineyard network that fermented wines popular in Carthage, Iberia, Italy, Provence, and Corsica. The early vintages prefaced island success at producing marsala, faro, moscato, and fragrant malvasia, made from fresh and dried grapes.

Literature preserved enthusiasm for diners on Sicilian food. Around 350 B.C.E., the Sicilian poet Archestratus rhapsodized over grilled bonito. In the 200s B.C.E., the poet Theocritus of Siracusa praised country beans, wine, and wild celery as the source of Sicilian cuisine. The island colonies provided Greek pantries with the best cheese, including savory balls of caciocavallo, a stretched curd cheese. Cooks grated goat and sheep's milk cheeses over baked dishes to brown into an au gratin (cheese crust).

Control under Augustus, the first Roman emperor after 27 B.C.E., resulted in an agrarian revival and profits from which the empire skimmed 10 percent. Sicilian goods filled military kitchens at outposts in Greece and Macedonia. To meet the demand in Rome for cereals, overseers ordered widespread seeding of land with lentils, pulses, and hard triticum durum wheat, the foundation of pasta. Roman traders imported citrons, cherries, and plums from the Middle East and introduced allspice, nutmeg, ginger, cardamom, and cinnamon to island cookery.

One long-lived recipe for egg drop soup illustrated a homey comfort food—broth dotted with balls of bread crumbs, cheese, and eggs.

Medieval Innovations

Christianity impacted the thinking of Sicilian cooks during the early Middle Ages, a period of innovation and prosperity marked by wedding and first communion feasts. Preparers made Easter cakes from scaldato (cottage cheese) and invented a dish combining sardines with fennel, raisins, and pine nuts. On March 19, bakers shaped and fried dough into sfingi, altar gifts to San Giuseppe (Saint Joseph), who shielded them from famine. Each December 13, a similar votive recipe for sweetened wheat gruel honored the blinded martyr Santa Lucia (Saint Lucy). In observance of fast days, cooks sliced boiled shrimp, octopus, and calamari into a seafood salad sprinkled with a lemon-based dressing and served clams over spaghetti.

In the 700s, pasta factories in Palermo produced the macaroni and noodles that Arabs added to chicken soup and cinnamon and raisin desserts. After 827, North African Arabs overran western Sicily at Palermo and planted banana, date palm, pistachio, and lemon groves, which they watered with irrigation canals. Palestinians imported currant bushes, a source of tiny raisins. Saracen cooks introduced sesame, saffron, cinnamon, coffee, couscous, handmade pasta in olive oil, and a mutton entrée seasoned with almonds and mint. Eastern recipes combined apricots with meat and rice, Persian style. Arab bergamot, jasmine, and sugar sweetened zabaglione (egg custard) and cannoli (tubes of sugary cheese) and flavored ice from Mount Etna for melon sorbet, the forerunner of gelato and granita.

Islanders adopted a fusion cuisine based on ethnic insurgent foodways. In 920, Arabs planted the first crocus beds, a source of saffron. From Arab gastronomy, Sicilians skewered kebabs, stuffed fish and poultry, baked one-pot rice entrées, and served caponata (Tunisian eggplant with capers), a favorite appetizer. Portuguese crusaders planted sweet blood oranges, shaddocks, limes, and tangerines, the source of candied rind, preserves, and salads sprinkled with anise and wine. Lombards brought seed for white arborio rice. Arab control after 947 revived the tradition of the kitchen garden, which the Greeks had introduced at Siracusa. At Palermo, home gardeners raised onions, pomegranates, and artichokes, an edible Berber thistle.

The Norman Conquest of 1060 made a few changes in Sicilian cuisine, notably rotisserie cooking and air-drying cod. From 1096 to 1204, crusaders settling in Sicily imported their taste for Arab specialties made with almonds, cinnamon, cumin, and pepper. Christian and Muslim immigrants lived peacefully together and generated a fusion cuisine flavored with melons, lemons, and oranges as well as figs, pine and pistachio nuts, pomegranates in syrup, and tahini paste made from roasted and ground sesame seeds.

After the accession of William II in 1166, Norman lords stripped peasant farmland of its wealth and generated a two-level caste system. Traders satisfied Norman demands for Middle Eastern foodstuffs, which they imported from Alexandria and Jerusalem for the pantries of the rich. By the 1300s, taxation on the peasantry suppressed ethnic cuisine and reduced the poor to subsistence foods, such as the winged pea and butter instead of cheeses.

Island Prosperity

At the high point of the Renaissance, voyagers introduced Sicilian ports to rice, the basis of sweet desserts mixed with egg custard and fruit. In the 1400s, Sicilian cheese proved profitable for dairy farms, as did sugar for Jewish investors. Abbeys and nunneries produced painted marzipan replicating the blush of island fruit.

Industrial ovens turned out white bread for the wealthy and black loaves for peasants. When food shortages ended the dominance of professional bakeries, the poor extended homemade bread with bean husks, berries, grass, leaves, nuts, parsnips, sawdust, seeds, squash, and wild radish and asparagus. After the expulsion of Jews in 1493 and the influx of Aragonese grandees, the ruling class continued to expand excessive banquet entrées with sunflower oil, chocolate, lima beans, corn, turkey, potatoes, cactus, chilies, and tomatoes from the New World.

The victory of Giuseppe Garibaldi over Spanish Bourbon overlords in July 1860 left Sicilians free to determine the future of their traditional cuisine. Many returned to the fresh produce of their heritage, such as basil, peppers, and zucchini, and revived the traditional family meal prepared by the female head of household. Fishermen prospered once more on profits from sardines and octopus. Housewives pureed tomatoes and dried them in the sun into a utilitarian paste. Pastry chefs baked amaretti, almond ovals served with coffee.

In the twenty-first century, Sicily relies heavily on agritourism, an economy based on the pleasing of travelers with homegrown produce. Tables spread with snails, chickpeas, pasta, pine nuts, rice and meatballs, porcini mushrooms, beans, prosciutto, and bluefin tuna attest to a lusty appetite among islanders. To entice guests to a feast, Sicilians display attractive tidbits—anchovies, cured ham, pecorino cheese, *bottarga* (dried mullet and tuna roe), radicchio, figs, Gaeta olives, and preserved lemons and lemon liqueur.

See also: Athenaeus; Fish and Fishing; Mediterranean Diet and Cuisine; Pasta; Rice; Trading Vessels.

Further Reading

Benjamin, Sandra. *Sicily: Three Thousand Years of Human History.* Hanover, NH: Steerforth, 2006.
Keahy, John. *Seeking Sicily.* New York: St. Martin's, 2011.
Robb, Peter. *Midnight in Sicily: On Art, Food, History, Travel and la Cosa Nostra.* New York: Macmillan, 2007.

Sierra Leone Company

A colonial enterprise on the Grain Coast of West Africa, the Sierra Leone Company, established in 1792, added a permanent colony to Great Britain's holdings and an important new source of produce for Europe.

The creation of a settlement for London's black poor began in May 1787 as a reward for loyalists who fought for the redcoats during the American Revolution. The group, organized by the Committee for the Relief of the Black Poor, consisted of black Nova Scotians and immigrants from Bengal and the West Indies. Most were farmers, fishermen, and artisans. An expedition of 411 men, women, and children, arranged by English abolitionist and reformer Granville Sharp and escorted by administrators and ministers of the St. George's Bay Company, founded Granville Town, a utopian effort at Fourah Bay known as "the Province of Freedom." Commerce introduced the New World freedmen to the Bambara, Fula, Hausa, Mandinka, Soso, Wolof, Yoruba, and other native African traders. The community survived until an assault by the Temne, rival traders, in December 1789. Destroyed by arson, the town was a total loss.

In 1790, Sharp issued a second call to former slaves to colonize free African territory. His backers intended the newcomers to establish a link in Britain's global food trade to supplant the slave trade. He anticipated 500 applications but received over 1,100. Incorporated by parliament, the settlers met opposition from slave traders in Bristol, Lancaster, Liverpool, and London.

In January 1792, sea captain John Clarkson guided 1,196 black Nova Scotians aboard 15 ships and sailed from Halifax to Sierra Leone. They founded Freetown on March 11, 1792, and received allotments of land—20 each for men, ten for women, and five for children. The location suited commerce because of the natural harbor, which the British chose as a naval base for its antislave trade patrol.

Liberated blacks raised rice, a luxuriant crop sown in June and reaped the next October. A less demanding commodity, cassava grew over a four-month period but could remain in the fields for gradual harvesting of roots. Freetown gardens also produced bananas, cashew nuts, castor oil, cocoa, cola, corn, eddoes, millet, okra, palm wine, peanuts, plantain, potatoes, sweet potatoes, and yams for subsistence and sale. Fruits, herbs, and tender vegetables grew abundantly—apples, breadfruit, cardamom, cream fruit, figs, guava, limes and oranges, melons, pawpaws, pigeon peas, pineapples, plums, pumpkins, squash, tallow tree fruit, and tamarinds, all easily sold at the vegetable market. Their meals featured abundant greens—callaloo, purslane, and sorrel—and two local spices, *barreliera* and *mabeck*. The ambitious produce growers sought immediate profits from arrowroot, camwood, coffee, cotton, ginger, gum, hemp, honey and wax, palm oil, pepper, and rice. They also saw promise in cinnamon, mahant for nets and rope, sesame, sugarcane, and a short-stemmed variety of nutmeg (*Piper guinense*).

In the colony's beginning, land clearing drained the "born-again Africans" of energies for commercial agriculture and orchardry. Their main objective lay in feeding and protecting their families. The absence of farm-to-market roads from the dense interior inhibited the sale of such perishable goods as cherries, grapes, and tomatoes. To speed foods to customers, women ventured into Freetown and hawked fresh produce along the streets and harbor. Until competitive tribes ended Freetown's barter with the African heartland, dealers used rum or tobacco rather than currency as a medium of exchange.

During British hostilities with France, the Sierra Leone Company encountered business setbacks from naval incursions and piracy. In late September 1794, Freetown suffered the same demise that had ended Granville Town. After soldiers from five French warships pillaged and burned the community and uprooted gardens, colonists fled to sanctuary with Pa Demba, the headman of a small village. Survivors relied on trade with American merchants for supplies to rebuild. They returned to raising cattle and poultry and fruit and vegetables for export and to supplying the 200 natives who came daily from 80 miles (130 kilometers) away to buy their food products.

In a gesture to the United States, from 1794 to 1799, Scots abolitionist Zachary Macaulay, the governor of the colony, offered American ex-slaves parcels of free land. Bearing testimonials of good character, the newcomers agreed to seek British citizenship and to devote two years to clearing at least one-third of their land. In 1807, the Sierra Leone Company became the African Institution, a haven for former slaves. As of January 1, 1808, Sierra Leone flourished as a Crown Colony. In the 1820s, Freetown grew into a West African commercial nexus, a magnet for trade caravans.

Further Reading

Clifford, Mary Louise. *From Slavery to Freetown: Black Loyalists After the American Revolution.* Jefferson, NC: McFarland, 2006.

Megill, Esther L. *Sierra Leone Remembered.* Bloomington, IN: AuthorHouse, 2004.

Walker, James W. St. G. *The Black Loyalists: The Search for a Promised Land in Nova Scotia and Sierra Leone, 1783–1870.* Toronto: University of Toronto Press, 1992.

Wilson, Ellen Gibson. *John Clarkson and the African Adventure.* London: Macmillan, 1980.

Silk Road

A romanticized web of land and sea routes from Europe and the Persian Gulf to China and Malaysia, the Silk Road (or Silk Route) introduced Western society to the delights of the East. Stretching from the Mediterranean over the Levant and Afghanistan around the Taklimakan Desert and along the Great Wall of China, the track reached the venerable city of Xi'an in east-central China. The cultural nexus occasioned the world's first great venture into globalized cuisine. For nearly two millennia, armies, missionaries, nomads, pilgrims, and tradesmen traversed 4,000 miles (6,400 kilometers) by camel, donkey, horse, and yak, each bearing up to 700 pounds (320 kilograms) of goods. Western dealers trafficked in Eastern dyes, fabrics, food therapies and medicines, fragrances and ointments, lapis lazuli, spices, and Tibetan jade. Along the way from Izmir on the Aegean Sea to the Chinese terminus, goods changed hands rapidly, rising in value with each leg of the journey. In lieu of a common currency, strangers bargained through hand gestures with bolts of silk.

Adventures in meals and beverages encompassed a span of foodstuffs and kitchen crafts. A parallel sea route from Vietnam connected the Far East with Ceylon, India, and Egypt. Along the way, knowledge of history and geography, of religion—Buddhism and Zoroastrianism—and of technology—block printing, carpet weaving, glass blowing, making gunpowder, mirror and paper making, sericulture, silversmithing, wine making, wood carving, and wool weaving—from ancient China, India, and Persia influenced the civilizations of the Middle East and the Mediterranean. The result was the forerunner of fusion cuisine, the merger of tastes and cooking methods from disparate cultures. One popular example, the concept of breaking down gluten in dough, encouraged the stretching of noodles into thin strands for soup, *lumpia* (fried strips), and stuffed dumplings, which entered menus as far west as Sicily and Spain. Another unique taste,

Recipe: Lemon Pickles

Boil 25 whole lemons in 5 cups of water for three minutes and drain. Quarter the fruit and season with 4 teaspoons of salt and 1 teaspoon of asafetida powder. Grind into a paste 30 black peppercorns and 15 cloves with 3 tablespoons each of salt, sugar, and vinegar. Add to this paste 1 tablespoon of white cumin and 2 teaspoons each of black cardamom and red chili powder. Rub the paste into the quartered lemons. Pack into a jar. Moisten with the juice of ten lemons and set in the sun to hasten pickling.

asafetida root from southern Bactria impressed Greek buyers with its utility as a treatment for respiratory ills and indigestion and as a condiment, meat marinade and rub, and pickling spice.

Merger of Tastes

In the second century B.C.E., the Asian frontier separated two distinct cultures, the settled agrarianism of the Fertile Crescent and the seminomadic pastoralism of the Steppes. In 138 B.C.E., ambassador Zhang Qian (Chang Ch'ien), an explorer and representative of the Chinese Emperor Wudi (Wu Di), extended the markets of vendors from the Han dynasty. To enhance business with Afghanistan, India, Parthia, Turkestan, and Uzbekistan, Chang recorded data for the imperial court on trade items, particularly bamboo canes and cloth, and on exotic foodstuffs—caraway, coriander, eggplant, figs, sugar beets, and wines—available from central and western Asia. A major flavoring breakthrough, garlic added pungent smells and boosts to the immune system as well as flavoring for marinade, meat and fish rubs, pickles, and sauces. Chang also enlightened millers on the Persian technique of expressing oil from sesame seed and of grinding soft, easily blended flour from wheat. Upon his return in 125 B.C.E., China established commercial relations with Persia, which dispatched up to ten Eastern expeditions per year.

Along the Silk Road, Chang's mission preceded a flood of food swapping. From India, the Chinese acquired basil, black pepper, cardamom, curry, oranges and pomelos, and spinach. From the Persians, China began importing cucumber and marigold seed, fenugreek, grapes, pomegranate and quince bushes, sour cherry and sour plum stock, sumac, walnut and pear trees, and horses. Persian alfalfa seed aided Chinese horse breeders with a nitrogen-fixing forage and a pollinator for bees and provided pharmacists with an herbal digestive tea that treated arthritis, edema, and kidney disease. Under the Han Emperor Ling in 156 C.E., the Chinese domesticated sesame for pasta, seed cakes, and oil for saucing. Among court aristocrats, sesame became the era's fad food.

Fed by the lucrative silk trade, the east-west conduit traversed deserts, mountains, and bandit enclaves to enlighten isolated peoples to the innovations of great cities and empires. Caravans to China delivered Armenian apricots, Ethiopian coffee, Samarkand honey, Somalian aloe, and Persian dates, pistachio nuts, and saffron. From the Chinese, the Indians adopted anise, cassia, cinnamon, leeks, licorice, onions, pepper, red and yellow rice, rhubarb, and sesame oil as well as bananas and citrus fruit. Indian pharmacists learned to cook beetles in hot brine and to prescribe curative meals of baked or pickled silkworm pupae, caterpillars, green bottlefly larvae, and water bugs, all available at Beijing restaurants. Silkworm cocoons required soaking in water before scrambling them with chicken eggs or saucing them with onions. At Chinese commercial centers in Hangzhou (Hangchow) and Kaifeng, snack vendors steamed savory ping cakes, a holiday fruitcake. Visitors strolled along specialized markets for grain, pork, and vegetables. Butcher shops sold cuts to order. Specialty stalls displayed beans, oranges, and preserved fish, essentials to China's extensive catering businesses. In northern China, Peking chefs began incorporating imported millet in dairy and meat dishes and wheat into dumplings and noodles; to the south and in Szechuan, cooks balanced fruit and vegetables with fish and pork for peppery rice-based entrées. In imitation of Chinese cuisine, Indian and Persian cooks turned rice into a basis for their hybrid cookery.

Rome and the Rise of the Silk Route

After 100 C.E., the Roman Empire tapped Silk Road commodities in Alexandria, Egypt, and generated the first international cuisine. For expedience, the Emperor Trajan established the first Chinese embassy and posted legionaries along the east-west highway. Roman staples—beans and lentils, bread, oil, olive, and wine—accommodated additions of beer, butter, meat, and milk and flavorings with cabbage, celery, dill, kale, and parsley. Soldiers marching to distant postings carried in their knapsacks the elements of Rome's newfound cookery. By expanding varieties of peaches from Greece and tart orange and yellow apples from Kazakhstan throughout the provinces, Roman arborists introduced methods of espaliering, grafting, and pruning. Resultant strains of cooking and snacking apples and fragrant varieties for saucing and beverages expanded Roman demand for pome fruit. Italian traders satisfied the chef's need for cinnamon, galangal, and turmeric. Stocks of cardamom, ginger, and white pepper rose dramatically in cost because of a 25 percent import tax, but Romans willingly paid the tariff to acquire spices that they deemed powerful antidotes to food poisoning. The empire achieved its own renown as the source of Falernian and Opimian cult wines, which they produced at a rate of 1,600 gallons per acre.

Over the next 500 years, east-west trade reached its golden era. Arab traders educated farmers in Iberia, Italy, and North Africa on rice culture, a landmark of the global food market. Additional cross-fertilization of food staples through oasis towns introduced African melegueta pepper, okra, and watermelons and Middle Eastern barley, chickpeas, figs, dates, grapes, olives, pine nuts, and wheat to the Far East. From Kashmir came saffron; India contributed cardamom. Indonesia produced the most succulent oranges. By increasing stocks of domesticated pack animals, Islamic traders enlarged dissemination of pantry and produce staples to include aubergine, cucumber, spinach, and sugarcane, the source of a pan-European dessert craze. Chinese cooks experimented with stewing, flavoring meat with cinnamon, fermented black beans and soybeans, galangal, ginger, and mustard. The development of wok stir-frying added heady aromas and savors from coconut milk, dates, lotus seed, and mango and a final topping of Turkish alcohol.

The popularity of tea drinking dates to the eighth century and Lu Yu's treatise *Ch'a Ching* (*The Classic of Tea,* ca. 760 C.E.), a guide to purchasing filters, rollers, and sieves for drying, storing, and steeping tea leaves. Green tea fascinated Arab and Bactrian merchants, who reached Xi'an and immediately sought relaxation in teahouses. By way of cultural exchange, Western merchants impressed the Chinese with glazed Islamic tableware colored inside and out. Alongside opulent cups and platters, they set glass carafes and goblets and serving dishes embossed with copper, gold, and silver. They contributed to China's tables the Turkish grilled meat, halvah confections, kebabs, noodle soup, wheat cereal, and yogurt. Jewish merchants returned home with Chinese carp, a specialty fish revered by the Ashkenazim of southern Europe. Arriving from China to Afghanistan, carrots influenced the color, flavoring, and texture of Arab and Persian cookery.

Dynamic Dishes

Invigorated interest in cuisine increased food commentary and menu critiques. Travelers noted variations on Eastern recipes, particularly flatbread, mare's milk butter and cheese, soups, and *mantou,* a fried or steamed bun or dumpling. In 1027, the Emperor Zhao Zhen (Renzong) saved the poor from hunger by importing lentils from India and a fast-ripening Vietnamese rice. Chinese publishers distributed recipes in food compendia and food remedies in compiler Su Song's 21-volume *Ben Cao Tu Jing* (*The Illustrated Basic Herbal,* 1061), a compendium of 780 drugs and 634 herbs. During the Song dynasty, banqueting attested to the wealth and cultivation of aristocrats, who vied for the most opulent table settings. Meanwhile, the rise of the nomadic Mongols introduced wild game cookery to the West. By boiling bear, boar, tiger, and wolf haunches with berries, fruits, greens, and tubers, they produced uniquely flavored stews. Mongol sophistication increased with the import of the *tannur,* a clay oven from India, and of lamb-based recipes employing generous use of chickpeas, ghee (clarified butter), and parsley. At the fragmentation of the Mongols after 1271, the Chinese rejected lamb as a political protest to northern insurgents.

Late in the Middle Ages, Eurasian cross-fertilization increased along the transcontinental food chain, China's main channel of communication with the West. Cookbooks described 43 kitchen techniques for 42 meats, 50 grains, and 68 fish varieties. In 1279, Kublai Khan rejuvenated overland trade from its lapse following the fall of the Tang dynasty. Marco Polo's expedition to China, which ended in 1295, revealed the unique use of charcoal for cookery. He observed service of delicate wines and rice in fine porcelain bowls, the extrusion of macaroni,

and the salt-making industry. His dictated writings described the world's first fast food, curdled mare's milk fermented into koumiss, a dairy innovation first processed by the Scythians.

By the fifteenth century, the speed and safety of sea routes replaced slower, more treacherous overland travel and the haphazard packing of food on dray animals. So dazzled were European navigators by the promise of a rich global food trade that they began plotting new water routes to the Spice Islands, a yen that directed Christopher Columbus toward the New World. In 1526, the founding of India's Mughal Empire promoted the fusion of central Asian cookery with pilaus spiced with cinnamon and nutmeg, cloves, nut and yogurt toppings and with sweets scented with rose petals. By 1550, China joined the rest of the world in adopting Dutch snow peas, Portuguese watercress, and American specialties—beans, chili peppers, guava, squash, tomatoes, and turkey. Propagation of sweet and white potatoes relieved famine conditions with crops that required less hand labor than rice and which flourished on marginal farmland. Corn and peanuts bolstered nutrition with foods that could be baked, boiled, or milled. Even Mexican cactus fruit, chayote, and jicama appeared in Far East recipes.

See also: Ibn Battuta; Polo, Marco; Trade Routes; Trading Vessels.

Further Reading

Kelley, Laura. *The Silk Road Gourmet.* New York: iUniverse, 2009.

Kuz'mina, E.E. *The Prehistory of the Silk Road.* Philadelphia: University of Pennsylvania Press, 2008.

Mack, Glenn Randall, and Asele Surina. *Food Culture in Russia and Central Asia.* Westport, CT: Greenwood, 2005.

Wood, Frances. *The Silk Road: Two Thousand Years in the Heart of Asia.* Berkeley: University of California Press, 2002.

Slave Diet
See African Slave Diet

Sloane, Hans (1660–1753)

An Irish physician and archivist, Hans Sloane summarized the strengths of the West Indian diet and introduced milk drinkers to chocolate milk.

Born in Killyleagh, County Down, Sloane collected curiosities from nature, a lifelong hobby. In London and Paris, he studied botany and pharmacy. After completing a medical degree at the University of Orange in Vaucluse, France, he practiced medicine in Jamaica, where he advocated smallpox vaccinations and the treatment of malaria with quinine. He championed pure water and the regular hydration of the body with water rather than wine or ale.

Upon opening a practice in 1689 in Bloomsbury, Sloane became one of London's most respected doctors. As head physician at Christ's Hospital, president of the Royal College of Physicians, and governor of the Foundling Hospital, he used his prominence to campaign for pure drugs and food and to promote a two-year regimen of breastfeeding to combat high infant mortality. His written report on mother's milk was one of the earliest to cite hospital statistics to prove his theory.

Sloane foresaw the commercial exploitation of drugs and foodstuffs from the West Indies. In the ethnobotany, *Natural History of Jamaica* (1707–1725), he characterized arum, corn, plantain, sorghum, and yams as nourishing foods relegated to livestocks and slaves. He mounted samples of valuable food commodities, including the kidney bean and peanut, examples of the influence of West African slaves on the North American diet. In addition to cataloging 800 Caribbean plants, he published *A Voyage to the Islands Madera, Barbadoes, Nieves, St. Christophers, and Jamaica* (1707). The text described the milling of cacao nuts with Indian pepper and the separation of froth from the oil. He recommended chocolate as a digestible "simple" promoting nourishment and well-being.

Sloane disliked the native drink of cocoa mixed with pepper and water because of its bitterness. He chose milk as a base, added chocolate liquor and sugar, and introduced England to his sweetened drink. Doctors prescribed chocolate for consumptives and as a treatment for dysentery, inflammation, and kidney stones. Sloane warned that overindulgence could worsen frail health.

Aficionados bought chocolate milk ready mixed from druggists Nicholas Sanders and William White and in powder form from a Birmingham chocolate and cocoa factory, where Quaker brothers John and Richard Cadbury packaged cocoa in tins. The chocolate recipe appeared in cookbooks and influenced service in chocolate houses.

In addition to his fame for inventing milk chocolate, Sloane gained a professional reputation as president of the Royal Society, a founder of the British Museum, and the physician to Queen Anne, George I, and George II and to the British army. The British Museum houses his tin-glazed ceramic chocolate cups from Italy.

Further Reading

Grivetti, Louis, and Howard-Yana Shapiro, eds. *Chocolate: History, Culture, and Heritage.* Hoboken, NJ: John Wiley & Sons, 2009.

MacGregor, Arthur. *Sir Hans Sloane: Collector, Scientist, Antiquary, Founding Father of the British Museum.* London: British Museum, 1994.

Slow Food

A contemporary eco-culinary movement that protects aboriginal food culture, heritage, and tradition, Slow Food advocates celebrate the quality and flavor of food and wine worldwide. Founded in Langhe, Italy, in 1986 by gastronomic activist Carlo Petrini of Barolo, the Slow Food initiative began with a protest of a McDonald's opening along Rome's Spanish Steps. From a single public brouhaha grew his media and Internet war against cosmetically enhanced, shippable foodstuffs and unnatural, out-of-season meals.

Petrini's outreach to world cuisine embraced Indian tandoori, Korean noodles, and innovations in falafel, lady apples, ostrich, souvlaki, and tacos. Recalling the husbandry of rural foodstuffs after World War II, he mocked Carrefour and Tesco supermarkets as wasteful and warned of the spiritual sterility of a distracted eat-and-run lifestyle. On behalf of smallholders and farmer's markets, he proclaimed Monsanto's patenting of seeds a form of biopiracy against Third World developers of heritage fruits and vegetables. His campaign gained the support of chefs Mario Batali and Graham Kerr, *Saveur* magazine, and winemaker Robert Mondavi.

Rather than a luxury for the rich and privileged, Petrini envisioned food service as a daily act of joy, a celebration of gusto. He scorned big name television cookery as "pornographic" and urged career chefs to offer sensory training to children and to feed patients in hospitals and retirement homes out of a reverence for satisfying meals. In place of strutting before audiences, he harangued food experts to plant school gardens and to rescue Argentine amaranth, Canadian Red Fife wheat, Chiapas coffee, Cornish salted pilchards, Dutch lobster, Greek and Polish cheeses, Malaysian rice, and Moroccan argan oil—all acts of sharing, collegiality, and "virtuous globalization."

In a revolt against banality and capitalistic factory foods, the movement fought the genocide of taste. Members promoted not only freshness and savor but also the environment and animal and human rights. The project "Ark of Taste" took as a model Noah's Ark and the shielding of rare cultivars. Slow Foodists professed a philosophy of leisurely conviviality and vowed to maintain table conversation and pleasure to humanize the younger generation.

The concept spread to France, Germany, and Switzerland by 1993. Writers and journalists praised the movement with rhapsodic essays; travel companies began organizing Slow Food tours. In 1996, Slow Food crusaders issued the periodical *Slow,* which focused on global health as well as fair pay for producers and accessible prices for consumers. In Africa, members pledged to create 1,000 community vegetable gardens from Morocco to Madagascar. Growers began sharing their experiences and coordinating green methods of controlling pests and boosting harvests.

Eco-gastronomists joined producers to protect sustainable, quality food crafts as regional assets. Members supported wild food collection and local "foodsheds," the

Italian author and gastron-omist Carlo Petrini (*left*) founded the international Slow Food movement in the 1980s. American restaura-teur, chef, and activist Alice Waters (*right*) pioneered the organic food movement. *(Paul Sakuma/Associated Press)*

venues of agrarian and oceanic biodiversity. In 2001, European members launched a "No GM Wine" appeal to halt the marketing of genetically modified (GM) grapes. They also defended raw milk cheeses as living museums of dairy history. With tastings and potlucks, consortia recognized terroirs, the geographical locales of the best in dairy, farm, orchard, smokehouse, and vineyard produce. On the movement's twentieth birthday, donors sent funds to the Louisiana food communities devastated by Hurricane Katrina in August 2006. The U.K. Slow Food chapter focused on salvaging cheddar and perry, traditional British products. The following year, reformers in Munchberg, Germany, saluted "Slow Bier."

Slow Food events in 153 countries bring together locavores involved in maintaining food standards. In April 2011, Grandmother's Day throughout Ireland honored inherited skills, such as baking sponge cake for tea and cooking boysenberries, loganberries, raspberries, and tayberries into jam. A month later, food promoters recruited Canadian youth for the Perth County Terra Madre assembly to demonstrate camp cookery, gardening, and pig roasting. A May gathering in De Haere, Holland, offered a symposium on slow eating. In Genoa, Italian fishermen and consumers attended a conference on sustainable species and marketing.

In June 2011, the Sami of Jokkmokk, Sweden, organized a delegation to study traditional knowledge and language of indigenous people. A similar training session at Darlington, New South Wales, presented Australian cuisine, spotlighting Aunty Beryl Van Oploo's kangaroo curry and pies. On Fyn Island, Danes hosted

Germans and Swedes at a gastronomic fair displaying artisanal baked goods, cheese, fruit juices, and seafoods. A July initiative in Springfield, Illinois, hosted "Kid's Day at the Farm." In October, Viennese Slow Food fans held a diversity market, a concept repeated that same month in Wolfville, Canada, and Tours, France. Basque chefs presented culinary programs in December in Bilbao, Spain, in opposition to homogenized, industrialized food.

See also: Agriculture; Nomad Diet and Cuisine; Pit Cookery; Theophrastus; Wine.

Further Reading

Honoré, Carl. *In Praise of Slowness: How a Worldwide Movement Is Challenging the Cult of Speed.* Toronto: Vintage Canada, 2004.

Petrini, Carlo. *Slow Food: The Case for Taste.* New York: Columbia University Press, 2001.

———, ed. *Slow Food: Collected Thoughts on Taste, Tradition, and the Honest Pleasures of Food.* White River Junction, VT: Chelsea Green, 2001.

Smoked Food

After the control of fire for cooking in 498,000 B.C.E., the smoke from burning dung, plants, and wood increased the savor and lengthened the shelf life of a variety of edibles—almonds, beans, cheese, garlic, peppers, prunes, pumpkin seeds, radishes, and whiskey. The most common smoked goods involve meat—chipped beef, cod, frankfurters, geese, kielbasa, mackerel, pastrami, roe, salami, and turkey breast. Hot smoking cooks tissues while preserving them. Cold smoking fumigates and increases temperatures, but it does not heat foods enough to alter delicate textures, such as the sirloin cuts used in Italian chevon (goat) sausage and brewed ales, lagers, porters, and stouts tinged by smoke in Australia, Austria, Brazil, Canada, Denmark, England, Finland, Holland, Italy, Japan, New Zealand, Sweden, and the United States.

As a partial preservative, smoke vapor permeates exterior tissues with hydrocarbons, such as the woody gases that preserve Barbary ducks from Nantes, the tea smoking that flavors game hens in China, and the brief smoking of Pandora moth caterpillars by Paiute Indians. Curing over a fire reduces the risk of trichinosis from bacon infested with trichinae (roundworms). The smoke also kills bacteria and fungus on the surface of fish and meat but not on the interior.

Smoking increases long-term storage time, as in the case of sweet *lap cheong* pork sausage lightly cured in southwestern China and dry Australian sausage stuffed with kangaroo meat, a high-protein, low-fat trail food. In Corsica, five days of smoking dries the pork liver in *figatelli* sausage until it is safe for eating for up to 30 days. For Czechs, Danes, Dutch, Germans, Poles, and Swedes, the smoking process turns oily eel meat into a gourmet item for canapés served on brown or black bread. The Sami of Finland smoke reindeer for daily consumption, setting aside smoked tongue as a delicacy.

In prehistory, smoking may have evolved as a means of thwarting flying insects during the drying of fish and game. From 100 B.C.E., German brewers dried malt over an open flame to make *Rauchbier* (smoked beer), a specialty in Bamberg. The unique kiln process imparted a sweet, musky accent. Roman dairiers smoked cheese to impart a woody taste. In northern Italy in 1000, the curing of pork butt into *andouille* sausage set a standard of flavor and texture for smoked meat. Louisiana settlers transported the preservation method from Europe and contributed smoked meats to both Cajun and Creole recipes.

The Industry

For traditional home smoking, after the invention of the flue chimney in the twelfth century, Manx, Northumberland, and Scots families hung deer sides and kippered herring inside the chimney in free-flowing smoke. Herring required two full days of vapor treatment. At Grimsby, a fishing center on England's east coast from the 1100s, the availability of cod and herring fillets fresh from the Faroe Islands, Iceland, and Norway turned into a business the preservation of seafood over smoldering sawdust fires. After the arrival of the railroad in 1848, Grimsby's smoked fish flourished along with the rest of the sea-fishing industry.

The British fish market preceded by four decades a similar growth of the smoked, salted haddock business begun in Arbroath, Scotland. Arbroath smokies, a popular processed fish, required beheading, cleaning, brining, and suspending on wooden dowels over a smoking barrel. East of London, Jews from Poland and Russia introduced the curing of Baltic and Scottish salmon, a popular fatty fish on deli and restaurant menus. The spread of Romanian Jews to Montreal around 1890 imported the salting and curing of spiced beef brisket for

Preserving meats, fish, and berries since humans first gained control of fire, smoking provides a universal means of enhancing flavor. Here, filleted salmon hangs in a smokehouse in British Columbia, Canada, for cold or hot smoking. *(Sarah Leen/ National Geographic/Getty Images)*

pastrami, a mainstay of Canada's kosher delis for service on bagels.

A cold smoke bath flavored Danish and German cheese, meats, oysters, salmon, and scallops, which then required further cooking. The curing of applewood cheese, cheddar, Gouda, Gruyère, mozzarella, and *scamorza* by the cold process could take up to 30 days. Hot smoking combined the processes of flavoring and cooking over a smoldering fire, thus shrinking tissues by evaporating moisture. To prevent complete desiccation—such as the roasting of pheasant and venison—cooks placed a pan of plain or herbed water over the flame to maintain tenderness. The most thorough smoking resulted from barbecuing or pit roasting, which raised the meat temperature to a safe level for consumption. Industrial smoking ensured the edibility of salmon by adding a purifying gas to wood vapors.

Techniques

Different types of fuel impart uniqueness to cured edibles, such as the burning of rice bran to cure and harden bean curd for smoked tofu. Forest Indians of North America chose fruitwoods and maple for preserving trout and whitefish. Alaskan and Pacific Coast tribes in British Columbia and Washington State preferred hickory or oak chips for smoking wild salmon for jerky or for drying fillets and nuggets for glazing with honey. Southern pit farmers saved corncobs and savory sassafras roots for smoking bacon, ham, and ribs before flavoring the meat with cinnamon, honey, maple, molasses, or red pepper. Curing reduced hams to 75 percent of their kill weight and fish to 33 percent of their catch weight. The poor valued soul food seasoned with smoked bacon and ham hocks, which stretched their meat budgets by up to 200 percent.

For Mexican and Tex-Mex grilled fish and steaks, roasted chicken and pork, and sea salt, slow-burning mesquite added flavor. A specialty, chipotle (smoked jalapeño peppers) fueled a fad for canned adobo marinade as well as ground and whole peppers for use in condiments and salsa. After 1915, immigrant brewers from Austria, Czechoslovakia, and Germany at Shiner, in south-central Texas, applied the same vapor principle to the smoking of Spoetzl beer, giving it a caramelized quality.

Combustibles, according to experts, also influence the outcome of curing. Currently, Scandinavians flavor beer with juniper vapor. Eurasians burn alder and oak, such as the alder wood that permeates salt from the Black Sea, oak sawdust for smoking York ham, and oak smoke flavoring for Spanish paprika, which cures for 14 days. In Luxembourg, brined ham smokes for a week over a blend of beech and oak chips. Peat gives a complex aftertaste to Imperial Russian Stout and Scotch ale and whiskey. In Germany, Black Forest ham absorbs savor from smoldering fir, as opposed to Westphalian ham, cured over a blend of beechwood and ground juniper.

New Zealanders smoke beer and fish by burning tea tree, which yields antibacterial sap. Japanese processors pickle daikon radishes after curing them over cherrywood. In China and Taiwan, smoked plums bolster wine fermented from oolong tea and plum liquors. Lapsang souchong tea from Fujian, China, internalizes a smoky flavor from the burning of cedar or pine tar as a desiccant, which complements the natural strength of black tea.

Home grillers and commercial preparers of smoked foods may enhance flavor by atomizing liquid smoke, a condensation of the gases of wood combustion, or adding a few drops to marinades. Health food specialists condemn liquid smoke and smoke-flavored oils, especially from beech and poplar, for raising the risk of colorectal and stomach cancer in otherwise safe comestibles, such as jalapeño peppers and lamb. In 2010, the European Food Safety Authority studied 11 smoke flavorings to determine levels of toxicity but reached no conclusion as to danger from eating artificially smoked cheese, fish, and meat.

See also: Arctic Diet and Cuisine; Horses; Salt; Sausage; Scandinavian Diet and Cuisine; Travel Food.

Further Reading

Oster, Kenneth V. *The Complete Guide to Preserving Meat, Fish, and Game.* Ocala, FL: Atlantic, 2011.

Saberi, Helen, ed. *Cured, Fermented and Smoked Foods.* Totnes, UK: Prospect, 2011.

Snodgrass, Mary Ellen. *Encyclopedia of Kitchen History.* New York: Fitzroy Dearborn, 2004.

Toussaint-Samat, Maguelonne. *A History of Food.* Hoboken, NJ: Wiley-Blackwell, 2009.

Snack Food

A between-meal phenomenon, snack food is a product of hunger pangs and availability. Portable snacks, such as fruit, seeds, insects, and nuts, existed in prehistory as pack food for travel and hunting. Yogurt, which the Sumerians coagulated in 6000 B.C.E., produced a handy power drink. After 1200 B.C.E., almonds, chestnuts, hazelnuts, pistachios, and walnuts satisfied the empty stomachs of Phoenician seamen.

Asian cooks mastered the production of convenience eats. From 400 C.E., at Xiamen (Amoy) in Fujian Province, China, a regional pancake enfolded bean sprouts, cooked filling, seaweed, and hot mustard or plum sauce. In 156 C.E., the Chinese domesticated sesame for seeded dough strips. At commercial centers in Hangzhou and Kaifeng, street hawkers steamed fruit and dough into savory *ping* cakes. In the same era, along the Silk Road, tea with dim sum (dumplings) relaxed traders in Guangdong. The bite-size morsels of pork and seafood fit neatly in the hand. Wrappings of bamboo or lotus leaves prevented mess.

For all-day theatrical performances, Greeks took breaks with pies and wine coolers purchased from street stalls. Families in Crete, Greece, Italy, the Levant, and Magna Graecia (Sicily and southern Italy) roasted *erebinthos* (chickpeas), a high-protein grain with satisfying mouthfeel. Roman laborers who lived in kitchenless apartments relied on snack shops for apples, nuts, olives, and tarts filled with eels, goat meat, shellfish, and songbirds. Aristocrats, who disapproved of eating in public, consumed their snacks at the public baths.

Worldwide, cooks based finger food recipes on local ingredients. Berbers in the Sahara toasted locusts for snacks, while Palestinians preferred chickpea paste and *halwa* (hard jelly). In 6 C.E., Tamil laborers took a break with *idli,* a spongy dal. Australian Aborigines preferred raw or grilled witchetty, a large white grub. For medieval laborers leaving home at early hours without time for breakfast, leftover cold cuts and oatcakes sufficed until the late afternoon meal.

New World

In the Western Hemisphere, Native Americans ate cherries and plums and relied on jerky and sliced pemmican for a packable snack reduced in weight from lengthy evaporation of moisture. After 950 B.C.E., the Inca ground nuts into peanut paste, a forerunner of peanut butter, a power spread still popular with the Dutch, British, Filipinos, and Indonesians. The Quechua of Argentina, Bolivia, Chile, Colombia, Ecuador, and Peru turned raw or coal-roasted caterpillars and larvae into light repasts. When Spanish conquistadors invaded Mexico in 1519 C.E., they discovered the penchant of Emperor Montezuma II and his advisers for munching on peanuts. Spaniards became the first Europeans to encounter two more American treats, popcorn and foamy *xocolatl* (chocolate), a caffeinated beverage spiked with chili pepper.

American settlers brought from Europe the know-how to make English fruit puddings and apple turnovers, Scots scones, and German pretzels, a tasty hot or cold treat they shared with Indians. In 1728, William Byrd, the founder of Richmond, Virginia, obtained an energy boost from dried bouillon. Colonial mothers satisfied discontented children with maple syrup drizzled on snow and with fruit leather, a berry or pome fruit puree spread thin for drying. In the South, the growth of sporting events and festivals connected citrus drinks and fried pork rinds with fun.

In the 1800s, frontier women relaxed with teatime, a late afternoon opportunity to visit and share tidbits prepared in cabins and sod huts from berries and nuts, such as cranberry preserves and sugared hickory nuts. Children anticipated an evening of sipping cider and popping corn in a wire basket over a log fire. In Charleston, South Carolina, in 1832, John Mathews marketed the first carbonated sodas, the impetus to sarsaparilla, a nonalcoholic beverage available from coast to coast. After 1853, the "Saratoga chip" ousted other potato snacks as the potato chip, a fabricated nibble processed from dried potato flakes or flour.

Starving Confederate troops ravaged fields for "goobers," a common slave food named for the Angolan word *nguba*. Soldiers returning from the American Civil War turned peanuts into a street snack on a par with the Roman chickpea, Russian sunflower seed, and Renaissance roasted chestnut. As the costs of sugar and chocolate fell, factories churned out sweet lozenges shaped in molds.

The American melting pot welcomed new snacks, such as the Scandinavian gingersnap. Just as Italian Americans relished their pepperoni rolls and Sicilian Americans revered pizza slices, Jewish immigrants and factory laborers embraced the dill pickle for its convenience and zip and the knish for its thick potato filling and availability from ghetto pushcarts. Likewise, the Pennsylvania Dutch satisfied between-meal cravings with pickled beans, eggs, gherkins, and root vegetables.

Commercial Fare

The late nineteenth and the early twentieth century saw a change in eating habits and times. Americans could choose from a host of tempting snacks, beginning with Cracker Jack in 1893, Hershey bars in 1900, Popsicle ice pops in 1905, Oreos and Life Savers in 1912, Kool-Aid in 1920, Fleer bubble gum in 1928, and Toll House cookies and Hostess Twinkies in 1930. Families gobbled handfuls of popcorn, an inexpensive stomach filler during the Great Depression and a substitute for confections during the rationing of sugar in World War II. Movie theaters enhanced the smell of popping corn with butter-flavored salt to entice patrons to munch during the film. The saltier the batch, the more likely the audience would buy sodas.

At cafés, late-afternoon hors d'oeuvre menus featured nachos, a crunchy snack of tortilla triangles topped with savory cheese and jalapeño peppers. In 1932, Southwestern innovators of Tex-Mex recipes created the Frito pie, made from corn chips invented by Elmer Doolin of Frito-Lay in Atlanta, Georgia, and Memphis, Tennessee. Emulating the flavor of tostados (fried tortillas), the Frito chip combined easily with beef chili and beans, jalapeños, onions, and shredded cheese for a variant of nachos. A second boost to salted snacks, the end of Prohibition in 1933 revived saloon and lounge traffic. Barkeeps enticed drinkers by offering salted gherkins, pickled eggs, and crackers. For street festivals and fairs, Hawaiian cuisine contributed shaved ice, an icy ball topped with flavorings of coffee, lime, peach, pineapple, and satsuma, a seedless tangerine.

U.S. airlifts to the Burma Road in April 1942 ferried C rations, tins packed with the homey flavors and textures of chocolate squares, biscuits, instant coffee, and sugar cubes. After World War II, veterans returned home with a yen for chocolate, an emerging giant of comfort foods.

At the end of World War II rationing, Americans and Europeans celebrated by reaching for taffy, nougat bars, and gumdrops at soda shops, theater lobbies, and candy stores. Factory extruders, invented to shape nuggets of feed for livestock, pushed out corn curls, the first squeezed-out snack.

In the 1950s, televised jingles and cartoons touted sweets with smiling actors enjoying Juju Babies, Mary Janes, M&Ms, PEZ, and Tootsie Pops, all unsuited to a balanced diet and dental health. British snack tables offered hearty spiced finger foods—shrimp *satay,* spicy cheddar bites, curried corn fritters and deviled eggs, and lamb wontons. The 1970s brought Carnation Instant Breakfast and power bars, a packable cereal snack.

New Alternatives

Health food advocates took a new look at popcorn in the 1980s and reclaimed it as a fiber food, a low-calorie filler reducing hunger and satisfying the urge to chew. Modern versions of poppers ejected a kernel exploded with air rather than hot oil. In 2003, Illinois Governor Rod Blagojevich declared popcorn the state snack, a gesture of support for the prairie corn culture. After 2006, the calorie-conscious demanded reduced trans fats. Frito-Lay led the rush to retool and reformulate grain and potato snack production, all previously processed with oil at high heat. Nutritionists examined the marketing of junk food to schoolchildren at ages when they established eating habits.

Holiday and party food writing devoted newspaper columns and whole cookbooks to dips and munchies for tailgate eating, Super Bowl snacks, study night breaks, and New Year's Eve trays. Cookbooks even included pet snacks, such as liver and soy cookies and peanut butter snaps. The shift to weight consciousness in the 2000s resulted in additions to the packaged snack canon—carrot and sweet potato chips, granola bars, yogurt drinks, jalapeño poppers, frozen grapes, and hummus. Proponents of healthful snacks recommend small meals of fruit and raw vegetables to promote satiety and a sustainable body mass.

See also: Corn and Maize; Crackers; Fast Food; Jerky; Kebabs; Lunch; McDonald's; Soft Drinks and Juices; Street Food; Tortillas; Voegtlin, Walter L.

Further Reading

Allen, Gary, and Ken Albala. *The Business of Food: Encyclopedia of the Food and Drink Industries.* Westport, CT: Greenwood, 2007.

Lusas, Edmund W., and Lloyd W. Rooney, eds. *Snack Foods Processing.* Boca Raton, FL: CRC, 2001.

Smith, Andrew F. *Fast Food and Junk Food: An Encyclopedia of What We Love to Eat.* Santa Barbara, CA: Greenwood, 2011.

Stern, Jane, and Michael Stern. *The Lexicon of Real American Food.* Guilford, CT: Lyons, 2011.

Soft Drinks and Juices

The production of refreshing beverages parallels ingenious methods of pressing and liquefying sweet fruit pulp. In the Western Hemisphere, the extraction of juice from fruit by hunter-gatherers predates agriculture as a source of satisfaction for sweet pulpy liquids, such as that of agave, cranberries, barrel cactus, crab apples, and prickly pear as well as saguaro juice, a ceremonial drink to bring rain. Significant to the appeal of fruit nectars, their perishability conferred an image of delicacy and pleasure and an appreciation of juice as a tonic for toddlers and the sick. Natural yeasts that initiated fermentation extended the view of fruit juice as magical.

From 5000 B.C.E., Middle Eastern date palms provided pulp for fruit syrup and date wine, an intoxicant denounced by abstemious Hebrew priests. Persians and Syrians upped the light taste of fruit drinks with the raw juice of sweet oranges, which blended with pomegranate juice into a crimson thirst quencher. Orange growing migrated by traders to Iberia and Provence, where the French dubbed the refresher *jus d'or* (golden juice).

In the seventh century C.E., the banishment of alcoholic drinks from Muslim households elevated fruit juice as a refresher and mealtime drink suitable for adults and children. When Islam arrived in Indonesia, it promoted the consumption of passion fruit juice, a restorative drink also common in Australia, Ecuador, Costa Rica, India, and Kenya. In the eleventh century, Viking hosts offered crowberry, bilberry, and cowberry juice as welcoming refreshers to guests. A similar rise in juice consumption occurred in the late sixteenth century, when Spanish dealers planted citrus groves in colonial St. Augustine, Florida, and introduced oranges to the Dutch.

North Americans made tribal tonics and teas from a prodigious variety of extracts of rose hips, canyon grapes, pokeberries, milkweed, cream berries, Solomon's seal, gooseberries, wolfberries, Ponderosa pine, dewberries, tickseed, and sumac. In the far north, gatherers favored Alaskan rhubarb, mooseberries, and mountain sorrel, which preparers added to seal blubber. Blackfoot husbands and favorite sons received special attention from ceremonial chokecherry juice. Apache women pounded honey mesquite beans into a pulpy nectar consumed like milk; Mendocino children dried silverpuff juice into gum. The Cherokee treated guests to passionflower drinks. The Navajo prized saskatoon juice as a marinade and juniper juice as a famine food.

Industrialized Beverages

From the conception of carbonated drinks in 1767, manufacturers have varied the original two-ingredient formula—carbon dioxide and water—with birch bark, fruit pulp and juice, herbs, spices and wine. In 1820, Townsend Speakman, a Philadelphia pharmacist, distributed Dr. Physick's Soda Water, a fizzy health tonic.

Distributors stored cork-topped bottles on their sides to prevent the drying of cork and release of gas. The invention of the church key opener in 1892 simplified cap removal with a portable gadget.

Nineteenth-century diners favored berry and fruit ades, fruit juices combined with sugar and water. Lower in calories than marmalade, cool pitchers of fruit ade accompanied teatime scones as well as children's lunches and family picnics. Urban snackers patronized the soda fountain and popularized ginger ale, fermented ginger beer, and phosphate soda, an extension of carbonated fruit drinks with phosphoric acid. First aid manuals recommended ginger ale for queasy stomachs and inflamed throats. Bartenders found greater use for ginger ale for mixing with alcohol for cocktails and punch.

A drugstore specialty, the phosphate came in egg, malt, and fruit flavors and remained popular until the 1930s, when pure juices in cans rose in consumption. Eroding the popularity of carbonated drinks between 1890 and 1910, the invention of inexpensive pasteurized grape and orange juice (*Citrus sinensis*), a sweet antiscorbutic, gave consumers a wider choice between fizzy and nonbubbly beverages for breakfast. Home refrigerators kept juice cold for impulse drinking. Teetotal church congregations welcomed Charles Welch's pressed grape juice as an alternative to wine. In Australia in 1926, the sale of fresh-squeezed Sunkist lemon and orange juice at 4¢ per drink introduced the Pacific world to carbonated citrus beverages. South Africans promoted honey beer and the nectars of wild fruit, which vendors purchased from as far inland as Lesotho and Swaziland for blending with millet porridge. In the last decade of the phosphate fad, cardboard six-pack cartons enabled buyers to carry six bottles with ease. In the same period, vending machines served chilled bottles in bus and train depots and food stores and at beach and tourist sites.

Vegetarians in the mid-1900s popularized smoothies, an iced fruit or vegetable juice cocktail available at juice bars. Pre–World War II consumption of fruit juice reached 45 million cases, with grapefruit the front-runner over pineapple. In 1942, the U.S. Army Subsistence Research and Development Laboratory identified fruit juice as a necessary health boost to motorized desert units. By the late 1990s, worldwide commerce in juice reached 13.2 billion gallons (50 billion liters), with orange outranking apple, grape, and pineapple in sales.

Designer Waters

The mid- to late 1900s generated patronage of sports drinks, a source of rehydration and restoration of electrolytes lost from exertion and sweating. Unlike V-8 and cranberry tonics, sports beverages offered controlled formulas designed by physiatrists. Athletes combated fatigue during training and competition by sipping isotonic drinks balanced in salt and sugar to reflect body chemistry. Cups of sports beverages reputedly protected runners and team players from heat stroke. In 1965, Stokely-Van Camp began distributing Gatorade, a 50-calorie fluid replacement formulated at the University of Florida to fortify the stressed athlete with sugars, potassium, and sodium.

In the late 1990s, fruit water and vitamin water promoted a feeling of health through the blending of vitamins B, C, and E with mineral water or tea and fructose. Litigation against Vitaminwater by England's Advertising Standards Authority declared nutritional fruit-flavored soft drink manufacturers misleading in their claims to promote endurance and recovery from exertion. In 1998, the Center for Science in the Public Interest published *Liquid Candy: How Soft Drinks Are Harming Americans' Health,* a warning that makers of designer drinks—Hoist, OXYwater, KonaRed, and Thirst for Greatness, known as T4G—conceal the dangers of artificial coloring and sweeteners to health, especially that of children. The alert stressed the parallel rise in soft drink consumption with incidence of obesity, diabetes, kidney stones, degenerated bone mass, low potassium, eroded tooth enamel, and dental caries.

See also: Carbonation and Carbonated Beverages; Cider; Fast Food; Guar; Packaging; Snack Food; Vinegar; Wild Food.

Further Reading

Hamilton, Alissa. *Squeezed: What You Don't Know About Orange Juice.* New Haven, CT: Yale University Press, 2009.

Hawkins, Richard. *A Pacific Industry: The History of Pineapple Canning in Hawaii.* New York: I.B. Tauris, 2011.

Shachman, Maurice. *The Soft Drinks Companion: A Technical Handbook for the Beverage Industry.* Boca Raton, FL: CRC, 2005.

Soul Food

A reminder of slavery, African and Southern culture, and a history of making do, soul food showcases the intimate kitchens and heritage cuisine of African Americans.

Triangular slave trade from the late sixteenth to the early nineteenth century introduced to the New World the black abductees who worked plantations as well as mills and mines. To the New World diet, African newcomers brought okra and peanuts, the bases of Creole, Caribbean, and Southern specialties, notably, gumbo, peanut brittle, and pralines. Cabin staples—chestnuts, clabber (buttermilk), hot sauce, molasses, rice, sorghum—combined with cabbage, collards and pot likker, corn, manioc, poke, turnips, and yams to produce survival meals for blacks newly introduced to freedom. Family and church celebrations allied shared spreads with fellowship, horseshoes, hymn singing, and juba dancing.

During the protracted Jim Crow era, meats for black sharecroppers and poor whites tended toward the rejected cuts and scraps—"chitlins and cracklins',", guinea hen, ham hocks, oxtails, pig's feet and skin, and tripe—along with river bottom feeders, carp and catfish. Hunters and trappers added groundhog, opossum, rabbit, raccoon, squirrel, and wild turkey to rural meals. Coastal Gullah tradition contributed gastronomy based on lowland crab, oysters, shrimp, and turtles. From the Mississippi River delta came recipes for black bean soup and hoppin' John, a savory combination of black-eyed peas, ham bone, onion, peppers, and rice. Home food preservation involved the young in coring pears for pear preserves, drying slices for fried apples pies, and scalding tomatoes for canned soup mix.

Southeastern native tribes—Cherokee, Chickasaw, Choctaw, Creek, and Seminole—added alligator, terrapin, and smoked venison to serve with field peas, green beans, lard cakes, and wilted lettuce. Pone, grits, and hominy (corn soaked in lime) influenced indigenous inventions—cornmeal dumplings, hoecake, liver mush and souse, and succotash. A simple child pleaser, hush puppies (corn fritters) paired with coleslaw at fish fries and with fried fatback in knapsacks and pockets as travel food. Jack Daniel's Tennessee Whiskey, a sour mash drink introduced in 1866, rounded out good eating and fellowship.

From legacy recipes such as sweet potato pie and watermelon pickles, Malinda Russell issued *A Domestic Cookbook: Containing a Careful Selection of Useful Recipes for the Kitchen* (1866). A 49-year-old mulatto cook, Abby Fisher, an illiterate former slave in South Carolina and Alabama, compiled a revered soul food cookbook, *What Mrs. Fisher Knows About Old Southern Cooking* (1881). Rufus Estes, an emancipated slave and Pullman redcap, collected another version, *Good Things to Eat* (1911). Blacks who rode the rails to the Freedom Belt in the North opened soul food stands and cafés in Chicago, Detroit, New York, and Philadelphia. During the Harlem Renaissance, food and music lured whites to "speakeasies," where bootleggers plied customers with fish sandwiches, fried green tomatoes, pinto beans, corn bread, and moonshine.

Southern black cooking styles traveled to the Freedom Belt and thrived in Chicago, Detroit, New York, and Philadelphia. Popularized in the 1960s, soul food equated with ethnic comfort food, such as blackberry cobbler, pork brains and eggs, chicken feet, fried country ham and redeye gravy, hog jowls, muscadine wine, and ribs. The flavor and aroma of bay leaf, garlic, onion, sesame, and thyme enhanced beet and dandelion greens, Jerusalem artichokes, purslane, shad roe, she-crab soup, and shrimp grits, the subjects of *The Taste of Country Cooking* (1976) by Edna Lewis, a Virginia-born chef at Café Nicholson, a Manhattan eatery. The unpretentious recipes stimulated the five senses and satisfied the appetite much as slave-era meals soothed the anguish of bondage and repression.

Recipe: Mrs. Fisher's Jumberlie (Jambalaya)

"Take one chicken and cut it up, separating every joint, and adding to it one pint of cleanly-washed rice. Take about half a dozen large tomatoes, scalding them well and taking the skins off with a knife. Cut them in small pieces and put them with the chicken in a pot or large porcelain saucepan. Then cut in small pieces two large pieces of sweet ham and add to the rest, seasoning high with pepper and salt. It will cook in twenty-five minutes. Do not put any water on it."

In the 1980s, the media placed greater emphasis on the high incidence of diabetes, heart attack, and stroke among poor folk, notably residents of Mississippi and Louisiana who consumed a diet high in inexpensive commodities—banana pudding, wild-gathered creasy greens (cress), lard, pork neck bones, rhubarb pie, sugary home-canned peaches, and sweet tea. Around 1995, Lewis ignored attempts to replace Southern ingredients with tofu and yogurt and formed the Society for the Revival and Preservation of Southern Food. Her example of historical sustenance survives in the documentary *Fried Chicken and Sweet Potato Pie* (2006) and in the field trips and oral history projects of the Southern Foodways Alliance, affiliated with the Center for the Study of Southern Culture at the University of Mississippi.

See also: African Slave Diet; Cajun Diet and Cuisine; Cookbooks; Mustard; Pork; Restaurants; Whiskey.

Further Reading

Harris, Jessica B. *High on the Hog: A Culinary Journey from Africa to America.* New York: Bloomsbury, 2011.

Jones, Wilbert. *The New Soul Food Cookbook: Healthier Recipes for Traditional Favorites.* New York: Citadel, 2005.

Reed, Dale Volberg and John Shelton Reed. *Cornbread Nation 4: The Best of Southern Food Writing.* Athens: University of Georgia Press, 2008.

Williams, Lindsey. *Neo Soul: Taking Soul Food to a Whole 'Nutha Level.* New York: Avery, 2007.

Soup Kitchens

Soup kitchens, like homelessness and underemployment, have existed throughout world history to provide on-site meals for the needy. Around 2200 B.C.E., Ptahhotep, an Egyptian vizier under King Isesi, recognized the danger of discontent of those with empty bellies, who threatened the social order. On festival days around 1100 B.C.E.,

Egypt's royal pantry managers opened their stores to the public for a general distribution of meat and bread and all the beer that petitioners could drink. In the Torah, Exodus 16:3 records how Hebrew slaves took part in Egypt's public dole. Ethiopians, according to the Greek traveler and historian Herodotus, established a similar reputation for charity at Carthage. As he described, around 551 B.C.E., the Persian king Cambyses I sent spies to report on "the table of the sun," a meadow outside the city where volunteers boiled meat each night for service throughout the following day. According to Ethiopian ethics, the earth yielded meat for sharing with all.

Food Charities Through the Ages

In the Middle Ages, handouts became a staple during the rise of religious missions and monasteries. A Christian saint in central Germany, Elizabeth of Hungary, became the patron of bakers and the homeless after distributing grain to the impoverished in the 1220s. She also caught fresh fish and made rosemary tea for the hungry. In Florence, Italy, in 1244, Pier Bossi led the Misericordia charitable order in relieving bouts of starvation among the poor and providing transportation to medical centers and burial for the dead. Dispatched from the Piazza del Duomo, they appear in a painting by Domenico Ghirlandaio in 1472 alongside stacks of bread and vats of wine, where three agents filled the empty pitchers of destitute peasants.

Other faiths pursued the feeding of the poor as a humanitarian obligation. In 1545, the Fatih mosque of Istanbul hosted 3,000 paupers twice a day and served meals of bread, chickpeas, mutton soup, plums, and yogurt. The location housed a laundry and clinic serving hygiene and medical needs. In the mid-1500s, Angad Dev, second of the ten orthodox Sikh gurus, set up a communal *langar* (soup kitchen) in Khadur Sahib, India, to feed all who sought food, whatever their caste, race, or religion. At the end of each meal, he organized outdoor sports to encourage physical stamina among street beggars.

When horticulturist Edward Richard Gardiner wrote *Profitable Instructions for the Manuring, Sowing and Planting of Kitchin Gardens* (1603), he subtitled his book "Very profitable for the common wealth and greatly for the helpe and com-fort of poore people." Gardiner struck to the core of malnutrition by abandoning table dainties for hearty soups made from beans, cabbage, and carrots. His dictum implied that salad greens and herbs were luxuries belonging only on the tables of the well fed, a belief in keeping with status-based Renaissance nutritional standards. The unfortunate needed more satisfying root crops, which cooks made palatable by simmering them in broth.

Nineteenth-Century Initiatives

The concept of an ongoing network of civic altruists and moral reformers thrived in New York City after 1802,

when the Humane Society opened its first soup kitchen. To prevent abuse of the system, volunteers distributed tickets to paupers. Breadlines of the down-and-out concerned conservatives, who blamed the soup kitchen for drawing criminals to the area. In the 1820s, a backlash in Chicago against social reform aimed at forcing derelicts and tramps to seek work and support themselves rather than rely on churches and food pantries to provide a daily meal.

The Irish Potato Famine (1845–1852) turned world attention to the social dangers of poverty, which escalated to epidemic, rootlessness, and rebellion. In the introduction to his *Treatise on Food for People* (1850), Bavarian theologian Ludwig Andreas Feuerbach challenged evangelists to inveigh against hunger rather than preach on sin. Charles Elmé Francatelli, Queen Victoria's personal cook, added an entry to his compendium, *A Plain Cookery Book for the Working Classes* (1852), encouraging more people to make soup for the poor, especially during the winter, when scanty food supplies prevented common laborers from doing their jobs. After the spread of the Salvation Army to Australia, England, France, Ireland, Scotland, and the United States in 1880, the Protestant charity took as its symbol the soup kettle.

In the United States, altruism flourished in large cities during the rise of the home economics movement. American essayist Rebecca Blaine Harding Davis championed late-nineteenth-century asylums, charity schools, missions, and slum kitchens, feeding stations that also provided medical care. The emergence of messianic zeal in the late 1800s restructured domestic school curricula to meet the needs of mendicants and low-income immigrants. Popular lecturer Sarah Tyson Rorer, an educator at the Boston Cooking School, urged Christians to feed the poor and upgrade humble homes with cookery classes and recipes for inexpensive soups. Instructor Maria Parloa predicted that such hygienic instruction would reduce the number of felons and orphans. The Cooking Teachers' League elevated food distribution to a "religion of right living."

During the Panic of 1873, Commodore James Gordon Bennett, owner of the *New York Herald*, set up eight soup kitchens in the city. The chain dispersed 2,000 meals a day, prepared by Charles Ranhofer, head chef at Delmonico's restaurant. A critique in *Frank Leslie's Illustrated Newspaper* acclaimed the gourmet-quality soup from immaculately clean kettles. Staff served the public in neat rooms similar to the scientific laboratory at chemist Ellen Richards's New England Kitchen, a facility that sustained malnourished refugees of European wars and trained them in American-style meal planning and cookery.

At the height of interest in public kitchens, German army Captain M.P. Wolff, author of *Food for the Million: A Plan for Starting Public Kitchens* (1884), studied the penny kitchens that fed the poor in Scotland and England. In collaboration with English designer William White,

Wolff planned an idealized soup kitchen and dining hall. Food preparation took place in a sanitized area equipped with steamers and roasters, hot plates, meat slicing station, and specialized hotel kitchen larder and scullery. Clients could wash up, receive food at the serving window, and eat at trestle tables on the premises or buy carryout meals, which servers placed in vessels lined with a hot water cell to maintain temperature.

Twentieth Century: War on Hunger

Political instability increased the demand for soup kitchens. In 1931, in the novel *The Good Earth,* Pearl Buck reflected on her life in China, where she grew up on the Presbyterian mission field with her parents. From her memories of turmoil accompanying the Boxer Rebellion of 1900, she described the terror of southern refugees to Kiangsu Province, presumably in Nanking. They carried begging bowls and sought public kitchens, where aid workers cooked huge cauldrons of rice for distribution. A security force halted exploiters from buying cheap food for slopping hogs.

During World War I, refugees from Galicia overran Vienna, forcing Austrians to come to terms with hungry families roaming the city. Social reformers Sophie Grünfeld and Hermine Kadisch opened kosher soup kitchens featuring menus of beans, dumplings, potatoes, sausage, and soup. A sliding scale distributed cost to the poor and middle class, who paid what they could afford. Kadisch stretched supplies during the lean times of 1917–1918, when a volunteer staff served 13 million low-cost meals and 3 million free dinners.

In the 1930s, with North America in the throes of the Great Depression, food insecurity plagued the lowest class and the newly dispossessed. In contrast to the private charity system that had weathered a 16 percent jobless rate during the depression of the 1890s, the 30 percent unemployed during the Depression ate up resources. Food doles and soup kitchens, such as the one that Marjorie Merriwether Post subsidized in New York City's Hell's Kitchen and the Gleaners' Aid shelter and kitchen that radio evangelist Rosa Artimus "Mother" Horn opened at 132nd Street and Madison Avenue, survived the first two winters by feeding more than 48,000 people. The protracted demand on relief rolls ultimately exhausted the system.

Volunteers serve dinner to the homeless at a soup kitchen in San Jose, California, during the economic recession of 2008–2009. Most associated with the Great Depression of the 1930s, on-site meal service for the needy actually dates to ancient times. *(Christian Science Monitor/Getty Images)*

Another altruist of the time, reformer Dorothy Day, a founder of the Catholic Worker Movement and author of *House of Hospitality* (1939), led a reform drive to ease the suffering of New York City's poor. In 1934, she launched St. Joseph's House of Hospitality, a Christian waystation to succor wanderers of the city's Bowery. In a challenge to readers, she referred to her public kitchen as a "Christ's room." The establishment of Day's Chrystie Street Shelter initiated the opening of 30 rescue missions nationwide to dispense hot meals.

Recent Outreaches

The tradition of staffing and supplying public kitchens remained a form of charitable outreach to the world's underfed throughout the last decades of the twentieth century. Between 1980 and 1990, with New York City's homeless population escalating rapidly, nongovernmental agencies staffed 136 public pantries and 104 soup kitchens distributing more than 78,000 meals per week to stem the crisis. To expand the offerings of feeding stations, volunteers such as Gleaners and Second Harvest collected surplus groceries and restaurant donations.

In the 1990s, the American Dietetic Association studied emergency food programs to assess the quality of service to the poor. Despite the guidelines of the 1989 Recommended Dietary Allowances for adult males, staff ignored hand washing, thawing, and reheating standards before ladling up meals at five locations near New York University in midtown Manhattan. Menus dependent on donated items varied in nutrition, typically low in carbohydrates, folic acid, and vitamin C and high in fat and protein. Observers concluded that charitable institutions needed the services of dietitians to ensure food purity and nutritional content.

Worldwide, altruism has taken numerous forms to end the obscenity of starvation amid plenty. In Ajmir, India, locals honoring the anniversary of a saint held a scramble feast. They set up two cauldrons to cook rice and butter for distribution to beggars. The giveaway concluded with volunteers who wrapped themselves in thick coverings and climbed into the pots to scrape out the remains of the meal. An effort organized in Sofia, Bulgaria, to aid orphans, pensioners, the disabled, elderly, and jobless began with the social activism of Donka Paprikova, Bulgaria's Mother Teresa. On October 21, 1996, her team of volunteers started a soup kitchen with donations of garden vegetables and offered bread, fruit, soup, and yogurt to more than 200 recipients twice a week. Among the Bushmen of the Nyae Nyae Conservancy of Botswana, the cooking and distribution of soup and bread to children at Schmidtsdrift early in 2001 provided fuel to help pupils attend class. Those who skipped class did not eat.

Amid plenty in the United States, on Super Bowl Sunday in January 1990, Brad Smith, a second-year seminarian and intern at Spring Valley Presbyterian Church in Columbia, South Carolina, originated the Souper Bowl of Caring, a religious and laic campaign to pass the soup kettle and collect food for the hungry. The annual project, supported by a toll-free number and Web site, channeled some of the enthusiasm for sport into a will to nurture and uplift. Advocated by former presidents and first ladies, the National Football League, and a host of celebrities, donations for soup kitchens exceed $10 million annually.

See also: Rumford, Count; Soups; Soyer, Alexis.

Further Reading

Glasser, Irene. *More Than Bread: Ethnography of a Soup Kitchen.* Tuscaloosa: University of Alabama Press, 2010.

Kusmer, Kenneth L. *Down & Out, on the Road: The Homeless in American History.* New York: Oxford University Press, 2002.

Rumble, Victoria R. *Soup Through the Ages: A Culinary History with Period Recipes.* Jefferson, NC: McFarland, 2009.

Stettner, Larry, and Bill Morrison. *Cooking for the Common Good: The Birth of a Natural Foods Soup Kitchen.* Berkeley, CA: North Atlantic, 2010.

Soups

Whether cold or hot, thick or clear, soups offer cooks a flavorful, aromatic menu item to suit a variety of meals and snacks. Ancient pottage recipes hold so high a reputation that historians refer to the cradle of human life as "primordial soup."

Ancient Fare

A fireside staple from 7000 B.C.E., the first liquid meals emerged from pit cookery or stone boiling, the dropping of heated stones into pouch hides, wood troughs, turtle shells, or the stomachs of large animals. Analysis of residue in pottery containers identified acorns, animal bones, chestnuts, grains, lentils, and root crops as standard ingredients softened by boiling. An ancient classic, pea soup, involved the mashing of the peas to absorb herbal, meat, and vegetable flavorings.

By the Iron Age and the invention of heat-proof, leak-proof cookware, soup filled bellies along the Mediterranean and in Europe, China, India, Japan, Korea, and Nigeria. Herodotus, the fifth-century B.C.E. Greek historian, viewed the Scythians at an economic fireside ritual heating ox flesh in the paunch over a fire of the ox bones. In 200 B.C.E., Chinese bitter-and-sour soup concocted from bean curd and vegetables cost only a pittance. Herbalists recommended its healing properties. Roman home cooks specialized in fish soup flavored with herbs and wine, which paired with salad, a classic complement.

Soups Through the Ages

To save fuel and squeeze food value from sparse ingredients, medieval chefs retained Byzantine pottage recipes, which flourished in Catalonia, England, France, and Italy. A cauldron occupied the fireplace hob and remained bubbling day by day, replenished with leftovers from the last cooked meal. Peasants fished out chunks of meat and vegetables with their fingers and tipped bowls toward the mouth to drain the juice. A messier version of sipping, the sopping of bread crusts in broth rescued the dregs from the bowl. In the 1450s, Turkish consumers sipped cups of soup as handy snacks, particularly in blustery weather.

During the Renaissance, vendors ladled bowls of restorative broth or soup in France. In 1765 in Paris on the Rue Bailleul, four blocks north of the Île de la Cité, vintner A. Boulanger opened a bistro devoted to bouillon and *pot-au-feu* under the title *restaurant* (restoring), a dispenser of *restoratifs*. Refined buyers dipped soup from a tureen and ate their servings with long-handled soupspoons. Asian and Baltic dessert makers simmered their own savory blend from adzuki beans, bananas, coconut, melon, and tapioca. Iberian gazpacho reduced elements of a salad—cucumbers, onions, peppers, tomatoes—into a chilled slurry seasoned with oil and vinegar, pepper, and salt. Scandinavian chefs diversified northwestern Asian and European dinner recipes with fruit soup simmered from prunes and raisins and dressed with cream, dumplings, spices, and wine.

In the late 1700s and early 1800s, high-minded British relief workers in London and Glasgow attempted to raise the standard of living for the destitute and refugees with daily handouts. A recipe from optician William Kitchiner's *Apicius Redivivus: The Cook's Oracle* (1817) yielded 250 gallons (950 liters) of soup by flavoring stewed beef strips and knucklebones with black pepper, celery, flour, leeks, salt, and split peas. The cauldrons fed 600 families.

The American Melting Pot

Waves of immigrants to North America added a variety of cooking styles, from creamy French seafood bisques, bouillabaisse, and veloutés to Chinese egg drop soup, Greek lemon chicken soup, Hungarian goulash, Tamil mulligatawny, Italian minestrone, English curried carrot soup, Russian borscht, and hearty Newfoundland seacoast chowders, thick with clams, crabs, and fish. National dishes featured distinctive ingredients—hominy and tripe in Mexican menudo, stewing hens in Scots cock-a-leekie, bean curd in Japanese miso, potatoes in French vichyssoise, peanuts and pumpkin in African purees, and celeriac in Dutch *snert*. Among the Pennsylvania Dutch, a steaming tureen of soup symbolized community and sharing a one-dish meal with guests. The North American elite adopted soup at the opening course of a heavy meal as a civilized method of arousing the appetite.

In the 1750s, while woodsmen had the luxury of cooking an outdoor hunter's stew, explorers and naval provisioners purchased portable soup, or pocket soup, a defatted, dehydrated paste of boiled meat, rice, and vegetables topped with died salt pork and peppercorns. Galley cooks reconstituted the pantry staple in a stockpot by adding a quart of water. A forerunner of bouillon cubes, canisters of portable soup traveled with Captain James Cook to the South Seas in 1768 and Lewis and Clark to the Pacific Coast in 1804. By the 1850s, canned soups had expanded the selection of quick meals for cowboys, frontier cavalry, and hospital patients.

In 1897, John Thompson "Jack" Dorrance, a chemist trained at the Massachusetts Institute of Technology and Göttingen University, revolutionized convenience foods by inventing the first condensed soups in Camden, New Jersey, for the Joseph A. Campbell Preserve Company (later renamed the Campbell Soup Company). Campbell's became one of the most respected brands in U.S. history. The reduced bulk of condensed soup lowered the cost of canning and transporting. For 10¢ per can, homemakers could choose water or milk as the liquid that reconstituted one of 21 varieties of prepared soup and add individual touches to the mix, such as chopped boiled egg, minced onion, or orzo pasta.

In May 1900, Campbell's soups won a bronze medal at the Paris Exposition, where soup makers exhibited equipment for extracting flavor from meat. Four years later, company publicists connected soup with children and motherhood by publishing a "Campbell Kids" ad campaign. During World War I, Dorrance added his food acumen to the three-year effort of the U.S. Food Administration to reduce waste and increase nutrition in army rations. In 1917, the company shipped 45 percent of its soups to Europe.

During the Great Depression on the South Carolina coast, shore restaurants had limited access to the ingredients of their signature dish, she-crab soup, made from crab and roe. The cook often resorted to the burrowing gopher tortoise, called "Hoover's chicken," for the makings of soup. After 1939, instant soup reduced the cumbrous work of chopping and stirring the ingredients of nutritious broth. Within five years, when Lipton offered three flavors of soup mixes at under 10¢ each, revenue from soup sales rose by 750 percent.

Recent History

The salad bar, first advertised in 1951 in Springfield, Illinois, began offering the soup-and-salad combination, a satisfying meal light on calories and cost. Gradually, buffet items included chili and soup garnishes—bacon bits, bamboo shoots, black olives, croutons and melba toast rounds, grated cheese, green onion slices, and a sprinkle of red pepper. The appeal of fragrant hot soup increased restaurant traffic for retirees and couples with young children, who relished soft vegetables in broth.

In the heyday of space travel, astronauts rehydrated and squeezed soup from tubes packed in Estonia, such

Recipe: Chicken Noodle Soup

In 2 quarts of boiling water, poach four boneless chicken breasts. Remove the chicken pieces. Chop three of the chicken breasts and return them to the stock. Cool the fourth piece. Add to the pot 1 tablespoon each of freshly chopped parsley and rosemary and 1 teaspoon each of dill weed and sea salt. While the soup is simmering, sprinkle the surface with black pepper and granulated flour and stir vigorously. Add 1/2 cup of slivered baby carrots and one celery heart with its leaves. Shred the cooled chicken breast in a food processor and blend it into the soup. Shortly before serving, stir in 1 cup of thin egg noodles and simmer until tender.

as the borscht dispensed aboard the Soviet Soyuz 19 mission in 1975. By the start of manned U.S. Apollo missions in the late 1960s, hot water dispensers made moistening dried foods and spooning cream of chicken "moon soup" from bowls easier and more normal. The Japanese Aerospace Exploration Agency made its own advances, including ramen noodles. For meals of black bean and lentil soup, special trays held pouches and utensils in place. Thermostabilization destroyed enzymes and microbes that could cause spoilage and debilitate the crew.

In the 1990s, the growth of the soup industry derived from the convenience store and workplace microwave, where consumers could heat ramen with water or ready-to-eat soup in plastic bowls. Cooking magazines and ads from Campbell and Knorr featured canned and dry soups as additives to roast meats and vegetable casseroles, such as the classic holiday green bean dish dressed with cream of mushroom soup and topped with french fried onions.

To accommodate the health conscious, soup manufacturers in the 2000s offered a variety of low-sodium or salt-free servings, as well as vegetarian fare and soups free of trans fat. The Slow Food movement introduced young couples to the ease of electric slow cooker preparation, which extended over the workday the simmering of a one-pot dish—a boon to two-wage-earner households.

See also: Arctic Diet and Cuisine; Chowder; Crackers; Cussy, Louis, Marquis de; Rumford, Count; Soup Kitchens; Soyer, Alexis.

Further Reading

Clarkson, Janet. *Soup: A Global History.* London: Reaktion, 2010.
Rumble, Victoria R. *Soup Through the Ages: A Culinary History with Period Recipes.* Jefferson, NC: McFarland, 2009.
Shea, Martha Esposito, and Mike Mathis. *Campbell Soup Company.* Charles, SC: Arcadia, 2002.
Solley, Patricia. *An Exaltation of Soups: The Soul-Satisfying Story of Soup, As Told in More Than 100 Recipes.* New York: Three Rivers, 2004.

Sourdough

A complex microbiological union of fermentation and leavening in wet grain, sourdough demonstrates the value of experimentation from the beginning of bread history. In Egypt in the twenty-sixth century B.C.E., wild yeast from vineyards or gardens drifted into dough, producing a light texture and memorable piquance. In the port of Alexandria, the world's first commercial ovens produced thousands of loaves per day. At the Great Pyramids in Giza, commercial distributors fed 30,000 laborers on bread cooked in earthen jars over pit fires. According to Exodus, around 1450 B.C.E., some 600,000 Hebrew workers fled Egypt by night, leaving behind their sourdough starter.

In the Bronze Age, Sumerians thrived on sister skills—brewing and baking yeast bread. Commercially, the mixing of sourdough required a bacteria-rich inoculum, or starter, from previous batches or from beer or wine. To keep the starter viable, preparers fed the mass fresh leavening. By 800 B.C.E., the souring of dough reached Western Europe. For tart savor and fragrance, Greek and Roman bakers permeated the mass with lactic acid from the acetobacteria on grapes and allowed the flora to develop spontaneously for up to 24 hours. For loft and crumb, they relied on *Candida* and saccharine yeasts, which boosted the volume of dough by metabolizing sugar. The concept spread as far west as Morocco and Iberia, east to Arab lands and India, and south to Ethiopia, home of teff pancake bread.

After the barbarian invasions of the sixth century C.E., public bake ovens disappeared until twelfth-century monastic kitchens revived artisanal breads. Medieval European sourdough versions—German *sauerteig,* Polish rye, Italian *biga*-flavored ciabatta and *panettone,* braided Jewish challah, and nutty-tasting Belgian *desem*—accelerated the method of leavening with natural microflora with quick-acting compressed yeasts. During a grain shortfall in 1443, rye sourdough, reputedly named for the Swiss baker Pumper Nickel, substituted mixed-grain bread for pure-wheat loaves.

The popularity of sourdough bread after the 1849 California gold rush emerged from the makeshift cookery of pioneers and gold panners. Carried up the Pacific Coast to the Yukon and Alaska, starter bore a value equal to tobacco or flint and steel for fire making. Borne in buckskin pouches close to body heat or in wooden kegs jouncing in chuck wagons, the dough remained unfrozen, ready for the day's bread and cake baking or flapjack making.

One of San Francisco's pioneer entrepreneurs, Isidore Boudin, fed hungry gold seekers from his French bakery, which employed native wild yeast. He followed artisanal Burgundian techniques to produce a crusty loaf. The Boudin family operated the nation's largest sourdough industry. During the 1906 San Francisco earthquake, his wife, Louise Erni Boudin, saved the "mother" dough containing the original leaven.

Into the twenty-first century, San Francisco maintains fame as the sourdough capital. White doughs soured by the original *Lactobacillus sanfranciscensis* yield the familiar tangy accompaniment to chili and clam chowder. Health advocates promote sourdough biscuits, coffee-cakes, loaves, and rolls as more nutritionally complete and more easily digested than industrialized gluten breads.

See also: African Diet and Cuisine, Sub-Saharan; Beans and Legumes; Bread; Chowder; Fermented Foods; Wheat.

Further Reading

Hui, Yiu H., ed. *Handbook of Food Products Manufacturing: Principles, Bakery, Beverages, Cereals, Cheese, Confectionary, Fats, Fruits, and Functional Foods.* Hoboken, NJ: Wiley-Interscience, 2007.

Preedy, Victor R., Ronald R. Watson, and Vinood B. Patel. *Flour and Breads and Their Fortification in Health and Disease Prevention.* Boston: Academic Press, 2011.

Rayner, Lisa. *Wild Bread: Hand-Baked Sourdough Artisan Breads in Your Own Kitchen.* Flagstaff, AZ: Lifeweaver, 2009.

South American Diet and Cuisine

South American foodways remain anchored in ancestral patterns of edibles from sea, river, and land. From 10,000 B.C.E., indigenous peoples relied on chayote, peanuts, beans, squash, tomatoes, yucca, oca tubers, dried sea bass, amaranth, chilies, and sweet potatoes for sustenance. Guava, mangos, papayas, passion fruit, and melons contributed natural sweets to drinks and snacks.

In the Andes highlands, alpaca and llama meat and game dried readily into jerky. The Amazonian heartland teemed with rain forest acai palms and cashew nuts and the world's largest array of fresh water fish, including dorado, baitfish, bass, and catfish. Regional dependence on corn and potatoes and military rations of quinoa preceded the post-Columbian explosion in New World starches on European menus, the first east-west fusion cuisine from the Western Hemisphere.

To bland carbohydrates, South Americans added chili peppers, roasted guinea pigs, corn beer, and clams and goat meat steamed in a *huatia* (pit oven). The addition of toasted ants derived from a closeness with nature and the incorporation of insects into a heavily vegetarian diet. Colonial sugar plantations enhanced beverages with rum and honeyed desserts with a granular sugar and molasses. Wheat, chickpeas, oats, lentils, and rice from Spain expanded sources of bread and hot porridge.

Into the twenty-first century, South Americans rely on cassava for flour. The growth of coffee in Brazil, producer of 33 percent of the world's beans, supplies the region with a full-bodied beverage, which they brew strong and blend with evaporated milk. Three alternatives, chamomile tea, passionflower tea, and yerba maté (*Ilex paraguariensis*) with milk and sugar, promote wellness and boost immunity.

Family-centered lunches stress sociability and shared dining on heavy entrées—*ajiaco* (potato soup) and corn fritters or empanadas (meat turnovers) for starters. The second course pairs grilled beef with rice and black beans and leafy sorrel. The day ends with a leisurely dinner that draws guests and family into conversation. Flan, milk cake, fried bananas, or berries and cheese satisfy appetites without overfilling.

In the north, Colombian and Venezuelan restaurants display a New World preference for traditional corn *arepa* (griddle cakes) and plantain chips alongside the western Mediterranean influence of cheese, garlic and parsley, onion, and olive oil, particularly in chicken or beef stew. Brazilian cooks fry chorizo (sausage) and cassava and steam collards to serve with *feijoada*, a one-pot fusion dish consisting of black, red, or white beans, cabbage, carrots, tomatoes, palm oil, and meat and based on cooking styles from Africa and India. Guyana absorbed from African slaves and Asian and Portuguese colonists a preference for flatbread, Caribbean pepper pot stew, and curried rice. Andean cuisine depends on some 200 types of potatoes for entrées and finger food and a topping of chopped fresh *aji* (pepper) and onion into a salty salsa.

Farther south, Argentine beef dominates menus with *asado* (barbecue), grilled sweetbreads, and prime cuts, especially baked flank steak, a national entrée. Because of heavy immigration from Europe, native restaurants advertise Italian pasta and polenta, German schnitzel and lager, Dutch gin, Caribbean coconut rice, and Chinese *yakisoba* and ramen noodles. Tea rooms offer British tea served with *dulce de leche* (milk caramel), whipped cream, and scones. Patagonian menus feature king crab, lamb, goat, and venison seasoned with *chimichurri,* a condiment of garlic, cilantro, and vinegar, and bilberry or strawberry desserts. The Pacific Coast cooks claim their native heritage in ceviche, shrimp and fish marinated in citrus juice.

See also: Beef; Chocolate; Corn and Maize; Inca Diet and Cuisine; Peppers; Potatoes; Tortillas.

Further Reading

Civitello, Linda. *Cuisine and Culture: A History of Food and People.* 3rd ed. Hoboken, NJ: John Wiley & Sons, 2011.

Janer, Zilkia. *Latino Food Culture.* Westport, CT: Greenwood, 2008.

Jefferson, Ann, and Paul Lokken. *Daily Life in Colonial Latin America.* Santa Barbara, CA: ABC-Clio, 2011.

Lovera, José Rafael. *Food Culture in South America.* Westport, CT: Greenwood, 2005.

Soyer, Alexis (1810–1858)

London's Reform Club chef Alexis Benôit Soyer turned food service into rescue efforts during the Irish famine and the Crimean War.

A native of Meaux-en-Brie, France, Soyer apprenticed in restaurant kitchens in Paris at age 11 and advanced to deputy chef at the French Foreign Office. At age 20, he began cooking for British royalty and Members of Parliament. His innovations ranged from oven thermometers, steam dumbwaiters, and gas stoves to pantry chambers chilled with circulating water. In June 1838, he catered a breakfast for 2,000 following Queen Victoria's coronation. Soyer compiled 2,000 recipes, including such comforts for invalids as nettle soup, and composed basic instructions on how to get ten servings from each fowl and how to carve beef or lamb to get the leanest slices. For beverages, he praised tea for encouraging sobriety in England and mocked British efforts to make coffee. A review in the London *Times* lauded the cook for stressing that good food is a pleasure and a boon to health.

Soyer inveighed against England's rejection of vegetables from the menu. His fruit and vegetable selection showcased the firm red potato and promoted young and tender brussels sprouts, carrots, mangels, onions, and turnips. For fruit jelly, he preferred isinglass (from fish air bladders) as a jelling agent and sought to retain as much of the natural fruit color as possible. He recommended endive and spinach for good health and cacao, Irish moss, and kelp for economy. For variety, he encouraged the use of continental favorites, such as Jerusalem artichokes, salsify, and truffles, which he simmered in champagne. His instructions for cooking artichokes and white haricot beans followed the French style of flavoring with fines herbes (chervil, chives, parsley, and tarragon) or sorrel. His writings about ancient cookery impressed on readers the importance of lentils to human nourishment.

At the onset of the Irish Potato Famine of 1845, Soyer mustered volunteers to devise an orderly feeding system to replace mismanaged relief efforts. While Quakers transported 180 gallons (680 liters) of soup daily to the countryside, for city meal service, he devised barrows and soup carts, the first urban soup kitchens to feed the starv-

ing. In a 200-foot (60-meter) mobile kitchen set up opposite the Royal Barracks in Dublin, he housed an oven and boiler, where he conserved funds by steaming vegetables. On a tight budget, he introduced swedes (rutabagas), a much-neglected root crop. From a giant cauldron, his staff distributed quart servings of soup to 26,600 people, who lined up for hand washing and daily meals. A phalanx of tables held 100 quart-sized bowls alongside spoons attached by chains. From April 6 to August 14, 1847, he distributed 1,147,279 meals. The British government purchased his mobile kitchen for the use of Dublin's South Union Relief Committee. Based on his experiences, Soyer published a monograph titled *Charitable Cookery, or The Poor Man's Regenerator* (1847). Among his recommendations for the poor, he stressed the value of brown bread, cornmeal, fish, and ox heart and liver, cheap foods that the proud Irish were embarrassed to purchase.

A celebrity cook, Soyer remained active in kitchen design and in food service to the needy. He summarized simple meal planning in *A Shilling Cookery for the People* (1854), in which he regretted that the poor relied more on bread and cheese than on wholesome vegetables. In support of soldier wellness, morale, and food safety, Soyer traveled to Turkey to organize the British army hospital kitchen at Scutari during the Crimean War. In addition to demonstrating low-budget recipes and training regimental cooks, he designed a field stove for feeding 2,000 British soldiers in two hours. The stove remained a field staple until the Gulf War of 1990. Late in his career, he lectured on the need for dietary reform for the military. He sketched plans for a mobile field canteen and planned a model kitchen at Wellington Barracks in London. Despite some commercial success, such as Crosse & Blackwell marketing his signature sauce and relishes, Soyer died broke at age 48 from alcoholism.

See also: Breakfast; Cookbooks; Famine; Seacole, Mary Jane.

Further Reading

Arnold, Ann. *The Adventurous Chef: Alexis Soyer.* New York: Farrar, Straus and Giroux, 2002.

Brandon, Ruth. *The People's Chef: The Culinary Revolutions of Alexis Soyer.* New York: Walker, 2004.

Cowan, Ruth. *Relish: The Extraordinary Life of Alexis Soyer, Victorian Celebrity Chef.* London: Phoenix, 2007.

Fraser, Evan D.G., and Andrew Rimas. *Empires of Food: Feast, Famine, and the Rise and Fall of Civilizations.* New York: Simon & Schuster, 2010.

Spices

The rage for spices transformed culinary history, sending Asian and European fleets around the world in search of intriguing taste sensations.

After 10,000 B.C.E., Neolithic hunter-gatherers prized mustard seeds and juniper berries to deodorize corpses for burial. The two flavorings entered culinary use as an afterthought. From as early as 3000 B.C.E., Assyrians imported cassia from southern India and revered sub-Saharan sesame as a divine flavoring. Egyptians honored dead pharaohs with peppercorns in the nostrils and spiced embalming salts for permeating the torso cavities and soaking the limbs and skull. Nile residents also cooked curative and aromatic dishes with cumin, marjoram, calamus (sweet flag), and anise to increase well-being and longevity. From 2580 to 2560 B.C.E., desert overseers allotted Asian spice to laborers to promote steady work on Cheops's pyramid, the tomb of the Pharaoh Khufu.

Spice purchasing involved lengthy travel by ship, caravan, or a combination of the two. Traders bore fenugreek and *mahlab* (dried cherry stones) from Turkey, licorice root and star anise from China, poppy seed from the Middle East, mastic resin (gum arabic powder) from Chios, calamus from Egypt, sumac from Iran, and caraway from the Sahara. The most varied stock came from India, where markets sold *amchur* (powdered mango), red *kokum* (mangosteen) and tamarind rind, *ajwain* (carom seed), nigella (black cumin), orrisroot oil, and zedoary, a bitter rhizome.

The Fertile Crescent developed a cuisine tinged with foreign flavorings. After 2400 B.C.E., Sumerians traded to the Moluccas for cloves, cubeb pepper, and galangal, a rhizome cooked into a tonic. Syrians coveted Asian spices as aphrodisiacs around 1700 B.C.E., at the same time that spice cultivators in Crete plucked the stigmas from crocus blooms to extract sweet saffron, a yellow colorant

from Kashmir that Assyrians applied to 90 diseases. Around 1230 B.C.E., Hebrews anointed the Ark of the Covenant with cassia oil (aromatic cinnamon) from the Malabar coast, India's southwestern trading nexus.

In 950 B.C.E., northern Arabs led camel and donkey trains through India to China over the Incense Route to buy goods marketable to Greeks. Evolving land and maritime routes joined Arabia and Baghdad with spice depots in Malabar, Guangzhou, and the Spice Islands. Thus, Arabs controlled the world's commerce in the most valuable comestibles, including delicate yellow mace, the powdered aril of the nutmeg.

After 600 C.E. Chinese and Arabic gourmands envisioned heaven as a grand orgy of aromas and flavors as disparate as aromatic aloeswood and cardamom, a flavoring for sweets. Alexander the Great redirected spice profits from the Far East through Alexandria, the center of Mediterranean commerce. Silphium, one of the standard flavorings, traveled along Greco-Roman trade routes as far north as Gaul. Balance of trade drained off much of Roman wealth to Egyptian and Arab merchants until Roman sea captains mastered trade winds and journeyed safely to India and back with pepper.

Rise of European Cuisines

After the fall of Rome and the rise of Islam in 622 C.E., Muslims spread their religion over old spice routes and revived Arab commerce. Returning crusaders found Europe in a gastronomic slump that resurrected warriors' memories of Palestine and Cyprus. Soldiers embroidered tales of Middle Eastern pleasures with samples of cinnamon, jasmine, sugar, nutmeg, and artemisia, a bitter flavoring. As much as Christendom longed to reclaim the

A spice vendor in the southwestern Indian state of Kerala displays pepper, ginger, cinnamon, and star aniseed. Kerala and the Malabar Coast have been a major source of high-quality spices and a vital stop on Asian trade routes since 3000 B.C.E. *(EyesWideOpen/ Getty Images)*

Hebrew capital of Jerusalem from Saracen control, Christians lusted for Eastern luxuries, which the wealthy deemed their birthright. Recoiling from such greed, the Benedictines esteemed the unadorned plain food of peasants as a sign of true Christian humility and poverty.

To relieve the monotony of medieval boiled trout and peacock pie, chefs generated savor with cinnamon, fenugreek, nigella, sugar, mace, and nutmeg. Recipes for meat marinade called for soaking haunches in honey spiced with cloves, ginger, and black pepper. Spice added new interest to condiments, jam, and sauces and to such sweets as gingerbread and gingersnaps, cookie recipes that crusaders brought from the Middle East. Meals ended with hippocras, an after-dinner wine tinged with cinnamon and heated as a nightcap.

Dynasties gambled huge investments on the planting of new spice-growing colonies in the Indian subcontinent and Java; British, Dutch, Swedish, and Portuguese power mongers jockeyed for control of trading routes to Sumatra and Malabar. In 1271, Marco Polo journeyed from Venice to China to investigate trade possibilities. The scramble for dominance of cassia, black pepper, ginger, cloves, mace, cinnamon, sugar, and nutmeg in Venice, Lisbon, and Amsterdam produced the first global culinary conflict and possibly spread *Yersinia pestis,* the vector of the Black Death that followed sailors to European port cities.

Spice marketing became the domain of pharmacists, whom Italians called *speziali* (spice dispensers). After Spanish explorer Hernán de Cortés discovered vanilla in Aztec Mexico in 1519, German doctors prescribed the aromatic bean as a cure for impotence. Medicinal recipes listed mastic, cloves, and Indian sesame among apothecary simples that purified foods and treated coughs, gastric ills, headache, and toothache. Physicians advised cooks on the appropriate balance of food with additives such as Persian asafetida, a flu fighter, and allspice, a Jamaican dried fruit that corrected gustatory excesses threatening sleep, digestion, and sexual potency. The more cures attached to spices, the greater the rush to profit from them.

Routes to Spice Markets

At the beginning of the age of discovery, travelogues tweaked European curiosity about Javanese mace and Indonesian pepper vines. Tales from *The Travels of Sir John Mandeville* (1357) inspired Genoan navigator Christopher Columbus to petition the Spanish court of Ferdinand and Isabella for funding to explore new spice routes to the Orient. His sole encounter in 1492, *aji* (chili or green pepper), seemed insignificant in comparison with the flavorings of India and Sumatra. With a more pragmatic eye for profit and avoidance of Ottoman monopolies, Portuguese explorer Vasco da Gama worked his way around southern Africa toward caches of spice in India and Malaysia. The resultant stampede to grow spices in

the Americas aroused another world evil, slavery, the source of labor for plantations in Jamaica, Barbados, and Brazil.

The late Renaissance advanced medieval interest in taste with a burst of sense impressions from fragrance and color. Reformulated recipes boosted the price of fragrant sandalwood, aloeswood, and yellow turmeric and saffron, the two chief additives to rice and cream desserts. Aristocrats and parvenus flaunted wealth with a display of spiced rotisserie meats for entertainment and ambassadorial receptions. To corner the market on trans-European spice dispersal, Venice outflanked the merchant republics of Florence, Genoa, and Pisa, turning a small marine village into a world commodities player. Into the holds of Venetian galleys tumbled goods traveling northwest from Tripoli and Tyre, Crete, and Alexandria.

While chili peppers gained slow recognition for enlivening bland cuisine, stores of saffron and nutmeg commanded high prices in Tudor England. In 1603, physicians prescribed the yellow and brown powders to treat bubonic plague. The difficulty in pollinating vanilla left Mexican planters in control of a new fad in aromatic cookery, especially the preparation of hot chocolate, a trendy drink throughout Europe. Similarly, Brazilian vendors monopolized the flow of annatto, an exotic flavoring and food coloring for rice dishes.

In 1748, Bengal (now Bangladesh) fell to the British East India Company (BEIC), the beginning of the collapse of Dutch East India Company control of commercial traffic in cloves, pepper, cinnamon, nutmeg, and mace from Bengal, Malabar, Persia, and Surat, India. The BEIC outdistanced French and Portuguese commercial efforts, usurped Danish trade depots, and, in 1798, monopolized global food marketing. In 1813, the Swedish East India Company capitulated to the BEIC control of cinnamon, pepper, ginger, and anise, source of a flavored aperitif. By 1839, the British flag flew over warehouses in Burma and Aden, from which clipper ships delivered spices, sugar, and tea around the world.

In the United States, McCormick & Company, a Baltimore distributor, marketed a mélange of aromas and tastes in its array of spices, including liquid mint, maple, rum, and lemon flavoring, beginning in 1896. A handy source of chili and tempura spices, enchilada and fajita spice, crab boil, tagine mix, orange peel, and sweet-and-sour and Thai rice flavorings, the McCormick family of products sold under one label the world's most-sought-after ingredients. Similarly comprehensive, the products of British Pepper & Spice, the largest spice retailer in the United Kingdom, supplied the grocery chains of Tesco, Sainsbury, and Marks & Spencer with Mexican, Indian, Thai, Malaysian, and Mediterranean taste enhancers, including gourmet peppers—Sumatran *lampong, sarawak* from Borneo, and Ceylonese *sambal* chili.

The availability of spices in the modern era belied the struggles and one-upmanship of past centuries.

Grocery stores stocked unassuming bottles of goods as disparate in provenance as Choctaw *filé* powder from the North American sassafras tree and Jamaican jerk spice, a dry rub combining pepper with allspice, a Central American berry. Internet sales made available the unique smells and tang of idiocuisine—the fragrant *merkén* of Chile, Australian aniseed myrtle and fruit-flavored olida, and African Grains of Selim, a pungent pod from Senegal. Asian specialties—Vietnamese coriander, wasabi (Japanese horseradish), Chinese five-spice powder, Szechuan pepper, and garam masala, an Indian blend of pepper, cloves, mace, cumin, cardamom, nutmeg, anise, and coriander—enrich the culinary range of chefs dedicated to multicultural cuisine.

In 2012, studies of spice restored respect for ancient recipes and natural medicines. Nutritionists reclaimed nutmeg as a treatment for swollen joints and cloves as a temporary first aid for toothache. Bacteriologists recognized the antimicrobial strength of allspice and oregano against salmonella and listeria.

See also: Abreu, António de, and Francisco Serrao; British East India Company; Crusaders' Diet and Cuisine; Dutch East India Company; Gama, Vasco da; Maritime Trade Routes; Pastry; Portuguese Diet and Cuisine; Salt; Silk Road; Tudor Diet and Cuisine.

Further Reading

Alcock, Joan Pilsbury. *Food in the Ancient World.* Westport, CT: Greenwood, 2006.

Freedman, Paul H. *Food: The History of Taste.* Berkeley: University of California Press, 2007.

Krondl, Michael. *The Taste of Conquest: The Rise and Fall of the Three Great Cities of Spice.* New York: Random House, 2007.

Wilkins, John M., and Shaun Hill. *Food in the Ancient World.* Malden, MA: Wiley-Blackwell, 2006.

Standish, Miles (ca. 1584–1656)

One of the founders of Massachusetts and New England's first soldier, Miles Standish pioneered the North American corn trade.

A native of Duxbury, Lancashire, (or possibly the Isle of Mann), Standish entered the military at age 17. In Holland during the English and Dutch war against Spanish invaders, he advanced to the rank of captain. In summer 1620 at Leiden, he accepted the post of military adviser to 102 Pilgrims, who sailed aboard the *Mayflower* to Cape Cod, Massachusetts, in search of freedom from religious persecution. After the nine-week Atlantic crossing, a shortage of food and beer forced the company to abandon plans to sail to the Hudson River. On November 11, Standish signed the historic Mayflower Compact,

a social contract among 41 male passengers intended to safeguard the colony from dissension and disorder.

As a likely spot for settling, Standish chose Plymouth, on the cape's western shore, a former Indian compound abandoned after plague wiped out the residents. Standish's efforts helped save the English immigrants from malnutrition. At Patuxet, Massachusetts, on November 16, 1620, the newcomers rejoiced in the discovery of broiled herring in an empty wigwam and a mound of sand adjacent to a harvested cornfield. Inside they dug out a basket containing cranberries and three or four bushels of an unfamiliar grain—husked Narragansett corn, a dried staple that the aborigines of southern New England had grown since 700 B.C.E. Reconnoitering two Indian houses, Standish commandeered beans and more corn and led hunters who shot an eagle, ducks, and geese. A year later, the Pilgrim settlers learned that the Wampanoag bore a grudge against them for food pilferage, which tribes ranked as a serious crime.

Standish proved his leadership of the citizens' militia during the winter, when only a handful of colonists remained healthy. In February 1621, as more Pilgrims fell sick from exposure and starvation, he chopped wood and cooked for the ailing. Among the victims, his wife Rose died. He buried her alongside other colonists, of whom only 55 survived. Standish used corn as an exchange medium when he purchased his first dairy cow from Edward Winslow, the colony's first cattle agent. On April 2, the Wampanoag donated parched corn, roasted fish, and venison as tokens of friendship. The English reciprocated with biscuit, butter, and "strong water," a general term for fermented beverages.

In spring 1621, Squanto joined Chief Massasoit in training the Pilgrims in fishing and in growing and storing corn. The English planted their first garden on 20 acres (8 hectares) of thin, rocky soil. By placing kernels in hills, the newcomers improved corn pollination. Squanto demonstrated burying a dead herring or shad in each mound to help stalks produce ears. The pilgrims also sowed 6 acres (2.4 hectares) in barley and peas. Squanto introduced the colonists to New England traditions—digging for clams and tapping maple trees for sap.

After a season of half rations, plentiful clams, eels, lobster, and various game ensured survival. The sharing of food with the Wampanoag in early October 1621 set the model for Thanksgiving, a uniquely American holiday. Before the feast, four sharpshooters went fowling for birds. In anticipation of a treaty with the Indians, Standish invited Massasoit, Samoset, and Squanto to a celebration. The Indians, in accordance with tribal custom, brought their whole clan of 90 people. To supply a three-day feast, Massasoit donated Canada geese, five deer, grape wines, shellfish, and wild plums. Standish introduced the chief to dining at a trestle table instead of on floor mats.

With the arrival of 93 more colonists in July 1621, the Pilgrims enlarged their cornfields. Until the next harvest, they subsisted on berries and venison. Standish abandoned the communal living style and encouraged cultivation of individual plots. In February 1623, he traveled by boat down the coast to a distant tribe at Namasket (Middleborough) to barter for corn, his introduction of New England's coastal food trade. A successful harvest in 1624 set up the colony to barter for Indian furs, which vessels carried back to England. The following year, Standish negotiated a buyout of the colonial contract that freed the Pilgrims of London investors. Throughout the 1630s, the colony enjoyed high commodity prices. Standish remarried and retired to his farm, where he died at age 72.

See also: Dried Food; Fish and Fishing; Wine.

Further Reading

Bunker, Nick. *Making Haste from Babylon: The Mayflower Pilgrims and Their World: A New History.* New York: Random House, 2010.

Philbrick, Nathaniel. *Mayflower: A Story of Courage, Community, and War.* New York: Penguin, 2007.

Stratton, Eugene Aubrey. *Plymouth Colony: Its History and People.* Salt Lake City, UT: Ancestry, 1986.

Storage, Food

Whether in a box chest, calabash, granary, in-ground urn, pantry, springhouse, or hillside lean-to, food storage preserves staples and extends shelf life for emergencies as predictable as blizzards, floods, hurricanes, and typhoons and as unexpected as earthquakes, volcanic eruptions, acts of terrorism, and nuclear war.

The Harappans of the Indus Valley practiced food preservation as early as 2500 B.C.E. by separating types of beans and grains into bins and ventilating them. From 100 B.C.E. to 100 C.E., the sheds that the Iceni Celts of Great Britain attached to longhouses held domestic supplies and smoked meats and fish. In this same era, Roman households erected iron stands to hold sealed amphorae of fish sauce, oil, olives, vinegar, and wine. In medieval Russia, the icehouse added more options for food variety, such as caviar, corned beef, and sturgeon.

Gervase Markham's compendium *The English Huswife* (1615) lauded the hovel, a simple shed, lean-to, or shelter constructed from eight crotchets or braces topped with spars. He suggested that builders craft semipermanent shelters to guard hearth fuel, herd animals, and grain bags and bales and urged roofing the pantries in bracken, brush, and furze. For the smallholder, his ideal storage shed suited stacks of pease and vetch, a common famine food from the early days of the Fertile Crescent. In *The Land of England* (1979), British domestic expert

Dorothy Hartley added that makeshift thatching could come from heather, rough grass, or willow bark. Tight casks and tin or japanned canisters kept biscuit, cheese, rye, sugar loaves, and yeast safe from moisture.

To shelter foodstuffs at the height of quality and flavor, Native Americans found unique methods of storage in a woven mocuck (bark box), hide saddlebag, or parfleche, a rectangular pouch used for travel. The Pee-Posh of the lower Colorado River, the Yukon of northwestern Canada, and the Hare of Alberta, added pantries to the hogan, igloo, or lodge as storage space for baskets of berries and grain or as a shelter for buffalo chips, firewood, dried fruit and herbs, fodder, smoked meats and fish, and vegetables, such as camassia and wild carrot root. Before 600 C.E., the Maya of Cerén, El Salvador, suspended ropes of onions and peppers and pots of food from ceilings and stacked bags of goods on rafters. Hawaiians recycled coconut shells into lard safes and tropical leaves into *poi* wrappers.

The Menominee chose bark buckets to protect maple sap or wild rice; the Chumash lined grass canisters with asphaltum to hold seabird eggs. The Carib of the West Indies built sheltered food storage near their homes and vented open-air drying, roasting, and smoking through the unthatched sides. A lean-to increased by 50 percent the floor space of the Mexican *jacal*, a one-room thatched mud hovel built by farmers and preferred by Texas *mestizos* and cowboys living at the edge of ranches. Likewise, the Iroquois loft and the underfloor of the Seminole *chickee* reduced the clutter of living space while shielding bagged perishables from rats and thieves.

Frontier Food Preservation

On the New World frontier, the add-on, meat closet, root cellar, saltbox, and indoor well house offered makeshift relief to crowded cabins and sod huts. In colonial York, Maine, the extra space of a lean-to or potato cache was a step saver that placed staples near the hearth. The nearness to a chimney assured the cook dry beans as well as sliced rounds of pumpkins and winter squash. Emulating the ramadas of Southwestern Indians, prairie farmers constructed brush arbors and slatted sheds on the south side as the need arose for storing firewood, dried meat, grain, and molasses. Among Quebec bakers, the one- or two-story lean-to sheltered a semi-indoor oven, which faced the outside and attached through the wall to the central chimney. Flues and roofing protected the dwelling from smoke and sparks by sequestering the shed from prevailing winds. Rising heat dried bean pods and grain sheaves to ward off mildew and kept canned salmon and sausage and rounds of hard cheese from freezing.

As meager bush cabins took shape on the Australian frontier, squatters chose survival over luxury. For a food safe, they suspended crates from trees. After outfitting their homes with a fireplace, bucket, shovel, and ax, some thrived enough to hammer together a crude cookout hut or kitchen lean-to. To these structures, they added bread tables, water filters, and meat safes, their bulwarks against ants, flies, and human and animal predators. For a similar purpose, in Scotland and the Hebrides, where fishermen and crofters relished dried and stewed seaweed as a vegetable or condiment and as forage for sheep, shelving required ample space. In storage sheds, they draped dulse and carrageen for drying.

Work Station and Storage

In Japan, the miso room once abutted the farmhouse kitchen. An unheated outer closet, it held fermenting pickles and soy products and flour in stoppered bamboo cylinders. Householders stored homemade condiments, blended from soybeans, barley, rice yeast, and salt for flavoring soup. Flat-bottomed wood barrels held rice yeast, a slurry of wheat, soy sauce, soybeans, and salt that gradually seeped into a bamboo filtration cylinder for ladling into noodle broth or stew. Lidded baskets secured dried sardines and shiitake mushrooms. In conical baskets, housewives mounded tofu, a curd formed of cooked soybeans and bittern extracted from sea salt. The typical Kyushu housewife, aided by a daughter-in-law, did the cooking in a dirt-floored lean-to at a stove situated on the outside wall for maximum protection of stored goods from fire.

The Agta of the Philippines constructed pantry sheds from wood and branches. Women sat together under the shade to pound corn between stones and secure it in bags. Similarly, near Rara Lake in Chhapru, Nepal, people in multifamily residences flailed barley and winnowed it from baskets before storing it in rooftop lean-tos. Malaysian families typically built a house, then nailed up an auxiliary cooking space. Their needs tended toward Asian simplicity—slatted baskets for storing rice, a mortar and pestle for grinding dried spices, and a wok and stirring paddle for cooking meat and vegetables.

In the 1980s, industrialized nations, strapped for fossil fuels, added lean-to greenhouses, hoop houses, solaria, and sunrooms to their homes. Part of the impetus came from tax breaks on passive solar energy. In addition to storing warmth in stone and concrete floors, frame buildings, made of tempered glass and extruded aluminum, heated space for cultivating and drying herbs and growing a year-round supply of salad greens. In Ireland and Scandinavia, where the growing season is limited, greenhouse advocates readied seedlings for the spring kitchen garden.

See also: Amerindian Diet; Bamboo; Caching; Cooking Schools; Famine; Middens; Olives and Olive Oil; Pemmican; Seaweed; Vinegar; Yeast.

Further Reading

Astyk, Sharon. *Independence Days: A Guide to Sustainable Food Storage and Preservation.* Gabriola, British Columbia, Canada: New Society, 2009.

Cordes, Lyndsee Simpson. *Simple Recipes Using Food Storage.* Springville, UT: Cedar Fort, 2008.

Pond, Catherine Seiberling. *The Pantry: Its History and Modern Uses.* Salt Lake City, UT: Gibbs Smith, 2007.

Street Food

Convenience meals and portable snacks sold on the street have a long and colorful history. From the 500s B.C.E., the agora of Athens teemed with sellers of nuts, sweets, lentil soup, cheese pies, *koulouri* (sesame buns), and wheat and barley cakes, especially during holidays and after theatrical performances. In Rome and Pompeii, vendors sweetened scoops of snow with grape must and honey. As an enticement to dock workers and soldiers, vintners accompanied wine carafes with dishes of olives and toasted chickpeas.

In the Middle Ages, a grassroots food culture appealed to crowds at fairs, bazaars, and agricultural markets. The circulation of coins simplified impulse purchases of drinks and tidbits, such as charcoal-grilled fish, roasted chestnuts, and semolina snacks in Constantinople and Smyrna. In 1100, Japanese peddlers hawked quail eggs to passersby. Easily accessible Korean food stands displayed squid and octopus for consuming with rice cakes, a boon to the poor who had no kitchens.

Between 1096 and 1204, crusaders to the Holy Land purchased honeyed pastries and soup from food stalls and bought pocket snacks of almonds, apples, chickpeas, melons, pistachios, and walnuts from portable kiosks. At Cairo in 1326, Muslim travel writer Ibn Battuta observed drink and snack sellers doing business with Iraqi and Syrian refugees along the Nile. Ready-to-eat fare across the Middle East ranged from hearty grilled eggplant and sardines to child-pleasing snacks of almond cookies rolled in sesame seeds.

During the Renaissance, convenience food sold well as travelers and shoppers lined up to buy calzone in Naples, pomegranate seeds in Malta, and honey-nut morsels in Marrakech. In bazaars, purchasers watched street cooks roast meat and baste it with vinegar sauce. On Christian holidays, Europeans selected from scones and *gaufres* (waffles) marked with religious symbols. In India in the 1500s, enterprising cooks shaped fermented dal and rice into *dosas* (crepes) and offered coriander or tamarind chutney as condiments.

A thorough survey of New World street commerce reached Europe after 1519. Spanish conquerors of Montezuma II perused the food court of Tlatelolco, where Aztec shoppers bought seafood empanadas, corn on the cob, corn bread, bird and fish paté, and eggs as well as cashews and peanuts. Historian Bernardino da Sahagún reported the popularity of tortillas filled with ants, fish, *huitlacoche* (corn fungus), locusts, maguey worms, and snails. Buyers topped the main filling with raw vegetables and hot pepper sauces, a Mesoamerican innovation.

Curbside cuisine took advantage of place, time, and milieu. After 1550, Portuguese voyagers to Benin, Gambia, and Ghana found local vendors organizing food stalls along the coast. In Ethiopia in 1627, travelers could escape desert heat with melon slices and fruit ades sweetened with sugar. New Yorkers began patronizing pushcart food in 1691, when Italian immigrants sold marinated olives and Jewish cooks hawked knishes and dill pickles. In Jamaica after 1728, aloo balls of cumin-flavored mashed potatoes emerged from deep fryers for eating hot. In the 1800s, Hong Kong street chefs deep-fried *char siu* (barbecue pork) turnovers, ling balls, skewered meatballs, and vegetarian spring rolls. Laborers and stevedores in Victorian England took advantage of penny pies and sheep's trotters, which purchasers consumed standing up.

The turmoil of war advanced the need for unorthodox food service. During the American Civil War, soldiers bought liquor and luxury items from mobile sutlers (civilian merchants). Noncombatants emptied home pantries to set up canteens at railroad stations to feed incoming wounded and their military attendants. From 1861 to 1865, black marketers and profiteers answered the demand for cheap meals. Food preparers overcame devalued currency and shortages by clever budgeting and eking out supplies with wartime recipes, such as vinegar pie and ersatz coffee.

Agritourism established itself in the late 1800s as an appeal to gourmands interested in exotic and regional dishes, including Thai papaya salad in Bangkok; barbecued iguana in Baja, Mexico; and the stuffed pancakes of Xian, China. At the Philadelphia Centennial International Exhibition of 1876, fairgoers sipped ice cream treats from an arctic soda fountain. Neighborhood vendors on bicycles or pushing carts profited from foot traffic at train stations and hotels. At the 1893 Columbian Exposition in Chicago, innovative food dealers marketed chili from stalls and hot dogs from self-contained barrows and wienie vans.

The street venue prospered in large cities at sports arenas, landmarks, beaches, and public parks. Typically staffed by individuals or families, the outdoor food business offered financial security during hard times, especially for children, women, immigrants, and the underemployed. In the 1920s, entrepreneurs developed corn dogs, a wiener on a stick that succeeded in Argentina, Australia, Canada, New Zealand, and Vietnam. Chinese shoppers bought tofu curds simmered in soy sauce as a midday meal. The taste and smell introduced outsiders to a cultural staple as authentic and diverse as Hopi fry bread, and the aromas of hot dishes drew buyers to such specialties as the cassava chips of Mozambique, Barbadian pineapple slices, Thai steamed fish, and Peruvian coconut desserts. Sumatran vendors brushed turmeric sauce on *satay padang* (beef kebabs), a favorite with on-the-run eaters. Turkish meat sellers sliced doner kebabs from rotating vertical spits and sold side dishes of eggplant, peppers, pilaf, and tomatoes folded into flatbread.

In Africa and Asia in the twenty-first century, up to 50 percent of urban snacks consist of street purchases of oil-cooked peanuts and yams. In urban areas, mobile dim sum and dumpling bars, pita sandwich and gyro carts, and falafel and taco stands provide 40 percent of the nourishment consumed by the homeless and low-income patrons. In Tanzania, schoolchildren buy fried bananas and cassava at midmorning break. The Food and Agricultural Organization of the United Nations monitors the role of quick snacks on the diets of children and the underclass. The World Health Organization sets sanitation and safety standards to reduce the merchandizing of unclean or toxic ingredients.

See also: Chili; Curry; Fast Food; Finger Food; Grilling; Insects; Kebabs; Tortillas; Wine.

Further Reading

Ferguson, Clare. *Street Food.* Alexandria, VA: Time-Life, 1999.

Hester, Elliott. *Adventures of a Continental Drifter: An Around-the-World Excursion into Weirdness, Danger, Lust, and the Perils of Street Food.* New York: St. Martin's, 2005.

Kime, Tom. *Street Food.* New York: Penguin, 2007.

Sugar and Sweeteners

The incorporation of sugar and sweeteners in food increases its palatability and satisfaction to human taste buds. In New Guinea, Malaysians domesticated sugarcane around 8000 B.C.E. and passed the plant to traders from northern India. The Sanskrit language identified the white crystals as *sharkara* (grains or gravels), a reference to the crystalline structure of dried juice, which snackers could suck from the chewed cane. Indian ambassadors ferried gifts of sugar to Chinese emperors and touted its value as an aphrodisiac.

The sweet cane impressed Darius the Great of Persia, who invaded India in 510 B.C.E. and studied the growing of sugarcane along the Indus River east of Pakistan. According to field reports by the Macedonian admiral Nearchus, head of the Indus River fleet, Alexander the Great made a similar observation of the Indus Valley in 327 B.C.E., when he chewed sweet cane. On Alexander's march west, he introduced Greece to imported jaggery, a crude form of sugar.

Around 70 C.E., Greek pharmacist Dioscorides, a specialist in the curative nature of honey, recognized sugar as a tonic for the alimentary canal and renal system. According to the Roman historian Arrian, the sugar trade thrived along the Red Sea by 95 C.E. Around 300, India competed with the Persians by extracting cane juice from the chaff and boiling the sap into a sweet syrup. After 606, the Chinese adopted sugarcane as a money crop and studied India's crystallizing technology.

Muslim expansion in 641 revealed the Persian source of cane and the milling of granular sugar. From the Fertile Crescent, Arabs and Berbers spread sugarcane cultivation and refinement west to Egypt, Sicily, Morocco, and Iberia. In the 800s, Sicilian brokers exported powdered sugar throughout the region. By the mid-tenth century, additional sugarcane fields produced moneymaking crops in Afghanistan, Cyprus, and Zanzibar and along the Caspian Sea. Venetian planters bought Lebanese plantations in Tyre operated by slaves from the Black Sea and dispersed bulk sugar from warehouses into central Europe.

European Sugar Mania

After 1000, Arab entrepreneurs invested in sugar factories in Crete and transported sacked goods by caravan. After 1096, crusaders to the Holy Land chewed cane for its flavor. Letters home reported on the wonder of the sweet juice, which soldiers categorized as a luxury spice. By 1099, supplies arrived in England, encouraging trading voyages to Asia. Apothecaries dispensed sugar at exorbitant prices. In France, sugar duties in 1153 raised tariff income in Marseilles and Narbonne.

During the reign of William II in Palermo, Sicily, in the mid-1170s, Theobald, the head of the Benedictine Abbey of Monreale invested in sugar milling, which became a foundation of marzipan, a popular money raiser. Similarly, in 1191, the Knights Hospitallers of Saranda Kolones Castle in Paphos, Cyprus, milled cane in the basement as a source of tax-free revenue from buyers at Acre, Israel. After Richard I the Lionheart outmaneuvered the Muslim general Saladin in September 1192, Richard claimed among his spoils spices and sugar, which he ranked with precious metals.

The fourteenth century saw standardization in the eastern Mediterranean sugar market and new plantations in Andalusia and Portugal. Factors in Egypt, Cyprus, Jordan, and Syria identified their wares under the headings of basket, block, cone, fine granule, loaf, raw, rock, rose, and violet sugar. Within the 1300s, sugar appeared to outdistance honey as a sweetener in recipes, an ingredient in medicines, and a source of confections, candied citrus peel, molasses, and Iranian rum. Improved technology increased cane yield from heavier presses, thus elevating the profitability in sugar.

In the 1400s, Venetians established refineries to reduce transport costs of raw sugar and competed with government-subsidized Sicilian operations and Iberian enterprises funded by Flemish and Genoan bankers. In 1493, Christopher Columbus thought so highly of sugarcane that he transported the pricey commodity to Santo Domingo on his second voyage. His foresight began a monocrop industry that thrived in the humid clime. Portuguese colonists transplanted his agricultural plan to Brazil, where planters imported slaves to oversee sugarcane fields.

The cuisine of the 1500s advanced sugar from a spice to a prime ingredient for baked goods, meat marinades, and fruit ades. Growers increased the trade in slaves from Africa, who labored as sugarcane cultivators and harvesters in Cuba, Surinam, Barbados, Guadeloupe, and Jamaica. The Dutch East India Company joined the sugar trade in Java in 1615. Demand for workers grew as the toll on slaves from burns and fevers reduced labor forces, cutting British imports of 4 million slaves by 90 percent to 400,000 by 1838.

Tudor England imported the best sugar from Madeira, Morocco, Cape Verde, and the Canary Islands and added it to sack (dry wine). Diners indulged so heavily in sweet desserts, preserved pears, and hypocras (spiced wine) that high consumption rotted their teeth. Into the sixteenth century, pirates listed stores of sugar as valuable swag. New plantations in the tropical Americas competed with monopolies over Sicilian and Venetian trade routes. To boost profits, British and French entrepreneurs promoted stronger sugarcane cultivars for planting in eastern Asia and the Mediterranean. In the late 1700s, the craze for sweetened chocolate for candies and drinks increased demand for sugar.

Competitive Substitutes

In the mid-eighteenth century, British treasury agents exacted high taxes on sugar from the nation's 120 factories. Government officials pressed the British East India Company to augment plantations with more fields in Bengal. Counter to hopes for a steady source of British revenue, the refining of beets into a cheaper sweetener during the Napoleonic era placed the French in control of an emerging Continental industry.

In the late 1800s, watermills, steam engines, centrifuges, and the vacuum evaporator invented in 1843 by American engineer Norbert Rillieux boosted plantation profits. Technological upgrades reduced the loss of slaves to industrial accident, exhaustion, and disease. Market revenues tempted Pacific islanders in Australia, Fiji, Hawaii, and Mauritius to plant their own sugarcane fields tended by coolie labor. Because of increased competition, wholesale prices of sugar dipped enough to allow smallholders to invest in bakeries, confectionaries, and street food sales.

In 1957, the formulation of high-fructose corn syrup introduced a cane sucrose substitute for soft drinks and processed cereals and fruit preserves. The discovery of aspartame in 1965 at G.D. Searle & Company in Skokie, Illinois, offered a replacement for saccharin, a late-nineteenth-century sweetener that leaves a bitter aftertaste. With the abandonment of cyclamate sweeteners in the 1970s to prevent bladder cancer, the sugar substitute xylitol, a product of corn and hardwood, resulted from Finnish studies of its benefits to teeth, bones, and insulin levels and control of yeast infections.

In 1976, the British marketing of Splenda, a sucralose sweetener, raised questions about false advertisements that concealed the chlorination of sugar molecules. Industrial food processors rejected Splenda because of its inability to brown and caramelize in confections and baked goods. In 2008, the U.S. Food and Drug Administration approved stevia, an herbal derivative of sunflowers long consumed in Japan, Australia, Russia, Singapore, and South America.

See also: Dutch East India Company; Honey; Liebig, Justus von; Medieval Diet and Cuisine; Mozambique Company; Proust, Joseph-Louis; Seaweed; Soft Drinks and Juices; Theophrastus.

Further Reading

Eagen, Rachel. *The Biography of Sugar.* New York: Crabtree, 2006.

Gudoshnikov, Sergey, Lindsay Jolly, and Donald Spence. *The World Sugar Market.* Boca Raton, FL: CRC, 2004.

Richardson, Tim. *Sweets: A History of Candy.* New York: Bloomsbury, 2002.

Schmitz, A., T.H. Spreen, W.A. Messina, and C.B. Moss, eds. *Sugar and Related Sweetener Markets: International Perspectives.* Gainesville: University of Florida Press, 2002.

Supermarkets

Self-service grocery emporia simplify shopping for food and household items by offering bar, bakery, deli, floral, pet, and pharmaceutical items along with cleaning, kitchen, and school supplies as well as beauty items, video rentals, cash machines, and gas stations. The supermarket concept deviated from the frontier trading post and the dry goods or general store, where clerks took orders at a counter. The clerk rather than the customer fetched and weighed the items, bagged the goods, and totaled the cost by hand.

Small stores contributed to their own downfall. They offered a limited variety of commodities, purchased without the advantage of a cooperative buying agency. The one-on-one nature of shopping reduced the number of selections that multiple customers could make at one time and the number of bundles that wagoneers could deliver to homes. Low-volume sales on credit raised prices to cover the cost of labor and overhead.

In an effort to automate grocery buying on a cash-only basis, on September 6, 1916, grocery wholesaler Clarence Saunders developed the first true supermarket at 79 Jefferson Avenue, one block from the Mississippi River in Memphis, Tennessee. He deliberately piqued consumer interest with a whimsical rhymed name, Piggly Wiggly. His merchandising featured name-brand goods, the beginning of consumer identification of foods by industrial processor and media advertising claims. Clean, self-serve shelving presented the entire inventory and individual prices at eye level for customer inspection.

The Great Atlantic & Pacific Tea Company (A&P) began in 1859 as a small retailer of tea and coffee in New York City. By the turn of the century, it emerged as America's first grocery chain, with nearly 200 stores. This one dates to about 1890. *(The Granger Collection, New York)*

Shoppers carried in-house peach baskets and advanced through a turnstile in one direction through a series of aisles. Weekly specials and candy racks developed the tension between shopping to save money and to satisfy the urge to buy on impulse. At the checkout stand in the front of the store, customers carried items to uniformed cashiers, who totaled them on a mechanical register. Within a decade, Saunders's patented concept of independent ownership and supply from 36 centralized warehouses spread to 2,660 stores in 22 states.

By the end of the 1920s, food emporia added fresh eggs, fish, fruit, meats, and vegetables in refrigerated cases to displays of dry goods—bottled ketchup, boxed crackers, canned pork and beans and soups, and jars of mayonnaise and pickled vegetables. Large stores featured discount deals and parallel aisles arrayed by department. The addition of wheeled frames to shopping baskets encouraged browsers to buy more than they had intended.

An Idea Grows

By the turn of the twentieth century, meanwhile, the Great Atlantic and Pacific Tea Company (A&P), initiated in New York City by wholesalers George Gilman and George Huntington Hartford, had grown from a local distributor of prepackaged tea to a thriving chain of old-style groceries throughout the United States and Canada. In the succeeding decades, as the stores converted to self-serve shopping, merchandisers boosted enthusiasm by selling store brands—A&P fruit preserves and powdered milk, Ann Page canned beans and spaghetti, Eight O'Clock and Red Circle coffees, Jane Parker peanut butter and potato chips—and by issuing store premiums from S&H Green Stamps, redeemable in merchandise. A similar marketing style in Great Britain brought success to Sainsbury, a supermarket chain offering house brand bacon, baked beans, biscuits, and cereals.

From August 4, 1930, until his death on April 24, 1936, Irish American salesman Michael Joseph Cullen of Jamaica, Queens, operated King Kullen, an iconic supermarket competing with American Stores, Big Bear, Kroger, Ralph's, and Safeway. Following the stock market crash of October 24, 1929, the rise of Cullen's expansive grocery empire coincided with a severe lull in the sale of farm crops and a spike in unemployment and vacant warehouses and workshops. Recognizing the importance of the automobile to women's household chores, Cullen began locating stores in low-rent districts and offering ample free parking and evening hours. To create one-stop shopping, he added automotive and home hardware products to the inventory. Admirers dubbed him the founder of the supermarket industry.

To appeal to the bargain hunter during the Great Depression, Cullen's circulars and two-page newspaper advertisements guaranteed low prices by selling 300 items at wholesale price and 200 items at cost plus 5 percent. One popular example, Campbell's tomato soup, cost 7¢ in most stores and 4¢ at King Kullen. The economic model improved the quality and variety of the American diet while reducing food costs by 8 to 15 percent and pharmaceuticals by 10 percent. By 1932, Cullen's eight locations in the Bronx and Long Island sold $6 million in groceries, as opposed to a neighborhood grocer's average sales of $25,000.

Cullen, known as the "price crusher," bought quantities of commestibles at discount and sold at lower prices than small grocery stores could match. His competitors launched blimps to promote grocery specials. Lobbyists for the "little man" fought heavy discounting to supermarkets by backing the Robinson-Patman Act of 1936, called the "Anti-Chain-Store Act" for intervening in the sale of food from manufacturers directly to supermarket chains. The Miller-Tydings Retail Price Maintenance Act of 1937 echoed the Robinson-Patman Act, which halted the underselling of branded merchandise by legitimizing fixed retail prices. The U.S. Supreme Court negated state statutes that allowed price fixing as violations of the Sherman Antitrust Act of 1890. Nonetheless, President Franklin Delano Roosevelt supported Miller-Tydings in shielding small business through authorized price fixing.

The success of supermarkets paralleled the death of the mom-and-pop service market and the growth of agribusiness, especially the sale of produce with the longest shelf life. Chains targeted fiscally healthy communities rather than ethnic enclaves and ghettos. Preferred customer cards allowed computers to keep track of what age group in what neighborhood relied on specials and which buyers ventured into gourmet and table-ready foods, such as barbecued ribs and rotisserie chicken. Centralized purchasing and distribution succeeded at Target and Walmart superstores in the United States; Tesco in Great Britain as well as China, the Czech Republic, Ireland, Japan, Malaysia, Poland, South Korea, and Turkey; and Zellers, a subsidiary of the Hudson's Bay Company in Canada.

Hyperstores, which combined groceries with department stores, profited from satisfying the average customer rather than the gourmand seeking culinary adventures, such as imported game. By courting familiar edibles, supermarkets threatened the variety of regional cuisines. A backlash by Earth Fare, Fresh Market, New Seasons, and Trader Joe's established a niche for local and organic produce; Avanza, Marukai, and Viva offered ethnic goods for the minority shopper. Whole Foods, a chain established in Austin, Texas, in 1980, profited from acquiring natural foods stores with the appealing names of Bread of Life, Food for Thought, Fresh Fields, Nature's Heartland, Wellspring, and Wild Oats. In England, Whole Foods introduced American concepts of pure, wholesome diet by purchasing seven Fresh & Wild stores.

See also: African Food Trade; Clipper Ships; Cooperatives, Food; Hudson's Bay Company; Industrial Food Processing; Markets and Marketing; Russian Diet and Cuisine.

Further Reading

Bowlby, Rachel. *Carried Away: The Invention of Modern Shopping.* New York: Columbia University Press, 2002.

Burch, David, and Geoffrey Lawrence, eds. *Supermarkets and Agri-Food Supply Chains.* Northampton, MA: Edward Elgar, 2007.

Longstreth, Richard W. *The Drive-in, the Supermarket, and the Transformation of Commercial Space in Los Angeles, 1914–1941.* Cambridge, MA: MIT Press, 2000.

Seth, Andrew, and Geoffrey Randall. *The Grocers: The Rise and Rise of the Supermarket Chains.* London: Kogan Page, 2001.

Swedish East India Company

From 1731 to 1813, a golden era of Nordic commerce, the Swedish East India Company (*Svenska Ostindiska Companie,* or *SOIC*) competed with the Dutch and English for trade in Bengalese silk and Chinese foodstuffs, drugs, porcelain dishes, spices, and tea.

Scots trader Colin Campbell negotiated with Swedish brokers Henrik König and Niclas Sahlgren on forming an import-export business directed by Swedish nobles. In the wake of the Ostend Company, which closed in March 1731, the SOIC received a 15-year charter to carry copper, iron, lumber, and silver for trade with Asian markets. Setting out from the city-fort of Göthenburg, on the Göta River, on 20-month ventures, the 25 East Indiamen made use of an ice-free port established by herring fishermen. The ships, all built in Stockholm Terra Nova shipyard, bore about 100 armed crewmen to ward off pirates.

The SOIC initiated its customs-free business on June 14, 1731, from Japan south and west to the Cape of Good Hope. The SOIC charter limited competition with established trading centers and kept secret all transactions. Wholesalers vied for the goods at public auction in Göthenburg, returning a profit as high as 60 percent. Food sellers in Amsterdam, Antwerp, and Ghent, such as Johannes Josephus Moretus of Antwerp, specialized in Swedish teas, making Sweden one of northern Europe's largest tea suppliers.

On the maiden expedition of the *Friedericus Rex Sveciae* and the *Ulrika Eleanora*—named for King Frederick and Queen Ulrica, respectively—Campbell took the role of Sweden's first ambassador to the Chinese emperor. Captain Georg Herman von Trolle loaded a fresh cow, goats, and pigs to feed the crew and embarked on February 9, 1732. He avoided deaths from scurvy by distributing lemon juice and sauerkraut, both antiscorbutics. The ships reached Guangzhou (Canton) in September 1732 and made the first purchase from *hong* (security or duty) merchants of Chinese spices and 430,000 porcelain butter boxes, rice and sugar bowls, soup tureens, mustard pots, salt containers, ewers, dessert dishes, fishplates and strainers, and chocolate, coffee, and tea services. Delayed by a Dutch inspection at Batavia, the expeditioners reached port on August 27, 1733. Chests of cinnamon and ginger turned such a profit that investors reaped a 25 percent dividend. Swedish pietists feared that such riches tempted citizens away from staunch Christian values and introduced them to an exotic cuisine and luxury chinoiserie—silk, taffeta, satin, damask, mother of pearl, japanned tea canisters and toilette tables, and blue-and-white porcelain tea services—that weakened the appeal of Scandic foods and customs.

A renewed 15-year charter and an increase of vessels to 36 continued a steady commerce with Guangdong Province and Surat, India. Within two decades, the SOIC imported 30,488 tons (27,653 metric tons) of tea. In its 82-year history, shippers completed 132 voyages, lost five East Indiamen, and turned into sizable wealth for capitalists a variety of foods—Asian galangal, a basic flavoring of Indonesian and Vietnamese cuisine, along with pepper, rhubarb, rice, sago flour for baking and puddings, tea, cinnamon and ginger, and arak, an anise-flavored aperitif and ingredient in Swedish punch distilled from rice and sugarcane.

Because Scandinavia had not developed a taste for tea, smugglers peddled contraband tea through the Channel Islands, thus avoiding heavy port duties and excise taxes. Despite threats of imprisonment and confiscation of ships, Swedish dealers extended profiteering by underselling English wholesalers of Bing, Bohea, Congou, Hyson, Hyson Skin, Pekoe, Singloe, and Souchong varieties. The illicit trade, one of the causes of the Seven Years' War, introduced lower-class English and Scots to a drink once limited to the British aristocracy.

Further Reading

Dickson, David. *Irish and Scottish Mercantile Networks in Europe and Overseas in the Seventeenth and Eighteen Centuries.* Ghent, Belgium: Academia, 2007.

Fur, Gunlög Maria. *Colonialism in the Margins: Cultural Encounters in New Sweden and Lapland.* Leiden, Netherlands: Brill, 2006.

Swedish West India Company

An ambitious undertaking, the Swedish West India Company (*Svenska Västindiska Companiet*) made limited inroads on the Dutch and English domination of New World trade in corn, furs, liquor, and tobacco during the seventeenth century.

William Usselincx, creator of the Dutch West India Company, collaborated with King Gustav Adolph and Chancellor Axel Gustafsson Oxenstierna in 1624 to form a Swedish stock company. Despite interest from key investors, subscriptions lagged at first. The projected colonization of Brazil and Guinea stalled after the king's death in battle, at Lützen on November 6, 1632. During the reign of Queen Christina, in summer 1635, Peter Minuit proposed that the Swedes join the Dutch in settling the Delaware, New Jersey, and Pennsylvania area and in exporting goods to Iberian and Prussian ports. In 1637, Chancellor Oxenstierna, speaking for the 11-year-old queen, decided to colonize the Atlantic Coast of North America and equipped the first Swedish expedition with Minuit at its head.

In early November 1637, the first 20 settlers traveled from Göthenburg on the sloop *Fågel Grip* and the armed merchantman *Kalmar Nyckel*. The pair of ships arrived on March 29, 1638, to Swede's Landing across the Delaware River from Dutch-controlled territory. Arrivals immediately distinguished themselves from more militant Europeans by launching friendly, honest talks with local Indians, whom the Swedes suspected of being cannibals. With acreage purchased from the Lenni Lenape and Susquehannock, the first pioneers of Nya Sverige (New Sweden) made their home at Fort Christina (Wilmington), on the west bank of Delaware Bay in north-central Delaware. In a climate much warmer and drier than that of Sweden, they intended to raise their own food, evaporate sea salt, refine whale oil, and trade beaver furs, liquor, lumber, and tobacco in European markets. At the time, tobacco seemed the most likely cash crop because it began selling well in Sweden as a medicine for inhalants, painkillers, and poultices and as a recreational smoke.

Corn vs. Tobacco

While Minuit governed New Sweden, the colony reached a population of 600 with the addition of Dutch, Finn, and German volunteers. On February 7, 1640, the *Kalmar Nyckel* made its second voyage to the New World, arriving on April 17 with the provincial governor Peter Hollandare and a few cows and oxen. The Finns acclimated to the land by building pole wigwams, conical Lapp dwellings that they equipped with a central fire and cauldron suspended from a crossbar and adjustable wooden hook. Swedes preferred the log cabin and hearth cookery in the great room, which set a standard of New World dwellings. A third expedition in 1641 brought cloth, fishing net, grain, muskets, tools, and wine malt plus chickens, horses, and sheep. Finnish grain farmers planted a cash crop of tobacco and cultivated corn as the region's staple food.

Because the Finns and Swedes found New World agriculture more rigorous than they expected, they established trade with the Lenni Lenape for corn, fish, hops, and venison. The Indians were generous with chestnuts, grapes, peaches, plums, walnuts, and watermelons. They misunderstood why the Swedes considered apple orchards private property and why removing apples without permission constituted a crime. According to the writings of Quaker philosopher William Penn, the Indians, using a Unami form of pidgin English, taught settlers how to beat dried corn and boil it in water to produce hominy. Native women demonstrated how to crush corn kernels in a hollow log mortar. By placing a flat stone on top of the corn and pounding with a stone pestle, they reduced labor and waste and produced an evenly crushed meal. Native cooks mixed the meal with water and shaped the dough into corn cakes for wrapping in shucks and baking in ashes. A kind of travel bread involved mixing cornmeal with tobacco juice, which boosted energy and quenched thirst.

In 1642, Swedish traders began supplying Indians with European axes, cloth, fish hooks, guns, kettles, knives, and liquor in exchange for beaver pelts, corn, and wampum, a shell-based adornment that doubled as currency. To get through the winter, colonists shot deer and geese and wove baskets, graters, pepperboxes, and sieves as well as slippers from birch bark. For drinking at Christmas and for sale, the Swedes fermented various varieties of wild grapes into a blended wine. At hearthside cauldrons, they brewed a thick ale by boiling and steeping six measures of barley, seven of hops, and seven of water and adding fir cones, yeast, and honey before storing the brew in casks. They reserved their stock of French wine for the sick.

Indian Commerce

To meet the demand of spring and fall barter on the Schuylkill River, the Lenni Lenape moved closer to trading posts in 1643. In addition to subsistence gardens of beans, melons, pumpkins, and squash and stores of wild Indian potato, they increased their cultivation of corn from a subsistence staple for *samp* (porridge) and a source of beer to a barter crop. For marketing, they stored beans and corn in hemp bags in caves and underground caches and transported up to 225 bushels (7,930 liters) of corn in each log canoe. In lieu of minted currency, pelts and wampum served as media of exchange. The arrival in March 1644 of equipment for a sawmill and gristmill plus leather-topped wooden shoes, bricks, and barrels of brandy, flour, salt, and wine increased the settlement's self-sufficiency. Colonists also imported ginger, pepper, and vinegar as condiments to flavor their bland diet. At a low point in trade, trappers depleted the beaver, a fire destroyed a fort and storehouses, and the Swedes imported fewer trade items. In 1645, the Lenni Lenape pondered slaughtering their partners in commerce to rid the valley of Europeans.

The Swedes stepped up their cash income by depending entirely on Indian corn, increasing their investment in sheep and swine, and turning cornfields to tobacco cultivation. By 1647, traders exported 6.5 tons (5.9 metric tons) of tobacco from New Sweden, yet the colonists chose to stress agriculture over commerce. A Lutheran minister scolded them for putting more energy into stockpiling skins, building river vessels, clearing new fields, planting orchards, and brewing than into converting Indians to Christianity. Diligence proved beneficial to the colony. Three years later, after acquiring plow oxen from the Dutch, Swedish settlers raised for sale 100 barrels of barley, corn, and rye and added the Dutch and English to their trading partners.

Agrarian Diversity

In 1650, debt incurred during the Thirty Years' War plus competition with the Dutch and epidemics and hard times in North America wilted the fervor of New Sweden, which suffered from despair, illness, and limited diet. The population shrank to 100 as colonists deserted to Maryland. At the direction of Governor Johan Björnsson Printz, farmers lowered their ratio of tobacco to food crops to ease colonial famine. Because corn grew better than European grain, New Sweden invested heavily in corn cultivation, warehousing kernels for human consumption and cobs, husks, and stalks for livestock feed. The Lenni Lenape taught farmers how to plant corn among stumps and downed timber at the rate of six or seven seed grains to the hill. On August 31, 1655, the Dutch, led by Peter Stuyvesant, the director-general of New Netherland, directed cannon fire from seven ships at New Sweden's Fort Casimir (New Castle), which surrendered the next day. Nonetheless, the Swedish Crown sent another expedition in March 1656 to pursue lucrative trading partnerships with English, German, and Scotch-Irish settlers. With a spurt of Finnish immigration to New Sweden, the population rose to 1,000. The Dutch divided the land into two colonies, which remained under Dutch control until the English seized the area on September 8, 1664.

By 1693, exports of bread, flour, grain, and oil to neighboring islands established the Swedish yeomen as minor players in the New World food trade. In the early 1700s, reports of Swedish-American cuisine noted a heavy noon meal of bacon or pork, wheat dumplings, and pudding flavored with butter or molasses. Balancing the day's intake, breakfast consisted of pop robbin pudding, an egg batter boiled in milk, and an evening meal of mush or hominy.

Recipe: Pop Robbin Pudding

For pop robbin (a milk porridge also called heifer's delight, Indian hasty pudding, or lumpy dick), heat 1 quart of milk with salt and 1 cup of maple syrup. Knead a stiff batter of 1 cup of wheat flour, 1/4 teaspoon of cream of tartar, 1/2 teaspoon of baking soda, and one egg. Drop an acorn-sized lump of the batter into the hot milk. When the "robbin" pops to the surface, it is done. Serve with butter and cinnamon.

In New Sweden, this recipe was popular for a winter breakfast or afternoon treat and made good use of extra milk. The sweet, fat-free dumplings suited the needs of the sick, especially those suffering from dysentery.

The colonists of New Sweden maintained a reputation for intoxication from homemade cider, mead, metheglin (spiced mead), perry, and punch and from rum and liquor imported along with Madeira wine and confections. Swedish celebrations favored treats of wild game and chocolate sweetened with maple sugar, but no coffee or tea, a custom that had not flourished in Scandinavia. In the 1770s, the Swedish carbohydrate-rich diet increased in variety with additions of beans, cabbage, peas, potatoes, rye bread, and turnips.

Further Reading

Dickson, David. *Irish and Scottish Mercantile Networks in Europe and Overseas in the Seventeenth and Eighteenth Centuries.* Ghent, Belgium: Academia, 2007.

Fur, Gunlög Maria. *Colonialism in the Margins: Cultural Encounters in New Sweden and Lapland.* Leiden, Netherlands: Brill, 2006.

Swiddens

From Neolithic times to the present, the clearing of agricultural lands and pasturage created by slashing and burning scrub, brambles, and woodlands dates historically to farmland around the globe. Swiddening contributed directly to the rise of civilization. As prehistoric hunter-gatherers shifted from nomadism and a heavy wild game and meat diet to one based on domestic animals, dairying, small game and birds, and berry and grain cultivation, around 9000 B.C.E., they clear-cut wood for fuel and charcoal and left open areas for up to four weeks to dry out for a thorough labor-saving burning. By 5000 B.C.E., swidden agriculture dominated food production, especially in the tropics and subtropics, including Brazil, Cambodia, Colombia, Ecuador, Guatemala, Jordan, Laos, Lower Danube, Mexico, New Guinea, Panama, the Philippines, and Vietnam. The system dominated agriculture into the twentieth century, when commercial food production overtook subsistence farming in importance.

As a communal effort, swidden cultivators such as the Olmec and Maya and the slaves of the British Caribbean zigzagged over the ground and applied torches to underbrush and diseased vegetation. The effort cleared fire-fallow ground of galls, pests and insect eggs, weeds, roots, and stumps. Cultivation required only a dibble (digging stick) or hoe. The firing method, still in use by some 500 million people, saves on slave purchase and peonage, pesticides and fertilizer, and the expense of earth-clearing machinery and fossil fuels. Swiddens, set aflame before the rainy season, rids a patch of its competitive flora and fertilizes the loam with nitrate- and potassium-rich ash, which improves the uptake of calcium and magnesium.

In an age-old division of labor, men drill the soil with dibbles, while women seed the holes and slide soil in place with bare feet. Children sometimes pile stones to one side for other uses. Seedlings, slips, and suckers from earlier swiddens at least two years old supply transplants of select species, such as coconut palms or paper mulberry, which farmers fertilize with night soil. Traps stop rats and birds from destroying new food plants.

A controversial land-management concept, slash-and-burn techniques require the purchase of extra land for alternation of fallowing and cultivation. Swiddening contributes to deforestation and destabilization of the watershed from loss of root structures. Burning releases carbon into the atmosphere through smoke that chokes bee colonies and renders denuded soil susceptible to wind and water erosion, which savvy farmers combat by outlining the area with logs or a greenbelt of shrubs and trees. Overgrazing and poorly managed swiddens can clear too broad an area for cultivation of a single crop, such as corn, rice, sorghum, or sugarcane. Infringement on natural growth patterns compromises ecosystems and increases the danger of desertification, notably, the advancing Sahara of northern Africa. The rapid settlement of Acre and Rondonia, Brazil, deprives the region of its forest canopy and limits the number of game species for table use. Among the plants destroyed by early swiddens, grasses, artemisia, Alpine sorrel, sea-buckthorn, and dwarf birch and willow disappeared, depriving early farmers of edible seeds for cereals, artemisia leaves for flavoring and brewing, birch berries and sorrel nuts to prevent scurvy, sea-buckthorn for syrup, and willow leaves for fever-reducing teas.

Eastern Asia and Indonesia perpetuate the swidden system, especially in Cambodia, Laos, Malaysia, Thailand, and Vietnam. In the mid-1980s, northern Vietnamese followed a five- to-eight-year cycle that supported a two-crop system. During the fallow period, trees and shrubs enriched the soil, particularly nitrogen-fixing legumes, a soil enhancer also favored by the ancient Timucua of Florida. Acidity levels evened out, allowing for improvement of soil moisture, structure, and texture. Soil acquired earthworms and valuable fauna that nurtured grasslands. Seed production and insects attracted birds and mammals for hunting.

In the Philippines, the Hanunóo of southern Mindoro Island apply slash-and-burn methods to croplands for corn and rice and live adjacent to their fields to protect them from pillagers, both human and animal. In choosing forest canopy for removal, they log the largest species and leave edible ferns, bamboo, and fruit and nut trees and vines undisturbed by their bush knives. Among rice stands, the Hanunóo intercrop—beans, betel, corn, and sugarcane—and plant empty swiddens with high diversity—bananas, bitter melons, cannas, cassavas, cucumber, eggplant, lemon grass, millet, papayas, peppers, squash, sweet potatoes, and wild yams. Cooks prepare the produce for courtship feasts and ritual spirit offerings to the dead. Over three- to five-year periods, farmers such as the Hanunóo allow swiddens to return to the wild and move on to uncleared land before reclaiming swiddens in a cycle of fallow followed by slash and burn.

See also: African Food Trade; Agriculture; Hunter-Gatherers; Las Casas, Bartolomé de; Manioc; Taro; Wild Food.

Further Reading
Dressler, Wolfram. "Disentangling Tagbanua Lifeways, Swidden, and Conservation on Palawan Island." *Research in Human Ecology* 12:1 (2005): 21–29.

Padoch, Christine, Kevin Coffey, Ole Mertz, Stephen J. Leisz, Jefferson Fox, and Reed L. Wadley. "The Demise of Swidden in Southeast Asia? Local Realities and Regional Ambiguities." *Danish Journal of Geography* 107:1 (2007): 29–41.

Whitmore, Thomas M., and Billie Lee Turner. *Cultivated Landscapes of Middle America on the Eve of Conquest.* New York: Oxford University Press, 2001.

Symbolism, Food

Food and drink, the sustainers of life, carry unique significance in world customs and rituals. Ethnography epitomizes hunger and thirst as cyclical urges, evidence of human frailty and the need for cooperation and social relationships. Commensality—the practice of eating together—brought people together around fire, a source of light, heat, and cooking. According to the theories of French ethnologist Claude Lévi-Strauss, initial technologies of boiling and roasting food earned reverence for combining the powers of fire and water to produce palatable dishes. Thus, cooking, eating, and worship shared ground in the human ethos.

Around 23,000 B.C.E., Stone Age civilizations in Anatolia, Mesopotamia, and the Western Hemisphere recognized the female breast and ample belly and thighs as sources of human survival. In some societies, the voluptuous female body epitomized well-being, dignity, and potential. More than the birthing and feeding of a family, maternal nourishment, symbolized by goddess cults, shielded the clan and tribe from seasonal scarcities and famine through mystic intervention with natural disasters, particularly floods and droughts.

The control of ingredients established the uniqueness of the female as food provisioner for the household. A corollary damned the woman who poisoned comestibles or who worked magic spells and curses through inedibles, such as poisonous fish, herbs, berries, mushrooms, and reptiles. The perversion of womanly roles required the destruction of the witch/poisoner, an antidote to the threat of consuming toxic foods. Similarly upsetting to social order, the loss of a staple food—notably a declining herring or salmon run, persistent rust blight on wheat, or the destruction of the North American buffalo herd—required amended mythologies and economic and religious restructuring to legitimize a serious or permanent shift in diet.

Gendered food symbols set patterns of mythology and social interaction. In 8000 B.C.E. among the Cochise culture of Arizona and a millennium later among the Basketmakers of the Rio Grande, worshippers feminized the planet as the Earth Mother and deified pit cookery as the steaming of agave, tubers, fish, and game within a female heart. Mongolian nomads identified tea as a gesture of hospitality feminized with camel's or mare's milk. Persian cooks took a realistic approach to the New Year with string egg noodles, an emblem of vulnerability and unavoidable entanglements of both genders.

Meal consumption elicited contemplations of power and family stability. For Mediterranean meals, the triad of bread, olives, and wine represented a varied diet promoting fullness and health. To impart these virtues to the newborn, parents planted an olive tree, a tangible equivalent of the human lineage. When Xerxes led Persian forces against Athens in 480 B.C.E., he ordered a conflagration in the olive grove on the Acropolis, a contemptuous attack on the Greek goddesses Athena and Nike, deities governing military power and victory. His blasphemy against female deities and a staple crop contributed to the Greek perception of all things Persian as perverse and contrary to nature.

In peacetime, food symbolism promoted civilized behaviors. In Japan before 200 B.C.E., the fermentation of rice into sake (or saki) generated an icon of the joy in sharing. At nuptials, couples sipped sake in oneness as a prophecy of the happy home. The filling and emptying of sake cups in holy processions and Shinto rituals served monks and priests as propitiatory gifts to the *kami* (nature gods). The rice drink stocked the court pantry as evidence of fealty to the imperial family. Between rounds, the emperor's guests ate abalone, chestnuts, squid, pickled apricots, and seaweed, proofs of nature's bounty. New Year's celebrants recalled food insecurity in past eras by serving *awabi* (mussels), an ancestral famine food.

Greek food symbolism embodied a parallel mark of the good life, as exhibited by cheesecake and roast lamb, a celebratory banquet meat honoring heroes. A bride baked flatbread to prove her wifely worth. Draped in marjoram, a badge of fulfillment, she encircled the hearth to embrace her feminine obligations to her husband. As signs of blessing on matrimony, the wedding party tossed dried figs and nuts, storable supplies that warded off shortages.

In harmony with Greek ideals, Roman priests blessed wedding food as a manifestation of harmony and marital felicity. Guests threw almonds and coins as palpable wishes for fertility and prosperity. At his threshold, the groom blessed his mate with a lighted torch and carafe of water, emblems of housewifely duties and the power of the female to both kindle flame and douse it with water. Significant to the husband's responsibilities, the blood sacrifice of meat and the presentation of prime tidbits at the household shrine echoed the masculine emphasis on maleness and reverence to Mars, Rome's patron god.

Judeo-Christian Images

Judeo-Christian iconography established the Torah as the basis for food analysis. Hebrews reverenced Adam and Eve, the progenitors of humankind, and their raw food diet as chaste beginnings. As signs of nonviolence and satiety in nature, their uncooked meals reflected simple expectations and unity with Jehovah in the Garden of Eden. Sin and corrupt living precipitated the flood and Noah's escape. His family became the first full-time carnivores, pioneers of a new beginning in a land where animals and humans assumed adversarial roles.

Jewish food lore reached a height of metaphor at Passover seders. Families consumed dishes signifying their history as recorded in Exodus: matzoh (affliction), bitter herbs (slavery), fruit and nuts (labor in Egypt), eggs and lamb (sacrifice), and parsley (rebirth). With all dishes, diners drank wine, the anticipatory gift reserved for Elijah, the legendary prophet and defender of the faithful against the flesh-eating adherents of Baal. For the Jewish mourners' meal during shivah, family members ate bagels, eggs, and lentils, round foods equating with the life cycle.

For Christians, the sacrament of Holy Communion joins celebrants in a shared meal reminiscent of Christ's last act of earthly leadership of the 12 apostles. The Eucharist betokens finality before the martyrdom of Christ on a Roman cross. Medieval Italian bakers empowered communion loaves with religious talismans—crosses, stars, pentecostal flames, and the Chi-Rho (XP), an abbreviation of Jesus's deification as the Christos, the anointed savior. After the 40-day Lenten fast, the blessing of Easter eggs foretokened new life and the promise of heavenly rewards concealed in the shells.

In memory of Jesus's miracle in feeding 4,000 followers with five loaves and two fish, early Christians sanctified the Greek *ichthus* (fish). For Easter and Pentecost, French and Italian confectioners shaped marzipan and sweets with fins and tails. Classical vegetarianism lost its following as fish dinners reminded the devout that Jesus proclaimed his disciples "fishers of men." Extending the image, church designers called the heart of the sanctuary the *nave,* a Latin term for "boat" that recalls the lowly status of the fishermen who supported Jesus's ministry.

Medieval Food Culture

In the Middle Ages, families raised swine as an indication of a prosperous, well-fed household. For English holidays, preparers roasted a boar's head and browned the skin with a basting of broth, butter, and herbs. Significant of plenty, garnishes of rosemary, mustard, and a lemon in the pig's mouth also attested to a varied, satisfying diet. Bakers and confectioners illustrated salvation by inscribing cookies with *XP* and *IHS,* abbreviations of the Greek Christos and Iesous, and *INRI,* the Latin slogan "Jesus of Nazareth, King of the Jews."

The post-Columbian confrontation between American Indians and Europeans shattered beliefs on both sides about the significance of edibles. When Spanish conqueror Hernán de Cortés arrived at the court of Aztec Emperor Montezuma II in 1519, he discovered corn, a staff of life to the Mexica. Preparers of court meals shaped corn cakes into beasts and butterflies, reminders that the spirits of heroes eventually return to nature. Both the Aztec and Maya reverenced cacao beans as icons of godliness and earthly treasure, a prophetic assessment of Europe's response to chocolate.

During the mid-1500s, Catherine de' Medici, the teenage bride of Henry II, transformed French dining rituals with signs of elegance and savoir faire, elements of the role of food in determining social class and political power. She introduced the artichoke as a status vegetable and demonstrated table manners and the use of the fork, a delicate three-tined implement used by men and women. In 1564, her *laiteries* (dairies) at Fontainebleau and Saint-Maur outside Paris elevated rural virtues, patriotism, and the feminine essences of fecundity and maternity.

Later meetings of East with West advanced knowledge of global cuisines. On Captain James Cook's voyage to Tahiti aboard the *Endeavour* in 1769, he recognized breadfruit as a ceremonial totem for Pacific islanders. Because of its assurance of food security, the newcomers interpreted the breadfruit as a token of a pastoral Eden. Similarly representative, from the Carolinas to the Caribbean, the pineapple appeared as a table centerpiece and carved affirmation of New World hospitality.

As Europeans expanded their interaction with other cultures, they recognized ethnic foods as more than sustenance. The Mexican tortilla, Cree pemmican, Chinese mooncake, Acoma fry bread, Inuit seal meat, Hawaiian rice balls, and Ceylonese curry bespoke ancestral ties to Earth's abundance. Supernatural attachments to nature enabled cultures to place themselves in the scheme of things and to bless the nutriments that dispelled human impermanence. The roles of the fisherman, herder, farmer, marketer, butcher, and cook generated an understanding of personal productivity and its effect on the social and economic order.

In American sociologist David Riesman's survey of food consumption in *The Lonely Crowd* (1961), mealtime and social drinks establish for the individual a place in an increasingly complex, fragmented milieu. As conventional conformity breaks down in metropolises with fast food, coffee breaks, and snacks, the isolation of the individual diminishes the comfort of table rituals and shared cooking and serving. Riesman and his followers recognized that to cling to shreds of ancestral food sharing, city dwellers tend to flee the urban diaspora and return home for Easter, Passover, Eid al-Fitr, Thanksgiving, Corn Festival, and Christmas. In the familiarity of baked ham, roast lamb, challah, pecan pie, *pulque,* or turkey and dressing, the loner renegotiates a lost consciousness of home and reclaims the assurance of belonging to a human family.

See also: Afterlife and Food; Bread; Feasting; Portuguese Diet and Cuisine; Russian Diet and Cuisine; Shellfish; Taboos, Food; Vegetarianism.

Further Reading

Albala, Ken. *Eating Right in the Renaissance.* Berkeley: University of California Press, 2002.

Bendiner, Kenneth. *Food in Painting: From the Renaissance to the Present.* London: Reaktion, 2005.

Cheung, Sidney C.H., and Tan Chee-Beng, eds. *Food and Foodways in Asia: Resource, Tradition, and Cooking.* New York: Routledge, 2007.

Helstosky, Carol. *Food Culture in the Mediterranean.* Westport, CT: Greenwood, 2009.

Macbeth, Helen M., and Jeremy MacClancy, eds. *Researching Food Habits: Methods and Problems.* New York: Berghahn, 2004.

Szechuan Diet and Cuisine

One of China's four great culinary traditions—along with Cantonese, Shangdong (or Lu), and Jiangsu—Szechuan (Sichuan or Szechwan) cuisine marries the fresh and aromatic to the tangy and spicy. The style of cooking originated in China's south-central Szechuan province.

From the 2100s B.C.E., the region evolved a cuisine noted for hot pot working-class meals and for robust taste in dried, pickled, and salted dishes. Situated on the trade route to India, Nepal, and Tibet, Szechuan prospered in commerce that proceeded east down the Yangtze River, thus linking western, central, and eastern China. Abundant in crayfish, oxen, rice, sugarcane, sweet potatoes, and wheat, area farms produced anise, bamboo shoots, bitter melon, chili peppers, citrus fruit, grapes, leeks, peaches, and radishes, the variants that add flavor, scent, and texture to dry braising sea cucumbers and turtle, saucing green vegetable tips, and steaming duck with pickled cabbage.

Regional cooks ventured outside Chinese norms with the addition of prickly ash powder and greater quantities

The spicy hot pot is the signature dish of Szechuan cuisine and the focal point of a group meal. Diners cook bits of meat, seafood, or vegetables in a simmering broth spiced with hot pepper oil or chilies and flavor the morsels with dipping sauces. *(China Photos/Getty Images)*

than normal of garlic and ginger. From sacrificial cookery came twice-cooked pork, an entrée originally prepared for the gods. By 420 C.E., the Szechuan diet had acquired permanent culinary techniques and lasting influence. With the local well salt from Zigong, around 620 C.E., a 50-volume recipe book captured regional specialties. In the late 1600s, the importation of hot peppers from South America added the fiery heat for which the province is famous.

Local dishes display the significance of the mountainous province and regional tastes. Szechuan cuisine balances the fish and seafood focus of Shanghai with the hearty beef entrées of the interior. Preparation offers variety from poaching or steaming with flour gravy to quick stir-frying, which generates more mouth appeal. Recipes impose mythic qualities from the legends that surround their provenance. A specialty, Kung Pao chicken, originated around 1865, preserves the name of a provincial governor. Central to the entrée, the deep-frying of cashews or peanuts precedes the addition of marinated chicken cubes flash-fried in sesame oil. The layered flavors derive from balsam, black vinegar, lemony peppercorns (prickly ash berries), and red chili pepper plus varying amounts of chopped carrot, celery, Chinese cabbage, okra, scallions, and water chestnuts.

In the diverse Szechuan province, vegetarians find alternatives to the ever-present pork and poultry in bean curds and peanuts, Chinese cabbage hearts, cold bean jelly, cucumbers in mustard dressing, fried sweet potato cakes, hot soybean milk, lettuce in sesame sauce, marbled eggs, and vegetable wontons. Mapo tofu, a hot main dish, became known for numbing the mouth with pep-

pers. The recipe dates to a female chef, Mrs. Chen Liu, who operated a restaurant in Chengdu, the provincial capital, in 1870. To achieve the sweet-and-sour flavor, the cook parboils cubed tofu, then emboldens the bland meat substitute with sautéed minced ginger, douban paste (fermented and spiced broad beans), chili flakes, green onions, peppers, rice wine, and soy sauce. According to herbalists, the pungent combination relieves aching joints by making the body sweat.

Famine taught the Chinese to avoid waste. Street peddlers served a piquant lunch or zesty snack of rice dumplings, squid in broth, or dan dan mein, a fragrant noodle dish topped with pickled mustard greens, pea sprouts, pepper, pork, scallions, and vinegar. For the poor, since the 1930s, *fuqi feipian* has made use of beef offal and organ meats heavily spiced with peppercorns. Essential to both entrées are cooking temperatures, fresh ingredients, and the slicing style for lamb, lotus root, wasabi, and other fibrous staples. In May 1958, Joyce

Recipe: Szechuan Grilled Sweet Potatoes

Brush sweet potato rounds with sesame oil and sprinkle with sea salt. Grill on both sides. Arrange in a casserole. Top with 3 tablespoons of brown sugar and 1 tablespoon of ground Szechuan peppercorns blended with 1/3 cup of melted butter. Bake at 400 degrees Fahrenheit for 25 minutes.

Chen, a restaurateur from Beijing, set exacting standards for the Szechuan menu she imported to four restaurants in Cambridge, Massachusetts. In 1977, the opening of Yang Chow in Los Angeles's Chinatown introduced California diners to slippery shrimp, a fried specialty in a cornstarch crust.

See also: Feasting; Hot Pots; New World Commodities; Silk Road; Tea.

Further Reading

Chiang, Jung-feng, and Ellen Shrecker. *Mrs. Chiang's Szechwan Cookbook: Szechwan Home Cooking.* New York: HarperCollins, 1987.

Dunlop, Fuchsia. *Land of Plenty: A Treasury of Authentic Sichuan Cooking.* New York: W.W. Norton, 2003.

Lo, Eileen Yin-Fei. *The Chinese Kitchen: Recipes, Techniques, Ingredients, History, And Memories from America's Leading Authority on Chinese Cooking.* New York: William Morrow, 1997.

Taboos, Food

The banning of edibles from consumption derives from a variety of cultural, ethical, hygienic, and religious reasons. Taboos may be tacit agreements of animists, as with Irish Celts who banned the eating of sweets designated as "fairy food" and the exclusion of fish and waterfowl from the diet by the Apache, Navaho, and Zuni. Another class of proscriptions lists codified regulations and canonical writing—for example, forbidding the eating of cattle and dogs by Hindus and the drinking of tea and coffee by Mormons. From 8000 B.C.E., Jainism in India ruled out root vegetables as well as figs because of the number of life-bearing seeds contained in each one. Out of reverence for life, Jains preferred leafy vegetables for their simplicity. In Greece around 540 B.C.E., Pythagoras's followers adhered to his abstinence from beans, which he believed contained elements of human souls.

The pagan logic of excluding foods from the diet also reflected locale, such as the reverence for the beaver among the Oconee Valley Indians of Georgia. People in temperate zones relished dairy products that tropical cultures banned, primarily because dairy animals failed to thrive where they could not pasture. Similarly, the eating of live insects in Central America resulted from the variety of edible species, which the Aztecs tucked into tacos. Groups with a European background were more likely to recoil from grub and locust consumption because their region lacked palatable insect species.

Jewish Dietary Laws

Israelite health ordinances in the priestly books of Deuteronomy (after 641 B.C.E.) and Leviticus (after 538 B.C.E.) codified *kashruth* from preexisting food prejudices. Scripture approved the consumption of only clean, unspotted edibles already killed for the table. Dietary laws permitted ruminants, the animals that digested tough green fiber. Some *treif* (forbidden edibles) comprised a singular category, such as bats, camels, cats, catfish, crocodiles, eels, elephants, hares, horses, insects, reindeer, or swine. Additional considerations listed a distinct class—carrion-eating birds, such as buzzards and rooks; the blood of any mammals; or a species, specifically bonefish (herring and marlin), crustaceans, reptiles, and rodents. In current times, the pollution of clean food with proscribed emul-

sifiers, enzymes, gelatin, glycerin, or rennet also negates processed items from use.

The Hebraic revulsion of pork may have derived from the inability of swine to adapt to deforestation and desertification in the Middle East. Sociologists account for the loathing of pigs as a demonstration of enmity between sedentary farmers and pastoral Hebrews, whose nomadic lives were unsuited to tending swine. The distaste for pigs grew so virulent in Egypt that priests outlawed the approach of swineherds to temple grounds. Nineteenth-century interpretations substituted clinical logic for desert lore. The educated Jew acknowledged the danger from trichinosis, which flourished in pork. A host of internal pathogens thrived in blood; likewise, shellfish bore typhoid toxins, which early Jews identified only as fever. These scientific views on treif corroborated centuries of arbitrary injunctions.

Taboo Details

Less doctrinal considerations have determined individual cases, notably the social consumption of alcohol and salt by Methodists and Rastafarians and the slaughter of companionable dogs or horses as entrées in Scandinavia. In southern Asia from 2600 B.C.E., monastic house rules governed the diet of priests and temple servants, such as Brahmins and Buddhist priests, who ate no garlic, mushrooms, onions, or pepper. During the Christian meat fasts of Lent, the sacred period from Ash Wednesday to Holy Saturday established after 190 C.E., French monasteries allowed the eating of the laurice (unborn rabbit), which Pope Gregory I declared a fish. From 630 C.E., Muslims agreed to ban consumption of blood and to fast throughout daylight hours during Ramadan, the most sacred celebration. However, Islamic sects clashed over consumption of meat: Shia forbade catfish, eel, rabbit, and shark from Muslim tables; Sunni allowed them. At present, Sinhalese Buddhists refuse to slaughter cattle, to prevent the waste of a useful animal that gives milk and pulls the plow and wagon.

Other regulations determined gendered situations, such as the fasting of Saulteaux girls of Canada during menarche and the eating of duck wings and avoidance of raw meat by Eskimo mothers during the first five postpartum days. The avoidance of papaya and mango by pregnant or lactating women in southern India for fear of spontaneous abortion coincided with rejection of saffron lest it turn the fetus's skin lighter. Chinese women feared crab claws, fish, and turtles, reputed to cause miscarriage. In Africa, rules governing daily meals denied eggs to young children and fish and green vegetables to some pregnant women. Separate dicta in Australia governed the diet of uninitiated Aboriginal boys, such as the proscription of totemic crows or hawks to Euahlayi youth of northwestern New South Wales.

Cultic taboos traditionally emerged from specific situations, such as the arbitrary ban on consumption of sacrificial foods from Israelite and Greek holy altars and the Iroquois taboo against eating a bear, eel, heron, sandpiper, turtle, or wolf, an animal that named a clan. A required reciprocity forced gift giving of yams to keep growers from consuming their own produce. Specifics governed limitations of foods to specific persons: the eating of animal testicles by Plains Indian warriors, the hunting of lizards for snacks by Papuan boys, Aztec rituals for devouring the palpitating heart of an enemy, and the consumption of an infant's placenta in Chinese Nu Bao (herbal) pharmacopoeia and Vietnamese midwifery.

Many regulations are class specific, such as the reservation of swan for English royalty only and of gorilla feet and hands for guests in the Congo. According to Hindu social dicta prescribed in the Dharma Sutra (after 200 C.E.), Brahmins could not eat food offered by the lower castes except in cases of illness or famine. According to religious laws, those who disobeyed returned in the next life as worms. In the early 1500s, the court of Montezuma II in Tenochtitlán declared chocolate so strong an aphrodisiac that no woman or priest could risk being inflamed by it. In the nineteenth-century southeastern United States, the eating of carp, opossums, pickled pig's feet, ramps, and shad occurred mostly among the isolated poor, whom urbanites ridiculed.

Historic Taboos

Individual tribal separations of food into the edible and the forbidden occurred among people for unique reasons, as with the seasonal separation of caribou and walrus meat among the Eskimo and the avoidance of fish by Cushites of Egypt, Eritrea, Ethiopia, Kenya, Somalia, and Tanzania. Among the Kikuyu of Kenya, men and women dined apart to restrict women from seeing men cook and eat meat. Among the nomadic Masai herders of East Africa, food service was labor and gender specific—virile hunters depended on blood, meat, and milk, the sources of manhood; women, children, and elderly men ate mostly vegetables. The Middle East, dominated by Islam, separated meat cookery into seafood, which the Koran allows, and the flesh of four-footers, which scripture condoned except for pork, an abomination to Muslims.

Currently, moral consumerism resolves issues apart from dogma—the esthetic worth of songbirds, the ethics of eating animal fetuses, and the sustainability of endan-

gered Apache trout, blue whale, bonobo, Chinook salmon, crocodile, sea turtle, and whale shark meat. A moot category limits consumption of exotica—fertilized eggs, offal, road-kill, and snails, all repugnant in some societies but eaten as delicacies in others.

As a gesture to animal rights, ethicists promote the sale of free-range over caged poultry for both meat and eggs and of ocean fish caught by netters who avoid harm to dolphins. Situations allow the exemption of taboo or repulsive sustenance during famine or danger of starvation, when survivors accept decaying garbage, insects, cats and dogs, rodents, and even human flesh as food. Other considerations, as with the infection of beef with mad cow disease and the bush rat with monkeypox and leptospirosis, precipitate trade barriers against targeted animals.

See also: Alcoholic Beverages; Cannibalism; Customs, Food; Halal; Kosher Food; Paula Marín, Francisco de; Shellfish; Temperance.

Further Reading

Allen, Stewart Lee. *In the Devil's Garden: A Sinful History of Forbidden Food.* New York: Ballantine, 2002.

Civitello, Linda. *Cuisine and Culture: A History of Food and People.* 3rd ed. Hoboken, NJ: John Wiley & Sons, 2011.

Deutsch, Jonathan, and Rachel D. Saks. *Jewish American Food Culture.* Westport, CT: Greenwood, 2008.

Lindgreen, Adam, and Martin K. Hingley, eds. *The New Cultures of Food: Marketing Opportunities from Ethnic, Religious, and Cultural Diversity.* Burlington, VT: Gower, 2009.

Whitehead, Harriet. *Food Rules: Hunting, Sharing, and Tabooing Game in Papua New Guinea.* Ann Arbor: University of Michigan Press, 2000.

Taillevent (ca. 1310–1395)

A flexible, efficient Norman-French master of late medieval gastronomy, Taillevent produced a period overview of Capet and Valois food service with *Le Viandier* (*The Provisioner,* ca. 1375), a sourcebook of medieval cuisine during the Hundred Years' War. Rising from potboy and frycook to master chef, Guillaume Tirel of Pont-Audemer, on Normandy's north shore, is the only medieval cook known by name and career. Later called Taillevent ("chopwind" or "jibsail"), he apprenticed in turning spits and prepping vegetables in royal households.

From boyhood service in Paris to Queen Jeanne d'Évreaux, wife of Charles IV, Taillevent advanced at age 26 to royal chef of Philip VI de Valois, who called his servant "our beloved cook." In 1347, the master cook moved on to south-central France to serve the Dauphin de Viennois for eight years as kitchen manager. His employment as provisioner coincided with staff shortages and a severe dearth in foodstuffs, following the Black Death of 1348 and the famine of 1351. By 1355, Taillevent's salary included wages of 15 livres plus a travel allowance and hay for his horses during the scouring of the countryside for royal groceries.

At his peak, Taillevent cooked for Charles V, a low-key monarch who maintained friendly relations with his staff. One of the cook's innovations, the introduction of cabbage recipes, upgraded a food usually relegated to peasants. He also proposed balancing cooking flavors by mingling vinegar with sweetened wine. He abandoned spice for spicing's sake and recommended specific flavorings for specific tasks, such as reducing the smell of rot in a wine cask with the addition of ginger.

From chef to head chef and provisioner, Taillevent achieved the rank of sergeant at arms, an unusual appointment to knighthood, and directed a household security force. For quality service, the king awarded him 100 gold francs and a home in Paris called Larchière. In 1392, the cook's titles included *Maistre des Garnisons de Cuisine du Roi* (master caterer to the king). Still in service to the Valois household in his mid-80s, he continued to work for Charles VI as kitchen supervisor.

In Taillevent's recounting of cookery, France's earliest-known cookbook, the author cites the intricacies of beef bouillon and the use of bird giblets and boiled sauces. His refined tastes demanded saffron for coloring entrées and slow cookery on heated tiles. The cook revealed his experiences in day-to-day kitchen problems with advice on how to leach salt from cod and vegetable ragouts by steaming a cloth over the pot and how to remove the scorched taste of burned entrées with yeast. Taillevent's cooking vocabulary—plucking, dismembering, grinding, infusing, parboiling, fricasseeing, crisping, straining—displayed practical knowledge of hearthside techniques as well as a command of domestic and imported aromatics. An arbiter of taste to royalty and prelates, he de-emphasized spicing and allowed chief ingredients to unleash natural flavors, a philosophy that returned to favor in the 1970s with nouvelle cuisine.

The chef moved effortlessly from simple rabbit stew to the glazing of bitterns, calf tripe, mallards, rays, suckling pig, and turtledoves. His finishes—an incised fleur-de-lis, gold and silver leaf, pomegranate seeds, almonds fried in butter and set in a pattern, and a final dusting of powdered sugar—reflected an obsession with plating done right. For these skills, he achieved an annual salary of 55 livres, the equivalent of 55 pounds of silver.

In his 100-page handbook, the royal chef named briskly, but inexactly, the ingredients of each concoction. While he omitted measurements, he disclosed personal preferences, such as the sautéing of greens and tasty nibbles in bacon grease. His versatility in creating fresh or spiced eel dishes and bracing hot caudles for the sick indicated an intellectual curiosity into dietetics.

An anonymous addendum, *Du Fait de Cuisine* (*On Cookery,* 1420), inserts menus that explain the order of

Recipe: Subtil Brouët d'Angleterre

For a rich English broth, Taillevent described a labor-intensive preparation: "Peel and boil a quantity of chestnuts, and then pound them in a mortar with the yolks of hard-boiled eggs, and a piece of calf's liver, moistening them from time to time with luke-warm water; pass through a hair sieve; flavour with pepper and saffron; then put in your broth and boil together."

service for meat and meatless days on the ecclesiastical calendar. Into the seventeenth century, Taillevent's text remained a standard of food innovation. His nickname became a synonym for excellence.

See also: Cod; Cookbooks; Fish and Fishing; Grilling; Poultry; Salad and Salad Bars; Wine.

Further Reading

Adamson, Melitta Weiss, ed. *Regional Cuisines of Medieval Europe: A Book of Essays.* New York: Routledge, 2002.

Bober, Phyllis Pray. *Art, Culture, and Cuisine: Ancient and Medieval Gastronomy.* Chicago: University of Chicago Press, 2001.

Redon, Odile, Françoise Sabban, and Silvano Serventi. *The Medieval Kitchen: Recipes from France and Italy.* Chicago: University of Chicago Press, 2000.

Scully, D. Eleanor, and Terence Scully. *Early French Cookery: Sources, History, Original Recipes, and Modern Adaptations.* Ann Arbor: University of Michigan Press, 2002.

Taro

A hardy native of Indo-Malaysia, taro (*Colocasia esculentum*) balances a meat diet with a vitamin-rich starch and provides growers with leaves, roots, and stems for a versatile famine food. Because of the tuber's lengthy shelf life and transportability at sea, it may be Earth's oldest edible crop. Evidence of taro in the Solomon Islands dates to 28,000 B.C.E., when Austronesian seafarers chopped the wild plant with stone tools. Tropical Asians began cultivating the tubers before 8000 B.C.E.

In 7000 B.C.E., Indonesian farmers managed taro fields by the swidden method, using calcified shells for weeding and cutting tools and burning fields clear of chaff. The peelings, returned to the roots, fertilized the next crop. In New Guinea, the cropping of bananas, coconuts, sago, taro, and yam provided a substantial and varied diet. Highlanders advanced taro fields at greater altitudes by burning forests and scraping out ditches with digging sticks. In the Ryukyu Islands, fishermen and traders eased into farming after discovering how to plant tubers.

The eastern Chinese grew tubers in irrigated paddies. Crop tenders developed an integrated diet of adzuki beans, rice, soy, and taro as accompaniments to chicken and the fish they netted from rivers and in taro turnovers, steamed cakes, and dessert soups. Although taro corms and leaves required soaking and cooking to counter the toxicity of calcium oxalate, it produced a digestible staple suitable to the feeding of infants and invalids. A diet enriched by fried and steamed taro launched a population explosion.

Global Foodstuff

From India, Malaya, and New Zealand, taro migrated to Madagascar and Kenya under the name *cocoyam.* Cooks served breadfruit and taro with roasted doves. In West Africa, growers called taro greens "callaloo," which they prepared with okra, pepper, tomatoes, and shrimp. The recipe followed slaves to the Caribbean. Subsequent migrations introduced into standard English the Polynesian terms *taro* and *poi,* a nutritious fermented paste or cream of baked taro corms.

Serious drought in 4000 B.C.E. forced sub-Saharan natives into the tropical lakes and rivers of southern Mali. Seminomadic growers domesticated taro and yams to eat with the meat of gazelles and oryx. From market contacts, in 2000 B.C.E., the African taro passed to the Fertile Crescent of western Asia and west into the Levant.

After 400 B.C.E., Japanese growers planted taro tubers in paddies as a pantry staple. The vegetable anchored the diet until the cultivation of rice. On Cyprus and Icaria in Roman times, cooks simmered taro with celery and coriander and seasoned the stew with lemon juice. In Roman kitchens, cooks stocked the roots that shippers imported from Egypt. Recipes by Apicius in *De Re Coquinaria* (*On Cookery,* ca. 35 C.E.) suggested ways of complementing meat and tangy sauce with bland boiled taro, a forerunner of the Peruvian potato in European gastronomy.

After 1000 C.E., taro cultivation supported population surges and intensified farming. On New Year's morning, Japanese cooks presented red rice with taro soup, which they prepared the previous night to prevent cooking on a holiday. An unusual bridal menu on May 12, 1192, for King Richard I the Lionheart of England and Queen Berengaria of Navarre introduced guests at Limassol, Cyprus, to platters of hash meat and taro.

In Hawaii, some 300 varieties of taro bore the ritual respect of the men who prepared it for human food and pig fodder and the women who baked it in *imus* (earth ovens). At the royal estate at Nuuanu Valley, King Kamehameha III hosted the largest luau on July 31, 1847, when 10,000 guests ate fish, pork, and taro, which preparers wrapped in ti leaves and steamed over hot rocks. Royal cooks rounded out the banquet with *kulolo,* a baked taro pudding sweetened with grated coconut. On June 11, 1871, a royal decree honored the king's deceased grandfather, Kamehameha I, with a traditional banquet featuring taro grated into poi as a side dish for roast pork and fish wrapped in taro leaves. Despite the place of taro in national dishes, nutritional standards gradually declined as imported bread, rice, tea, and tinned meat replaced fresh fish and taro.

Modern Uses

In the twentieth century, Samoan chefs enlivened breadfruit and taro recipes with brown sugar or curry, a luxury spice from India. Cooks built feasts around boiled taro or rice steamed in coconut milk. Dishes of breadfruit, crayfish, green bananas and papayas, seaweed, and taro leaves in coconut cream complemented the starchy entrée. Between China and India, the Bhutanese supplemented grain harvests with avocado, bamboo shoots, and taro. Filipinos grew taro to stew with pork or shrimp or to mix with jackfruit and sago for dessert. Egyptians flavored soup with cooked taro leaves and added them to lamb stew.

The popularity of poi in the 1980s resulted from a low-fat regimen, the Waianae diet, a source of energy and stamina from traditional Hawaiian foods. To a bland entrée, Hawaiian chefs added poultry and seafood and side dishes of arrowroot, bananas, berries, fern, pickled seaweed, sea salt, and yams. Reports that taro prevented cancer increased its value, as did the use of taro flour in diabetic cookery, gluten-free baking, and vegan diets. Monopolies grabbed Hawaiian taro and other unusual commodities for hoarding and profit. In aquaponic plantations, taro greens thrived in a flowing water garden.

Currently, New Guineans grow some 600 taro cultivars but prefer the red tuber for its buttery taste. Indian and Nepalese chefs serve taro in pancakes and as complements to dal to piquant condiments—curry, green chili chutney, mustard, pickles, and tamarind. Lebanese diners prefer taro with tahini; Maldivians fry the roots into chips. Cook Islanders prepare taro greens (also called dasheen or eddo) in coconut milk and serve it with chicken, octopus, parrotfish, and suckling pig. Hotels in the Pacific as well as Disneyland and Sea World emulate the Polynesian feast by plating slices of roast pig with poi and taro chips. In the Azores and China, chefs add sugar to pureed taro for dumplings, ice cream, and pie filling.

Because it lacks the nutrients of corn, rice, potatoes, and wheat, taro can only supplement meals, such as the taro greens added to Vietnamese pumpkin in coconut milk or sweet-and-sour fish soup. Traditional Hawaiian cuisine features poi made from the "royal" pink-fleshed tubers and forced through a ricer to add to bread, muffins, pancakes, and pudding. Some prefer it naturally soured by lactic acid and yeast. Island healers maintain that taro contributes to wellness by warding off fevers and malaria. Because of its digestibility, poi nourishes endangered infants. It also strengthens athletes by boosting the immune system to reduce inflammation.

See also: African Food Trade; Curry; Hot Pots; Luau; Polynesian Diet and Cuisine; Wild Food.

Further Reading

Friedlaender, Jonathan Scott, ed. *Population Genetics, Linguistics, and Culture History in the Southwest Pacific.* New York: Oxford University Press, 2007.

Mager, Marcia Zina, Muriel Miura, and Alvin S. Huang. *Hawaii Cooks with Taro.* Honolulu: HI: Mutual, 2007.

Nesbitt, Mark. *The Cultural History of Plants.* New York: Taylor & Francis, 2005.

Watson, Ronald R., and Victor R. Preedy. *Bioactive Foods in Promoting Health: Fruits and Vegetables.* Burlington, MA: Academic Press, 2010.

Tea

The world's most popular brewed beverage, tea (*Camellia sinensis*) anchors daily food consumption and official and social events. As a drink and as a medicine and vegetable, it derives from a wild evergreen that flourishes in tropical and sub-tropical highlands of Burma, China, India, Java, Laos, Sri Lanka, Thailand, Tibet, and Vietnam. Whether hot or cold, tea's most intense flavor comes from tiny shoots, which crown the bush during the growing season. The distinctive oolong, or red tea, from Fujian, China, acquires stronger bouquet, color, and sweetness from the end leaves plus the next four on the stem.

Interplanted with jasmine and mallow, the tea plant absorbs surrounding aromas, which contribute to refreshing, transcendental qualities. Packagers blend black, green, oolong, and white teas to ensure first-crop quality and to protect invigorating caffeine and tannins. Refiners augment flavor and scent with additions of bergamot orange rind, caramel, cardamom, honey, lemon, lotus, masala, mint, and vanilla. Because of its mellow taste and gentle stimulation of the body, *tea* has become one of the most common terms in world languages.

Early History

Tea drinking began in China before 2700 B.C.E. with the chance discovery of stimulating flavor by the mythic Emperor Shennong, an amateur herbalist. Around 700 B.C.E., practitioners of Taoism honored a gracious tea ritual for invigorating the mind and spirit. The charred bud tips, first embraced as an imperial pleasure, gained popularity around 200 C.E. in China as an exhilarating tonic. By the early 600s, tea advanced to Japan and Korea as a relaxing drink and ritual offering during ancestor worship.

Sichuan tea reached Tibet in 641 after the union of a Chinese princess with Tibetan King Songtsan Gambo. Supplied with low-grade "border tea" over the Tea Horse Routes, Himalayan tribes traditionally churned their refreshment with rock salt and rancid yak butter, which foamed to the top. *Tsamba,* the staple travel food of Tibetan nomads, began with popping barley like popcorn and forming a dough with butter-tea to the consistency of oatmeal. Tea, tsamba, and yogurt produced a satisfying meal for family and guests. The thrifty Tibetans reserved the tea leaves for feeding horses.

Chinese merchants distributed leaves in brick form for grinding and boiling in clay kettles or in rolls of darkened *pu'er* tea wrapped in bamboo husks. Traders bore packages from Yunnan Province along southwestern borders and, as early as 750, introduced tea drinking in northern India. In the 900s, Moorish travelers carried the tea custom to Islamic nations. Beginning in 960 during the Song dynasty, Chinese beverages made from compressed tea cakes encouraged catering services, exotic food clubs, restaurants, social clubs, and teahouses. In repose, refined guests heard poetry recitations and storytelling and negotiated business deals while nibbling finger food, such as quail eggs and bean curd rolls.

Trade and Commerce

Around 1250, Chinese food processors altered traditional steam-treating methods by roasting loose tea leaves for brewing rather than boiling. As a commodity, bags of the loose tea traveled along the Silk Road to Arabia and North Africa. In the 1500s, widening sea routes introduced mariners to the tea of Macau. In 1610, the first boatload of tea impressed elite Dutch visitors to the Hague, where they tinged each cupful with milk.

Over the next half century, tea gained a reputation for curing headaches, preventing consumption, and relieving fatigue. Traders carried the commodity to Germany and, in 1670, to colonists in Massachusetts and New York. Quakers promoted enthusiastic tea consumption in Philadelphia. To the north, black tea arrived in Russia in the late 1600s, when courtiers and aristocrats blended it with vodka and wholeheartedly adopted it as a national beverage. To the south, Persians received tea from the Tartars and extolled it as a tavern drink for maintaining stamina.

In London in 1657, restaurateur Thomas Garraway touted tea to his coffeehouse customers as a treatment for anemia, dropsy, and scurvy. The beverage gained fame in 1662 as the favorite of Queen Catherine of Braganza, the Portuguese wife of Charles II. British drinkers developed a taste for tea with milk, which produced a creamier, less astringent beverage.

The British Crown recognized the tea fad as a source of steady income, and by 1684, authorities imposed a duty that boosted the price by 500 percent. Thomas Twining, distributor of Earl Grey tea, opened London's first tearoom in 1706, where customers sipped steaming drinks while reading newspapers and conversing with fellow tea fans. Eastern Europeans developed their own tea culture from Lapsang souchong, a tea dried in bamboo baskets over pinewood fires. The strong, smoky leaves traveled by camel caravan on a 6,000-mile (9,600-kilometer) route through Russia, raising prices for supplies of chai tea.

Varieties

The 1800s brought demand for distinctive varieties, such as the aged leaf steamed in Korean court ceremonies in the late Joseon dynasty and the iced black tea consumed in the American South. In Hong Kong, diners took Chinese congou or souchong tea with dim sum, a variety of snack buns, dumplings, steamed rolls, and tarts. After Europeans began trading with the Maghreb (northwestern Africa), Moroccans imported Chinese green tea, which hosts steeped with sugar into a syrup and served with ambergris, citron, lemon verbena, mint, pine nuts, and wormwood.

After 1840, tea drinking by British colonials and soldiers in Bengal and Nepal energized demand for darjeeling, a light, floral drink made from indigenous bush leaves. Ceylon tea, first shipped to England in 1873, competed with coffee as a major import. Scots entrepreneur Thomas Lipton bought up Ceylonese coffee plantations and replanted them in tea for dispensing in sealed packets. A specialty estate tea, limited to high-quality black Keemun leaves from Anhui, China, and sold by Twinings, came from the royal blend made for Prince Edward of Wales. The smoky, plum-scented drink contributed to the merchandising of English Breakfast Tea, a favorite of Edward's mother, Queen Victoria, during her residency at Balmoral Castle, Scotland.

In the 1920s, after the collapse of the Ottoman Empire, coffee became too expensive in postwar Turkey. Rize tea from the Black Sea coast received the blessing of President Mustafa Kemal Ataturk as a replacement beverage grown on Turkish soil. Served full-strength in glasses with beet sugar, the rich red liquid came to table in bazaars and homes with a separate pot of hot water for diluting to individual taste.

Leaves, Bags, Bottles, and Cans

Following World War II, tea sales shifted to suit convenience in snacks and meals. In 1953, Tetley, a major tea distributor in India, began bagging and selling leaves in one-cup servings throughout Britain. Tea experts charged bag makers with cloaking substandard crumbled leaves and tea dust rather than whole leaves and with limiting the action of hot water in extracting savory oils. The

A plantation worker picks tea leaves in India's northeastern Assam state, which accounts for more than 70 percent of the nation's tea industry. Long the world's top producer, India now ranks second to China. Fine-leaf tea is still hand-plucked. *(Anupam Nath/Associated Press)*

discovery that the epichlorohydrin paper coating caused cancer further discredited bag tea.

Connoisseurs heaped more scorn on instant tea, popularized in the 1950s, for overpowering delicate flavor with additions of fruit, honey, powdered milk, and vanilla. The least favored product, bottled and canned tea, first distributed in Japan in 1985, offered a wan version of fresh tea sparkle. Fans chose it as an alternative to soft drinks and in response to claims of health benefits. Aficionados turned to traditional pu'er tea for lowering bacteria count and cholesterol, and promoted oolong, a variety reputed to aid in weight loss, reduce blood pressure and tooth decay, relieve stress, and lengthen life.

See also: Art, Food in; Clipper Ships; Herbs; Silk Road; Swedish East India Company; Tea Ceremony; Trading Vessels; Wild Food.

Further Reading

Heiss, Mary Lou, and Robert J. Heiss. *The Story of Tea: A Cultural History and Drinking Guide.* New York: Random House, 2007.

Mair, Victor H., and Erling Hoh. *The True History of Tea.* New York: Thames & Hudson, 2009.

Martin, Laura C. *Tea: The Drink That Changed the World.* Rutland, VT: Tuttle, 2007.

Moxham, Roy. *A Brief History of Tea: The Extraordinary Story of the World's Favorite Drink.* Philadelphia: Running Press, 2009.

Rose, Sarah. *For All the Tea in China: How England Stole the World's Favorite Drink and Changed History.* New York: Viking, 2010.

Tea Ceremony

A dynamic emblem of cultural identity, the traditional Japanese tea ceremony expresses community and belonging through a simple, powerful taking of refreshment. The *chado* or *sado* (way of tea) ritual had its roots in Zen Buddhism as a religious or medicinal drinking of *matcha,* a bitter green tea. The aesthetic evolved from an appreciation of beauty and order in cyclical mundane events, and the elements of the ritual mimic the physics of the universe: wood into charcoal, charcoal set afire, fire heating metal, and metal causing water to boil.

In keeping with Buddhism, the ritual celebrates the sacred within. For this reason, participants need no religious icons or statuary. Each experience produces its own mood and positive outcomes, from sober to peaceful or glowing with hospitality and camaraderie. As a result of practitioners' enthusiasm for formal tea drinking, the ceremony has fundamentally influenced the Japanese ethos—its religion, clothing, etiquette, architecture, art, gardening, calligraphy, and philosophy. As a unifier of society, the ceremony has perpetuated citizenship and ideal behavior.

Order and Discipline

Motivation for the ceremony grew out of the high value placed on a rare and expensive commodity. Rigidly programmed, often after a light meal, the ritual welcomes honored guests to a microcosm of order—a ceremonial room, teahouse, or rustic shed in a garden. Each space features a raised platform in a rectangle no larger than 9 square yards (7.5 square meters). Entrance through the 3-foot (0.91-meter) door requires a humble crouch from participants, who number no more than five.

Guests kneel in front of the niche for a ceremony that can last up to four hours. In an ambience sweetened with incense, the host sounds a gong and carries in the prescribed utensils—a water jar, bamboo ladle and stand, lid rest, bowl washer, bamboo whisk, spatula, and tea caddy. The ritual begins with the passing of sweets, then the crushing of either thin or heavy tea leaves for stirring into water heated in a charcoal brazier or a sunken hearth. The tea, served in a communal bowl, passes from guest to guest, with the last participant finishing the remainder. After polite exchanges, the host removes the implements and the guests depart.

From the Monastery to Martyrdom

The tea cult got its start late in the 1190s, when Zen monks made tea their customary drink. They pulverized expensive green leaves, poured on boiling water, and whisked the powder with a bamboo beater. Daily, they sipped tea to keep them from nodding off during meditation. In the 1400s, the ritual evolved into a meeting of friends to sip tea and talk in sacred space at an isolated spot. The quiet, hospitable sharing of tea appealed to all levels, military leaders as well as aesthetes.

Influenced by Buddhist priest-poet Lu Yu's three-volume *Ch'a Ching (The Classic of Tea,* ca. 760 C.E.), Murata Shuko, tea master at the court of the Shogun Ashikaga Yoshimasa of Kyoto, initiated the use of a quiet tea building removed from town and reserved for meetings between heads of state, courtiers, and dignitaries. The antithesis of the resplendent palace hall, the tea hut enforced civility and equality before a steaming kettle. Just as the kettle shaped and controlled steam, the ambience constrained behaviors.

By blending Chinese and Japanese styles, Shuko perfected a spiritual ritual and gave lessons to others in the Zen of intimate, personal tea service. Under his influence, tea became a social and meditational medium. An outgrowth of feudalism, the act of participating in a ceremonial tea, like European banquets, regulated and suppressed negative urges. Ritual promoted consensus and peace among belligerent lords, who approached the table unarmed and composed for a polite exchange. By association, the Japanese equated formalized tea drinking with refinement and international peace.

The classical Japanese tea ceremony, with roots in Zen Buddhism, ritualizes the preparation and pouring of green tea. A form of spiritual discipline and aesthetic contemplation, the rite cultivates both the sacred within and the national cultural identity. *(Sankei/Getty Images)*

In the 1580s, Japan produced its first tea master, Sen Rikyu, a cultured intellectual who thrived at court. In addition to being the unifier of Japan, he built a teahouse near Kyoto and standardized the simple ritual as a time of quiet forbearance. In defiance of royal displays of wealth and attainment, Rikyu stressed harmony, respect, cleanliness, and tranquility. For his effrontery, the emperor ordered Rikyu's ritual suicide on February 28, 1591, a martyrdom that elevated the tea master to a cultural deity.

In ordinary homes, adherents of Rikyu built light, fragile tearooms screened with paper and a lattice transom. The ceremony became the goal of the bride-to-be, who concentrated on her role as hostess. The ritual took on an allure of the peerless East and encouraged importers to sell beverages and matching tea services. In 1894, the World Food Fair in Boston featured home economist Sarah Tyson Rorer's Japanese luncheon and foreign table settings. The ritual took on marital significance in Joshua Logan's film *Sayonara* (1957), which dramatized the melding of races in wedlock. Other staged versions include *The Teahouse of the August Moon* (1956) and *The Last Samurai* (2003), a Hollywood fantasy.

Today, the Japanese tea ceremony follows the rules of Sen Rikyu. In January, celebrants boil the year's first kettle of tea; the year draws to a close with the austere November ceremonies and ends with December's last boiling of the kettle. The service enhances a contemplation of the passage of time, symbolized by antique implements passed down through family. In mid-June 2011 at the Hotel Duval in Tallahassee, Florida, a benefit for survivors of an earthquake and tsunami in Fukushima, Japan, chose a tea ceremony as a means of raising funds and honoring Japanese culture.

See also: Art, Food in; Tea.

Further Reading

Chiba, Kaeko. *Japanese Women, Class and the Tea Ceremony.* New York: Routledge, 2010.

Kalman, Bobbie. *Japan: The Culture.* New York: Crabtree, 2009.

Kato, Etsuko. *The Tea Ceremony and Women's Empowerment in Modern Japan.* New York: Routledge, 2004.

Okakura, Kakuzo. *The Book of Tea.* Philadelphia: Running Press, 2002.

Temperance

Temperance, the self-regulation of behavior, applies to various areas of human life, especially food and drink. The world's religions through history—Buddhism, Christianity, Confucianism, Islam, Jainism, Wovoka and the Ghost Dancers, and Zoroastrianism, among others—have targeted extreme consumption, especially the flaunting of costly, luxurious, and rare edibles and potables to the detriment of a wholesome life. Governments typically leave questions of consumption to communities, where alcohol plays an integral role in ritual and celebration, such as wine at a Jewish bris and a Greek Orthodox Eucharist. In 1644, the Scots added a new slant on consumption by instating the first alcohol levy, a governmental profiteering on intemperance.

From the early 1600s, ale, cider, liquor, and wine dominated beverage choices among settlers of the Western Hemisphere. Within a century, Boston, Jamaica, and Philadelphia rum traders turned distilling into profit. By the American Revolution, abstainers recognized the need for a national movement to control riotous drinking. In

1791, U.S. legislators mooted the question of nationally enforced temperance by passing a whiskey tax.

In the early 1800s, U.S. women made temperance a gender issue, forming phalanxes of teetotalers who disrupted public tippling and pressured elected officials to ban distilling and the sale of beer and liquor. In 1813, Boston reformers formed the Massachusetts Society for the Suppression of Intemperance, a crusade for community restraint. They focused on the neighborhood saloon as the fount of wasted wages and cruelty in men who used bingeing as an excuse for neglecting and abusing wives and children.

Politically, control of controversial diet elements produced unforeseeable results. The drive for sobriety generated xenophobia against immigrants, particularly German, Italian, and Polish Catholics, for whom beer and wine defined cuisine and culture for men, women, and children. In an unusual political pairing, mine owners and factory owners backed temperance as a means of eliminating absenteeism and on-the-job drinking and of raising productivity among immigrant workers.

As consumption of brandy, gin, rum, and whiskey reached 7 gallons (26.5 liters) per year per capita, the reform movement spread worldwide. In the 1830s, Australian men and women who were mockingly called Wowsers crusaded for sobriety and the closing of grog shops. A drive by Presbyterians and Catholics in England, Ireland, Quebec, and Silesia involved the signing of total abstinence pledges and the opening of temperance inns, which stocked no alcohol in their kitchens. Chefs revamped recipes, substituting applesauce or molasses for brandy in mincemeat pie and fruit juice for hard cider in Christmas punch. By 1840, general consumption fell to less than half that of the previous two decades.

Sober wives and mothers surmised that inadequate home cooking increased men's thirst for alcohol. For guidance on ridding the home of intoxicants, abstainers turned to the anonymous *Total Abstinence Cookery* (1841) and the *Temperance Cook Book: Containing Practical Receipts for Plain and Rich Cooking Without the Use of Wine, Cider, or Alcoholic Liquors* (1841), published by the *Christian Herald*. Mormons and other zealous nondrinkers carried to extremes the ridding of the home of stimulants, including coffee, tea, and meat, an alleged spur to carnal appetites. In 1851, Maine set a national example of statewide prohibition, which passed to 12 states.

In the 1860s, defenders of Native Americans challenged the unregulated sale of alcohol on Indian reservations in the United States and Canada. According to Susan Allison, author of *A Pioneer Gentlewoman in British Columbia* (1976), indulgence in strong drink retarded the advance of civilization by debauching Indians. Canadians, taking a moderate view, passed the Canada Temperance Act of 1864, which left up to individual counties the choice of being wet or dry. Swedes in Gothenburg experimented in 1865 with a local monopoly on the sale and service of aquavit in city public houses. In Paris, the Academy of Medicine formed a temperance union in 1871 as an adjunct to health and sanity.

In 1877, First Lady Lucy Webb Hayes forbade the stocking of wine in the White House larder. Dubbed "Lemonade Lucy," she backed Frances Elizabeth Willard in the spread of the Woman's Christian Temperance Union (WCTU), which campaigned across the Midwest and Northeast. Author Hester M. Poole compiled *Fruits, and How to Use Them: A Practical Manual for Housekeepers* (1890), a nonalcoholic handbook that honored the WCTU by substituting fruit for sherry.

Passage of the Eighteenth Amendment to the U.S. Constitution on January 17, 1920, tested the practicality of superintending the individual's alcohol intake. Repeal by the Twenty-First Amendment on February 21, 1933, unleashed drinkers from artificial controls and restored voluntary restraint to drinkers besotted with illicit booze in speakeasies and drugstores. The formation of Alcoholics Anonymous in 1935 in Akron, Ohio, offered a workable compromise by placing the responsibility for imbibing on the reformed drinker.

Through the mid-twentieth century, the lingering effects of Prohibition continued to impinge on the American wine and beer industries, which lagged until the revival of aesthetic wine tasting in the 1970s and craft beers in the 1980s preceded the revival of the martini in the 1990s. In a counter drive to protect teens, in Sacramento, California, in 1980, Candy Lightner organized Mothers Against Drunk Driving. In 2000, U.S. legislators set a blood-alcohol concentration of 0.08 as an arbitrary definition of drunkenness.

See also: Alcoholic Beverages; Beer; Charlemagne; Durante, Castor; Lunch; Religion and Food; Taboos, Food; Wine.

Further Reading

Beyer, Mark. *Temperance and Prohibition: The Movement to Pass Anti-Liquor Laws in America.* New York: Rosen, 2006.

Blocker, Jack S., David M. Fahey, and Ian R. Tyrrell. *Alcohol and Temperance in Modern History.* Santa Barbara, CA: ABC-Clio, 2003.

Fletcher, Holly Berkley. *Gender and the American Temperance Movement of the Nineteenth Century.* New York: Routledge, 2008.

Gately, Iain. *Drink: A Cultural History of Alcohol.* New York: Gotham, 2008.

Slavicek, Louise Chipley. *The Prohibition Era: Temperance in the United States.* New York: Chelsea House, 2009.

Tex-Mex Diet and Cuisine

A fiber-filled cuisine melding cowboy tastes with cantina cookery, Tex-Mex fare fuses beef with the recipes and hearth techniques of Monterrey and interior Mexico.

Touted as America's oldest and most popular national cuisine, Tex-Mex got its flair in the early-eighteenth-century mission era around San Antonio. It took its name in 1875 from the chartering of the Texas-Mexican Railway, dubbed the "Tex-Mex."

Original Tex-Mex cuisine incorporated smaller divisions, beginning with Az-Mex spiced chocolate and ranging to the Pacific and Atlantic shores for Baja-Mex fish tacos and veracruzana ceviche and red snapper. Farther from the Texas-Mexican border lay the more recent Cali-Mex and New Mex, which contributed Pueblo corn dishes and elevated hamburger and pork above shredded beef in entrées. Additional elements drew on galleon traffic between Acapulco and Manila from 1561 to 1815, the source of rice dishes.

The Innovators

The first trans-Pecos food sharing derived from Apache and Pueblo cooks, Mexican *norteños*, and Tejanos, Hispanics born in Texas who make up 60 percent of the populace. Beginning in the 1820s with work-a-day meals of agave cacti, black beans or *frijoles refritos* (kidney beans well fried in lard), chorizo sausage, limes, onions, squash, sweet and mild chilies, and tomatoes and tomatillos, innovators added Texas beef to create dishes doubly rich in protein. Early experimenters tended to omit other Mexican staples—jicama, nopales, and prickly pears. In 1864, bakers adopted Austrian-French bread during the occupation by Emperor Maximilian I, introducer of the *bolillo,* a short loaf that emulated the hard-shelled French baguette.

In the style of Middle Eastern pitas and Indian naan, Mexican tortillas, the *masa harina* (cornmeal) or flour rounds used as edible containers, surrounded a variety of foods. Salsas and *moles* (sauces)—*adobado* (marinated in chili sauce)*,* bitter chocolate, guacamole, *mole poblano, pipian* (pumpkin seed sauce)—demonstrated Central American know-how at blending healthful vegetarian mixtures to complement entrées. Quesadillas, cheese turnovers flavored with the Nahuatl herb *epazote,* required layering and toasting on a griddle or deep-frying in lard.

Cookery focused on baking in a *horno* (oven) and grilling over mesquite coals for *barbacoa* (barbecue) and *carnitas* (braised meats) as well as the steaming of corn-on-a-stick with lime and of husk-wrapped tamales, a self-serve item created by pre-Hispanic Aztecs. Because of its blending of minced vegetables with small amounts of goat or beef, chili con carne earned the name "Southwestern pemmican" as a survival food for the poor. From 1880 to 1937 at the Military Plaza in San Antonio, the chili queens peddled their "bowl o' red" for a dime to cattle drovers and soldiers. Spanish priests denounced the hot stew as a devilish aphrodisiac. The health department halted the al fresco dish-up because of poorly washed utensils. The spicy bean-and-tomato dish fed non-Texans in 1893 at the Chicago World's Fair.

Hispanic cooks introduced fusion dishes to please Texans and Southwestern visitors. Pulitzer Prize–winning novelist Larry McMurtry demonstrated the crossover of Mexican and Texas cuisine in *Lonesome Dove* (1958), filmed for television in 1989. Around 1876, the fictional Mexican cook Bolivar feeds wranglers of a border cattle company on Texas meat and vegetables served Mexican style with chilies and *pan de campo* (wheat bread).

Commercial Fare

The outback fare predates by a decade Tula Borunda Gutierrez's ancestral meals in Marfa, Texas, at the Old Borunda Cafe, the first Tex-Mex vendor. She assured authentic flavor by importing mesquite wood from Fort Davis for slow simmering. O.M. Farnsworth of San Antonio followed Tula's example in 1900 with the Original Mexican Restaurant, which added fish to her beef-based menu. The dynamics of the gastronomic hybrid earned praise from *Texas Monthly* as "soul-binding, brotherhood food," a source of multicultural harmony. Less enthusiastic reviews hailed William Gebhardt's commercial chili powder and canned chili con carne, manufactured in San Antonio.

Additional cross-fertilization around El Paso coincided in 1916 with the flight of Pancho Villa's fighters out of range of capture. The expedient exile north of the Rio Grande introduced demands for the heritage cuisine of Spanish California—*albondigas* (meat dumplings), alligator pear (avocado) salad, chili verde, *cojets de leche* (caramels), flan, ranchera sauce, *sopa* Azteca (tortilla soup), Spanish rice, tamale pie, and tomato gravy. Revolutionary spirit charged mestizos with pride in their *indigenismo* and authentic native dishes.

In 1920, the *Los Angeles Times* concluded a 15-year effort to honor Southwestern foodways through cooking contests and recipe collections featuring the sour cream of German-American dairies and kumquats and oranges,

Recipe: Sopa Azteca

Cut 12 stale corn tortillas into strips and fry them in 2 tablespoons of oil. Drain. Roast six plum tomatoes over an open flame and remove the blackened peel. Heat two ancho poblano or pasilla chilies, two avocado leaves, 1/2 cup chopped onion, and one chopped garlic clove in a skillet. Mash all of the vegetables, moistening with 1/2 cup of water and seasoning with one sprig of *epazote* and sea salt. Boil the pulp in 1 tablespoon of oil. Add 4 pints of vegetable stock and cook for 30 minutes. Serve soup over tortilla strips and top with grated Chihuahua *queso fresco,* lime juice, chopped cilantro, and avocado slices.

pomegranates, and walnuts, all grown in California. Dish names captured the flavor of the Old West: Arizona enchiladas, chili Colorado, eggs à la Mme. Murrillo, Mariposa pudding, Navarino salad, and rice à la Valenciana. The unpretentious cooking style favored fritters, hash, omelets, moles, soups, and stews accompanied by Navajo fry bread with honey-dipped churros and sopapillas for dessert.

International Cuisine

In 1945, more than a century after the fusion of Anglo tastes with Mexican cookery, the term "Tex-Mex cuisine" appeared in print, creating a demand for authentic cookbooks. Chefs reorganized ingredients of the burrito, rolled enchilada, and taco meal in the 1950s in Tucson, Arizona, to include chimichangas, a blend of potatoes and spices with chopped beef. In 1964, a concessionaire in Dallas served the first nachos to attendees of the Texas State Fair.

The blended cuisine gained a champion in food maven Diana Southwood Kennedy, the British author of *The Cuisines of Mexico* (1972), who defined the mixed plates in terms of ethnic origins and alternative ingredients. Tex-Mex reached fad status and spread from the American Southwest throughout North America to Asia, Europe, the Middle East, and South America. From Austin and Houston in 1973, the standard entrée menu acquired fajitas, a sizzling plate of marinated skirt steak with grilled peppers and onions washed down with a Mexican beer or tequila.

The development of chalupas, margaritas, and tortilla and yucca chips with salsa, three U.S. twists on south-of-the-border recipes, applied American ingenuity to gastronomic evolution. A Middle Eastern flair for cumin compromised the original Central American herb battery of chili powder and epazote. In the late 1960s, two other Anglo specialties—tacos and taco salad—harmonized Hispanic basics with lettuce and tomato, the makings of a restaurant side salad, topped with cheese and salsa or *pico de gallo,* a chunky tomato relish.

By the twenty-first century, salsa outsold ketchup as a condiment for the freshness and the nutritive value of tomatoes cubed with cilantro, onion, and peppers, all rich in vitamins A and C. The mainstream recipe alters the piquant Mexican salsa, made from chipotle, roasted *ricado* spice, and tomatillos. Innovative American salsas venture from vegetables to blends of chilies and sweet syrup with citrus fruit, mango, papaya, passion fruit, and pineapple. Vegetarians promote much of Tex-Mex innovation for its antioxidants, natural cancer fighters.

See also: Agriculture; Chili; Cookbooks; Grilling; Lunch; Packaging; Smoked Food; Tortillas.

Further Reading

Albala, Ken. *Beans: A History.* New York: Berg, 2007.

Kennedy, Diane. *Oaxaca al Gusto: An Infinite Gastronomy.* Austin: University of Texas Press, 2010.

Stacy, Lee. *Mexico and the United States.* New York: Marshall Cavendish, 2003.

Walsh, Robb. *The Tex-Mex Cookbook: A History in Photos and Recipes.* New York: Broadway, 2004.

Theophrastus (ca. 371–ca. 287 B.C.E.)

The ancient Greek scientist, encyclopedist, and educator Theophrastus, whom Carolus Linnaeus called the "Father of Botany," introduced classical concepts of physiology and nutrition to plant science.

Born at Eresus on the west side of the island of Lesbos, Theophrastus bore the birth name Tyrtamus. He studied under Leucippus and at Athens under Plato and Xenocrates, a protopsychologist, and became a reader of Empedocles's writings on the elements and nature. At age 17, the young savant became a disciple of Aristotle, the tutor of Alexander the Great. To acknowledge Tyrtamus's eloquent language, Aristotle renamed him Theophrastus (spoken by God).

Mentor and pupil traveled to Lesbos in 347 B.C.E. to study the island's animals and plants. In 322 B.C.E., Aristotle's will left Theophrastus the philosopher's library, his manuscripts, and the guardianship of his children. As the lecturer at the Lyceum, a combination garden and covered *stoa* (portico), Theophrastus taught a lifetime total of 2,000 pupils, including the dramatist Menander, and succeeded as principal of the school from age 49 until his death at age 85. He maintained a botanical herbarium and studied Asian plants—banyan, cinnamon, cotton, frankincense, myrrh, and pepper—that Alexander's troops imported to Greece from as far east as Persia, Afghanistan, and the Indus Valley. His systematic examination of plant foods introduced the Greeks to the argun palm, banana, cardoons, citron, jackfruit, jujube, mango, pistachio, and tamarind.

Drawing heavily on his mentor's concepts, around 300 B.C.E., Theophrastus compiled two botany textbooks—the ten-volume *Historia Plantarum* (*Enquiry into Plants*) and the eight-volume *De Causis Plantarum* (*On the Causes of Plants*)—covering 550 species in all. The compendia influenced *Historia Naturae* (*Natural History,* ca. 79 C.E.), the Latin encyclopedia of Pliny the Elder, and remained valued reference sources throughout the Middle Ages. In *Historia Plantarum,* Theophrastus summarized the style of container gardening and horticulture in Greece and its environs. He touched on orchards—pruning and grafting—as well as culinary arts, such as the use of raw garlic and onions in salad dressings and sauces. He stated a preference for such wild collectibles as arbutus, cumin, dandelion, fennel, fern, lettuce, mint, parsley, rocket (arugula), truffles, and water chestnuts. The marsh mallow (*Althea officinalis*) he valued in sweet wine as a treatment for cough and sore throat. He had a sweet tooth for such treats as the medlar and myrtle and yew berries, suggested pounded gladiolus bulbs as a sweetener for bread dough. The papyrus he particularized as a source of sweet juice for desserts.

Theophrastus studied botany as both a science and an element of the Greek economy. His survey warned of such common poisons as hellebore, hemlock, nightshade, and wolfsbane, which could sicken or kill herd animals. He promoted thick-seeded barley, heavy-bearing fig bushes and stone fruit, and such annual summer vines as cucumbers and gourds. For the home gardener, he described irrigation with well water as an effective way to increase succulence and sweetness in vegetables. In addition to evaluating cereals and pulses made from fava beans, lentils, millet, and sesame, he compared the yield for Babylonian and Greek farms and named chickpeas, lupines, millet, sesame, and vetch as the plants historically stockpiled as famine food.

Theophrastus savored his meals and recommended slow simmering as the best cooking style. He explained the aromatic appeal of apples, pears, and wine and the influence of fragrance on taste in carob and Phoenician cedar. He enumerated aphrodisiac foods and listed as culinary additives anise, bay leaves, and dill. For root vegetables, Theophrastus recommended the squill bulb and chopped asphodel mixed with figs, but he banished the turnip to peasant cuisine. His text recognized the value of cabbage grown in salty soil and proposed boiling cabbage leaves in *nitron* (sodium) to improve their color and flavor. In reference to high-end cuisine, he cautioned that the perfuming of dishes could spoil food and that storing herbs and spices near heat destroyed their flavor. *De Causis Plantarum* described the dual work of plants—producing seeds for reproduction and food for humankind.

In a lost treatise *On Sense Perception,* Theophrastus argued that taste and smell overlap. The brain is the seat of perception, he maintained, thereby linking the intellect with enjoyment of pleasant mealtime aromas, colors, tastes, and textures. He proposed that the cooking and digestion of such herbs as rue cause chemical changes that are detectible in the odors of breath and sweat. He warned of belching and flatulence caused by "vulgar" radishes and pondered at length on the body's need to rid itself of salt. The text covered appetite, fatigue, and stamina as well as the value of honey as a food and a wound dressing.

See also: Beans and Legumes; Cereal; Greek Diet and Cuisine; Plant Disease and Prevention; Poisonous Foods; Pulses.

Further Reading

Dalby, Andrew. *Food in the Ancient World from A to Z.* London: Routledge, 2003.

Inwood, Brad. *Oxford Studies in Ancient Philosophy.* Oxford, UK: Oxford University Press, 2009.

Theophrastus. *De Causis Plantarum,* 3 vols. The Loeb Classical Library. Cambridge, MA: Harvard University Press, 1976–1990.

Tofu

A bland, low-fat curd of soymilk, tofu supplies the diet with a healthful alternative to meat. A Chinese vegetable food processed with calcium or magnesium salt or vinegar, bean curd took its name from the Chinese for "fermented bean." Archaeologists have identified the Liao River valley in northeastern China as the region's prime producer of soybeans. Legend from 164 B.C.E. during the Han dynasty connects the processing of soymilk with the scholarly Prince Liu An, who may have experimented with bean curd in imitation of an Indian or Mongolian curdling method.

Tofu, or soybean curd, is a high-protein cheeselike food sold in blocks in Taiwan (*shown here*) and across East Asia. Itself bland in taste, tofu absorbs other flavors well and blends easily. It can be prepared in myriad ways, in virtually unlimited combinations. (*Patrick Lin/AFP/Getty Images*)

The technology for making the cheesy substance spread to Korea and reached Japan after 710 C.E., then passing to Southeast Asia, Indonesia, and Pacific island clusters. The acceptance of tofu coincided with Zen Buddhist proselytizing, which required a nondairy, nonmeat diet. Monastery and temple kitchens may have been the original distributors of bean curd.

Late medieval Japanese recipes identified various forms of tofu—frozen and grilled curd, skewered in kebabs, and stewed in a broth. Tofu advanced in ritual importance in the sixteenth century, when ceremonial tea service included such curd foods as dried tofu with plum sauce as models of humility and austerity. During the Edo period around 1575, tofu appeared on the menu in Kyoto at the first restaurant, Nakamura-ro, as an element of haute cuisine. Chefs served *dengaku,* curd blocks topped with egg or nut miso and charcoal broiled to enhance a creamy texture and sweetness.

A century later, Okutan Vegetarian Restaurant, one of the nation's most famous tofu venues, featured stewed curd, a popular dish with pilgrims who frequented Kyoto's Zen Temple. Chefs prepared a traditional Zen recipe by arranging boiled tofu on a tray of soy dips and vegetables. During the eighteenth century, Japanese tofu makers departed from coarse Chinese soyfood recipes to create soft, white curd cheese prized for its delicacy. The first soy curd cookbook, *Book of Tofu* (1782), cataloged 230 dishes. Its success created demand for a second volume, issued in 1783.

American tofu had its beginnings in the San Francisco Bay area in 1878 with the first soy milk shop, Wo Sing & Company at 708 1/2 Dupont Street. That venue and a second factory, Sing Hau Lee's Quong Hop & Company, catered to tofu aficionados in Chinatown and to Chinese laborers. Vegetable cheese surged to popularity in Sacramento and across California and, in 1923, spread to H. Iwanaga Daufu at 1031 Aala Street in Honolulu, Hawaii. Tofu, called *fromage végétal* (vegetable cheese) in French, found favor in Paris in May 1911 with Li Yu-ying's customers.

In 1929, Seventh-Day Adventist and manufacturer Theodore A. Van Gundy became the first Caucasian to process soy milk into cheese, which he first encountered at the 1915 World's Fair in San Francisco. His La Sierra brand of canned tofu required the addition of pimiento to keep the curd from graying. Until Van Gundy's death in 1935, health food stores hawked his products as cures for arthritis and ulcers.

During the 1940s, the Japanese military substituted tofu for meat in army rations. Ironically, in the 1970s, when postwar Japanese were serving tofu steaks with barbecue sauce to American tourists, Chinese Communists were rationing soyfood after prioritizing the use of soybeans for oil. In the 1980s, the curd came to Chinese markets more liberally as flour, noodles, rolls, sheets, and

Recipe: Dengaku

Cut 1 pound of firm tofu into 1-inch cubes. Lightly brown the surfaces evenly. Whisk over low heat 1/2 cup of miso paste with 4 tablespoons of sake, 3 tablespoons each of sugar and water, and two egg yolks. Spread the sauce over the tops of the tofu cubes. Top with chopped walnuts or sesame seeds and broil until the surface browns.

squares and as a common street food simmered in soy sauce. At all social levels, tofu, served with cabbage and rice, became part of daily fare in southeastern China. Healers recommended tofu's phytoestrogens to women suffering from hot flashes and osteoporosis.

Depending on the amount of moisture extraction and preparation, tofu varies in density and texture, including smoked and deep-fried curd. Flavorings determine the role of tofu in a meal, whether mixed with chili sauce, dried shrimp, onion, or soy sauce for breakfast or blended with palm syrup as a sweet snack, a Filipino delicacy. The addition of black beans or edamame to the original curd turns tofu into a vegetable blend suited to a low-cholesterol diet. American recipes for tofu burgers, cheesecake, hotdogs, mayonnaise, meatballs, sausage, tamales, and imitation tuna salad increase acceptance of the Asian specialty.

See also: Asian Food Trade; Freeze-Drying; Grilling; Hot Pots; Mandarin Diet and Cuisine; Noodles; Szechuan Diet and Cuisine.

Further Reading

Du Bois, Christine M., Chee Beng Tan, and Sidney Wilfred Mintz, eds. *The World of Soy.* Urbana: University of Illinois Press, 2008.

Evans, K. Lee, and Chris Rankin. *Giant Book of Tofu Cooking.* New York: Sterling, 2000.

Hagler, Louise. *Tofu Cookery.* Summertown, TN: Book Publishing, 2008.

Murray, Michael T., Joseph Pizzorno, and Lara Pizzorno. *The Condensed Encyclopedia of Healing Foods.* New York: Simon & Schuster, 2006.

Tortillas

Literally "small cakes" in Spanish, tortillas anchor the eating style of Central Americans and Pueblo Indians. The term originally identified a Spanish egg-and-potato omelet. For Mesoamericans, *tortilla* referred to a utilitarian toasted flatbread, made with corn, wheat, or occasionally sorghum, that contained or wrapped food. Aztecs made the first tortillas in 10,000 B.C.E., when the rounds began their way to prominence as a national dish. As both utensil and staple, the tortilla became a constant dietary presence, *el pan de cada día* (our daily bread), the food of millions.

Preparation began with a complex chemical process. *Nixtamalization,* the soaking of kernels in boiling slaked lime water or wood ash, moistened the endosperm and dissolved the pericarp, the tough outer hull. Culinary historian-anthropologist Sophie Dobzhansky Coe created the neologism from the Aztec *nixtamal,* the milky solution of corn with lime developed in Guatemala around 1500 B.C.E. At the same time that the transformation made the grain elastic, the process introduced calcium, protein, and vitamin B for the body's use and prevented kwashiorkor and pellagra, both dietary deficiency diseases. The use of juniper ash also imparted an evergreen flavor and aroma. In *America's First Cuisines* (1997), Coe credited nixtamalization with the expansion of Mesoamerican culture from village to empire and the rise of Paleo-Indians of the Mississippi River valley.

With the arrival of Hernán de Cortés and his 7,000 conquistadors in 1519, the Spanish changed the name of the flat cakes from the Nahuatl *tlaxcalli* to tortilla. The salted disks required heavy female labor for the crushing of kernels by mano and metate (stone roller and tray) and the baking of tortillas on a *comal* (griddle stone) for approximately 20 seconds per side. Women took pride in the individuality of a food that seemed to vary little from house to house and century to century.

Spaniards enjoyed filling the rounds with cheese, guacamole, *picadillo* (spiced meat sauce), and *pico de gallo* (chunky relish). Schoolchildren and field laborers packed lunches of tortillas and leftovers. Newly converted natives expressed their Catholic leanings by marking tortillas with a cross or crown of thorns. In the absence of communion wafers, priests served *santas tortillas* (sacred tortillas).

According to Renaissance encyclopedist and linguist Bernardino da Sahagún, the "Father of Ethnography and Culinary History" and author of *Historia General de las Cosas de Nueva España* (*General History of the Things of New Spain,* 1540–1569), tortillas flourished in homes and as street food. Mexica peasants customized the palm-sized pancake with available fillings—ants, fish, *huitlacoche* (corn fungus), locusts, maguey worms, and snails. Diners chose from a variety of raw vegetables and hot *moles* (sauces). They developed a handhold that cradled the tortilla with the thumb and index finger, leaving the little finger to crook upward and seal the end to keep the contents from spilling. Tortillas also shaped easily into rolls and scoops for dipping or for tearing into strips to dunk into soup.

The back- and shoulder-punishing labor of tortilla making ended for women in the first third of the twentieth century. On April 25, 1930, inventors Antonio Boué

simplified manual tortilla making by patenting laminated rollers. The machine forced the *masa* (dough) through a cutter that standardized size and shape. An upgrade in March 1936 by Boué and Teodoro Gómez added a wire that scraped the tortilla from a cylinder and dropped the pancake onto a conveyor belt. Further tinkering altered rolling to pressure injection, the mechanism of commercial *tortilladoras.* By making flatbread readily available, industrialization revived mestizo cuisine in Mexico and Guatemala. In October 1956, Oscar Verástegui Santoscoy combined operations in an automatic tortilladora that mixed, extruded, and baked identical rounds 8 inches (20 centimeters) in diameter and 1/8 inch (0.3 centimeters) thick.

Whether patted out by hand or extruded from machines, tortillas have become prominent on the American baked grain market, becoming the second-most-popular bread after sliced wheat loaves. T. Coraghessan Boyle's satire *The Tortilla Curtain* (1995) uses the Mexican bread as an emblem of the Tex-Mex border, the dividing line between a have and have-not nation. Researchers estimate that Mexicans, for both cultural and economic reasons, continue to consume tortillas at an average daily rate of 325 grams (11.5 ounces) per person.

Tortillas figure in a variety of specialties—the burrito, enchilada, quesadilla, taco, tostado, and *totopo,* a fried tortilla. To spur the growth of the $7 billion industry, makers introduced flavored flour rounds by adding cheddar cheese, jalapeño, lime, onion, tomato, and spinach. Tex-Mex, the Americanized version of Mexican cuisine, added the tortilla chip, a crisp strip that mounds into nachos and garnishes salads and soups.

See also: Aztec Diet and Cuisine; Corn and Maize; Genetically Modified Food; Religion and Food; Tex-Mex Diet and Cuisine.

Further Reading

Bauer, Arnold J. *Goods, Power, History: Latin America's Material Culture.* Cambridge, UK: Cambridge University Press, 2001.

Counihan, Carole. *A Tortilla Is Like Life: Food and Culture in the San Luis Valley of Colorado.* Austin: University of Texas Press, 2009.

Inness, Sherrie A., ed. *Pilaf, Pozole, and Pad Thai: American Women and Ethnic Food.* Amherst: University of Massachusetts Press, 2001.

Muñoz, Carolina Bank. *Transnational Tortillas: Race, Gender, and Shop-Floor Politics in Mexico and the United States.* Ithaca, NY: Cornell University Press, 2008.

Trade Routes

The maze of routes by which food reaches consumers combines transport by air, river, road, and sea as well as overland portages and canals. After 4100 B.C.E., the

Fertile Crescent initiated waterborne trade over rivers and canals in obsidian for kitchen knives and resins for sealing storage baskets and jars. Longer distances increased the opportunity for profit as well as the swapping of ideas.

From 3300 B.C.E., the Via Maris (Way of the Sea) connected Egyptian merchants with the Levant and Mesopotamia. The ancient commercial artery gained respect during the Crusades as a caravan route and pilgrim pathway. The success of intercontinental commerce valorized the skills of accountants, linguists, and cartographers.

After the domestication of the camel in 1500 B.C.E., Persian caravans traveled known arteries connecting west-central Asia with Arabia, the Levant, Phoenicia, and North Africa. Heavy traffic raised the importance of commercial centers in Alexandria, Egypt, and at Palmyra, Syria, and Petra, Jordan. Within 250 years, the networks expanded east to China and India, supplying rice, spice, and tea to the western Mediterranean. Around 1000 B.C.E., Chinese junks traveled the Strait of Malacca to Sri Lanka, India, the Persian Gulf, and Axum, the capital of Ethiopia on the Red Sea. Chinese merchants also established a route east from Guangzhou to the Solomon Islands to trade in dolphin, shark, swine, and turtle meat.

Because sea transport became safer, surer, and swifter than desert or mountain crossings, Athenian and Egyptian food dealers increased reliance on sea-lanes. To the west, Berber caravans trekked through Tuareg country in Algeria and Libya, a source of camels and goat meat as well as dried butter and cheese, dates, and millet. Pack trains crossed the Sahara Desert to access salt fish from the Songhay of the Sahel and the kola nuts and salt of Bamako, a business nexus on the Niger River in southwestern Ghana. Local potentates filled their coffers with duties and tolls from steady traffic of cattle and slave buyers.

From the 700s B.C.E. to 100 C.E., Greeks expedited commerce by crossing the Diolkos, a portage over the Isthmus of Corinth that linked the Bay of Corinth with the Aegean Sea. Sailors dragged their merchantmen across 4 miles (6.4 kilometers) of limestone track and returned them to sea to carry fresh provisions to the military. Similar shipping shortcuts on the Nile River delta at Alexandria sped dhows, small lateen-sailed coasters, from the river to the Mediterranean. Additional saltwater commerce east on the Red Sea supplied Egypt with spices from Arabia and coffee and millet from the Horn of Africa.

To feed the cosmopolitan region around Rome, merchants dominated Mediterranean commercial arteries and pressed north to German and Slavic territory as far as the North Sea. In addition, aqueducts directed water from highlands by gravity to consumers, flour mills, and food processors, including makers of *garum* (fish sauce), a major Roman export. From Egypt across the Sinai to Aqaba, Jordan, the King's Highway directed traffic south and east, the future artery of Islamic food commerce to north-

western Africa. Paralleling land transport of grains, seeds, and wines, the Spice Route took Chinese cargo vessels south to Java and east along Indian Ocean ports to India to sell cardamom, cassia, cinnamon, ginger, pepper, and turmeric, an essential of Indian cuisine and food coloring.

Across southern Asia, Roman engineers fortified the Grand Trunk Road, which accessed rice and spices through the Khyber Pass and southeast along the Ganges River through Delhi to Calcutta. Simultaneously, Roman merchants traveled to the British Isles as far north as the customs inspection site at Hadrian's Wall, begun in 122 C.E. On safe Roman roads, haulers bore Gallic and Iberian olive oil, olives, and wine to exchange for Gallo-Belgic dinnerware, cattle, hunting dogs, oysters, and salt.

Medieval Commerce

From the 700s to the 1000s, Varantian (Scandinavian) traders approached Eastern Europe emporia via the Dnieper, Don, and Volga rivers. Waterways carried their long ships down the Dnieper to the Black Sea and Byzantium and to warehouses on the Caspian Sea and Baghdad. With stocks of furs, honey, and meat, Varantian traders bartered for bread and spices.

During the eleventh-century clash between Christians and Muslims, the rise of the Italian maritime republics of Amalfi, Ancona, Genoa, Pisa, and Venice increased competition for military food contracts in the Holy Lands. Beginning in 1096, Italian city-states enriched themselves on army provisions for the Crusades, which required barley, beans, chickpeas, dried fruit and meat, lentils, and wine. Provisioners boarded sea transport to complete deals at entrepôts in Christian-held ports at Alexandria, Antioch, Constantinople, Corfu, Crete, Cyprus, Dalmatia, and Istria. The busy sea-lanes crisscrossing the Mediterranean enticed Cilician pirates, who offloaded foodstuffs from captured vessels to supply the enclaves of privateers in southern Turkey.

In times of famine, Christian armies avoided high prices in Turkey by holding out until European supply ships arrived at Joppa, Israel, and Nicaea, Turkey. On return over the direct sea route around Iberia to northern Europe, vessels carried Mediterranean goods—citrus fruit, figs, nuts, palm oil, pepper, pomegranates, sesame seeds, spices, and wines. The arrival of exotic foodstuffs spurred British, Belgian, Dutch, and Iberian trade to the Middle East, fueling the trade wars of the sixteenth and seventeenth centuries for dominance of major trade routes.

In South America, the roadways of the Wari Empire from 600 C.E. served as the template for Qhapaq Ñan, the Inca highway, an advanced coast road linking Cuzco and Quito, Ecuador, with Santiago, Chile. Ranging up to 13 feet (4 meters) wide, the system traversed Andes fens and slopes with stone highways and reed and stone bridges. Llama caravans brought craft items, herbs, meat, and vegetables to lowland villages and inland to Argentina and Bolivia. The route to Machu Picchu, Peru, carried corn, fruit, potatoes, and sweet potatoes for barter at livestock markets.

On the other side of the globe, Henry the Lion of Saxony founded the Hanseatic League, which functioned in Lübeck from 1159 to 1630 as a price stabilizer for German resins, rye, salt, and wheat. Because the Catholic Church tightened its Lenten requirements, the herring preserved by net fishermen in Scania, Sweden, gained economic importance as a nonmeat protein transported throughout the Christian world. Along the northern sea routes, Livonia and Prussia contributed butter, grain, and horses. Trading vessels journeyed east to merchant guilds in Danzig, Riga, and Novgorod and west to Hamburg, Brügge, and London. Throughout the Baltic region, the league suppressed piracy against slow-moving grain barges by dispatching armed guards aboard commercial convoys.

From the late 1500s to the early 1800s, triangular trade linked African, American, Caribbean, and European sites in transatlantic commerce based on slavery. The northern route took Southern corn and Canadian salt cod to England for exchange with woolen manufacturers. Profits paid for the purchase of black abductees and convicts from the Bight of Benin and west-central Africa. The Middle Passage carried slaves northwest from the port city of Elmina, Ghana, to Barbados, British Guiana, Jamaica, Puerto Rico, Santo Domingo, and Trinidad for sale to cacao, coffee, and sugar plantations. Return loads of sugar and molasses traveled up the Atlantic Coast to New England stocked distilleries selling rum. The sale of rum in Africa yielded cash for the lading of more slaves for American corn, cotton, and tobacco producers.

North American traders took advantage of major waterways, turning the Chicago, Des Plaines, Ohio, Mississippi, and Missouri rivers and the St. Lawrence Seaway into commercial arteries. Lacking cash, Indians bartered for horses in exchange for corn, dried meat, pemmican, and pumpkins. Along the Great Lakes, a lively trade in salmon, smelt, trout, and walleye encouraged swaps with the Cree and Erie for furs, meat, and nuts.

Beginning in the 1850s, frontier families took wagon trains from barge wharfs in St. Louis over the Oregon Trail and the Santa Fe Trail to the American Southwest. Freight wagons, pulled by horses, mules, or oxen, followed settlers crossing the Rocky Mountains to commercial centers in Virginia City, San Francisco, Salt Lake City, Portland, Seattle, and Vancouver. A string of forts guarded the routes and escorted families through dangerous passes. Indigenous tribes profited from the flow of settlers by trading food for liquor, livestock, and metal knives and cook pots.

Rail Routes and Beyond

The establishment of commercial rail networks followed ancient trails with more safety and speed than dray animals and wagons of previous centuries. In England, the 1844 Railway Act linked cities with outlying farm and herding areas in commerce governed by William Gladstone, president of the Board of Trade. Similarly, in 1856, the Rock Island Railroad and the Illinois Central, the world's longest track, linked Cairo, Illinois, with New Orleans, the heart of the U.S. slave and sugar trade.

Beginning in May 1869, the Union Pacific transcontinental rail line to Sacramento, California, benefited commerce as never before, restoring Southern sales of cotton, molasses, rice, sugar, and syrup to the former Union states and the far west. In the boom years, prairie farmers and ranchers supplied northeastern restaurants with fresh beef and grain from the heartland. A complementary boost in rail-to-barge trade via the Mississippi River from New Orleans to Cairo, Illinois, lowered prices throughout the Mississippi valley.

A parallel link in California enhanced business in dried fish, pineapples, rice, and sugar from Honolulu and Lahaina, Hawaii, via regular steamer service to the islands and Australia. The success of transpacific trade preceded the 1875 Reciprocity Treaty between Hawaii and the United States for exclusive rice and sugar trade rights. The alliance of entrepreneurs with the U.S. government ensured extensions of intercontinental trade via direct routes to Yokohama, Japan, and Shanghai.

The advance in rail lines established new trade routes. The extension of the Baltimore & Ohio and the Pennsylvania Railroad in 1886 sped canned goods, Eastern fruits, meats, processed foods, and vegetables throughout the Ohio River valley. The completion of the Canadian Pacific Railway in 1885 from Thunder Bay on Lake Superior to Winnipeg advanced trade with Vancouver. At both Atlantic and Pacific outlets, fast service boosted agricultural profits from Canadian wheat.

Railroad engineering enabled Asians to augment their diet with global imports. In March 1891, Nicholas II, Russia's future czar, initiated the building of the Trans-Siberian Railway, which connected Moscow across Siberia to Vladivostok and by sea to Japan. The addition of the Chinese Eastern Railway from Chita, Siberia, to Harbin, China, increased the flow of foodstuffs to Russia's frozen east.

In the twenty-first century, the flow of foodstuffs from industrialized countries by air, land, and water profits from containerized freight, refrigerated dairy products, eggs, fish, fruits, and vegetables transhipped in cellular loads by crane from ships' holds and rail flatcars to trucks for rapid transfer to small towns. The concept, initiated as Sea-Land Service, in 1955 by shipper Malcolm Purcell McLean of Winston-Salem, North Carolina, and engineer Keith Walton Tantlinger of Orange, California, defeated the ancient and medieval concepts of static trade routes by increasing outreach to isolated locales. Shifting needs from small piers to container equipment reduced the importance of the choked Strait of Sunda and Strait of Malacca; shut the ports of Liverpool, London, Manhattan, and San Francisco; and transferred trade route destinations to larger facilities at Felixtowe, England; Rotterdam, Holland; and Oakland, California.

See also: Abreu, António de, and Francisco Serrao; African Food Trade; Caravans; Clipper Ships; Hudson's Bay Company; Maritime Trade Routes; Peppers; Silk Road; Trading Vessels.

Further Reading

McLaughlin, Raoul. *Rome and the Distant East.* New York: Continuum, 2010.
O'Brien, Patrick Karl. *Atlas of World History.* New York: Oxford University Press, 2002.
Pons, Frank Moya. *History of the Caribbean: Plantations, Trade, and War in the Atlantic World.* Princeton, NJ: Markus Wiener, 2007.
Smith, Richard Lee. *Premodern Trade in World History.* New York: Routledge, 2009.

Trading Vessels

Since the end of the first millennium B.C.E., the expansion of the global food market has relied on stout merchant vessels. Shipwrights designed the first cargo carriers to transport fish, grain, meat, produce, spices, and wine along oceans and major water routes, primarily the Danube, Nile, Rhone, Tigris and Euphrates, and Yalu rivers. The reciprocal exchange of agricultural goods and food technology between peoples liberated regions from limits on cuisine and improved the choices for farmers and herders through the importation of seeds, plants, and livestock, such as the fast-growing South African Dorper sheep to Australia and the soft Spanish Merino sheep to Sweden. Because sea transport outpaced overland hauling over desert or mountainous terrain, ancient Athenian, Egyptian, and Phoenician food dealers preferred ships to caravans. They developed the shallow coaster for short hauls of fish, grain, and wine to ports surrounded by reefs and shoals. As early as 2500 B.C.E., the Egyptians risked sailing by coaster southeast to the unidentified land of Punt (probably Eritrea) to trade for shorthorn cattle. Other ventures by Arabs, Chinese, Indians, Malaysians, and Persians focused on aromatics, jewels, and metals, but less often on food.

The Phoenicians earned acclaim as the earliest masters of commercial trade routes as far away as Cornwall in southwestern England. Because of rocky soil unsuited to growing grain, Cretan farmers around 1200 B.C.E. exploited commerce in fine olive oil and rich wines in exchange for wheat from Israel and Judah. Trade increased demand for coins, the medium of exchange that facilitated quayside dealing in perishable goods. Beginning in 1000 B.C.E., larger Mediterranean freighters bore bales, resin-sealed jars, and sacks of trade items for sale at a distance from their provenance. Period modifications to naval biremes and triremes (galleys with two and three rows of oars on each side) enabled captains to haul livestock for auction in distant ports. Around 400 B.C.E., cargo vessels ventured as far as Egypt, Hispania, Lydia, and Mauretania (present-day Morocco).

The growth of the Athenian state economy depended on further improvements to fleet speed and naval technology, such as the adjustable deck canvas to protect baskets of fruits and vegetables from sun and wind. By 600 B.C.E., Athens led the Mediterranean in marketing olive oil and wine, both of which shippers transported in 3-foot (1-meter) clay amphorae, each holding 6 gallons 7 pints (26 liters) of dry or wet foods.

Shipbuilders rigged coasters with sails to free the space usually filled by rowers and oars for cargos of *defrutum* (fruit paste or syrup), figs, *garum* (fish sauce), grain, honey, nuts, oil, and *mustum* (crushed grape pulp and skins), and such exotica as capers, mushrooms, oysters, and truffles. Lading of amphorae (tall jugs) required nestling each jar point-first between the shoulders of the bottom row and packing the spaces with straw to absorb the ship's roll. A molded terra-cotta bas-relief from Pompeii depicts two slaves bearing a jar, which they had tied with a thong that they slung over a pole. By shouldering their burden, the bearers allowed the jar to swing freely on its way up the gangplank and into the hold. Around 300 B.C.E., four Greek sailors could load and maneuver an entire shipload of 400 amphorae of oil and wine to Cos, Cyprus, Samos, and Rhodes.

Perils at Sea

Theft dogged sea-lanes. For Chinese and Japanese junks, in 400 B.C.E., freebooters created havoc at the straits between Singapore and Indonesia. Paralleling commercial routes, piracy shadowed the most successful routes of Greek and Roman super-galleys, especially along the eastern Mediterranean south of Cilicia and Illyria, off the islands of Crete and Delos, and throughout the Red Sea shoreline. In 230 B.C.E., the Roman Republic underwrote 200 ships and 20,000 marines under Consul Gnaeus Fulvius to annihilate the Illyrian mercenaries who preyed on convoys from Egypt, North Africa, and Sicily of grain for the army. Within two years, Fulvius swept clean the eastern Mediterranean pirate sanctuary. The action freed merchants to engage in transoceanic trade and rid Rome of its fear of famine. The suppression of seagoing outlaws improved Roman trade to the Black Sea and between the Arabs and Somalis along the Red Sea. Under the implementation of the *annona* (poverty relief) during the reign of Augustus, Rome's first emperor, the nation had to import 14 million bushels (500 million liters) of wheat per year to stave off hunger from the plebeian class. Lest the nation founder from an unfavorable trade balance, Roman shippers engaged in ongoing trading voyages, even during the dangerous winter months, the period that saw the greatest loss of sailors, goods, and vessels.

In the Middle Ages, port cities dominated the food trade. Of 86 imported agricultural goods, 44–51 percent were spices. In the 900s C.E., Viking trade networks sped longboats beyond the Baltic and North seas. The development of holds to accommodate bulk stowage increased sale of dried Norwegian cod from Ribe in Jutland to buyers in Asia, Greenland, and Western Europe. Following the decline of the Byzantine Empire, Muslim and Slavic pirates raided the dockside warehouses of Rome and Venice with hit-and-run tactics, driving down profits and raising prices on imported herring, salt, seeds, spices, and tallow. Merchants lowered overhead around 1000 C.E. by increasing the cargo capacity of vessels to more than 20 tons (18 metric tons). Among German grain dealers, formation of the Hanseatic League by Henry the Lion of Saxony in Lübeck in 1159 stabilized prices by evening out surpluses and crop failures of rye, salt fish, and wheat.

Technological Breakthroughs

During a peak in commerce in spirits in the late 1200s, ships arrived in the port of London carrying as many as 200 barrels of beer or wine each. The addition of hops to brewed beverages lengthened the time that sea captains could transport fresh batches before they soured. By 1340, the convenience of slewing cranes that rotated horizontally over European harbors sped the loading of baskets, pallets, wine barrels, and wooden crates. Agricultural surpluses in cheese, ham, oats, rye, and vegetables increased the activity of vessels between England and Scandinavia.

During hostilities between Denmark and Sweden in 1392, a pirate guild called the Vitalienbrüder (Victual Brothers) focused on clumsy fish- and grain-laden cogs (large-hulled cargo ships) and returned with the spoils to Stockholm, then under siege. Open season on freighters threatened the region's economic stability. Because of the success of the *Seetiger,* captained by Klaus Störtebeker of Gotland, the herring trade on the Baltic Sea collapsed within two years and remained suppressed to 1440 as far north as Bergen, Norway, and south to Iberia.

In the fifteenth century, navigational advances in lateen sails and stern rudders resulted in the easily steered, adaptable caravel, which prefaced a golden era of sea trade. The ship's speed and broad beam enabled Iberians to make longer sea voyages and to carry 130 tons (118 metric tons) of trade goods. Portuguese writer Duarte Barbosa, who sailed with navigators Pedro Alvares Cabral and Ferdinand Magellan from 1500 to 1521, observed the value of trading vessels to world culinary exchange. At the port of Mogadishu, Somalia, Barbosa remarked on the availability of barley, fruit, horses, meat, spices, and wheat delivered by traders from western India. The speed and safety of sea voyages replaced slower, more treacherous overland travel from Europe over the Silk Road to China and the haphazard packing of cardamom, ginger, sesame seed, and white pepper on camels and donkeys. However, adventurers paid the price of daring. Attackers, marooning, reefs, scurvy,

and storms took the lives of many men who risked all to enrich themselves on the global trade in coffee, spices, sugar, and tea.

East Indiamen, the largest cargo vessels, served European commercial ventures by the British, Dutch, and Swedish, who organized convoys to protect valuable goods. Warships and auxiliary cruisers sometimes escorted trader fleets through the most treacherous sea-lanes. The rich global food trade influenced Portuguese navigators to plot new water routes to the Spice Islands around the opposing currents of Africa's Cape of Good Hope. The lure of instant fame and wealth directed Christopher Columbus toward the New World. The Chinese and Spanish trade with Luzon, in the Philippines, in the early 1500s extended commerce in bird's nests for soup, cinnamon and ginger, honey, porcelain dinnerware, table linens, and benzoin and caribou horn for medicines.

In *Suma Oriental que trata do Mar Roxo até aos Chins* (*Survey of the East, from the Red Sea up to the Chinese,* 1512–1515), Portuguese explorer Tomé Pires reported steady seagoing traffic by Arabs, Burmese, Chinese, Filipino, Indians, Japanese, Malays, and Thais to the international port of Melaka (Malacca), Borneo, on the shortest run between China and India. To facilitate harbor transactions, the Melakans insisted on standard coins and weights and measures. At Sumatra alone, Pires marveled at trade in oil, rice, shad, and wine and in durian and tampoy, two luscious fruits. At Java, he remarked on the availability of cardamom, oil, pepper, tamarind, and wine. In exchange for Javanese goods, the Portuguese introduced islanders to butter and cheese, which were unknown.

British Sea Power

During the 274 years that the British East India Company (BEIC) dominated commerce in Asian foods and beverages (1600–1874), the firm made no advances in the speed or size of its vessels. Mercantile agents chartered heavy noncombatant merchantmen to navigate routes between London and central and eastern Asia. Under the leadership of Admiral James (or John) Lancaster, skipper of the 600-ton (540-metric-ton) *Red Dragon,* the BEIC launched its first voyage from Tor Bay, Sumatra, on February 13, 1601. For some 30 annual expeditions from the Far East around South and West Africa to England, loaders packed company holds with alum for pickling and baking powder, areca nuts, jaggery (black sugar), cardamom, China root (sarsaparilla), cinnamon, cloves, coconuts, ginger, pepper, rice, tamarinds, turmeric, and wax for sealing preserves. To protect valuable cargoes from capture, King James I fought piracy in 1604 by ordering the impounding of the privateers' lands and cargoes. In April 1608, William Hawkins navigated the *Hector* past Madagascar and the Seychelles to Gujarat, becoming the first English trader on the Indian subcontinent. In 1609, a company dockyard at Deptford on the River Thames built swifter freighters but not in time to save Hawkins and his load of pepper from Algerian pirates.

To protect valuable trade in molasses, sugar, and tobacco from North and Central American shores, the British admiralty outfitted merchant vessels with cannon and light armaments. To save money, shipwrights painted fake loopholes and simulated defensive weaponry by disguising equipment as artillery. In 1700, brisk Atlantic trade between Great Britain, the West Indies, and the American ports of Charles Town, Boston, Newport, New York, and Philadelphia required constant surveillance to protect stores of dried and pickled fish, flour, rice, rum, sugar, tobacco, and wheat. On transpacific voyages in the 1770s, shippers who included stops at Lahaina, Hawaii, got more for their money, while loading up on fish, fruit, meat, tallow, taro, and whaling products. In exchanges with Europeans, Hawaiians acquired cattle, chickens, goats, and sheep as well as liquor, which debauched all classes of islanders. The importation of grazing animals turned the island economy toward success in livestock husbandry.

The BEIC set world records for success in intercontinental commerce. At the exchange market at Singapore, trade in betel nut, black pepper, cardamom, fish, medicinals, red cane sugar, rice, salt, and tea borne by Cantonese and Siamese junks from 1800 to midcentury was lucrative for both parties. With the introduction of *Camellia sinensis* tea from Assam, India, in 1823, the BEIC purchase of American clipper ships with hydrodynamically efficient clipper bows sped global food distribution in half the time required by deep-draft merchantmen, thus delivering fresher produce to market. Until competition from private companies forced the disbandment of the BEIC in June 1874, the British monopoly commanded the planet's largest merchant navy and controlled half of world trade in such commodities as beer and porter, coffee and tea, pickles and salt, rum and molasses, and wine and cheese.

The New Superpower

By the 1860s, during an era of New World transportation breakthroughs, the U.S. merchant marine seized dominance of global shipping with the largest, sturdiest, and most specialized vessels afloat. The square-rigged, three- or four-masted clipper ship, in the final decade of its control of light freight before the advent of steamers, maintained swift trade in opium, spices, and tea between North America and Asia. In China's harbors, flat-bottomed sampans carried tea chests to the waiting clippers for the dash to London. A more capacious tall ship, the four- or five-masted windjammer, built in Finland, France, and Germany, carried barley, rye, and wheat typically from Australia or South America to Europe from the 1870s into the early 1900s.

The production of steel by the Bessemer process replaced wood, cast iron, and wrought iron parts for steamers, a technological advance that inhibited fires at sea and hold damage by woodworms. Stronger, more flexible steel suited the demand for boilers, steam engines, gears, propellers, and ships' keels and masts. Improved manageability enabled navigators to avoid icebergs, a common doom of freighters rounding Tierra del Fuego, at South America's southern tip. Consumers profited from refined shipbuilding—the finer the machining of boilers and pistons for use at high pressure, the lighter the hulls and the greater the fuel efficiency. Because steamers lowered hauling rates, shoppers enjoyed reduced food prices on such imported goods as coffee, rice, spices, and tea.

During the 1860s, U.S. merchants strove for global shipping routes and the hiring of merchant mariners. Inland ships and barges carried supplies, passengers, newspapers, and the U.S. mail over the Great Lakes and into the American heartland. River transport to the Upper Missouri River carried New Orleans commerce as far north as the Arctic Circle. By 1866, northwestern wharves received an annual freight of 4,441 tons (4,028 metric tons) distributed as far west as Walla Walla, Washington. As a result of post–Civil War commerce, Honolulu thrived from shipping and whaling traffic. Occidental and Oriental shipping from Australia through the Hawaiian Islands to California increased the flow of investors to Pacific Coast orchards, ranches, strawberry fields, and vegetable farms. In southern California, citriculture turned Duarte and National City into lemon and orange packing and shipping centers. In 1870, the United Fruit Company, one of the first multinational corporations in the Americas, began monopolizing transport of bananas from Costa Rica, Guatemala, and Honduras to the United States. The 1876 Centennial Celebration in Philadelphia boosted the banana to national prominence, thus introducing a lucrative market to American produce shippers.

World trade advanced to an exchange of fresh foodstuffs unprecedented in the planet's history. After the opening of the Suez Canal on November 17, 1869, food carriers lopped 36 days from the ocean route between London and Calcutta, metaphorically shrinking the globe and speeding Indian wheat to England at a low price. Humanitarians lauded the shortened routes to sites of Third World disasters, where the offloading of food and pure drinking water prevented mass deaths in Brazil, China, Ethiopia, India, Russia, Sudan, and Tanganyika.

World Wars I and II plagued global merchantmen with danger from German U-boats armed with torpedoes. Allied forces made double use of escorted convoys and air cover. Provision supply ships eased the scarcity of necessities while luring German submarines to Allied battleships. Use of depth charges, barrels filled with explosives, enabled the battleships and cruisers to destroy U-boats and free the convoys to replenish dwindling coffee, meat, medicines, and sugar for Allied regiments.

High-Tech Shipping

Twentieth-century technology upgraded U.S. merchant marine fleets, which expanded under the Shipping Act of 1916. This act regulated food shipments by Great Lakes and oceangoing barges and merchant vessels. In the late 1940s, technology on reefer ships designed by the United Fruit Company improved refrigeration, which Scots shipwright Robert Duncan had introduced in 1874 with the building of the three-masted clipper *Dunedin*. In the mid-1900s, cargo chilling answered a demand for highly perishable goods, such as fresh asparagus, avocados, caviar, milk and butter, poultry, seafood, and strawberries, especially from Australasia and South America. Use of Bell Coleman equipment, a four-stage refrigeration system, assured the cleanliness and purity of frozen meat from New Zealand to Great Britain.

To decrease chances of spoilage of beef and mutton, hares, pork, and poultry from New Zealand, shippers built abattoirs adjacent to docks in Port Chalmers. In 1948 aboard the SS *Yaque*, the first of nine in the United Fruit Company fleet, sealed compartments allowed carriers to individualize air cooling and humidity to slow the ripening process in apples, bananas, citrus fruit, and kiwis by forcing them into artificial hibernation. Bins designed to hold hanging bunches of bananas gradually gave place to hand-packed storage boxes stacked on pallets and loaded on strong gratings through side doors rather than from above by crane. A double-skinned hold encouraged even cooling and freezing via circulated air and ongoing defrosting by powerful heating coils. A quality-control system monitored the ventilation and temperature control required by each food and released ethylene to inhibit pathogens and kill insects; however, lowered oxygen content in compartment atmosphere threatened crew with suffocation.

Another post–World War II advance, container freight, invented in 1953 by trucker Malcolm Purcell McLean of Maxton, North Carolina, shortened the time necessary to empty train and truck contents into ships' holds by loading the entire container without jostling or repositioning the goods. A revolution in merchant hauling, the container freight system of shipping allowed transporters of perishable goods, such as bananas, grapes, peaches, pineapples, plums, melons, and other tender fruit, to complete the delivery with less handling damage and delay. Dole Fresh Fruit International adapted refrigerated technology by applying the containerized freight concept aboard reefers, such as those offloaded at the Dole trucking yard in San Diego harbor. By supplying grocers with fresh tomatoes and fruit from the Northern and Southern hemispheres, freighters extended the range of produce availability and opened new markets for food growers.

See also: British East India Company; Clipper Ships; Dutch East India Company; Gama, Vasco da; Maritime Trade Routes; Portuguese Diet and Cuisine.

Further Reading

Berggren, Lars, Nils Hybel, and Annette Landen, eds. *Cogs, Cargoes, and Commerce: Maritime Bulk Trade in Northern Europe, 1150–1400.* Toronto: Pontifical Institute of Mediaeval Studies, 2002.

Crothers, William L. *The American-Built Clipper Ship, 1850–1856: Characteristics, Construction, and Details.* Camden, ME: International Marine, 1997.

De La Pedraja Tomán, René. *The Rise and Decline of U.S. Merchant Shipping in the 20th Century.* New York: Twayne, 1992.

Trans Fat

An unsaturated fatty acid, trans fat contributes to cardiovascular disease by elevating cholesterol and triglycerides in the body. The sticky nature of trans fat clogs arteries with plaque, restricting blood flow to major organs and heightening risks of heart attack and stroke. Trans lipids increase belly fat and raise levels of triglycerides in the blood, encouraging atherosclerosis or hardening of the arteries.

In 1883, although Canadian officials banned margarine, a Newfoundland spread producer hydrogenated fish, seal, and whale oil and bootlegged the product throughout Canada at half the price of butter. The presence of harmful fat in the diet from beef, cocoa butter, coconut oil, dairy foods, mutton, palm and palm kernel oil, and pork increased after the hydrogenation of margarine and vegetable oil in the 1890s by French chemist Paul Sabatier. By treating substances with hydrogen, he solidified margarine for the table as a cheap, shelf-stable substitute for butter. The chain of saturated fats made chicken legs and fried fish crisper and biscuits, cheese, ice cream, and popcorn more flavorful.

By the twentieth century, some 40 percent of supermarket products contained dangerous saturated fats. In 1909, production of solidified fats in England and the United States preceded the creation of Unilever's Spry and Crisco, Procter & Gamble's hydrogenated shortening made in part from cottonseed oil. Crisco rapidly replaced animal lipids—beef tallow, butter, and lard—in American recipes. Consumers preferred margarine for table use because of its spreadability, even when cold. As a result of increased intake of trans fat, 7 percent of human breast milk in Canada and the United States consisted of harmful fatty acids that may have contributed to the onset of Alzheimer's disease, cancer, depression, diabetes, infertility, liver failure, and obesity. In 1947, physiologist Ancel Benjamin Keys began studying cholesterol and its role in the rise of fatal heart attacks in American men.

Preliminary research into trans fat health hazards in the 1940s and 1950s preceded analysis in the 1990s, which confirmed ties to coronary disease from regular intake of chocolate, doughnuts, hamburgers, macaroons, pastry, peanut butter, and yogurt. Gradually, according to the Mayo Clinic, industrial food companies began to identify less harmful fat—avocado, canola, olive, and peanut oils—on the label. In 1994, health experts charged trans fat with causing 20,000 deaths annually from clogged and inflamed arteries and overworked heart muscles and insisted on the listing of harmful fat in food contents. On July 10, 2002, the Institute of Medicine challenged the nation to reduce its trans fat intake to zero.

Negative publicity began the downfall of trans fat in processed foods. By 2004, Unilever's Canadian markets featured only margarine products free of trans fat. In 2006, the National Institutes of Health and the U.S. Department of Agriculture rejected palm oil as a substitute for trans fats. A year later, the U.S. Food and Drug Administration coerced Procter & Gamble to reduce trans fat in Crisco to no more than 7 percent. The company created a new shortening from palm, soybean, and sunflower oils.

Public demand for reduced trans fats forced the reformulation of baked and fried goods, fast food, and snacks. Other products following low-trans-fat formulations included Girl Scout cookies, Oreos, and menu items from Arby's, Burger King, Kentucky Fried Chicken, Chick-fil-A, McDonald's, Taco Bell, Walt Disney Company, and Wendy's. In 2011, New York City banned trans fats from restaurant fare. In September 2011, Monsanto announced a breakthrough in lessening of fatty acids in the genetic modification of low-fat soybeans.

Further Reading

Dijkstra, Albert J., Richard J. Hamilton, and Wolff Hamm, eds. *Trans Fatty Acids.* Ames, IA: Blackwell, 2008.

Hobbs, Suzanne Havala. *Get the Trans Fat Out: 601 Simple Ways to Cut the Trans Fat out of Any Diet.* New York: Three Rivers, 2006.

Julien, Ronni Litz. *The Trans Fat Free Kitchen: Simple Recipes, Shopping Guides, Restaurant Tips.* Deerfield Beach, FL: Health Communications, 2006.

Shaw, Judith, and Jeffrey M. Aron. *Trans Fat: The Hidden Killer in Our Food.* New York: Pocket Books, 2004.

Watson, Stephanie. *Trans Fats.* New York: Rosen, 2008.

Travel Food

The selection and packing of travel food has affected the military, pilgrimages, sailing, and trading throughout history. During the Neolithic revolution around 12,000 B.C.E., the large seeds of einkorn wheat produced digestible, easily chewed roasted grains for campfire meals. Pouches of charred or roasted grain bore a tasty, fragrant, and lightweight pocket meal easily loaded and eaten out of hand without further cooking or worry of spoilage.

Into the Middle Ages, travel food developed character and variety. Yogurt, first coagulated naturally in Sumer in 6000 B.C.E., dehydrated into a nomad's snack. Armenians and Egyptians wind-dried camel and goat meat for *pastirma,* a spiced packable meal for unhurried chewing. In the first century B.C.E., Apicius, a Roman culinary writer, chose *mulsum* (honeyed wine) to fill his flask. At taverns and roadside stops in Iberia, canteens of cider gained respect as a sweet, energizing thirst quencher.

During the Crusades, journeyers to Jerusalem bought baklava and soup from street vendors, peach turnovers and meat pies at inns, and sacks of almonds, chickpeas, melons and apples, pistachios, and walnuts at food stalls. By the fifteenth century, the speed and safety of sea travel replaced slower, less comfortable overland routes and the awkward loading of food and drink on dray animals. During the Renaissance, European pilgrims packed cheese wedges and flatbread for outdoor repasts and evening possets of valerian for untroubled sleep. In the 1830s, Dutch Voortrekkers of South Africa rubbed desiccated ostrich or venison strips with vinegar, salt, and herbs to make biltong, a rock-hard cured meat similar to jerky.

The New World produced unique road food. The Inuit valued slices of bear and seal as high-energy meals for snowy journeys. In Argentina, Brazil, Chile, Peru, and Uruguay, meal sellers hyped the portability of jerky, which campers could boil in water for a hearty broth. The Canadian Huron relied on dried berries, corn, and sweet prairie turnips (*Psoralea esculenta*), an ingredient in fry bread.

Farther south, travel food derived from home gardens and from nature. California Indians preferred corn mush with grass seed or sunflower seeds. Desert wanderers cored saguaro cactus and chewed the cortex for moisture. Southwestern Indians carried corn in backpacks and tucked sacks of cornmeal in woven belts. European settlers of the Great Plains centered cookery on ashcake, johnnycake, mock oysters (corn fritters), and pone, all convenient corn foods for long passages. A simple kitchen staple, hush puppies (cornmeal fritters) paired with fried fatback in knapsacks and pockets and served children as snacks for long treks to and from school.

Luxury Travel

Pleasure travel became famous for exquisite cuisine. Europe's transcontinental rail line, the Simplon-Orient Express, ran for eight decades from central France to Constantinople, beginning in 1883 with a maiden passage from Paris to Varna, Bulgaria, then by steamer over the Black Sea to Constantinople. Preordered meals eaten from baskets or from the passengers' stores required only cutlery, glasses, napery, and tables from the rail stewards. In 1877, the Simplon-Orient company added a restaurant car, which drew a privileged clientele for the quality of its decor and five-star food service. Meals took on the glamour of top restaurants. Lunch consisted of partridge, fruit, a Turkish pumpkin dessert, chopped almonds in rose syrup, and Turkish coffee. At formal dinners, 42 passengers at a time shared space in the dining car for ten-course meals, beginning with soup and hors d'oeuvres and continuing with capon, goose liver, lobster in aspic, oysters,

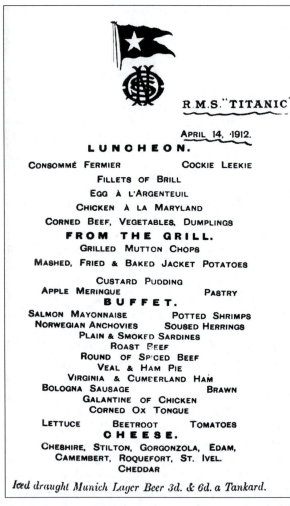

R.M.S. "TITANIC"

APRIL 14, 1912.

LUNCHEON.

CONSOMMÉ FERMIER   COCKIE LEEKIE

FILLETS OF BRILL

EGG À L'ARGENTEUIL

CHICKEN À LA MARYLAND

CORNED BEEF, VEGETABLES, DUMPLINGS

FROM THE GRILL.

GRILLED MUTTON CHOPS

MASHED, FRIED & BAKED JACKET POTATOES

CUSTARD PUDDING

APPLE MERINGUE   PASTRY

BUFFET.

SALMON MAYONNAISE   POTTED SHRIMPS

NORWEGIAN ANCHOVIES   SOUSED HERRINGS

PLAIN & SMOKED SARDINES

ROAST BEEF

ROUND OF SPICED BEEF

VEAL & HAM PIE

VIRGINIA & CUMBERLAND HAM

BOLOGNA SAUSAGE   BRAWN

GALANTINE OF CHICKEN

CORNED OX TONGUE

LETTUCE   BEETROOT   TOMATOES

CHEESE.

CHESHIRE, STILTON, GORGONZOLA, EDAM,
CAMEMBERT, ROQUEFORT, ST. IVEL.
CHEDDAR

Iced draught Munich Lager Beer 3d. & 6d. a Tankard.

Travel food reached the pinnacle of luxury on the ill-fated maiden voyage of the RMS *Titanic* in 1912. As evidenced by this luncheon menu for April 14—the afternoon before the ship struck an iceberg and sank—even second-class passengers dined in high style. *(UniversalImagesGroup/ Getty Images)*

saddle of venison, smoked trout, truffles, turtle soup, and woodcock. Wait staff completed the meal with fresh vegetables, green salads, elaborate pastries, sorbets, cheese, and fruit baskets, all served with appropriate wines.

Combat halted the Orient Express route for five years during World War I, but the famed rail line resumed service in April 1919, carrying the wealthy and elite to spas and seasonal retreats at Belgrade, Calais, Lausanne, Sofia, Trieste, Venice, and Zagreb. By 1947, upgrades to service brought full kitchens, freezers, and a bakery, which turned out 100,000 pastries and cakes per month, and an upscale buffet. In the 1990s, the line served breakfast privately in cabins and maintained a bar car and dinner menu rivaling cruise ships.

Aboard the *Titanic*

One of culinary history's most momentous travelers' meals, the last dinner aboard the RMS *Titanic* served diners bound from Southampton, England, west to New York City. An Edwardian pantry required cargo loaders, crane operators, dockworkers, and stevedores to stow around 4,000 bales, bundles, and cases. The fresh items accompanying the maiden voyage of the *Titanic* consisted of a staggering quantity of the finest comestibles, including: 37.5 tons (34 metric tons) of meat, plus 12.5 tons (11.3 metric tons) of game and poultry and 3.75 tons (3.4 metric tons) of ham and bacon; 7.5 tons (6.8 metric tons) of fish, plus 305 gallons (1,154 liters) of oysters and 25 cases of sardines; 40 tons (36 metric tons) of potatoes; 5 tons (4.5 metric tons) of sugar; 3 tons (2.7 metric tons) of butter; 63 cases of champagne; and 1,000 bottles of wine. Brine-cooled refrigeration chilled beef chambers, cold lockers, and wine and beer caves. Two carbon dioxide machines churned out ice.

Lavish stocking of the pantries of the Ritz, the hotel-sized restaurant on B deck, met the expectations of moneyed passengers and the critical eye of manager Gaspare Luigi Gatti, who had formerly managed Oddening's Imperial Restaurant in London. First- and second-class passengers selected gourmet dishes from à la carte menus. Steerage class passengers, who traditionally had carried their own food and dishes aboard ocean liners, ate plain, but hearty porridge, beef with gravy, cheese, pickles, rice, smoked herring, and stewed figs, all prepared in a separate galley and served in the dining saloon on D deck.

The *Titanic*'s spacious cooking area featured an unprecedented array of worktables and utilities for preparing 60 recipes. Separate refrigeration units held dairy items, eggs, fish, meat, fruit, and vegetables. Supervisors heading individual staffs labored at one specialty each—frozen desserts, kosher meals, pastry, roasting, salad, saucing, seafood, soup, and vegetables. Before dawn each day, workers prepared the day's specialties and readied dough for fresh breakfast buns and breads, managed by Walter Belford, the night baker.

The first-class luncheon for April 14, 1912, featured brill fillets, corned ox tongue, egg à l'Argenteuil, eight cheeses, galatine of chicken, Norwegian anchovies, potted shrimp, salmon mayonnaise, smoked sardines, soused herring, and the standard cruise highlight, a steamship round of roast beef carved to each diner's taste. The evening menu equaled a *table d'hôte* meal from a fine hotel: shrimp canapés and raw oysters in vodka with lemon and hot sauce consommé or barley soup; poached salmon with mousseline sauce; filet mignon with foie gras and black truffles or chicken lyonnaise or minted lamb, glazed roast duck or beef sirloin, served with potatoes; mint tea timbales, and creamed carrots; sorbet made from champagne, orange juice, and rum; roast squab on watercress; asparagus-champagne-saffron salad; chocolate eclairs, French vanilla ice cream or jellied peaches, and assorted fresh fruits and cheeses.

The *Titanic* sank at 2:20 A.M. on April 15, 1912, after striking an iceberg less than three hours earlier. Chief baker Charles John Joughin assigned his staff to stock each lifeboat with bread. Of the liner's staff of 685, only three galley employees survived. After the discovery of the submerged hull on September 1, 1985, survey crews reported that dishes and plates remained in meticulous stacks alongside pots and pans and unopened bottles of Monopole champagne, port, sherry, and Bordeaux, Burgundy, Mosel, and Rhine wine.

Luxury Air Service

In a class with spectacular ocean liners such as the *Titanic* and rail service aboard the Orient Express, the elegant airships of the 1930s expanded choices in transportation. Within five compartments, passengers enjoyed light inflight refreshments, including grenadine and kirsch cocktails. By 1931, the spectacular *Graf Zeppelin* scheduled passenger Pacific flights from Japan to Los Angeles and an Atlantic itinerary across France and Spain, down the western coast of Africa, and west to Recife de Pernambuco, Brazil. Although space was cramped, passengers dined well on a snack menu of cold cuts, chicken, and champagne. A dinner meal, created by the Los Angeles Biltmore Hotel and prepared on two hot plates and an electric oven, began with beef consommé and advanced to marrow dumplings, roast gosling, salmon, and after-dinner brandy, but no cigars.

On a new breed of faster, more commodious zeppelins in 1936, the *Hindenburg* offered bar service in a sealed, pressurized smoking lounge. Deck B housed a dumbwaiter that hoisted meals from the plating area to the serving pantry above. An after-lift-off supper of cold cuts, salads, and hot biscuits satisfied appetites on the departure from Frankfurt. For three daily meals and afternoon tea, the dirigible's crew loaded the galley with 800 eggs, 440 pounds (200 kilograms) of potatoes, 220 pounds (100 kilograms) of cheese and butter, and heaps of smoked meat, cheese wheels, and mineral water, superintended by Chef Xavier Maier, formerly of the Ritz Hotel in Paris. At a fare of $405 one way, the airship promised contentment. The *Hindenburg*'s menu offered fresh fruit, sausages, and hot buns at breakfast and a lunch of Westphalian ham and roast beef sandwiches. At dinner, passengers could choose sole, duckling, ham with asparagus, veal, or venison. A white-coated steward took orders for food and French and German wines and brought the first course, bowls of clear soup.

Beyond Earth

Space travel presented new challenges to meal planners and nutritionists. In 1998, the planning of the International Space Station (ISS) for low Earth orbit included food service for researchers and crew. Before takeoff, most of their meals arrived to the pantry canned, frozen, or refrigerated for maximum purity. Each occupant cooked packeted stores in the galley in two food warmers and rehydrated supplies with either cold or heated water. Plas-

tic bags held drinks and soups for sipping through straws. A fork and a knife attached to each tray to prevent the utensils from floating away in zero gravity.

Laminated retort pouches retained sterility of varied dishes and drinks, including brownies, irradiated beef steak, granola bars, rice pilaf, scrambled eggs, and tortillas. Limitations on condiments reduced choices to ketchup, liquid salt, mayonnaise, mustard, and pepper paste. In 2007, to appeal to Japanese engineer Koichi Wakata, provisioners added adzuki beans with wild greens, curry, egg soup, mackerel in miso, ramen, and rice balls, all available with green tea. When Korean astronaut Yi So-yeon joined the crew in April 2008, she brought *kimchi,* her country's national dish of fermented cabbage. Jewish Canadian engineer Gregory Errol Chamitoff added sesame bagels. Russian fliers selected from black currant juice, borscht, curds, goulash, and jellied pike.

In July 2011, the last ISS mission departed aboard the shuttle *Atlantis,* the end of a 30-year space program. To stimulate space-inhibited appetites, celebrity chef Emeril Lagasse supplied the ISS pantry with jambalaya, mashed potatoes with bacon, green beans with garlic, and rice pudding. The space food developer explained that appetizing meals at the rate of 3.8 pounds (1.7 kilograms) per day raised morale and ensured wellness during extensive weightlessness. To ensure nutrition in future missions, space scientists experimented with kitchen gardening, producing cabbage, carrots, herbs, lettuce, onions, peppers, radishes, spinach, strawberries, and tomatoes.

See also: Animal Husbandry; Biscuit; Crackers; Dried Food; Hunter-Gatherers; Ibn Battuta; Jerky; Nomad Diet and Cuisine; Pemmican; Polo, Marco.

Further Reading

Brüssow, Harald. *The Quest for Food: A Natural History of Eating.* New York: Springer, 2007.

Croce, Erica, and Giovanni Perri. *Food and Wine Tourism: Integrating Food, Travel, and Territory.* Cambridge, MA: CABI, 2010.

Holland, Leandra Zim. *Feasting and Fasting with Lewis & Clark: A Food and Social History of the Early 1800s.* Emigrant, MT: Old Yellowstone, 2003.

Tudor Diet and Cuisine

From 1485 to 1603, an era of status-raising displays of pomp and wealth in England, Tudor diet and cuisine verified the provider's ability to serve an elegant meal. Unusual demand raised urban food prices and stripped the countryside of its best produce. In April 1486, to relieve the treasury of costly state meals, King Henry VII went on an extended royal progress to Pontefract and York in the northern and western parts of his realm. According to the *Croyland Chronicle* (1486), the royal entourage placed the burden of feeding on social climbers and rural aristocrats seeking the prestige of serving the royal table.

For peace talks between Henry VIII of England and French King Francis I at the Field of the Cloth of Gold, near Calais, France, in June 1520, workers erected two red wine fountains. A brick oven produced bread for 12,000 attendees, all of whom had table rights to dine at the king's expense. Cooks distributed mutton from 2,200 sheep and served 70 jars of strawberry jam on 1,350 pastries. Gamekeepers contributed coneys, geese, larks, pigeons, partridges, snipe, and woodcocks.

Hampton Court

Hampton Court Palace, a Thames-side estate in East Molesey, Surrey, remains the primary model of food service surviving from Tudor England. Its owner, chief minister Thomas Wolsey, the archbishop of York, doubled the floor plan to one of the three grandest courtier residences in England. For serving guests in the 45 apartments, the kitchen garden produced chicory, endive, fennel, mallow, purslane, rocket, and smallage (wild celery).

Until Wolsey's fall from favor in 1528, he treated guests to feasting on Dutch lettuce salad, the favorite of Queen Catherine of Aragon, first of the six wives of Henry VIII. A featured meat, turkey, newly imported from the New World in 1525, treated the discriminating English to a costly bird that came to the table plumper and juicier than pheasant. With knives and fingers, diners ate the gilded entrées, which chefs scented with lemons and Seville oranges, perhaps as a gesture to the queen's Iberian heritage. The use of citrus juices as flavorings appeared less fashionable after Catherine's replacement in the king's affections by Anne Boleyn in the late 1520s.

Food as Exhibition

When Henry VIII bought the Hampton Court palace in 1529, he further remodeled the property to house 1,200 people for grand entertaining. At its completion in March 1532, a wine fountain in Base Court spouted drink for holiday visitors. The complex included two butteries (bottlers), two dressers, saucery, larder, flesh larder for meat, dry larder, pastry office in charge of tarts and crusts, confectionery for making marzipan and gingerbread, chandlery, spicery, and two plating counters. On the main kitchen wall, a brick shelf with grates above charcoal burners reduced the size of fires needed for individual dishes.

At one end of the great kitchen, a hearth five times the size of a sitting room fireplace held a giant cauldron and spits for roasting whole oxen. Behind a screen, one of a crew of seven spit boys sat at a four-legged stool away from direct heat to rotate and baste roasting meats with pan drippings and piquant sauces and gravies made from bone marrow, ginger, and wine. For beverages, the estate

offered a privy cellar to serve the royal table. For guests, butlers drew on a drinking house for storing leather ale jugs and a three-stage wine cellar holding the annual reserve of 300 barrels imported from Burgundy and the Rhinelands.

For fiscal supervision, the Board of the Greencloth, administrators of the kitchens and pantry, checked in deliveries of candles, charcoal, rushes for strewing the floors, and spice, the costliest food outlay. Provisioners limited wheat to the high-quality grain harvested on the king's farmlands for baking soft cheat (loaf bread) and manchet (soft rolls). A wet larder stored saltwater fish in barrels of seaweed; fresh water bream and carp remained live in the palace moats and ponds until removed for cleaning and cooking.

Staffing Extravaganza

At Henry's new Great Hall, service to England's royalty and aristocrats required a lord steward to look after the pantry and food service. In addition to the great kitchen adjacent to the main hall, the designer established larders beyond the kitchen, a confectory within the confines, and a pastry house and poultry scalding and plucking area outside the walls as a precaution against fire and odor. The kitchen brigade, which had access to the nation's first printed cookbook, *A Noble Boke of Cookery for a Pryncis Household* (ca. 1500), outlined impressive menus for meals at 7 A.M., 10 A.M., and 4 P.M., plus a late-night snack after 8 P.M. Both the king and queen engaged personal cooks. Pero Doux served the king as master chef; head cook John Bricket prepared household meals.

For maximum temperature control of dishes, the serving counters lay within easy walk to the high table and to the watching chamber, where officials ate. In the kitchen wall at a hatch resembling a modern restaurant service window, servants collected hot food for groups of four to share, including cooked salad ingredients dressed with oil, red wine, and sugar. Bread and drink came up the back stairs from the buttery and cellars below the main hall.

For private meals, Henry VIII had a separate kitchen near his quarters. His daughter, Elizabeth I, preferred even stricter privacy at mealtime. She chose to share any untouched entrées with her ladies in waiting.

Royal Diet

Meat comprised 75 percent of palace cuisine, which reached as high as 5,000 calories per day. In one year, the staff cleaned, dressed, cooked, and served 8,200 sheep, 2,330 deer, 1,870 pigs, 1,240 oxen, 760 calves, and 53 wild boar. Most came from the royal estates or from local farms and markets. During Lent and on Christmas, Easter, Ascension, Assumption, Midsummer, and other fast days, the staple dish consisted of salt kippered herring, pickled and smoked, or fresh fish and eels, some sold by local fishermen. In 1541, Henry abandoned 70 percent of holy fast days. He abolished absolute fasting by increasing ingredient choices to include dairy items and eggs on Lenten menus.

After the death of King Edward VI in 1553, his half sister, Mary I, reverted to Catholic food customs and upheld fast days to shield the fish industry from financial ruin. Entrées continued to feature fish each Friday and Saturday. Cooks baked, boiled, fried, and grilled a variety of species, from ordinary cod and dace to crayfish, ling, loach, sturgeon, and whale. Leftovers passed to the wait staff and kitchen help; their leavings went to beggars.

During the 45-year reign of Elizabeth I (1558–1603), she more than tripled household budgets from her father's £16,000 to £55,000. State dinners for as many as 600 required two sittings, constituting the first separation of the dining chamber from food service in European history. The lord steward organized a liveried staff of 200 men consisting of a master chef, 12 sous-chefs, 12 cook's aides, and a serjeant of the cellar, William Abbott, with a staff of ten for each subsidiary kitchen.

High Renaissance menus departed from the heavy black puddings and meat haunches of early Tudor times in favor of more delicate recipes. They grilled birds and steaks flavored with healthful broths, coriander, lemon, mint, parsley, and wine. At the queen's direction, cane sugar, once imported from the West Indies as a curative, sweetened vegetables, meats, and desserts. Pastry chefs decked elaborate display pieces with candied violets, fruit paste, ginger crystals, gold leaf, licorice, marmalade, and rosewater.

Commoner's Food

While Elizabeth imported Flemish gooseberries for pies and anchovies, artichokes, asparagus, capers, fish egg relish, and Greek olives from the Mediterranean, the gentry imitated her example by arranging for intimate gourmet dinners cooked by their French chefs. An expensive paste, blancmange involved shredding chicken for mixing with almond milk, rice, and sugar. Baskets of manchet established the status of any family that could afford fine white flour, which bakers sifted and resifted through fine linen.

In contrast to aristocrats and the upwardly mobile, who could afford New World kidney beans in tomato sauce, spiced pumpkin soufflé, and sweet potatoes boiled in wine, peasants relied on staid English fare. The poorest of England's 4 million subjects fed on maslin (brown bread) or horse bread, barnyard loaves made from ground dried peas. They raised sheep for milk and mutton, which they ate from common plates or trenchers, thick bread slices the size of a platter for soaking up gravy. As a side dish for venison, a grain pudding called frumenty, either homemade or purchased from a cookshop, combined almond milk and egg yolks. Cooks surrounded bacon with pureed beans to absorb the excess salt that preserved pork. Both adults and children drank ale and beer. In Ireland, where cuisine standards suffered, crude cookery

of boiled cabbage with mutton and pork entrails relied on cowhides for pots and straw for strainers.

Stale bread undergirded the simplest recipes. A common sauce, *cameline,* resembling the napped surface of camel hair, consisted of bread crumbs, nuts, and raisins blended with cinnamon, cloves, ginger, and vinegar. In the 1590s, when harvests disappointed farmers, strapped rural families stretched Scandinavian or Russian stockfish and boiled meat by grinding them into *mortrews* (mortared stew), a paste thickened with bread crumbs and eggs and flavored with inexpensive bay salt.

By autumn 1596, food riots threatened in Oxfordshire. The poor, who lived in wattle and daub huts, had no oven and only a cauldron for cooking one-pot meals. The most common dish, that of the landless carter or drover, depended on pottage or vegetables boiled in barley or oat grain with mustard and vinegar as condiments. The pickling of surplus vegetables required verjuice, a vinegar pressed from rotted crab apples. To escape malnutrition, desperate people worked as apprentices or in great houses as servants and wet nurses, both of whom received adequate meals. In 1601, passage of the Elizabeth Poor Law set an almoner over parish food relief for poorhouses in England and Wales.

Further Reading

Colquhoun, Kate. *Taste: The Story of Britain Through Its Cooking.* New York: Bloomsbury, 2007.

Jones, Norman, and Robert Tittler. *A Companion to Tudor Britain.* New York: John Wiley & Sons, 2007.

Weir, Alison. *Henry VIII: The King and His Court.* New York: Ballantine, 2008.

Tull, Jethro (1674–1741)

An English experimental agronomist and amateur engineer, Jethro Tull invented a seed drill and plow that modernized agriculture.

Born in Basildon, Berkshire, Tull studied law at Oxford University and Gray's Inn until pulmonary disease ended his career plans. After marriage, at age 25, he joined his father in farming the chalky, unpromising fields at Howbery near Wallingford and northwest of London. Costs and operational waste frustrated Tull from the outset. In 1701, to prevent the waste of seeds in the process of broadcasting them at random and leaving them on the surface for birds to peck, he invented a hopper and cylinder that turned against a spring-loaded tongue to plant sanfoin, a French pasture grass. He dubbed the mechanized method the "vineyard technique." By directing seeds through grooves into a funnel, the device regulated distribution along three rows at a time. The placement of beans and peas at controlled intervals and depths preceded covering with soil by a harrow, to leave space for tillage.

Two years after settling on Prosperous Farm at Hungerford, Oxford, Tull advanced from gentleman farmer to innovator. He promoted the use of the horse to replace oxen as draft animals. He championed innovation and adapted his drill for the planting of potatoes and turnips, two food crops gaining primacy in Europe. Although his employees rebelled and covertly sabotaged his equipment, he earned regard for growing wheat 13 seasons in the same field without adding manure. In 1713, he toured the vineyards of France and Italy to study Continental farming methods. The following year, he upgraded his planting mechanism to stir the soil more thoroughly. With the aid of three plowwrights, Tull engineered a four-coultered disc plow, which cut into sod. The moldboard plow, an experimental soil breaker, overturned weeds and left their roots to dry in the sun. He also invented a horse-drawn hoe for pulverizing dirt clods to release minerals into wheat and forage plants. The system reduced irrigation and seed costs as well as the labor of sowing and weeding. Tull joined a farming cooperative that founded the Norfolk system, a scientific approach to planting and cultivation by replacing fallow farming (allowing fields with depleted soil to lie fallow) with the soil enrichment of clover and turnips. Tull's treatise, *The New Horse-Hoeing Husbandry* (1731), proposed contour plowing to form terraces to catch water runoff and theorized that the use of manure as fertilizer caused a bad taste in vegetables.

Although the Tullian system won approval in Scotland and the advocacy of philosopher Adam Smith, English critics initially charged row cropping with wasting strips of land between furrows. A virulent critic, editor Stephen Switzer denigrated Tull's concepts by issuing a monthly journal, *Practical Husbandman and Planter* (1733–1774), which charged Tull with undermining the classical methods taught in Virgil's *Georgics*. Nonetheless, Tull's work remained a touchstone of modern agriculture and passed through five editions. He published an expanded version in 1733, a supplement in 1735, addenda in 1738,

and a conclusion the following year, all aimed at the interests of aristocratic landowners. The introduction of soil fertility methods broke the dung-fodder cycle, by which farmers had grown more fodder to feed more stock to make more manure. A 1750 translation by Henri-Louis Duhamel du Monceau introduced Tull's farming concepts at experimental fields in France and won encyclopedist Denis Diderot and philosopher Voltaire to Tullian methods. In 1759, distribution of the English version of Duhamel's six-volume *Traité de la Culture des Terres Suivant les Principes de M. Tull* (*Treatise on Agriculture according to the Principles of Jethro Tull,* 1756) revived interest in Tull's farming methods. Despite a resurgence of agrarian disputation for the next 15 years, historians acclaimed Tull as the "Father of British Agriculture" and originator of the "New Husbandry."

The fifth edition of Tull's work, completed by Aaron Brachfeld and Mary Choate in 2010, defended Tull's reputation from period charges that he generated unemployment of farm laborers and depressed wages by industrializing agriculture. The text recommended turnips, a recent addition to English farms for intercropping with barley, oats, and wheat. Instead of importing low-calorie fruits and vegetables from the Continent, the fifth edition proposed that the English boost nutrition and health by growing their own. The editors promoted a balanced diet, including beans and whole grains, the basis of an antitoxic diet that included cranberries, kelp, and thistle.

See also: Agriculture; Beans and Legumes; Eliot, Jared; Wheat.

Further Reading

Brachfeld, Aaron, and Mary Choate. *The Horse Hoeing Husbandry by Jethro Tull, Esq.* Agate, CO: Coastalfields, 2010.

Fussell, G.E. *Jethro Tull: His Influence on Mechanized Agriculture.* Reading, UK: Osprey, 1973.

Porter, Roy. *The Cambridge History of Science: Eighteenth-Century Science.* New York: Cambridge University Press, 2003.

Vanilla

A sultry, intoxicating aroma and flavor associated with chocolate, vanilla derives from a succulent tropical vine native to Mesoamerica. The dried bean entered world cuisine in the Totonac diet of Veracruz in Mexico's Valley of Mazantla, a volcanic crater, long before the Spanish conquest in the early sixteenth century. Purists credited the flavor of Mexican vanilla to terroir, the complex ecology of climate and soil. The vine flourished in the Gulf Coast jungle understory of *cocuite* and *pichoco* trees.

In Belize, the Maya interplanted vines with amaranth, corn, tomatillos, and tomatoes and harvested vanilla beans for trade. Cooks toasted pods on a *comal* (flat clay or cast-iron griddle) and cooked crushed beans in bread pudding and stewed squash or pumpkin. In Brazil, Ecuador, Guiana, Honduras, and Peru, an inferior species produced a coarser scent and taste valued mainly by the perfume industry.

After the Aztec king Itzcoatl overthrew the Totonac in 1427, the conquerors levied a vanilla bean tax. When Hernán de Cortés first observed the Aztec diet on November 14, 1519, Emperor Montezuma II consumed countless cups of hot chocolate flavored with honey and the vanilla bean (*Vanilla planifola*), a revered neurological stimulant and aphrodisiac. By 1700, introduction of vanilla in European coffee, confections, medicinal powders and tinctures, luxury sauces, and tobacco jolted Mexican farmers to monetary success. In 1789, Thomas Jefferson, the U.S. envoy to France, brought home to Monticello enough vanilla beans to flavor ice cream, rice pudding, and syrups.

At the end of a boom in cacao markets, vanilleries gained investors hoping to profit from New World flora. Planters of the vanilla vine in other humid climes failed to connect the centrality of hummingbirds and the Melipona bee to the pollination of flowers. Javanese planters in Krawang and Preanger were the first to try—and fail—to rival the Mexican bean; German colonists made another attempt in East Africa. By emulating bee action, Belgian horticulturist Charles François Antoine Morren broke the impasse in 1837 by introducing artificial propagation in French colonies.

Indonesia and Madagascar entered the vanilla market after 1841, when a 12-year-old slave, Edmond Albius of Réunion, pioneered hand pollination by smearing pollen from anther to stigma with a bamboo sliver. Fields of vanilla cuttings, cultivated by black slaves and laborers imported from China and India, required tree trunks or crutch-shaped stands to lift vines and beans into sunlight. Harvesting occurred one bean at a time when the green sheath split and the pod pulled free of its stem. Curing began with blanching in hot water and sun-drying. The yield hovered at 1 pound (0.45 kilogram) of dried vanilla from 4 pounds (1.8 kilograms) of beans. Workers, overwhelmed by the intoxicating scent, suffered an illness known as vanillism, manifested in headache, hives, and malaise.

For farmers in the Comoros Islands, Madagascar, and Réunion, experimental pollination increased observation time and field labor. The work was worth the effort because it boosted profits from the world's second-most-expensive flavoring after saffron. In 1850, the first liquid vanilla extract, made by chemist Joseph Burnett, traveled from Paris to Boston and gained fame among New York chefs for its vibrance. Additional vanilla plantations thrived in Australia, Costa Rica, Fiji, Guadeloupe, Guatemala, India, Jamaica, New Guinea, Sri Lanka, Tonga, Uganda, and Vanuatu. Prices fluctuated according to yield during cyclone season in the Indian Ocean and around French Polynesia.

Pure vanilla, the only fruit produced by an orchid, remained popular as a flavoring for ice cream, liqueurs, soft drinks, and sweets as well as in medicines. In 1858, Nicolas-Theodore Gobley first isolated the source of the bean's sweetness and complex fragrance, which derives from 171 aromatic compounds. In 1874, industrial chemists at Haarmann & Reimer in Holzminden, Germany, synthesized the flavoring from pine bark and clove oil, thus threatening the primacy of Madagascar as the world's top vanilla producer. Two decades later, the French firm of Rhone-Poulenc Pharmaceuticals competed with German synthesizers.

In the 1990s, high prices influenced the Costa Rican government to introduce vanilla propagation in the rural communities of Puerto Jimenez and Quepos. After weathering viral infection and a hurricane, planters in 2000 began marketing oversized pods, with premium-grade beans reaching 11 inches (28 centimeters). Mexican farmers ruined their reputation for quality by mixing vanilla with coumarin, a carcinogen derived from tonka beans that endangers the kidneys and liver. As a result, Indian planters in Karnataka, Kerala, and Tamil Nadu moved

Recipe: Chocolate-Vanilla Pie

Bake a pie shell and set aside to cool. Stir 1 cup of sour cream into 2 cups of water and whisk until the liquid thickens. In the top of a double boiler, combine the slurry with the powdered mix of a 5-ounce carton of dark chocolate pudding (not instant). Turn the heat on low and continue stirring. Add one 4.4 ounce (125 grams) Lindt dark chocolate bar, coarsely chopped, plus 2 teaspoons of pure vanilla extract and 1 tablespoon each of butter and espresso coffee powder. Continue cooking and stirring until the chocolate bar has melted and the filling is a smooth consistency. Pour into the pie shell and cool. Garnish with chocolate curls and mint leaves.

into first place with 16 tons (14.5 metric tons) of premium quality beans by 2002, outselling Madagascar's harvests. Mexican productivity dropped to 5 percent of the global vanilla market, which reached a height of demand in Australia, Canada, France, Germany, and Japan. From 2004 to 2010, prices fell from $500 per kilo to $20, the result of competition from vanillin, an imitation taste synthesized from an aldehyde used in 95 percent of the world's vanilla flavoring.

See also: Biscuit; Blenders and Food Processors; Chocolate; Greenhouse Horticulture; Mail-Order Food; Polynesian Diet and Cuisine.

Further Reading

Havkin-Frenkel, Daphna, and Faith C. Belanger, eds. *Handbook of Vanilla Science and Technology.* Ames, IA: Wiley-Blackwell, 2011.

Karner, Julie. *The Biography of Vanilla.* New York: Crabtree, 2006.

Rain, Patricia. *Vanilla: The Cultural History of the World's Most Popular Flavor and Fragrance.* New York: Jeremy P. Tarcher, 2004.

Veganism

An avoidance of animal products in the diet, veganism professes a respect for animals and a desire to nourish the body on micronutrients from fruits, nuts, and vegetables. The concept of passive resistance to violence dates to the meatless diet of sixth-century B.C.E. Greek Orphism and Pythagoreanism and to Jainism, an Indian religion that abhors the exploitation of animals and violence to any living being. Strict observers thus reject factory farming and cleaning products and cosmetics tested on animals. The vegan regimen excludes, among other items, gelatin,

honey and beeswax, fur and leather, silk and wool clothing, and carmine, the red dye in cider and chewing gum derived from the *Dactylopius coccus,* an insect that infests the opuntia cactus in Central and North America.

In 1944, English reformer Donald Watson coined the term *vegan* to describe nonmeat eaters who also reject dairy foods and eggs. Notable vegans have included Renaissance polymath Leonardo da Vinci, Transcendentalist educator Bronson Alcott, pop singers k.d. lang and Sinéad O'Connor, actors Brad Pitt and Sandra Oh, writer and feminist Alice Walker, civil rights activist Coretta Scott King, pacifist author Brigid Brophy, Vietnamese Zen monk Thich Nhat Hanh, and César Chávez, founder of the first migrant labor union in the United States. Carol J. Adams, an animal rights advocate, issued the bibles of vegans, *The Sexual Politics of Meat* (1990) and *The Pornography of Meat* (2004), which blame detachment from animal slaughter for promoting a meat diet. She and other vegans blame meat diets for damaging and consuming Earth's resources.

The popularity of cruelty-free eating increased in 2009 after the American Dietetic Association found the

A member of People for the Ethical Treatment of Animals (PETA) rallies the public to adopt a vegan diet and lifestyle. Vegans avoid the consumption of animal products for ethical and environmental reasons as well as for personal health. *(Vincent Thian/Associated Press)*

vegan diet to be low in fat, high in fiber, and suitable to virtually all periods and activities in human life, including infancy, pregnancy and lactation, and professional athletics. Vegan cooking involves substitutions for standard ingredients—nondairy butter (replacing butter), soy or almond milk and coconut cream (cow's milk), tofu (eggs), applesauce (honey), and vegetable broth (meat-based broth).

Followers of the plan avoid food-borne bacteria from livestock—campylobacter, *Escherichia coli* (*E. coli*), listeria, mad cow disease, and salmonella, all sources of illness that can kill. Vegans also experience fewer incidents of arthritis, cancer, coronary disease, diabetes, hypertension, obesity, and osteoporosis, though they risk iron-deficiency anemia and insufficient intake of vitamins D and B12.

A more stringent vegan diet consists only of raw foods, primarily fresh beans, grains, fruits, nut pastes and seeds, plant oils, sea and land vegetables, sprouts, and juices made from such ingredients. Another meatless variant, macrobiotics, stresses whole grains and limits consumption of avocados, beets, eggplant, peppers, potatoes, spinach, and tomatoes. A similar regimen, the Edenic diet follows the book of Genesis by excluding all meat and shellfish, salt and spice, sugar, coffee and tea, and alcohol.

See also: Child, Julia; Fructarianism; Gourmet Cuisine; Kitchen Lore; Raw Cuisine; Vegetarianism.

Further Reading

Lamey, Andy. "Food Fight! Davis Versus Regan on the Ethics of Eating Beef." *Journal of Social Philosophy* 38:2 (Summer 2007): 331–348.

Patrick-Goudreau, Colleen. *Vegan's Daily Companion.* Beverly, MA: Quarry, 2011.

Stepaniak, Joanne. *Being Vegan: Living with Conscience, Conviction, and Compassion.* Los Angeles: Lowell House, 2000.

Stepaniak, Joanne, and Virginia Messina. *The Vegan Sourcebook.* Los Angeles: Lowell House, 2000.

Vegetarianism

The avoidance of animal products in the diet, called vegetarianism, aims to improve health and increase longevity through the avoidance of ingesting animal blood, marrow, and fatty muscle tissue.

The concept made its impact on human history after the second great food revolution. The first, at the end of the Paleolithic age, turned weapon-making omnivores to carnivores when hunters realized they could bring down large mammals for food with clubs, spears, darts, pits, deadfalls, axes, hooks, knives, nets, and poison. The former diet, based on foraging for plants and mollusks and snaring birds and small animals, gave place to a daily intake of large haunches of meat. Much of the world's diet

Types of Vegetarians

Type	Diet
Buddhist vegetarians	no animal products, garlic, or onions
fructarians	fruit, nuts, and seeds
granivores	grain and seed
herbivores	plants
lactarians	plants and dairy food
liquidarians	plant juices
macrobiotic vegetarians	primarily beans and whole grains
modified vegetarians	no flesh and no fowl that eat fish
ovo-lactarians	plants, eggs, and dairy food
ovo-vegetarians	plants and eggs
pescetarians	plants and fish
pollotarians	plants and poultry
pollo-pescatarians	plants and white meats
raw vegans	fresh fruit, nuts, seeds, and vegetables
semi-vegetarians	plants, no mammal meat
vegans	plants, no dairy, eggs, or honey
vegetarians	no fish, flesh, or fowl
vitarianism	fruit, raw milk products, and vegetables

still centers on sizable mammals cooked into meat dishes. However, despite the shift from wild greens to meat, vegetarians insist that meat avoidance is more natural to human anatomy, which lacks the carnivore's powerful jaws and the short gut associated with rapid digestion of animal protein.

A major shift from a carnivore diet to grains and legumes occurred with the beginning of agrarianism. Lentils, a high-protein Stone Age crop, entered the human diet in 9500 B.C.E. in southeastern Turkey, followed in 9000 B.C.E. by the harvesting of wild einkorn wheat. By cultivating grains and other feed crops, growers could raise domesticated livestock and poultry and also supply a vegetarian diet. Globally, meat eaters dominated Europe; vegetable eaters settled most of Asia.

The Pious Diet

Vegetarianism prevailed in controversies among Asian theologians. Although there is no proof that Buddha was a vegetarian, the abstemious Buddhists of Tibet ate animals only if beasts accidentally died or other beasts slaughtered them. As early as 2000 B.C.E., Aryan Hindus set harsh strictures against cattle slaughter. The *Atharvaveda* (ca. 800 B.C.E.), a normative guidebook attributed to the mythic sage Atharvan, a son of Brahma, specified that only Brahmins could sacrifice a cow to the gods as a holy offering. Peasant esthetics gradually supplanted the burning of haunches of meat with flowers, fruit, incense, oil, and vegetables, all more easily attainable and less wasteful of herd animals.

Buddhist, Hindu, and Jainist scripture set the tone and style of the peasant diet. Around 800 B.C.E., the Baudhayana Sutra, a collection of manuals on behavior, warned the devout to keep silent, sit with crossed legs each night, and eat sparingly of barley, dairy products, oil cake, and rice. In a travelogue issued around 415 C.E., Fa Xian, a Chinese Buddhist monk who toured Nepal, India, and Ceylon, condemned the herding and breeding of domestic animals as a sinful abuse of creation prefacing slaughter and meat eating.

Concurrently, Jainism, a pacifist sect originating in northwestern India, evolved dietary monastic vows. Laws in the Anga kingdom of eastern India (ca. 450 B.C.E.) required nonviolence to people and animals, cyclical fasts, and the eating of "innocent" food. Jain kitchen rules for monks and laypersons exceeded even the severity of orthodox Hinduism. Jain cuisine authorized the eating of ginger and other rhizomes but declared the harvesting of root crops a form of killing.

Gradually, Jainist, Hindu, and Buddhist abstinence from violence won out over ritual killings. Buddhism became less dogmatic than Hinduism or Jainism. For the sake of health, Buddhist monasticism advised the teacher to avoid intoxication and health-threatening seven-day fasts from meat, salt, and grains. Abstinence from meat was not obligatory until the third century B.C.E. At Bihar, in northeastern India, Ashoka the Great, the Mauryan emperor (r. ca. 270–232 B.C.E.) and patron of Buddhists, ordered his subjects to refrain from harming animals and to revere an all-vegetable diet for themselves and for feeding their flocks. In Gujarat, Ashoka's first command incised on the Girnar Edict Stones forbade the type of widespread animal slaughter that once preceded kingly feasts. In response, Buddhists banned meat from their kitchens and avoided contact with butchers and fishermen.

Subsequent Hindu law held it a crime in the food industry to kill, butcher, buy, sell, cook, or eat animal flesh. For sacramental gifts, the devout purchased milk products rather than meat. A passage in the *Mahabharata* (ca. 200 B.C.E.), the Indian epic, warned that violators would rot in hell for the number of years equal to the hairs on the slaughtered beast. Another entry promised sound memory, beauty, health, and longevity plus strong character and spirituality to vegetarians.

Jews, Christians, and Confucians

Judaism systematized meat slaughter, food purchase, kitchen cleanliness, and cookery but did not require vegetarianism. As illustrated in Genesis, Jehovah created humankind—Adam and Eve—as vegetarians or possibly fructarians. Their holistic diet reflected nonviolence and a perfect harmony with nature, symbolized by residence in the Garden of Eden, the metaphoric "Peaceable Kingdom." The mythic first couple remained fructarian or vegetarian until after their expulsion from paradise for violating a dietary constraint. Under a concession from the divine creator, Noah and his family became the first followers of Yahweh to kill animals for food. Based on biblical example, the Hebrews, unlike the Babylonians, hunted no animals with weapons and fished only with large nets, never spears.

According to Josephus's *Antiquities* (94 C.E.), the first-century Essenes embraced vegetarians and centered communal dining on bread loaves, the focus of the Eucharist. Other early Christians preferred fish to meat because of the symbolism of the Greek anagram *Ichthus* (fish) for "Jesus Christ, Son of God, Savior." By popularizing fish entrées, Christ cults eroded classical Greek vegetarianism.

The meatless diet held a minor role in the Chinese Taoist cult, which sanctioned only vegetarian gifts to honor dead ancestors. The source of chi (energy or life force), some cultists declared, derived from the cypress or pine tree and peaches. Taoist proto-pharmacist Ge Hong (Ko Hung), who lived near Nanjing, compiled a philosophical text called *Pao-p'u Tzu* (*The Master Who Embraces Simplicity,* ca. 317 C.E.) that advised on lifestyle. The text blended Confucius's ethics with Taoist metaphysics, including charms, magic recipes made from crane eggs and tortoise shell, and the "elixir vitae," the tonic of life. To earn extra days of life, his followers practiced self-control and sexual continence but abandoned reliance on herbalism, which incorporated toxic plants. The neo-Taoist strand eventually abandoned its narrow regimen to follow a healthful lifestyle based on earthly contentment and the hope of heaven. The reshaping of Taoism took another direction in 415 C.E., when Kou Qianzhi (K'ou Ch'ien-Chih) reformed the creed by removing the extremes of breath control and sexual ritual and taxes to support the priesthood. With the aid of Emperor Tai Wudi (T'ai Wu Ti), Kou reestablished the faith as a state religion, a decree that remained in force until 448 C.E., when northern schismatics reinstated the cult of longevity based on medicine, herbs, and vegetarianism.

In the late third century C.E., Porphyry of Lebanon, a Neoplatonist philosopher educated in Athens, vigorously opposed human consumption of animal flesh by warring with ancient dietary theorists. His writings lauded the vegetarianism of Pythagoras, the Samian philosopher of the late 500s B.C.E. who refused to eat meat on the grounds that departed human spirits transmigrate to animal form. A soulful nature lover, Porphyry justified a vegetable diet in *De Abstinentia* (*On Abstinence from Animal Food,* ca. 275 C.E.) on the basis of his compassion for animals, which he described as sensitive to human anger and cruelty. He forbade bloody sacrifices to God. His ideals refuted those of Roman philosopher Aulus Cornelius Celsus, author of

De Medicina (On Medicine, ca. 15 C.E.), who promoted a diet of bread and meat over vegetables and fruit because he believed that human physical structure called for analogous tissue from animal torsos and limbs. In agreement with Porphyry, the eleventh-century medical school dietary guide *Regimen Sanitatis Salerni (Healthy Salernian Diet)* treated depression with dairy products and fresh fruit and an avoidance of red meat.

Early Medieval Vegetarianism

Into the Middle Ages, church fathers condemned a meat- and wine-rich cuisine for its association with wealth, prominence, and the tormenting of beasts. In the third century, Clement of Alexandria and Tertullian opposed consumption of animals as evidence of carnal lust. After concurrence by Saint Jerome and Saint John Chrysostom in the next century, the monastic hierarchy evolved rules concerning what foods to proscribe. The fount of Christian hospitality, Saint Benedict the Great of Nursia, Italy, author of *Regula Monachorum (Rules for Monks,* ca. 515), excluded four-footed animals from allowable cuisine for monks but made no comment on the substitution of birds or fish for meat. He based his ideal of a noncarnivorous, nonalcoholic diet on a belief that costly red meats and wines violated vows of poverty and encouraged sexual debauchery. On meatless days, monks ate fish, frogs and other water creatures, eggs, snails, and the tender unborn fetuses of rabbits, which had not yet become meat.

From the Monastery of Saint Denis, France, twelfth-century scholar and teacher Pierre Abélard urged a similar restraint in his wife, Héloïse, a Benedictine nun and abbess at Argenteuil. Around 1135, she refuted his assertion that women might be sexually aroused from meat in the diet but yielded to his antimeat stance by formulating statutes basing diet on vegetables and grain.

In subsequent centuries, the heretical Cathars of Languedoc forbade the carnal corruption that they believed was caused by consumption of meat, eggs, cheese, and milk, all foods produced by animal coition and containing a soul. Some extremists rejected honey as another

form of animal food. Out of a misunderstanding of the reproduction of fish, Cathar regulations allowed the cooking of swimming creatures as animals created by spontaneous generation.

Meatlessness in the Late Middle Ages

As monastic discipline eroded, monks who once served butchered meat only to invalids extended the privilege to all infirmary patients. Cistercians followed a rule of 1240, which allowed monastery kitchens to prepare no meat except for the sick and workmen. Even though the Decretals (church laws, 1234) by Pope Gregory IX forbade meat entrées, abbeys created a dispensation between infirmary and refectory that sanctioned meat on the table. In 1335, Pope Benedict XII relented because he could not enforce the prohibition of meat. He conceded that monks could serve meat up to four times a week except during holy fast days. As a control on excess, he allowed only half the brotherhood to abandon vegetarianism. Monastic cooks at Kirkstall Abbey in Leeds, England, prepared meat in a separate hall, the misericord, and later in a two-story refectory, with meat service allowed only on the lower level and vegetarian entrées served upstairs.

During the Nara era of the eighth century, when Japan turned to Buddhism, citizens embraced vegetarianism and abstained from consuming oxen or horses, which they revered as dray animals, helpers of humanity. In place of mammals in the diet, the Japanese cultivated their national staple, rice, along with barley, beans, millet, and sorghum. In the twelfth century, Zen Buddhist records introduced tofu, a soybean curd that simulated meat in cooked dishes. Around 1600, Jesuit proselytizer Matteo Ricci, an Italian missionary to Nanking, lambasted Buddhist asceticism as pagan, but his harsh dictum failed to halt Zen extremes of self-denial.

Over time, the sustenance of religious groups varied according to broad or narrow interpretations of scripture, canon law, and local practice. Japanese clergy ignored the past norm of Buddhist monks and nuns and ate meat. Thai brothers of the Thammayut sect rejected meat; the pragmatic Mahanikai brotherhood accepted meat when almsgivers offered it. Tibetan monasteries allowed meat in the diet according to the dictates of the individual conscience. Chinese Buddhists cooked only vegetables in home kitchens, in part because of the Confucian ideal—a parallel to classical Greek Pythagoreanism—that an animal may be a reincarnated human soul.

Influential Vegetarians

Because of persuasive dietary guidebooks, numerous philosophers and wellness authorities have applauded the vegetarian diet, either as a life's regimen or as a temporary measure to restore health. Syrian theologian Gregory Bar Hebraeus, author of a philosophical encyclopedia,

Recipe: Snail-Stuffed Mushrooms

Cap two dozen large white mushrooms. Stir-fry for one minute in oil and cool. Mince the mushroom stems and one small onion and sauté in oil. Fold in one beaten egg, 1 tablespoon of chopped chervil or parsley, 1 tablespoon of chopped tarragon, 2 tablespoons of white wine, and a handful of toasted breadcrumbs. Fill each mushroom cap with a snail and top with the seasoned stuffing. Broil and serve with a sprinkle of vinegar and sea salt.

Hewath Hekhmetha (*The Cream of Science,* ca. 1285), covered issues of fasting and vegetarianism. He admired both the anchorite who limited himself to bread, salt, and water and the monk who ate dairy products, eggs, and fish. Reformer Thomas Moffett, author of *Health Improvement; or, Rules Comprizing and Discovering the Nature, Method, and Manner of Preparing All Sorts of Food Used in This Nation* (1655), warned that diners dug their graves with their teeth when they ate meat.

From a humane perspective, artist Leonardo da Vinci; philosopher Ralph Waldo Emerson; reform leader Mohandas Gandhi; Sylvester Graham, inventor of the graham cracker; and playwright George Bernard Shaw hated meat because it caused the deaths of mammals, which shared awareness and sensation with humankind. English nutritionist Thomas Tryon, author of *The Way to Health, Long Life and Happiness* (1683), wrote so persuasively on vegetarianism that he influenced American statesman Benjamin Franklin to give up meat temporarily. Franklin observed a meatless diet until age 17. While traveling by boat from Boston to Philadelphia, he observed the cook cleaning fresh fish and frying them for passengers. Franklin noted that the larger fish had a smaller one in its belly. Reflecting on nature's method of feeding larger animals on smaller ones, he abandoned vegetarianism as contrary to nature.

During the colonial era, Europeans in India observed the privilege of the Brahmin class, which followed a vegetarian diet. In his travelogue *Travels of a Philosopher: or, Observations on the Manners and Arts of Various Nations in Africa and Asia* (1770), Pierre Poivre, a botanist and biopirate, studied the effects of vegetarianism on the Indian subcontinent. He described the Hindus of Malabar in southwestern India as pacifists and eaters of butter, fruit, and grain and pulses, but nothing that enjoyed an animal life. He approved nursing mothers feeding infants spoonfuls of sesame oil and admired particularly the vining Chinese spinach and orchards of bananas, cocoa, guavas, and mango as sources of wholesome produce. Publications spread Asian concepts, including the *Health Journal,* issued in 1842 by Mary Gove Nichols and Henry Wright, and, the following year, the British publication *The Healthian,* edited by Wright.

Fad Turned Lifestyle

On September 30, 1847, when English abstainers formed the Vegetarian Society at Ramsgate, they formalized the term *vegetarianism* to encompass all life deliberately sustained without meat consumption. The following year, they offered advice in their magazine, *The Vegetarian.* In 1908, other national antimeat societies formed the International Vegetarian Union in Dresden, Germany.

One proponent, Russian novelist Leo Tolstoy, became an ascetic in his declining years, promoting meatless eating among Russian intellectuals as a moral issue. In his opinion, the overall perfection of individual moral-ity naturally resulted in vegetarianism. Attracted to nonviolence and animal rights, Tolstoy praised all-vegetable cookery as an adjunct to health. He deliberately isolated himself from meat preparers to cook and eat *kasha,* a Russian cereal that linked him with peasants.

In the United States, reform movements touched on the meatless diet as a key to health. William A. Alcott, a respected Boston physician and teacher, proclaimed the vegetable diet the basis of social reform. In June 1843, his cousin, idealist Amos Bronson Alcott, and English reformer Charles Lane founded a vegetarian retreat, Fruitlands, a transcendentalist "new Eden" on a 90-acre (36-hectare) parcel at Harvard, Massachusetts. The experiment collapsed in January 1844 from lack of interest in an austere vegan regimen that also rejected eggs and dairy products from communal kitchens. Alcott's contemporary, New York newspaper editor Horace Greeley, hosted a vegetarian banquet and welcomed such dignitaries as feminists Susan B. Anthony, Amelia Bloomer, and Lucy Stone. In 1850, William Alcott zealously toasted the initial session of the American Vegetarians Society as the promotion of an ideal undergirding all civil, moral, religious, and social betterment.

The mid-nineteenth century brought a mass swing toward vegetarianism in the United States and Europe. Meatless and antimeat cookbooks abounded, many from California, the kitchen garden of America. Educator and domestic expert Catharine Beecher's *Domestic Receipt-Book: Designed as a Supplement to Her Treatise on Domestic Economy* (1846) raised an objection to animal fat, which she labeled the home's most injurious food. Christian reformer John Smith published *Fruits and Farinacea the Proper Food of Man* (1853), subtitled "Being an attempt to prove, from history, anatomy, physiology, and chemistry, that the original, natural, and best diet of man is derived from the vegetable kingdom." Straying from biblical injunction to scientific theory, Smith advised self-control, re-education, and gradual dietary adaptation along with a guarantee that fruits, vegetables, and grains sustain human nutritional needs. His work, still read in the twenty-first century, erred in the dismissal of legumes as minimally valuable to health.

Nutritional Debate

Gradually, Asian concepts of what is allowable on the menu earned favor with other reformers, notably, the Salvation Army and temperance workers. When the first vegetarian restaurant opened in Leipzig, Germany, in 1875, followed by others in Liverpool, London, Manchester, and Portsmouth, England, and in Sydney, Australia, passersby thought the menu eccentric. Those uninitiated into meatless cookery often ordered a meal out of curiosity and found choices lower in price than standard commercial fare. Because menus favored Indian curries or Mediterranean vegetable ragouts, customers ate with a spirit of adventure. However, carnivorous home cooks considered vegetarians and teetotalers nuisances because their feeding demanded a separate menu and imaginative restructuring of traditional entrées.

Another food writer and instructor, Jules Arthur Harder, head chef at San Francisco's Palace Hotel, acquired experience during his tenures at Saratoga's Grand Union Hotel and New York City's Union Club and during a decade at Delmonico's steak house in Manhattan. He initiated a huge undertaking, which he called *The Physiology of Taste: Harder's Book of Practical American Cookery* (1885). His proposed six-volume compendium launched an exhaustive study of herbs and vegetables based on culinary science. In his catalog of 300 fruits, herbs, and vegetables, he explained when and how to buy fresh produce and how to prepare it. He compiled a large collection of recipes for boiled, braised, fried, parboiled, puréed, and stuffed lettuce and cited opinions on the best way to dress lettuce salad. Because his pompous, judgmental air made few converts, the first volume ended the project.

Extremes of Opinion

One alarmist, San Francisco journalist Daniel O'Connell, declared late-nineteenth-century abstemiousness foolish and shortsighted. In a diatribe, *The Inner Man: Good Things to Eat and Drink and Where to Get Them* (1891), he accused ascetic theologians of interfering with pleasures of the table by fettering individual freedom of choice. He attacked beliefs that followers of Asian religions maintain muscle and strength without eating meat. By his reasoning, no vegetarian nation had produced any lasting good in contrast to the achievements of Peter the Great, Dr. Samuel Johnson, Friedrich von Goethe, William Wordsworth, and other meat eaters. O'Connell warned youth that abandoning meat robbed them of strength. For anecdotal evidence, he pointed to the Harvard University rowing crew, who ate only vegetables while training for a race against meat eaters from Oxford University, and blamed the Americans' loss on specious dietary beliefs.

In 1897, the Theosophical Publishing Company in Wheaton, Illinois, issued Constance Wachtmeister and Kate Buffington Davis's *Practical Vegetarian Cookery,* one of the first U.S. vegetarian guidebooks. The text warned that disease in cattle revolted the home cook, who turned to vegetables in search of purer foodstuffs. Theosophists added that clean cooking and dining readied the astral body for the afterlife by liberating the spirit from earthly dross to rise to heaven. The authors also characterized salt and alcohol as poisons and valued steaming over boiling for preserving nature's goodness. Divided into 37 subheadings, the compendium covered home cooking for family and invalids, whom it tempted with arrowroot, creamed gruel, and rice foam.

In Tennessee in 1904, Eugene Christian, author of *The Encyclopedia of Diet* (1916), and his wife, Mollie Griswold Christian, published *Uncooked Foods and How to Use Them: A Treatise on How to Get the Highest Form of Animal*

Energy from Food. An unusual tack of these nature-food proponents was the claim that a return to a natural diet would end kitchen drudgery for American women, to whom they dedicated their work. They typified the home kitchen as a source of vassalage, where the housewife stood over a miniature furnace and inhaled the toxic smell of broiled and frying flesh. The melodramatic description of preparing lunch and dinner placed the woman of the house in charge of a blazing firebox topped by greasy cookware. The authors fantasized that the home cook, like a pirate, unfurled a dishrag over blood and bones.

A Californian, Edward Giles Fulton published a similar warning, *Vegetarian Cook Book: Substitutes for Flesh Foods* (1910), which advised meat-eaters that they were chewing themselves into an early grave. In place of flesh dishes, he proposed natural entrées rich in fruits, grains, nuts, and vegetables. To stave off cravings for meat, he compiled nut-based substitutes—ersatz chicken soup, meatless sausage and hamburger steak, mock whitefish, and vegetarian salmon fillets. Pantry provisions called for nut gravy, nut loaf, nuto cero, nuttolene, and protase, all patented meat substitutes common in markets of the era.

Twentieth-Century Innovations

In the early 1950s, a Japanese couple, Aveline and Michio Kushi, popularized macrobiotics, a health regimen that forbids dairy products, meat, and processed foods. They based the nutritional system on a theory of the Greek physician Hippocrates, who coined the term *macrobiotics* to mean quality health and longevity. The couple asserted that a meat-heavy diet disturbed international harmony and undermined global peace by supporting aggressive behaviors. Aveline Kushi first studied a controlled environment in the writings of philosopher Georges Ohsawa, founder of the macrobiotic movement. Until her death in 2001, she educated individuals and families on the place of diet in nurturing stamina and wellness. As a source of organic and natural foods, she founded the Kushi Institute, a world center for macrobiotic education. Her proponents foster the One Peaceful World Society, an international network and support system for people seeking to cook and eat macrobiotic foods and to cure ailments with alternative medicine.

From her home in Boston and Erewhon, Kushi's shop in Brookline, and a sister school in Amsterdam, Holland, Aveline Kushi counseled clients and trained hundreds of cooking teachers and natural foods chefs. Aided by macrobiotic counselor Wendy Esko, Kushi also published *Introducing Macrobiotic Cooking* (1988), *Quick and Natural Macrobiotic Cooking* (1989), and *Aveline Kushi's Complete Guide to Macrobiotic Cooking* (1989). Her texts explained the how and why of vegetarianism, such as control of fats, and emphasized whole grains and green leafy vegetables. Kushi spotlighted miso soup, an enzyme-rich soybean soup that promotes digestion, and aduki beans for cleansing the system. The Smithsonian Institute accepted her collected works for display at the National Museum of American History.

In 1991, South African journalist Margaret Visser summarized the effort of cooking vegetarian style in *The Rituals of Dinner: The Origins, Evolution, Eccentricities, and Meaning of Table Manners.* While establishing what does and does not constitute a meal, she ruled out tea and biscuits and questioned the service of cold plates. In her opinion, history has conditioned people to expect a meal to include hot foods, especially roasted meats. From the cook's point of view, according to Visser, vegetarian entrées cost less, require less toil and cleanup than meat, and encourage sharing of portions. She concluded that, for those unfamiliar with vegetarian cuisine, meatless cooking requires more imagination and effort to convince diners that they receive a full and satisfying meal.

Avoiding Meat

British families began deserting the traditional beef roast in 1986, when bovine spongiform encephalopathy, or mad cow disease, first began and spread to 14 European nations. The rise of hoof-and-mouth and mad cow disease in Europe late in 2000 and into 2001 turned some cautious diners from red meat to fish, ostrich and kangaroo flesh, and vegetarianism. Italy experienced a 40 percent decline in beef consumption; in Germany, the percentage fell nearer to 80 percent. A poll of English eating habits in April 2001 turned up a sudden switch by 1.5 million carnivores to a nonmeat diet. While Continental restaurateurs assured patrons that their kitchens served only safe Argentine beef, diners began lining up for a table at Margutta Vegetariano restaurant in Rome and other vegetarian establishments throughout the continent. Cautious families bought vegetarian cookbooks and sought the advice of the Vegetarian Society on how to alter diet and cookery to satisfy those more accustomed to hamburgers and standing rib roast than hummus and moussaka.

On May 1, 2001, Hindu attorney Harish Bharti and others in Lynnwood and Seattle, Washington, filed a class-action suit in the state as well as in California and British Columbia against the McDonald's fast-food chain. They and Jewish, Muslim, and Sikh groups charged false advertisement that violated the sacred norms. After 1990, when the company announced a switch from frying french fries in beef fat to all-vegetable oil, religious ascetics patronized the restaurants to eat what they thought were fries untainted by animal fats. When editors of *India West* newspaper revealed McDonald's duplicity in April 2001, Hindus raged at false advertisement. In India, protesters smashed McDonald's restaurant windows; Hindu politicians demanded that the government oust the chain. Company official Walt Riker denied the charge of fraud and declared that french fries sold in India and Fiji were all vegetable. He added that the company never misrepresented itself as a vegetarian restaurant. The company requited the claims in 2005 with checks ranging from $50,000 to $1.4 million.

In February 2011, in an article for the *Journal of Agricultural and Food Chemistry,* biochemist Duo Li of Zhejiang University publicized the results of a three-decade study of veganism and vegetarianism. Research credited a meatless diet with building the immune system, avoiding diabetes, and controlling blood pressure, body weight, and cholesterol. New data also indicated that vegetarians increased the risk of heart disease, macular degeneration, and senile dementia. The lack of omega-3 fatty acids and vitamin B12 elevated chances of atherosclerosis and blood clots. Vegetarians advocated an increase of nuts to supply omega-3 and of eggs, milk, yogurt, and yeast extract spreads such as Vegemite or Marmite to supply vitamin B12. The report ignited a twenty-first-century round of arguments as old as Hippocrates.

See also: Daubenton, Louis Jean-Marie; McDonald's; Polo, Marco; Pulses; Raw Cuisine; Theophrastus; Tofu.

Further Reading

Bourette, Susan. *Meat, a Love Story: Pasture to Plate, a Search for the Perfect Meal.* New York: Penguin, 2009.

Kushi Institute. www.kushiinstitute.org.

Preece, Rod. *Sins of the Flesh: A History of Ethical Vegetarian Thought.* Vancouver, Canada: University of British Columbia Press, 2008.

Roberts, Holly. *Vegetarian Christian Saints: Mystics, Ascetics, and Monks.* San Francisco: Anjeli, 2004.

Walters, Kerry S., and Lisa Portness, eds. *Religious Vegetarianism: From Hesiod to the Dalai Lama.* Albany: State University of New York Press, 2001.

Verrazzano, Giovanni da (1485–1528)

The Italian explorer of the Atlantic Coast from Newfoundland to Florida and the Antilles, Giovanni da Verrazzano (or Verrazano) produced the first report on American Indian lifestyle and diet since the logbooks of Christopher Columbus.

Born at Val di Greve, south of Florence, Verrazzano chose to sail as a freebooter for France to the eastern Mediterranean and west to Newfoundland, a North American landmass familiar to fishermen and whalers. To pit the French against the competition of Spain and Portugal for new lands, in 1522 he convinced Francis I that exploration to the west might open French markets in Asia. Aboard *La Dauphine* (the Princess) at Dieppe, he and a crew of 50 set off for Cathay (China) in April 1523 in a four-caravel convoy. Eluding a blockade manned by the Portuguese and Spanish, he sailed from Madeira on January 17, 1524. His provisions included enough food for an eight-month voyage. After seven tough weeks of navigation through storms, on March 1, Verrazzano arrived ashore at a country he called Francesca and anchored south of the Cape Fear delta off North Carolina. By April 17, he had maneuvered upcoast, where native craft plied the shore. Historians surmise that his expeditions' contact with a virgin soil population decimated aborigines by spreading European pathogens.

In his letters to Francis I, Verrazzano admired the beauty of the land and its fertility. During a three-day visit to the Pamlico Sound beginning July 8, 1524, he reported on a 25-man foray to shore for fresh water at Hatteras, North Carolina. Farther north, near Chesapeake Bay, the woodlands produced cherry and plum trees as well as fruits new to the explorer. In houses built of woven mats covering bent saplings, some 30 residents composed a single family. In the style of hunter-gatherers, they lived on abundant beans and on birds, deer, and fish that they shot with arrows or snared with nets. Verrazzano determined that the Wampanoag survived long and well because of their lifestyle. Their congeniality enabled them to taste shipboard cooking of meats, but they set a limit on fraternization between the crew and native women. Verrazzano compared the wild grapes that grew upward into the trees with the wine stock of Lombardy. He named the region Bacchus Island and, despite the Indians' ignorance of fermentation, predicted that the nomadic Wampanoag could cultivate European grapes, grain, and olives.

The convoy departed on May 6, hugging the coast of Sandy Hook, New Jersey, and Cape Cod and Nantucket, Massachusetts. An encounter with the Munsee of New York bay ended in an unforeseen retreat from gale winds. At Refugio (Narragansett Bay, Rhode Island), Verrazzano rested for 15 days and enjoyed another exchange of foods with aborigines. He judged Narragansett corn the continent's best, which natives honored with ritual harvest observances. At Casco Bay, he encountered the Abenaki of Maine, who survived on fish and game as well as an unidentified root. Judging by their draping of pelts for garments, Verrazzano deduced that the natives hunted bear, lynx, and wolf. Because of the foul manners of the Abenaki, the voyagers moved on toward the Canadian Maritimes and named the region Arcadia. In July 1524, they departed Cape Breton Island for Dieppe. Food historians credit Verrazzano with carrying corn to Italy, from where it spread to France and Hungary, competing with the potato as inexpensive peasant fare.

After his voyage to Brazil and Newfoundland in 1526, Verrazzano sought the patronage of Philippe de Chabot, admiral of France. The navigator turned a profit from the import of brazilwood, a source of red dye. In 1527, the cartographer Vesconte de Maggiolo published a map of the journey.

In March 1528, aboard *La Flamenque,* Verrazzano left Dieppe a third time for India. After locating Florida and sailing south into the Caribbean Sea, at Guadeloupe, he encountered the Carib, cannibals who may have mistaken him for more of Columbus's crew, the perpetrators of massacres on Indians. The man-eaters dismembered and ate the captain and six men of his crew. His brother, cartographer Girolamo da Verrazzano, returned home to report the catastrophe and to bear maps, gold and silver, and spices to the royal court. In 1556, Italian geographer Giovanni Battista Ramusio issued Verrazzano's commentary in a collection of correspondence by voyagers.

Further Reading

Horwitz, Tony. *A Voyage Long and Strange: Rediscovering the New World.* New York: Henry Holt, 2008.

Quinn, David Beers. *Explorers and Colonies: America, 1500–1625.* London: Hambledon, 1990.

Wroth, Lawrence C. *The Voyages of Giovanni da Verrazzano, 1524–1528.* New Haven, CT: Yale University Press, 1970.

Vinegar

A bright, tart condiment, foodstuff, and pickling liquid made by the biotransformation of alcohol, vinegar, or acetic acid, figures in food writing over much of culinary history. Around 8500 B.C.E., grape juice fermented into wine during storage. After a short period, wine lost its sweetness and soured into vinegar. To halt the transformation, vintners added terebinth berries and resin to the batch. Egyptians stored vinegar in urns in 3000 B.C.E. and added the liquid to embalming fluids to preserve human cadavers. According to a Chinese food classic, Shen Nong's *The Divine Farmer's Herb-Root Classic* (ca. 220 C.E.), vinegar originated in East Asia in 2800 B.C.E. for use in food and pharmaceuticals.

A food conservation method dating to Mesopotamia in 2400 B.C.E., pickling imported cucumbers in brine prevented spoilage by replacing natural liquids with preservatives. A vinegar solution excluded oxygen while producing an acid marinade that soured by lacto-fermentation. The natural process required a warm, dark storage area. In the Fertile Crescent, pickling with date palm fruit vinegar or acidic figs or grapes made available such seasonal vegetables as cucumbers and cauliflower for long sea voyages and lemons and peaches for nomadic journeys.

In place of expensive red wines, Greek commoners drank *fouska* (diluted vinegar). After 400 B.C.E., Hippocrates, the Greek physician, dosed patients with vinegar to cure coughs and heal wounds. In 79 C.E., Roman encyclopedist Pliny the Elder wrote of the cooling effects of vinegar on the skin and as a treatment for hiccups, nausea, and sneezing as well as dog and spider bites and leprosy. Galen and the Moorish doctors of North Africa diluted vinegar in water to ease consumptives.

Roman cooks soaked artichokes in cold vinegar and slowed the spoilage of sardines by marinating them in hot vinegar. Laborers in the fields and legionaries on the march refreshed themselves with *posca*, a drink of watered down vinegar valued as a defense against malaria. Punishment of unruly soldiers and jailed prisoners involved flogging, following by soothing the flesh with oil and preventing infection with vinegar.

African and Asian acetification of foods received little commentary in early culinary texts. By 221 B.C.E., commercial vinegar made from salted plums achieved popularity and contributed to the five tastes of classical Chinese cuisine. In the eighth century C.E., Japanese samurai drank vinegar to boost stamina and strength. The Japanese and Koreans joined the Chinese in making soured rice wine a standard recipe flavoring.

Technological Advances

In the Middle Ages, French vintners in Orléans solved the mystery of vinegar making by adding "mother," or a bacteria-rich starter, to ventilated barrels of beer or wine. In the presence of oxygen, over a period of 90 days, fermentation took place at a steady temperature of 85 degrees Fahrenheit (29 degrees Celsius). Eleventh-century vinegar makers at the Benedictine monastery of Spilamberto, Italy, courted royal patrons by sending barrels of their product to kings.

In Modena and Reggio, Italy, after 1000 C.E., the Este wine makers created the first balsamic vinegar as an aromatic and healing liquid related to "balm," a medical soother. After heating with hot bricks, vinegar fermented for five years in casks of ash, cherry, chestnut, mulberry, or oak. The wood imparted an outdoorsy flavor that paired well with salad greens. Barrels of Este vinegar gave false hope to victims of bubonic plague that the tart liquid could kill germs.

Throughout the Renaissance, the French prospered at commercializing vinegar, which they flavored with basil, cherries, clover, fennel, garlic, lemons, peppercorns, raspberries, rose petals, and tarragon. Specialty shops stocked 150 varieties, each for a unique purpose, including tenderizing vegetables. Minorcans blended pepper and vinegar to season pilau; Cubans and Filipinos creamed vinegar and spices into a paste to make pork adobo sauce. In England in 1673, a growing vinegar industry prompted Parliament to tax output.

Into the colonial period in North America, the Chippewa of the Great Lakes region soured maple syrup to add to maple sugar for sweet-and-sour meat glaze and to use as a condiment and preserver of cucumbers and flavoring for milkweed pods. The Menominee favored maple sap vinegar as a liquid basis for greens cooked in cornmeal and pork fat. The Algonquin of Quebec ground cardamine root into relish flavored with vinegar. The Eskimo fried greens and meat in vinegar as a hot salad.

Canadian and U.S. vintners earned three times the profit from vinegar that they received from cider. In fishing villages, cafés offered crab boil, a steaming of crabs over hot vinegar. Housewives retained the flavor of flowers and fruit by pickling mangoes and peaches whole with cloves and preserving nasturtiums first in cold, then boiling vinegar. Similar efforts produced ginger beer, tenderized game, and kept berry and cucumber ketchup, chicken, chili sauce, nuts, oysters, and watermelon rind safe in stone jars.

Commercial Varieties

During the Industrial Revolution, food processors used fruit and vegetable waste or B-grade wine to make vinegar. They sieved the liquid through wood chips to add a woodsy flavor and aroma. Forcing oxygen into the mix, an innovation of Dutch scientist Herman Boerhaave, sped up the souring process. By skimming the acetobacters that floated on the liquid, processors could initiate subsequent batches, thus increasing their profits. Barbecuing used ample quantities of vinegar to tenderize tough cuts of beef, chicken, and pork. In slave quarters in the Western Hemisphere, Africans turned chitterlings and pig's feet into edible meat by stewing in hot pepper and vinegar.

The British navy preserved vegetables in vinegar to prevent scurvy. Fish and chips stalls, which date to Joseph Malin's London venue in the 1860s, served vinegar in squeeze packets for sprinkling with salt. In the United States, pioneers packed casks of pickled vegetables to vary their diet on the way west. A shortage of medicines during the Civil War turned physicians to old-time disinfection of wounds with vinegar. An understanding of bacterial action on wine occurred in 1864 with the studies of French researcher Louis Pasteur. Temperance workers applauded the diversity of vinegars, which supplanted alcoholic beverages in such seasonal recipes as cranberry sauce and fruit shrub.

Over time, vinegar makers fermented pungent batches from bamboo, beech sap, beets, cane, champagne, coconuts, dates, honey, kiwis, malt, melons, molasses, palm flowers, persimmons, raisins, and whey. Chinese and Japanese vinegar makers began with rice wine; Spaniards initiated vinegar batches with sherry; Greeks used *oxos* (sour wines). Europeans preferred grape vinegar; on the island of Quemoy, vinegar makers specialized in sorghum flavor. In Indonesia, vinegar makers chose pineapple; Filipino vintners used coconut wine to make a marinade for "cooking" fish into kinilaw, a finger food flavored with chili, ginger, and onions. Mesoamericans opted for prickly pear cactus vinegar, a central ingredient in salsa and flavoring for toasted pumpkin seeds. White grapes, the source of balsamic vinegar, produced the mellowest vintages; beer, cider, and wine yielded the strongest flavor. Rice wine lay somewhere in the middle of the rankings.

Today, vinegar is a key ingredient in processed chutney ketchup, mayonnaise, mustard, salad dressing, and vinaigrette. In the American South, vinegar stabilizes the tang in canned pickles, cole slaw, collard greens, potato salad, and vinegar pie. British and North American chip makers use chives and vinegar to add savor to deep-fried potato slices. The tart flavor also enhances the blander flavors of Irish lamb, Japanese sushi rice, and Russian beet salad.

See also: Cider; Condiments; Pickling; Wine.

Further Reading

Chiarello, Michael. *Michael Chiarello's Flavored Oils and Vinegars.* San Francisco: Chronicle, 2006.

Giudici, Paolo, and Lisa Solieri. *Vinegars of the World.* New York: Springer, 2009.

Hoffman, Susanna, and Victoria Wise. *The Olive and the Caper: Adventures in Greek Cooking.* New York: Workman, 2004.

Muscatine, Doris. *The Vinegar of Spilamberto.* Washington, DC: Shoemaker & Hoard, 2005.

Virginia Company of Plymouth

A joint stock venture chartered by James I of England in April 1606, the Virginia Company of Plymouth (also the Plymouth Company or Virginia Bay Company) anticipated the settlement of the Atlantic Coast from Maine to the Potomac River.

Investors made vague plans for the enrichment of England by mapping a water route to Asian spice markets. On May 31, 1607, stockholders, backed by entrepreneur Ferdinando Gorges, equipped the *Gift of God* and a supply ship and dispatched 125 volunteers to found Popham Colony on the Kennebec River delta at present-day Phippsburg, Maine. Along the way, they discovered the teeming waters of Newfoundland's Grand Banks and filled their boats with cod. After landing safely on August 13, they awaited the arrival of a sister ship, the *Mary and John,* which beached on August 16.

The company built Fort Saint George, dug a moat, diverted a stream into an artificial lake, and completed a compound of 12 cabins, a chapel, and storehouse. President George Popham, the customs agent at Bridgewater, Somerset, assured the king of ample cinnamon, mace, and nutmeg, trade goods that the colonists intended to exploit along with abundant furs, alum deposits, nuts, cedar, and oak. Settlers made wine from wild grapes and began gathering the roots of the vining smilax, also called greenbrier. The English had first received the flavorful root from Mexico in 1536 to compound into sarsaparilla, a pleasing drink and a tonic or tea to treat eczema, impotence, psoriasis, rheumatism, and syphilis. Because the colonists arrived too late to harvest a crop, more than half sailed back to England on December 1, 1607, aboard the *Mary and John.*

The Virginia Company of Plymouth succeeded but not at trade. From local lumber, colonists built North America's first seagoing ship, the 30-ton (27-metric-ton) pinnace *Virginia.* Popham's successor, Admiral Raleigh Gilbert, failed to establish a commercial relationship with Skitwarroes, the local Abenaki chief. Because of hostile Abenaki and a disastrous fire the following spring, the colonists abandoned their settlement. Boarding the *Gift of God* and the *Virginia,* the remaining 45 adventurers returned home with their furs and dried sarsaparilla.

The collapse of the Popham experiment proved beneficial to the Pilgrims, who learned from the returning colonists how to prepare for difficult winters by setting up fishing stations to provide enough cod and shellfish to sustain a colony until spring. Amid squabbles and litigation, stockholders of the Virginia Company of Plymouth dissolved the venture in 1609. The failure of the intended cod and spice trade also caused the English to reassess their hopes of immediate wealth from New England.

See also: Dried Food; Shellfish.

Further Reading

Boyer, Paul S., Clifford E. Clark, Jr., and Sandra McNair Hawley. *The Enduring Vision: A History of the American People.* Boston: Wadsworth/Cengage Learning, 2010.

Pflederer, Richard L. "Before New England: The Popham Colony," *History Today* 55:11 (January 2005): 10–18.

Rice, Douglas Walthew. *The Life and Achievements of Sir John Popham: 1531–1607: Leading to the Establishment of the First English Colony in New England.* Madison, NJ: Fairleigh Dickinson University Press, 2005.

Voegtlin, Walter L. (1904–1975)

In 1975, Seattle gastroenterologist Walter Lyle Voegtlin proposed that people revert to the protein-heavy diet of Paleolithic humans, who lived from about 2,000,000 to 8,000 B.C.E. Voegtlin served in the Department of Physiology and Pharmacology at Northwestern University in Evanston, Illinois, and taught biophysics and physiology at the University of Washington. In addition to publishing articles on gall bladder complaints, in the late 1940s, he created a treatment for chronic alcoholism involving an aversion response to vomiting. From his observation at the Shadel Sanitarium in Seattle, Washington, of alimentary canal ailments—colitis, Crohn's disease, indigestion, and irritable bowel syndrome—he deduced that humankind could improve digestion and lengthen life by adopting the Paleo diet, the ancestral food of carnivores.

Only months before his death at age 71, Voegtlin shared his theories of food and health in *The Stone Age Diet: Based on In-Depth Studies of Human Ecology and the Diet of Man* (1975), a work he paid to publish at Vantage Press. Along with meticulous comparisons of the human digestive tract to that of dogs and sheep, he detailed the effects of eating on human functions. In chapter one, he complained about the diet of "citified" humans: "Our foods are chemically preserved, sweetened, colored, and flavored; they are canned, dehydrated, frozen, pasteurized, Fletcherized, fortified, ground, juiced, instantized, Osterized, precooked, prepackaged, puréed, pickled, salted, strained, and swallowed whole." In addition to battling low digestibility of food, he shocked readers by claiming the legitimacy of eugenics, the controlled breeding of superior examples of the human species and the extermination of the defective and weak.

Voegtlin made specific lists of beneficial foods. In place of beans, bread, dairy products, pasta, rice, and sugar, he promoted fish and grass-fed meats, grubs and reptiles, nuts and berries, sprouts and roots, mushrooms, and fruits and vegetables. Among the foods from the Stone Age, he recognized the particular value of acorns and almonds, amaranth and sunflower seeds, pecans, pine nuts, and prickly pear fruit. He insisted that, by adopting the foodways of hunter-gatherers, his patients could rid themselves of the modern curses of alcoholism, allergy, autoimmune disease, cancer, depression, diabetes, heart disease, obesity, osteoporosis, sprue (celiac disease), and stroke.

Voegtlin equated postindustrial malaise with the products of wealth and ease—sedentary lifestyle, overeating, indulgence in alcohol and smoking, and reliance on salty and sweet processed snacks. He concluded that diseases of civilization flourish where the diet focuses on refined flour and sugar, corn and potatoes, cheese, and ice cream. In their place, he promoted meals of cress and other greens, eggs, fruit, game, herbs, mushrooms, nuts, seafood, spices, and vegetables, the foods available to hunter-gatherers.

Debate arose in the late 1980s among anthropologists and nutritionists who challenged Voegtlin's summation of the strengths of a high-fiber Stone Age diet. At issue was the omission of brown rice, peanuts, potatoes, skim milk, vegetable oils, and whole-grain bread and pasta. Less dogmatic dieticians declared that stringent exclusion of carbohydrates and milk, two core foods, startled the body and generated cravings.

Voegtlin's theory, which he based on the elements of evolution, rested on clinical evidence from research into anatomical changes over time. After the rise of agriculture in 8000 B.C.E. and the addition of cereals to cuisine, humans declined in body mass and well-being. Anthropologists have noted a decrease in human height and the size of the bite as well as a spurt in dental decay.

By studying pockets of Stone Age tribalism in the Alaskan Nunamiut, the Gwi of Botswana, and Austronesians of the Trobriand Islands, researchers refuted Voegtlin's diet and charged that the modern lifestyle defeats health by creating an imbalance between stored calories and burned energy. Additional questions from experts about overpopulation, socially disruptive farming, and restrictive diet implied that Voegtlin's proposed food intake oversimplified the root causes of modern ills.

Despite its rigid notions of edible food and the value of human life, the Paleo diet gained followers. Loren Cordain, a specialist in health and exercise at Colorado State University, popularized Voegtlin's regimen in *The Paleo Diet: Lose Weight and Get Healthy by Eating the Food You Were Designed to Eat* (2002). After reading about the diet in 1990 and practicing its food constraints, Cordain reported improvements in acne, arthritis, and breathing problems and gains in muscle mass. In *Primal Body, Primal Mind* (2009), nutritionist Nora T. Gedgaudas related the caveman diet to hormonal balance and the slowing of cellular aging.

See also: Allergies, Food; Ice Cream; Paleolithic Diet.

Further Reading

Audette, Ray, and Troy Gilchrist. *Neanderthin: Eat Like a Caveman to Achieve a Lean, Strong, Healthy Body.* New York: Macmillan, 2000.

Cordain, Loren. *The Paleo Diet.* Hoboken, NJ: John Wiley & Sons, 2011.

Keith, Lierre. *The Vegetarian Myth: Food, Justice and Sustainability.* Crescent City, CA: Flashpoint, 2009.

McClatchy, Anna Tong. "Back to the Cave: No Processed Foods Are Allowed in Neanderthal Paleo Diet." *Hamilton* (Ontario) *Spectator,* August 29, 2010.

Water

Covering some 70.1 percent of the global surface, water sustains humankind and its food sources. From prehistory, people have sheltered near abundant fresh water—the Mesopotamians between the Tigris and Euphrates rivers, Chinese along the Yalu, and Amerindians on the Amazon and Mississippi. Irrigation ditches spread water from creeks and precipitation across fields, sometimes directing 90 percent of potable sources to sustain crops, orchards, and livestock. In addition to rehydrating the body with about 2.5 quarts (2.4 liters) per day, water supplies to kitchens serve as solvents for making beverages, soaking husks from and steaming grains, and stewing fruit, meat, and vegetables into palatable cooked dishes.

Water permeates scripture with alerts to impurity. In India, the Vedas, Sanskrit scriptures begun in 1500 B.C.E., instructed the devout to choose cooking and drinking water only from rainwater, springs, streams, and wells. The Sutras (800–350 B.C.E.) advised Hindus to filter drinking supplies. Jainism reverenced water as a symbol of life; priests advocated a stringent regimen of boiling and straining water every eight hours before using it for cooking or for relieving thirst during fasts. Buddhists consumed only rainwater and grew lotus in their cisterns so that the roots and leaves would purify and the flowers perfume the contents.

Armies depended on large quantities of water to replenish marching men and dray animals. In 342 B.C.E., Alexander the Great learned from Aristotle, his teacher, to keep the Macedonian military hydrated and healthy by purifying field water supplies. The heating, evaporating, and cooling regimen anticipated distillation, a scientific method of ridding water of pathogens that can cause cholera, cryptosporidiosis, *Escherichia coli* (*E. coli*), gastroenteritis, giardiasis, and typhoid fever. Around 370 C.E., Hypatia of Alexandria, a Greek mathematician and inventor, devised a distillery to ensure an uncontaminated supply of water.

After the fall of Rome in the sixth century C.E., hydrology declined from municipal control to guesswork. Medieval cooks chose between boiled or well water and supplies from questionable sources, usually buckets of lake, moat, or pond water. Monastery recipes composed by apothecaries often specified fountain or spring water as a guarantee of potability.

Some believers connected water with holiness and salvation. Muslim pilgrim Ibn Battuta, author of the travel memoir *On Curiosities of Cities and Wonders of Travel* (1354), described the significance of water to his once-in-a-lifetime hajj (pilgrimage) to the Arabian holy site of Mecca. Among other hajjis entering the great city, he prayed at the curtains of the Kaaba, the holy of holies, and drank at the well of Zamzam. Sacred water, he declared, quenched thirst and cured illness. He concluded with high praise to Allah, who blessed those visiting his shrine with unlimited sips from a holy thirst quencher.

For 20 percent of the world's people in the twenty-first century, water engineering provides businesses and habitations with the piping, filtration and purification equipment, and storage tanks for convenience and sanitation. Developing nations rely on less sophisticated means of securing supplies from aquifers, lakes and canals, and aqueducts and reservoirs. The least convenient, village standpipes and wells, require hand-carrying of buckets and jerry cans.

The dispensing of water through kitchen spigots became safer and easier to control from the invention of the single-handle union tap, the design of plumbing fixture pioneer Alfred M. Moen of Seattle, Washington. After burning his hands in water from a two-handled faucet while studying mechanical engineering at the University of Washington, he decided to improve on standard plumbing fixtures. In the 1940s, he created the one-control mixer, an ingenious simplifier and reducer of kitchen clutter.

Out of range of kitchen taps, bottled water offers immediate access to supplies, whether in jugs in electric coolers or in glass or plastic bottles carried to campsites and on tour buses. One liability of faddish water bottles is packaging in polyethylene terephthalate, which litters parks and highways and clutters local recyclers and landfills. However, the distribution of packaged water at disaster sites—earthquakes, fires, floods, wars—inhibits unsanitary conditions from spreading contagion. According to industry estimates, the global consumption of bottled water more than doubled between the years 2000 (over 100 billion liters, or 26.4 billion gallons) and 2010 (over 200 billion liters, or 52.8 billion gallons). Soda and sparkling water bottlers—Coca-Cola, PepsiCo, Perrier—also offer beverages fortified with caffeine, fruit flavors, vitamins, and minerals.

As nations face issues of variability in water supplies, scientists predict that threats to urban hydration will precipitate sectional conflicts and wars. The countries most at risk dot the African continent—Kenya, Mozambique, Sudan, and Uganda. An alarming shift in control in Australia and New Zealand allowed the privatization of water. To restore supplies to the public trust, the United Nations General Assembly in July 2010 declared sanitation and water justice as human rights. Proposals for alleviating human suffering from catastrophes and droughts and resultant epidemics and famine include abandoning field agriculture in favor of hydroponics, building desalination plants, investing in solar disinfection of water supplies, and even transporting icebergs to arid locales.

See also: Agroecology; Aquaponics; Desalination; Irrigation; Nutrition; Rice; Sanitation.

Further Reading

De Villiers, Marq. *Water: The Fate of Our Most Precious Resource.* Boston: Houghton Mifflin, 2001.

Shiva, Vandana. *Water Wars: Privatization, Pollution and Profit.* Cambridge, MA: South End, 2002.

Solomon, Steven. *Water: The Epic Struggle for Wealth, Power, and Civilization.* New York: Harper Perennial, 2011.

Whaling

Since 6000 B.C.E., whaling in all the world's oceans has accessed meat and oil from cetaceans, the earth's largest mammals. Whales and sea animals form the basis of foodways among the Aleut and Inuit of Alaska, the Pacific Northwest, and Greenland. From prehistory, natives subsisted on hunting coastal whales and harvesting meat from stranded belugas, narwhals, porpoises, and three-ton pilot whales driven ashore by fishermen in small boats. Off Vancouver Island, the Kwakiutl pursued the 6-ton (5.4-metric-ton) orca. In contrast, in the Bering Sea, Eskimos tracked the 60-ton (54-metric-ton) bowhead in kayaks and umiaks made of walrus hide. The slayer of so vast a meat supply earned the prestige of a chief.

From the Middle Ages, whaling in the North Atlantic off the coasts of Denmark, the Hebrides, Iceland, Orkney, and the Shetlands has supplied communities with meat. Between Iceland and Scotland in 1000 B.C.E., Faeroe Islanders made dolphins, porpoises, and long-finned pilot whales a staple of their cuisine. Villagers carved carcasses on the beach and along fjords into blubber for boiling and steaks for salting, air-drying, and serving with dried fish.

By 800 C.E., the Japanese began regular whale hunts for meat, which they valued as a luxury food. Pacifist Buddhists advocated whale consumption over shrimp because one animal's death could feed many. Priests promoted the distribution of tougher cuts to the poor. In the 1570s, the Japanese organized in-shore hunts by raising watchtowers and dispatching harpooners and netters to slay the 35-ton (32-metric-ton) gray, 30-ton (27-metric-ton) humpback, 9-ton (8.2-metric-ton) minke, and 100-ton (90-metric-ton) right whale.

Cash Business

Flensers stripped flesh from bone, separated fat from meat, and transported perishables to meat-processing warehouses. Cookbooks listed 70 cuts for kitchen use. At the end of the nineteenth century, Juro Oka, the father of modern Japanese whaling, introduced Norwegian stalking methods and technology from Finnmark County to Nihon Enyo Giyogo, his Nagasaki whaling firm. The successful venture made Japan the only nation to hunt whales primarily for human consumption rather than for cometic oils and pet food.

Simultaneous with Asian whaling industrialization, eleventh-century Basque fishermen from Bayonne, France, established a whaling consortium off Red Bay, Labrador, and St. Anthony, Newfoundland. After killing a right whale, they hoisted cauldrons on board their ships to cook blubber down to oil, a forerunner of the cod liver oil business. In the Arctic Sea and along the New England shore, Dutch and Newfoundland hunters focused on the bowhead; Icelanders preferred the larger right whale. In 1803, the capture of Boston armorer John Rodgers Jewitt by Nootka off Woody Point, British Columbia, introduced him to the diet of Northwest Indians. In addition to clams and herring, they ate gray whale blubber and oil, which they stirred into servings of wild strawberries.

The market for margarine and inexpensive canned meat and meat cakes in the 1880s increased the strain on the baleen whale population—bowhead, gray, and right whales—until cotton and vegetable oils replaced animal sources. Oslo processors led commercialization by advertising whale meat as tasty as beef at one-third the price. World War I reduced supplies of beef, mutton, and pork and caused U.S. government leaders to advocate replacing familiar protein sources with whale meat.

By 1917, San Francisco restaurants ordered canned whale meat in 100-pound (45-kilogram) boxes. In Victoria, British Columbia, clerks advertised "sea beef" for use in meat rolls, shepherd's pie, steaks, and stew. New York restaurateurs proclaimed whale meat as the nouvelle cuisine favorite for hors d'oeuvres, *pot-au-feu* (stew), and plank steaks cooked on a hickory or oak plank. In 1918, department stores in Toronto and Winnipeg advertised canned whale meat as a Christmas specialty.

Marketing

To meet demand around Gibraltar, whalers opened a winter operation in 1921 on Iberia but failed to profit from canned or smoked whale meat, which they sold in the Congo. German whalers increased merchandising in

Japanese fishermen slaughter a Baird's beaked whale at one of the few ports at which whaling is allowed for "research" purposes. The Japanese have actively resisted an international moratorium on commercial whaling that went into effect in 1986. *(Koichi Kamoshida/Getty Images)*

the mid-1930s with the processing of blubber fiber, liver meal, and meat extract for kitchen use and other parts for feeding household pets and mink raised on ranches. In anticipation of another global conflict, both England and Germany processed whale blubber into margarine and stockpiled edible fats. To make meat more flavorful, processors soaked cubed blubber in soda ash solutions.

Because whale meat tastes more like venison than fish, it pleased Asian diners but not many Americans or Canadians. After the devastation of World War II, the Japanese refused to kill dolphins but depended on whale meat for half of their protein and much of school lunch diets. On May 19, 1946, nine months after the country's surrender to the United States, one-quarter-million Japanese launched a Food May Day before the Imperial Palace. Because of food scarcity, they demanded that General Douglas MacArthur, head of Allied occupation forces, rescind antiwhaling restrictions. In August, he authorized a deep-sea whaling hunt to Antarctica. The relaxation of sea hunting laws, for the first time, made whale consumption a daily part of Japan's cuisine. The stalking of the 180-ton

(165-metric ton) blue whale and other baleen whales along migration routes from the Antarctic increased kills to a height of 220,000 tons (200,000 metric tons) of marketable meat in 1962.

Monitoring Slaughter

At Bournemouth, England, in 1986, international restrictions on overhunting by the International Whaling Commission placed a moratorium on annual catches that exceeded the species' ability to reproduce. Laws destabilized the traditions of coastal peoples—Ainu, Aleut, Chukchi, Haida, Inuit, Klallam, Kwakiutl, Makah, Nootka—further suppressing their aboriginal rights to subsistence hunting. Protests emerged from Iceland, South Korea, and the Soviet Union.

In the 1990s, Norwegians in Reine contested U.S., British, and German controls on hunting minke whales, which flourished in larger numbers than the endangered blue whale. The Japanese fishing industry fought the ban by advertising the low-fat, high-omega-3 food value of minke meat as an ideal seafood for schoolchildren.

Preservation of the practice of catch sharing bolstered a distribution system that had ensured community solidarity since feudal times.

Currently, meat markets in the Arctic, Iceland, Japan, and Norway stock whale meat. Unlike the meat cutters of the early 1800s, who divided the kill into 70 different cuts, today's preparers offer mainly belly and fluke cuts. Eskimos prefer fluke fat, a prime cut they award to the successful whaling captain. When offered in food stores, fluke meat costs three times the price of belly cuts. On a beach haul of a bowhead kill at Barrow or Kaktovik, Alaska, Eskimo families gather *muktuk* (skin) to heat on a pot for all viewers to taste, a communal ritual dating to prehistory.

Worldwide, menus featuring whale meat offer bacon and jerky, other cured or marinated meat, grilled blubber, *udemono* (boiled organs), and cartilage salad. The Japanese choose whale meat for New Year's feasts and for honoring ancestors at the Shinto home altar during the August All Souls' Festival. In Osaka, *nabe* (skin stew) is a specialty served with mizuna (peppergrass). Sashimi (sliced raw whale meat) refers to marbled dorsal fin, flipper, jaw, or red (muscle) meat.

In schools in Kyoto, Nara, Osaka, and Tokyo, beginning in 2006, lunch programs doubled the stocking of whale meat in school meat lockers. A countermove by environmentalists the following year declared sperm whale meat too polluted with dioxin and heavy metals for frequent consumption. Whaling in Iceland virtually collapsed. In 2008, Faeroe Islands medical authorities altered the national diet by declaring the pilot whale too toxic from dichlorodiphenyltrichloroethane (DDT), mercury, and polychlorinated biphenyls (PCBs), which accumulate in whale blubber.

See also: Arctic Diet and Cuisine; Endangered Species; Japanese Diet and Cuisine; Trading Vessels.

Further Reading

Bortolotti, Dan. *Wild Blue: A Natural History of the World's Largest Animal.* New York: Thomas Dunne, 2008.

Dolin, Eric Jay. *Leviathan: The History of Whaling in America.* New York: W.W. Norton, 2008.

Kalland, Arne. *Unveiling the Whale: Discourses on Whales and Whaling.* New York: Berghahn, 2009.

Morikawa, Jun. *Whaling in Japan: Power, Politics and Diplomacy.* New York: Columbia University Press, 2009.

Wheat

Domesticated wheat, one of the eight founder crops of paleoagriculture, introduced a basis for world cuisine and a major source of vegetable protein from the Fertile Crescent to most points of the globe. The earliest wheat preparation occurred at a grinding stone at an archaeological dig in the Rift Valley of Israel around 17,000 B.C.E. During the Neolithic revolution around 12,000 B.C.E., acorn consumption declined. In its place, self-pollinating wheat proved easy to grow, gather, and store. In contrast to acorns, threshed grain provided digestible, easily chewed grains for roasting. Pouches of charred or roasted wheat bore a fragrant, savory, and stable travel food easily packed and consumable without further cooking.

After the settlement of Abu Hureyra in western Mesopotamia (Syria) around 11,050 B.C.E., a dry millennium forced inhabitants to cultivate grain fields and to select natural free-threshing hybrids with the largest grains. As the population density increased from 1 to 15 persons per square mile (less than 1 to about 9 persons per square kilometer), protofarmers domesticated einkorn and emmer wheat along with barley, bitter vetch, chickpeas, flax, lentils, and peas. From the Karacadag Mountains south and east, Syrians made grain their primary foodstuff. Benefits of wheat growing included forage for domesticated herds and thatch for roofing shelters.

In Mycenae, Sumer, and Troy from about 10,500 B.C.E., wheat processing contributed to the replacement of flatbread in urban baking styles. Sumerians made the first sourdough to form light risen loaves. Cultivation in Jordan and Turkey spread across the Balkans to Serbia, the Danube River delta, the mouth of the Rhine; as far west as northern Italy and Valencia, Spain; and north to Denmark and Britain. From the Mediterranean shores to the northern coniferous forests, single-grain einkorn wheat (*Triticum monococcum*) flourished as one of the first domesticated crops cultivated in the Neolithic period. Dating to 9800 B.C.E., emmer (*Triticum dicoccum*), which grew wild in Israel and on the West Bank of the Jordan River valley, provided the most nutritious and palatable grain and the easiest to harvest in prehistory.

According to ethnobotanical studies, at 80 percent of excavated sites, wheat fed the Assyrians, Babylonians, and Egyptians. Professional bakers in the Nile River delta developed wheat loaves into the first commercial food enterprise. Spreading to Cyprus, Germany, Iberia, India, and Scandinavia, wheat served brewers as a basis for beer and cooks as a source of high-fiber bread and a thickener for soup. Its chewy texture and nutty flavor satisfied hunger and introduced dietary fiber while supplying calcium, iron, magnesium, protein, and vitamins A and C. Because of its improvement to the human diet, grain cultivation on settled farmland rapidly replaced rigorous and risky hunter-and-gatherer nomadism.

Developments in Consumption

By 7000 B.C.E., natural selection in central Europe resulted in durum wheat (*Triticum durum*), a free-threshing grain that yielded 15 percent protein, as contrasted with soft wheat, which contained 10 percent protein. Durum, the second-most-common commercial wheat, became the source of Iberian noodles, Italian macaroni and pizza,

North African couscous, Syrian pilaf, and Turkish bulgur, a high-fiber, low-glycemic (sugar-producing) grain. Cooks in Armenia, Bulgaria, Greece, and Iran also favored durum flour for stuffings and tabbouleh.

The invention of the horse collar in 3000 B.C.E. simplified the job of plowing by not pressing on the draft animal's throat. The gentler harness increased the acreage that one wheat farmer could cover. By 2000 B.C.E., wheat production advanced beyond the Caspian Sea as the Chinese adapted traditional cuisine to include wheat. Chinese, Japanese, and Vietnamese Buddhists welcomed steamed wheat gluten as a staple of vegetarian dishes.

A standard rural meal among pastoral Europeans involved the boiling of flour at the hearth with salt or *siraion* (wine must) and either milk or water to produce sweetened porridge. According to Hippocrates's *Regimen II* (ca. 400 B.C.E.), Greek cooks traditionally baked wheat into unleavened cakes. More elaborate recipes for *diepnon* (the main or evening meal) called for frying wheat batter into drop biscuits or pancakes, baking in crockery or under layers of ash, or stirring in an urn into sweetened *maza* (porridge), the main Greek dish. More sophisticated cuisine replaced traditional cookery after 300 B.C.E., when Greek kitchen styles influenced Roman cooks.

Because Rome grew into an urban metropolis, citizens formed 75 percent of the daily diet around wheat gruel. The devout revered wheat for funeral meals and grave gifts. Consumers, who grew no crops, depended on Egypt, the ancient world's major grain seller, to stave off food shortages. In 230 B.C.E., because of the burgeoning population of the Roman Republic and its reliance on wheat imports, Consul Gnaeus Fulvius suppressed Illyrian pirates, who had been commandeering grain convoys from Egypt, North Africa, and Sicily. Within two years, Fulvius ensured wheat imports by quelling piracy around the Black Sea and along the Red Sea. Unhampered imports restored wheat to Roman military provisions and rid the citizenry of cyclical grain shortages.

To feed the plebeian class, Augustus, Rome's first emperor, instituted the *annona* (poverty relief), for which he annually imported 14 million bushels of wheat. More than four centuries later, the Gothic siege of Rome in September 408 C.E. drove the city into a food panic. The reduction of the daily wheat ration from one-half to one-third wrecked the Roman Empire. For the next four centuries, Rome's population shrank by 90 percent from hunger and disease.

Previous military occupation introduced parched wheat into the diet of Celtic Britain. In the 700s C.E., einkorn *hwaete* (wheat) became the main Anglo-Saxon cereal crop as well as a form of currency for requiting monetary court judgments. Unlike Arab and Indian reception of grains, Britain's agrarian traditions shifted slowly toward bread wheat, in part because of culinary habit and resistance to agrarian and nutritional imports from Asia.

After the Spanish colonization of Peru in the sixteenth century, Spanish settler María de Escobar, a benefactor of the Inca, introduced grain cultivation in the Andes Mountains. On the South American frontier at Cuzco in 1535, she sowed a half sack of grain she imported from Spain. In Cañete Valley southeast of Lima and south of Machu Picchu, she taught the Inca the value of barley and wheat. For three years, she distributed 20–30 seeds each to other colonists for introducing in Peru and Chile. At the Dominican church, established after Pizarro arrived in 1534, some wheat growers used the harvest as an altar offering, a parallel to the reverence of wheat in Egypt and Rome.

Agrarian Revolution

As new varieties of wheat evolved, farmers adopted easily milled hull-less grain and practiced crop rotation and fertilization, both boons to yield. In 1713, British agronomist Jethro Tull's invention of the seed drill and four-coultered disk plow augmented wheat growing at the harvest rate of eight times the number of sowed grains. The colonial age added new wheat farms in Argentina, Australia, and North America. The application of guano to fertilization in 1830 boosted nitrogen in depleted European soil.

During the Industrial Revolution, cooks popularized soft wheat, which gave bread and pastries more elasticity and a springier texture. The formulation of fertilizer in 1909 by Carl Bosch and Fritz Haber of BASF, a German chemical firm, replaced dwindling sources of imported guano for field revitalization. In the Great Plains of North America from 1901 to 1918, Mark Alfred Carleton, a botanist at Kansas State University and the U.S. Department of Agriculture, rejuvenated dryland agriculture by introducing American farmers to durum wheat, which eventually flourished in half of Kansas's wheat fields and in Montana and North Dakota. The collapse of Russian wheat farming at the end of World War I produced a doubling of wheat farming in Kansas to meet global demand. The invention of the tractor reduced acreage needed for draft animals, thus freeing 25 percent more land for wheat growing.

The International Maize and Wheat Improvement Center (CIMMYT), formed in Spain in 1943, developed more resilient strains of wheat for nourishment and commerce. While assisting Japan in rebuilding its economy in 1945, U.S. General Douglas MacArthur appointed wheat specialist Samuel Cecil Salmon to collect indigenous grains, including Norin 10, a large-eared, semidwarf wheat raised in Iwate, in northeastern Honshu. Orville A. Vogel, a wheat breeder in Washington State in 1949, crossed short-strawed grains that yielded 25 percent more output than conventional varieties. Because the 2-foot (60-centimeter) stalks survived high winds, the cultivar assisted global developers of sustainable farming. Ample wheat harvests engendered a protein-rich diet for the

Green Revolution in Afghanistan, Bangladesh, China, Colombia, Ethiopia, Georgia, India, Iran, Kazakhstan, Kenya, Nepal, Turkey, and Zimbabwe.

Into the late 1970s, agronomist Norman Borlaug's dissemination of higher-yielding short-strawed wheat crops advanced nutrition worldwide. He began with Mexico in the 1940s, boosting its wheat harvests six times its former yield. In March 1963, he spread hybrid seed to the Punjab, followed by the Philippines and Africa. On the basis of wheat production, India became self-sufficient in 1974, disproving dire predictions of mass starvation. The application of DNA suppression by ethyl methane sulphonate (a mutagen) and by thermal neutrons and X-ray in 1983 enabled botanists to genetically modify wheat seed predictably and enhance grain diversity. By 1984, world grain yields had increased by more than 250 percent, raising food security in India and Pakistan by staving off a likely famine and malnutrition. Responding to conservationists who complained about increased use of pesticides, Borlaug declared them elitists who had no experience with world hunger. He projected that food security from high-yield wheat would boost the populations of Burkina Faso, Mali, Niger, Somalia, Uganda, and Yemen, necessitating 35 percent more calories to feed the next generations.

Genetic modification of corn, rice, and soybeans began the eclipse of wheat as a global crop in 1998, when the Atkins, Dukan, and South Beach diets vilified carbohydrates from bread. By 2007, wheat ranked third after corn and rice as the world's most cultivated grain. British scientists furthered interest in wheat modification in 2010 by decoding the grain genome. As corn and rice prices rose, according to the International Grains Council, a major glut on the wheat market in Australia, Canada, India, Kazakhstan, Russia, Ukraine, and the United States in 2011 eased shortages and reduced prices.

See also: Einkorn Wheat; Emmer Wheat; Fertile Crescent Diet and Food Trade; Pasta; Pastry.

Further Reading

Bakels, C.C. *The Western European Loess Belt: Agrarian History, 5300 B.C.–A.D. 1000.* New York: Springer, 2009.

Gressel, Jonathan, ed. *Crop Ferality and Volunteerism.* New York: Taylor & Francis, 2005.

Nevo, Eviatarl, Abraham B. Korol, Avigdor Beiles, and Tzion Fahima. *Evolution of Wild Emmer and Wheat Improvement.* New York: Springer, 2002.

Prance, Ghillean T., and Mark Nesbitt. *The Cultural History of Plants.* New York: Taylor & Francis, 2005.

Whiskey

For more than a millennium, aged whiskey, a satisfying fermented intoxicant of barley, corn, rye, and wheat, has added sparkle to entertainment and friskiness to social interaction. Distilling in Gaelic and Highland monasteries began before 1000 C.E. with barley beer, a compromise in the British Isles, a region that could not sustain grape growing for wine. Physicians prescribed whiskey for sufferers of bowel complaint, infection, smallpox, surgical pain, and tremors. Farmers and herders flaunted whiskey as a source of cash and recycled grain mash for livestock feed and as a class symbol of defiance of intrusive English nobility.

Monks and pharmacists became the original potion distributors. Peace officers attempted to enforce spirit licensing after 1367, but the Irish scoffed at Edward III and the Statutes of Kilkenney. The lower class chose distilling as a source of income over lace and woolen manufacture. The insolent openly danced jigs and sipped whiskey smuggled by underground distributors and dealers. First referred to by the Latin *aqua vitae* (water of life), whiskey in the anonymous Irish *Annals of Clonmacnoise* (1408) reputedly killed a chief, Richard Magranell of Leitrim, who overindulged on Christmas 1405. The chronicler made a macabre jest of *aqua mortis* (water of death).

The Scots Exchequer Rolls of 1494 identifies Brother John Cor as a Benedictine maltmaster at Lindores Abbey near Fife, the legendary birthplace of Scotch whiskey. Under royal contract from James IV of Scotland, Cor distilled 1,500 bottles of malt whiskey on June 1, 1495. The king, an imbiber of Highland, Islay, and Lowland stock, drew on bottled beverages controlled by the Guild of Surgeon Barbers in Edinburgh, the sole licensee to make whiskey. His subjects continued to flout the guild monopoly and trade laws and imbibed bootleg whiskey, the country's most popular drink.

An illustrated distilling manual, *Liber de Arte Distillandi* (*Book on the Art of Distilling,* 1500) by Hieronymus Brunschwig, a military surgeon from Strasbourg, France, established the methods by which fermentation turns grain into alcohol, a valuable drug therapy. After Henry VIII seized monastic properties in 1536 and forced monks to take lay jobs, they set up distilleries as cottage industries that marketed smooth aged whiskey.

On March 8, 1608, James I of England charged Bishop Andrew Knox of Argyll and the Isles of Scotland with improving Irish behavior. Knox declared that the chiefs' barbarity and feuding was an outcome of their love of "aquavite." To curb spirited Gaels, Knox's Statutes of Iona banned the importation of spirits for peasants but issued monopolies allowing landowners and the rich to make and drink Irish whiskey. The first licensee, Charles Waterhouse of Munster, received Ireland's first seven-year whiskey patent for operations in County Antrim in northern Ireland. Waterhouse's sublicensee, Thomas Phillipps of Ulster, owner of Old Bushmills, distilled yeast-fermented oat mash into Irish *usquabach* (whiskey).

Following the Act of Union with England in 1707, Scotland set the example of a whiskey culture that refused taming by British excisemen and antismuggling raids. A Hogmanay (New Year's Eve) bash involved service of St. Andrews cakes and Scotch whiskey. On Burns's Night each January 25 since 1801, Scots have celebrated the birthday of plowman-poet Robert Burns with clapshot (mashed potatoes and turnips), haggis (stuffed sheep stomach), and traditional whiskey. Peat-smoking of raw barley for 30 hours combined the dehydration of moist grain with the fumigation of insects and the extermination of microbes in pungent malt whiskeys, such as Douglas Laing from Glasgow, Longrow from Argyll, and Talisker from the Isle of Skye. In northern Scotland, highland dairiers made crowdie, an unaged cream cheese that Viking raiders had clotted from skim milk in the eighth century C.E. and sealed in black pepper and oatmeal. At wedding celebrations, soft crowdie coated the stomachs of whiskey drinkers to ward off nausea.

American Whiskey

In 1783, the *Parliamentary Register of Ireland* denounced pubs as a nuisance and blamed cheap drink with the ruination of the Irish. Meanwhile, immigrants were transporting usquabach, the key ingredient in Irish coffee, to North America. In a lush agricultural setting, newcomers produced a distinctive male tippling culture based on an Old World ethic.

Both the Dutch and English colonials cleared land for barley fields and sold their surplus to Irish distilleries, which turned field corn into grain alcohol and bourbon whiskey, a corn-based enterprise allegedly invented in 1783 by T.W. Samuels at Samuels Depot, Kentucky, the home of Maker's Mark. The establishment of Hudson's Bay Company trading posts among the Great Lakes tribes and the Inuit expanded the natives' addiction to European brandy and whiskey. Traveler François de la Rochefoucauld predicted in *Travels Through the United States of North America* (1800) that intoxication would thin out indigenous peoples until none survived.

Upon retirement from the military to Mount Vernon in 1785, George Washington operated five copper stills to distill 11,000 gallons (41,600 liters) of barley, corn, and rye whiskey per year, a kitchen business that provided most of his income. Bottled stock had numerous applications as curatives and flavorings. For curing meat, whether applied at low or high temperatures in the closed quarters of a metal chamber smoker or a walk-in smokehouse, whiskey-soaked hardwood chips imparted unique savors. Because Scots-Irish smallholders in western Pennsylvania rejected a federal excise tax levied in 1794, backwoods distillers raised a no-tax banner, the prelude to the Whiskey Rebellion on July 16. Three months later, President Washington suppressed the revolt by dispatching militia from Maryland, New Jersey, Pennsylvania, and Virginia.

In 1823, the first sour mash whiskey introduced controlled acidity during fermentation. Throughout the American Southwest, pioneers relied on whiskey to ease suffering from labor pains and wounds. Coexisting with Western medical practice, Chinese acupuncturists and herbalists treated the Asian population with opium in a whiskey solution to combat dysentery and influenza.

Spirits figured in a number of historic scenarios. When slave owners wanted to encourage harder work during planting and harvest, they doled out rum and whiskey from the big house to field hands. Sea-to-sea freighters to the California goldfields during the 1849 gold rush transported food staples, laudanum, and whiskey via steamer around Argentina, a treacherous dividing point between Atlantic and Pacific. Before breakfast and after dinner, ships' stewards on naval warships measured 4 ounces (118 milliliters) of grog or, during combat, of whiskey. On September 1, 1862, U.S. congressional action ended the sailor's grog ration.

The mid-1860s yielded acknowledgement of whiskey's significance to American society. Recipes for the absinthe cocktail, flaming Blue Blazer, Manhattan, Old Fashioned, Tom and Jerry, whiskey skin, whiskey punch, and whiskey sour appeared in the nation's first drink manual, Jeremiah P. "Jerry" Thomas's *The Bar-Tender's Guide* (1862). Mary Ann Bickerdyke, chief nurse and dietician under General Ulysses S. Grant, turned medicinal whiskey into a combat restorative. On April 7, 1862, she assuaged survivors of the Battle of Shiloh with dollops of whiskey in coffee or tea, a stimulant similar in purpose to wine distributions by nursing brotherhoods during the Crusades. In 1865, Congress repealed other temporary levies but retained the alcohol tax, which helped finance war debts.

On the frontier, whiskey came cheap at 12.5 cents a shot. Saloons became popular places to drink, play cards, smoke, and order from menus that offered whiskey-soaked pot roast and steak. Jack Daniel's Tennessee Whiskey, a sour mash drink first marketed from Lynchburg, Tennessee, in 1866, rounded out the fellowship. Maryland barbecuers sauced slow-roasted pork with fruit chutney blended with bourbon whiskey and onions. New Orleans restaurants topped meat entrées with whiskey sauce. For Southern ambrosia, a Christmas specialty, cooks layered shredded coconut with orange slices, sprinkled on confectioner's sugar, and topped the mix with Southern Comfort, a sweet whiskey liqueur introduced in New Orleans in 1874.

In the 1880s, a plague of the American vine louse (*Phylloxera vastatrix*) that blighted British and French vineyards ruined the wine market, leaving the French to the mercy of dealers in *liqueur spiritueuse*. With fine brandies gone from competition, makers of blended and sour mash whiskeys commanded the market in the United States, while distillers of light, smooth rye whiskey in Canada seized a large share of international commerce. Contributing to British profits in Bristol and Liverpool, in 1880, Parliament repealed the tax on malt, sprouted barley, or other cereal grains that yielded enzymes to turn starch into sugar.

Prohibition and Beyond

On October 28, 1919, when the U.S. Congress passed the National Prohibition (or Volstead) Act, federal agents intervened in the manufacture, transport, and sale of any beverage containing more than 0.5 percent alcohol. Appalachian rebels fought regulation by moonshining, a covert distillation by night initiated in 1725 by Scots avoiding the English malt tax. Speakeasies survived on cases of Canadian and Mexican booze shipped on rumrunners, fast cutters that showed no running lights as they breached borders.

With shot glasses and cigarettes, women adopted coarse male exhibitionism at the bar as a declaration of gender independence. Country-western singer Tex Ritter popularized "Rye Whiskey," a 1933 plaint acknowledging the addictive power of alcohol. Although wine, brandy, and moonshine headed the list of private U.S. stock and home curatives, "dry" pressure groups such as the Woman's Christian Temperance Union (WCTU) cheered the defeat of "demon rum" and attendant corruption from brothels and gambling.

When Prohibition failed in 1933, spirits returned to respectability for dining, entertainment, and sports events. Bars profited from drinks by the shot, a trend that burgeoned after World War II. Gay bars later helped boost the gay, lesbian, and transgender population to public attention and to break down prejudices against uncloseted homosexuals.

See also: Alcoholic Beverages; Curative Foods; Prohibition; Smoked Food; Temperance.

Further Reading

Black, Rachel, ed. *Alcohol in Popular Culture: An Encyclopedia.* Santa Barbara, CA: Greenwood, 2010.

Gately, Iain. *Drink: A Cultural History of Alcohol.* New York: Gotham, 2008.

Hopkins, Kate. *99 Drams of Whiskey: The Accidental Hedonist's Quest for the Perfect Shot and the History of the Drink.* New York: St. Martin's, 2010.

Kosar, Kevin R. *Whiskey: A Global History.* London: Reaktion, 2010.

MacLean, Charles. *Whiskey.* New York: Dorling Kindersley, 2008.

Wild Food

Wild birds, fish, mammals, and plants provide a full range of edibles that grow at the whim of nature. Studies of the Paleolithic era as early as 98,000 B.C.E. authenticate the use of preagricultural foods for rural sustenance—bird eggs, bugleweed, fiddlehead ferns, grubs and earthworms, maple sap, minnows and river mussels, snails, snakes, sphagnum moss, and thistles.

In the Iron Age, Celtic hunter-gatherers from the British Isles to Eastern Europe depended year-round on seaweed and heather tea. They cooked currants into pudding and rowan berries into soup and baked medlars in season. For winter, they stored beechnuts and hazelnuts, flax, and dried bilberries, dewberries, and hawthorn and juniper fruits in sealed containers and preserved taproots of horseradish, salsify, and wild carrots in peat and sand. Herbs suspended in warm, airy environments remained flavorful for adding to crab apple vinegar and sloe and wild plum wine.

North America

Nineteenth-century westering in North America offered European newcomers alternatives in bird and mammal entrées, especially wild turkeys and buffalo, and in bulbs, herbs, nuts, and wild fruits and vegetables, including blueberries, camassia tubers, cattails, elderflowers, muscadines, nettles, pecans, and prickly pear fruit. In pioneer days in Indiana, frontier families improvised new recipes and reformulated old ones by incorporating into their diet birch catkins, miner's lettuce, mustard greens, and wild persimmons, plums, and strawberries. Cooks ate watercress and violet salads and baked with amaranth and bullrush flour. In a pinch, they drank chicory when coffee ran out and added birch sap or meadowsweet buds to tea as a sugar substitute. Healers acquired respect for indigenous cures, such as cranberry juice to stem bladder infection, blackberries for kidney disease, mullein tea and sarsaparilla to relieve coughing, and wild blueberries for diarrhea, eye problems, poor circulation in the extremities, and chest pain.

In the twentieth century, food writers enlarged public awareness of the free harvest in the wild. In the 1960s and 1970s, outdoorsman Euell Gibbons's *Stalking the Wild Asparagus* (1962) and naturalist Richard Mabey's *Food for Free* (1972) encouraged gatherers to examine Stone Age and Amerindian diets for clues to wellness from wild edibles. In the United Kingdom, the availability of wild rose hips offered a free source of pulp rich in vitamin C. Northern Pacific cuisine featured in Margaret Craven's young-adult novel *I Heard the Owl Call My Name* (1967) introduced outsiders to *gluckaston,* a Kwakiutl seaweed stew cooked with corn.

Multiple-Source Diet

Worldwide, people strategize their livelihood from a combination of sources—herding, raising crops, hunting bushmeat, and combing fields and shores for available produce. Gendered food chores often relegated fishing and hunting to adult males, while women and children gathered bird eggs, mollusks, seeds, and fruit. The sources met at the dinner table, where wild grapes and piñon nuts flavored venison or salmon and wild oats and yams thickened pones. In India, foraging sustained a starving populace during the food shortages of 1965 and 1987.

Throughout the famine of 1984 in Darfur, Sudan, an area suffering chronic ecological decline, the Sudanese depended on patches of wild food to flavor the small amount of millet and sorghum they could afford to buy at the market. Without the watermelon seeds and wild grasses and barley that made up 96 percent of their alternative diet, they risked starvation. Migration decreased chances of survival when refugees entered crowded camps among unfamiliar edible plants and sickened themselves on poisonous greens and berries. The most viable families relied on elders who had survived similar hunger crises in the 1940s.

Contemporary Foraging

Into current times, the persistence of wild plants during agroecological change returns degraded or war-torn areas to productivity. The canals of China that water overused rice fields sustain alga, locusts, fish, and frogs, all of which are edible. Eroded farmland in Kenya and Tanzania generates gullies in which wild legumes and gourd vines sprout. The clear-cutting of forests in Brazil and Zimbabwe increases opportunities for fungi and edible mosses to reproduce.

Parts of the world—central Australia, the Himalayas, Mesoamerica, Southeast Asia, and southern Africa and the Sahel—flourish with the flora and fauna that adapt to fallow swiddens and arid, jungly, and swampy settings. Botswana produces 100 animal species and 126 plants that nourish the Tswana, an agropastoral people. Between China and India, the Bhutanese supplement agrarian harvests with wild avocados, bamboo shoots, orchids, and taro; in northern Peru, the seminomadic Aguaruna subsist on wild birds, boar, monkeys, prawns, sago flour, and tender shoots. In Mali, the Gourma store millet to feed them during the dry season; foraged greens rate a double value as vegetables and tonics. During periods of food insecurity in Turkana, a region overlapping Ethiopia and Kenya, the Ngiboceros increase their foraging from 25 percent to 42 percent. They refer to their gatherings as famine food.

Hobby Foraging

Today, Western survivalists and backpackers cultivate a knowledge of edible flora and fauna from the wild. They favor the plants that have nourished indigenous peoples from prehistory, such as the wild rice that centered the Ojibwa diet and the restorative wild grapes, mesquite and tepary beans, and Indian tea (*Ephedra fasciculata*) of the Pueblo. For the hiker, cacti, honeysuckle flowers, spruce gum, and spearmint, wintergreen, and clover or gorse tea with wild honey quench thirst when potable water is scarce. One ubiquitous example, wild spinach, tops the list of nutritious leafy plants for its fiber, potassium, and vitamins A and C. A versatile vegetable, it produces leaves for salads and sandwiches, steamed greens, and toppings for pizza and tacos.

Uninformed foraging carries dangers, particularly the appeal of poisonous mushrooms and nightshade berries and the collecting of hallucinogenic datura seeds and peyote buttons or picking blackberries or other fruits from polluted slopes. Young hikers, such as Boy and Girl Scouts learning orienteering, need guidance in selecting icicles and pond ice for potable water and in rinsing chickweed, clams, and daylily bulbs of grit.

In animals and plants, the stage of growth may determine safe consumption. Adult hares harbor parasites. Plants such as milkweed pods and pokeweed shoots are edible in early spring but not after they reach full size. Raw dandelion greens reach a bitter stage that can irritate the bladder and intestines. Only certain parts of some plants are safe to eat and those may require special preparation. Elderberry leaves and stems contain cyanide; rhubarb stems can be eaten but not the leaves. Calcium oxalate makes the jack-in-the-pulpit toxic, though the root is edible if properly dried or cooked.

See also: Blueberries; Buffalo; Bushmeat; Cacti; Fish and Fishing; Paleolithic Diet; Seaweed; Shellfish.

Further Reading

Brill, Steve. *The Wild Vegetarian Cookbook.* Boston: Harvard Common, 2002.

Kallas, John. *Edible Wild Plants: Wild Foods from Dirt to Plate.* Layton, UT: Gibbs Smith, 2010.

Parrish, Christopher C., Nancy J. Turner, and Shirley M. Solberg, eds. *Resetting the Kitchen Table: Food Security, Culture, Health and Resilience in Coastal Communities.* New York: Nova Science, 2008.

Runyon, Linda. *The Essential Wild Food Survival Guide.* Shiloh, NJ: Wild Food, 2002.

Wine

A sine qua non of thirst quenching and social lubrication since the Neolithic era, wine has figured in farming, nutrition, healing, ritual, and commerce. Wine grapes (*Vitis vinifera sylvestris*) grew wild in the Caucasus Mountains near Shulaveri, Georgia, around 6000 B.C.E. Babylonians originated the fermentation of the juice of wild vine fruits through the action of natural yeast, which transformed sugar into alcohol. In the Zagros Mountains in 5400 B.C.E., Sumerian technologists at Godin Tepe and Hajji Firuz Tepe sank six large jars into mud brick floors. During the annual pressing and fermentation, workers added terebinth resins to grape juice as a preservative while the jars lay stoppered on their sides. By the 900s C.E., the wine of Shiraz, Persia, earned distinction as sherry, a prized wine of the Middle East.

In Armenia in 4100 B.C.E., vintners produced sacred red wine for rituals and for sale in Anatolia, Palestine, and Syria. Bottlers strained the latest vintage through metal sieves into goblets and passed them to wine tasters to sample. From this period of wine appreciation, Greeks allied bread and wine with heavenly blessings and spirituality. Athenians honored both foods through festivals, hymns, and sacred performances, the foundations of Western drama.

By 3000 B.C.E., China, Egypt, and Sumer operated profitable commercial plantations. Juice preservation involved methods of eliciting aroma, taste, and viscosity by encouraging formation of tartaric acid, which prevented spoilage and enhanced transportability. Nomadic oenophiles valued fermented juice as a way to preserve fruit for famines and hard winters. Derived from Eastern grape preservation, the Mediterranean triad—grain, grapes, and olives—got its start with the fermentation of overripe grapes or raisins. To lengthen the shelf life of grape drinks, vintners introduced retsina, a resinated drink that Greek travelers introduced in the Crimea, Cyprus, Dalmatia, France, Italy, Lesbos, Rhodes, and Sicily.

Throughout the ancient world, vendors set up at city gates to sell surplus table grapes and skins of wine. Traders navigated the rivers to bear edibles to nearby commercial centers and followed Nile tributaries into central Africa to introduce their beverages in new territory. In the Nile River delta, amateur vintners learned to train vines on trellises and ferment grape juice. The Egyptians reserved their vintages for bureaucrats, priests, and royalty. Mourners supplied five ritual wines to the dead at mausoleums at Abydos and Saqqara, near Mem-

phis. Vintners advanced industrial by-products by turning soured wine into vinegar, a pantry staple. Ceramic wine jars in the tomb of King Tutankhamen, sealed in 1323 B.C.E., attested to the boy king's preference for red wine.

To the northeast around 1200 B.C.E., because of rocky soil unsuited to growing grain, Phoenician (or Canaanite) farmers exploited commerce in fine olive oil and rich wines in exchange for wheat from Israel and Judah. The Phoenicians stored liquids in amphorae, two-handled jars crafted with a knob at the bottom for ease of pouring. They also imported barley, livestock, and wine from Egypt, Greece, Mesopotamia, Sardinia, Sicily, and the Atlantic coast of Iberia and reverenced wine as a suitable altar gift.

The adventurers and interharbor transporters of the ancient world, Phoenician shippers plied coastal waters and the Atlantic Ocean. In cedar plank ships, they disseminated wine from Aleppo, Beirut, Byblos, Sidon, and Tyre as far north as Cornwall, in southwestern England. The best, Bybline wine, earned a reputation in Greek poetry for bouquet and sparkle, perhaps evidence of muscat grape stock, a source of sweet dessert beverages.

The Etruscans, Greeks, Romans, and Phoenicians flourished at winemaking for medicinal use as well as dining. Around 850 B.C.E., Homer referred to fermentation methods, techniques that recurred in the poet Hesiod's *Works and Days* (700 B.C.E.) and viticulture expert Columella's 12-volume *De Re Rustica* (*On Agriculture,* ca. 50 C.E.). Workers stamped on raisin clusters and stored the *passum* (pulp) in clay amphorae sealed with gypsum. In the fifth century B.C.E., Enotria Tellus (land of wine), a vineyard network throughout Magna Graecia in Sicily and Italy from Calabria to Paestum, succeeded in

At a winery in Italy's Tuscany region, renowned for its dry, red Chiantis, the vintner tastes a sample from an oak barrel during the fermentation stage. Viticulture emerged as a true agrarian science in the classical civilizations of the Mediterranean. *(David Lees/Time Life Pictures/Getty Images)*

marketing premium wines in Iberia, Italy, Provence, and Corsica.

Greek navigators peddled local wines through the Dodecanese to Pontus on the Black Sea and, after 500 B.C.E., from Massalia (Marseilles), the Greek colonial port on the French Riviera. While caravans delivered Mediterranean wines to China, the first water cargo carriers—round skin coracles—ferried casks of date palm wine along the Danube, Euphrates and Tigris, Nile, Rhone, and Yalu rivers. Within a millennium of honing transport methods and boosting sales, Athens led the Mediterranean in commercial wines, which vintners distributed in 3-foot-high (0.9-meter-high) terra-cotta jars, each holding 6.9 gallons (26 liters).

Everyday Consumption

From as early as 850 B.C.E. through the Talmudic period ending in 500 C.E., Hebrew imbibers celebrated Purim with honey and fruit turnovers eaten with wine. Jewish dealers in Gaza, Israel, and Jordan identified wine amphorae with clay inspection labels specifying date of filling and the vintner's identity. As dramatized in Homer's *Iliad* (eighth century B.C.E.), wearied Achaian soldiers during the Greek siege on Troy shared Pramnian wine in possets, a restorative blended with barley and honey and dressed with grated goat cheese. For Greek and Roman infantry and seagoers, supply trains ensured daily distribution of green olives, sourdough biscuits, beer, and *posca,* a drink of watered sour wine valued as a defense against malaria.

At home dinners, Greeks celebrated camaraderie with aperitifs. The loving cup, a two-handled sipping *krater* (bowl), bore hippocras, mead, or vermouth, an herbed wine. After meals, servers freshened cups with one-fourth to one-half water to pure wine to accompany fruit and nuts and small honey cakes.

During the same period, Chinese sage Confucius (551–479 B.C.E.) warned that drunkenness was socially inappropriate, an opinion unshared by the ordinary diner who relished vintages made with grapes from Dayuan in central Asia. By the second century B.C.E., dealers on the Asian frontier contemplated a beverage dealership with the west. In 138 B.C.E., ambassador Zhang Qian (Chang Ch'ien), an explorer and representative of the Emperor Wudi, extended vintage marketing from the Han dynasty to the Fertile Crescent and the seminomadic pastoralists of the Steppes. Chang recorded trade accounts for the imperial court on business with Afghanistan, India, Parthia, Turkestan, and Uzbekistan.

In imperial Rome, the wine industry upgraded technology with coopering, glass bottles from Syria, and screw presses. From the national food industry, Apicius, a first-century C.E. epicure, evolved recipes for beans served with celery, *caroenum* (wine concentrate), and fish pickle. His innovations included rue-flavored wine, a forerunner of Italian grappa, a distillate of pulp, seeds, skins, and stems.

For common travel fare, he specified creamy hot mayonnaise and the preparation of *mulsum* (honeyed wine), a Roman favorite for stall-feeding swine.

Some of the encyclopedia articles of Pliny the Elder, Apicius's contemporary, elevated viticulture to an agrarian science and an element of medical treatment. His 37-book *Historia naturae* (*Natural History,* ca. 77 B.C.) summarized the planting and pruning of prime grapes, the source of popular Opimian wine. He particularized the use of cedar, pine, and terebinth resins for stabilizing wine to prevent its souring into vinegar. Like Confucius, Pliny disdained overt drunkenness, especially where married women shared tables with men. He warned, *"In vino veritas,"* indicating that truth emerges from a brain befuddled by strong drink.

The Roman Empire generated the first international cuisine by trading olives and wine from Italia for exotic imports. After 100 C.E., the Roman military consumed Gallic wines fermented in Bordeaux and tapped Silk Road commodities in Alexandria, Egypt. Buyers extolled Falernian and Opimian vintages, which Roman vineyards produced at the rate of 1,600 gallons per acre (2,450 liters per hectare). During economic depressions, Rome's senatorial class handed out grain, oil, pork, and wine among ghetto dwellers in the Suburra as a sop to political unrest. The empire's promotion of viticulture supported much of the food trade until the 600s. Ironically, while Muslims forced converts to abandon the fermentation and imbibing of spirits, the Christian Eucharist ensured perpetuation of Roman technology.

Late in the eleventh century, brandy and wine transportation demanded planning by provisioners of the Crusades. Because distillation concentrated flavors and removed fluids from brandy, it required smaller containers. In August 1096, the first Christian regiments marched from France, abandoning estate vineyards to monks in exchange for ongoing prayers for victory over the Saracens who overran Jerusalem. Some warriors left vineyards in their wills to prelates, who agreed to petition for salvation for the deceased in purgatory. Within three centuries, Benedictine and Cistercian brothers managed the largest grape-growing plantations in France and Germany.

During the First Crusade, combat interrupted supply trains from the West. In October 1097, according to William of Tyre, crusaders foraged around Antioch in northern Syria for more than seven months for pantry goods and Sidonian wine. Into 1098 along the Orontes River through Lebanon, Syria, and Turkey, the Calabrian Captain Bohemond, Robert of Flanders, and Tancred of Normandy led 20,000 men on grain and wine raids. In a winter of epidemic typhoid fever and near starvation, throughout the Holy Lands, nursing brothers treated sick pilgrims and crusaders with cups of wine as restoratives and tonics. By the twelfth century, London merchants stocked Babylonian palm oil, pepper, spices, and

Mediterranean wines, which returning soldiers popularized for their revitalizing effects.

Consumer statutes got their start in the Middle Ages with official strictures governing the quality and sanitation of foods and wine. Along the network of old Roman highways, food service at coach inns and pubs followed official dictates concerning fermented beverages. Rules covered sales in the eastern third of the Czech Republic, where hosts toasted guests with artisanal beers and wines. The wide selection influenced the foodways of Austria, eastern Bohemia, Silesia, and Western Slovakia.

Wine surveillance derived from multiple sources. Kosher housewives patronized a network of grocers and wineries that obeyed rabbinic edicts. In 1291, stringent French statutes forbade the concealment of original wine casks, the mixing of two wines, and the marketing of shipments by false name or vintage. During a peak in commerce in spirits in the late 1200s, ships arrived upriver to London carrying as many as 200 barrels of beer or wine each, a massive cargo for port authorities to inspect.

Travelogues and cookbooks treated oenology as serious science. Marco Polo's expedition to China, which ended in 1295, outlined the unique service of delicate Asian wines. Taillevent, the Norman-French master of late medieval gastronomy, proposed balancing cooking flavors by mingling vinegar with sweetened wine. The Renaissance set European event planners in search of aperitifs, brandies, cordials, and sparkling wines to accompany elegant menus. In 1501, Portuguese voyager Vasco da Gama identified India's coconut wine as a beneficial shipboard beverage.

In England, the Tudors revered hippocras, a wine cordial flavored with coriander and heated with a hot poker plunged into the serving carafe. For peace talks at the Field of the Cloth of Gold between Henry VIII of England and French King Francis I in June 1520, guests filled goblets at two red wine fountains. At Henry VIII's completion of Hampton Court in March 1532, a wine fountain spouted drink to refresh state guests. After 1573 at the court of Henry III of France, the royal *bottigliere* (cellar master) poured aperitifs onto ice and snow in each glass to make the forerunner of frozen daiquiris.

Global Exchange

The European discovery of Mesoamerica introduced aborigines to wine. On February 19, 1519, Hernán de Cortés set out for Yucatán with 600 soldiers and 20 horses and food and drink unfamiliar to indigenous peoples. Upon encountering the Maya, he welcomed them to food and wine. His arrival introduced Spanish grapes, the ancestral vines of the Central American wine industry. Latin American vineyards yielded an essential of evangelism at Franciscan and Jesuit missions along the Baja and California coast and into the Sierra Nevada lowlands.

Wine influenced the success of settlement to the northeast. To avoid scurvy, in 1620, Captain John Smith, Virginia's founder, listed as galley provisions lemon juice, marmalade, and wine, a source of ascorbic acid. At Patuxet, Massachusetts, in early October 1621, the sharing of food between Pilgrims and the Wampanoag set the model for Thanksgiving. To mediate a treaty with the Indians, Captain Miles Standish invited Massasoit, Samoset, and Squanto to a feast. To provision a three-day open house, Massasoit donated game and grape beverages.

Worldwide, wine commanded a place in daily cuisine. Chinese and Japanese vinegar makers cultured their stock from rice wine. Coastal chowder in Europe and North America lost some of its fishiness from the quality of wine thinning the broth. In the West Indies, papaya chutney dominated table relishes with the zest of lime juice and rice wine vinegar. The British sweetened apple wine by pressing the sugary juice of dessert fruit. In Germany, the making of *apfelwein* (apple wine) from Bramley and Granny Smith cultivars required the addition of astringent serviceberries (*Sorbus domestica*) for flavoring. Sauces, rubs, pastes, and red wine marinades determined the flavor of Carolina and Texas barbecues.

Rules and Restrictions

Compelled by the religious fervor of the late 1800s, sobriety activists advocated replacing spirits with coffee. Local statutes typically left governance of wine consumption to community standards of celebration and ritual, such as a Jewish *bris,* Greek Orthodox confirmation, and Scandinavian wedding. Among North American zealots, the demand for temperance aroused xenophobia against German, Italian, and Polish Catholic immigrants, for whom beer and wine defined festivals and fellowship among whole congregations. Prohibition gained momentum after the 1917 declaration of war against Germany. In England, the War Prohibition Act of November 1918 halted the production and sale of beer, liquor, and wine until demobilization as a redirection of labor and supplies from luxuries to necessities.

In the United States, vintners lost business from the passage of the National Prohibition (Volstead) Act on October 28, 1919, until its repeal on December 5, 1933. The absence of wine lists in restaurants ended table service of dinner beverages and champagne. More people fermented home brew and served wine from private cellars. The revival of aesthetic wine in the 1970s coincided with the purchase of investment labels. In public displays of refinement and expertise, gourmets frequented wine and cheese tastings offering niche labels and exotic flavor combinations, such as Stilton cheesecake iced with Madeira or port wine gelée. Worldwide, France, Italy, and Spain led the world in wine production, with France also number one in consumption.

In the late twentieth century, specialty menus paired dishes with distinctive vintages. Soul food turned blackberry cordial and muscadine wine into heirloom beverages served with apple dumplings and peach cobbler.

In 1986, Slow Food advocates promoted unique dishes and wines from global markets. Chefs Mario Batali and Graham Kerr, *Saveur* magazine, and winemaker Robert Mondavi applauded the efforts of locavores to restore demand for drinks from regional vineyards, including the newcomers from Australia. In 2001, European members rallied against genetically modified (GM) grapes under placards demanding "No GM Wine," an unstated support of heirloom vine varieties.

See also: Cussy, Louis, Marquis de; Fermented Foods; Greek Diet and Cuisine, Ancient; Mediterranean Diet and Cuisine; Plant Disease and Prevention; Pliny the Elder; Prohibition; Sicilian Diet and Cuisine; Silk Road; Temperance; Travel Food; Yeast.

Further Reading

Blocker, Jack S., David M. Fahey, and Ian R. Tyrrell. *Alcohol and Temperance in Modern History.* Santa Barbara, CA: ABC-Clio, 2003.

Fraser, Evan D.G., and Andrew Rimas. *Empires of Food: Feast, Famine, and the Rise and Fall of Civilizations.* New York: Simon & Schuster, 2010.

McGovern, Patrick E. *Ancient Wine: The Search for the Origins of Viniculture.* Princeton, NJ: Princeton University Press, 2003.

Meacham, Sarah Hand. *Every Home a Distillery: Alcohol, Gender, and Technology in the Colonial Chesapeake.* Baltimore: Johns Hopkins University Press, 2009.

Pinney, Thomas. *A History of Wine in America.* Berkeley: University of California Press, 2007.

World Trade

Global commerce in food dominates world finance, creating the need for agricultural consensus, food security, international purity and quality distinctions, and the policing of airports and deep waters to prevent biopiracy and the smuggling of potentially harmful goods. Since the development of the Silk Road after 125 B.C.E., expansion of the Hanseatic League in the 1390s, and round-the-world voyages in the sixteenth century, food has traveled to far-flung markets, introducing outlanders to foreign cuisines and farmers to new money crops. Rapid transit of rations by air, land, and sea allows diners in remote locales to enjoy perishables, from lettuce and strawberries in Alaska and Iceland to bananas and Chinese shrimp in Antarctic commissaries and the International Space Station. The most active shippers rely on fruits, grain, meat, processed foods, seafood, and vegetables for up to 80 percent of their total exports.

From 1948 to 1994, the World Trade Organization (WTO), a specialized international agency of 153 members administered by the United Nations, set and supervised rules of market access. To prohibit cultural imperialism and new sources of global conflict, the WTO defined food categories and proposed duty concessions on a case-by-case basis. Members based their elimination of trade discrimination on the economic protectionism that impaired food distribution before World War II. Concerned experts worked toward an integrated system free of cultural, political, and religious prejudice. A consensus regarding exploitation and oppression of labor turned international attention to issues of child labor and enslavement among migrant harvesters, notably grain reapers in Uzbekistan, grape and lettuce pickers in the American Southwest, and tea sorters in China.

Disputes arose thereafter as agrarian and fishing competition escalated. At issue lay the trade barriers in Japan, Mexico, and South Korea against the importation of apples from France and the United States, the world's leading exporters of fresh pome fruit. As opposed to nations marketing their fruit internally, the United States maintained that a broad range of global apple cultivars—Fuji, Granny Smith, Macintosh, Rome, Yellow Delicious—enhance biodiversity. Technology introduced pricklier topics for conciliation—chemical hazards, classification of additives and dyes as carcinogens, genetic modification, heirloom seeds, organic growing conditions, and packaging. A serious threat to small growers, proprietary hybridization funneled profits from single-use seeds distributed by Bayer, Calgene, Dow, DuPont, Monsanto, and Syngenta. Another troubling issue involved "like products," a loose cataloging of processed foods derived from dairy, fish, meat, and vegetable products, such as cheese sticks, imitation crab meat, and unpasteurized fruit juice and yogurt drinks.

In a potentially explosive confrontation, the European Union (EU) controverted free trade in meat and dairy products in 1985 by prohibiting the use of growth hormones in cattle. Four years later, the EU banned Canadian and U.S. imports of beef treated with synthetic growth stimulants. A prolonged dispute arose in the WTO based on international accords on adulterated meat. To compensate for losses to the food trade, the United States imposed tariffs on meats imported from the EU. The levy inflicted hardship on European merchants, who imported more food than any other global area. Subsequent dispute resolution centered on the hidden agendas of agricultural interests to suppress free trade in such goods as bottled mineral water, honey, and infant food.

To reconcile issues that affected prosperity and precipitated hunger and malnutrition, in 1995, a multilateral trade consortium negotiated formation of the General Agreement on Tariffs and Trade (GATT). The smaller signatories—Argentina, Australia, Bolivia, Brazil, Canada, Chile, Colombia, Congo, Costa Rica, Guatemala, Indonesia, Malaysia, New Zealand, Pakistan, Paraguay, Peru, the Philippines, South Africa, Thailand, and Uruguay—protested onerous regulation of fresh produce and seafood, both high-income markets. Lesser competitors charged big nations with the distortion of commodity supplies and prices by the internal quotas and subsidies of industrialized countries, principally U.S. legislation protecting corn and cotton prices and subsidizing the soybean and sugar industries. To boost global welfare, diplomacy enabled members to lower trade barriers and countermand export restrictions—for example, rejection of eggs from Tanzania, blackberries and snow peas from Guatemala, and shrimp from Bangladesh based on microbial contamination and environmental pollutants.

Since November 2001, the Doha Development Round, launched at the GATT conference held in Qatar, has continued to address world marketing of coffee, grain, oil seeds, and tea as it applies to developing nations. In committee, Brazil, China, India, and South Africa represent preindustrial countries. Contention over agricultural imports of beef, chicken, and rice and serious concern for transnational food security and market access for farmers from the poorest nations involved mediators from China, India, and the United States into late 2008.

Subsequent negotiations indicate agreement that prosperous markets protect all growers and sellers. On June 4, 2011, Japan donated $278,368 to the Standards and Trade Development Facility fund, which the World Bank created in September 2002. The purpose of grants and financial aid is to help have-not nations upgrade their border analysis of animal and plant health. With technologically advanced food labs, small countries identify and suppress substandard goods that contain pesticides and veterinary drugs or that spread food-borne *Campylobacter*, *Escherichia coli* (*E. coli*), listeriosis, bovine spongiform encephalopathy (mad cow disease), and salmonella.

See also: Abreu, António de, and Francisco Serrao; Biopiracy; British East India Company; Clipper Ships; Gama, Vasco da; Ice; Lapérouse, Jean François Galaup; London Virginia Company; Mail-Order Food; Maritime Trade Routes; New World Commodities; Roman Diet and Cuisine, Ancient; Vanilla.

Further Reading

Bermann, George A., and Petros C. Mavroidis, eds. *Trade and Human Health and Safety*. New York: Cambridge University Press, 2006.

Hawkes, Corinna, Chantal Blouin, Spencer Henson, Nick Drager, and Laurette Dubé. *Trade, Food, Diet and Health: Perspectives and Policy Options*. Ames, IA: Blackwell, 2010.

Hinkelman, Edward G., and Karla C. Shippey. *Dictionary of International Trade: Handbook of the Global Trade Community*. Novato, CA: World Trade, 2004.

Krissoff, Barry, Mary Bohman, and Julie A. Caswell. *Global Food Trade and Consumer Demand for Quality*. New York: Kluwer Academic/Plenum, 2002.

Yeast

A fungus generating bubbles and froth in sugar, yeast raises bread and ferments beer, two cereal products that date to the beginnings of culinary history. Yeast takes two forms—ferment in such liquids as honey and molasses and leaven in solids, particularly grains and tubers. A mystery in the ancient world, the energetic organism grew naturally in sugary materials with a low pH (high acidity), including grape and peach skin and berries, and in fermented vegetables and starch

Beer, koumiss (fermented mare's milk), liquor, and wine acquire ethanol from the action of yeast on sugar, which feeds the fungal colony. The fermentation of coconut sap into toddy and of agave juices into *pulque* happens naturally from the action of airborne spores on saccharides (carbohydrates). The first sippers of such fermented drinks felt euphoria, and mystic interpretations of inebriation turned the beverages into holy gifts from the Greek deities Bacchus and Dionysus and the Aztec goddess Mayahuel.

The action of yeast on fruit processing occurred in the Caucasus in 8000 B.C.E. and subsequently in Armenia, Iran, and Macedonia. Greek cooks used yeasty grape must to make *oinoutta,* a moist anise- and cumin-flavored wine cake that Roman writer Cato the Elder exalted in *De Agri Cultura (On Farming,* ca. 160 B.C.E.). Egyptian, Phoenician, and Roman wineries turned processed grape juice into a profitable export, which they sealed into amphorae (two-handled pottery jars). The spread of Catholicism in the early second century C.E. encouraged wine making for use in the Eucharist.

The same gas-emitting action in bread and pastry intensified during rising and baking. In ancient times, wheat gluten offered a strong foundation for the growth of yeast colonies, which increased the versatility of high-protein dough for macaroni and noodles. The leavening produced air pockets in bread dough that lightened the crust and gave it a springy crumb and nutty flavor. Egyptian experimenters became the first to cultivate yeast and dry it for storage.

In the 1300s, English bakers recycled ale barm as a leavening for bread and for an egg batter fried into "cryspeys," a forerunner of the bagel, doughnut, fritter, and funnel cake. In Romania, Easter risen cakes celebrated Good Friday, an anticipation of the resurrection of Christ.

The addition of the potato to European cuisine in the late 1400s offered a simple medium for growing yeast for home use.

For good reason, medieval brewers fermented more reliable ales by building their vats next to bakeries. By inoculating subsequent batches with yeasty mash from past successes, they cultured their ales with select strains of microorganisms. Experts developed a purification method of growing spores in boiled cane sugar. The method killed other ferments that yielded odd flavors in the finished wort. For its stability during travel, ale raised a devoted following among the New England Pilgrims, who imported ale casks to Plymouth, Massachusetts, in July 1620 as a daily beverage.

Viewed under a microscope for the first time in 1680 by Dutch scientist Anton van Leeuwenhoek, yeast came on the market in 1780, when the Dutch commercialized fermentation solutions for bakers. By 1825, the substance was available in cake form. Bakeries gained clientele for the light puffiness of their loaves; the Parker House Hotel in Boston earned a reputation for its delectable yeast roll.

The organic nature of the fungus remained a mystery until 1857, when French microbiologist Louis Pasteur identified the globules as living one-celled organisms. Specialists isolated yeasts by type. By eliminating wild yeasts and spoilage bacteria, food processors applied pure spores to particular needs, such as potato bread and pilsner beer, a pale lager.

To replace haphazard homemade starters, Czech immigrant brothers Charles Louis and Maximilian Fleischmann of Riverside, Ohio, unveiled an American yeast to consumers in 1876 at their Model Vienna Bakery, an exhibit at the Centennial Exposition, held in Philadelphia. The commercial brand produced a tender, aromatic crumb and consistent quality. The Fleischmann Yeast Company fostered a demand for granulated yeast and advanced to the world's top yeast marketer.

Yeast has a history of fortifying the malnourished, beginning in the Middle Ages with the feeding of beer sediment to anemic infants. Public health nurses distributed brewer's yeast in the American South in the early 1900s to combat pellagra, a deficiency of B vitamins. In 1902 in Australia, England, New Zealand, South Africa, and Sri Lanka, a British yeast extract called Marmite offered a savory, nutritious spread for bread.

During World War I, German peasants consumed yeast as a famine food for its protein and minerals. After World War II, refugees required a regimen of strength building, which included yeast. In 1943, English hematologist Lucy Wills, a pathologist for the Emergency Medical Service, found that commercially processed yeast bolstered the hemoglobin level in anemic pregnant women, improving their chances of producing healthy infants.

See also: Alcoholic Beverages; Beer; Bread; Seaman's Diet and Cuisine; Sourdough; Wine.

Further Reading

Hornsey, Ian Spencer. *A History of Beer and Brewing.* Cambridge, UK: Royal Society of Chemistry, 2003.

McFarland, Ben. *World's Best Beers: One Thousand Craft Brews from Cask to Glass.* New York: Sterling, 2009.

McGovern, Patrick E. *Ancient Wine: The Search for the Origins of Viniculture.* Princeton, NJ: Princeton University Press, 2003.

Murray, Michael T., Joseph Pizzorno, and Lara Pizzorno. *The Condensed Encyclopedia of Healing Foods.* New York: Simon & Schuster, 2006.

Sumner, Judith. *American Household Botany: A History of Useful Plants, 1620–1900.* Portland, OR: Timber, 2004.

Yogurt

A tangy semisolid dairy food, yogurt illustrates the height of bacterial fermentation of milk, a parallel to fermenting grape juice into wine. Originally a product of buffalo, camel, cow, ewe, goat, reindeer, or yak milk, yogurt first coagulated naturally in 6000 B.C.E. from the enzyme chymosin, or rennin, accumulating in the pouches that Sumerian nomads made from sheep stomachs. The smooth texture of yogurt combined well with wild herbs for Balkan sour soups and in bulgur (cracked wheat) and millet balls, a combination favored by the Fulani of Nigeria. Russians sipped it like buttermilk.

Yogurt won devotees because of its benign flavor and a smooth texture. It answered the needs of infants and invalids, stimulated the immune system to fight infection, and dried well for travel food and winter storage. Mughal palace cooks turned yogurt into a binding agent for stew and a garnish for fruit and vegetable dishes. It also cooled the tongue after a bite of hot chilies. In Sumatra, enthusiasts cultured buffalo's milk into yogurt in bamboo tubes and served the velvety results over rice with chili sauce.

Cultured milk rapidly became a culinary staple for its versatility and long shelf life. Across the Caucasus, Balkans, and Indian subcontinent, the daily diet incorporated kefir, a yogurt drink valued for longevity and well-being. Persians paired honey with yogurt in 500 B.C.E. for a pleasing balance of flavors. In the southern Himalayas, yogurt provided cooks with a basis for desserts.

A versatile product, yogurt also served Greece and the eastern Mediterranean as a hair and body wash and as a treatment for enteritis. In the Balkans, Greece, and Turkey, recipes for salads, cold soups, and dips enhanced yogurt with cucumbers, dill, garlic, lime, mint, sea salt, and walnuts. In India, the addition of carrot, ginger, papaya, and pineapple produced a sweet blend. In 1215, Genghis Khan credited koumiss, yogurt made from mare's milk, with boosting the efficiency of his soldiers, who conquered Mongolia.

In a 1904 study of cultured milk, Bulgarian microbiologist Stamen Grigorov isolated *Lactobacillus bulgaricus,* the bacteria in lactic acid, and recommended the consumption of yogurt to suppress ulcers and tuberculosis. In 1919 at a shop in Barcelona, a Spanish physician, Isaac Carasso, commercialized pure cultured yogurt, the beginning of the Dannon brand. He popularized it as a preventative of dairy food intolerance and gastrointestinal distress, an antidote he developed from the research of Ukrainian microbiologist Ilya Ilyich Mechnikov, winner of the 1908 Nobel Prize in Physiology or Medicine. In 1933, the addition of fruit jam in Prague increased the selections of flavored yogurt in Czech grocery stores.

In the United States, yogurt became a model of the assimilation of ethnic food into American cookery. During the Great Depression, Armenians Rose and Sarkis Colombosian in Andover, Massachusetts, began selling glass carafes of Colombo yogurt door-to-door to Greek, Lebanese, and Syrian immigrants. In the 1960s, health food gurus championed yogurt as a boost to the immune system and a source of calcium and milk protein for the lactose intolerant. Aficionados cultured their own batches at home with the aid of electric culturing machines.

Recipe: Beef in Yogurt Gravy

Flour 20 ounces of thin beef strips and pound them with a mallet. Panfry the strips in 1 cup of canola oil. Set the beef aside to drain. In enough pan drippings to cover the bottom of a skillet, deglaze with 1/2 cup of Burgundy wine at high heat. Sprinkle the deglazed drippings with granulated flour, sea salt, and a generous dusting of pepper. Continue cooking over high heat, stirring until the mixture browns. Whisk together 1 cup of plain yogurt and 1/2 cup of water. Add this to the pan, scraping the bottom to incorporate flavorful bits. Return the beef strips to the gravy and simmer until tender, about 20 minutes. Serve over salted egg noodles.

Throughout western Asia and the Balkans, children come of age on yogurt drinks flavored with chilies, mint, or salt. In Arab countries and India, strained yogurt reduces the proportion of whey to solids and yields a thick spread for pita and sandwich bread and as a cream base for meat and onion pies. In the twenty-first century, despite its higher price, natural Greek-style yogurt, which makers strained to remove some of the whey for a thicker product, gained popularity in the Americas and Australia as a staple in weight loss diets by replacing sour cream.

See also: Blenders and Food Processors; Fermented Foods; Guar; Tea; Travel Food; Vegetarianism.

Further Reading

Allen, Gary, and Ken Albala. *The Business of Food: Encyclopedia of the Food and Drink Industries.* Westport, CT: Greenwood, 2007.

Chandan, Ramesh C., Charles E. White, Arun Kilara, and Yui H. Hui, eds. *Manufacturing Yogurt and Fermented Milks.* Ames, IA: Blackwell, 2006.

Clark, Stephanie, Michael Costello, MaryAnne Drake, and Floyd Bodyfelt, eds. *The Sensory Evaluation of Dairy Products.* New York: Springer, 2009.

Shurtleff, William, and Akiko Aoyagi. *History of Soybeans and Soyfoods in Canada (1831–2010).* Lafayette, CA: Soyinfo Center, 2010.

Yildez, Fatih, ed. *Development and Manufacture of Yogurt and Other Functional Dairy Products.* New York: Taylor & Francis, 2010.

Chronology

B.C.E.

500,000–250,000 Control of fire increases the palatability of food and releases more nutrients into human metabolism from cooked meals.

200,000 The Paleolithic diet centers on wild food.

100,000 Neanderthal mourners supply meals for the dead as nourishment for a netherworld.

38,000 Spit roasting and pit cookery in North America increase flavor, texture, and aroma of meat haunches.

30,000 In Mesopotamia, flax serves human needs for dye and linseed oil.

25,000 Feral beasts adapt to human presence as a source of protection from wild predators.

18,000 Homo sapiens make the first use of grinding stones to separate husks from digestible tissues of nuts and grains.

17,000 In the Rift Valley of Israel, seeds of the self-sowing hulled emmer wheat satisfy hunger and introduce dietary fiber and high nutrition.

13,000 Cave paintings in Bicor, Spain, depict the collection of wild honey.

Neolithic farmers hybridize fruit and grain, beginning with Chinese and Indian strains of rice.

12,000 Hunter-gatherers embrace farm life by planting einkorn wheat on the western end of the Fertile Crescent.

11,050 Drought forces early Palestinians to water sheep herds, irrigate home gardens, and cache grain in storage pits as famine food.

10,500 At Nevali Cori, Turkey, the historic transition from hunting and gathering to domesticated einkorn wheat begins the shift in cookery from pit-roasted meats to bread, flour, noodles, and pasta.

10,000 The Nordic Sami follow reindeer herds, producers of milk and venison cooked over pit fires.

Brazilians and eastern Peruvians elevate manioc to a trade commodity along the Lower Amazon, Orinoco, and Guianas rivers.

9500 In southeastern Turkey, Syria, and Lebanon, lentils add a high-protein pod plant to the human diet.

9000 Neolithic cuisine in southeastern Turkey contributes cooked legumes to a meat diet and relies on herding and dairying as a reliable source of food.

8500 Syrians first cultivate barley as a cereal grain and source of bread and beer.

8000 Herders in India raise zebu for meat and evolve dairy foods from cows.

Egyptians begin baking flatbread.

7500 The chickpea adds protein to the diet in the Jordan Valley, Israel, and southeastern Turkey.

7000 Worldwide, farming and animal husbandry improve under formalized methods and strategies, including the cultivation of bitter vetch as a forage crop.

Babylonian farmers enhance revenues by making new beverages from dates and palm sap and by diverting malted grain to brewing 26 different beers.

The Maya of the Yucatán Peninsula develop a corn-centric diet.

6000 Yogurt coagulates naturally in the pouches that Sumerian nomads shape from sheep stomachs.

Wine grapes originate in the Caucasus Mountains.

Pea cultivation in the Middle East adds a nitrogen-fixer to garden plants.

5000 At Ur, Sumerians achieve state-run agriculture.

The Mediterranean diet begins forming in the Middle East.

The potato enters cultivation in the Lake Titicaca area of Peru.

4500 Ukrainian herders gentle the horse, a major contribution to streamlining field labor.

4100 A cave winery in Areni, Armenia, produces sacred beverages reserved for ritual.

4000 Drought forces farmers from the Sahel south to Mali, where they adapt to bushmeat and wild food.

From Texas to Manitoba and Saskatchewan, Amerindian stone mallets reduce buffalo muscle to meat flour for pemmican.

The first curry is derived from the mortars and pestles of the Mohenjo Daro, whose occupants add mustard seed grown in the Indus Valley.

Sumerian farmers augment agriculture by planting fruit and pistachio trees.

3600 Amerindians discover popcorn.

3100 Egyptian peasants maintain one of the highest standards of living in North Africa.

3000 The Maya of the Yucatán Peninsula chew chicle as a thirst quencher.

India's healers develop Ayurveda, a unified dietary system featuring wellness as its goal.

The use of 40 percent of Babylonian cereal grains to make beer introduces drunkenness and the attendant ills of alcoholism.

The first maritime trade route carries dates, grain, and oil from Babylon to Bahrain and the Harappa culture on the Indus River to barter for sorghum and millet.

2838 Herbalist Shen Nung, the "Father of Chinese Medicine," names preserved soybeans as a curative food.

2600 Episodes from the *Epic of Gilgamesh* urge the hero to feast among good company and good food as a way to enjoy life at its fullest.

2500 Central Asians add the double-humped Bactrian camel and the yak to agrarian investments in meat animals.

2400 The first organized beekeeping begins in clay pipes throughout Lower Egypt.

2100 Healers in southwestern Asia develop dietary treatments from herbs and honey.

2000 A miniature Cypriot wine jug simplifies infant feeding.

The Maya invent *pozol,* a fermented corn drink.

The orchardists of Crete first cultivate olive orchards.

1700 Persian cooks keep ice sheds and subterranean caches of frozen chunks for making sorbet.

1550 At Luxor, Egypt, the Ebers papyri list chants and herbal dosages that improve blood flow to the heart.

1400 Egyptians build the first physic garden at Karnak and learn the art of espaliering branches along garden walls.

1323 Jars in the tomb of King Tutankhamen attest to the boy king's preference for red wine and Turkish almonds.

1250 Pharaoh Ramses II places the Hebrew Joseph, the vizier of Egypt, over granaries of emmer wheat.

1184 The Greeks pickle soft feta cheese.

1150 The Aztec cultivate *chinampas,* floating gardens that farmers anchored in lake bottoms.

1050 In the earliest era of acorn, barley, and oat refinement in England, hand-grinding dominates much of the homemaker's day.

1000 Persia grows into the ancient world's largest empire and the most noted for abundant dining and charity.

Capitalism from Middle Eastern agriculture enables cities to muster standing armies.

Chinese traders develop sea routes to cassia merchants in Southeast Asia.

The mechanical press raises profits for Iberian and Phoenician olive growers.

590 Chinese sausage makers develop a complex recipe for long-lived fermented minced meat.

551 Zoroastrians boil gift eggs to celebrate the New Year and to honor the birthday of Asho Zarathushtra, the Persian sage and founder of the faith.

550 Samian mathematician Pythagoras of Croton, the "Father of Vegetarianism," sets the example of healthful eating for his disciples.

538 The book of Leviticus begins the codification of Jewish kosher laws.

500 The Chinese turn soybean mold into an antibiotic. Pythagoreans invent dietetics for Olympic athletes.

450 The Greek poet Philoxenos describes cheesecake, made with curdled milk and honey.

428 Herodotus investigates the grain production on land watered annually by the Nile River's overflow.

360 Hippocrates, the Greek "Father of Medicine," proposes desalination by straining boiled water through a cloth bag.

332 Alexander the Great serves iced fruit ades to Macedonian soldiers.

323 Most Greeks ridicule the importation of Persian food fads.

300 The Indian Kautilya's *Arthashastra* (*Statecraft*) authorizes the penalizing of marketers who adulterate food. For longevity, the Chinese *Tao-te Ching* (*The Classic Way*) recommends eating herbs, mushrooms, nuts and seeds, and seaweed.

200 Roman buyers solve their national wheat crises by looking to Berbers in Numidia for emergency supplies. Chinese cooks ferment seasonal fish and mix rice with frozen milk for an early sherbet.

164 During the Han dynasty, scholarly Prince Liu An experiments with bean curd to make the first tofu.

162 Roman cuniculture and the invention of the capon circumvent the fattening of hens, forbidden by the Lex Faunia, an austerity law limiting gluttony.

146 The concept of suppressing future agriculture takes shape in Pope Boniface VIII's plowing and sowing of the town of Palestrina, Italy, in salt.

125 China establishes commercial relations with Persia, which dispatches up to ten eastern expeditions per year over the Silk Road.

55 Britons in the Wey Valley of south-central England accept Roman watermills as a shortcut to producing flour.

54 In Britannia, Julius Caesar discovers venues selling sharp cheddar cheese.

52 On the march of Roman legions into Gaul, provisioners take along the pheasant, a source of eggs and meat.

27 The Roman Empire generates the first international cuisine.

C.E.

30 The Roman Emperor Tiberius's garden staff plants Armenian gherkins in portable barrows, forerunners of container gardening.

35 Apicius compiles *De Re Coquinaria* (*On Cookery*), making Rome one of the few ancient cities to have codified its cuisine.

70 As an act of dominance in Palestine, the Emperor Titus orders Roman legionaries to fell olive groves.

77 Encyclopedist Pliny the Elder's *Historia Naturae* (*Natural History*) warns of adulterated grain from Tunisia and recommends grapes as integral to a healing diet.

100 The Aztec and Maya revere cacao beans as aphrodisiacs, food, money, and symbols of deity.

190 Greek table customs separate dining from drinking bouts.

390s In Rome's declining days, after the failure of taxation and the economy, food transportation ceases.

410 Alaric I ransoms Rome in exchange for 1.5 tons (1.4 metric tons) of pepper, the prime ingredient in Gothic sausage.

476 Christian convents and monasteries engage in beekeeping, taking over the apiaries once maintained by Roman farmers.

500 Across the Mediterranean and Polynesia, the coconut contributes a form of food currency.

534 Agroecologist Jia Sixie, a governor in Shandong Province, compiles one of the world's oldest agricultural monographs.

638 Bedouins trapped by hunger and epidemic seek help at food rationing stations at Medina, Arabia.

650 The Koran specifies the table luxuries awaiting those who win favor with God by eating only halal (permissible) foods on Earth.
Arab notables dine on exotic wild foods from Africa.

700 In Toledo, Spain, Arab confectioners introduce marzipan.

794 Frankish King Charlemagne superintends food pricing and standardizes market weights and measures.

800 The Japanese begin regular hunts for whale meat, which they value as a luxury food.

840 *De Cultura Hortarum* (*On Gardening*), by Walafrid Strabo, a Frankish monk, prioritizes cures for the stomach, the "king of the body."

875 When a rebellion threatens Henan Province with a military coup, hungry Chinese soldiers turn to cannibalism.

900 Arab insurgents in Iberia introduce the Spanish to Jordanian and Lebanese dishes.
Christian monks in Paris revive Roman technology for processing mustard.

1010 Persian historiographer Firdawsi's *Shahnameh* (*The Book of Kings*) balances sober laws and moralizing with commentary on merry Zoroastrian feasting.

1075 Jewish nutritionist Symeon Seth's *On the Properties of Foods* illustrates Byzantine interest in diet and cuisine.

1086 England supports 6,000 milling operations.

October 1097 Crusaders ravage Antioch, Syria, for edible plunder.

1099 Returning crusaders bring the recipe for gingerbread to Europe.

1100 The Japanese domesticate quail as a source of attractive entrées and tiny eggs, exotic plate adornments, and street food.

1152 Hildegard of Bingen, a German abbess, incorporates aromatic plants, spices, and wines in her *Physica* (*Medicines*) and advises correct dosages of simples for various diseases.

1159 Among German grain dealers in Lübeck, formation of the Hanseatic League stabilizes prices by evening out food gluts and compensating for crop failures.

1190 The Japanese tea cult, begun by Zen monks, symbolizes social order.

1200s On the eve of the Persian New Year, Iranian cooks make fine egg noodles.

1200 The Inca of the Andes in Bolivia and Chile propagate quinoa.

1215 Genghis Khan credits koumiss, yogurt made from mare's milk, with boosting the efficiency of his soldiers, who conquered Mongolia.

1226 Baghdad cookbook compiler Mohammad Ibn al-Hasan proclaims gastronomy the height of the noble life.

1245 London's first pharmacy stocks ground pine nuts and colored sugar flavored with attar of roses and violets for spicing wine.

1260 Huou, Chinese chef of Kublai Khan, originates fusion cuisine.

1275 In Tibet, Marco Polo observes the stamping of salt cakes with the khan's imperial logo as a form of currency.

1300s Mongol nomads teach the Chinese *kao* cuisine, toasting kebabs over charcoal grills.
To save energy, Japanese families warm their feet on the charcoal pot that cooks their dinner.

1350s With the liberality of the coming Renaissance, diners achieve some choice in their food intake.

1354 Travel writer Ibn Battuta notes that late medieval Arab dining follows a regimented social order.

1441 Korean inventor Jang Yeong-sil's rain gauge and water gauge enable farmers to compute the best allotment of stored water.

1486 When the Spanish learn about a four-day Aztec human flesh–eating festival, they coin the term *cannibal* to indicate a revolting blood crime.

October 28, 1492 In Cuba, Christopher Columbus encounters the potato, which reminds him of the taste of chestnuts.

December 26, 1492 After the Taíno of Santo Domingo offer Columbus chili peppers, he plans to deliver them to Spain by the shipload.

April 2, 1494 In the West Indies at Santo Tomás, Christopher Columbus introduces European food technology by building a gristmill.

July 8, 1497 Portuguese voyager Vasco da Gama redirects the Arab–Venetian spice monopoly from the Spice Road to a sea route around Africa.

1500s Spanish colonists add milk products to the largely vegetarian Aztec regimen.

July 7, 1503 At Jamaica, Christopher Columbus makes another culinary discovery for the Europeans, a wild turkey.

November 7, 1504 Christopher Columbus arrives back in Spain with details of Jamaican style barbecuing, the first source of chocolate seen in Europe, and samples of chili pepper and Jamaican allspice.

1511 Explorer António de Abreu secures a Portuguese monopoly on spices from Indonesia, Ceylon, and Malabar, India.

August 1519 Spanish observers note the consumption of cacti among the Nazca of Peru and the Maya in Tlaxcala, Mexico.

Aztec King Montezuma II introduces invader Hernán de Cortés to New World foodstuffs—beans, cherries and figs, corn cakes, fish, and roast turkey.

November 8, 1519 The soldiers of Hernán de Cortés readily adopt avocado, beans, corn, pineapple, squash, sweet potatoes, tomatoes, and tomatillos and relish foaming mugs of hot chocolate, spiced with chilies and vanilla.

1520 Spanish chronicler Bernal Díaz writes of shaping corn tortillas into tacos that diners filled with pork and dipped into clay dishes of *mole* (sauce).

1521 Portuguese voyager Ferdinand Magellan takes corn and tomatoes to the Philippines.

In the North American Southwest, Catholic missionaries outlaw the eating of hallucinogenic mushrooms and peyote.

1533 Catherine de' Médici introduces Tuscan cuisine to the French.

1534 French explorer Jacques Cartier learns from the Algonquin of Montreal how to cure scurvy with plants rich in vitamin C.

1535 Peruvian settler María de Escobar introduces the cultivation of barley, lucerne, oats, and wheat in the Andes Mountains.

May 1535 In Baja at La Paz Bay, Hernán de Cortés introduces Spanish grapevines, the beginnings of the Central American wine industry.

1542 Oxford-trained physician Andrew Boorde recommends breakfast for English day laborers.

At the end of Europe's longest foray into native America to date, Hernando de Soto's expedition proves the value of dried fruit, ground corn, and nuts to future conquistadors.

1550 Spanish explorer Gonzalo Jiménez de Quesada introduces Iberia to the Colombian potato, which ultimately saves Europe from famine.

1559 Spanish historian Bartolomé de Las Casas extols peanuts and the Caribbean pepper as indispensable to Aztec cookery.

1578 In Baffinland, the Canadian Eskimo store fish and meat under stone cairns, a method of supplying Arctic males on their return treks from hunting grounds.

1585 Italian botanist Castor Durante compiles an A-to-Z study of more than 900 plants and their value to nutrition and healing.

1591 Venetian botanist Prospero Alpini introduces Europeans to the date palm, a staple Egyptian food and a source of wine.

1599 In Leiden, Holland, French botanist Jules Charles de L'Ecluse builds the first greenhouse.

August 1607 The first Christian harvest festival, held at the Popham colony in Maine, predates the American custom of Thanksgiving.

1617 Peruvian ethnohistorian Garcilaso de la Vega enlightens Europeans about the New World diet.

1620s When moralist William Vaughan settles in Newfoundland, he inveighs against alcohol consumption for deforming fetuses.

1622 British beekeepers in Virginia spread the European bee and honey-making techniques to the Americas.

February 20, 1627 Dutch settlers on Barbados initiate the raising of poultry and the planting of sugarcane from Surinam.

1643 Roger Williams observes how Atlantic Coast Indians carry corn in burden baskets as travel food and secure cornmeal in leather belts.

1644 Chinese Manchus ensure agrarian abundance by improving efficiency of flood control and grain storage.

1653 Naturopath Nicholas Culpeper compiles home recipes to treat common ailments in *The Complete Herbal.*

1660 The restoration of Charles II to England's throne reinstates the ritual gala, where royalty and courtiers dine at public feast tables while their subjects watch in silence.

1670 Planters in Barbados and Jamaica establish the first New World growth of Africa's green wealth in black-eyed peas, okra, and greens.

Formation of the Hudson's Bay Company earns profits for Great Lakes Indian women, who taught white males to make pemmican, Canada's first processed food.

1687 The supervision of food service on slave transport vessels reduces the mortality rate from 33 percent to 13 percent.

1690s Portuguese traders introduce manioc in Angola and the Congo.

1700s China's Qing emperors enter the golden age of famine relief.

1704 Creole cuisine of Louisiana Territory evolves from the blending of African okra and Choctaw sassafras leaves (*filé*) with classic French and Italian gastronomy.

1714 Scots-French explorer Amédée François Frézier introduces Europeans to the Pacific Coast strawberry.

1728 Germans near Weisbaden bottle and cork seltzer water and sell 600,000 stoneware jugs per year.

1730 Virginia slaves add African specialties to plantation menus.

1749 In North America, the natural crossbreeding of a cow with a buffalo produces sturdier stock to withstand extremes of drought and blizzards.

1750s Sweet French dessert cheeses and festive custard and berry ice cream recipes in London cookbooks migrate to colonial America.

1750 Portuguese monks complete a unique kitchen at Alcobaca Monastery by diverting the Alcoa River through the premises.

1753 The concern of James Lind, a Scots physician, for diet and pure drinking water improves well-being for the Royal Navy.

1757 Swedish ethnographer Carolus Linnaeus, the "Father of Biological Taxonomy," studies the risks of hunger among commoners.

1761 Agronomist Jared Eliot of the Connecticut Colony aids farmers in producing greater wheat yields.
Prussian analytical chemist Andreas Sigismund Marggraf produces loaves of beet sugar, a slave-free commodity.

1769 In Tahiti, English sea captain James Cook combats shipboard scurvy by dispensing malt wort, portable soup, and sauerkraut.

1771 In Bengal, India, British mismanagement of rice distribution allows profiteers to elevate prices to ten times the normal cost and thugs to seize food shipments for sale to the highest bidder.

May 10, 1773 The Tea Act enables the British East India Company to ship Chinese tea duty-free to the American colonies, thus underselling colonial food marketers and, in 1776, fomenting the American Revolution.

1783 The Hudson's Bay Company spreads its control of trade among the Cree, Eskimo, Ojibwa, and Slave from the Dakotas to Ontario and Quebec.

1785 French anatomist Louis Jean-Marie Daubenton notes the slowing of digestion in aging humans and recommends vegetarianism to prevent dyspepsia and flatulence.

1788 English colonists in Australia reject island wild food.

October 17, 1788 Letters from French explorer Jean François de Lapérouse acquaint the Western world with the native foods and diet of Pacific Coast aborigines.

1794 Creole planter Jean Étienne de Boré of New Orleans founds the Mississippi Delta sugar industry.

1796 Under taoism, Chinese poet Yuan Mei, author of Shih Tan (The Menu), advocates inspection of pigs and chickens for disease.

1797 Thomas Malthus's Essay on the Principle of Population warns that the global population will outpace the food supply.

1798 British Crown colonies rule world food commerce.

1802 Herb collector Jules Paul Benjamin Delessert introduces beet sugar refining to the Napoleonic Empire.

1807 Frederic Tudor of Boston acquires a monopoly on the ice trade to the West Indies.

1809 French inventor Nicolas Appert perfects vacuum canning.

1820s Andalusian horticulturist Francisco de Paula Marín introduces 65 edible species to Hawaii.

1820 Analytic chemist Friedrich Christian Accum, apothecary to George III, issues A Treatise on the Adulterations of Food and Culinary Poisons, a jeremiad, subtitled "There is death in the pot."

1821 The Hudson's Bay Company spans North America and dominates the food trade.

1824 Mary Randolph compiles America's first cookbook, The Virginia House-Wife.

1825 Protosociologist Jean Anthelme Brillat-Savarin issues the gourmet's bible, Physiologie du Goût (The Physiology of Taste), which captures the complex stimuli of the table.

1830 Australian colonists export salt beef to England.

1832 In Charleston, South Carolina, American inventor John Mathews enhances the popularity of bottled carbonated drinks.

1833 Marie-Antoine Carême's death leaves unfinished his five-volume encyclopedia L'Art de la Cuisine Française (The Art of French Cuisine), a compendium of baroque table settings, menus, and recipes.

1834 The British East India Company launches a fleet of clipper ships to speed Indian foods to Europe and the Americas.

1837 Lea & Perrins offers Worcestershire sauce, a liquid condiment fermented at apothecary shops, as an appetite stimulant.

February 10, 1840 French club chef Alexis Soyer caters a breakfast for 2,000 following Queen Victoria's coronation.

1842 The Treaty of Nanking opens five Chinese ports to trade with Great Britain.

1843 Food historian Louis, Marquis de Cussy declares gastronomy and hospitality as tokens of a nation's greatness.

1845–1852 The Irish Potato Famine results during English domination of starving smallholders.

September 30, 1847 English abstainers from meat form the Vegetarian Society at Ramsgate.

1848 The Pennsylvania Dutch publish America's first ethnic cookbook, Die Geschickte Hausfrau (The Housewife's Tale).

1850 Thomas Wakley, editor of The Lancet, England's primary medical journal, establishes the Analytical and Sanitary Commission, which vilifies chemical enhancement of 2,500 foodstuffs.

1851 The importation of Chinese laborers to Australian cotton plantations and gold mines introduces Asian vegetables to island cuisine.

1852 Advances in rotary printing make catalog advertising profitable and adaptable to food commerce, beginning with wines from Aristide Boucicaut's Paris store Au Bon Marché.

1861 King Kamehameha IV imports honeybees to Hawaii, experiments with hybrid rice seed, and adds a waterworks to ensure even distribution of fresh water.

1862 In the United States, contract farming replaces subsistence farms with more advantageous methods of sharing risk in producing eggs and meat.

Gail Borden's production of canned milk in vacuum pans enlarges the pantry with stable, safe milk and dairy products.

1863 In Richmond, Virginia, Mary Jackson leads women from the Belvidere Hill Baptist Church in a two-hour bread riot at Capital Square.

1864 British tea boutiques become a London fad.

1867 German chemist Justus von Liebig's Registered Concentrated Milk Company in London ships artificial mother's milk to American and European markets. Pharmacist Henri Nestlé of Vevey, Switzerland, formulates baby food from sweetened condensed milk and malted wheat rusks.

1869 Tabasco pepper, a local specialty from Avery Island in Iberia Parish, Louisiana, becomes a regional condiment. French chef Felix Urbain Dubois popularizes the presentation of dinner in separate courses on individual plates rather than grand displays.

1870 The grapefruit thrives as a commercial crop in Orange County, Florida.

1872 Naturalist Charles Darwin's theories of the struggle, adaptaion, and survival of living organisms revolutionize science.

October 1872 The cultivator of the Red Delicious apple, Indiana fruit grafter Jesse Hiatt, propagates one of the world's preferred health foods.

1873 North American corn cultivation expands to more than 34 million acres (14 million hectares).

1876 The F. & J. Heinz Company bottles and markets tomato ketchup.

1877 The Quaker Mill Company of Ravenna, Ohio, makes cooked oats a staple of the American breakfast menu.

1878 The North American buffalo are too sparse in number to warrant tracking.

February 2, 1880 The freighter *Strathleven* brings the first frozen meat from Melbourne and Sydney, Australia, to London.

1880s English caterer Agnes Marshall turns the food business into a successful conglomerate.

1884 Naval physician Takaki Kanehiro treats beri-beri, a disease caused by too little vitamin B1 in the rice-heavy diet of Japanese sailors.

1890 Georges Auguste Escoffier, the "Father of Modern French Cuisine," brings order to public dining with the first à la carte menu.

1893 Richard Warren Sears of Stewartville, Minnesota, prints the first Sears, Roebuck catalog, initiating the world's most successful groceries-by-mail service.

1895 At the Cordon Bleu cooking school in Paris, chefs prepare the ornate, refined menus of the era.

1896 Dutch industrialist Martinus van der Hagen's Nutricia foods first commercialize prepared infant foods resembling mother's milk.

1897 Freda Ehmann initiates the California ripe olive curing industry.

1900s American Reform Judaism abandons kosher rules, which tend to isolate Jews within mainstream society.

1901 Biochemists Ellen Swallow Richards and Alpheus Grant Woodman warn of unscrupulous dealers in adulterated foods.

1906 The U.S. boom in breakfast cereals brings fame to Battle Creek, Michigan, from which the Kellogg brothers ship 1,000 cases of bran, corn, and wheat flakes a day.

June 30, 1906 President Theodore Roosevelt signs the Pure Food and Drug Act into law, requiring the accurate labeling of foods and drugs and prohibiting interstate trade in adulterated foods.

1907 Henry Perry, a Tennessee-born steamboat cook, initiates barbecuing in Kansas City, Missouri.

1908 Japanese chemist Kikunae Ikeda isolates monosodium glutamate, a salt that mimics *umami,* the taste of meat.

1910s Fructarianism gains popularity as a solution to human drudgery.

1911 Agronomist Elizabeth Coleman White hybridizes blueberries at a plantation in Burlington County, New Jersey.
107 brands of cornflakes are available to U.S. shoppers.

1912 Salish author Mourning Dove reports on the annual hunger that struck native families each February in Washington State.

1914 The Hudson's Bay Company distributes wheat and frozen meat to Belgium and France.

August 1914 The Panama Canal enables oceangoing vessels to deliver food cheaply, dependably, and speedily.

1915 A small ice compartment in Frigidaires enables homemakers to insert their own metal ice trays for freezing.

1917 George F. Doran patents the first U.S. nitrite curing process, a system that enhances meat savor.
In lieu of currency, isolated Russian peasants exchange pots of jam for goods and services.

October 28, 1919 The U.S. National Prohibition Act, also known as the the Volstead Act, prohibits the sale of alcohol.

1920 Colombia and Panama develop resilient sheep herds.
The Hudson's Bay Company in the eastern Arctic at Inukjuak trades in whale blubber and oil and salt fish.

1922 West African trade in peanuts makes Alhassan Dantata the region's richest merchant and founder of private enterprise among Nigerian peasants.
U.S. Grain Future Acts shield the heartland from grain price instability.

1925 Italian agronomist Nazareno Strampelli attempts to free Italy from reliance on imported food.

1930 The United States exports $2 billion per year in farm goods.

May 1933 The Agricultural Adjustment Act, the first modern U.S. farm bill, pays farmers for not planting and for slaughtering excess livestock to avoid food surpluses.

1940s Plant geneticist Norman Ernest Borlaug introduces semidwarf, thick-stemmed wheat in Chapingo, Mexico, as a means of shortening growing seasons and boosting yield.

1940 During rationing, the British minister of food forces dairiers to slaughter herds to free pastures for growing grain and vegetables.

British philosopher Christopher James Northbourne, the "Father of Organic Agriculture," champions environmental sustainability through traditional farming.

1941 Earle R. MacAusland's *Gourmet: The Magazine of Good Living* publishes up-to-the-minute commentary on U.S. restaurants and recipes.

1942 U.S. agronomist Gordie Consyntine "Jack" Hanna develops a tomato that can hold up to mechanical picking.

April 1942 The U.S. Air Force launches air relief over the eastern Himalayas to supply Chiang Kai-shek's Chinese troops.

1943 Price gouging, panic buying, warehousing, wartime inflation, and military provisioning precipitate starvation in rural Bengal, India.

1944 English reformer Donald Watson coins the term *vegan* to describe nonmeat eaters who also reject dairy foods and eggs.

1945 California orchardists field 2 million of botanist Luther Burbank's hybrid plum trees and distribute fresh fruit and prunes worldwide.

May 1946 Food allotments in Tokyo average only about 520 calories per person, leaving the Japanese to forage for wild food.

June 4, 1946 The U.S. National School Lunch Act guarantees markets for eggs, meat, and milk.

June 28, 1948 The first sortie of 32 U.S. C-47s delivers 80 tons (73 metric tons) of flour, medicine, and milk along with CARE packages to Berlin, Germany.

1949 The U.S. Food and Drug Administration initiates government inspection of processed foods.

1950s Kudo Kazuyoshi, a Japanese master at bamboo implement manufacture, designs creels for draining seaweed, transporting salt for pickling eels, and trapping and storing live fish in water.

Television ads spur enthusiasm for Jell-O, TV dinners, and frozen fish sticks and vegetables.

The growth of fast food and patio cookouts increases the eating from hand of buns and rolls with meaty fillings and of fish sticks and kebabs.

Hybrid cultivars, drip irrigation, recirculated water, acrylic tunnels, and plastic film for quonset huts increase possibilities for the global gardener and university research centers.

Gourmet food co-ops welcome imported exotica and wild foods.

1950 Gastronomer Elizabeth David's *A Book of Mediterranean Food* popularizes the sensual pleasures of regional dining.

1952 Advertisers introduce consumers to the first diet soft drink.

1955 John H. Davis, a Harvard professor of agriculture and marketing, creates the term *agribusiness* to describe the evolution of subsistence farming into a commercial complex.

1956 The U.S. La Leche League encourages mothers to return to natural breastfeeding for at least a year.

1958–1961 China incurs a devastating famine that kills 45 million.

January 1, 1958 The U.S. Food Additives Amendment identifies 700 safe food substances and bans cyclamates, lead, and halogenated compounds.

1960s New Orleans chef Leah Chase creates a meatless Creole special for Lent, Gumbo z'Herbes, a puree of mustard greens, spinach, and turnips based on West African pot greens and the French *potage aux herbes*.

1960 U.S. politician George McGovern proposes a consortium of civilian-led food aid programs organized by the United Nations.

Geneticists introduce miracle seeds and chemical fertilizers into the Indian subcontinent.

French food critics Henri Gault and his colleague Christian Millau revive the term *nouvelle cuisine* for pared down, uncomplicated menus.

1961 To stimulate world trade and global prosperity, 34 countries convene the Organisation of Economic Cooperation and Development.

February 11, 1963 On WGBH-TV in Boston, Julia Child debuts as *The French Chef*.

1970s The effect of fast-food psychology on students, office workers, and drivers erodes the notion of the home breakfast table.

Gourmet cuisine abandons cultic French dishes for international foods.

Tokyo greenhouses yield marketable vegetables.

The U.S. Food and Drug Administration bans time-release diethylstilbestrol (DES) pellets from ear implants in cattle and sheep.

1970 In the United States, no commercial grower picks tomatoes by hand.

1971 The U.S. Food and Drug Administration recommends the addition of iron to breakfast cereals and baby foods.

October 12–16, 1971 Reza Pahlavi, the shah of Iran, recalls the splendors of ancient Asia by hosting an elaborate international celebration of the 2,500th anniversary of the Persian Empire.

1972 The U.S. Department of Agriculture establishes the Women, Infants, and Children Program, which distributes iron-fortified infant formula and cereal to some 88,000 applicants.

The U.S. Food and Drug Administration's studies of nitrosamines prove that bologna, corned beef, hot dogs, pepperoni, and salami contain carcinogens.

1973 The Endangered Species Act protects imperiled amphibians, birds, fish, and mammals, as well as crustaceans and mollusks.

The first genetically modified bacteria prove the feasibility of engineering animal life.

1975 Seattle gastroenterologist Walter Lyle Voegtlin promotes a Stone Age, or Paleolithic, diet as the ideal sustenance for human wellness and stamina.

Ancel Keys and Margaret Haney Keys's *How to Eat Well and Stay Well the Mediterranean Way,* a commentary on degenerative ills, is published.

1975–1979 Global emergency aid to Cambodia feeds refugees displaced by tyranny and mass killings under Pol Pot and the Khmer Rouge.

1976 Chef James Beard enlivens service at Windows on the World, a tower restaurant in the World Trade Center.

1980s Food snobbery elevates pink peppercorns, pineapple chutney, and sushi as the exotica of the moment.

1983 British biochemists create a high-fiber, low-starch bread intended to control appetite and cholesterol while emulating the mouthfeel and satisfying quality of ordinary bread.

1984 Agronomist Norman Borlaug introduces intense monoculture in famine-plagued Ethiopia.

1986 The Slow Food initiative begins with a protest of a McDonald's opening along Rome's Spanish Steps.

Restrictions enforced by the International Whaling Commission place a moratorium on the overhunting of whales.

British families began deserting the traditional beef roast this year, when bovine spongiform encephalopathy, or mad cow disease, first threatens meat eaters and spreads to 14 European nations.

1988 Studies of breast milk at Baffin Island and Nunavik, Canada, reveal methylmercury in seal, walrus, and whale blubber.

1989 The European Union issues a ban on synthetic hormones.

1990s The slang term *grazing* refers to sampling varied finger foods.

July 3, 1992 A multinational effort supplies 179,910 tons (163,178 metric tons) of goods to Sarajevo, Bosnia.

1993 The U.S. Food and Drug Administration mandates nutritional labeling on all edibles.

1994 A Colorado firm hybridizes and patents the Enola bean, a yellow legume originated in Mexico.

1996 To stave off malnutrition, French pediatrician André Briend concocts Plumpy'nut, a nutritive peanut paste of milk, oil, peanuts, and sugar.

1998 In New Delhi, India, philosopher Vandana Shiva begins a national movement to empower women in the green movements in Africa, Asia, Europe, and Latin America.

Filipina ecofeminist Neth Daño campaigns against bioengineered foods.

1999 Ecologist Dickson Despommier at Columbia University creates the Genesis system, a soilless root enclosure misted with water and nutrients.

2000s The world's largest greenhouse, the Eden Project, opens in Cornwall, England.

25 percent of American cornfields produce bioengineered grain.

U.S. meat inspectors apply the Hazard Analysis and Critical Control Point law to meat testing by using scientific measures of pathogens.

U.S. teens gravitate toward veganism.

September 22, 2000 In the United States, Kraft Foods recalls $10 million worth of genetically modified foods.

2001 Walter Willett, chair of the department of nutrition at Harvard School of Public Health, blames a heavy carbohydrate diet for causing diabetes, obesity, and early death.

January 2001 Dole Food Company, the world's largest fruit and vegetable seller, enters organic marketing.

2002 Pfizer, a British firm, pays royalties for hoodia, an appetite suppressant discovered by the Khoi and San bush people of South Africa.

During guerrilla warfare in Angola, women network the transport and caching of edibles.

The Cuny Center honors engineer Frederick C. Cuny by expediting disaster relief with practical solutions.

2003 AquaBounty Farms of Waltham, Massachusetts, sells the first chinook salmon raised on growth hormones.

2004 Specialized seagoing vessels increase the profits for investors in the food trade.

July 29, 2005 The United Nations begins a 23,000-ton (21,000-metric-ton) food airlift to Maradi, Niger.

August 23, 2005 After Hurricane Katrina devastates the Mississippi Delta coastline and farms, chef John Besh joins other food specialists in restoring Louisiana's economic basis.

2005–2011 Africa's agricultural commerce increases by 92 percent.

2007 Allura red dye comes under scrutiny in England for lowering IQs in children and increasing hyperactivity.

2008 The Mayo Clinic announces that the Mediterranean diet reduces risk for Alzheimer's disease, breast cancer, and Parkinson's disease.

2009 62 percent of U.S. farm earnings—$180.9 billion—come from the government.

The United Kingdom and the United States restore subsidies and erect barriers to free trade with Australia and New Zealand.

2010 In Australia and Canada, urban aquaponics reduce the distance that crops travel to market.

Food researchers find saffron beneficial in the treatment of Alzheimer's disease, macular degeneration, and retinitis pigmentosa.

The United Fresh Produce Association Foundation of Washington, D.C., campaigns to open a salad bar in every school.

The documentary *Kuru: The Science and the Sorcery* dramatizes the danger of cannibalism, which can cause kuru, a degenerative brain disorder related to mad cow disease.

Peppersmith reintroduces minted chicle gum in Great Britain and Holland under claims that sweetening with xylitol remineralized damaged tooth enamel.

January 1, 2010 The International Food Policy Research Institute predicts that environmental degradation and water mismanagement could reduce sustainability in Burkina Faso, Chad, and Niger.

April 2010 Environmental researchers link the polyethylene terephthalate in soft drink bottles to endocrine disruptors.

June 30, 2010 The Center for Science in the Public Interest recommends banning yellow food dye for its disruption of children's behavior and for possibly causing cancer.

July 2010 The United Nations General Assembly declares water justice and sanitation to be human rights.

2011 The United Nations's Food and Agriculture Organization predicts that Africa holds the key to world food security.

In the United States, empty calories cost less than nutritious food, tempting the poor to spend food dollars on beer, carbohydrates, and snacks.

March 2011 China forbids millers from bleaching wheat flour.

March 15, 2011 At Magaria, Sudan, 6,200 starving children require hospitalization.

May 2011 The Chelsea Flower Show promotes edible flowers.

June 2011 The U.S. Department of Agriculture issues MyPlate, the second update of the food pyramid, a pictorial guide to healthful consumption.

July 2011 Transgenic fish appear biologically and chemically indistinguishable from native species.

July 25, 2011 A world airlift begins importing emergency rations to Mogadishu and border airports in Dolo, Ethiopia, and Wajir, Kenya.

August 2011 Vandals opposed to genetically modified foods destroy bioengineered wheat warehoused for distribution to victims of famine in Somalia.

August 29, 2011 Social media and the Canadian government network to raise famine awareness worldwide.

October 2011 The 21-nation Asia-Pacific Economic Cooperation pledges to create the world's largest free-trade area.

February 29, 2012 North Korea bargains for food aid by agreeing to a moratorium on nuclear development.

Appendix: Herbal Foods and Uses

Herb	Food Use	Curative Use, Health Benefits
agar	soup, sauce, jelly, dessert	constipation, malaise, obesity
alecost	flavoring, soup, salad, game, poultry, stuffing, fruitcake, beer	cold, congestion, cramp, pain, sunburn
alexander	flavoring, fritters, salad, stew, fish, candy	poor appetite
alfalfa	tea	arthritis
almond	candy, liqueur, cake, marzipan	constipation, cough, sunburn
angelica	crystallizing, syrup, tea, beverage, fruit salad, ice cream	flatulence, nausea, rhinitis, indigestion
anise	fruit salad, garnish, soup, cake, bread, pie, candy, sauce, cheese, pickles, curry, fish, liqueur, stew	colic, congestion, cough, nausea, poor lactation, flatulence
artemisia	stuffing, tea	infection, rheumatism
arugula	syrup, snack seed, salad, sauce, vegetable, garnish	cough
balm	tea, beverage	fever, cold, headache, cramp
balsam	flavoring	bleeding, healing, kidney disease, worms, scabies, hemorrhoids
bamboo	salad, garnish	edema, fever, tension
basil	salad, vegetable, soup, flavoring	insomnia, muscle cramp, rhinitis, sinusitis, fever, nausea, dysentery
bay	*bouquet garni,* marinade, stock, pâté, stuffing, curry	indigestion, rheumatism, sprain
bearberry	tea	urinary and venereal disease
beech	nut, oil, potherb	burn, infection, worms, tuberculosis, diabetes
benzoin	flavoring, beverage	sores, healing, croup, laryngitis, chap
bergamot	salad, tea, beverage, wine, stuffing, jam, jelly, meat, milk	congestion, flatulence, insomnia, menstrual pain, sore throat
betel palm	nut, salad	malaise, indigestion, gum disease, tapeworm
bistort	roasted rhizome, soup, flour, salad	enteritis, dysentery, skin irritation, bleeding
black birch	candy, oil	sore muscles, pain
black locust	tea	anemia, headache, stomach pain
black mustard	salad, condiment	bronchitis, congestion
blackberry	beverage, vinegar, wine, jelly, pudding, ice cream, meat sauce	edema, skin ulcer, sore throat, urinary infection
boneset	tea	flu, malaria, kidney disease, typhus, sweating
borage	salad, candy, garnish, beverage, yogurt, cheese, pickles, sandwich, stuffing, tea, wine	bruise, dry skin, fever, urinary pain, tension, inflammation

Herb	Food Use	Curative Use, Health Benefits
bouncing bet	beer	constipation, acne, boil, poison ivy, kidney pain
buckthorn	broth	constipation, bleeding, wart
bugloss	cordial, candy	headache, inflammation, malaise, rhinitis, tension
burdock	salad, vegetable, soup	rheumatism, gout, leprosy, sores
burnet	salad, butter, garnish, vegetable, vinegar, dressing, beverage	enteritis, dry skin, edema, bleeding, rheumatism, hemorrhoids, poor appetite, gout, plague, indigestion
calamint	tea	bruises, colic, cough, flatulence
calendula	food coloring, flavoring, cheese, yogurt, butter, cake, milk, bread, fish, game, garnish, fruit salad, pâté, stew	cracked nipples, halitosis, inflammation, sores, varicose veins, wound
camphor tree	veneer, candy, soap, soft drink, potpourri	hysteria, heart pain, epilepsy, bruise, rheumatism, emphysema, gout, sprain, cold
cañaigre	tea	sore throat, enteritis, bleeding
caraway	meat, game, soup, bread, cake, biscuit, pie, fruit, cheese, snack food, candy, liqueur	flatulence, halitosis, spasm, indigestion, poor appetite
catnip	meat, tea, salad, herb	bruise, colic, fever, toothache, insomnia, headache, upset stomach
celery	soup, stock, sauce, salad, oil flavoring	malaise, flatulence, scurvy, jaundice
chamomile	tea	arthritis, chapped skin, dandruff, eczema, gingivitis, indigestion, insomnia, malaise, menstrual pain, morning sickness, sore eyes, teething, windburn
chaparral	tea	cough, arthritis, cancer
chat	tea	malaise
chervil	omelette, salad dressing, roast fowl, eggs	congestion, poor appetite, poor circulation
chickweed	salad, vegetable, herb	constipation, eczema, hemorrhoids, inflammation, psoriasis, skin disease, sores, ulcer, tumor, sore eyes
chicory	salad, pickles, vegetable, beverage, coffee flavoring, soup, stew	edema, constipation, gallstone, inflammation, urinary infection, poor lactation, jaundice, kidney stone, swelling
Chinese lantern	jam, jelly	kidney stone, gout, infection, typhoid, worms
chives	salad, soup, poultry, meat, potato, cooked vegetable, fish, spread	congestion, hypertension
chocolate tree	candy, beverage, soap	skin irritation, burn
clary	wine, flavoring, potpourri, beer, omelet, soup	eye irritation, upset stomach, splinter
cleavers	coffee or tea substitute, soup	kidney stone, bladder pain, wounds, scurvy, malaise, psoriasis
clove	spice, flavoring, tea	toothache, nausea, athlete's foot, hernia, flatulence, enteritis
clover, red	vegetable	insomnia, spasm, acne, cough, cold, burn
clover, sweet	cordial, sausage, meat, stuffing, beef, cheese, tea	cut, headache, indigestion, infection, pain, sore eyes, wound, spasm
coca shrub	beer	high blood pressure, pain, malaise

Herb	Food Use	Curative Use, Health Benefits
coffee	beverage, candy, flavoring	heart pain, malaise, headache
coltsfoot	salad	asthma, cough, flu, rhinitis
comfrey	tea, salad, vegetable	cough, diaper rash, dry hair, infection, skin damage, varicose veins, wound, bronchitis, psoriasis, broken bone
coriander	stir-fry, soup, sauce, cookies, vegetable, poultry, aperitif	indigestion, rheumatism, soreness, tension
cotton seed	oil	childbirth pain, menstrual pain
couch grass	coffee or tea substitute, grain	urinary disease
cow parsnip	vegetable, salt substitute	headache, toothache, acne, epilepsy
cowslip	jam, wine, pickles, salad, dessert, stuffing, vegetable	cough, headache, insomnia, tension, wound
cress	salad, sauce, garnish	infection
culver's root	tea	blood thinner, tuberculosis, enteritis, liver disease, constipation
cup plant	tea, chewing gum	cold, neuralgia, bleeding, menstrual flooding, compress
dandelion	tea, salad, wine, coffee	constipation, dry skin, eczema, edema, gout, hypertension, insomnia, kidney or gallbladder pain, sallow skin
dianthus	salad, pie, sandwich, flavoring, jam, vinegar, wine, syrup	tension
dill	salad, pickles, apple pie, salmon, herbed butter, oil, mayonnaise, mustard, soup, flavoring, bread	colic, flatulence, hiccups, indigestion, stomach cramp
dittany	tea	fever, kidney stone, stomach cramp
dock	salad	toothache, itch, acne
dog rose	syrup, jelly	rabies, skin inflammation, fever, poultice
elderberry	wine, syrup	cough, skin inflammation, constipation, congestion, kidney disease
elecampane	candy, wine	indigestion, congestion, asthma, spasm, inflammation
English holly	tea substitute	jaundice, malaria, fever, malaise
eucalyptus	syrup	bronchitis, infection, asthma, cough
European alder	smoking fish or meat	inflammation, fever, lice, scabies
European chestnut	nut, flour, soup, bread, cake, oil	enteritis, cough, cold, inflammation
evening primrose	vegetable, pickles, salad, aperitif	hypertension, menstrual pain, multiple sclerosis
eyebright	tea	red or sore eyes, eyewash, inflammation
fennel	fish, salad, vegetable, bread, tea, herb	chapped skin, constipation, flatulence, infection, obesity, sore eyes, toxicity, cataract, poor lactation, cough, blindness
fenugreek	salad, vegetable, roast meat, curry, chutney, spice	bruise, cough, enteritis, poor appetite, poor lactation, flatulence, inflammation, sciatica, swollen gland, tuberculosis, sore throat, impotence, malaise

Herb	Food Use	Curative Use, Health Benefits
feverfew	soup, stew, flavoring, tea	arthritis, fever, insomnia, malaise, migraine, sore throat, vertigo, impeded menstrual flow, bee stings, hysteria
fireweed	potherb, soup, vegetable, salad, tea substitute	spasm, skin disease, asthma, cough, hiccups
flax	snack food	boil, constipation, inflammation, lung infection
four-o'clock	tea	obesity, joint pain
garlic	salad, dressing, marinade, grilled meat, fish, spread	infection, cough, cold, snakebite, high blood pressure, kidney disease, plague, worms
geranium	sauce, custard, jelly, ices, soup, syrup, jam, vinegar, cake, wine, tea, pâté, fish, pastry, sandwich	dermatitis, dry skin, eczema, edema, premenstrual tension, herpes
ginger	spice, flavoring, tea, oil	cold, flu, cough, hangover, malaise, sore muscle, sinusitis, cramp, kidney pain, flatulence
ginseng	tea, candy	anemia, congestion, cough, malaise, poor appetite, tension, impotence
golden orach	salad, vegetable, soup garnish	gout, jaundice, sore throat
goldenrod	tea	dropsy, bruise, colic, sweating, flatulence, kidney disease
goldenseal	tea	morning sickness, eyewash, stomachache, ulcer, vaginal infection, tuberculosis, cancer
Good King Henry	flour, gruel, vegetable, salad, casserole, stuffing, soup, pie	cough, sores
goosefoot	vegetable, potherb, salad	sores, constipation, anemia, kidney disease
gum arabic	wax, candy	sore throat, enteritis, cough, chap
heather	liqueur, sweetener	snakebite, kidney stone, insomnia, cough
heliotrope	food fragrance	epilepsy, hysteria, cough, convulsion
hibiscus	tea	menstrual cramp, indigestion, asthma
highbush cranberry	jelly, dried fruit	cramp, mumps, spasm, palpitation, childbirth pain
hops	flavoring, beer, salad, soup, vegetable	indigestion, inflammation, insomnia, pain, poor appetite, toothache
horehound	candy, tea	cold, asthma, snakebite, poor lactation, hysteria, jaundice, constipation
horseradish	salad, roast meat, fish, slaw, dip, pickles, cheese, mayonnaise, stuffing	chapped skin, cough, edema, sore muscle, worms, rheumatism, sciatica
horsetail	tea	infection, split fingernail, thin blood
houseleek	salad	burn, corn, cut, sore throat, stings, ulcer, wound
hyssop	tea, seasoning, salad, oil, stew, pâté, pie, soup, pulses, fish, game, liqueur, wine	bruise, cough, indigestion, bronchitis, cut, poor appetite, skin disease, rheumatism
Iceland moss	vegetable	malaise, poor appetite, bronchitis, asthma
Irish moss	thickening, vegetable, stew, jelly	chap, constipation, sore throat, skin irritation
jack-by-the-hedge	meat, cheese, sandwich, sauce	edema

Herb	Food Use	Curative Use, Health Benefits
juniper	pâté, marinade, stuffing, gin, sauerkraut, ham, game dressing, stew	plague, leprosy, cold, worms, dropsy, cystitis, stomachache, sores, scurvy, childbirth pain
karaya tree	dressing, cheese, dessert	infection, constipation
kava	beverage	heart pain, malaise, urinary disease, nerves, infection
kelp	vegetable, salt substitute	asthma, skin irritation, arthritis, constipation, radiation poisoning
khella	toothpicks	heart pain, bronchitis, kidney stone, allergy, asthma
knotweed	meal	skin irritation, kidney pain, hemorrhoids
kola nut	beverage, soft drink	obesity, heart pain, nausea, headache, asthma
lady's bedstraw	cheese, food coloring	insomnia, malaise
lady's mantle	salad	enteritis, menstrual dysfunction, pain
laurel	tea, herb, food fragrance	rheumatism, headache, pain
lavender	candy, garnish, oil	asthma, enteritis, eczema, hypertension, hay fever, headache, insomnia, stroke, nausea, oily hair, sallow skin, sinusitis, sprain, swelling, tension, fainting
lavender cotton	oil	snakebite, infection, worms, itch
lemon	beverage, salad, poultry, stir-fry, baking	congestion, cough, fever, rheumatism, rhinitis, headache, infection
lemon balm	beverage, salad, custard, roast meat	congestion, cough, fever, headache, sores, stings, tension
lemon grass	salad, tea	oily skin, tension
lettuce	salad, soup	allergy, congestion, insomnia
licorice	candy, flavoring, beer, sweetening, tea	congestion, constipation, cough, fever
lovage	meat, pâté, broth, cheese, stew, candy, salad, bread, pastry, poultry, tea, soup, vegetable	edema, rheumatism, menstrual pain, halitosis, flatulence
marjoram	soup, pasta, fish, game, sausage, meat loaf, tea, vegetable, omelette, cheese, stuffing, herb	chill, hay fever, muscle cramp, tension, upset stomach, toothache, itch, snakebite, flatulence
marsh marigold	vegetable, food dye, pickles	wart, rheumatism
marshmallow	cheese, salad, vegetable	burn, cough, enteritis, inflammation, insomnia, skin disease, teething
maté	beverage	malaise, fatigue
mayapple	fruit	liver cancer, constipation
meadowsweet	beer, wine, mead, herb, flavoring, jam, fruit	enteritis, edema, fever, gastritis, inflammation, heartburn, pain, tension, ulcer, skin
milkweed	vegetable	asthma, insomnia, ringworm, dropsy, poison ivy, venereal disease
mint	sauce, syrup, vinegar, tea, potato, cream cheese, yogurt, dessert, pastry, candy, garnish, liqueur	acne, enteritis, flu, halitosis, muscle pain, sinusitis, indigestion, morning sickness, nausea, oily hair

Herb	Food Use	Curative Use, Health Benefits
moonseed	soft drink	tuberculosis, lymph infection, arthritis, malaise, constipation, kidney disease
mormon tea	beverage	syphilis, cold, fever, headache, sores, burn, bleeding, asthma, sunburn
motherwort	beverage	palpitation, cramp, rabies, childbirth pain, convulsion
mouse-ear	tea	liver disease, intestinal pain, asthma, sore throat, nosebleed
mountain ash	pie, jelly, jam, wine	enteritis, hemorrhoids, scurvy, inflammation
mugwort	tea, herb	sore feet, childbirth pain, palsy, menopause, tension, epilepsy
mulberry	jam, wine	constipation, edema, weakness
mullein	liqueur	congestion, cough, earache, hoarseness, migraine
mustard	spread, flavoring, eggs, mayonnaise, sandwich, salad, pickles, syrup	arthritis, chapped skin, chill, pain, laryngitis, pleurisy, congestion, inflammation, sciatica, poison
myrtle	beer, soup, stew, grilled and roast meat, barbecue, flavoring	bruise, hemorrhoids, infection, psoriasis, sinusitis, upset stomach
nasturtium	salad, flavoring, garnish, sauce	rhinitis, scurvy
nettle	salad, soup, beer, tea, vegetable	acne, edema, indigestion, scrofula, bleeding, gout, oily skin, inflammation, menstrual pain, tuberculosis
oats	cereal, flour, beer	indigestion, spasm, skin inflammation, depression, high cholesterol
onions	vegetable, herb, flavoring, salad, pickles	high blood pressure, wart, acne, infection, flatulence, kidney disease, diabetes, pneumonia
oregano	pizza, chili, eggs, cheese, vegetable, fish, stuffing, barbecue	cough, gallbladder disease, menstrual pain, headache, irritability, rheumatism, stiff neck, seasickness, toothache, upset stomach
Oswego tea	oil, tea	cold, sore throat, sinus pain
pansy	candy, salad, garnish	congestion, toxins, skin inflammation
papaya	juice, fruit wrap, meat tenderizer	back pain, anticoagulant
parsley	salad, garnish, *bouquet garni,* sandwich, soup, fried fish, eggs	acne, dandruff, dry hair, dry skin, halitosis
pepper, black	condiment, oil, flavoring	flatulence, heart pain, kidney disease, infection
pepper, chili	flavoring, salad, pickles	bursitis, rheumatism, infection, poor circulation
periwinkle	tea	cancer, stings, eye pain, congestion, sore throat
pine nut	snack, thickener	bronchitis, eczema, constipation, enteritis
pineapple	fruit, beverage, tenderizer	skin inflammation, abscess, ulcer, anticoagulant
pipsissewa	root beer, candy	kidney stone, sore eyes, leg swelling, rheumatism, infection

Herb	Food Use	Curative Use, Health Benefits
poppy	bread, cake, biscuit, soup, oil, garnish, condiment, food dye, wine, pastry	cough, enteritis, pain, insomnia
prickly lettuce	salad, vegetable	poor lactation, chapped skin, kidney disease
pumpkin	vegetable, oil, snack, pie, fruit butter	worms, burn, urinary pain
purslane	salad, vegetable, soup, pickles, flavoring	edema, poor appetite
pussytoes	chewing gum	cough, fever, skin irritation
quassia	dessert	malaise, liver disease, gall bladder pain, leukemia
raspberry	syrup, tea, fruit, jam, jelly	spasm, plaque on teeth, heart disease, childbirth pain, cramp, cold, fever, enteritis, skin irritation
rose	pickles, pie, salad, garnish, liqueur, wine, tea, syrup, jam, sauce	conjunctivitis, poor circulation, tension
rosemary	roast meat, game, pâté, bread, vinegar, orange, sausage, herb, oil, potato	asthma, chill, dandruff, gout, rheumatism, indigestion, infection, soreness, baldness, malaise, oily hair, toothache, poor circulation
rue	milk, cheese, marinade, eggs, fish, sauce	diabetes, edema, epilepsy, worms, spasm, fever, hysteria, wound, poor lactation, rheumatism, skin ulcer, menstrual pain
safflower	cooking oil, food dye	edema, hypertension, skin disease, fever, constipation
saffron	food coloring, curry, cake	Alzheimer's disease, tumor, depression, breast cancer, antihistamine, immunity
sage	cheese, dip, soup, vinegar, bread, biscuit, omelette, vegetable, tea, beer, herb	dirty pores, dry hair, fever, sweating, tension, sore throat, menstrual pain, dysentery, halitosis, poor lactation, colic
sagebrush	liqueur	enteritis, flatulence, sores, bullet wound
Saint-John's-wort	salad, tea	anemia, bruise, headache, insomnia, pain, ulcer, rheumatism, tension, varicose veins, wound, tuberculosis, depression
sassafras	tea, oil, syrup, root beer	malaise, blood disease, syphilis
scurvy grass	herb, salad, potherb	scurvy, gout, rheumatism, kidney stone, acne
sea holly	vegetable	cystitis, malaise, prostatitis, sexual dysfunction, urethritis, wound
sea onion	stock, vinegar	congestion, cough, kidney problems, heart disease, poison
seneca snakeroot	syrup, tea, candy	pleurisy, cough, cold, asthma, infection
sesame	snack food, bread, oil, vegetable, casserole, sauce, pâté, biscuit	constipation, hemorrhoids
shepherd's purse	vegetable, salad, stew, herb	bleeding, hemorrhoids, skin inflammation
silverweed	vegetable, tuber	cramp, indigestion, sore gums, sore throat, toothache
skirret	stir-fry vegetable, meat, stew, pie, pickles, salad	edema, indigestion, jaundice, urinary disease

Herb	Food Use	Curative Use, Health Benefits
slippery elm	tea	kidney disease, childbirth pain, enteritis, skin disease, diphtheria
smallage	salad, cheese, poultry, stuffing, garnish, fish, soup	colic, diabetes, flatulence, indigestion, insomnia, kidney disease, poor appetite, urinary disease
smartweed	seasoning, food coloring	cholera, earache, epilepsy, toothache, skin irritation, contraception
soapwort	garnish, fruit salad, beer, salad	acne, psoriasis
sorrel	sauce, soup, meat, salad, fish, poultry, eggs, flavoring, vegetable, herb	boil, dry skin, fever, kidney disease, liver disease, gout, sunburn, ulcer, wound, constipation
soursop blueberry	fruit, tea	bladder disease, diabetes, worms, skin irritation
speedwell	tea substitute	congestion, skin irritation
spicebush	spice, tea	cold, malaise, worms, dysentery, bruise, rheumatism, menstrual pain
spikenard	root beer, syrup	malaise, rheumatism, gout, deafness, syphilis, earache, broken bone, angina
summer savory	beans, sauce, roast meat, soup, vinegar, beverage	indigestion, nausea
sundew	syrup	cough, spasm, tuberculosis
sunflower	snack food, oil, salad, sandwich, vegetable	cough, kidney disease
sweet cicely	stew, fruit, jam, salad, cake, pudding, fruit salad, stir-fry, dressing, sweetener	indigestion, inflammation, poor appetite
sweet flag	candy	cramp, flatulence, malaise, fever, toothache
sweet herb	sweetener, potherb	diabetes
sweet woodruff	beverage, wine, cordial, herb	stomach pain, tension, poison, wound
sweetgum	flavoring	congestion, infection, ringworm, herpes, acne, hemorrhoids
tansy	stew, flavoring, sausage, meat, pie, omelette, food coloring, stuffing	bruise, sprain, rheumatism, menstrual pain, cold, stomachache, spasm
tarragon	fines herbes, sauce, soup, fish, vegetable, eggs, roast chicken, grilled meat	indigestion, poor appetite, menstrual pain, scurvy, toothache, malaise
thistle	vegetable, oil, salad, tea	cancer, rhinitis, skin ulcer, fever, liver disease, contraception
thyme	bouquet garni, meat, fish, game, meat, vegetable, fruit salad, jam, oil	arthritis, chill, dandruff, hay fever, indigestion, infection, malaise, poor appetite, nightmares, sore throat, athlete's foot, enteritis
trefoil	tea	nerves, spasm
turmeric	pickles, mustard, food dye	bruise, gas, worms, skin lesion, infection, liver disease, arthritis
valerian	soup, stew	cramp, exhaustion, headache, insomnia, tension
vervain	liqueur, stew	bruise, exhaustion, fever, liver disease, sore throat, urinary infection

Herb	Food Use	Curative Use, Health Benefits
violet	garnish, candy, cake, food dye, ice cream, salad, syrup, pudding, punch	bruise, constipation, cough, pleurisy, jaundice, headache, insomnia, stress, epilepsy, skin cancer, kidney disease
water lily	stir-fry vegetable, boiled tuber	enteritis, skin irritation, excessive libido
watercress	salad, soup, sandwich, garnish	scurvy, malaise, cough, asthma, acne, contraception
white oak	nut, tea	sores, wound, skin irritation, hemorrhoids
wild cherry	syrup, jam, jelly, wine, gin	enteritis, lung inflammation, worms, ulcer, abscess
wild ginger	candy, flavoring	menstrual pain, flatulence, malaise, fever
wild licorice	sugar substitute, candy	pain, earache, fever, ulcer, rheumatism, cough, childbirth pain, arthritis
wild strawberry	meat, gravy, fruit, jam, candy, cake, pie, syrup, cordial, liqueur, tea	anemia, enteritis, edema, poor appetite, fainting, fever, gout, kidney disease
willow	mashed vegetable	pain, nausea, cold, fever, insomnia, indigestion, inflammation
winter savory	vegetable, jelly, herb, flavoring	fever, flatulence, indigestion, pain, sore throat, stings
wintergreen	beverage, tea, candy	headache, infection, pain, rheumatism, sore throat, skin disease, inflammation
witch hazel	snack seed, oil	strain, fever, bruise, bleeding, menstrual pain, hemorrhoids, eyewash, postpartum soreness, acne
wormwood	liqueur, bitters, wine, beer, food dye, flavoring	gout, malaise, bruise, worms, swelling, menstrual pain
woundwort	tuber, vegetable, pickles	wound, bleeding, vertigo, dysentery
yarrow	tea, spice, food dye	cystitis, flu, hangover, hypertension, infection, oily hair, oily skin, wound, earache
yellow bedstraw	food dye, cheese, beverage	sore feet, bleeding, styptic, kidney disease, epilepsy

Glossary

aeroponics a soilless horticultural system that encloses plant root systems and supplies nutrients and water through misting; a variant of hydroponics. *See also* hydroponics.

agribusiness the totality of buying and selling involved in bringing food crops to the table, involving farmers and herders along with financiers, equipment manufacturers, seed suppliers, livestock marketers, and food processors and distributors, a system that the United Nations encourages in preindustrial countries.

agroecology the integration of food production into a sustainable whole by allying scientific knowledge of the systems of nature with farming and herding, such as balancing Brazilian livestock pasturage with preservation of the rain forest.

anthropophagy cannibalism; the ingestion of human flesh by their own kind, a food culture once observed by Australian Aborigines and other native peoples.

aperitif a spiritous appetite stimulant served before a meal, such as the herbal bitters drunk in the 1200s to ward off cholera.

apiculture the keeping of bee colonies in apiaries as a source of honey, pollen, and wax, a form of husbandry that the ancient Romans passed to medieval farmers.

appetizer a preface to the eating and digestion of a satisfying meal, such as the *mezes* that Arabs serve before a heavy dinner.

aquaponics a sustainable food production system that applies a simulated habitat to the controlled growth of fish and plants, a food business in Japan.

asceticism self-denial of luxury beverages and foods as well as normal comforts, a monastic self-discipline that trained Christians in stoicism.

bain-marie a version of the double boiler that heats delicate custards and egg dishes to a fixed temperature over boiling water without drying out ingredients, the invention of Florentine alchemist Maria de' Cleofa in the early 1500s. Catherine de' Médici brought the device to France on September 2, 1533, as part of her trousseau.

barbecue the slow-cooking of meat over a smoky fire, a culinary technology invented by the Caribbean Arawak, Carib, and Taíno peoples.

biopiracy the theft and control of indigenous fungi, livestock, plants, and seeds for commercial exploitation, notably food plants from Africa for sale by industrialized nations.

bottarga mullet roe, a Byzantine forerunner of caviar, which the Egyptians called *batarekh.*

bouquet garni a string-tied bundle of bay leaf, parsley, and thyme, three essential herbs that Pierre La Varenne introduced to the cooking stage of soup, stew, and stock. The string enabled the server to remove the bundle before plating the dish.

charcuterie the curing and preservation of fresh pork as bacon, confit, forcemeat, *galantine,* ham, pâté, or terrine, all French specialties. *See also* confit.

colloid a gas, liquid, or solid dispersed within another substance, the physical principle behind homogenized milk. *See also* emulsion.

compressor the device in a refrigerator that reduces refrigerants into hot, high-pressure vapor for lowering temperatures.

confit a meat preserved in salt and cooked in its own fat, such as *confit de canard,* a duck recipe developed by early Louisiana Cajun cooks.

congee a cooked cereal such as rice thinned with broth or milk, a staple of Chinese cuisine.

coprolite charred, dried, or frozen feces or excrement, which bears evidence of food types and diversity as well as cooking styles. Archaeologists analyze coprolites to determine the foodways and nutrition of prehistoric diners.

cordial a sweet aperitif, tonic, or soft drink that spurs appetite, such as the elderflower beverage distributed to guests in ancient Rome.

coshering the paying of landlords in food-rents of cattle and grain, a feudal economic system between the aristocracy and tenant farmers.

cuisine du pauvre a planned diet for soup kitchens and feeding stations, conceived in 1790 by Count Rumford to relieve the beggars of Munich, Germany.

curd a gel or coagulant of milk; a source of cheese, including tofu, a vegetable cheese derived from soybean curds.

curing the processing of fish and meat by smoking or flavoring with salt and sugar plus nitrates or nitrites to preserve fats and proteins. Charcuterie is the French subspecialty of curing pork.

dairy food products derived from processing the milk of buffalo, camels, cows, goats, horses, sheep, and yak, including koumiss from mare's milk and ewe's milk cheese.

dal a split pulse made from a husked bean, lentil, or pea. Variants of dal recipes identify the cookery of parts of India and Sri Lanka.

debitage the rock fragments, flakes, and shattered or damaged materials of stone tool manufacture, such as chert, flint, or obsidian skinning, flaying, and deboning knives and burins for carving bone and wood eating utensils and bowls.

desalination any process removing salt from water to make available potable water for household use and crop irrigation, a boon to utilities in Dubai, Israel, and other arid countries.

deviled an eighteenth-century term for seasoning a dish or ingredient with the hottest mustards and spices, such as deviled lobster, a coastal English specialty flavored with cayenne.

dietetics the study of food consumption and the effects of nutrients on human health, an outgrowth of the U.S. home economics movement of the 1910s and 1920s.

dioxin a toxic chemical compound that threatens human health, particularly breast milk.

Edenic diet a stringent form of veganism that follows the scriptural model in the book of Genesis by excluding all meat and shellfish, salt and spice, sugar, coffee and tea, and alcohol. *See also* veganism.

emulsion a mixture of two incompatible liquids, such as oil and vinegar in vinaigrette and oil and egg in mayonnaise.

endangered species a plant or animal that sinks too low in numbers to survive. The threat of extinction heightens depletion of the world's food diversity, such as the loss of shark, tilapia, and whale from seafood.

endore to gild or glaze the crust of a presentation piece with savory egg yolk and saffron mixtures. In the early Renaissance, chefs extended endoring with real gold leaf and other metallic finishes hardened in lidded tureens or before metal screens.

entomophagy the consumption of insects for food, such as the Aztec consumption of live crickets in tacos and the Chinese sale of scorpions on skewers as street food.

entremets palate cleansers served between courses of banquets, as described in Taillevent's *Le Viandier* (*The Provisioner*, ca. 1375), a sourcebook of medieval cuisine.

epicure an individual whose discriminate taste focuses on fine dining and table luxuries, the defining characteristic of restaurant critic James Beard.

espaliering spreading shrubs and trees horizontally over a flat plane while inhibiting shoots branching obliquely or vertically, a plant technology that boosted fruit and berry production in Renaissance kitchen gardens.

estate tea an unblended tea picked from a single variety of bushes grown in a distinct terroir, such as Prince of Wales tea, a favorite of Edward VIII.

Eucharist a Christian sacrament involving ritual consumption of bread and wine, commemorations of the body and blood of the martyred Christ. The medieval elevation of the sacrament dignified the professions of bakers and vintners.

factor a dealer or commercial agent of a stock corporation, such as the Hudson's Bay Company or the Dutch East India Company.

fermentation a chemical phenomenon that converts carbohydrates into acids or alcohols, a source of flavor and texture in Inuit buried salmon.

fertigation the injection of soluble fertilizer directly into an irrigation system, a method that applies nutrients to an aquaponics garden such as those in Barbados and Australia.

filtre a love potion or tonic, a focus of ancient literature, such as the myth of Tristan and Isolde, who mistakenly drink a charmed wine intended for King Mark.

food justice the opposition to patent abuse that strips smallholders of food sovereignty, such as the planting of hybrid corn in Angola.

food sovereignty the human right to produce food through farming, fishing, and herding, a liberty promised to Indian tribes in the Northwest.

foodie neologism for a food hobbyist, such as the gourmands who form exotic food clubs.

forcemeat a puree of ground meat emulsified with fat as found in pâté and sausage, a preservation method pioneered by German butchers.

four humors an ancient Greek scientific term for blood, phlegm, black bile, and yellow bile, the extremes of human chemistry that cooks sought to balance with specific food combinations.

fricassee a juicy dish of meat or poultry sliced into chunks and stewed in gravy or pan drippings, a favorite in ancient Persia.

frugivore a fructarian or fruit eater, such as the early hominoids, who subsisted on fruit and nuts.

gastronome an intellectual who studies the sensual elements of nourishment, an interest of Greek and Persian sybarites.

gene bank the protected storage of genetic resources, such as the collected seeds and plant material of Seed Savers Exchange near Decorah, Iowa.

genetically modified food the integral modification of ova or seeds through recombinant DNA technology, a reordering of the essential material that establishes the uniqueness of a plant or animal, such as corn, rice, or sheep.

germplasm a collection of genetic resources for an organism, such as food plants cataloged and distributed by the Royal Botanic Gardens Millenium Seed Bank.

gourmand an individual who takes pleasure in eating and drinking, a description of the courtiers of Henry VIII.

gourmet an expert on the best in food and drink, such as Julia Child, a proponent of French cuisine.

Green Revolution post–World War II scientific initiatives—notably the work of Norman Borlaug—that boosted the world's agrarian yield. *See also* genetically modified food.

groats hulled whole barley, buckwheat, oats, or cracked wheat, an ingredient in tabbouleh, a Middle Eastern salad of grains, mint, and parsley.

halal a term for food deemed permissible and fit for consumption under Islamic law.

heritage foods an authentic regimen of cooking and eating for a particular population or culture, such as the Aleut of Alaska.

hippocras heated wine spiced with cinnamon, a common nightcap during the Middle Ages.

hippophagy the consumption of horse meat, which eighth-century popes forbade as a form of idolatry in pagan Germans.

hybridization the crossbreeding, mating, or interbreeding of living things to produce dissimilar offspring or stock. Through hybridization, California agronomist Luther Burbank pioneered 800 innovations in truck farming and orchardry to increase the supply and quality of the world's food.

hydroponics the cultivation of plants in water, a source of pesticide-free organic produce such as that pioneered aboard the space station.

idiocuisine food containing the ingredients and recipes indigenous to a household, such as the unique recipes and canning of English apple growers.

insectivory *See* entomophagy.

intraspecific within a single species, such as hybrids of the wild blueberry.

irrigation the artificial watering of soil and vegetation to increase the success of dryland farming and areas incurring inadequate rainfall, such as sub-Saharan Africa.

kosher the detailed regimens for food selection and cleanliness dictated by *kashruth,* Torah dietary law, particularly the avoidance of swine and pork products.

leaven an ingredient mixed into bread dough that ferments or releases CO_2 bubbles to create a light texture, such as compressed yeast and baking powder in Southern angel biscuits.

libation a sacred beverage poured on an altar to reverence a deity, the task of male householders in ancient Rome.

linctus a homemade cough syrup made by blending herbs and root extracts into sugar syrup.

liquidarianism a fruit diet that excludes pulp and seeds and relies solely on alternating fasting with fruit juices; hydrorianism.

local food movement a grassroots encouragement of consumers to subsist on area harvests of flora and fauna within a 100-mile (160-kilometer) area, a campaign that flourishes in Australia's outback and shores.

locavore a consumer of locally grown produce, including the fish and vegetables raised on aquaponic farms.

macrobiotics a diet that stresses whole grains and limits consumption of avocados, beets, eggplant, peppers, potatoes, spinach, tomatoes, seafood, and other animal products. *See also* veganism.

Maillard reaction a chemical change in browned foods producing identifiable flavors, including bread crust, fried steak, and roux, a Creole cooking staple of fried flour that enriches gravies and stews.

mandoline a kitchen device that slices, crinkle-cuts, and juliennes fruits and vegetables.

mano and metate a stone tray and cylindrical crushing bar used by North American peoples to pulverize seeds, grains, and manioc roots to make flour, such as corn for *pulque* or tacos.

mezzaluna a single or double semicircular blade rocked back and forth for dicing herbs or cutting blubber, the favorite meat of Eskimos.

mocuck a lidded bark storage box used by forest Indians to store nuts and tubers.

moulinette a French food mill for pureeing vegetables, as described in Elizabeth David's *French Country Cooking* (1951).

mouthfeel the chemical and physical element of chewing solids and swallowing liquids. Effects involve difficulty of mastication, viscosity, moisture, density, and aftertaste. Russian cooks refine the mouthfeel of meat pies by cooking them in beef broth.

national dish a food that characterizes a nation and its foodways and illustrates the ingenuity of an ethnic group in readying local ingredients for the table, such as passion fruit drinks in Costa Rica and *poi* in Hawaii.

neutriceutical an edible that combines the benefits of nutrition and prevention of disease, such as freeze-dried lactobacillus and fish oil capsules.

omnivore animal species that eat animals and plants, a description of early hominids.

open pollination the propagation of a plant by insects or wind rather than human intervention, the Aztec method of corn production.

organic foods edibles near their original form that come to market in a pure state without additives, dyes, fertilizer, genetic modification, irradiation, and pesticides, including leaf greens and farm-raised catfish.

orthorexia an eating disorder in people obsessed with health food regimens, such as fasting, liquid diets, and raw foodism. *See also* raw foodism.

osmazome the flavor of roasted meat, which Japanese biochemists identify as *umami. See also* umami.

parfleche a rawhide food bag in which Amerindians packed travel foods, such as dried berries, jerky, and pemmican.

pastillage the creation of figures, symbols, and scenes from sugar dough and gum-based paste, the artistic medium of Nicolò della Pigna, a sixteenth-century pastry chef.

patent an official monopoly of trade over other competitors, such as the legal control that Monsanto places over genetically engineered seed.

pathogen any microorganism that can cause disease in a plant or animal, such as coffee rust, peach leaf curl, or gray mold on squash.

PCBs (polychlorinated biphenyls) toxic organic compounds that endanger the human endocrine and nervous systems.

permaculture the creation of permanent landscaping with berry bushes and fruit and nut trees, a sound ecological investment providing food security.

pisciculture the raising of fresh water fish in farm ponds, a common source of protein at monasteries during the Middle Ages. *See also* aquaponics.

pome fruit tree fruit with a fleshy mesocarp, notably, the apple and pear, both onetime ingredients in ketchup.

prazo a semifeudal African plantation supervised by Portuguese overseers, such as the estates exploiting native resources of the Zambezi River valley.

rationing the allotment of foods during wars and national emergencies, a method of preventing the hoarding and black marketing that emerged during the Korean War.

raw foodism (or rawism) consumption of only raw foods, primarily beans and grains, fruits and vegetables, juices, nut pastes and seeds, plant oils, sea vegetables, and uncooked meats.

reduction a sauce or stock boiled down to the consistency of gravy, such as raspberry dressing for chocolate mousse, a standard dessert in nouvelle cuisine.

rococo an extreme of decoration that marked banquet centerpieces during the 1700s.

roux a cooking basis blended from flour in hot bacon fat, butter, or olive oil. As a result of the Maillard reaction, a small amount of roux imparts a nutty taste to meat and vegetables. *See also* Maillard reaction.

salmi a highly flavored ragout of roast bird and mushrooms, such as that prepared for the late-eighteenth-century Lapérouse expedition in the South Pacific.

service à la russe the presentation of dinner in separate courses on individual plates rather than in grand rococo displays. In 1856, Felix Urbain Dubois began shifting formal meals away from *service à la Française,* which treated cuisine as a demonstration of wealth and largesse. *See also* rococo.

shaduf a counterweighted dip bucket, an early Egyptian technology that enabled a farmer to maintain an even flow of water in irrigated vegetable beds.

shuttle breeding the cultivation of the same crop at different altitudes and latitudes, such as short-stemmed wheat in the plateaus and piedmont of Mexico and paddy and dryland rice in Cambodia.

sofrito a Latin American and Spanish condiment combining annatto seed, chili pepper, cilantro, garlic, ham, onion, and oregano sautéed in lard. In Puerto Rico, cooks use sofrito as a seasoning for beans and rice.

sutler a freelance itinerant grocer, such as the wagoneers who marketed liquor and luxury foodstuffs to soldiers during the American Civil War.

sybarism indulgence in luxuries and pleasures, a description of the self-indulgent eating style in France under Louis XVI and Marie Antoinette.

synesthesia the merger of sensual delights, particularly aroma and flavor in the consumption of vanilla, an early ingredient in hot chocolate.

tagine a Berber pot fashioned from clay into a saucer and cone-topped lid, a source of liquid condensation that tenderizes mutton and lamb.

tartare mammal meat or fish chopped raw for service on rusks, such as Sicilian carpaccio or Peruvian ceviche.

terroir the complex influence of geography, climate, and temperature on local foods, particularly monofloral honey and coffee, tea, vanilla, and wine representative of a limited region, such as the volcanic soil of Mexico's Mazatlán Valley and the Chinese provinces that produce estate teas.

umami a fundamental flavor of meat first isolated in Tokyo in 1908 and added to the basic savors of bitter, salty, sour, and sweet. *See also osmazome.*

understory vegetation that grows under the forest canopy, a source of mushrooms, truffles, and fiddlehead ferns.

veganism the avoidance of animal products through a diet of fruits, nuts, and vegetables.

vegetarianism the avoidance of crustaceans, fish, domesticated animals, game, poultry, and shellfish in the diet. Extreme vegetarians also abstain from meat by-products, including gelatin and rennet, a curdling element employed in cheese making.

vermifuge a purgative substance that rids the body of intestinal parasites, such as tansy, clove, and artemisia.

zoonosis a disease that can pass between animals and humans, such as Ebola, which humans can contract from handling or eating primate bushmeat.

Bibliography

Primary Sources

Accum, Friedrich Christian. *A Treatise on Adulterations of Food and Culinary Poisons.* London: Longman, 1820.

al-Warraq, ibn Sayyar. *Annals of the Caliphs' Kitchens: Ibn Sayyar al-Warraq's Tenth-Century Baghdadi Cookbook.* Boston: Brill, 2007.

Athenaeus. *The Learned Banqueters.* Ed. and trans. S. Douglas Olson. Cambridge, MA: Loeb Classical Library, 2011.

Baegert, Jacob. *Observations in Lower California.* Ed. and trans. M.M. Brandenburg and Carl L. Baumann. Berkeley: University of California Press, 1952.

Beard, James. *Beard on Food: The Best Recipes and Kitchen Wisdom from the Dean of American Cooking.* Ed. José Wilson. New York: Bloomsbury, 2007.

Bicknell, A.S. "Hippophagy: The Horse as Food for Man." *Journal of the Society of Arts* 16:801 (March 27, 1868): 349–359.

Billings, John Davis. *Hardtack and Coffee.* Boston: G.M. Smith, 1887.

Borlaug, Norman E. "Ending World Hunger: The Promise of Biotechnology and the Threat of Antiscience Zealotry." *Plant Physiology* 124:2 (October 2000): 487–490.

Bradford, Gamaliel. "Madame de Maintenon." *Virginia Quarterly Review* 6:1 (Winter 1930): 65–83.

Buell, Paul D., and Eugene N. Anderson. *A Soup for the Qan: Chinese Dietary Medicine of the Mongol Era as Seen in Hu Szu-Hui's* Yin-shan Cheng-yao. New York: Kegan Paul International, 2000.

Cannon, O.S., and G.C. Hanna. "New Disease Resistant Tomatoes." *California Agriculture* 13:3 (March 1959): 7.

Chardin, Jean, and Ina Baghdiantz McCabe. *Du Bon Usage du Thé et Des Épices en Asie: Réponses à Monsieur Cabart de Villamont.* Paris: L'Inventaire, 2002.

Child, Julia, and Alex Prud'homme. *My Life in France.* New York: Anchor, 2006.

Cieza de León, Pedro de. *The Second Part of the Chronicle of Peru.* London: Hakluyt Society, 1883.

Cranz, David. *The History of Greenland.* London: Brethren's Society for the Furtherance of the Gospel Among the Heathen, 1767.

Diefendorf, Mary Riggs. *The Historic Mohawk.* New York: Putnam, 1910.

Dittman, M.E. "The Olive: Shasta County's Symbol of Peace and Prosperity." *Sunset, the Pacific Monthly* 33:1 (July 1914): 170–174.

Doran, John. *Table Traits, with Something on Them.* London: R. Bentley, 1854.

Eckhardt, Linda West, and Katherine West Defoyd. *Half-Scratch Magic.* New York: Clarkson Potter, 2003.

Egede, Hans. *A Description of Greenland.* London: T. & J. Allman, 1818.

Ellis, George Edward. *Memoir of Sir Benjamin Thompson, Count Rumford, with Notices of His Daughter.* Boston: Estes and Lauriat, 1871.

Eyles, John. *A View of the Greenland Trade and Whale-Fishery.* London: J. Roberts, 1722.

Fisher, M.F.K. *The Measure of Her Powers: An M.F.K. Fisher Reader.* Ed. Dominique Gioia. Washington, DC: Counterpoint, 2000.

Frezier, Amadée François. *A Voyage to the South-Sea and Along the Coasts of Chili and Peru in the Years 1712, 1713, 1714.* London: Jonah Bowyer, 1717.

Gault, Henri, and Christian Millau. "Vive La Nouvelle Cuisine Française." *Nouveau Guide Gault-Millau* 54 (October 1973).

Grigson, Jane. *Jane Grigson's Fruit Book.* Lincoln: University of Nebraska Press, 2007.

Hale, Sarah Josepha. *The New Household Receipt-Book.* London: T. Nelson and Sons, 1854.

Harland, Marion, William Henry Milburn, Francis E. Clark, Sarah Knowles Bolton, and Helen Hunt Jackson. *Young People's New Pictorial Library of Poetry and Prose.* New York: N.D. Thompson, 1888.

Hasselquist, Frederick. *Voyages and Travels in the Levant in the Years 1749, 50, 51, 52.* London: L. Davis and C. Reymers, 1766.

Hearn, Lafcadio. *La Cuisine Creole.* New Orleans, LA: F.F. Hansell & Bro., 1885.

Herodotus. *The Landmark Herodotus: The Histories.* Ed. Robert B. Strassler and Andrea L. Purvis. New York: Anchor, 2009.

Heyerdahl, Thor. *Fatu-Hiva: Back to Nature.* Garden City, NY: Doubleday, 1974.

Holt, Vincent M. *Why Not Eat Insects?* London: Field & Tuer, 1885.

Homans, Isaac Smith. *A Cyclopedia of Commerce and Commercial Navigation.* New York: Harper & Brothers, 1858.

Jefferson, Thomas. *Thomas Jefferson's Garden Book.* Ed. Edwin Morris Betts. Chapel Hill: University of North Carolina Press, 2002.

Johnson, Amandus. *The Swedish Settlements on the Delaware.* Philadelphia: University of Pennsylvania, 1911.

Kennedy, Diane. *Oaxaca al Gusto: An Infinite Gastronomy.* Austin: University of Texas Press, 2010.

Keys, Ancel, and Margaret Keys. *How to Eat Well and Stay Well the Mediterranean Way.* New York: Doubleday, 1975.

Kitchin, G.W., ed. *Compotus Rolls of Obedientiaries of St. Swithun's Priory, Winchester.* London: Simpkin & Co., 1892.

Koninckx, Christian. *The First and Second Charters of the Swedish East India Company (1731–1766).* Kortrijk, Belgium: Van Ghemmert, 1980.

La Pérouse, Jean François de Galaup. *The Journal of Jean François de Galaup de la Pérouse, 1785–1788.* Ed. and trans. John Dunmore. London: Hakluyt Society, 1994.

La Varenne, François Pierre de. *The French Cook.* Lewes, UK: Southover, 2001.

Lang, George. *Nobody Knows the Truffles I've Seen.* New York: iUniverse, 1998.

Lind, James. *An Essay on Diseases Incidental to Europeans in Hot Climates.* Philadelphia: William Duane, 1811.

Livingston, A.W. *Livingston and the Tomato: Being the History of Experiences in Discovering the Choice Varieties Introduced by Him, with Practical Instructions for Growers.* Columbus, OH: A.W. Livingston's Sons, 1893.

The Los Angeles Times Cook Book. Los Angeles, CA: Times-Mirror Company, 1905.

Lovell, M.S. *The Edible Mollusks of Great Britain and Ireland.* London: Reeve, 1867.

Lyman, Joseph Bardwell, and Laura E. Lyman. *The Philosophy of Housekeeping: A Scientific and Practical Manual.* Hartford, CT: S.M. Betts, 1859.

Maclear, G.F. *St. Augustine's, Canterbury: Its Rise, Ruin, and Restoration.* London: Wells Gardner, Darton, 1888.

Mansfield, George E. *History of Butte County, California.* Los Angeles, CA: Historic Record, 1918.

Markham, Clements R., ed. *The Voyages of Sir James Lancaster, Kt., to the East Indies.* London: Hakluyt Society, 1877.

Merrill, Elmer Drew. *Emergency Food Plants and Poisonous Plants of the Islands of the Pacific.* Washington, DC: U.S. War Department, 1943.

Mims, Stewart L. *Colbert's West India Policy.* New Haven, CT: Yale University Press, 1912.

Molokhovets, Elena. *Classic Russian Cooking: Elena Molokhovets' A Gift to Young Housewives.* Ed. Joyce Stetso Toomre. Bloomington: Indiana University Press, 1992.

Monaghan, Gail, Eric Boman, and George Lang. *The Entrees: Remembered Favorites from the Past.* New York: Rizzoli, 2010.

———. *Lost Desserts: Delicious Indulgences of the Past: Recipes from Legendary Restaurants and Famous Chefs.* New York: Rizzoli, 2007.

Montagné, Prosper. *Larousse Gastronomique: The World's Greatest Culinary Encyclopedia.* Ed. Jennifer Harvey Lang. 3rd ed. New York: Clarkson Potter, 2001.

Morton, John. *Morton's Sixpenny Almanack and Diary with Compendium.* London: Simpkin, Marshall, 1876.

North Borneo Company. *Handbook of North Borneo.* London: William Clowes & Sons, 1890.

Northbourne, Christopher James. *Look to the Land.* London: J.M. Dent & Sons, 1940.

Ovington, John. *An Essay upon the Nature and Qualities of Tea.* London: R. Roberts, 1699.

Parker, Arthur C. "Iroquois Uses of Maize and Other Food Plants." *New York State Museum Bulletin* 144 (November 1, 1910): 5–115.

Pavy, F.W. *A Treatise on Food and Dietetics, Physiologically and Therapeutically Considered.* London: Churchill, 1875.

Petrini, Carlo. "Endangered Species: Slow Food." *The New York Times,* July 26, 2003.

———, ed. *Slow Food: Collected Thoughts on Taste, Tradition, and the Honest Pleasures of Food.* White River Junction, VT: Chelsea Green, 2001.

———. *Slow Food: The Case for Taste.* New York: Columbia University Press, 2001.

Plain Words About Food: The Rumford Kitchen Leaflets (no. 1–20), 1899. Boston: Whitcomb & Barrows, 1904.

Poivre, Pierre. *Travels of a Philosopher: or, Observations on the Manners and Arts of Various Nations in Africa and Asia.* Glasgow, UK: Robert Urie, 1770.

Polo, Marco. *Travels of Marco Polo.* New York: Harper & Brothers, 1845.

"Portable Soup." *Lady's Companion* 1:6 (1753): 35–36.

Porter, George Richardson. *The Tropical Agriculturist.* London: Smith, Elder, 1833.

Prescott, William Hickling. *The Conquest of Mexico.* New York: Henry Holt, 1922.

Randolph, Mary. *The Virginia Housewife: Or, Methodical Cook.* Baltimore: Plaskitt, Fite & Company, 1838.

Richards, Ellen H. "Count Rumford and His Work for Humanity." *American Kitchen Magazine* 8:6 (March 1898): 203–208.

Robinson, Conway, and R.A. Brock. *Abstract of the Proceedings of the Virginia Company of London, 1619–1624.* Richmond: Virginia Historical Society, 1888–1889.

Salerno, John P., and Linda West Eckhardt. *The Silver Cloud Diet.* New York: Madison Lexington, 2010.

Saunders, Simon M. *Domestic Poultry.* New York: Orange Jude, 1866.

Seacole, Mary. *Wonderful Adventures of Mrs. Seacole in Many Lands.* 1857. New York: Kaplan, 2009.

Sloane, Hans. *A Voyage to the Islands Madera, Barbadoes, Nieves, St. Christophers, and Jamaica.* London: B.M., 1707.

Soyer, Alexis. *A Shilling Cookery for the People.* London: George Routledge, 1854.

Stelzle, Charles. *Why Prohibition!* New York: George H. Doran, 1918.

Vega, Garcilaso de la. *El Reino de Los Incas del Perú.* Ed. James Bardin. Boston: Allyn and Bacon, 1918.

Velho, Alvaro, João de Sá, and Ernest Georg Ravenstein, eds. *A Journal of the First Voyage of Vasco da Gama, 1497–1499.* London: Hakluyt Society, 1898.

Von Liebig, Justus. *Chemistry of Food.* London: Taylor & Walton, 1847.

Willett, Walter C., and Patrick J. Skerritt. *Eat, Drink, and Be Healthy: The Harvard Medical School Guide to Healthy Eating.* New York: Free Press, 2001.

Wills, C.J. *Persia As It Is, Being Sketches of Modern Persian Life and Character.* London: S. Low, Marston, Searle, & Rivington, 1886.

Wilson, Robert A. *Mexico and Its Religion.* New York: Harper & Brothers, 1855.

World Food Programme. *Hunger and Markets.* Sterling, VA: Earthscan, 2009.

Young, Warren R. "An Epic for Epicures." *Life* 51:16 (October 20, 1961): 16, 18.

Secondary Sources

Aberle, Elton David, John C. Forrest, David E. Gerrard, and Edward W. Mills. *Principles of Meat Science.* Dubuque, IA: Kendall/Hunt, 2001.

Abramson, Julia Luisa. *Food Culture in France.* Westport, CT: Greenwood, 2007.

Abulafia, David. *The Great Sea: A Human History of the Mediterranean.* New York: Oxford University Press, 2011.

Adamson, Joni, and Scott Slovic. "The Shoulders We Stand On: An Introduction to Ethnicity and Ecocriticism." *MELUS* 34:2 (June 1, 2009): 5–24.

Adamson, Melitta Weiss, ed. *Regional Cuisines of Medieval Europe: A Book of Essays.* New York: Routledge, 2002.

Adamson, Melitta Weiss, and Francine Segan, eds. *Entertaining from Ancient Rome to the Super Bowl.* Westport, CT: Greenwood, 2008.

Agrios, G.N. *Plant Pathology.* 5th ed. San Diego, CA: Academic Press, 2005.

Aguilar-Moreno, Manuel. *Handbook to Life in the Aztec World.* New York: Oxford University Press, 2007.

Aidells, Bruce. *Bruce Aidells' Complete Sausage Book.* New York: Ten Speed, 2000.

Aidells, Bruce, and Lisa Weiss. *Bruce Aidells's Complete Book of Pork.* New York: HarperCollins, 2004.

Akbari, Suzanne Conklin, and Amilcare A. Iannucci, and John Tulk, eds. *Marco Polo and the Encounter of East and West.* Toronto: University of Toronto Press, 2008.

Aksoy, M. Ataman, and John C. Beghin, eds. *Global Agricultural Trade and Developing Countries.* Washington, DC: World Bank, 2005.

Albala, Ken. *The Banquet: Dining in the Great Courts of Late Renaissance Europe.* Urbana: University of Illinois Press, 2007.

———. *Beans: A History.* New York: Berg, 2007.

———. *Eating Right in the Renaissance.* Berkeley: University of California Press, 2002.

———, ed. *Food Cultures of the World Encyclopedia.* Santa Barbara, CA: Greenwood, 2011.

———. *Food in Early Modern Europe.* Westport, CT: Greenwood, 2003.

Albertson, Ellen, and Michael Albertson. *Temptations: Igniting the Pleasure and Power of Aphrodisiacs.* New York: Simon & Schuster, 2002.

Alcock, Joan Pilsbury. *Food in the Ancient World.* Westport, CT: Greenwood, 2006.

Alexander, Leslie M., and Walter C. Rucker, eds. *Encyclopedia of African American History.* Santa Barbara, CA: ABC-Clio, 2010.

Alford, Jeffrey, and Naomi Duguid. *Beyond the Great Wall: Recipes and Travels in the Other China.* New York: Artisan, 2008.

Allaby, Michael. *Plants: Food, Medicine, and the Green Earth.* New York: Facts on File, 2010.

Allen, Gary, and Ken Albala. *The Business of Food: Encyclopedia of the Food and Drink Industries.* Westport, CT: Greenwood, 2007.

Allen, Stewart Lee. *In the Devil's Garden: A Sinful History of Forbidden Food.* New York: Random House, 2002.

Allhoff, Fritz, and Dave Monroe. *Food & Philosophy: Eat, Drink, and Be Merry.* Malden, MA: Blackwell, 2007.

Alt, Carol, and David Roth. *Eating in the Raw.* New York: Clarkson Potter, 2004.

Ames, Glenn Joseph, ed. *Em Nome de Deus: The Journal of the First Voyage of Vasco da Gama to India, 1497–1499.* Boston: Brill, 2009.

———, ed. *Vasco da Gama: Renaissance Crusader.* New York: Pearson/Longman, 2005.

Amussen, Susan Dwyer. *Caribbean Exchanges: Slavery and the Transformation of English Society, 1640–1700.* Chapel Hill: University of North Carolina Press, 2007.

Amyx, Elise. "Farming Subsidies Often Do More Harm Than Good." *Detroit News,* August 16, 2011.

Anderson, Eugene N. *Everyone Eats: Understanding Food and Culture.* New York: New York University Press, 2005.

Andoh, Elizabeth. *Washoku: Recipes from the Japanese Home Kitchen.* Berkeley, CA: Ten Speed, 2005.

Antol, Marie Nadine. *Confessions of a Coffee Bean: The Complete Guide to Coffee Cuisine.* Garden City Park, NY: Square One, 2002.

Aoyama, Tomoko. *Reading Food in Modern Japanese Literature.* Honolulu: University of Hawaii Press, 2008.

Appelbaum, Robert. *Aguecheek's Beef, Belch's Hiccup, and Other Gastronomic Interjections: Literature, Culture, and Food Among the Early Moderns.* Chicago: University of Chicago Press, 2006.

Araton, Harvey. "Agent or No Agent?" *The New York Times,* December 18, 2009.

Arnold, Wayne. "Surviving Without Subsidies." *The New York Times,* August 2, 2007.

Ashley, Bob, Joanne Hollows, Steve Jones, and Ben Taylor. *Food and Cultural Studies.* New York: Routledge, 2004.

Asimov, Eric, and Kim Severson. "Edna Lewis, 89, Dies; Wrote Cookbooks That Revived Refined Southern Cuisine." *The New York Times,* February 14, 2006.

Astyk, Sharon. *Independence Days: A Guide to Sustainable Food Storage and Preservation.* Gabriola, British Columbia, Canada: New Society, 2009.

Aubet, Maria Eugenia. *The Phoenicians and the West: Politics, Colonies, and Trade.* Trans. Mary Turton. Cambridge, UK: Cambridge University Press, 2001.

Audette, Ray, and Troy Gilchrist. *Neanderthin: Eat Like a Caveman to Achieve a Lean, Strong, Healthy Body.* New York: Macmillan, 2000.

Avramescu, Catalin. *An Intellectual History of Cannibalism.* Princeton, NJ: Princeton University Press, 2009.

Ayto, John. *An A–Z of Food and Drink.* New York: Oxford University Press, 2002.

Bakels, C.C. *The Western European Loess Belt: Agrarian History, 5300 B.C.–A.D. 1000.* New York: Springer, 2009.

Baker-Clark, Charles Allen. *Profiles from the Kitchen: What Great Cooks Have Taught Us About Ourselves and Our Food.* Lexington: University Press of Kentucky, 2006.

Bakken, Gordon Morris, and Brenda Farrington, eds. *Encyclopedia of Women in the American West.* Thousand Oaks, CA: Sage, 2003.

Bakker, Henk. *Food Security in Africa and Asia: Strategies for Small-Scale Agricultural Development.* Cambridge, MA: CABI, 2011.

Banerji, Chitrita. *Eating India: An Odyssey into the Food and Culture of the Land of Spices.* New York: Bloomsbury, 2007.

Barbosa-Cánovas, Gusatavo V., Enrique Ortega-Rivas, Pablo Juliano, and Hong Yan. *Food Powders: Physical Properties, Processing, and Functionality.* New York: Kluwer/Plenum, 2005.

Barrett, Christopher Brendan, and Daniel G. Maxwell. *Food Aid After Fifty Years: Recasting Its Role.* New York: Routledge, 2005.

Bartholomes, D.P., R.E. Paull, and K.G. Rohrbach, eds. *The Pineapple: Botany, Production, and Uses.* Oxford, UK: CABI, 2003.

Basan, Ghillie. *The Middle Eastern Kitchen.* New York: Hippocrene, 2006.

Batmanglij, Najmieh. *A Taste of Persia: An Introduction to Persian Cooking.* London: I.B. Tauris, 2007.

Baumbusch, Brigitte. *Food in Art.* Milwaukee, WI: Gareth Stevens, 2005.

Baylor, Ronald H., ed. *Multicultural America: An Encyclopedia of the Newest Americans.* Santa Barbara, CA: ABC-Clio, 2011.

Behnke, Alison. *Vegetarian Cooking Around the World.* New York: Lerner, 2002.

Beier, Ross C., Suresh D. Pillai, and Timothy D. Philips, eds. *Preharvest and Postharvest Food Safety: Contemporary Issues and Future Directions.* Chicago: IFT, 2004.

Belasco, Warren James. *Meals to Come: A History of the Future of Food.* Berkeley: University of California Press, 2006.

Belasco, Warren James, and Roger Horowitz, eds. *Food Chains: From Farmyard to Shopping Cart.* Philadelphia: University of Pennsylvania Press, 2009.

Belasco, Warren James, and Philip Scranton. *Food Nations: Selling Taste in Consumer Societies.* New York: Routledge, 2002.

Bellwood, Peter. *First Farmers: The Origins of Agricultural Societies.* Malden, MA: Blackwell, 2005.

Benac, Nancy. "US Panel Rejects Calls for Warning Labels on Link Between Food Dyes and Hyperactivity." *Canadian Medical Association Journal* 183:9 (June 14, 2011): 183–191.

Bendiner, Kenneth. *Food in Painting: From the Renaissance to the Present.* London: Reaktion, 2005.

Bendrick, Lou. *Eat Where You Live.* Seattle, WA: Skipstone, 2008.

Bennett, Todd D. *Kosher.* Herkimer, NY: Shema Yisrael, 2005.

Benson, John, and Laura Ugolini. *A Nation of Shopkeepers: Five Centuries of British Retailing.* London: I.B. Tauris, 2003.

Benton, A.A. "The Classical Cook." *Sewanee Review* 2:4 (1894): 413–424.

Berggren, Lars, Nils Hybel, and Annette Landen, eds. *Cogs, Cargoes, and Commerce: Maritime Bulk Trade in Northern Europe, 1150–1400.* Toronto: Pontifical Institute of Mediaeval Studies, 2002.

Bermann, George A., and Petros C. Mavroidis, eds. *Trade and Human Health and Safety.* New York: Cambridge University Press, 2006.

Bernstein, William J. *A Splendid Exchange: How Trade Shaped the World.* New York: Atlantic Monthly, 2008.

Berriedale-Johnson, Michelle. *Food Fit for Pharaohs: An Ancient Egyptian Cookbook.* London: British Museum, 2008.

Berzok, Linda Murray. *American Indian Food.* Westport, CT: Greenwood, 2005.

Besh, John. *My New Orleans: The Cookbook.* Kansas City, MO: Andrews McMeel, 2009.

Bess, Nancy Moore, and Bibi Wein. *Bamboo in Japan.* New York: Kodansha International, 2001.

Betrán, Javier, Edward C.A. Runge, and C. Wayne Smith, eds. *Corn: Origin, History, Technology, and Production.* Hoboken, NJ: John Wiley & Sons, 2004.

Bettoja, Jo. *In a Roman Kitchen: Timeless Recipes from the Eternal City.* Hoboken, NJ: John Wiley & Sons, 2003.

Beyer, Mark. *Temperance and Prohibition: The Movement to Pass Anti-Liquor Laws in America.* New York: Rosen, 2006.

Bienvenu, Marcelle, Carl A. Brasseaux, and Ryan A. Brasseaux. *Stir the Pot: The History of Cajun Cuisine.* New York: Hippocrene, 2005.

Biliardis, Costas G., and Marta S. Izydorczyk. *Functional Food Carbohydrates.* Boca Raton, FL: Taylor & Francis, 2007.

"Biopiracy: A New Threat to Indigenous Rights and Culture in Mexico." *New England Journal of International and Comparative Law* 7 (April 2001): 1–6.

Bitterman, Mark. *Salted: A Manifesto on the World's Most Essential Mineral, with Recipes.* New York: Random House, 2010.

Bjorklund, Ruth. *Food Borne Illnesses.* New York: Marshall Cavendish Benchmark, 2006.

Black, Michael, J. Derek Bewley, and Peter Halmer, eds. *The Encyclopedia of Seeds: Science, Technology and Uses.* Wallingford, UK: CABI, 2005.

Black, Rachel, ed. *Alcohol in Popular Culture: An Encyclopedia.* Santa Barbara, CA: Greenwood, 2010.

Blatt, Harvey. *America's Food: What You Don't Know About What You Eat.* Cambridge, MA: MIT Press, 2008.

Blay-Palmer, Alison. *Food Fears: From Industrial to Sustainable Food Systems.* Burlington, VT: Ashgate, 2008.

Blech, Zushe Yosef. *Kosher Food Production.* Ames, IA: Wiley-Blackwell, 2008.

Board on Science and Technology for International Development, National Research Council. *Lost Crops of Africa.* Vol. 2, *Vegetables.* Washington, DC: National Academies Press, 2006.

Bober, Phyllis Pray. *Art, Culture, and Cuisine: Ancient and Medieval Gastronomy.* Chicago: University of Chicago Press, 2001.

Boesche, Roger. *The First Great Political Realist: Kautilya and His Arthashastra.* Lanham, MD: Lexington, 2002.

Bohstedt, John. *The Politics of Provisions: Food Riots, Moral Economy, and Market Transition in England, c. 1550–1850.* Burlington, VT: Ashgate, 2010.

Boi, Lee Geok. *Classic Asian Noodles.* Singapore: Marshall Cavendish, 2007.

Bortolotti, Dan. *Wild Blue: A Natural History of the World's Largest Animal.* New York: Thomas Dunne, 2008.

Bourette, Susan. *Meat, a Love Story: Pasture to Plate, a Search for the Perfect Meal.* New York: Penguin, 2009.

Boutenko, Victoria. *12 Steps to Raw Foods: How to End Your Dependency on Cooked Food.* Berkeley, CA: North Atlantic, 2007.

Bowden, Jonny. *The 150 Healthiest Foods on Earth: The Surprising, Unbiased Truth About What You Should Eat and Why.* Gloucester, MA: Fair Winds, 2007.

Bowen, Dana. "A New Tasting Menu in the Baby Section." *The New York Times,* August 2, 2006.

Bowen, H.V., Margarette Lincoln, and Nigel Rigby, eds. *The Worlds of the East India Company.* Woodbridge, UK: Boydell, 2002.

Bower, Anne L., ed. *African American Foodways: Explorations of History and Culture.* Urbana: University of Illinois Press, 2009.

———, ed. *Reel Food: Essays on Food and Film.* New York: Routledge, 2004.

Bowlby, Rachel. *Carried Away: The Invention of Modern Shopping.* New York: Columbia University Press, 2002.

Brachfeld, Aaron, and Mary Choate. *The Horse Hoeing Husbandry by Jethro Tull, Esq.* Agate, CO: Coastalfields, 2010.

Brandon, Ruth. *The People's Chef: The Culinary Revolutions of Alexis Soyer.* New York: Walker, 2004.

Branen, A. Larry, P. Michael Davidson, Seppo Salminen, and John H. Thorngate, eds. *Food Additives.* 2nd ed. New York: Marcel Dekker, 2002.

Braund, David, and John Wilkins, eds. *Athenaeus and His World: Reading Greek Culture in the Roman Empire.* Exeter, UK: University of Exeter Press, 2000.

Bray, Tamara L., ed. *The Archaeology and Politics of Food and Feasting in Early States and Empires.* New York: Kluwer Academic, 2003.

Brennan, Georgeanne. *The Mediterranean Herb Cookbook.* San Francisco: Chronicle, 2000.

Brenner, Robert. *Merchants and Revolution: Commercial Change, Political Conflict, and London's Overseas Traders, 1550–1653.* London: Verso, 2003.

Brennessel, Barbara. *Good Tidings: The History and Ecology of Shellfish Farming in the Northeast.* Lebanon, NH: University Press of New England, 2008.

Bridgewater, Alan, and Gill Bridgewater. *The Self-Sufficiency Handbook: A Complete Guide to Greener Living.* New York: Skyhorse, 2007.

Brill, Marlene, Paul D. Buell, and Eugene N. Anderson. *Soup for the Qan: Chinese Dietary Medicine of the Mongol Era.* Leiden, Netherlands: Brill, 2010.

Brill, Steve. *The Wild Vegetarian Cookbook.* Boston: Harvard Common, 2002.

Brink, Jack. *Imagining Head-Smashed-In: Aboriginal Buffalo Hunting on the Northern Plains.* Edmonton, Canada: Athabasca University Press, 2008.

Brock, Wendell. "Critic's Notebook: Films as Feasts for the Senses." *Atlanta Journal-Constitution,* January 7, 2001.

Brock, William H. *Justus von Liebig: The Chemical Gatekeeper.* New York: Cambridge University Press, 2002.

Broomfield, Andrea. *Food and Cooking in Victorian England: A History.* Westport, CT: Greenwood, 2007.

Brostoff, Jonathan, and Linda Gamlin. *Food Allergies and Food Intolerance.* Rochester, VT: Healing Arts, 2000.

Brown, Amy C. *Understanding Food: Principles and Preparation.* Belmont, CA: Wadsworth, 2011.

Brown, Paul. *Britain's Historic Ships: A Complete Guide to the Ships That Shaped the Nation.* London: Conway, 2009.

Brown, Vincent. *The Reaper's Garden: Death and Power in the World of Atlantic Slavery.* Cambridge, MA: Harvard University Press, 2008.

Bruinsma, Jelle, ed. *World Agriculture: Towards 2015/2030: An FAO Perspective.* London: Earthscan, 2003.

Brush, Stephen B. *Farmers' Bounty: Locating Crop Diversity in the Contemporary World.* New Haven, CT: Yale University Press, 2004.

Brüssow, Harald. *The Quest for Food: A Natural History of Eating.* New York: Springer, 2007.

Bsisu, May. *The Arab Table: Recipes and Culinary Traditions.* New York: HarperCollins, 2005.

Buesseler, Cathryn Anne Hansen. *Scandinavian and German Family Cookery.* Madison, WI: Goblin Fern, 2005.

Buglass, Alan J., ed. *Handbook of Alcoholic Beverages: Technical, Analytical and Nutritional Aspects.* Hoboken, NJ: John Wiley & Sons, 2011.

Burch, David, and Geoffrey Lawrence, eds. *Supermarkets and Agri-Food Supply Chains.* Northampton, MA: Edward Elgar, 2007.

Burgess, Kelly. "What's Cooking in the Melting Pot?" *Ancestry* 25:6 (November/December 2007): 23–29.

Burnett, John. *England Eats Out: A Social History of Eating Out in England from 1830 to the Present.* Harlow, UK: Pearson/Longman, 2004.

Caballero, Benjamin, Lindsay Allen, and Andrew Prentice, eds. *Encyclopedia of Human Nutrition.* Boston: Elsevier, 2005.

Calhoun, Creighton Lee. *Old Southern Apples: A Comprehensive History and Description of Varieties for Collectors, Growers, and Fruit Enthusiasts.* White River Junction, VT: Chelsea Green, 2010.

Campbell, Cheryl. *Edible: An Illustrated Guide to the World's Food Plants.* Washington, DC: National Geographic, 2008.

Campbell, Susan. *A History of Kitchen Gardening.* London: Frances Lincoln, 2005.

Campbell-Platt, Geoffrey. *Food Science and Technology Textbook.* London: Blackwell Science, 2005.

"Can Biotech Food Cure World Hunger?" *The New York Times,* October 26, 2009.

Cantú, Norma Elia, ed. *Moctezuma's Table: Rolando Briseño's Mexican and Chicano Tablescapes.* College Station: Texas A&M University Press, 2010.

Capatti, Alberto, and Massimo Montanari. *Italian Cuisine: A Cultural History.* Trans. Aine O'Healy. New York: Columbia University Press, 2003.

Carney, Judith Ann. *Black Rice: The African Origins of Rice Cultivation in the Americas.* Cambridge, MA: Harvard University Press, 2001.

Carney, Judith Ann, and Richard Nicholas Rosomoff. *In the Shadow of Slavery: Africa's Botanical Legacy in the Atlantic World.* Berkeley: University of California Press, 2009.

Carpender, Dana. *1000 Low-Carb Recipes: Hundreds of Delicious Recipes from Dinner to Dessert.* Gloucester, MA: Fair Winds, 2010.

Carrington, Damian. "Insects Could Be the Key to Meeting Food Needs of Growing Global Population." *The Guardian* (London), August 1, 2010.

Carroll, Sean B. "Tracking the Ancestry of Corn Back 9,000 Years." *The New York Times,* May 24, 2010.

Carter, Mia, and Barbara Harlow, eds. *Archives of Empire: From the East India Company to the Suez Canal.* Durham, NC: Duke University Press, 2003.

Cartwright, Peter. *Consumer Protection and the Criminal Law: Law, Theory, and Policy in the UK.* New York: Cambridge University Press, 2001.

Cary, Nancy, ed. *Hunger and Thirst: Food Literature.* San Diego, CA: San Diego City Works, 2008.

Casid, Jill H. *Sowing Empire: Landscape and Colonization.* Minneapolis: University of Minnesota Press, 2005.

Caton, Mary Anne, ed. *Fooles and Fricassees: Food in Shakespeare's England.* Washington, DC: Folger Shakespeare Library, 2000.

Cauvain, Stanley P. *Bread Making: Improving Quality.* Boca Raton, FL: CRC, 2003.

Cech, Thomas V. *Principles of Water Resources: History, Development, Management, and Policy.* Hoboken, NJ: John Wiley & Sons, 2010.

Chakraverty, Amalendu, ed. *Handbook of Postharvest Technology: Cereals, Fruits, Vegetables, Tea, and Spices.* New York: Marcel Dekker, 2003.

Chandan, Ramesh C., Charles E. White, Arun Kilara, and Yiu H. Hui, eds. *Manufacturing Yogurt and Fermented Milks.* Ames, IA: Blackwell, 2006.

Chapman, Pat. *India: Food & Cooking: The Ultimate Book on Indian Cuisine.* London: New Holland, 2007.

Chen, Nancy N. *Food, Medicine, and the Quest for Good Health: Nutrition, Medicine, and Culture.* New York: Columbia University Press, 2009.

Chen, Teresa M. *A Tradition of Soup: Flavors from China's Pearl River Delta.* Foreword by Martin Yan. Berkeley, CA: North Atlantic, 2009.

Cheung, Peter C.K., ed. *Mushrooms as Functional Foods.* Hoboken, NJ: John Wiley & Sons, 2008.

Cheung, Sidney C.H., and Tan Chee-Beng, eds. *Food and Foodways in Asia: Resource, Tradition, and Cooking.* New York: Routledge, 2007.

Chiba, Kaeko. *Japanese Women, Class and the Tea Ceremony.* New York: Routledge, 2010.

"Chicle Quest Beats Highway to Tropics." *Popular Mechanics* 41:3 (March 1924): 406–411.

Cho, Susan Sungsoo, and Priscilla Samuel, eds. *Fiber Ingredients: Food Applications and Health Benefits.* Boca Raton, FL: CRC, 2009.

Chopra, V.L., and K.V. Peter, eds. *Handbook of Industrial Crops.* Binghamton, NY: Haworth Reference, 2005.

Choy, Sam, and the Makaha Sons. *A Hawaiian Luau.* Honolulu: Mutual, 2003.

Civitello, Linda. *Cuisine and Culture: A History of Food and People.* 3rd ed. Hoboken, NJ: John Wiley & Sons, 2011.

Clapp, Jennifer. *Food.* Malden, MA: Polity, 2012.

Clark, Melissa. "Once a Villain, Coconut Oil Charms the Health Food World." *The New York Times,* March 1, 2011.

———. "Tiny Come-Ons, Plain and Fancy." *The New York Times,* August 30, 2006.

Clark, Stephanie, Michael Costello, MaryAnne Drake, and Floyd Bodyfelt, eds. *The Sensory Evaluation of Dairy Products.* New York: Springer, 2009.

Clarkson, Janet. *Menus from History: Historic Meals and Recipes for Every Day of the Year.* Santa Barbara, CA: Greenwood, 2009.

———. *Soup: A Global History.* London: Reaktion, 2010.

Clay, Edward J., and Olav Stokke, eds. *Food Aid and Human Security.* Portland, OR: Frank Cass, 2000.

Cloutier, Marissa, and Eve Adamson. *The Mediterranean Diet.* New York: Avon, 2004.

Coe, Andrew. *Chop Suey: A Cultural History of Chinese Food in the United States.* New York: Oxford University Press, 2009.

Coff, Christian. *The Taste for Ethics: An Ethic of Food Consumption.* New York: Springer, 2006.

Cole, Martin B. "Trends in Food Safety Management." *Microbiology Australia* 25:3 (July 2004): 6–9.

Collingham, Lizzie. *Curry: A Tale of Cooks and Conquerors.* New York: Oxford University Press, 2006.

Collins, Geneva. "Where Settlers, Slaves and Natives Converged, a Way of Eating Was Born." *Washington Post,* May 9, 2007.

Colpitts, George. *Game in the Garden: A Human History of Wildlife in Western Canada to 1940.* Vancouver, Canada: University of British Columbia Press, 2002.

Colquhoun, Kate. *Taste: The Story of Britain Through Its Cooking.* New York: Bloomsbury, 2007.

Conklin, Alfred R., and Thomas C. Stilwell. *World Food: Production and Use.* Hoboken, NJ: Wiley-Interscience, 2007.

Constantine, Nathan. *A History of Cannibalism: From Ancient Cultures to Survival Stories and Modern Psychopaths.* Edison, NJ: Chartwell, 2006.

Cooke, Elise. *The Grocery Garden: How Busy People Can Grow Cheap Food.* Denver, CO: Outskirts, 2009.

Coppens, Linda Miles. *What American Women Did, 1789–1920.* Jefferson, NC: McFarland, 2001.

Coquery-Vidrovitch, Catherine. *The History of African Cities South of the Sahara: From the Origins to Colonization.* Trans. Mary Baker. Princeton, NJ: Markus Wiener, 2005.

Cordain, Loren. *The Paleo Diet.* Hoboken, NJ: John Wiley & Sons, 2011.

Cordes, Lyndsee Simpson. *Simple Recipes Using Food Storage.* Springville, UT: Cedar Fort, 2008.

Cornell, Kari A. *Holiday Cooking Around the World.* Minneapolis, MN: Lerner, 2002.

Cornell, Kari A., and Merry Anwar. *Cooking the Indonesian Way.* Minneapolis, MN: Lerner, 2004.

Coulombe, Charles A. *Rum: The Epic Story of the Drink That Conquered the World.* New York: Citadel, 2004.

Coulter, Lynn. *Gardening with Heirloom Seeds.* Chapel Hill: University of North Carolina Press, 2008.

Counihan, Carole. *A Tortilla Is Like Life: Food and Culture in the San Luis Valley of Colorado.* Austin: University of Texas Press, 2009.

Courtright, Nicola. "A Garden and a Gallery at Fontainebleau: Imagery of Rule for Medici Queens." *Court Historian* 10:1 (December 2005): 55–84.

Covey, Herbert C., and Dwight Eisnach. *What the Slaves Ate: Recollections of African American Foods and Foodways from the Slave Narratives.* Westport, CT: Greenwood, 2009.

Cowan, Brian William. *The Social Life of Coffee: The Emergence of the British Coffeehouse.* New Haven, CT: Yale University Press, 2005.

Cramer, Michael M. *Food Plant Sanitation: Design, Maintenance, and Good Manufacturing Practices.* Boca Raton, FL: CRC, 2006.

Croce, Erica, and Giovanni Perri. *Food and Wine Tourism: Integrating Food, Travel, and Territory.* Cambridge, MA: CABI, 2010.

Crosby, Alfred W. *The Columbian Exchange: Biological and Cultural Consequences of 1492.* Westport, CT: Greenwood, 2003.

Cullather, Nick. *The Hungry World: America's Cold War Battle Against Poverty in Asia.* Cambridge, MA: Harvard University Press, 2010.

Curry, Andrew. "Ancient Excrement." *Archaeology* 61:4 (July/August 2008): 42–45.

Da Silva, Chandra Richard. "The Portuguese East India Company, 1628–1633." *Luso-Brazilian Review* 11:2 (Winter 1974): 152–205.

Dalby, Andrew. *Dangerous Tastes: The Story of Spices.* Berkeley: University of California Press, 2002.

———. *Flavours of Byzantium.* London: Prospect, 2003.

———. *Food in the Ancient World from A to Z.* London: Routledge, 2003.

———. *Tastes of Byzantium: The Cuisine of a Legendary Empire.* London: I.B. Tauris, 2010.

Darling, Jennifer, ed. *Food Network Kitchens Cookbook.* Des Moines, IA: Meredith, 2003.

Davidson, Alan. *The Oxford Companion to Food.* Ed. Jane Davidson, Tom Jaine, and Helen Saberi. New York: Oxford University Press, 2006.

Davies, Glyn, and David Brown, eds. *Bushmeat and Livelihoods: Wildlife Management and Poverty Reduction.* Oxford, UK: Blackwell, 2007.

De Villiers, Marq. *Water: The Fate of Our Most Precious Resource.* Boston: Houghton Mifflin, 2001.

De Vita, Oretta Zanini. *Encyclopedia of Pasta.* Berkeley: University of California Press, 2009.

De Waal, Alexander. *Famine That Kills: Darfur, Sudan.* New York: Oxford University Press, 2005.

DeJean, Joan. *The Essence of Style: How the French Invented High Fashion, Fine Food, Chic Cafés, Style, Sophistication, and Glamour.* New York: Free Press, 2005.

DeLong, Deanna. *How to Dry Foods.* New York: Penguin, 2006.

Denker, Joel. *The World on a Plate: A Tour Through the History of America's Ethnic Cuisine.* Lincoln: University of Nebraska Press, 2007.

D'Eramo, Marco. *The Pig and the Skyscraper: Chicago, a History of Our Future.* Trans. Graeme Thomson. New York: Verso, 2002.

Derby, Mary Patricia. *Poison Control Center Foodborne Illness Surveillance.* Ann Arbor, MI: UMI, 2008.

Deutsch, Jonathan, and Rachel D. Saks. *Jewish American Food Culture.* Westport, CT: Greenwood, 2008.

Deutsch, Tracey. *Building a Housewife's Paradise: Gender, Politics, and American Grocery Stores in the Twentieth Century.* Chapel Hill: University of North Carolina Press, 2010.

Dijk, Wil O. *Seventeenth-Century Burma and the Dutch East India Company, 1634–1680.* Singapore: Singapore University Press, 2006.

Dijkstra, Albert J., Richard J. Hamilton, and Wolff Hamm, eds. *Trans Fatty Acids.* Ames, IA: Blackwell, 2008.

Dikötter, Frank. *Mao's Great Famine: The History of China's Most Devastating Catastrophe, 1958–1962.* New York: Walker, 2010.

Dincer, Ibrahim, and Mehmet Kanoglu. *Refrigeration Systems and Applications.* Hoboken, NJ: John Wiley & Sons, 2010.

Diski, Chloe. "Famous Foodies: Charles Darwin." *Manchester (UK) Guardian,* March 9, 2003.

Dixon, Jane. *The Changing Chicken: Chooks, Cooks and Culinary Culture.* Sydney, Australia: University of New South Wales Press, 2002.

Djurfeldt, Göran, ed. *The African Food Crisis: Lessons from the Asian Green Revolution.* Cambridge, MA: CABI, 2006.

Dolin, Eric Jay. *Leviathan: The History of Whaling in America.* New York: W.W. Norton, 2008.

Donahue, Brian. *The Great Meadow: Farmers and the Land in Colonial Concord.* New Haven, CT: Yale University Press, 2004.

Donkin, Robin A. *Between East and West: The Moluccas and the Traffic in Spices up to the Arrival of Europeans.* Philadelphia: American Philosophical Society, 2003.

Downie, David. *Food Wine Rome: A Terroir Guide.* New York: Little Bookroom, 2009.

Draper, A. "Blueberry Breeding: Improving the Unwild Blueberry." *Journal of the American Pomological Society* 61:3 (2007): 140–143.

Draycott, A. Philip. *Sugar Beet.* Ames, IA: Blackwell, 2005.

Dressler, Wolfram. "Disentangling Tagbanua Lifeways, Swidden, and Conservation on Palawan Island." *Research in Human Ecology* 12:1 (2005): 21–29.

Driskell, Judy Anne, and Ira Wolinsky, eds. *Energy-Yielding Macronutrients and Energy Metabolism in Sports Nutrition.* Boca Raton, FL: CRC, 2000.

Du Bois, Christine M., Chee Beng Tan, and Sidney Wilfred Mintz, eds. *The World of Soy.* Urbana: University of Illinois Press, 2008.

Dubin, Margaret Denise, and Sara-Larus Tolley, eds. *Seaweed, Salmon, and Manzanita Cider: A California Indian Feast.* Berkeley, CA: Heyday, 2008.

Duncan, Dorothy. *Canadians at Table: Food, Fellowship, and Folklore: A Culinary History of Canada.* Toronto: Dundurn, 2006.

———. *Nothing More Comforting: Canada's Heritage Food.* Tonawanda, NY: Dundurn, 2003.

Dunmire, William W. *Gardens of New Spain: How Mediterranean Plants and Foods Changed America.* Austin: University of Texas Press, 2004.

Dunn, P.M. "Sir Hans Sloane (1660–1753) and the Value of Breast Milk." *Archives of Disease in Children: Fetal and Neonatal Edition* 85 (2001): F73–F74.

Duram, Leslie A., ed. *Encyclopedia of Organic, Sustainable, and Local Food.* Santa Barbara, CA: ABC-Clio, 2010.

———. *Good Growing: Why Organic Farming Works.* Lincoln: University of Nebraska Press, 2005.

Eagen, Rachel. *The Biography of Sugar.* New York: Crabtree, 2006.

Edelstein, Sari, ed. *Food, Cuisine, and Cultural Competency for Culinary, Hospitality, and Nutrition Professionals.* Sudbury, MA: Jones and Bartlett, 2011.

Edwards, Mike. "The Adventures of Marco Polo." *National Geographic* 199:5 (May 2001): 2–31; 199:6 (June 2001): 20–45; 199:7 (July 2001): 26–47.

Egan, Timothy. "'Perfect' Apple Pushed Growers into Debt." *The New York Times,* November 4, 2000.

Eidlitz, Eliezer. *Is It Kosher?: Encyclopedia of Kosher Foods, Facts and Fallacies.* Nanuet, NY: Feldheim, 2004.

Elie, Lolis Eric, ed. *Cornbread Nation 2: The United States of Barbecue.* Chapel Hill: University of North Carolina Press, 2004.

Elliott, Charles. *The Potting-Shed Papers: On Gardens, Gardeners, and Garden History.* Guilford, CT: Lyons, 2002.

Ellis, Hattie. *Sweetness and Light: The Mysterious History of the Honeybee.* New York: Random House, 2006.

Entis, Phyllis. *Food Safety: Old Habits, New Perspectives.* Washington, DC: ASM, 2007.

Epps, Garrett. *Peyote vs. the State: Religious Freedom on Trial.* Norman: University of Oklahoma Press, 2009.

Erskine, William, et al. *The Lentil: Botany, Production and Uses.* Cambridge, MA: CABI, 2009.

Ettlinger, Steve. *Twinkie, Deconstructed.* New York: Plume, 2007.

Evans, K. Lee, and Chris Rankin. *Giant Book of Tofu Cooking.* New York: Sterling, 2000.

Evans, Kimberly Masters. *Endangered Species: Protecting Biodiversity.* Detroit, MI: Thomson Gale, 2007.

Evans, L.T. *Feeding the Ten Billion: Plants and Population Growth.* Cambridge, UK: Cambridge University Press, 2000.

Faas, Patrick. *Around the Roman Table: With More Than 150 Original Recipes: Food and Feasting in Ancient Rome.* Trans. Shaun Whiteside. Chicago: University of Chicago Press, 2005.

Fairburn, Christopher G., and Kelly D. Brownell, eds. *Eating Disorders and Obesity: A Comprehensive Handbook.* New York: Guilford, 2002.

Fairlie, Simon. *Meat: A Benign Extravagance.* White River Junction, VT: Chelsea Green, 2010.

Farnworth, Edward R., ed. *Handbook of Fermented Functional Foods.* Boca Raton, FL: CRC, 2008.

Farrer, Keith Thomas Henry. *To Feed a Nation: A History of Australian Food Science and Technology.* Collingwood, Australia: CSIRO, 2005.

Fedoroff, Nina V., and Nancy Marie Brown. *Mendel in the Kitchen: A Scientist's View of Genetically Modified Foods.* Washington, DC: Joseph Henry, 2004.

Feldman, George Franklin. *Cannibalism, Headhunting, and Human Sacrifice in North America: A History Forgotten.* Chambersburg, PA: Alan C. Hood, 2008.

Ferguson, Priscilla Parkhurst. *Accounting for Taste: The Triumph of French Cuisine.* Chicago: University of Chicago Press, 2004.

Fernández-Armesto, Felipe. *Near a Thousand Tables: A History of Food.* New York: Simon & Schuster, 2002.

Ferrara, Suzanne Alex. *The Raw Food Primer.* San Francisco: Council Oak, 2003.

Ferry, Jane. *Food in Film: A Culinary Performance of Communication.* New York: Routledge, 2003.

Field, L.T. "Valorous Traditions of Merchantmen." *The New York Times,* April 27, 1916.

Finch, Caleb E. "Herodotus on Diet and Longevity: How the Persians Fed on Dung and Lived to 80, While the Tall,

Handsome Ethiopians Ate Boiled Meat and Lived Beyond 120." *Journal of Aging, Humanities, and the Arts* 3:2 (2009): 86–96.

Finck, Henry Theophilus. *Food and Flavor: A Gastronomic Guide to Health and Good Living.* 1913. Bedford, MA: Applewood, 2010.

Findlay, Ronald, and Kevin H. O'Rourke. *Power and Plenty: Trade, War, and the World Economy in the Second Millennium.* Princeton, NJ: Princeton University Press, 2009.

Fischer, John. "Table Service." *Gastronomica* 1:3 (Summer 2001): 90–91.

Fisher, Carol. *The American Cookbook: A History.* Jefferson, NC: McFarland, 2006.

———. *Food in the American Military: A History.* Jefferson, NC: McFarland, 2010.

Fishkoff, Sue. *Kosher Nation.* New York: Random House, 2010.

Fitzgerald, Deborah Kay. *Every Farm a Factory: The Industrial Ideal in American Agriculture.* New Haven, CT: Yale University Press, 2003.

Fitzpatrick, Joan, ed. *Renaissance Food from Rabelais to Shakespeare: Culinary Readings and Culinary Histories.* Burlington, VT: Ashgate, 2010.

Flammang, Janet A. *The Taste for Civilization: Food, Politics, and Civil Society.* Champaign: University of Illinois Press, 2009.

Flandrin, Jean-Louis. *Arranging the Meal: A History of Table Service in France.* Trans. Julie E. Johnson. Berkeley: University of California Press, 2007.

Flandrin, Jean-Louis, and Massimo Montanari. *Food: A Culinary History from Antiquity to the Present.* Trans. Clarissa Botsford et al. New York: Penguin, 2000.

Fletcher, Nichola. *Charlemagne's Tablecloth: A Piquant History of Feasting.* New York: St. Martin's, 2005.

Fold, Niels, and Bill Pritchard. *Cross-Continental Food Chains.* New York: Routledge, 2005.

Ford, Andrea. "The Holes in America's Food-Safety Net." *Time* (September 30, 2008).

Ford, Brian J. "The Microscope of Linnaeus and His Blind Spot." *The Microscope* 57:2 (2009): 65–72.

Fortin, Neal D. *Food Regulation: Law, Science, Policy, and Practice.* Hoboken, NJ: John Wiley & Sons, 2009.

Foster, Debbie, and Jack Kennedy. *H.J. Heinz Company.* Charleston, SC: Arcadia, 2006.

Fowler, Damon Lee. *Classical Southern Cooking.* Layton, UT: Gibbs Smith, 2008.

———, ed. *Dining at Monticello: In Good Taste and Abundance.* Chapel Hill: University of North Carolina Press, 2005.

Fraioli, James O. *The Best Recipes from America's Food Festivals.* New York: Alpha, 2007.

Fraser, Evan D.G., and Andrew Rimas. *Empires of Food: Feast, Famine, and the Rise and Fall of Civilizations.* New York: Simon & Schuster, 2010.

Freedman, Jeri. *Genetically Modified Food: How Biotechnology Is Changing What We Eat.* New York: Rosen, 2009.

Freedman, Paul H. *Food: The History of Taste.* Berkeley: University of California Press, 2007.

Freidberg, Susanne. *Fresh: A Perishable History.* Cambridge, MA: Belknap Press, 2009.

Frewer, Lynn J., Einar Risvik, and Hendrik Schifferstein, eds. *Food, People and Society: A European Perspective of Consumers' Food Choices.* New York: Springer, 2001.

Frey, Darrell. *Bioshelter Market Garden: A Permaculture Farm.* Gabriola, Canada: New Society, 2011.

Frieda, Leonie. *Catherine de Medici: Renaissance Queen of France.* New York: Harper Perennial, 2003.

Fromartz, Samuel. *Organic, Inc.: Natural Foods and How They Grew.* Boston: Houghton Mifflin Harcourt, 2006.

Fruton, Joseph Stewart. *Fermentation: Vital or Chemical Process?* Boston: Brill, 2006.

Fussell, Betty Harper. *The Story of Corn.* Albuquerque: University of New Mexico Press, 2004.

Gage, Earle William. "Making Chewing Gum for American Chewers." *Popular Electricity and Modern Mechanics,* September 1914, 74–76.

Gardner, Marilyn. "Singles Forge New Holiday Traditions." *Fulton County (IN) News,* December 18, 2008.

Gast, Ross H. *Don Francisco De Paula Marin, a Biography; The Letters and Journals of Francisco De Paula Marin.* Ed. Agnes C. Conrad. Honolulu: University of Hawaii Press, 2002.

Gately, Iain. *Drink: A Cultural History of Alcohol.* New York: Gotham, 2008.

George, Donald W. *A Moveable Feast: Life-Changing Food Adventures Around the World.* London: Lonely Planet, 2010.

George, Raymond A.T. *Vegetable Seed Production.* Cambridge, MA: CABI, 2009.

Geraci, Victor W., and Elizabeth S. Demers. *Icons of American Cooking.* Santa Barbara, CA: Greenwood, 2011.

Gerbi, Antonello, and Jeremy Moyle. *Nature in the New World: From Christopher Columbus to Gonzalo Fernandez de Oviedo.* Pittsburgh, PA: University of Pittsburgh Press, 2010.

Germaine, Elizabeth, and Ann Burckhardt. *Cooking the Australian Way.* Minneapolis, MN: Lerner, 2004.

Gilbert, Sara. *The Story of McDonald's.* Mankato, MN: Creative Education, 2009.

Gilman, Sander L. *Diets and Dieting: A Cultural Encyclopedia.* New York: Routledge, 2008.

———. *Fat: A Cultural History of Obesity.* Malden, MA: Polity, 2008.

Gisslen, Wayne. *Professional Cooking.* Hoboken, NJ: John Wiley & Sons, 2007.

Giudici, Paolo, and Lisa Solieri. *Vinegars of the World.* New York: Springer, 2009.

Glasser, Irene. *More Than Bread: Ethnography of a Soup Kitchen.* Tuscaloosa: University of Alabama Press, 2010.

Gliessman, Stephen R. *Agroecology: The Ecology of Sustainable Food Systems.* Boca Raton, FL: CRC, 2007.

Gollner, Adam. *The Fruit Hunters: A Story of Nature, Adventure, Commerce, and Obsession.* New York: Simon & Schuster, 2008.

Goody, Cynthia, and Lorena Drago, eds. *Cultural Food Practices.* Chicago: American Dietetic Association, 2010.

Gopal, Lallanji, and V.C. Srivastava, eds. *History of Agriculture in India (up to c. 1200 A.D.).* New Delhi, India: Concept, 2008.

Gorman, James. "A Diet for an Invaded Planet: Invasive Species." *The New York Times,* December 31, 2010.

Grainger, Sally. *Cooking Apicius: Roman Recipes for Today.* Illus. Andras Kaldor. Totnes, UK: Prospect, 2006.

Gratzer, Walter Bruno. *Terrors of the Table: The Curious History of Nutrition.* New York: Oxford University Press, 2005.

Greenberg, Paul. *Four Fish: The Future of the Last Wild Food.* New York: Penguin, 2010.

Greenfeld, Karl Taro. "Wild Flavor." *Paris Review* 175 (Fall/Winter 2005): 7–26.

Gressel, Jonathan, ed. *Crop Ferality and Volunteerism.* New York: Taylor & Francis, 2005.

Griffith, Linda, and Fred Griffith. *Nuts: Recipes from Around the World That Feature Nature's Perfect Ingredient.* New York: St. Martin's, 2003.

Griggs, Lynden, Eileen Webb, and A.Y.M. Freilich. *Consumer Protection Law.* New York: Oxford University Press, 2008.

Grivetti, Louis, and Howard-Yana Shapiro, eds. *Chocolate: History, Culture, and Heritage.* Hoboken, NJ: John Wiley & Sons, 2009.

Grogan, Barbara Brownell, ed. *Food Journeys of a Lifetime: 500 Extraordinary Places to Eat Around the Globe.* Washington, DC: National Geographic, 2009.

Grotto, David W. *101 Foods That Could Save Your Life!* New York: Bantam, 2011.

Gudoshnikov, Sergey, Lindsay Jolly, and Donald Spence. *The World Sugar Market.* Boca Raton, FL: CRC, 2004.

Guest, Kristen, ed. *Eating Their Words: Cannibalism and the Boundaries of Cultural Identity.* Albany: State University of New York Press, 2001.

Gunderson, Gordon W. *The National School Lunch Program: Background and Development.* New York: Nova Science, 2003.

Gutman, Richard J.S. *The Worcester Lunch Car Company.* Charleston, SC: Arcadia, 2004.

Haber, Barbara. *From Hardtack to Home Fries: An Uncommon History of American Cooks and Meals.* New York: Free Press, 2002.

Haden, Roger. *Food Culture in the Pacific Islands.* Santa Barbara, CA: Greenwood, 2009.

Hagler, Louise. *Tofu Cookery.* Summertown, TN: Book Publishing Company, 2008.

Hailman, John. *Thomas Jefferson on Wine.* Jackson: University Press of Mississippi, 2006.

Hak, Marriaine. "Extreme Diets." *Vegetarian Times* 315 (November 2003): 74–75.

Hall, Colin Michael, and Liz Sharples. *Food and Wine Festivals and Events Around the World: Development, Management and Markets.* Burlington, MA: Elsevier, 2008.

Hall, Colin Michael, Liz Sharples, Richard Mitchell, Niki Macionis, and Brock Cambourne. *Food Tourism Around the World: Development, Management and Markets.* Amsterdam: Butterworth-Heinemann, 2002.

Halpern, Daniel, ed. *Not for Bread Alone: Writers on Food, Wine, and the Art of Eating.* New York: Ecco, 2009.

Halpern, Georges M. *Healing Mushrooms.* Garden City Park, NY: Square One, 2007.

Halweil, Brian. *Home Grown: The Case for Local Food in a Global Market.* Ed. Thomas Prugh. Washington, DC: Worldwatch Institute, 2002.

Hames, Gina. "Every Home a Distillery: Alcohol, Gender, and Technology in the Colonial Chesapeake." *Journal of Social History* 44:4 (Summer 2011): 1291–1292.

Hamilton, Alissa. *Squeezed: What You Don't Know About Orange Juice.* New Haven, CT: Yale University Press, 2009.

Hamilton, Cherie Y. *Brazil: A Culinary Journey.* New York: Hippocrene, 2005.

Han, Jung H. *Innovations in Food Packaging.* San Diego, CA: Elsevier Academic, 2005.

Hancock, James F., ed. *Temperate Fruit Crop Breeding.* Berlin, Germany: Springer, 2008.

Harris, Gardiner. "F.D.A. Panel to Consider Warnings for Artificial Food Colorings." *The New York Times,* March 29, 2011.

Harris, Jessica B. *High on the Hog: A Culinary Journey from Africa to America.* New York: Bloomsbury, 2011.

Harrison, Charles Hampton. *Tending the Garden State: Preserving New Jersey's Farming Legacy.* New Brunswick, NJ: Rivergate, 2007.

Hartel, Richard W., and AnnaKate Hartel. *Food Bites: The Science of the Foods We Eat.* New York: Copernicus, 2008.

Hasheider, Philip. *The Complete Book of Butchery, Smoking, Curing, and Sausage Making.* Minneapolis, MN: Voyageur, 2010.

Havkin-Frenkel, Daphna, and Faith C. Belanger, eds. *Handbook of Vanilla Science and Technology.* Ames, IA: Wiley-Blackwell, 2011.

Hawkes, Corinna, Chantal Blouin, Spencer Henson, Nick Drager, and Laurette Dubé. *Trade, Food, Diet and Health: Perspectives and Policy Options.* Ames, IA: Blackwell, 2010.

Hawkins, Richard. *A Pacific Industry: The History of Pineapple Canning in Hawaii.* New York: I.B. Tauris, 2011.

Hayes, Dayle, and Rachel Laudan, eds. *Food and Nutrition.* New York: Marshall Cavendish Reference, 2009.

Hayes, Joanne Lamb. *Grandma's Wartime Baking Book: World War II and the Way We Baked.* New York: St. Martin's, 2003.

Hefnawy, Magdy. *Advances in Food Protection: Focus on Food Safety and Defense.* New York: Springer, 2011.

Heine, Peter. *Food Culture in the Near East, Middle East, and North Africa.* Westport, CT: Greenwood, 2004.

Heiss, Mary Lou, and Robert J. Heiss. *The Story of Tea: A Cultural History and Drinking Guide.* New York: Random House, 2007.

Heldman, Dennis R., ed. *Encyclopedia of Agricultural, Food, and Biological Engineering.* New York: CRC, 2003.

Helphand, Kenneth. *Defiant Gardens: Making Gardens in Wartime.* San Antonio, TX: Trinity University Press, 2006.

Helstosky, Carol. *Food Culture in the Mediterranean.* Westport, CT: Greenwood, 2009.

Henderson, Mindy B. *The Great Southern Food Festival Cookbook.* Nashville, TN: T. Nelson, 2008.

Henningfeld, Diane Andrews, ed. *Genetically Modified Food.* Detroit, MI: Greenhaven, 2009.

Hess, John L., and Karen Hess. *The Taste of America.* Urbana: University of Illinois Press, 2000.

Hewitt, Aileen. "Squeezo Summer." *The New York Times,* September 5, 2008.

Hicks, Terry Allan. *Obesity.* New York: Marshall Cavendish Benchmark, 2009.

Higgins, Adrian. "Why the Red Delicious No Longer Is." *Washington Post,* August 5, 2005.

Higman, B.W. *How Food Made History.* Malden, MA: Wiley-Blackwell, 2012.

Hinton, Kerry. *Cool Careers Without College for People Who Love Food.* New York: Rosen, 2004.

Hjalager, Anne-Mette, and Greg Richards, eds. *Tourism and Gastronomy.* New York: Routledge, 2002.

Hobbs, Suzanne Havala. *Get the Trans Fat Out: 601 Simple Ways to Cut the Trans Fat out of Any Diet.* New York: Three Rivers, 2006.

Hoffman, Susanna, and Victoria Wise. *The Olive and the Caper: Adventures in Greek Cooking.* New York: Workman, 2004.

Hogan, Linda, and Brenda Peterson, eds. *The Sweet Breathing of Plants: Women Writing on the Green World.* New York: Farrar, Straus & Giroux, 2002.

Holland, Leandra Zim. *Feasting and Fasting with Lewis & Clark: A Food and Social History of the Early 1800s.* Emigrant, MT: Old Yellowstone, 2003.

Holley, Joe. "Entrepreneur Norman Brinker, 78, Pioneered Casual Dining, Invented Salad Bar." *Washington Post,* June 10, 2009.

Holy, Norman. *Deserted Ocean: A Social History of Depletion.* Bloomington, IN: AuthorHouse, 2009.

Honoré, Carl. *In Praise of Slowness: How a Worldwide Movement Is Challenging the Cult of Speed.* Toronto: Vintage Canada, 2004.

Hopkins, Kate. *99 Drams of Whiskey: The Accidental Hedonist's Quest for the Perfect Shot and the History of the Drink.* New York: St. Martin's, 2010.

Hornsey, Ian Spencer. *A History of Beer and Brewing.* Cambridge, UK: Royal Society of Chemistry, 2003.

Hosner, Kathleen S., and Linda Frazee. *Full Heart, Satisfied Belly.* New York: iUniverse, 2004.

Houston, Lynn Marie. *Food Culture in the Caribbean.* Westport, CT: Greenwood, 2005.

Howell, Jim. "On Waikaia Plains Station—Developing a Cuisine of Stewardship." *In Practice* 124 (March/April 2009): 8–11.

Hsu, Elizabeth. "Review: *A Soup for the Qan.*" *Medical History* 46:2 (April 2002): 285–286.

Hughes, Robert, "Still Fresh as Ever." *Time* 157:12 (March 26, 2001): 70–71.

Hui, Yui H., ed. *Handbook of Food Products Manufacturing: Principles, Bakery, Beverages, Cereals, Cheese, Confectionary, Fats, Fruits, and Functional Foods.* Hoboken, NJ: Wiley-Interscience, 2007.

———, ed. *Handbook of Food Science, Technology, and Engineering.* Boca Raton, FL: Taylor & Francis, 2006.

Hui, Yui H., et al., eds. *Food Drying Science and Technology: Microbiology, Chemistry, Applications.* Lancaster, PA: DEStech, 2008.

Hui, Yiu H., et al., eds. *Foodborne Disease Handbook.* Vol. 2, *Viruses, Parasites, Pathogens, and HACCP.* New York: Marcel Dekker, 2001.

Hui, Yiu H., et al., eds. *Handbook of Food and Beverage Fermentation Technology.* New York: Marcel Dekker, 2004.

Hull, Peter. *Glucose Syrups: Technology and Applications.* Ames, IA: Wiley-Blackwell, 2010.

Hurt, Ray Douglas. *Problems of Plenty: The American Farmer in the Twentieth Century.* Chicago: Ivan R. Dee, 2002.

Hutkins, Robert Wayne. *Microbiology and Technology of Fermented Foods.* Chicago: IFT, 2006.

Hutton, Wendy. *The Food of Love: Four Centuries of East–West Cuisine.* Singapore: Marshall Cavendish, 2007.

Iacobbo, Karen, and Michael Iacobbo. *Vegetarian America: A History.* Westport, CT: Greenwood, 2004.

Ilardi, A., and P. Marra. "A Chapter on Psychosomatic Medicine in the 'Tesoro della Sanita' of Castor Durante." *Rivista di Storia Della Medicina* 78 (July 1964): 172–182.

Imada, Adria L. "The Army Learns to Luau: Imperial Hospitality and Military Photography in Hawaii." *Contemporary Pacific* 20:2 (September 22, 2008): 329–362.

Inch, Arthur, and Arlene Hirst. *Dinner Is Served: An English Butler's Guide to the Art of the Table.* Philadelphia: Running Press, 2003.

"Indian Gum Makes Healthier Bread." *New Scientist* 97:1343 (February 3, 1983): 307.

Inglis, David, and Debra Gimlin, eds. *The Globalization of Food.* New York: Berg, 2009.

Ingram, Scott. *Want Fries with That? Obesity and the Supersizing of America.* New York: Franklin Watts, 2005.

Inness, Sherrie A., ed. *Pilaf, Pozole, and Pad Thai: American Women and Ethnic Food.* Amherst: University of Massachusetts Press, 2001.

———. *Secret Ingredients: Race, Gender, and Class at the Dinner Table.* New York: Palgrave Macmillan, 2005.

Isern, Neus, and Joaquim Fort. "Anisotropic Dispersion, Space Competition, and the Slowdown of the Neolithic Transition." *New Journal of Physics* 12:12 (December 3, 2010).

Iyer, Raghavan. *660 Curries.* New York: Workman, 2008.

Jackman, Ian. *Food Network Star.* New York: HarperCollins, 2011.

Jackson, Richard, and Stacy Sinclair. *Designing Healthy Communities.* San Francisco: Jossey-Bass, 2012.

Jadhav, Ujwala. *Aquaculture Technology and Environment.* New Delhi, India: PHI Learning, 2009.

James, Glyn. *Sugarcane.* Oxford, UK: Blackwell Science, 2004.

James, Kenneth. *Escoffier: The King of Chefs.* London: Continuum, 2006.

Janer, Zilkia. *Latino Food Culture.* Westport, CT: Greenwood, 2008.

Janick, Jules, and Robert E. Paull, eds. *The Encyclopedia of Fruit and Nuts.* Cambridge, MA: CABI, 2006.

Jansen, Kees, and Sietze Vellema, eds. *Agribusiness and Society: Corporate Responses to Environmentalism, Market Opportunities, and Public Regulation.* New York: Zed, 2004.

Johnston, Josée, and Shyon Baumann. "Democracy Versus Distinction: A Study of Omnivorousness in Gourmet Food Writing." *American Journal of Sociology* 113:1 (July 2007): 165–204.

———. *Foodies: Democracy and Distinction in the Gourmet Foodscape.* New York: Routledge, 2010.

Johnston, Ruth A. *All Things Medieval: An Encyclopedia of the Medieval World.* Santa Barbara, CA: Greenwood, 2011.

Joint FAO/WHO Expert Committee on Food Additives. *Evaluation of Certain Food Additives.* Geneva, Switzerland: World Health Organization, 2010.

Jones, Carl M., Charles M. Rick, Dawn Adams, Judy Jernstedt, and Roger T. Chetelat. "Genealogy and Fine Mapping of Obscuravenosa." *American Journal of Botany* 94:6 (June 2007): 935–947.

Jones, Carol. *Sausage.* Philadelphia: Chelsea House, 2003.

Jones, Wilbert. *The New Soul Food Cookbook: Healthier Recipes for Traditional Favorites.* New York: Citadel, 2005.

Kallas, John. *Edible Wild Plants: Wild Foods from Dirt to Plate.* Layton, UT: Gibbs Smith, 2010.

Karner, Julie. *The Biography of Vanilla.* New York: Crabtree, 2006.

Kato, Etsuko. *The Tea Ceremony and Women's Empowerment in Modern Japan.* New York: Routledge, 2004.

Katz, Solomon H., and William Woys Weaver, eds. *Encyclopedia of Food and Culture.* New York: Charles Scribner's Sons, 2003.

Kaufman, Cathy K. *Cooking in Ancient Civilizations.* Westport, CT: Greenwood, 2006.

Keith, Lierre. *The Vegetarian Myth: Food, Justice and Sustainability.* Crescent City, CA: Flashpoint, 2009.

Keller, James R. *Food, Film, and Culture: A Genre Study.* Jefferson, NC: McFarland, 2006.

Kelley, Laura. *The Silk Road Gourmet.* New York: iUniverse, 2009.

Kelly, Ian. *Cooking for Kings: The Life of Antonin Carême, the First Celebrity Chef.* New York: Walker, 2003.

Kerry, Joseph, and Paul Butler. *Smart Packaging Technologies for Fast Moving Consumer Goods.* Hoboken, NJ: John Wiley & Sons, 2008.

Kessler, Roman. "The Craze over Currywurst." *Wall Street Journal,* August 27, 2009.

Kijac, Maria Baez. *The South American Table: The Flavor and Soul of Authentic Home Cooking from Patagonia to Rio de Janeiro.* Boston: Harvard Common, 2003.

Kilman, Scott. "Crop Prices Erode Farm Subsidy Program." *Wall Street Journal,* July 25, 2011.

Kimball, Yeffe, and Jean Anderson. *The Art of American Indian Cooking.* New York: Lyons, 2000.

Kime, Tom. *Street Food.* New York: Penguin, 2007.

Kinchloe, Joe L. *The Sign of the Burger: McDonald's and the Culture of Power.* Philadelphia: Temple University Press, 2002.

Kingsbury, Noel. *Hybrid: The History and Science of Plant Breeding.* Chicago: University of Chicago Press, 2009.

Kiple, Kenneth F. *A Movable Feast: Ten Millennia of Food Globalization.* New York: Cambridge University Press, 2007.

Kiple, Kenneth F., and Kriemhild Coneé Ornelas, eds. *Cambridge World History of Food.* New York: Cambridge University Press, 2000.

Kirakosyan, Ara, and Peter B. Kaufman, eds. *Recent Advances in Plant Biotechnology.* New York: Springer, 2009.

Kittler, Pamela Goyan, and Kathryn Sucher. *Food and Culture.* Belmont, CA: Wadsworth/Thomson Learning, 2004.

Kole, Chittaranjan. *Oilseeds.* New York: Springer, 2007.

Koromilas, Kathryn. "Feasting with Archestratus." *Odyssey* (November/December 2007): 69–70.

Kosar, Kevin R. *Whiskey: A Global History.* London: Reaktion, 2010.

Krasner-Khait, Barbara. "The Impact of Refrigeration." *History* 1:3 (February/March 2000): 41–44.

Krissoff, Barry, Mary Bohman, and Julie A. Caswell, eds. *Global Food Trade and Consumer Demand for Quality.* New York: Kluwer Academic/Plenum, 2002.

Krondl, Michael. *Sweet Invention: A History of Dessert.* Chicago: Chicago Review Press, 2011.

———. *The Taste of Conquest: The Rise and Fall of the Three Great Cities of Spice.* New York: Random House, 2007.

Kurlansky, Mark, ed. *Choice Cuts: A Savory Selection of Food Writing from Around the World and Throughout History.* New York: Penguin, 2002.

———. *Salt: A World History.* New York: Penguin, 2002.

Kuz'mina, E.E. *The Prehistory of the Silk Road.* Ed. Victor H. Meir. Philadelphia: University of Pennsylvania Press, 2008.

La Boone, John A. *Around the World of Food: Adventures in Culinary History.* New York: iUniverse, 2006.

Lamey, Andy. "Food Fight! Davis Versus Regan on the Ethics of Eating Beef." *Journal of Social Philosophy* 38:2 (Summer 2007): 331–348.

Laszlo, Pierre. *Citrus: A History.* Chicago: University of Chicago Press, 2008.

Laudan, Rachel. "Review: A Soup for the Qan." *Journal of World History* 14:4 (December 2003): 563–566.

LeBesco, Kathleen, and Peter Naccarato, eds. *Edible Ideologies: Representing Food and Meaning.* Albany: State University of New York Press, 2008.

Leite, David. *The New Portuguese Table: Exciting Flavors from Europe's Western Coast.* New York: Clarkson Potter, 2009.

Lelieveld, H.L.M., et al., eds. *Hygiene in Food Processing.* Boca Raton, FL: CRC, 2003.

Lemon, Sarah. "Julia's Legacy." *Mail Tribune* (Medford, OR), August 9, 2009.

Levenstein, Harvey A. *Paradox of Plenty: A Social History of Eating in Modern America.* Berkeley: University of California Press, 2003.

Levine, Susan. *School Lunch Politics: The Surprising History of America's Favorite Welfare Program.* Princeton, NJ: Princeton University Press, 2010.

Li, Duo. "Chemistry Behind Vegetarianism." *Journal of Agricultural and Food Chemistry* 59:3 (February 2011): 777–784.

Li, Lillian M. *Fighting Famine in North China: State, Market, and Environmental Decline, 1690s–1990s.* Stanford, CA: Stanford University Press, 2007.

Liberman, Sherri, ed. *American Food by the Decades.* Santa Barbara, CA: ABC-Clio, 2011.

Liebreich, Karen, Jutta Wagner, and Annette Wendland. *The Family Kitchen Garden.* London: Frances Lincoln, 2009.

"*Life* Goes to a Luau in Hawaii." *Life* 19:9 (August 27, 1945): 103–106, 109.

Lindgreen, Adam, and Martin K. Hingley, eds. *The New Cultures of Food: Marketing Opportunities from Ethnic, Religious, and Cultural Diversity.* Burlington, VT: Gower, 2009.

Ling, Kong Foong. *The Food of Asia.* North Clarendon, VT: Tuttle, 2002.

Lipkowitz, Ina. *Words to Eat By: Five Foods and the Culinary History of the English Language.* New York: Macmillan, 2011.

Lipkowitz, Myron A., and Tova Navarra. *Encyclopedia of Allergies.* New York: Facts on File, 2001.

Liu, Yong. *The Dutch East India Company's Tea Trade with China, 1757–1781.* Leiden, Netherlands: Brill, 2007.

Lockie, Stewart, and David Carpenter, eds. *Agriculture, Biodiversity and Markets: Livelihoods and Agroecology in Comparative Perspective.* Sterling, VA: Earthscan, 2010.

Loewer, H. Peter. *Jefferson's Garden.* Mechanicsburg, PA: Stackpole, 2004.

———. *Seeds: The Definitive Guide to Growing, History, and Lore.* Portland, OR: Timber, 2005.

Long-Solis, Janet, and Luis Alberto Vargas. *Food Culture in Mexico.* Westport, CT: Greenwood, 2005.

Longstreth, Richard W. *The Drive-in, the Supermarket, and the Transformation of Commercial Space in Los Angeles, 1914–1941.* Cambridge, MA: MIT Press, 2000.

Lott, Dale F. *American Bison: A Natural History.* Berkeley: University of California Press, 2002.

Love, John F. *McDonald's: Behind the Arches.* Wake Forest, NC: Paw Prints, 2008.

Lovegren, Sylvia. "Barbecue." *American Heritage* 54 (June 1, 2003): 36–44.

———. *Fashionable Food: Seven Decades of Food Fads.* Chicago: University of Chicago Press, 2005.

Lovera, José Rafael. *Food Culture in South America.* Westport, CT: Greenwood, 2005.

Lucas, Fiona. *Hearth and Home: Women and the Art of Open-Hearth Cooking.* Toronto: J. Lorimer, 2006.

Lusas, Edmund W., and Lloyd W. Rooney, eds. *Snack Foods Processing.* Boca Raton, FL: CRC, 2001.

Lyle, Katie Letcher. *The Complete Guide to Edible Wild Plants, Mushrooms, Fruits, and Nuts.* Guilford, CT: Globe Pequot, 2004.

Macbeth, Helen M., and Jeremy MacClancy, eds. *Researching Food Habits: Methods and Problems.* New York: Berghahn, 2004.

Mack, Glenn Randall, and Asele Surina. *Food Culture in Russia and Central Asia.* Westport, CT: Greenwood, 2005.

Maclaran, Pauline, and Lorna Stevens. "Magners Man: Irish Cider, Representations of Masculinity, and the 'Burning Celtic Soul.'" *Irish Marketing Review* 20:2 (2009): 77–88.

MacLean, Charles. *Whiskey.* New York: Dorling Kindersley, 2008.

MacVeigh, Jeremy. *International Cuisine.* Clifton Park, NY: Delmar Cengage Learning, 2009.

Madavan, Vijay. *Cooking the Indian Way.* Minneapolis, MN: Lerner, 2002.

Maderia, Crystal. *The New Seaweed Cookbook: A Complete Guide to Discovering the Deep Flavors of the Sea.* Berkeley, CA: North Atlantic, 2007.

Mair, Victor H., and Erling Hoh. *The True History of Tea.* New York: Thames & Hudson, 2009.

Malaguzzi, Silvia. *Food and Feasting in Art.* Los Angeles, CA: J. Paul Getty Museum, 2008.

Malcolmson, Robert W., and Stephanos Mastoris. *The English Pig: A History.* New York: Continuum, 2001.

Maleki, Soheila J. *Food Allergy.* Washington, DC: ASM, 2006.

Mann, Charles C. *1493: Uncovering the New World Columbus Created.* New York: Random House, 2011.

Marchese, C. Marina. *Honeybee: Lessons from an Accidental Beekeeper.* New York: Black Dog and Levanthal, 2011.

Marcone, Massimo F. "Characterization of the Edible Bird's Nest the 'Caviar of the East.'" *Food Research International* 38:10 (December 2005): 1125–1134.

Mariani, John F. *How Italian Food Conquered the World.* Foreword by Lidia Bastianich. New York: Palgrave Macmillan, 2011.

Marianski, Stanley, and Adam Marianski. *Home Production of Quality Meats and Sausages.* Seminole, FL: Bookmagic, 2010.

Marianski, Stanley, Adam Marianski, and Robert Marianski. *Meat Smoking and Smokehouse Design.* Seminole, FL: Bookmagic, 2009.

Marks, Gil. *Encyclopedia of Jewish Food.* Hoboken, NJ: Wiley & Sons, 2010.

Marks, Henry. "Dining with Angels: Cuisine and Dining in the Eastern Roman Empire." *Medieval History Magazine* 2:1 (September 2004): 16–23.

Martin, Laura C. *Tea: The Drink That Changed the World.* Rutland, VT: Tuttle, 2007.

Martin, Meredith. *Dairy Queens: The Politics of Pastoral Architecture from Catherine de' Medici to Marie-Antoinette.* Cambridge, MA: Harvard University Press, 2011.

Mason, Laura. *Food Culture in Great Britain.* Westport, CT: Greenwood, 2004.

Matalas, Antonia-Leda, Antonis Zampelas, Vassilis Stavrinos, and Ira Wolinsky, eds. *The Mediterranean Diet: Constituents and Health Promotion.* Boca Raton, FL: CRC, 2000.

Mathews, Jennifer P., and Gilliam P. Schultz. *Chicle: The Chewing Gum of the Americas, from the Ancient Maya to William Wrigley.* Tucson: University of Arizona Press, 2009.

Maugh, Thomas H. "Ancient Winery Found in Armenia." *Los Angeles Times,* January 11, 2011.

Mazoyer, Marcel, and Laurence Roudart. *A History of World Agriculture: From the Neolithic Age to the Current Crisis.* Trans. James H. Membrez. London: Earthscan, 2006.

McCann, James. *Stirring the Pot: A History of African Cuisine.* Athens: Ohio University Press, 2009.

McDaniel, Rick. *An Irresistible History of Southern Food: Four Centuries of Black-Eyed Peas, Collard Greens & Whole Hog Barbecue.* Charleston, SC: History Press, 2011.

McFarland, Ben. *World's Best Beers: One Thousand Craft Brews from Cask to Glass.* New York: Sterling, 2009.

McGee, Harold. *On Food and Cooking: The Science and Lore of the Kitchen.* New York: Simon & Schuster, 2004.

McGinnis, J. Michael, Jennifer Appleton Gootman, and Vivica I. Kraak, eds. *Food Marketing to Children and Youth: Threat or Opportunity?* Washington, DC: National Academies Press, 2006.

McGovern, Patrick E. *Ancient Wine: The Search for the Origins of Viniculture.* Princeton, NJ: Princeton University Press, 2003.

———. *Uncorking the Past: The Quest for Wine, Beer, and Other Alcoholic Beverages.* Berkeley: University of California Press, 2009.

McGrath, Robin. *Salt Fish and Shmattes: The History of Jews in Newfoundland and Labrador from 1770.* St. John's, Newfoundland, Canada: Creative Book, 2006.

McLean, Alice L. *Cooking in America, 1840–1945.* Westport, CT: Greenwood, 2006.

McMillan, Sherrie. "What Time Is Dinner?" *History Magazine* 3:1 (October/November 2001): 21–24.

McNamee, Gregory. *Movable Feasts: The History, Science, and Lore of Food.* Westport, CT: Praeger, 2007.

McWilliams, James E. *Just Food: Where Locavores Get It Wrong and How We Can Truly Eat Responsibly.* New York: Little, Brown, 2009.

Meacham, Sarah Hand. *Every Home a Distillery: Alcohol, Gender, and Technology in the Colonial Chesapeake.* Baltimore: Johns Hopkins University Press, 2009.

Medina, F. Xavier. *Food Culture in Spain.* Westport, CT: Greenwood, 2005.

Méndez Montoya, Angel F. *Theology of Food: Eating and the Eucharist.* Malden, MA: Wiley-Blackwell, 2009.

Mercer, Lorraine. "I Shall Make No Excuse: The Narrative Odyssey of Mary Seacole." *Journal of Narrative Theory* 35:1 (2005): 1–24.

Mercuri, Becky. *Food Festival, U.S.A.* San Diego, CA: Laurel Glen, 2002.

Metcalfe, Dean D., Hugh A. Sampson, and Ronald A. Simon, eds. *Food Allergy: Adverse Reactions to Food and Food Additives.* Malden, MA: Blackwell Science, 2003.

Meyer, Arthur L., and Jon M. Vann. *The Appetizer Atlas: A World of Small Bites.* Hoboken, NJ: John Wiley & Sons, 2003.

Milton, Katharine. "Hunter-Gatherer Diets—A Different Perspective." *American Journal of Clinical Nutrition* 71 (2000): 665–667.

Minick, Jim. *The Blueberry Years: A Memoir of Farm and Family.* New York: Thomas Dunne, 2010.

Mink, Gwendolyn, and Alice O'Connor, eds. *Poverty in the United States: An Encyclopedia of History, Politics, and Policy.* Santa Barbara, CA: ABC-Clio, 2004.

Misiura, Shashi. *Heritage Marketing.* Burlington, MA: Elsevier, 2006.

Mitchell, Deborah. *Safe Foods: The A-to-Z Guide to the Most Wholesome Foods for You and Your Family.* New York: Signet, 2004.

Moerman, Daniel E. *Native American Food Plants.* Portland, OR: Timber, 2010.

Monroe, Jo. *Star of India: The Spicy Adventures of Curry.* Chichester, UK: John Wiley & Sons, 2005.

Moran, Joe. "Early Cultures of Gentrification in London, 1955–1980." *Journal of Urban History* 34:1 (November 2007): 101–121.

Morgan, James L. *Culinary Creation: An Introduction to Foodservice and World Cuisine.* Boston: Elsevier, 2006.

Morgan, Sally. *Superfoods: Genetic Modification of Foods.* Portsmouth, NH: Heinemann, 2003.

Morris, Scott A. *Food and Package Engineering.* Ames, IA: Wiley-Blackwell, 2011.

Moxham, Roy. *A Brief History of Tea: The Extraordinary Story of the World's Favorite Drink.* Philadelphia: Running Press, 2009.

Mudry, Jessica J. *Measured Meals: Nutrition in America.* Albany: State University of New York Press, 2009.

Muller, Mike. "Milk, Nutrition, and the Law." *New Scientist* 66:948 (May 8, 1975): 328–330.

Müller-Wille, Staffan, and Hans-Jörg Rheinberger. *Heredity Produced: At the Crossroads of Biology, Politics, and Culture, 1500–1870.* Cambridge, MA: MIT Press, 2007.

Muscatine, Doris. *The Vinegar of Spilamberto.* Washington, DC: Shoemaker & Hoard, 2005.

Mylne, R.S. "Ancient Peru." *Antiquary* 20 (January 1889): 14–18.

Nabhan, Gary Paul, ed. *Renewing America's Food Traditions: Saving and Savoring the Continent's Most Endangered Foods.* White River Junction, VT: Chelsea Green, 2008.

Nardo, Don. *Malnutrition.* Detroit, MI: Gale, 2007.

Nathan, Joan. *The Foods of Israel Today.* New York: Alfred A. Knopf, 2001.

Nelson, Max. *The Barbarian's Beverage: A History of Beer in Ancient Europe.* New York: Routledge, 2005.

Nenes, Michael F. *American Regional Cuisine.* Hoboken, NJ: John Wiley & Sons, 2007.

Neuman, William. "Nutrition Plate Unveiled, Replacing Food Pyramid." *The New York Times,* June 2, 2011.

Nevo, Eviatarl, Abraham B. Korol, Avigdor Beiles, and Tzion Fahima. *Evolution of Wild Emmer and Wheat Improvement.* New York: Springer, 2002.

Newton, David E. *Food Chemistry.* New York: Facts on File, 2007.

Nielsen, S. Suzanne. *Food Analysis.* New York: Springer, 2010.

Nunez, David G. *The Appetizer Is the Meal.* Bloomington, IN: AuthorHouse, 2011.

Nunley, Debbie, and Karen Jane Elliott. *A Taste of Virginia History: A Guide to Historic Eateries and Their Recipes.* Winston-Salem, NC: John F. Blair, 2004.

O'Connor, Kaori. *The Hawaiian Luau: A Cultural Biography, with Recipes.* New York: Kegan Paul International, 2008.

Oddy, Derek J., Peter J. Atkins, and Virginia Amilien. *The Rise of Obesity in Europe: A Twentieth Century Food History.* Burlington, VT: Ashgate, 2009.

Ojakangas, Beatrice. *Scandinavian Cooking.* Minneapolis: University of Minnesota Press, 2003.

Okakura, Kakuzo. *The Book of Tea.* Philadelphia: Running Press, 2002.

Oliver, Sandra Louise. *Food in Colonial and Federal America.* Westport, CT: Greenwood, 2005.

Ono, Tadashi, and Harris Salat. *The Japanese Grill: From Classic Yakitori to Steak, Seafood, and Vegetables.* New York: Ten Speed, 2011.

———. *Japanese Hot Pots: Comforting One-Pot Meals.* Berkeley, CA: Ten Speed, 2009.

Oppedisano, Jeannette, and Sandra Lueder. "Entrepreneurial Women and Life Expectancy." *New England Journal of Entrepreneurship* 5:2 (Fall 2002): 13–20.

Ormrod, David. *The Rise of Commercial Empires: England and the Netherlands in the Age of Mercantilism, 1650–1770.* New York: Cambridge University Press, 2003.

O'Rourke, Raymond. *European Food Law.* London: Sweet & Maxwell, 2005.

Orsini, Joseph E. *Italian Family Cooking: Unlocking a Treasury of Recipes and Stories.* New York: Thomas Dunne, 2000.

Oster, Kenneth V. *The Complete Guide to Preserving Meat, Fish, and Game.* Ocala, FL: Atlantic, 2011.

Owen, James. "Bottled Water Isn't Healthier Than Tap, Report Reveals." *National Geographic News,* February 24, 2006.

Owens, Gavin, ed. *Cereals Processing Technology.* Boca Raton, FL: CRC, 2001.

Padoch, Christine, Kevin Coffey, Ole Mertz, Stephen J. Leisz, Jefferson Fox, and Reed L. Wadley. "The Demise of Swidden in Southeast Asia? Local Realities and Regional Ambiguities." *Danish Journal of Geography* 107:1 (2007): 29–41.

Papadopoulos, Christos. "Post-Byzantine Medical Manuscripts." *Journal of Modern Greek Studies* 27:1 (May 2009): 107–130.

Paris, Harry S. "Paintings (1769–1774) by A.N. Duchesne and the History of *Cucurbita pepo*." *Annals of Botany* 85 (2000): 815–830.

Parrish, Christopher C., Nancy J. Turner, and Shirley M. Solbert, eds. *Resetting the Kitchen Table: Food Security, Culture, Health and Resilience in Coastal Communities.* New York: Nova Science, 2008.

Patrick-Goudreau, Colleen. *Vegan's Daily Companion.* Beverly, MA: Quarry, 2011.

Pegg, Ronald B., and Fereidoon Shahidi. *Nitrite Curing of Meat: The N-Nitrosamine Problem and Nitrite Alternatives.* Trumbull, CT: Food & Nutrition, 2000.

Pellechia, Thomas. *Garlic, Wine, and Olive Oil: Historical Anecdotes and Recipes.* Santa Barbara, CA: Capra, 2000.

Pendergrast, Mark. *Uncommon Grounds: The History of Coffee and How It Transformed Our World.* New York: Basic Books, 2010.

Pequignot, Amandine. "Une Peau entre Deux Feuilles, L'usage de L'herbier en Taxidermie aux XVIIIe et XIXe Siècles en France." *Revue d'histoire des science* 59:1 (January 2006): 127–136.

Petersen, David. "Chew on This." *Backpacker* 30:205 (June 2002): 29–33.

Peterson, James. *Sauces: Classical and Contemporary Sauce Making.* Hoboken, NJ: John Wiley & Sons, 2008.

Petrosian, Irina, and David Underwood. *Armenian Food: Fact, Fiction & Folklore.* Bloomington, IN: Yerkir, 2006.

Pettid, Michael J. *Korean Cuisine: An Illustrated History.* London: Reaktion, 2008.

Pflederer, Richard L. "Before New England: The Popham Colony." *History Today* 55:11 (January 2005): 10–18.

Pilcher, Jeffrey M. *Food in World History.* New York: Taylor & Francis, 2006.

Pimental, David, and Marcia Pimentel. *Food, Energy, and Society.* New York: Taylor & Francis, 2008.

Pinney, Thomas. *A History of Wine in America.* Berkeley: University of California Press, 2007.

Pollan, Michael. "You Are What You Grow." *The New York Times,* April 22, 2007.

Pond, Catherine Seiberling. *The Pantry: Its History and Modern Uses.* Salt Lake City, UT: Gibbs Smith, 2007.

Popper, Virginia. "Investigating Chinampa Farming." *Backdirt* (Fall/Winter 2000).

Potera, Carol. "The Artificial Food Dye Blues." *Environmental Health Perspectives* 118:10 (October 2010): A428.

Potterton, David, ed. *Culpeper's Color Herbal.* Foreword by E.J. Shellard. New York: Sterling, 2007.

Powell, Julie. "The Trouble with Blood." *Archaeology* 57:6 (December 2004).

Powell, Marilyn. *Ice Cream: The Delicious History.* New York: Penguin, 2009.

Prange, Sebastian R. "Where the Pepper Grows." *Saudi Aramco World* 59:1 (January/February 2008): 10–17.

Preece, Rod. *Sins of the Flesh: A History of Ethical Vegetarian Thought.* Vancouver, Canada: University of British Columbia Press, 2008.

Preedy, Victor R., Ronald R. Watson, and Vinood B. Patel, eds. *Flour and Breads and Their Fortification in Health and Disease Prevention.* Boston: Academic Press, 2011.

———. *Nuts and Seeds in Health and Disease Prevention.* Boston: Academic Press, 2011.

Prentiss, William C., and Ian Kujit, eds. *Complex Hunter-Gatherers: Evolution and Organization of Prehistoric Communities on the Plateau of Northwestern North America.* Salt Lake City: University of Utah Press, 2004.

Price, David Clive, and Masano Kawana. *The Food of Korea: Authentic Recipes from the Land of Morning Calm.* North Clarendon, VT: Tuttle, 2002.

Prince, Rose. "The French Cooking Bible Is Back—and Bigger Than Ever." *The Telegraph* (London), October 20, 2009.

Quinzio, Jeri. *Of Sugar and Snow: A History of Ice Cream Making.* Berkeley: University of California Press, 2009.

Rain, Patricia. *Vanilla: The Cultural History of the World's Most Popular Flavor and Fragrance.* New York: Jeremy P. Tarcher, 2004.

Rakocy, James E., Michael P. Masser, and Thomas M. Losordo. "Recirculation Aquaculture Tank Production Systems: Aquaponics—Integrating Fish and Plant Culture." *SRAC Publication* 454 (November 2006): 1–15.

Räsänen, Leena. "Of All Foods Bread Is the Most Noble: Carl von Linné (Carl Linnaeus) on Bread." *Scandinavian Journal of Food & Nutrition* 51:3 (September 2007): 91–99.

Ratti, Cristina, ed. *Advances in Food Dehydration.* Boca Raton, FL: CRC, 2009.

———. "Hot Air and Freeze-Drying of High-Value Foods: A Review." *Journal of Food Engineering* 49:4 (September 2001): 311–319.

Ravindran, P.N., ed. *Black Pepper: Piper Nigrum.* Amsterdam: Overseas, 2000.

Rayner, Lisa. *Wild Bread: Hand-Baked Sourdough Artisan Breads in Your Own Kitchen.* Flagstaff, AZ: Lifeweaver, 2009.

Reader, John. *Potato: A History of the Propitious Esculent.* New Haven, CT: Yale University Press, 2009.

Readicker-Henderson, E., ed. *A Short History of the Honey Bee: Humans, Flowers, and Bees in the Eternal Chase for Honey.* Portland, OR: Timber, 2009.

Redclift, M.R. *Chewing Gum: The Fortunes of Taste.* New York: Routledge, 2004.

Redman, Nina. *Food Safety: A Reference Handbook.* Santa Barbara, CA: ABC-Clio, 2007.

Redon, Odile, Françoise Sabban, and Silvano Serventi. *The Medieval Kitchen: Recipes from France and Italy.* Chicago: University of Chicago Press, 2000.

Reed, Dale Volberg, and John Shelton Reed, eds. *Cornbread Nation 4: The Best of Southern Food Writing.* Athens: University of Georgia Press, 2008.

Rees, Andy. *Genetically Modified Food: A Short Guide for the Confused.* Ann Arbor, MI: Pluto, 2006.

Regattieri, A., M. Gamberi, and R. Manzini. "Traceability of Food Products: General Framework and Experimental Evidence." *Journal of Food Engineering* 81:2 (July 2007): 347–356.

Reinfeld, Mark, and Bo Rinaldi. *Vegan Fusion World Cuisine.* New York: Beaufort, 2007.

Renfrew, Jane M. *Roman Cookery: Recipes & History.* London: English Heritage, 2004.

Riaz, Mian N., and Muhammad M. Chaudry. *Halal Food Production.* Boca Raton, FL: CRC, 2004.

Richardson, Philip S., ed. *Thermal Technologies in Food Processing.* Boca Raton, FL: CRC, 2001.

Richardson, Tim. *Sweets: A History of Candy.* New York: Bloomsbury, 2002.

Richman, Irwin. *The Pennsylvania Dutch Company.* Charleston, SC: Arcadia, 2004.

Richmond, Simon. *Trans-Siberian Railway.* Oakland, CA: Lonely Planet, 2009.

Ricotti, Eugenia Salza Prina. *Meals and Recipes from Ancient Greece.* Los Angeles, CA: Getty, 2007.

Riding, Alan. "Becoming Julia Child." *The New York Times,* May 28, 2006.

Rieger, Mark. *Introduction to Fruit Crops.* New York: Psychology, 2006.

Riley, Gillian. *The Oxford Companion to Italian Food.* New York: Oxford University Press, 2007.

Rimas, Andrew, and Evan Fraser. *Beef: The Untold Story of How Milk, Meat, and Muscle Shaped the World.* San Francisco: HarperCollins, 2009.

Rinella, Steven. *American Buffalo: In Search of a Lost Icon.* New York: Random House, 2008.

Rinsky, Glenn, and Laura Halpin Rinsky. *The Pastry Chef's Companion.* Hoboken, NJ: John Wiley & Sons, 2009.

Rizzuti, Lucio, Hisham Mohamed Ettouney, and Andrea Cipollina. *Solar Desalination for the 21st Century.* New York: Springer, 2007.

Roberts, Allison. "Carlo Petrini: The Slow Food Tsar." *The Independent* (London), December 10, 2006.

Roberts, J.A.G. *China to Chinatown: Chinese Food in the West.* London: Reaktion, 2002.

Robinson, Daniel F. *Confronting Biopiracy: Challenges, Cases and International Debates.* Washington, DC: Earthscan, 2010.

Robinson, Jane. *Mary Seacole: The Most Famous Black Woman of the Victorian Age.* New York: Carroll & Graf, 2005.

Robuchon, Joel. *New Concise Larousse Gastronomique: The World's Greatest Cookery Encyclopedia.* London: Hamlyn, 2007.

Roden, Claudia. *The New Book of Middle Eastern Food.* New York: Alfred A. Knopf, 2000.

Rodrigue, John C. *Reconstruction in the Cane Fields: From Slavery to Free Labor in Louisiana's Sugar Parishes, 1862–1880.* Baton Rouge: Louisiana State University Press, 2001.

Rose, Sarah. *For All the Tea in China: How England Stole the World's Favorite Drink and Changed History.* New York: Viking, 2010.

Rosenbaum, Stephanie. *Honey: From Flower to Table.* San Francisco: Chronicle, 2002.

Rosengarten, Frederic. *The Book of Edible Nuts.* Mineola, NY: Dover, 2004.

Rotberg, Robert I., ed. *Health and Disease in Human History.* Cambridge, MA: MIT Press, 2000.

Royle, Tony. *Working for McDonald's in Europe: The Unequal Struggle.* New York: Routledge, 2000.

Rubel, William. *The Magic of Fire: Hearth Cooking.* Berkeley, CA: Ten Speed, 2002.

———. "Thanksgiving by the Hearth." *Vegetarian Times* 315 (November 2003): 48–55.

Rubin, Lawrence C., ed. *Food for Thought: Essays on Eating and Culture.* Jefferson, NC: McFarland, 2008.

Rumble, Victoria R. *Soup Through the Ages: A Culinary History with Period Recipes.* Jefferson, NC: McFarland, 2009.

Runyon, Linda. *The Essential Wild Food Survival Guide.* Shiloh, NJ: Wild Food, 2002.

Russo, Ruthann. *The Raw Food Lifestyle: The Philosophy and Nutrition Behind Raw and Live Foods.* Berkeley, CA: North Atlantic, 2009.

Saberi, Helen, ed. *Cured, Fermented and Smoked Foods.* Totnes, UK: Prospect, 2011.

Sack, Daniel. *Whitebread Protestants: Food and Religion in American Culture.* New York: Palgrave Macmillan, 2001.

Sackett, Lou, Wayne Gisslen, and Jaclyn Pestka. *Professional Garde Manger: A Comprehensive Guide to Cold Food Preparation.* Hoboken, NJ: John Wiley & Sons, 2011.

Sackman, Douglas Cazaux. *Orange Empire: California and the Fruits of Eden.* Berkeley: University of California Press, 2005.

Saekel, Karola. "Julia Child: 1912–2004: TV's French Chef Taught Us How to Cook with Panache." *San Francisco Chronicle,* August 14, 2004.

Salau, Mohammed Bashir. "The Role of Slave Labor in Groundnut Production in Early Colonial Kano." *Journal of African History* 51:2 (2010): 147–165.

Sanchez, Priscilla C. *Philippine Fermented Foods: Principles and Technology.* Quezon City: University of the Philippines Press, 2008.

Sandler, Nick, and Johnny Acton. *The Sausage Book.* Lanham, MD: National Book Network, 2011.

Sarramon, Christian, and Carmella Abramowitz-Moreau. *Paris Patisseries: History, Shops, Recipes.* Paris: Flammarion, 2010.

Sarris, Alexander, and Jamie Morrison. *Food Security in Africa: Market and Trade Policy for Staple Foods in Eastern and Southern Africa.* Northampton, MA: Edward Elgar, 2010.

Satin, Morton. *Death in the Pot: The Impact of Food Poisoning on History.* New York: Prometheus, 2007.

———. *Food Alert!: The Ultimate Sourcebook for Food Safety.* New York: Facts on File, 2008.

Schehr, Lawrence R., and Allen S. Weiss, eds. *French Food: On the Table, On the Page, and in French Culture.* New York: Routledge, 2001.

Schenone, Laura. *A Thousand Years over a Hot Stove: A History of American Women Told Through Food, Recipes, and Remembrances.* New York: W.W. Norton, 2003.

Schiebinger, Londa L. *Plants and Empire: Colonial Bioprospecting in the Atlantic World.* Cambridge, MA: Harvard University Press, 2007.

Schinharl, Cornelia, and Michael Brauner. *Mushrooms.* San Francisco: Silverback, 2006.

Schlosser, Eric. *Fast Food Nation: The Dark Side of the All-American Meal.* Boston: Houghton Mifflin, 2001.

Schmidt, Arno, and Paul Fieldhouse. *The World Religions Cookbook.* Westport, CT: Greenwood, 2007.

Schmitz, A., T.H. Spreen, W.A. Messina, and C.B. Moss, eds. *Sugar and Related Sweetener Markets: International Perspectives.* Gainesville, FL: University of Florida, 2002.

Schneller, Thomas. *Meat: Identification, Fabrication, Utilization.* Clifton Park, NJ: Delmar, 2009.

———. *Poultry: Identification, Fabrication, Utilization.* Clifton Park, NY: Delmar, 2010.

Scholliers, Peter. *Food, Drink and Identity: Cooking, Eating and Drinking in Europe Since the Middle Ages.* New York: Berg, 2001.

Schulze, Richard. *Carolina Gold Rice.* Charleston, SC: History Press, 2005.

Scicolone, Michele. *Pasta, Noodles, and Dumplings.* New York: Simon & Schuster, 2005.

Scully, D. Eleanor, and Terence Scully. *Early French Cookery: Sources, History, Original Recipes, and Modern Adaptations.* Ann Arbor: University of Michigan Press, 2002.

Scully, Terence. *The Art of Cookery in the Middle Ages.* Rochester, NY: Woodbridge, 2005.

Serventi, Silvano, and Françoise Sabban. *Pasta: The Story of a Universal Food.* New York: Columbia University Press, 2002.

Seth, Andrew, and Geoffrey Randall. *The Grocers: The Rise and Rise of the Supermarket Chains.* London: Kogan Page, 2001.

Seth, Michael J. *A History of Korea: From Antiquity to the Present.* Lanham, MD: Rowman & Littlefield, 2011.

Shachman, Maurice. *The Soft Drinks Companion: A Technical Handbook for the Beverage Industry.* Boca Raton, FL: CRC, 2005.

Shapiro, Laura. *Julia Child.* New York: Lipper/Viking, 2007.

———. *Perfection Salad: Women and Cooking at the Turn of the Century.* Berkeley: University of California Press, 2009.

Sharma, S.D., ed. *Rice: Origin, Antiquity, and History.* Enfield, NJ: Science Publishers, 2010.

Sharma, Vinita, Harold T. McKone, and Peter G. Markow. "A Global Perspective on the History, Use, and Identification of Synthetic Food Dyes." *Journal of Chemical Education* 88:1 (2011): 24–28.

Shea, Martha Esposito, and Mike Mathis. *Campbell Soup Company.* Charles, SC: Arcadia, 2002.

Sheehan, Sean. *Endangered Species.* Pleasantville, NY: Gareth Stevens, 2009.

Shephard, Sue. *Pickled, Potted, and Canned: How the Art and Science of Food Preserving Changed the World.* New York: Simon & Schuster, 2000.

Sherman, Sandra, Karen Chotkowski, and Henry Chotkowski. *Fresh from the Past: Recipes and Revelations from Moll Flanders' Kitchen.* Lanham, MD: Taylor Trade, 2004.

Shi, John, Chi-Tang Ho, and Fereidoon Shahidi, eds. *Functional Foods of the East.* Boca Raton, FL: CRC, 2011.

Shillington, Kevin, ed. *Encyclopedia of African History.* New York: Taylor & Francis, 2005.

Shiva, Vandana. *Water Wars: Privatization, Pollution and Profit.* Cambridge, MA: South End, 2002.

Shurtleff, William, and Akiko Aoyagi. *History of Soybeans and Soyfoods in Canada (1831–2010).* Lafayette, CA: Soyinfo Center, 2010.

Sinclair, Pat, and Joel Butkowski. *Scandinavian Classic Baking.* Gretna, LA: Pelican, 2011.

Sinclair, Thomas R., and Carol Janas Sinclair. *Bread, Beer and the Seeds of Change: Agriculture's Impact on World History.* Cambridge, MA: CABI, 2010.

Singer, Amy, ed. *Starting with Food: Culinary Approaches to Ottoman History.* Princeton, NJ: Markus Weiner, 2010.

Skancke, Jennifer L., ed. *Genetically Modified Food.* Detroit, MI: Greenhaven, 2009.

Skrabec, Quentin R. *H.J. Heinz: A Biography.* Jefferson, NC: McFarland, 2009.

Slayton, Robert A. *Master of the Air: William Tunner and the Success of Military Airlift.* Tuscaloosa: University of Alabama Press, 2010.

Slemming, Brian. "The Best of the Wurst." *Rotarian* 179:5 (November 2001): 16–17.

Smith, Andrew F. *Eating History: 30 Turning Points in the Making of American Cuisine.* New York: Columbia University Press, 2009.

———. *Encyclopedia of Junk Food and Fast Food.* Westport, CT: Greenwood, 2006.

———. *Fast Food and Junk Food: An Encyclopedia of What We Love to Eat.* Santa Barbara, CA: Greenwood, 2011.

———, ed. *The Oxford Companion to American Food and Drink.* New York: Oxford University Press, 2007.

———. *Peanuts: The Illustrious History of the Goober Pea.* Urbana: University of Illinois Press, 2002.

———. *The Tomato in America: Early History, Culture, and Cookery.* Urbana: University of Illinois Press, 2001.

———. *The Turkey: An American Story.* Urbana: University of Illinois Press, 2006.

Smith, C. Wayne, and Robert Henry Dilday, eds. *Rice: Origin, History, Technology, and Production.* Hoboken, NJ: John Wiley & Sons, 2003.

Smith, Emma. "Living the Caveman's Good Life." *The Times* (London), October 12, 2008.

Smith, J. Scott, and Yui H. Hui, eds. *Food Processing: Principles and Applications.* Ames, IA: Blackwell, 2004.

Smith, Jane S. *The Garden of Invention: Luther Burbank and the Business of Breeding Plants.* New York: Penguin, 2009.

Smith, Richard Lee. *Premodern Trade in World History.* New York: Routledge, 2009.

Smith, Vanessa. "Give Us Our Daily Breadfruit: Bread Substitution in the Pacific in the Eighteenth Century." *Studies in Eighteenth Century Culture* 35 (2006): 53–75.

Snodgrass, Mary Ellen. *Encyclopedia of Kitchen History.* New York: Fitzroy Dearborn, 2004.

Sobey, Edwin J.C. *The Way Kitchens Work.* Chicago: Chicago Review Press, 2010.

Sohn, Mark F. *Appalachian Home Cooking: History, Culture, and Recipes.* Lexington: University Press of Kentucky, 2005.

Sokolov, Raymond. *A Canon of Vegetables: 101 Classic Recipes.* New York: William Morrow, 2007.

———. *Why We Eat What We Eat.* New York: Simon & Schuster, 1991.

Solley, Patricia. *An Exaltation of Soups: The Soul-Satisfying Story of Soup, As Told in More Than 100 Recipes.* New York: Three Rivers, 2004.

Solomon, Steven. *Water: The Epic Struggle for Wealth, Power, and Civilization.* New York: Harper Perennial, 2011.

Southgate, Douglas Dewitt, Douglas H. Graham, and Luther G. Tweeten. *The World Food Economy.* Malden, MA: Blackwell, 2007.

Spahr, David L. *Edible and Medicinal Mushrooms of New England and Eastern Canada.* Berkeley, CA: North Atlantic, 2009.

Spang, Rebecca L. *The Invention of the Restaurant.* Cambridge, MA: Harvard University Press, 2000.

Sparke, Kai, and Klaus Menrad. "Food Consumption Style Determines Food Product Innovations' Acceptance." *Journal of Consumer Marketing* 28:2 (2011): 125–138.

Spechtenhauser, Klaus, ed. *The Kitchen: Life World, Usage, Perspectives.* New York: Springer, 2006.

Spencer, Colin. *British Food: An Extraordinary Thousand Years of History.* New York: Columbia University Press, 2002.

Staller, John E., and Michael Carrasco, eds. *Pre-Columbian Foodways: Interdisciplinary Approaches to Food, Culture, and Markets in Ancient Mesoamerica.* New York: Springer, 2010.

Stamm, Mitch. *The Pastry Chef's Apprentice.* Beverly, MA: Quarry, 2011.

Standage, Tom. *An Edible History of Humanity.* New York: Walker, 2009.

Stanford, Craig B., and Henry T. Bunn, eds. *Meat-Eating & Human Evolution.* New York: Oxford University Press, 2001.

Stansfield, William D. "Luther Burbank: Honorary Member of the American Breeders' Association." *Journal of Heredity* 97:2 (2006): 95–99.

Stavely, Keith W.F., and Kathleen Fitzgerald. *America's Founding Food.* Chapel Hill: University of North Carolina Press, 2004.

Steckel, Richard H., and Jerome Carl Rose, eds. *The Backbone of History: Health and Nutrition in the Western Hemisphere.* New York: Cambridge University Press, 2002.

Steinkraus, Keith H., ed. *Industrialization of Indigenous Fermented Foods.* 2nd ed. New York: Marcel Dekker, 2004.

Stepaniak, Joanne. *Being Vegan: Living with Conscience, Conviction, and Compassion.* Los Angeles, CA: Lowell House, 2000.

Stepaniak, Joanne, and Virginia Messina. *The Vegan Sourcebook.* Los Angeles, CA: Lowell House, 2000.

Sterling, Richard. *Food: A Taste of the Road.* San Francisco: Travelers' Tales, 2002.

Stern, Jane, and Michael Stern. *The Lexicon of Real American Food.* Guilford, CT: Lyons, 2011.

Stevens, Laura J., Thomas Kuczek, John R. Burgess, Elizabeth Hurt, and L. Eugene Arnold. "Dietary Sensitivities and ADHD Symptoms: Thirty-Five Years of Research." *Clinical Pediatrics* 50:4 (April 2011): 279–293.

Stockton, Susan, and Jill Novatt, eds. *Food Network Favorites: Recipes from Our All-Star Chefs.* Des Moines, IA: Meredith, 2005.

Stonich, Susan C., ed. *Endangered Peoples of Latin America: Struggles to Survive and Thrive.* Westport, CT: Greenwood, 2001.

Strong, Roy C. *Feast: A History of Grand Eating.* London: Jonathan Cape, 2002.

Stuart, David C. *Dangerous Garden: The Quest for Plants to Change Our Lives.* Cambridge, MA: Harvard University Press, 2004.

Suas, Michel. *Advanced Bread and Pastry.* Detroit, MI: Delmar Cengage Learning, 2009.

Suddath, Claire. "A Brief History of Barbecue." *Time* (July 3, 2009).

Summers, William C. "Review: *A Soup for the Qan.*" *Journal of the History of Medicine and Allied Sciences* 56:2 (April 2001): 186–187.

Sun, Da-Wen, ed. *Modern Techniques for Food Authentication.* Boston: Elsevier, 2008.

Sutherland, Jonathan, and Diane Canwell. *Berlin Airlift: The Salvation of a City.* Gretna, LA: Pelican, 2008.

Swislocki, Mark. *Culinary Nostalgia: Regional Food Culture and the Urban Experience in Shanghai.* Stanford, CA: Stanford University Press, 2009.

Symons, Michael. *A History of Cooks and Cooking.* Urbana: University of Illinois Press, 2000.

Tal, Alon, and Alfred Abed Rabbo, eds. *Water Wisdom: Preparing the Groundwork for Cooperative and Sustainable Water Management in the Middle East.* New Brunswick, NJ: Rutgers University Press, 2010.

Tansey, Geoff, and Tasmin Rajotte, eds. *The Future Control of Food: A Guide to International Negotiations and Rules on Intellectual Property, Biodiversity, and Food Security.* Sterling, VA: Earthscan, 2008.

Tarantino, Jim. *Marinades, Rubs, Brines, Cures, and Glazes.* New York: Random House, 2006.

Tauger, Mark. *Agriculture in World History.* New York: Taylor & Francis, 2009.

Taylor, Judith M. *The Olive in California: History of an Immigrant.* Berkeley, CA: Ten Speed, 2000.

Taylor, Maureen A. "Everyday Gardening." *Ancestry* 23:5 (September/October 2005): 35–36.

This, Hervé. *The Science of the Oven.* New York: Columbia University Press, 2009.

Thorness, Bill. *Edible Heirlooms: Heritage Vegetables for the Maritime Garden.* Seattle, WA: Skipstone, 2009.

Thornton, William H. "Cannibals, Witches, and Slave Traders in the Atlantic World." *William and Mary Quarterly* 60:2 (April 2003): 273–294.

Tobias, Ruth. "Mealtime at the Movies: 15 Food Films." *World Literature Today* 83:1 (January/February 2009): 40–46.

Toensmeier, Eric. *Perennial Vegetables.* White River Junction, VT: Chelsea Green, 2007.

Toldrá, Fidel, ed. *Handbook of Fermented Meat and Poultry.* Ames, IA: Blackwell, 2007.

Tong, Anna. "Back to the Cave: No Processed Foods Are Allowed in Neanderthal Paleo Diet." *Hamilton (Ontario) Spectator,* August 29, 2010.

Toussaint-Samat, Maguelonne. *A History of Food.* Hoboken, NJ: Wiley-Blackwell, 2009.

Tracey, David. *Urban Agriculture: Ideas and Designs for the New Food Revolution.* Gabriola, Canada: New Society, 2011.

Trang, Corinne. *The Asian Grill: Great Recipes, Bold Flavors.* San Francisco: Chronicle, 2006.

Trehane, Jennifer. *Blueberries, Cranberries, and Other Vacciniums.* Portland, OR: Timber, 2004.

Trubek, Amy B. *Haute Cuisine: How the French Invented the Culinary Profession.* Philadelphia: University of Pennsylvania Press, 2000.

Tsuji, Shizuo. *Japanese Cooking, a Simple Art.* New York: Kodansha International, 2006.

Tucker, Gary, and Susan Featherstone. *Essentials of Thermal Processing.* Ames, IA: Wiley-Blackwell, 2011.

Tucker, Susan. *New Orleans Cuisine: Fourteen Signature Dishes and Their Histories.* Foreword by S. Frederick Starr. Jackson: University Press of Mississippi, 2009.

Turner, Jack. *Spice: The History of a Temptation.* New York: Vintage Books, 2004.

Ucko, Peter J., and G.W. Dimbleby, eds. *The Domestication and Exploitation of Plants and Animals.* New Brunswick, NJ: AldineTransaction, 2008.

Ungar, Peter S., ed. *Evolution of the Human Diet: The Known, the Unknown, and the Unknowable.* New York: Oxford University Press, 2006.

Uphoff, Norman Thomas, ed. *Agroecological Innovations: Increasing Food Production with Participatory Development.* Sterling, VA: Earthscan, 2002.

Vaccariello, Linda. "The Perfect Tomato." *Cincinnati Magazine* (July 2001): 58–59, 125–126.

Van Atta, Marian. *Exotic Foods: A Kitchen and Garden Guide.* Sarasota, FL: Pineapple, 2002.

Van Gelder, Geert Jan. *God's Banquet: Food in Classical Arabic Literature.* New York: Columbia University Press, 2000.

Van Zeist, William, Sytze Bottema, and Marijke van der Veen. *Diet and Vegetation at Ancient Carthage: The Archaeobotanical Evidence.* Groningen, Netherlands: Groningen Institute of Archaeology, 2001.

Vernet, Julien. "More Than Symbolic: Pierre Clement de Laussat's Municipal Council and French Louisianian Protest Against American Territorial Government." *French Colonial History* 4 (2003): 133–144.

Vinton, Sherri Brooks, and Ann Clark Espuelas. *The Real Food Revival: Aisle by Aisle, Morsel by Morsel.* New York: Jeremy P. Tarcher/Penguin, 2005.

Vivian, John. "The Three Sisters." *Mother Earth News* 184 (February/March 2001): 50–54.

Vossen, Paul. "Olive Oil: History, Production, and Characteristics of the World's Classic Oils." *Horticultural Science* 42:5 (August 2007): 1093–1100.

Wagner, Heather Lehr. *Hernán Cortés.* New York: Chelsea House, 2009.

Wahlqvist, Mark L., ed. *Food and Nutrition: Australasia, Asia and the Pacific.* Crows Nest, Australia: Allen & Unwin, 2002.

Waines, David. *The Odyssey of Ibn Battuta: Uncommon Tales of a Medieval Adventurer.* Chicago: University of Chicago Press, 2010.

Waldron, S.A., C.G. Brown, J.W. Longworth, and C.G. Zhang. *China's Livestock Revolution: Agribusiness and Policy Developments in the Sheep Meat Industry.* Cambridge, MA: CABI, 2007.

Walker, Jake, and Robert S. Cox. *A History of Chowder: Four Centuries of a New England Meal.* Charleston, SC: History Press, 2011.

Wallace, Emma Gary. "A Study of Period Crystal Ware." *The Jewelers' Circular* 75:9 (September 26, 1917): 97.

Walsh, Lorena Seebach. *Motives of Honor, Pleasure, and Profit: Plantation Management in the Colonial Chesapeake, 1607–1763.* Chapel Hill: University of North Carolina Press, 2010.

Walsh, Robb. *Legends of Texas Barbecue Cookbook: Recipes and Recollections from the Pit Bosses.* San Francisco: Chronicle, 2002.

———. *The Tex-Mex Cookbook: A History in Photos and Recipes.* New York: Broadway, 2004.

Walters, Kerry S., and Lisa Portness, eds. *Religious Vegetarianism: From Hesiod to the Dalai Lama.* Albany: State University of New York Press, 2001.

Warman, Arturo. *Corn & Capitalism: How a Botanical Bastard Grew to Global Dominance.* Chapel Hill: University of North Carolina Press, 2003.

Warner, Keith. *Agroecology in Action: Extending Alternative Agriculture Through Social Networks.* Cambridge, MA: MIT Press, 2007.

Watson, Ben. *Cider, Hard and Sweet: History, Traditions, and Making Your Own.* 2nd ed. Woodstock, VT: Countryman, 2009.

Watson, Ronald R., and Victor R. Preedy. *Bioactive Foods in Promoting Health: Fruits and Vegetables*. Burlington, MA: Academic Press, 2010.

Watson, Stephanie. *Trans Fats*. New York: Rosen, 2008.

Weaver, William Woys. *Country Scrapple: An American Tradition*. Mechanicsburg, PA: Stackpole, 2003.

———. "The Dark Side of Culinary Ephemera: The Portrayal of African Americans." *Gastronomica* 6:3 (Summer 2006): 76–81.

———. *Encyclopedia of Food and Culture*. New York: Charles Scribner's Sons, 2003.

———. *Pennsylvania Trail of History Cookbook*. Mechanicsburg, PA: Stackpole, 2004.

———. *Sauerkraut Yankees: Pennsylvania Dutch Foods & Foodways*. Mechanicsburg, PA: Stackpole, 2002.

———. "The Water Gate Inn: Pennsylvania Dutch Cuisine Goes Mainstream." *Gastronomica* 9:3 (Summer 2009): 25–31.

Wegren, Stephen K. *Russia's Food Policies and Globalization*. Lanham, MD: Lexington, 2005.

Weinberg, Bennett Alan, and Bonnie K. Bealer. *The World of Caffeine: The Science and Culture of the World's Most Popular Drug*. New York: Routledge, 2001.

West-Durán, Alan, ed. *Cuba*. Detroit: Gale-Cengage, 2012.

White, Jasper. *50 Chowders: One-Pot Meals: Clam, Corn & Beyond*. New York: Simon & Schuster, 2000.

Whitehead, Harriet. *Food Rules: Hunting, Sharing, and Tabooing Game in Papua New Guinea*. Ann Arbor: University of Michigan Press, 2000.

Whitney, Eleanor Noss, and Sharon Rady Rolfes. *Understanding Nutrition*. Belmont, CA: Thomson Higher Education, 2008.

Wild, Alan. *Soils, Land, and Food: Managing the Land During the Twenty-First Century*. Cambridge, UK: Cambridge University Press, 2003.

Wild, Antony. *Coffee: A Dark History*. New York: W.W. Norton, 2005.

Wilford, John Noble. "Columbus's Lost Town: New Evidence Is Found." *The New York Times*, August 27, 1985.

Wilk, Richard R., ed. *Fast Food/Slow Food: The Cultural Economy of the Global Food System*. Lanham, MD: Altamira, 2006.

Wilkins, John, and Shaun Hill. *Food in the Ancient World*. Malden, MA: Wiley-Blackwell, 2006.

Willer, Helga, and Minou Yussefi-Menzler. *The World of Organic Agriculture: Statistics and Emerging Trends 2008*. Sterling, VA: Earthscan, 2008.

Williams, Elizabeth M., and Stephanie J. Carter. *The A–Z Encyclopedia of Food Controversies and the Law*. Santa Barbara, CA: ABC-Clio, 2011.

Williams, Lindsey. *Neo Soul: Taking Soul Food to a Whole 'Nutha Level*. New York: Avery, 2007.

Williams-Forson, Psyche A. *Building Houses Out of Chicken Legs: Black Women, Food, and Power*. Chapel Hill: University of North Carolina Press, 2006.

Wilson, A.N. *Our Times: The Age of Elizabeth II*. New York: Macmillan, 2009.

Wilson, Carol. *Gypsy Feast: Recipes and Culinary Traditions of the Romany People*. New York: Hippocrene, 2004.

Wilson, Charles L., ed. *Intelligent and Active Packaging for Fruits and Vegetables*. Boca Raton, FL: CRC, 2007.

Winkler, Peter. *Feeding the World*. Washington, DC: National Geographic, 2003.

———. *Landscape Agroecology*. Binghamton, NY: Food Products, 2004.

Wolfe, David. *Naked Chocolate: The Astonishing Truth About the World's Greatest Food*. San Diego, CA: Maul Brothers, 2005.

———. *Superfoods: The Food and Medicine of the Future*. Berkeley, CA: North Atlantic, 2009.

Wolfe, Nathan D., Peter Daszak, A. Marm Kilpatrick, and Donald S. Burke. "Bushmeat Hunting, Deforestation, and Prediction of Zoonotic Disease." *Emerging Infectious Diseases* 11:12 (December 2005): 1822–1827.

Wood, Kate. *Eat Smart, Eat Raw*. Garden City Park, NY: Square One, 2006.

Woodside, Arch G., and Drew Martin, eds. *Tourism Management: Analysis, Behaviour, and Strategy*. Cambridge, MA: CABI, 2008.

Woolley, Benjamin. *Heal Thyself: Nicholas Culpeper and the Seventeenth-Century Struggle to Bring Medicine to the People*. New York: HarperCollins, 2004.

"The World Food Crisis." *The New York Times*, April 10, 2008.

Wrangham, Richard. *Catching Fire: How Cooking Made Us Human*. New York: Basic Books, 2009.

Wright, Clifford A. *Mediterranean Vegetables: A Cook's ABC of Vegetables and Their Preparation*. Boston: Harvard Common, 2001.

———. *Some Like It Hot: Spicy Favorites from the World's Hot Zones*. Boston: Harvard Common, 2005.

Wright, Julia. *Sustainable Agriculture and Food Security in an Era of Oil Scarcity*. Sterling, VA: Earthscan, 2009.

Wright, Simon, and Diane McCrea, eds. *The Handbook of Organic and Fair Trade Food Marketing*. Ames, IA: Blackwell, 2007.

Wu, David Y.H., and Sidney C.H. Cheung, eds. *The Globalization of Chinese Food*. Honolulu: University of Hawaii Press, 2002.

Yadav, Shyam Singh, Jerry L. Hatfield, Robert Redden, Hermann Lotze-Campen, and Anthony Hall, eds. *Crop Adaptation to Climate Change*. Ames, IA: Wiley-Blackwell, 2011.

Yildez, Fatih, ed. *Development and Manufacture of Yogurt and Other Functional Dairy Products*. New York: Taylor & Francis, 2010.

Zibart, Eve. *The Ethnic Food Lover's Companion*. Birmingham, AL: Menasha Ridge, 2001.

Zohary, Daniel, and Maria Hopf. *Domestication of Plants in the Old World: The Origin and Spread of Cultivated Plants in West Asia, Europe, and the Nile Valley*. Oxford, UK: Oxford University Press, 2000.

Zronik, John Paul. *The Biography of Rice*. New York: Crabtree, 2006.

Zweiniger-Bargielowska, Ina. *Austerity in Britain: Rationing, Controls, and Consumption, 1939–1955*. Oxford, UK: Oxford University Press, 2000.

Index

Page numbers in italics indicate illustrations;
italic page numbers followed by t indicate tables.

A

À la carte menus, **1**:212–213
À la française (in the French style),
  2:392
A.A. Libby & Company, **1**:60
Ab ovis ad mala (from eggs to apples),
  2:469
Abalone, **1**:195; **2**:463
Abattoirs. *See* Meatpacking industry
Abbasid dynasty, **1**:104, 140; **2**:423,
  444
Abbott, William, **2**:557
Abbott Laboratories, **1**:51
Abélard, Pierre, **2**:563
Abenaki, **1**:123; **2**:376t, 567, 569
Abernethy, John, **1**:68
Abernethy biscuit, **1**:68
Abigail (ship), **1**:354
Abolitionism, **1**:284
Aborigines, Australian
  biscuit, **1**:67
  bushmeat, **1**:86
  caching, **1**:89
  cannibalism, **1**:94
  cookware, **1**:147
  diet and cuisine, **1**:43–44, 292
  dried food, **1**:196
  food taboos, **2**:534
  grilling, **1**:265
  macadamia nut oil, **2**:402
  middens, **2**:376t
  pit cookery, **2**:427
  poultry, **2**:445
  snack food, **2**:505
  trade, **1**:97
Abraham (Hebrew patriarch),
  2:460
Abram (Jefferson's slave), **1**:325
Abreu, António de, **1**:3
Abruzzi region, Italy, **1**:108, 172;
  2:414
Absinthe, **1**:23
Abu Bakr, Sheikh, **1**:297
Abu Hureyra, Syria, **1**:28, 61, 232,
  291–292; **2**:574
Abu Inan Marini, Sultan (Morocco),
  1:299

Abu Ubaidah (governor of Syria),
  1:219
Abydos, **2**:402, 580
Abyssinia, food as currency, **1**:168
Academy of Medicine, **2**:541
Acadians, **1**:115
  See also Cajun diet and cuisine
Acalan province, Mexico, **1**:190
Acapulco, Mexico, **1**:130
Ac'cent, **2**:379
Accomplisht Cook, The (May), **1**:124,
  135
Accra, Ghana, **1**:11
Accum, Friedrich Christian, **1**:5
Aceh, Sumatra, **1**:313
Acetaria (Evelyn), **1**:275; **2**:478
Acetobacteria, **2**:513
Achaemenid Empire, **1**:218; **2**:422
Achiote, **1**:201
Ackee fruit (*Blighia sapida*), **1**:102;
  2:432
Acker, Finley, **2**:367
Acoma Pueblo, New Mexico, **1**:73, 91
Acorns
  caching, **1**:89, 90
  dried, **1**:194
  flour, **2**:398
  Neolithic diet, **2**:574
  noodles, **2**:388, 432
  preparation, **1**:152, 342–343;
    2:398, 432
  toxicity, **2**:432
  in Tuolumne Acorn Stew (recipe),
    1:343
Acqua di seltz (seltzer water), **1**:100
Acre, Brazil, **2**:528
Acre, Israel, **1**:161; **2**:522
Acropolis, Athens, Greece, **2**:529
Act for the Relief of the Poor
  (England, 1597), **1**:133
Act of Union (Great Britain, 1707),
  2:576–577
"Active packaging," **2**:410–411
Acton, Eliza, **1**:141
Acuera people, **1**:184
Adalia, Turkey, **1**:160
Adams, Abigail, **2**:484

Adams, Carol J., **2**:560
Adams, John, **1**:119, 208
Adams, Thomas, **1**:109, 110
Adams & Sons, **1**:110
Adams New York No. 1 (gum), **1**:109
Addis Ababa, Ethiopia, **2**:433
Addison, Joseph, **1**:340
Additives, food, **1**:4–5, 25, 177, 310;
  2:481
  See also Adulterated food; Dye,
    food; Guar; Hormones in food;
    Monosodium glutamate
Aden, Yemen, **1**:82; **2**:435, 517
Administration of Quality
  Supervision, Inspection, and
  Quarantine (China), **1**:313
Adobado (sauce), **2**:542
Adolf Fredrik, King (Sweden), **1**:348
Adrian, John, **1**:162
Adulterated food, **1**:5–7
  ancient Rome, **1**:5; **2**:468
  China, **1**:5, 15, 310, 312
  condiments, **1**:135
  consumer protection laws, **1**:137
  flour, **1**:5, 6; **2**:377
  grain, **1**:221
  industrial food processing, **1**:310
  inspection and safety, **1**:312; **2**:410
  Japan, **2**:481–482
  milk, **1**:6, 137, 312
  Pliny the Elder on, **1**:5; **2**:432
  punishment for, **1**:5
  world trade, **2**:583
Adulteration of Food, Drink, and
  Drugs, Act of (England, 1872),
  1:6
Adulteration of Tea and Coffee Act
  (Great Britain, 1724), **1**:131
Adventure, HMS, **1**:139
Advertising
  clipper ships, **1**:121
  coffee, **1**:127
  consumer protection laws, **1**:138
  deceptive practices, **2**:369, 507, 523,
    566
  fads, **1**:217
  French East India Company, **1**:247